C. I. Lewis

SUNY series in Philosophy

George R. Lucas Jr., editor

C. I. Lewis

The Last Great Pragmatist

Murray G. Murphey

State University of New York Press

Published by
State University of New York Press, Albany

© 2005 State University of New York
All rights reserved

Printed in the United States of America

For information, address State University of New York Press,
194 Washington Avenue, Suite 305, Albany, NY 12210–2384

Production by Michael Haggett
Marketing by Michael Campochiaro

Library of Congress Cataloging-in-Publication Data

Murphey, Murray G.
    C. I. Lewis : the last great pragmatist / Murray G. Murphey.
      P. cm. — (SUNY series in philosophy)
    Includes bibliography references (p.) and index.
    ISBN 0-7914-6541-1 (hardcover : alk. paper)
   1. Lweis, Clarence Irving, 1883–1964. I. Title. II. Series.

B945.L454M87 2005
191—dc22   2004027769

10 9 8 7 6 5 4 3 2 1

for Bruce Kuklick

Contents

Acknowledgments

When I was very young, I had the privilege of listening to C. I. Lewis lecture. My interest in him really began then, and was further stimulated by conversations with my classmate, Burt Dreben. So, many years later, I have written this book. I am deeply grateful to those who have helped me in this endeavor. Mr. Andrew Lewis, the son of C. I. Lewis, gave generously of his time and allowed me to quote from our discussions as well as his parents' writings, and afforded me access to papers I had not previously seen. I am most grateful to the Department of Special Collections at Stanford University for permission to use the manuscripts of C. I. Lewis archived there, and to Mrs. Polly Armstrong for her assistance. I am also grateful to the Harvard University Archives for allowing me to consult its Lewis material, and to Harvard University for permitting me to quote from Lewis's dissertation as well as that of William Parry. The Yale University Library generously granted me permission to quote from the Lewis material in the papers of Frederick Fitch. Kent Schnor provided important advice on the logic chapters. I am particularly grateful to Professor Max Cresswell for having shown me that a proof I had planned to use was wrong, and to Professor Ruth Marcus for allowing me to quote from two of Lewis's letters to her. Some of the material in Chapter 10 was previously published in the *Transactions of the Charles S. Peirce Society* 38:155–174 (2002), and I am grateful to Peter Hare for permission to use that material here. Bruce Kuklick has read several versions of this manuscript and made many helpful suggestions. To all of these, my thanks.

List of Abbreviations

_____

AKV   *An Analysis of Knowledge and Valuation* (LaSalle: Open Court, 1971)

CI&I   Mabel M. Lewis, *CI&I* (Privately Printed), 1956

CP   *Collected Papers of Clarence Irving Lewis*, eds. Goheen and Mothershead (Stanford: Stanford University Press, 1970)

GNR   *The Ground and Nature of the Right* (New York: Columbia University Press, 1955)

JP   *Journal of Philosophy*

JSL   *Journal of Symbolic Logic*

MWO   *Mind and the World Order* (New York: Dover Press, 1929)

OSI   *Our Social Inheritance* (Bloomington: University of Indiana Press, 1957)

PR   *Philosophical Review*

PPR   *Philosophy and Phenomenological Research*

S.C.   Special Collections, Stanford University Library

SL   *Symbolic Logic* with Cooper Harold Langford (New York: Dover Press, 1959)

SSL   *A Survey of Symbolic Logic* (Berkeley: University of California Press, 1918)

V&I   *Values and Imperatives*, ed. Lange (Stanford: Stanford University Press, 1969)

Introduction

The times that shaped C. I. Lewis are distant enough so that some description of the intellectual background from which he came is important for an understanding of his work. This description must be brief and is necessarily incomplete, but it will help to anchor the following analysis of his work in the world he knew.

The era preceding Lewis's work has often been referred to as the Golden Age of American philosophy. It was certainly a period of extraordinary intellectual productivity, and the reasons for that need to be understood. Pre-Civil War America was a vibrant time of economic and territorial expansion, political democratization, and bitter controversy over moral issues, yet some things did engender remarkable agreement. One of these was Protestant Christianity, which dominated the intellectual life of the country. Whatever the conflicts among different Protestant denominations and sects, the great majority of Americans espoused some form of Protestantism, and religious beliefs provided the fundamental tenets of the American worldview. Few challenged the literal truth of the Bible, and those who did based their views on issues of interpretation while reaffirming the general truths of Holy Writ. Educational institutions, from the common school to Harvard College, taught Protestant morality and often Protestant theology, and schoolbooks, from McGuffey Readers to the tomes on "Moral Science" studied by college seniors, were solidly orthodox.[1]

This was also an era in which the sciences were growing rapidly in the United States. Scientific training was on the rise, and new scientific

1

institutions, such as the Smithsonian and the U.S. Coast and Geodetic Survey, were being established.[2] But there was little if any conflict between science and religion. The Newtonian revolution had been absorbed with little difficulty by the churches, and the Natural Theology, which used science to demonstrate the existence and attributes of the Creator, bent science to the service of religion. Even the newer sciences like geology, which were beginning to raise religious problems in Europe, were not seen as posing any threat to orthodoxy here. In no small part, this was because the leading American scientists were devout believers in Christianity. Men like Benjamin Silliman, Louis Agassiz, Joseph Henry, Benjamin Peirce, and Dallas Bache—the men who dominated American science of that time—were convinced that science was the study of God's handiwork.[3]

In what today we would call the social sciences—economics, political science, and so on—there was also a broad consensus. The political theory hammered out between 1763 and 1788 had become canonical in the United States and no one seriously challenged it; to do so would have been regarded as unpatriotic. In economics, the theories of Adam Smith and his followers were generally accepted—not surprisingly, since they provided a rationale for the dynamic economy of the time. Disputes, of course, arose over issues such as protection, but these tended to be disputes within the Smithian framework. The texts on "political economy" that students read were uniformly Smithian in character. The remainder of what we would identify as social science fell under the rubric of "moral science" and was taught by philosophers who were ministers and ministers who were philosophers, and in both cases with a Scottish accent.

American philosophy of the era was the realism of the Scots. After Hume had shown that Locke's philosophy (or psychology—the two were hardly distinct) led to skepticism, it had been the Scottish thinkers—Reid, Stewart, Hutcheson et al.—who had developed an answer to Hume. In epistemology, they were realists, holding that what we knew was not just our own ideas but real objects as they truly were, known through the medium of sensations. But they also rejected Locke's belief that the mind was passive in knowing, holding that the active mind brought certain principles of common sense, such as the causal principle, to the act of knowing. In morality, they believed human beings were endowed with a "moral sense"—a perceptive faculty that allowed them to perceive the moral properties of acts. Thus, the model of empirical perceptual knowledge was extended to morality, but in a safe way; moral principles induced from the perceptions of the moral sense were not likely to lead to antinomian heresies.

Scottish epistemology had certain similarities to Kant's critical philosophy. Both asserted that the mind was active in knowing, that it contributed concepts and principles that made knowledge possible, and that Humean skepticism was fallacious. Not surprisingly, thinkers here and abroad began trying to wed the two philosophies. Sir William Hamilton, the last of the great Scottish thinkers, was the most successful in doing so, and Hamilton acquired many disciples in the United States. Thus, Kantian ideas were already in the air before the Civil War.[4]

Then came the war—an event that profoundly changed the United States. Never before had the nation witnessed such wholesale slaughter. Never before had it undertaken so great a managerial task as the support of armies of hundreds of thousands in the field. And never before had one entire section been conquered and occupied by an enemy. The war and the Constitutional amendments that followed it forever altered the relation of the state and federal governments, vastly increasing the power of the latter at the expense of the former. And the war accelerated the rise of corporate capitalism as men who had managed armies turned to business. By destroying the culture of the Old South, it made the culture of the North the new American culture, and it bequeathed to the nation the problem of the freed slaves.

These changes were upsetting enough, but it was not just the war that shocked the intellectual consensus of the prewar period, it was also the publication in 1859 of Darwin's *Origin of Species*. The impact of Darwin's work was enormous, and it reached far beyond the sciences. Before Darwin, most scientists had believed that species were immutable. This doctrine fit the account of creation in Genesis, and it also fit experience with hybrids, such as mules, that were infertile, for if species were not immutable, how could they change except by cross-breeding, and if hybrids were infertile, that avenue of change was closed. Furthermore, naturalists had devoted themselves for over a century to the task of finding the "natural" system of classification of plants and animals that would reveal the plan by which God had created the world, always assuming the species as the unit of classification. So pervasive was this orientation to nature that it was difficult for many to think in other terms. Some indeed had; Lamarck proposed an evolutionary theory using the inheritance of acquired characteristics, but his followers were few. Then Darwin published.

Darwin's theory allowed for a deceptively simple statement, with two major hypotheses. First, Darwin held that offspring differ from their parents by minute variations that are inheritable. Whatever the cause of these variations, they appear to observers as random. This was the principle of fortuitous variation. If it were true, the result over a large number of generations would be offspring differing from the original parents in every variety of characteristics. That, of course, is not what happens. To account for the fact that most variants are not found, Darwin introduced a second hypothesis—natural selection. Following Malthus, Darwin said that in any environment in which an organism can survive, it will reproduce much more rapidly than its supply of food and other necessities of life can be increased. The result must be a competition among the organisms for those necessities. In that competition, some organisms will find that they have inherited favorable characteristics; they will survive and reproduce and so transmit their good fortune to their progeny. Others will find that they have inherited unfavorable characteristics; they will die before they can reproduce and their unfavorable variations will die with them. This is not a theory in which organisms survive by adapting to their environment; they either are or are not adapted, depending on the variations they have inherited. The lucky make it; the unlucky do not.

As one would expect, Darwin's theory produced controversy within science. The theory had real weaknesses—particularly the lack of an adequate fossil record to support it and the absence of an adequate theory of inheritance. Yet Darwin's theory rapidly gained followers and within fifteen years captured the field. When Darwin's great opponent in the United States—Louis Agassiz—died in 1873, his own students had already embraced Darwin's views.

But although the controversy in science was relatively brief, the same was not true regarding religion. Darwin's theory was a fundamental challenge to the Christian religion on a variety of counts. Most obviously, Darwin proposed an origin for human beings that flatly contradicted the account in Genesis. For biblical literalists, that alone was sufficient reason to attack the theory of evolution as atheistic. But the Darwinian challenge went further. Natural Theology had attempted to deduce the attributes of the Creator from the orderliness of nature. But the order Darwin found in nature was not one that fit the needs of Natural Theology. If the natural order was one of the struggle for survival, if nature was "red in tooth and claw," then what did that imply about the character of the Creator? Certainly nature according to Darwin did not fit the picture of the wise, benevolent Creator of Natural Theology. But the fundamental challenge posed by the Darwinian theory was more profound. Christianity had always taught that humans had a dual nature: half animal and half angel. Although man had an animal body, he had an immortal soul. But in the Darwinian theory, man was a purely natural creature, the product of an animal ancestry. Darwin did not deny the existence of the soul; he simply showed that there was no reason to assume its existence. But if that were true, then there was no post-mortem reward or punishment, no immortality, no divine spark to elevate humans above the animal kingdom. And if *that* were true, Christianity was false.

That was, and is, the fundamental issue between Darwinian evolution and Christianity.

The controversy between Darwinian science and religion was long and bitter, and still continues. Some rejected evolution entirely and held to a literal interpretation of the Bible. Others sought various compromises. Some held that humans had evolved as Darwin said, but at some point in the process God had intervened to endow man with a soul. Others worked out providential interpretations of evolution, seeking a new Natural Theology that identified evolution with progress. Still others abandoned systematic theology and regarded Christianity as a program of social reform and good works. But for all believers in religion, the Darwinian theory posed critical problems. And given the degree to which religion had formed the basis of the pre-Civil War worldview, the result was intellectually traumatic as people found the "eternal truths" on which they had built their lives crumbling beneath them. The prewar worldview did not survive the shock.[5]

One should not, of course, attribute the intellectual trauma of late nineteenth-century America solely to the impact of evolutionary theory. The Civil War itself, with all the problems that followed in its wake, was profoundly unsettling. So was the rapid expansion of industrial capitalism that, like the war, forced an integration of the nation and brought a new economic and political order that appalled many. The flood tide of immigration and the rapid growth of large urban centers, along with large urban slums, further created wrenching problems. The American people found themselves in a period of rapid and radical change, whose nature was only dimly understood at the time but whose effects were both highly visible and deeply disturbing. That these economic, political, and social changes coincided with the shattering of the older worldview made matters even worse, for it deprived those who sought to understand and cope with their situation of the intellectual and moral certainties they needed to guide them through the chaos.

One result of this situation was an extraordinary outpouring of intellectual activity, as men sought desperately to put the worldview back together again. One of the most influential of these was not an American at all but an English engineer named Herbert Spencer. An advocate of evolution before Darwin published his work, Spencer was well placed to capitalize on the furor aroused by the *Origin of Species*, and, in 1860, announced his intention to construct a "synthetic philosophy" that would unify science and philosophy. Beginning in 1864 with *First Principles*, Spencer published volume after volume—*The Principles of Biology*, *The Principles of Psychology*, *The Principles of Sociology*, and so on. By the time Spencer died in 1903, he had sold 368,755 books in this country—a fantastic sale for the time and the nature of these works—and acquired a host of followers in the United States, ranging from Andrew Carnegie to Jack London, and publicists like E. L. Youmans, whose journals, *Appleton's Journal* and *Popular Science Monthly*, spread the master's teachings far and wide.

Spencer's synthetic philosophy was an attempt to integrate Darwin's evolutionary theory into the older worldview of Newtonian mechanics. Starting from the nebular hypothesis of LaPlace, Spencer projected a cosmic evolutionary process in which matter passed from a homogeneous distribution in space to ever more complex forms, eventuating in human beings. This process was mechanical, which meant that humans were material creatures, but it was also providential; evolution took the form of a linear progress toward an ideal state that looked remarkably like the perfect Smithian economic world. Thus, God was in his heaven directing events, even though Spencer held that we could never know anything more about him than that he existed, consequently on the one hand ruling out systematic theology while on the other reinstating it in the form of providential progress. Spencer was ingenious at yoking disparate scientific findings in such a way that they seemed to support his general theory, and his volumes on sociology and psychology contained many shrewd insights. They also included arguments all too appealing to late nineteenth-century readers, such as the claim that the "primitive" peoples were less evolved than the civilized. But most important was Spencer's psychology. He defined biological organisms as unstable material systems that sustained themselves by a continual adjustment of internal to external relations, but this adjustive process was conceived as automatic and mechanical. Human learning he took to be a direct copying of external sequences through association, so that the mind really consists in the power of memory and is completely determined by its environment. Thus, nature rules the mind; the determinism of mechanics binds the human will. The mind cannot turn back on the natural process that governs it, and any attempt to do so will have destructive consequences. Furthermore, men *ought* not to interfere with the working of the evolutionary process, for the process itself is good and will lead to the best possible results; interference will only create evil. Spencer was a man who had the courage of his convictions and did not flinch from their consequences.

It seems hard that widows and orphans should be left to struggle for life or death. Nevertheless, when regarded not separately but in connection with the interest of universal humanity, these harsh fatalities are seen to be full of benevolence—the same benevolence which brings to early graves the children of diseased parents, and singles out the intemperate, and the debilitated as victims of an epidemic.[6]

The vogue for Spencer was hardly universal, but he had great appeal, and the reasons are not hard to see. First, he integrated Darwin's disturbing new theory into a traditional mechanistic view that was familiar to most people. Second, he was no atheist; if he avoided theology, he nevertheless turned evolution into a providential design for human progress. Third, his ideal state toward which evolution led was one of natural rights politically and laissez-faire economics. Fourth, he assured his readers that evolution was good, that whatever was was right, and that all would come right in the end. For people struggling to understand a world turned upside down, Spencer had much to offer.[7]

But not everyone thought so. Those who argued for social reform found this theory appalling. Although American writers like William Graham Sumner championed theories very similar to Spencer's, there were others who rejected his determinism and argued that the human mind could in fact turn back on the process that produced it and modify it to fit our needs. The sociologist Lester Ward was one of the leaders of this reaction. "We are told," wrote Ward, "to let things alone and allow nature to take it course. But has intelligent man ever done this? Is not civilization itself with all that it has accomplished the result of man's not letting things alone, and of his not letting nature take its course?"[8] Ward rejected the claim that nature must rule the mind; human history, he held, proved just the opposite.

Given the terms of this debate, the appeal of Hegel, and of Idealism generally, in the United States, is not surprising. Modern Idealism has always been an effort to subordinate science to religion. Jonathan Edwards and George Berkeley both turned to Idealism to preserve the dominance of religion over Newtonian mechanics and Lockean psychology. Kant's effort to protect God, Freedom, and Immortality from science by giving them a separate realm could not keep his followers from reducing nature to the product of mind and so asserting the dominance of God and the soul over all. The same was true of Transcendentalism in this country. But of Idealists, Hegel had the singular advantage of having propounded an historical theory that depicted God as working through history to achieve His purpose. In the wake of Darwin, when theories of historical "development" were the order of the day, Hegel found a ready audience both here and in England. For many who felt their religious beliefs in jeopardy but who also believed in science, Idealism offered a viable position. If nature is the ideas of God displayed for our edification, then the study of nature cannot lead us astray, provided it is done with a due understanding of what it is we are studying.[9]

But Idealism offered more than a guarantee that God still reigned; it also wedded fact and value. One could debate whether the good was in the evolutionary process itself or external to it, but on Idealistic principles the world was a moral system and our knowledge of nature was therefore both a knowledge of fact and a knowledge of morality—indeed, the two were hardly distinct. Our ethical principles and our values were rooted in the nature of reality and were objective truths, just as the law of gravity was. Man was at home in a universe that cared about him and in which to be a moral actor was to be in harmony with the nature of things.

Among those who found in Idealism a congenial way of reconciling science and religion and who influenced Lewis deeply, was Charles Peirce. The son of the country's leading mathematician, Peirce was trained in the mathematical and physical sciences; although his degree from Harvard was in chemistry, he spent his professional life as a physicist working for the U.S. Coast and Geodetic Survey. Peirce thus had a thorough knowledge of the hard sciences, and was also an excellent mathematician; some of his most important contributions were made in mathematical logic. But, in addition, he was also a post-Kantian Idealist, and although the character of his Idealism changed as he grew older, he remained an Idealist throughout. The general character of his philosophy can best be described as an attempt to create an evolutionary cosmology on Idealistic principles that would support both science and religion.

Peirce is best known as the founder of Pragmatism and it was in this respect that he most influenced Lewis. In the early 1870s, Peirce and a group of friends who included William James, Chauncey Wright, and Oliver Wendell Holmes met in a discussion group that was called, half-jokingly, the Metaphysical Club. At this point, Peirce was developing a new theory of inquiry, and he presented a paper before the club that set it out. Apparently, in the discussion that followed, Peirce did use the term "pragmatism" to describe his theory, though he could not later recall having done so. In 1878, Peirce published a series of articles in *Popular Science Monthly* that outlined his theory of inquiry, and in one of them—"How to Make Our Ideas Clear"—he stated the famous maxim: "Consider what effects, which might conceivably have practical bearings, we conceive the object of our conception to have. Then, our conception of these effects is the whole of our conception of the object."[10] Nowhere in this, or any of his other papers of the period, did Peirce use the term "pragmatism," nor did he give this theory any particular designation. But, in 1898, William James, remembering the discussions of the early 1870s, quoted the maxim that he attributed to Peirce, and said Peirce had labeled it pragmatism.[11] Thus, Peirce became known as the founder of Pragmatism, a fact he found embarrassing because, by 1898, he had changed his position and did not agree with James's use of the term.

Although Peirce taught for a few years at Johns Hopkins, his career was made in the Coast Survey. Nevertheless, he exerted a considerable influence on William James and Josiah Royce, who were among Lewis's teachers at Harvard. James received an M.D. from Harvard Medical School, so he was a thoroughly trained biological scientist. Although he embraced evolution, he was appalled by the determinism of writers like Spencer, and this intellectual problem contributed to the profound depression he experienced in the late 1860s. According to his own account, he was rescued from this state of emotional collapse by reading Renouvier, whose argument convinced him to adopt the freedom of the will as a working hypothesis and to act on it. It also helped that in 1872 he became an instructor in anatomy and physiology at Harvard. But James was well aware that simply postulating freedom of the will did not constitute a proof that the will was free, and he was unable to find such a proof either in the materialists such as Spencer or in Idealism.[12]

Nothing better shows the genius of William James than his recognition that the fundamental issue of the evolutionary controversy was the nature of the human mind. In 1878, James began working on psychology; in 1880, he was appointed assistant professor of philosophy, and, in 1890, he published a 1400-page treatise entitled *The Principles of Psychology* that immediately became, and for decades remained, the leading work on psychology in the United States. This book provided the psychological frame of reference for all the Pragmatists who came after him. It was based on twelve years of research and a thorough grasp of the literature of the field. As was true of most psychologies of the time, it dealt extensively with cognition, but from a scientific point of view—that is, with *how* we know. This enabled James to explore issues of knowledge while at the same time to avoid philosophic questions as lying outside the scope of psychology. James also relied on both experimental results and introspection, and one of the strengths of the work was that James was an exceptional psychological observer. James justified his method by noting that awareness of mental states was simply a fact and, as such, constituted data for psychology.[13]

James considered an organism as a system for processing stimuli and responding to them. The mind is thus part of a physical system. Consciousness, James says, is "an organ added for the sake of steering a nervous system grown too complex to steer itself." James's famous chapter on the "stream of thought" is the key to the book. What he describes is the ever-changing stream of consciousness; what is in consciousness includes feelings, thoughts—all mental contents that we are aware of. James's ability as an observer is obvious in his attention not only to the focus of attention in the stream but to the fringe as well, to feelings of tendency, to variations in the rate of movement of the contents that he describes as "flights" and "perches," to the felt character of the stream as "mine," and to its continuity. The stream is a jumble of contents poured in by the senses, the body, thought itself, the emotions—all the receptors of the organism. There are no atomic units such as the simple ideas of Locke, no discrete impressions, but a continuous welter of contents.

It is the function of attention to carve a coherent world out of this on-rushing jumble. As James notes, the senses themselves are selective in what they admit. So, too, is attention selective in picking out some contents and ignoring others.

> The mind, in short, works on the data it receives very much as a sculptor works on his block of stone. In a sense the statue stood there from eternity. But there were a thousand different ones beside it, and the sculptor alone is to thank for having extricated this one from the rest. . . . Other sculptors, other statues from the same stone! Other minds, other worlds from the same monotonous and inexpressive chaos![14]

The mind makes it own world by selection, and the selection is governed by our interests and our purposes. Our knowledge is for action, and the conceptual structures we build are really plans for actions designed to satisfy our wants. There is thus no division between knowing and willing; to attend to this rather than that is an act of will. James takes voluntary action to be a psychological fact. Similarly, that some mental states signify existing objects is taken as a fact of psychology. In neither case does James feel compelled to provide philosophical justifications; he is doing psychology, not philosophy. Thus, the psychological picture James presents is that of a creature whose knowledge and purposes lead to intentional actions designed to solve the organism's problems. But there is no determinism here. James's human is a natural creature operating in an environment, but doing so freely and acting on the basis of individual values and purposes. There is indeed a sensory given, but each person creates his or her own world; the environment is not given but made. It should be obvious that James is very close to Idealism here, but by the pose of doing science rather than philosophy, he can avoid having to declare a philosophical position.

In the late 1890s, however, James realized that his psychology provided the basis for a philosophic position. Harking back to Peirce's doctrine of the 1870s, James turned what had been a theory of meaning into a theory of truth. An "idea" is true, James held, if its consequences are true—that is, if acting on the basis of the idea leads to the anticipated effects. Thus, he held that his idea of Memorial Hall was true if, following the plan involved in the idea, when he went to a particular place he saw what he expected to see. Truth, therefore, is a relation within experience, not a relation between experience and something beyond it. An idea is true if the experiences one predicts on the basis of the idea occur in the predicted manner; if they do not thus occur, the idea is false. This is not a copy theory of truth, and clearly James's psychology would permit no copy theory of truth.

As James elaborated his theory of truth, he found three criteria essential. The first is verification. An idea [proposition] has consequences; if it is true, then certain experiences must occur. The verification of the idea [proposition] consists in determining whether the predicted experiential consequences actually occur. The second criterion is assimilation. The idea [proposition] must be consistent with the body of knowledge we already have. If it is not, then something is wrong; either the idea is false or some part of our accepted structure of beliefs is wrong. Either way, an adjustment must be made to make our new belief consistent with our stock of established beliefs. These two criteria are primary; if both are satisfied by two alternative hypotheses, then the choice between them must be on grounds such as simplicity and elegance. Obviously, James is here laying down criteria that will square his theory with science. But James also says that the true is a species of the good. What James means by this is that since knowledge is for action, and action is for the purpose of attaining satisfactions or "goods," then truth itself is a good because it helps us to attain further goods. So far, James's theory would be acceptable to any scientist. But James went further. In "The Will to Believe," he tried to justify religious belief on the grounds that the consequences of believing in God were desirable. The argument is carefully hedged; it pertains to situations of vital importance in which one is forced to choose between competing hypotheses—that is, where not to choose is to choose—and where no evidence can decide the issue. But this was a long step beyond any scientific decision procedure.

There was a further problem for James. Having defined truth as a relation within experience, he appeared to have cut himself off from the external world, if there was an external world. James's answer to that was Radical Empiricism. There is, James said, nothing but experience. Taking an idea from his old Metaphysical Club partner Chauncey Wright, James claimed that experience by itself is neither subjective nor objective. We classify it as one or the other, depending on the relations in which it stands. If an experience is alterable at my will, exhibits regularities by association, and is recallable when I choose, I call it subjective; if it resists my will, stands in relatively invariable temporal and spatial relations to other experiences, and exhibits regularities of the sort we call natural laws, then we call it objective. But the same experience can be both subjective and objective, just as a point can lie on two lines at once. There is nothing but pure experience; everything else is constructed from that.

But this left James with two problems: what happens to the desk in the next room when no one experiences it? And how can two people know the same thing? James's answer to the first was panpsychism; the desk is alive and experiences itself. The answer to the second was continuity; the world consists of experiences that are continuous with each other and therefore sharable. That this created logical problems bothered James not at all; he renounced logic as a system of abstractions that falsified experience. Thus, James affirmed a type of Idealism, but a pluralistic Idealism that left room for human freedom, for moral striving, and for God.[15]

James was not the only Idealist at Harvard at this time. George Herbert Palmer, Hugo Munsterberg, and Josiah Royce were all Idealists.[16] But of them all, Royce was the preeminent figure. Royce was both an Absolute Idealist and profoundly religious, and some of his philosophic work was clearly theological. In *The Religious Aspect of Philosophy* in 1885, Royce gave the basic proof of his Idealism. Does error exist?, Royce asked. It must, for consider the statement "There is error." If the statement is true, there is error. If the statement is false, then there is error. Therefore, there is error. But what is error? A statement is in error if it does not correspond to its object. But what is the object referred to? A statement about a particular tree must correspond to *that* tree, not just to any tree. In other words, reference is intentional; the statement must correspond to its intended object. But for one to intend a given object, one must already know the object, and how can one be wrong about an object one already knows? Royce's famous example is the case of John and Thomas, each of whom refers to the other. But when John refers to Thomas, it is to Thomas as John conceives him that he refers, and John can hardly be in error about his own idea of Thomas, nor can Thomas be in error about his own idea of John. For error to be possible in this situation, a third knower is required who can compare John's idea of Thomas with real Thomas, and Thomas's idea of John with real John. But then we face a regress, for the third knower can only know his ideas of John and Thomas, and so we would need a fourth knower to guarantee the third knower's ideas, and so on. The solution, Royce held, is that John and Thomas are both ideas in the mind of the third knower, for about his own ideas the third knower cannot be in error. John and Thomas are therefore ideal; the third knower is the Absolute who knows not only what John and Thomas think but what they intended—namely, the real John and Thomas. This is possible in the same sense in which one can intend to recall a name one knows but cannot bring to mind. John and Thomas can intend each other as they really are, yet only be able to think of each other erroneously. But the Absolute, whose ideas John and Thomas are, also knows their unconscious intentions, and so can compare the two. This argument led Royce to conclude that whatever we can be wrong about, and so whatever we can make true statements about, must be ideas in the mind of the Absolute. The world is therefore Ideal.

Royce was also deeply interested in psychology and greatly influenced by James's great work. Royce, too, believed that knowing was a form of willing and that ideas are plans of action. In his own text on psychology, published in 1903, Royce used James's stream of consciousness and his view of ideas and will to create a psychological model that would underwrite his own theory of the human self and its conduct.

In 1901, Royce published *The World and the Individual*, which must rank as his major work. Royce drew a distinction between the internal meaning of an idea and its external meaning. By the internal meaning, Royce means the purpose or intention of the idea. But remembering here that ideas are plans of action, and that they summarize and epitomize our past experience, the internal meaning is a purpose in a special sense. Royce asserts that ideas always refer beyond themselves, that they seek something beyond present experience. The purpose of the idea as Royce conceives it is not just to find its referent but to synthesize experience in such a way as to create the sought-for referent. The external meaning of the idea is that sought-for referent that is the goal of the internal meaning. For since we are ideas of the Absolute, our ideas and actions are those of the Absolute, and the process of thought by which we seek out the external meaning is just that by which the Absolute creates this referent we seek.

The referent is, Royce says, an "individual." This term has a special meaning for Royce. No individual, he says, can be defined by concepts because concepts are always general. My idea of a hat is of a type of object, not a completely determinate individual. No complex of concepts can therefore define an individual; it would require an infinite series of determinations to create a completely determinate object. What serves as the principle of individuation is rather "exclusive interest"—in other words, love. This is an interest that distinguishes the object and denies the possibility of any equivalent object. Such an exclusive interest is an act of will, and the object so defined is the fulfillment of the purpose of the idea. Because such an individual is infinitely determinate, any process of inquiry by a finite being would have to be infinitely extended, so the true individual object can only be realized by the Absolute. We as finite minds contribute to the creation of these external meanings but what we are seeking is something only completed by the Absolute. Thus, Divine Love does individuate the world, and it is our privilege to contribute to that work.

But Royce found himself confronting a problem here. The English Idealist F. H. Bradley had argued that we cannot conceive how the Absolute combines the one and the many because such a combination involves the use of relations, and any relation dissolves into an infinite regress. Consider the relation aRb. What is the relation of R to a? There must be another relation R' linking a to R, so aRb becomes $aR'Rb$. But then the same issue arises regarding the relation of R' to a, and so on. In a supplementary essay to *The World and the Individual*, Royce argued that Bradley was wrong because the natural numbers provide just such an example of the combination of the one and the many. Consider the thought S. We can then define the series S, my thought of S, my thought of my thought of S, and so on. This series is infinite, having the same order as the series of natural numbers, but it is defined by the single resolve to be fully self-conscious regarding my thoughts. It is indeed the structure of self-consciousness, and so must characterize both human beings and the Absolute. That is possible since such a series can contain any number of subseries having the same infinite number of elements—for example, the even numbers are a subset of the natural numbers, but both have the same cardinality. What is notable here is Royce's use of the mathematical ideas of Dedekind and Cantor to solve his philosophical problem. No American philosopher except Peirce had done that before.

In the second volume of *The World and the Individual*, Royce returned to a question that he had previously struggled with—the difference between public knowledge and private. Some things we can describe in terms that others can grasp—for example, physical objects. Other things we cannot so describe—for example, private feelings. These two domains Royce labels the worlds of description and appreciation. Both are real, and are known to the Absolute, but we can only share the world of description with other human beings. Why? What is special about the world of description, Royce says, is that all its classifications are based on likeness and difference. These are reciprocal notions; to state that two books are different is to say they are both books; to say two girls look alike is to discriminate them as separate persons. Further, Royce argues that such discrimination has always a certain logical structure; between any two things discriminated, there is a third. Thus, the act of discrimination results in a dense series, like that of the rational numbers, whereas the world of appreciation is characterized by well-ordered series, as illustrated by self-consciousness. Here again, Royce is seeking to use mathematical notions to solve his problems.

Royce was fascinated by the new work in logic and mathematics that was appearing at this time, and followed these developments closely. Traditionally, such concepts as infinity had been associated with the divine. The fact that there were now mathematical theories of infinity suggested to Royce that it might be possible to develop a mathematical characterization of the Absolute, or at least of some aspects of the Absolute, and so reconcile the characterizations he had given of the worlds of description and appreciation. In 1905, Royce published a paper entitled "The Relation of the Principles of Logic to the Foundations of Geometry."[17] Building on the earlier work of the English mathematician Alfred Kempe, who had attempted a similar project in 1886, Royce set out his system in formal fashion. He defined a system, Σ, that contained n "elements," all of them "simple and homogeneous," and also contained all collections of these elements, all collections of those collections, and so on. As variables for elements, he used lowercase Latin letters, as variables for collections, Greek letters. Collections are also symbolized by enclosing the elements in parentheses—thus, "(a,b)" is the collection of the elements "a" and "b." Royce then defined his basic relation, the symmetric "O" relation, where "O" stands for "obverse." "O" collections are written as "$O(xy)$"; the order of the elements is immaterial, so "$O(xy) = O(yx)$." Any collection that is not an "O" collection is an "E" collection. Any two elements, "x" and "y," are called equivalent, written "$x = y$," if the substitution of one for the other in any "O" collection leaves the collection an "O" collection; if such a substitution changes the "O" collection into an "E" collection, the two elements are not equivalent.

Royce then gives six postulates for Σ.

I. $(\phi) (\psi) [O(\phi) \supset O(\phi\psi)]$
II. $(x) (\phi) (\psi) \{[(x \varepsilon \psi) \ \& \ O(\psi) \ \& \ O(x\phi)] \supset O(\phi)\}$
III. $(\exists x) (x \varepsilon \Sigma)$
IV. $(x) \{(x \varepsilon \Sigma) \supset (\exists z) [(z \varepsilon \Sigma) \ \& \ (x \neq z)]\}$
V. $(x) (y) \{(x \neq y) \supset (\exists z) [E(zx) \ \& \ E(zy) \ \& \ O(xyz)]\}$
VI. $(\exists x) (\phi) \{O(\phi x) \supset (\exists z) (O(\phi z) \ \& \ (w) [(w \varepsilon \phi) \supset O(xzy)])\}$

Postulates III through VI guarantee that there are an infinite number of elements in Σ. Royce then shows that all obverses of a given element are equivalent, that obverses of equivalent elements are equivalent, and that obverses of non-equivalent elements are non-equivalent. Since all obverses of a given element x are then equivalent, a single element can be chosen as representative of that class and called $\bar{x}$.

Royce proves a number of theorems about "O" collections. He then introduces the notion of an "F" collection, defined as

$$F(x/y) = df \ O(x\bar{y}) \qquad \text{or} \qquad O(\bar{x}y)$$

Of special interest are the triadic "F" collections, written as $F(xy/z)$ or $z \prec \substack{x \\ y}$. He then proves that

i. $(x)(z)(x \prec \substack{z \\ z})$
ii. $(x)(z)(z \prec \substack{z \\ x})$
iii. $(x)(y)(z)(w)\{[(x \prec \substack{y \\ w}) \ \& \ (y \prec \substack{z \\ w})] \supset (x \prec \substack{z \\ w})\}$

where w is referred to as the origin. After defining a "conjugate pair" of a collection θ, written $J(ps/θ)$, which are two elements bearing a unique relation to the collection θ, he turns to logic.

> It is now possible, without further difficulty, to point out that the elements of Σ possess the properties of a system of logical classes, or of entities to which the ordinary algebra of logic applies. Let the arbitrarily assumed origin y be taken as the 0 of the ordinary algebra of logic. Let $\bar{y}$ be taken as the 1 of that algebra. . . . Let the relation $p \prec_y q$ be regarded as the usual relation of logical antecedent to consequent; and let the subscript of the symbol $\prec_y$ be dropped, by virtue of that usual convention which regards the reference to 0, not as a reference to an arbitrary origin, but as such that $a \prec b$ has an invariant and absolute sense. So regarded, the system possesses an element, 0, such that whatever element x be chosen, $0 \prec x$; and also an element, 1, such that whatever element z be chosen, $z \prec 1$. The relation $\prec$ is transitive. If $a \prec b$ and $b \prec a$, then $a = b$. If $a \prec b$ and $a \neq b$, the relation $\prec$ is asymmetrical. Elements such as p and s may first be viewed as determined by some given pair of elements, e.g., by the pair (a,b). The element p is then called the *product*, the element s is called the *sum* of this pair; and, in the usual symbols, one may write
>
> $$ab = p; \qquad a + b = s$$
>
> The definitions of the operations of logical multiplication and of logical addition, may assume the form explained [above]. Obverses will now appear as elements each of which is what is ordinarily called the negative of the other.[18]

Royce's "F" relation allows him to define "betweenness," since "$F(xy/z)$" can be taken as "z" is between "x" and "y." Royce makes the point that this relation can be applied in logic, a fact he illustrates by the diagram

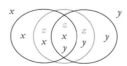

Here "$x \cap y \subset z \subset x \cup y$." Royce believed that whenever "$x \supset y$," then there existed a "z" such that "$x \supset z \supset y$." This is a point to which we will return. Royce also sought to show that by due selection of elements of Σ, he could obtain plane affine and projective geometry.

It is vital to recognize that the relation of logic and geometry to Σ is not one of logical deducibility. Rather, the relation Royce employs is modeled on that of the geometries in Felix Klein's Erlanger Program—a classification of the geometries in terms of generality in which the more general are presupposed by the less general. This is the relation that holds between logic and geometry. Both are obtainable from Σ when the appropriate selections of elements are made. But since all elements of Σ are "simple and homogeneous," there is no way of making that selection without the addition of postulates that will single out the required elements. This is not, one should note, a criticism of Royce's work, but a clarification of what he achieved.

Although Royce presented Σ as an abstract formal system, he had in mind from the beginning a particular interpretation of it. Thus, he says of the "O" relation that it "is the relation in which (if we were talking of the possible chances open to one who had to decided upon a course of action) any set of *exhaustive but, in their entirety, inconsistent choices* would stand to one another."[19] By 1914, Royce had developed this interpretation further; Σ applied, he said, to "certain possible modes of action that are open to any rational being who can act at all, and who can also reflect upon his own modes of possible action."[20] Thus, any mode of action has a negative—not so acting; for any two modes of action there is a logical product—doing both, and a logical sum—doing either or both. There is a zero element—doing nothing, and its contradictory—to act "in any way whatever which involves '*not doing nothing*.'"[21] The totality of modes of action cannot be defined without running into Russell's paradox, but a "logical universe" of modes of action can be defined "*in case* there is some rational being who is capable of performing some one single possible act"[22] and who notes every action he takes required by the performance of that act. This is, of course, the Absolute. Further, Royce believes that not only do the principles of logic apply to the modes of action, but so also does the betweenness principle. Apparently what Royce meant by this is that if a mode of action "x" implies a mode of action "y," then, since the doer of these action is a "rational being" who must be self-conscious, if doing "x" implies doing "y" it must first imply willing to do "y," which implies doing "y." One can then hold that if "x" implies willing to do "y", for such a reflective being it implies willing to will to do "y," and so on. This would result in a dense series. But the problem of reconciling description and appreciation is not thereby solved. Even if the well-ordered series of appreciation and the dense series of description are both obtainable from Σ by selection, the order of the one is not compatible with the order of the other. Royce's attempt to find a mathematical model of the mind of the Absolute did not succeed.

Royce's form of Absolute Idealism was a monism that the pluralist James found unacceptable, and for years the two men carried on a running argument. But Royce also characterized himself as a pragmatist, albeit an Absolute Pragmatist. With respect to the empirical claims of the sciences and the categorical concepts on which they were based, Royce could be as pragmatic as James. But other propositions for which truth was claimed had a different status. These include the propositions established by dialectical argument. Any such propositions "are known to us indeed both empirically and pragmatically (since we note their presence and learn of them through action); but they are also absolute. And any account which succeeds in telling what they are has absolute truth."[23] Moreover, Royce included among the principles of science certain propositions that he called "leading ideas." His best example of these was Virchow's definition of disease as "the course of the vital processes under altered conditions."[24] Such a proposition is neither confirmable or infirmable; it is a regulative principle that guides research. Such principles are decisions to interpret experience in a particular way and, although they are a priori, their justification is pragmatic.[25]

Among the philosophers Lewis studied with, Royce was the most theologically oriented; his *Sources of Religious Insight* was an attempt to define a type of synthetic grasp of many items in one whole that would yield a religious interpretation, and his *Problem of Christianity* was nothing less than an attempt to put an Idealistic floor under Christianity. But James was no less religious, as his *Varieties of Religious Experience* showed, and Palmer and Munsterberg were equally so. Santayana was the chief exception to this Idealistic and Christian consensus, and although Lewis took a course with Santayana on Greek philosophy, his own outlook was not influenced by him. This was the context in which Lewis began his college studies. Education at Harvard, as everywhere in the United States at that time, was still dominated by Christian beliefs and ideals, and Idealism was the reigning movement in American philosophy. The role of science in American college education was rapidly increasing, and the influence of Darwin was everywhere apparent, but Idealism had become the accepted answer of philosophy to the threat of evolutionary science. Pragmatism was one variant of Idealism that had become particularly influential at Harvard, where Lewis encountered it.

Biographical Note I

Early Years

Clarence Irving Lewis was born on April 12, 1883, in Stoneham, Massachusetts. His parents were from New Hampshire and, as Lewis himself remarked, "both by inheritance and in temperament, I am, I think, an up-country New England Yankee."[1] His greatgrandfather, Ebenezer Lewis, had been a blacksmith in Pelham, New Hampshire. His grandfather, Andrew Lewis, was born in Boston in 1817 but grew up in New Hampshire, where he, too, was a blacksmith. Lewis's father, Irving Lewis, was born in Pelham on March 18, 1852;[2] he became a shoemaker, but he was also a highly intelligent man and a reformer devoted to "good causes."[3] In the 1870s, he was a temperance advocate—a cause popular in New Hampshire that won him some acclaim. But when he later became an advocate of the Knights of Labor and actively participated in a strike, his popularity, and his job, and then his home, vanished. He was blacklisted, and for some years—years of severe poverty—had great difficulty in obtaining employment. Eventually he found work as a shoefinisher. This experience seems only to have intensified his beliefs and he became a committed Fabian Socialist. Lewis, of course, imbibed his father's views; he read Marx and Edward Bellamy at what he described as an "absurdly early age" and accompanied his father to meetings where he heard Samuel Gompers and Eugene Debs.[4] But Irving Lewis found that as time went on the socialist movement was taken over by "foreign agitators." He became disillusioned and embittered; although he still believed in the cause, he could not accept the way it was carried on.[5] How much his father's disillusion affected Lewis we do not know, but it may have been a factor in his later political conservatism.

Lewis's mother's family also came from New Hampshire. Her father, Edson Dearth, sired eight children, of whom the oldest, Samuel Willey Dearth, was the "Uncle Will" who played an important part in Lewis's early life. His mother was the fifth child—Hannah Carlin Dearth, though there is some question about her middle name. She called herself "Carrie," and signed her name "Caroline" or "Carolyn" as the spirit moved her, so "Carlin" may have been a misspelling for "Carolyn." The Dearths, like the Lewises, were very poor and received a rigorous upbringing. Lewis's wife recalled that "discipline in the family was strict. The children *stood* around the table at meals . . . and it was a *rule* that they did not speak, except to ask permission for this or that, unless spoken to."[6]

Clarence Lewis was the oldest of five children of this couple. His sister Mina (pronounced "Myna") was born on June 16, 1885, followed by brothers Edson, born December 12, 1887, Raymond, born September 16, 1890, and Paul, born July 9, 1893.[7] Lewis was devoted to his mother and father. He was fond of his sister Mina, a woman of considerable intelligence who worked problems in calculus for fun. She never married, and in later years Lewis helped her financially as she moved from one boardinghouse to another. Lewis was close to his brother Edson, who became a printer for the *Christian Science Monitor*, but not to his other brothers. Raymond became a truck driver and Paul a janitor. None of them achieved a higher education or any particular attainments in the course of their lives.[8]

When she married Irving Lewis, Hannah Dearth was fourteen years his junior, and evidently wanted more gaiety than she got. She stuck it out for forty years before finally divorcing him.[9] Her children were greatly distressed by the divorce, which, at that time and place, was certainly a traumatic event, and when she remarried a man named Billy Mills, whom her grandson described as a "simple hearty soul," her three younger children were very antagonistic. What Lewis thought of him we do not know. But all of her children seem to have remained devoted to her.[10]

As the eldest son, Lewis worked to help the family. At seven, he had a long paper route and collected coal for the family from along the railroad tracks and at the railroad roundhouse where the fireboxes were dumped after a run.[11] During the time he was in high school, he worked for four years at Pray's Sign Shop and for three years as a shoefinisher at John J. Page's Boot and Shoe Factory.[12] The money saved from these jobs enabled him to enter Harvard.

Lewis attended Haverhill public schools. After his family moved to Bradford, he went to Bradford High School, but when Haverhill and Bradford merged, he attended Haverhill High School, where he met Mabel Maxwell Graves, whom he fell in love with on first sight.[13] Mabel's parents, Harry Albert Graves and Mary Anna Maxwell, both came from

Nova Scotia. Her father was a carpenter and, although a good workman, made little money[14] so the financial position of the Graves was not that different from the Lewises. Mabel, however, had literary aspirations and was determined to obtain a college education, even though she knew she would have to pay her own way.

Lewis and Mabel were both outstanding students at Haverhill High School, though Lewis's grades suffered from his having to work as well as his efforts on the football team. When he applied to Harvard, Allison Tuttle, his teacher at Haverhill, wrote in his recommendation:

> We consider Mr. C. I. Lewis one of our most worthy and capable young men. His ability is far above the average and I have never seen or heard anything to criticize in his character.
> He has been one of the leaders of his class in scholarship and would have stood much higher but for the fact of working so hard to get money to take him through school and into college.[15]

It is to Harvard's credit that they took his recommendations more seriously than his grades—something that one doubts would happen today. Looking back years later, Lewis gave his high school good marks for the education he had received. He took Latin, Greek, and French, and received a good grounding in mathematics and physics. He believed that since he was working four hours a day in the shoe factory he could never have met the entrance requirements for Harvard had it not been for the excellence of his high school preparation. But even before he went to college, Lewis was already "bent upon philosophy." "At about the age of thirteen, I had found myself beset with puzzles which, as far as I could discern, came out of the blue and had no antecedents."[16] These were, as he himself noted, partly the result of the differences between his father's views and his mother's, but for a boy already reading the sort of fare he was captivated by, it is not surprising that puzzles about the nature and extent of the universe should have arisen. So, too, did questions about orthodox religion. In his early intellectual struggles, he found an unlikely ally.

> In the summer when I was fifteen I encountered, on the upland farm in Jackson, New Hampshire, where I was working, a little old lady who drew me out and encouraged discussion by confessing that she also was a heretic. I can still see her sprightly figure and little smile as we would sit on the porch at the end of the day, watching the mountains turn to black shadows in the twilight and comparing notes about the universe.[17]

Either from her or some other source, Lewis was inspired to read histories of philosophy. He records having read Marshall's *History of Greek Philosophy* and also Zeller's and at least looking into Ueberweg. This interest in Greek philosophy never left him, and his works are studded with references to Greek thinkers. He also read Herbert Spencer's *First Principles*—a book that made a lasting impression. In later years, Lewis assigned Spencer's works in his classes long after the great vogue for Spencer had passed.[18]

Lewis entered Harvard in 1902. Because his parents were not able to help him financially, he, like many others at that time, had to work to earn his tuition—then one hundred and fifty dollars a year.[19] During the summers, he worked in resort hotels in New Hampshire's White Mountains. In the summer of 1903, he was an assistant headwaiter at the Deer Park Hotel in North Woodstock, and in 1904 was promoted to headwaiter. In the summer of 1905, he worked at the Hotel Pilgrim, and, in the summer of 1906, was headwaiter at the Profile House in Franconia.[20] These were not cheap hotels; a tourist guide of the time described the Deer Park Hotel as "North Woodstock's leading house" with "all the attractions to be usually found in a first-class resort." Similar terms are used to depict the others.[21] During the school term, he worked as a waiter in the Randall dining hall at Harvard and did such odd jobs as he could find, including singing in church choirs.[22] But these were not enough. In 1905–1906 he was forced to take a leave of absence from Harvard and to work at Quincy High School teaching English—an experience that Lewis described as "miserable" and of which he remembered, "It was the low point of my career."[23] It did, however, enable him to graduate from Harvard.

Lewis remarked of his Harvard experience that "my chief interests at Harvard were Philosophy, English and Economics, in the order named."[24] But it was the philosophy department that most drew his interest—Royce, James, Munsterberg, Palmer, and Woods. He did not meet Santayana until his senior year and Perry was not yet at Harvard. Of his encounters with James and Royce, Lewis has left the following description:

> In my third and final year, I took the famous course in metaphysics which James and Royce divided between them and in which each gave some attention to shortcomings in the other's views. It was immense. James, I thought, scored the most points, but Royce won on a technical knockout. James's quick thrusts and parries, his striking apercus, and his stubborn sense of mundane fact were not well matched against Royce's ponderous and indefatigable cogency. Royce became then, and remained thereafter, my ideal of a philosopher.
>
> It also impressed me that James and Royce had more in common— particularly the voluntaristic strain—than either of them recognized; and I was later gratified by Royce's reference to what he called his "absolute pragmatism." I should be glad to think that the "conceptual pragmatism"

of *Mind and the World Order* had its roots in that same ground; indeed the general tenor of my own philosophic thinking may have taken shape under the influence of that course.[25]

The strain of trying to make ends meet while carrying a full course load was severe, and, after completing the required undergraduate program in three years, Lewis decided against going on, though with considerable regret. He particularly regretted not having taken more training in mathematics and science, and in German, in which he felt he lacked "real facility."[26] Probably because he was awarded his B.A. with "honorable mention in Philosophy and English," he received an appointment as Instructor in English at the University of Colorado in Boulder.[27] Lewis enjoyed Boulder; he liked the mountain environment and he liked the students, many of them working their way through college as he had. Lewis recognized in them qualities of self-reliance and independence that he valued from his own background.

At the end of his first term at Boulder, Lewis married Mabel.[28] After they had graduated from high school, Mabel had gone to work to earn enough money to enter Mount Holyoke. It took two years of cashiering in a china shop, but she did it and managed to complete her first two years, although she ran out of money before the end of her sophomore year and was able to finish only by the grace of a grant from the college and help from friends.[29] She identified strongly with Mount Holyoke, and ever after attended its reunions whenever possible.[30] But Lewis's proposal of marriage looked more attractive than the prospect of working several more years to earn enough to finish college, and she thought she would be able to complete her last two years at Colorado University. They were married on New Year's Day, 1907.

The young couple's financial position was precarious. They were so poor that on their return trip to Colorado after their wedding, they had to travel by scalper tickets—literally buying parts of tickets unused by others.[31] But despite Lewis's meager salary, they enjoyed hiking, camping, and exploring the surrounding mountains. Mabel had to learn to cook in the high altitude, and proudly mastered the art of making excellent sponge cake at six thousand feet—a feat she was never quite able to duplicate at lower altitudes.[32] Their first child, Irving, named for Lewis's father, was born in Boulder on October 19, 1907.[33] But Lewis was not enchanted by teaching English.[34] Even though in his second year he was appointed an assistant in philosophy in addition to his position as an instructor in English, this was not what he really wanted to do. With Mabel's support, he decided to return to Harvard in 1908 to pursue graduate work in philosophy.[35]

By 1908, the situation at Harvard had changed somewhat. James had retired and Perry had joined the staff. Perry was only seven years older than Lewis and the two became fast friends—a friendship that lasted a lifetime. Lewis continued his interest in Greek philosophy by taking Santayana's course on Plato, and he took Perry's course on Kant.[36] As Lewis later wrote,

> Kant compelled me. He had, so I felt, followed skepticism to its inevitable last stage, and laid his foundations where they could not be disturbed. I was then, and have continued to be, impatient of those who seem not to face the skeptical doubt seriously. Kant attracted me also by his intellectual integrity and by the massiveness and articulation of his structure. The evidence of Kant in my thinking ever since is unmistakable, however little I may achieve the excellences which aroused my youthful admiration.[37]

Perry taught a thorough course, requiring weekly summaries of the sections of the *Critique* assigned—a practice Lewis was to follow in his own courses on Kant throughout his career,[38] and one that many of his students then used in their own courses on Kant.

He also took Perry's seminar on epistemology; he described it as the "liveliest in which I ever have participated"[39] and one in which the issues of the day came to a focus. Looking back a half-century later, Lewis described the philosophic situation of that time as a three-way contest between the dominant school of Absolute Idealism, Pragmatism, and the rising movement of New Realism, of which Moore and Russell were the leaders abroad and Perry and Montague the leaders in the United States. Lewis claims that he found none of these positions acceptable. He tells us that he rejected Idealistic metaphysics,[40] but also found James's confusing of truth and validity unacceptable, while the New Realist's view of the nature of real objects struck him as inadequate. Lewis remarked:

> I also thought that, within the area in which the controversy was mainly waged, we could have it both ways—provided requisite distinctions are made. Absolute truth and the validity of such knowledge of the real as is achievable by humans, are two different things. The validity of acceptable empirical beliefs concerns a relation of them to their given premises; to the data on which they must be judged. Truth is, by contrast, a metaphysical notion—in current jargon, semantic.[41]

Once it was recognized that empirical knowledge can never be certain, Lewis believed there was no contradiction between the Pragmatist's view of knowledge as justified advice for action and of belief as attested by results and the

Idealist's insistence on rationality as the permanent critique of cognitive validity and on an ideal of absolute truth.

Furthermore, Lewis says,

> I did agree with Perry's main contention: the idealistic premises do not establish the idealistic metaphysical conclusion. There was no justification in them for the reification of the cognitive ideal as absolute mind. The idealists had reverted to a metaphysical *non sequitur* against which they should have taken warning from Kant: they had mistaken a valid regulative ideal for a constitutive metaphysical principle.[42]

What precisely did Lewis mean by this? In a book published a few years later, Perry wrote that "the new idealism gives 'constitutive' validity to that 'ideal of the Unconditioned,' to which Kant had attributed only a 'regulative validity.' "[43] For Kant, the idea of God is unconditioned[44]—it is a transcendental idea that admits of only regulative use: "I accordingly maintain that transcendental ideas never allow of any constitutive employment. . . . On the other hand, they have an excellent, and indeed indispensably necessary, regulative employment."[45] Specifically, the idea of God,

> like all speculative ideas, seeks only to formulate the command of reason, that all connection in the world be viewed in accordance with the principles of systematic unity—*as if* all such connection had its source in one single all-embracing being, as the supreme and all-sufficient cause.[46]

When Lewis said of his experience in Perry's seminar, "I had left idealistic metaphysics permanently behind,"[47] he meant that for him the idea of the world as a wholly rational system was a regulative ideal, not a constitutive one. What this means, as Lewis later noted, is that for an Idealist, reality must have an "essentially know*able* character,"[48] rather than being something actually known.

But in what sense can such a regulative idea be *valid*? The ideas of reason apply, not to sense experience directly, but to the understanding.

> The understanding is an object for reason, just as sensibility is for the understanding. It is the business of reason to render the unity of all possible empirical acts of the understanding systematic; just as it is of the understanding to connect the manifold of the appearances by means of concepts, and to bring it under empirical laws.[49]

But if such a priori ideas are to have validity, they must admit of a transcendental deduction. This deduction is not the same as that of the categories, but it is nevertheless a transcendental deduction. There is, Kant says, a difference between something being given to reason as an "object absolutely" or as an "object in the idea." In the first case, our concepts determine the object. In the second, there is only a schema that enables us to represent other objects in their systematic unity. Thus, the concept of a highest intelligence is a heuristic concept, or regulative principle: if "we declare, for instance, that the things of the world must be viewed *as if* they received their existence from a highest intelligence,"[50] we unify the world by viewing its contents as if they were the products of an intelligent cause. Thus, to use Kant's example, having successfully developed various classifications of objects of our experience, why should we still seek a more general classification that will subsume these in a higher unity? To do so is to follow a regulative rule of reason to seek maximum unity in our knowledge.[51] Following such rules enables us to expand our knowledge without introducing any inconsistency and demonstrates their validity. It should be noted that such a "proof" is really pragmatic, though Kant did not so label it and neither did Lewis.

It is hard to see how Lewis could have "left idealistic metaphysics permanently behind" if he had never held that view. Lewis very likely had been a Roycean Idealist prior to this. But the emphasis in the previous statement should be on the word "metaphysics." Lewis still saw himself as an Idealist at this point, and always retained a deep respect for Idealism. Years later he wrote of the Idealism of that day:

> no successor philosophic movement strikes me as having anything like equal depth and breadth. It remains as one of the most profound and impressive answers to perennial philosophic questions, though now largely neglected and forgotten. I wonder if we shall not someday see revival of it.[52]

Lewis took Royce's course on symbolic logic and his "Seminary" on logic in 1909–1910. His notes from the courses survive[53] and show that the course covered the latest work in the field. These notes make it clear that what Royce was teaching at this point was what would subsequently be published in the *Encyclopedia of Philosophical Sciences* in 1914.[54] This fact is important because it means that Lewis knew Royce's ideas when he wrote his own dissertation. It is therefore necessary to look briefly at some of the positions Royce advanced.

Royce defined logic as "*the General Science of Order, the Theory of the Forms of any Orderly Realm of Objects*, real or ideal."[55] He then divided his paper into three sections. The first deals with logic as methodology and attempts to show that modern science depends on the development of order systems. After briefly discussing the importance of classification, and of systems of classification, Royce considered the comparative and statistical methods, and argued that both depend on establishing ordering relations among the objects with which they deal. "The Concept of Order is thus a fundamental one both for the Comparative and for the Statistical Methods."[56] This led him to the problem of induction, which, following Peirce's arguments concerning probable inference, he tried to reduce to the problem of fair sampling. All that is required for the validity of induction, Royce held, is that the domain in question have a "determinate constitution" allowing the identification of its elements, and "fair"—that is, random—sampling; no assertions regarding the uniformity of nature are necessary.[57] Thus, Lewis was introduced early to the problem of induction.

Modern science, Royce held, involves the development of deductive theories that are tested indirectly—in other words, the hypothetical–deductive–inductive method. Such indirect testing is described as *"sampling the possible consequences of given hypotheses* concerning the constitution or the laws of some realm of natural phenomena, *or of sampling facts viewed with reference to their relation to such hypotheses."*[58] Royce stresses that the success of the method depends on the theory having "a precise order-system of its own" that permits exact quantitative predictions that can be compared with observational results.[59] Thus, for Royce, modern science depended essentially on such order systems.

Part II is entitled "General Survey of the Types of Order." It is devoted to a survey of the "forms of thought" or "logical constants" that are "constructions" of our "own rational will"; they are, Royce said, "the forms of all rational activity." These include relations and their properties, individuals, and classes and their laws. These are the fundamental "logical constants" on which logic is based, and their relations are "absolute."[60] On the other hand, particular classifications are arbitrary; "They are, namely, the expressions of *postulates*, or voluntary acts, since all classification involves a more or less arbitrary norm or principle of classification."[61] This blending of the absolute and arbitrary led Royce to remark that

> The only possible answer to the question of *how* the absoluteness of the logical principles is thus consistent with the arbitrariness of each of the classifications which we make, lies in saying that the logical principles define precisely the nature of the "Will to act in an orderly fashion" or in other words of the "Will to be rational."[62]

The final section of Royce's paper is entitled "The Logical Genesis of the Types of Order." Here Royce announced his "Absolute Pragmatism." On the one hand, although relational systems and classes are our constructions, they are absolute since any attempt to deny them leads to their reaffirmation.

> Whatever actions are such, whatever types of actions are such, whatever results of activity, whatever conceptual constructions are such, that the very act of getting rid of them, or of thinking them away, logically implies their presence, are known to us indeed both empirically and pragmatically (since we note their presence and learn of them through action); but they are also absolute. And any account which succeeds in telling what they are has absolute truth. Such truth is a "construction" or "creation," for activity determines its nature. It is "found," for we observe it when we act.[63]

On the other hand, particular classifications are arbitrary and determined by pragmatic factors—what leads to the best explanation of phenomena. But it is the absolute character of logic in which Royce saw a hope for a new "Deduction of the Categories" that would reveal what was implied "in the nature of our rational activity."[64] Royce briefly notes Russell's views of the basis of logic, but he points to the contradictions of class theory as raising doubts about Russell's approach. As an alternative, he suggests the approach of Kempe and his own system Σ, which he interprets as a calculus of the "modes of action."[65] But Royce does not fully develop this alternative, pleading limitations of space.

In the two courses Lewis took with Royce, much of the material in this paper was covered. Among the authors discussed were MacColl, Russell, Helmholtz, Kronecker, Dedekind, Cantor, Huntington, Couturat, Poincare, Clifford, Hilbert, Boole, Schroder, Peirce, Ladd-Franklin, Kempe, and Royce's own system Σ. There was extensive discussion of Peirce's theory of probable inference and of Absolute Chance, or tychism, and also of the problem of induction. The theory of order was clearly the centerpiece: Lewis wrote in his notes, "What are some of the most characteristic processes of thinking? And results of? How shall we define clearness, system, unity? *Order*, the answer." "We control phenomena so far as we get them into order. This order is determined by the nature of our thinking." Lewis's notes also show discussion of the non-Euclidean geometries and the Erlanger program. The notes echo Royce on the absolute character of logic. "Absolute truth we have. It is exactly the truth about the categories or forms of thinking, and is fundamentally mathematical. We understand the experience presented to us exactly so far as we identify some of these forms in it."[66] He also refers to the specification of position as a natural law, having the same form as $v = gt$, to the location of a specific color as a fraction of the spectrum, and to the spectrum and the three-dimensional system of defining position as a schema imposed on experience by the mind. As will be obvious, much of what was covered in this course showed up in Lewis's dissertation.

Lewis's graduate career at Harvard was highly successful; his work was excellent and he impressed a number of his professors as a man of exceptional gifts. But these were also difficult years in several ways. Lewis was desperately short of money. Palmer, who was a self-appointed guardian angel of graduate students, secured some fellowship money for him, but, even so, the Lewises were "always so hungry," as his wife recorded. During the school year, he worked at the Randall dining hall, and for a brief time made extra money by printing the menus, tutoring, and tending Palmer's furnace.[67] In the summer, they went to New Hampshire, where Lewis worked in 1909 at Sinclair House, a resort hotel in Bethlehem.[68] He also worked on his Uncle Will's farm in North Haverhill, which Lewis's son described as "the tiniest, little, rockiest, awful, New Hampshire farm you ever saw."[69] Nevertheless, Will Dearth was a highly intelligent man with great humor whom Lewis felt at ease with and to whom he was very close. Lewis's son recalled:

> a great deal of that hardscrabble New Hampshire environment survived in dad, and I remember as a kid when we would go back up there and all of a sudden he would be talking the New Hampshire dialect. He would speak of "down the rud," and as a kid this infuriated me to have this— what I took to be an imposture—why is my father pretending to belong here? But you know my father did belong here.[70]

Uncle Will was in fact an important influence on Lewis's life. His wife recorded that "consciously or not, C built himself into an image of Uncle Will, whom he physically resembled more than he did his own father. One could ask for no finer pattern."[71] From his background, his family, and particularly his uncle, Lewis had early on internalized the values of thrift, hard work, independence, and individualism that were to characterize him throughout his life. Lewis's later praise of New England farmers thus had a solid base in his own experience.

But although the Lewises managed to cope with financial privation, their marriage was in trouble. Lewis expected Mabel to be an academic wife—that is, to perform the domestic duties expected of women of that time and subordinate her wishes to his.[72] Mabel had intellectual aspirations of her own; she wanted to complete her college education, and dreamed of becoming an author.[73] Lewis was not receptive to her aspirations, and she felt increasingly unhappy. As she later wrote,

> He seemed oblivious to me as a person. I was no longer a pal—a partner in the great enterprise of getting his degree. Instead I felt as if I were just

a necessary appurtenance. His ambitious drive was crowding me out of his life.[74]

But, for the time being, Mabel suffered in silence.

In 1910, Lewis presented his doctoral dissertation and received his Ph.D. He has left the following well-known account of his graduate career.

> Of my teachers at Harvard, Royce impressed me most. His ponderous cogency kept my steady attention, even though I never followed to his metaphysical conclusions. James, I thought, had a swift way of being right, but how he reached his conclusions was his own secret. Royce was, in fact, my paradigm of a philosopher, and I was prone to minimize the difference from him of such convictions as I had. It was Royce himself, finally, with my doctor's thesis before him, who pointed out the extent of these differences. He concluded by saying, with his usual dry humour, "I thought you were principally influenced by Perry, but I find he thinks you are principally influenced by me. Between us, we agreed that perhaps this is original."[75]

This thesis was Lewis's first major work and so we should examine it with some care.

1

_____

Idealism and Epistemology

Lewis entitled his dissertation "The Place of Intuition in Knowledge." In the Introduction, he is careful to specify what he means by "intuition" since the term has been variously used. He does not mean "intuition" in the pre-Kantian sense of "an entirely non-sensuous faculty of the mind, which renders judgment immediately certain,"[1] nor does he mean the Kantian "pure intuition."[2] Rather, "intuition indicates the presentation to mind of that which is sensuously—or sensitively—specific or qualitative and not previously 'constructed by thought.'" "Whatever in knowledge is not produced by the activity of thinking, or is not what it is because the principles of the understanding are what they are—whatever in knowledge is real for some other reason that (sic) that a rational will demands its reality"[3] is the "given" or "intuition." This is, as Lewis notes, very close to Kant's sensuous intuition.

Lewis divides philosophical positions into two groups that he calls Intuitionism and Actionism.[4] This is, he says, "the great divide in epistemology."[5] Under Intuitionism he groups empiricism, nominalism, and phenomenalism; under Actionism he puts rationalism and realism, voluntarism and intellectualism.[6] Clearly, "actionism" here means those who believe the "world order" is constructed by the action of mind, whereas "intuitionism" refers to those who believe that at least some aspects of the "world order" are not so constructed. As to Pragmatism, Lewis says that "it splits into two contrasting portions, the synthesis of which it is not easy to grasp."[7] One may, I think, assume that Lewis means James and Royce here. Can these two positions be reconciled? That is what Lewis will attempt to do.

31

In the time-honored method of dissertations, Lewis reviews the major positions on each side of the controversy. In Chapter II, "Radical Actionism," he discusses T. H. Green's relationism and what Lewis calls Rationalistic Voluntarism, which, although he does not say so, is obviously Royce's Idealism. Taking the former first, Lewis presents extended quotations to show that Green holds that whatever is is constituted by its relations—"Abstract the relations from the thing and there is nothing."[8] But if all that is consists of relations, what is related? Green sees the problem; feelings or sensations would appear to be the obvious relata. Yet Lewis says Green confuses the feeling as presupposed by the relations with the feeling when made an object of thought by being related. The existence of the former is denied; "to suppose a primary datum or matter of the individual's experience, wholly void of intellectual determination, is to suppose such experience to begin with what (sic) could not belong to or be an object of experience at all."[9] Yet if the relata are themselves composed of relations, and their relata have the same character, this would appear to launch Green on a regress, and would—if he construed thought as the product of a single individual. His escape, Lewis says, is to see it as "the product of the world process"[10] so that no starting point in sensation is ever required.

Green's position, Lewis holds, leads to the following antimony:

> Thesis: the object of thought is through and through 'made' by the thinking, and can admit nothing which is, in any other sense, given. To hold that anything is 'given' and not 'made' is to contradict one's self.
>
> Antithesis: In some part the object of thought must be given, and not 'made' by the activity of thinking. For the activity of thought can produce only relations, and the relations presuppose a something related.[11]

Furthermore, Lewis holds that Green's account of knowledge is false to our experience, for "there is nothing of which we are more immediately aware than of feeling as such." Any account of our knowing process that fails to account for that fact cannot be true. If "knowledge" were redefined to exclude feeling and sensation, it would exclude perception, memory, and imagination, and would fail to be what we call knowledge.[12]

Lewis then turns to Rationalistic Voluntarism. Descartes's philosophy, he says, led to the egocentric predicament made famous by Perry that must be solved by any theory of knowledge.[13] Briefly, the egocentric predicament is this. Anything that can be known, say "x," stands in a relation "R" to some knower "E". "R" here can be any "form of consciousness that relates to an object"—for example, thinking, perceiving, desiring, and so on. The problem is, how does "x's" standing in "R" to "E" modify "x"? The problem admits of no solution, since any solution would require a comparison of "x"

when not modified by its relation "R" to "E" with "x" when so modified. But "x" can never be known except when it stands in "R" to "E". Therefore, we can never know to what extent, if any, "x" is modified by being known.[14] Rationalistic Voluntarism's answer to that is:

> An idea is not only a present experience; an idea is a purpose, intending its own object or other. And because an idea is such a purpose, its object must be a determinate existence. Only so far as we succeed in getting our ideas realized in experience, can we regard them as valid and say we have knowledge of the objects which they seek to express.[15]

That is, the "idea" postulates a determinate object that transcends present experience. The idea must be expressed in experience and "such expression would mean simply the completed determination of the intention itself."[16] This view legitimates sensuous experience, but only when fulfilling an idea. "Such a uniquely individual thing as a brute fact, being unique, could have no likeness, would be indefinable and hence unknowable."[17] The idea is the intention of the rational will, and only what fits that intention can be known. Clearly, what Lewis is discussing here is Royce's theory in *The World and the Individual.*

Lewis sees multiple problems with this view. Rationalistic Voluntarism offers no explanation of the origin of ideas, nor is an explanation regarded as necessary since the idea is the idea of the Absolute. Moreover, the process of determination that creates the object is infinite: therefore, "no object can be fully known in finite experience, and no object can be fully identified as that which any finite idea intends."[18] But in our experience, ideas do refer to finite objects.

> In a universe in which the rationally all possible was real, in which every thing, whose own essential nature did not involve a contradiction, existed, one would necessarily wait for the completion of the idea's infinite process of specification before any particular object could be identified. In a world of all possible hats, no finite being could honestly appropriate any hat at all. Admittedly, only an absolute mind could own hats in such a world. We must admit, further, that only an absolute mind could fully identify anything in *any* world in the sense of completing an ideal definition of it as a particular existence.[19]

If the process of determination is infinite, then at any given time the idea is general—an idea of a type, not an individual. But then at that given time, all hats of a certain type would be indistinguishable; in finite time there could be no individual. How then is it that Lewis knows his own hat?

Lewis gives a two-part answer. First, the idea does not fully specify the object as it appears in experience. The object is always found to have properties not involved in the idea; the experienced hat gets stained, or torn, or crushed, and such characteristics are as much properties of the object as any envisioned in the idea. It is therefore "something *given* and not the rational purpose *solely* which conditions that further specification of the idea."[20] But, second, in finite experience, the all-possible is not real; what exists is a limited selection from the all-possible. Since the "thats" that occur in experience are so limited, only partially explicit "whats" can denote them. Thus, the fact that there *could be* a hat indistinguishable from mine does not imply that there is such a hat, and even my partially indeterminate idea can therefore identify my hat.[21]

Furthermore, not all non-contradictory ideas have objects. An obvious example would be the geometric systems that do not describe real space. These are all clearly consistent ideas, but only one geometry can be true of real space; what is the status of the others? "Only some synthetic judgment can distinguish existence from the all which is rationally possible."[22] But such a synthetic judgment goes beyond the pure logic of intentions seeking their own specifications. Accordingly, that specification in the experience of a world that is a limited selection from the all-possible will require an empirical condition as well as a logical one. Hence, Lewis concludes that actionism cannot "meet the requirements of an epistemology which shall satisfactorily take account of individual thinkers in their relation to particular objects."[23] Actionism is trapped in a "cogitatio-centric predicament" just as fatal as the egocentric predicament.

Having rejected Radical Actionism, Lewis turns to Radical Intuitionism.

> But while voluntarism looks upon pure logic as an exhibition of the categorical ways of acting which belong to the logical will, the other view regards it as a system of relations among independent reals—'logical constants,' which are in another sense absolute variables.[24]

This view, which Lewis calls Logical Realism, is attributed to Bertrand Russell and G. E. Moore. It assumes, Lewis says, the transcendence of thought, holding that being, truth, and existence must be absolute. But instead of seeking to escape the egocentric predicament by appealing to the purposive nature of ideas, it asserts instead "the proposition that sentient experience can *make no difference* to such independent truth or being or existence."[25] As Lewis understands Russell and Moore, the universe is made up of concepts, some simple, some complex, and of propositional complexes. The relations in which these independent reals stand may be external relations rather than internal; the being of the object is not constituted by the external relations into which it enters. The noetic relation is one in which awareness implies its object, but the object does not imply awareness. The mind has no active role in knowledge: "the object of knowledge, both in content and in relations, is independent of mind and given, not constructed by any activity such as a synthesis of judgment."[26]

What there is, then, are concepts and propositional complexes of concepts that cannot be further analyzed. Even "existence" is a concept, since "A exists" is a proposition. Such a proposition "may be presented to a mind; and is presented always as just what it necessarily is."[27] But propositions given to us may be true or false; what is the difference between them? Since we do not know by inspection which propositions are true and which are false, these cannot be properties of propositions as presented to us but must consist in the relations of the propositions to the independent concepts of truth and falsity. Since in Russell's view relations are external, and since the fact that *aRb* does not forbid *a* standing in other relations, Lewis asks, "Is it possible that *aRb* may stand in certain immutable relations to truth and in the same, or analogous, and equally immutable relations to falsity?"[28] Given the independence of real entities from the mind and from each other, Lewis holds that such a contradictory result is perfectly possible, and fatal to the position.

The alternative form of Radical Intuitionism Lewis took to be that offered by Bergson, who held that the "true being" of external reality is to be found in pure duration, of which memory preserves portions that are germane to our present action. Lewis describes the central doctrine thus:

> We are, then, to regard our metaphysical object as a pure flow of qualitatively heterogeneous, unstable, interpenetrating reals, best conceived, perhaps, under the figure of a pure consciousness or experience. One moment in this movement seems to broaden out; the 'specious present' has its extension. And this extension seems to flow around a perception, a certain selection from it which stands forth as the expression of purpose in the activity of the subject. Mind or spirit is essentially the few bits of the part of the stream which is past, which are preserved in the body, adding themselves in a purposive fashion to the present action. *Abstract from* these, and the subject and the metaphysical object become partially identical in the intuition of the moment.[29]

But, Lewis says, selection from what? "That which is *selected from* seems hardly present to mind. It is already past." The flow of reality escapes us, leaving us with present perception and "bits" preserved in memory, but these cannot be added to reproduce the whole.[30] Any legitimate theory of knowledge, Lewis holds, must offer some solution to the egocentric predicament.

But this, Lewis holds, Bergson's theory does not do; rather it confines us within the present.

> If there is to be such a thing as knowledge, present experience must signify the existence of something beyond itself, and the problem of knowledge is soluble only when the validity of these signifying aspects of experience can be rationally affirmed. *The idea as purposive must be valid.* This is the *sine qua non* for epistemology. Since this is the case, no pure intuitionism seems likely to solve the problem.[31]

Accordingly, Lewis rejects Intuitionism.

Having reviewed these alternative positions of Intuitionism and Actionism, which Lewis takes as representing the extremes of the opposition between the claims that the mind makes reality and that reality is given, and found them both wanting, Lewis is ready to begin his own work. There are, Lewis says, two "moments" in knowledge—"a simple awareness and an activity of thinking."[32] Such a statement raises at once psychological questions. But Lewis declines to become involved in discussions of brain states or the nervous system; "we are concerned, then, with attention, purpose, activity, and awareness only so far as these may be identified by our direct inspection and reflection upon our own thinking."[33] Lewis finds his criterion for distinguishing awareness and attention in the will.

> If we can distinguish that which in knowledge stands for the activity of will itself, from something which does not represent such activity, we can, by the same token, distinguish the given from that which is the product of active thinking. Whatever in the object I can recognize as produced by my willing, will stand in opposition to whatever I must recognize as not so produced. If I find something which is in some sense the opposition of my willing, or the material upon which it is exercised, then I find something which can be called 'given' in opposition to what is 'made.'[34]

This is the distinction between awareness and active attention. Lewis explains:

> We actually find in consciousness, at any one time, a sensuous, qualitative content, an undifferentiated complex of that which is simply presented, and which no purpose of ours can create. We may open our eyes or close them, attend or refuse to attend, but so long as we have any content of consciousness at all, we shall have whatever content is in some sense given in our experience.[35]

"This moment of awareness" Lewis says, "does not exist by itself in the mind of any rational being." It always coexists with the moment of attention.

The latter, as Lewis puts it, is "superposed" on the former. What attention does is to discriminate the given "into 'objects,' or an 'object' and its surroundings or conjunctions."[36] Lewis's psychological model here is James's stream of thought, and James's distinction between the focus of attention on part of the stream and the "fringe" of less clearly apprehended content of the stream beyond the focus.[37] The bases for these discriminations are implicit in the given and are made explicit by attention. But the moment of attention does not change the qualitative character of the awareness when it is "superposed" on it. The sensuous "feel" of the given is not altered. Accordingly, we can "even in the attention moment itself, discriminate that which belongs to our activity and that which is given."[38] If attention focuses on certain aspects of the given, it does not in doing so create those aspects or alter them.

Lewis holds that attention is active and embodies our will and purpose. "Just as true purpose implies activity, so that activity is at bottom an integral part of the purpose itself, and only as such is it truly *our activity*."[39] This is not to say that the play of attention is always voluntary; sometimes experiences are forced on us quite against our will, or our attention is "caught" by something. But, in such cases, even if we must attend when we would rather not, "the purpose to *know* is still valid; the activity of attending still realizes its intent."[40] Our thinking is not aimless; attention is always purposive and directed toward something. That something is not just the given, nor the given as discriminated by attention. We have also to consider that the presentation of the object of thought is viewed in certain relations that have significance for the purpose our thinking seeks to fulfill.[41]

Lewis makes very clear his view that intuition alone is not enough for knowledge.

> For it is the first and fundamental characteristic of the finite knowledge which we seek to explain and to validate, that it forever refers beyond itself to what is transcendent of that which is just now clearly present in experience.[42]

If an undifferentiated given of intuition was all there was, knowledge could only be that of the enraptured mystic or esthetic contemplation. And any such "knowledge" would be "satisfied with the ego-centric or cogitatio-centric predicament."[43] In other words, it is the fact that knowledge seeks a transcendent object that provides the answer to the predicaments. This is the Idealistic answer to those problems.

But Lewis says that the given itself involves implicit distinctions that are the basis of the plurality we find in the "object-of-thought," by which he means not the real object, but the result of the superposition of attention on awareness. The object-of-thought contains a plurality; it is "itself a complex of discriminated elements."[44] Attention both discriminates elements that are implicit in the given awareness, and makes a synthesis "which holds them in the unity of an object of thought." But the object-of-thought, being discriminated from the field of awareness, also involves its relations to the context constituted by the rest of the field of awareness. To illustrate his point, Lewis uses the example of the orderly arrangement of a shelf of books. The books are objects-of-thought rather than real objects. Arranging the books requires comprehending their order relations in a single unity. At the same time, the shelf of books is related to other aspects of the field of awareness of which it is the focus. Thus, there is both diversity within the object-of-thought and unity resulting from one's synthesis, but also relations of the object-of-thought to its context in the field of awareness.[45]

Lewis then poses the problem of whether relations are given or made; "whether they should be, like qualities, attributed to intuition, or belong rather to a relating activity of thought."[46] His answer is, *some* are given. As examples of those that are, he cites spatial and temporal relations: as examples of those that are questionable, he cites the relation of friend to friend and of business conditions to the stock market.[47] The latter two then receive a discussion the point of which is that, to be known at all, these relations must have some aspect that is directly experienced. Lewis is not claiming that these relations are given: his point rather is that only as they "have some characteristic by which they are identified *in the experience of the moment* can I be sure that this is the relation which I *intend*, that it is the relation of *my* objects."[48] If friendship were not "felt," if there were no experience of friendship at all, I could never know it, and could never refer to it. Friendship, like any real thing, must transcend our experience, but it must also have some experiential aspect; otherwise, we could not recognize a case of friendship when we met one. This is a general principle for Lewis. The real must have some experiential aspect by which it can be identified.

But the discussion of friendship is a digression. All relations have some given aspect, but the contrast Lewis wants to draw is between those relations given in experience that permit the definition—by which he seems to mean "specification"—of something and those that do not.

> Defining requires a certain kind of abstraction, abstraction from all that is individual or of-the-moment in experience and reference to some standard situation or context of the thing defined, to which its relations are always the same.[49]

"In some cases,—that is, for some kinds of objects,—experience uniformly supplies us with such a standard context."[50] This context involves the spatial and temporal relations of the object. An object's extension is defined by its spatial relations—any change in the extension of a body is a change in its spatial relations. Is this also true of position? Lewis's answer is that although position is attributed to ideal entities such as points and lines, yet "if points and lines could not be thus identified in experience, they would be empty concepts." The boundary between two colored patches, Lewis says, is a line.

> The point and the line are *given in intuition*, even if reflection upon the physical nature of things convinces us that real objects cannot touch. Intuition is not *what* I see, but what I *see*, if there is to be a division of the two. Its *esse* is its *percipi*.[51]

However, Lewis says, the case of position is different from that of extension, for we experience position relative to our bodies, which are movable, and the same experienced characteristic may apply to different positions. With respect to position, "we must take some account of 'real space,' which, so far as knowledge goes, is constructed, by an ideal synthesis, out of such spaces as these given ones."[52]

This statement makes it clear that Lewis does not regard space as a form of intuition in the Kantian manner, but as something real, whose concept is synthesized from spatial relations given in intuition. He takes the same position with respect to time. *Ordinal* temporal relations are given in experience; we are aware of temporal succession, and all awareness involves temporal relations. Lewis summarizes:

> We may say that, in general, spatial and ordinal temporal attributes are such as to be adequately determined by relations to a context which must be given with them, or at least—when we remember the case of position—by relations of the *same kind* to a context of the *same kind*.[53]

Whatever is given in experience has temporal and spatial relations that are given with the experience.

But with respect to "secondary" qualities, the situation is very different. Taking color as his example, Lewis claims there is nothing in its given context "which determines that particular hue in the sense of making it possible for someone who cannot 'share my experience' to identify it by its relations."[54] In this case, thought must supply the context. "Such a context as is definitive can be secured only by reference to some *standard experience* or set of relations or context, which is more or less arbitrarily selected to serve as a *schema* for definition."[55] Thus, we might define colors by their relations to wavelengths of light, and such a definition will do for scientific purposes, but this context is not given in experience as spatial and temporal relations are.

> Only in the case of certain spatial and temporal attributes do we find that experience furnishes us with such uniform relations of object of thought to context as are required for defining that object. For all other attributes, the activity of thinking must supply the context by which adequate determination is secured.[56]

Not all contexts supplied by thought are adequate for definition. Thus, if we call something "rough" or "good," what is meant is relative to some purpose that leads to the predication. Such contexts determine something "more or less" but not with precision.

How then does definition differ from predication? Citing Plato, Lewis says that "the only adequate definitions are laws, and the only proper classes of phenomena are mathematical groups. Or to view it from another side, all completely determinate predication signifies the same *uniformity of relations* which appear as law."[57] This requires a rather extended notion of law by which fixing the position of a point by three coordinates would qualify as a law, but Lewis endorses it. Applied to colors, "that hue equals a certain fraction of the length of the spectrum, ordinally considered."[58] Just what a fraction of an ordinal array might be, Lewis does not tell us. But his point is the claim that the only uniformities that can define something are quantitative relations and ordinal temporal relations, and that all quantitative relations derive from spatial relations. The echoes of Royce are obvious here.

Lewis compares his view to Russell's views on order,[59] which exclude any appeal to temporal or spatial ideas. But, Lewis says, "Mr. Russell has not asked himself what orders are *given in experience*, and which represent our purposive activity." Taking Russell's independent orders (magnitude, numbers, wholes and parts, instants, points on a straight line, colors of the spectrum, and pitches of sound) one at a time, Lewis tries to show that we can think them only as represented in space and time. Indeed, Lewis claims "order cannot be otherwise imagined." Thus, Lewis concludes that there are two contexts for the object-of-thought: "a given context which is only in some aspects germane to the purposes of knowing, and a context which is supplied by our purposive activity in ordering our own experience." As Lewis points out, his argument is intended to restore "space and time to that unique position which they held for Kant," yet to do so in such a way as to avoid the objections that have been raised against "pure intuition."[60]

Definition, according to Lewis, requires reference to "some standard situation or context of the thing defined." That context, he says, is the rest of the field of awareness. All objects-of-thought stand in spatial relations to the rest of the field, and are before or after some elements of it. So the claim is that whatever can be experienced is experienced as having such relations. Extension (spatial or temporal) is taken to be the basic property of such objects-of-thought, and Lewis assumes that everyone's experience has these characteristics. With regard to intensive quantities, however, this is not true; one would have to share my particular experience to know the hue of a given red patch. Here, the context must be created by thought for a particular purpose, and this is done by relating it to a particular place in the spectrum or to a particular wavelength of light. The contrast Lewis wants to emphasize is between relations given in experience itself regardless of our purposes, and relations introduced by thought to serve our purposes.

But Lewis goes much further than this in claiming that only quantitative and ordinal temporal relations can define anything, and that "all quantitative relations must be derived from extensive spatial relations. It is only as extensive space relations that they can be exhibited in experience. *The only schematization which is adequately determinate, is correlation with certain spatial and temporal complexes.*"[61] What he means by definition here is exact specification or determination of the object-of-thought, which is given by its spatial and temporal relations to the rest of the field of awareness. Lewis is not claiming here that quantitative relations are *logically* derived from spatial or temporal relations; he was well aware that mathematical systems could be developed deductively from postulates with no appeal to spatial or temporal relations. What he *is* claiming is that quantitative relations can only be "exhibited in experience" in spatial and/or temporal terms. Thus, he says that

> *Order cannot be otherwise imagined.* Let the reader attempt to represent to himself any order—not a single entity and a relation, or pair of relations—without representing it either temporally or spatially. Such an attempt, I think, cannot possibly succeed.[62]

So, for example, a series of weights would have to be presented in temporal sequence or in some sort of spatial array; how else could they be presented in experience? And since knowledge arises from the interpretation of experience, his objective is to show that *epistemologically* we derive our quantitative ideas from spatiotemporal relations and that therefore these relations given in experience have a fundamental status similar to that which Kant gave them, although they are not based on any such "pure intuition" as Kant supposed.

Lewis then turns to the relation of intuition to the real world. Our purposive activity is a purpose to know,[63] to understand the given presentation. The idea does denote the presentation—the object-of-thought—but it also denotes the real object. The presentation is, Lewis says, "the *sine qua non* of knowledge" for without it the real object could never be identified in experience, but "the presentation can be understood only as it belongs to that complex which we call the real object."[64] That is, what it means to understand a presentation is to interpret it as an aspect of a real object. But before clarifying just what this means, Lewis turns to certain objections that he thinks will be raised to this claim. Namely, what about those ideas that appear to lack such a presentational element—abstract ideas? Ideas of the past and future? Ideas without sensory content? and symbolic ideas?

With respect to abstract ideas, Lewis turns to Berkeley's analysis of the real variable. There is, he says, no abstract idea of a triangle that is not an idea of some particular triangle, but "we can take a particular triangle and *neglect* all those features which are peculiar to it." The particular triangle can thus stand for any triangle, because the only characteristics of it to which we attend are those found in every triangle. But if the particular triangle we so use were "truly without any intuitional character," we would fail to recognize a triangle when we met it in experience. This leads Lewis to remark that "*Every* idea comprehends no more than certain characters of its real object." In finite experience, we can never attain the complete determination necessary to its full individual specification. Our ideas therefore remain partially indeterminate, but since our experience is not that of the all-possible but a highly selected subset of the possible, *some* of our ideas are specific enough to denote only one object in our experience.[65]

Memory and imagination, Lewis says, are patently intuitional; memory is a recall of past experiences and imagination is chiefly a presentation of images. We distinguish memory from other kinds of awareness because "memory is marked by the quality of 'pastness,'" though just what this quality is Lewis does not explain. The imaginary is distinguished from the non-imaginary by "a certain lack of coherence with the movement of awareness in general"[66]—that is, compared to other experience.

Symbolic thought Lewis says *is* a presentation of something in experience. The numeral "4" for example "is the presentation of a number or of the numerical attribute of something." We only think it is not when we stop thinking of what the symbol stands for and start thinking about the symbol itself. To a bookkeeper, Lewis says, numbers "are *presentations* of *real objects* . . . they are certain characteristics of those objects."[67]

"For every idea," Lewis says, "there must be a presentation which is, in part, that real object which the idea denotes."[68] Thus, Lewis here claims that the presentation in our experience *is* the real object as presented in our experience. This claim solves the problem of how the idea can denote both the presentation and the real object: the presentation is identical with some aspect of the real object. Accordingly, an idea without an intuitional presentation would not be an idea *of* anything. "Every real must be at least imaginable, if we use imagination in a loose way to denote the possibility of a presentation which is intuitional in character." Without this intuitional character, no object could be identified in experience. But if the idea contained nothing but intuition, it would not be knowledge, for "*Knowing* requires not only that something be presented, but that it be *understood*."[69] The real object Lewis holds is transcendent.

> We never know any object in such a way that there is nothing further to be found out about it. It is an imperative of our nature as thinking beings that we so regard any presentation and every synthesis of such. For only thus do we secure the unlimited possibility of valid activity of knowing. The possibilities of reality, for knowledge, must be inexhaustible.[70]

This is, Lewis says, a "necessary postulate."[71] "The unity of the object is the unity of our purpose to know,"[72] Lewis states. In order to know, to understand and explain our presented experience, we invoke "the postulate of the transcendent real,"[73] which is known only partially in our awareness of it. The transcendent character of the real object belongs to it because we postulate the real object to be such that it has these characteristics. We will, of course, find that it has other characteristics that we have not specifically postulated but that show up in our experience of the object. But if the presentation is to be understood, "it must be referred to some object that is real for some category."[74] That is, when we classify a presentation as a presentation of a real object, say a house, whatever further experience shall reveal with respect to that object must be consistent with its being a house, and not, for example, a horse.

"Whatever given is unreal, is unreal only *relative to the purposes to understand it in a certain way*." That is, if the presentation I seek to understand is not the presentation of a real house but an hallucination, it is a *real* hallucination. "The purpose to *understand* the presentation of any object, is the purpose to apprehend it in such categorical relations as it may have."[75] To classify correctly is the beginning of wisdom. And to classify some *x* correctly implies that what is true of members of the class into which we have put *x* will be true of *x*. The real is, then, the given, plus what is implied by our classification of it.

Here again Lewis is drawing on Royce. "Every intuition," Lewis says, "is the presentation of an object which is real for *some* category."[76] In discussing the uniformity of nature, Royce gave the example of St. Paul's being bitten by a viper. The "barbarians" expected Paul to die; when he did not, they pronounced him a god. The reasoning of the barbarians, Royce says, "was crude, but not extraordinary." They expected that, since Paul was a man, he would die when bitten by the viper. He did not. "Well then, what followed? Not that one changed one's description of man, but that one looked for another class with another description, wherein to place Paul."[77] Lewis uses the same argument. If the house I think I see turns out to be an hallucination, it is a real hallucination.

But what does it mean to say the real object is transcendent? We postulate the real object in order to explain our experience. This means that, if the object is real, there must be other possible experiences of it. These experiences must fit the classification of the real object we have made, and they must be experiences that involve intuitional presentations, since only such presentations would constitute experience for us. They also cannot contradict the experiences appropriate to the classification we have made; otherwise, we should have to reclassify it. But our experiences may contain many features not predicted, as long as these do not affect the classification.[78]

But what does "possible experience" mean here? It cannot mean simply possible for me, because my limitations as a finite being would then restrict possible experience to my lifetime. It is not my actual ability that defines what is possible but my way of knowing. "By possible experience, I must mean, then, that there can be, in the nature of the real objects, nothing which transcends my way of knowing and of identifying objects in experience."[79] That is, a possible experience is one that any finite being could have by following the methods of investigation we use. Whatever can be known must be known by yielding intuitional experience, since otherwise we could have no experience of it at all. Yet Lewis does not construe this requirement narrowly. The other side of the moon and the planets beyond Neptune are known indirectly—the one as inferred from the classification of the moon as a solid object, the other from the perturbations of Neptune and the theory of gravity. But however indirect the process and however long the chain of reasoning, the connection to intuition is essential.

But is the *specific* intuitional experience that I have of the real object essential to our knowledge? Suppose that where I see red, you see green— would that matter? Lewis's answer is that it would not, and indeed given individual variations in sensory acuity and the impossibility of ever comparing the intuitional experience of different people, there can be no reason to believe that such variations do not occur. What is essential for knowledge, however, is the "correspondence of our *ways of acting*, for only here can we discover surely the ground of common knowledge."[80] As long as we distinguish colors in the same way, it will make no difference which colors we discriminate. But if where I discriminate red from green, you see no difference all, it will make a difference in our actions—for example, with respect to traffic lights. "You must find a relation where I find one, so far as we know the same reality; and your relation and mine must belong to the same category, to the same system of relations."[81] This isomorphism of relations is important for action and signifies common knowledge, not the specific intuitional character of the relata.

What then is the place of intuition in knowledge? It furnishes the material that gives content to our thought and makes possible the identification of an object in experience. Together with "the necessary postulate of intelligibility," it permits us to distinguish the real from all that is conceivably possible. Although the real object transcends our experience, "as an object in its essential nature intelligible to our finite way of knowing," it must be presented in experience. "The limits of intuition are the limits of intelligibility."

> Yet this significance of intuition for us still lies, at every step, in its connection with our purposive activity; only by regard for the intuitional characters of experience can we be guided in our logical ways of acting. Without our activity, intuition has no significance; without intuition, our activity has no ground or meaning.[82]

Why must the object be intelligible? Our purpose is to know, to explain the intuitive element of our experience and give it significance. To do this, we postulate the real object as the cause of our intuitions; that is what explains our intuitions as intuitions of something. Without intuition, there is nothing to explain and our purpose to know is meaningless. Without our activity in explaining them, intuition has no significance.

Lewis added an appendix to his dissertation entitled "Intuition and the Non-Euclidean Geometries." Given the importance of geometry for Kant, and the excitement caused by the discovery of non-Euclidean geometries in the intellectual world of the nineteenth century, Lewis's interest in this question is hardly surprising, but the specific issue here is to use the various geometries as tests of his theory of intuition. He cites Couturat as his authority in holding that the Kantian view of pure intuition has been discredited by modern logic and mathematics. From this modern standpoint, mathematics is an abstract system whose statements are purely analytic. Given the primitive ideas, postulates, definitions, and rules of the system, all the theorems follow without appeal to construction or intuition. This view, Lewis remarks, is very similar to that of Leibnitz—an analogy that he would develop eight years later in the *Survey*.[83]

All the geometries are equally consistent. "But which of these shall be true of existence?"[84] Couturat's answer, Lewis says, is an appeal to "a principle of rational convenience." But this is in no sense an appeal to a pragmatic criterion, or to anything involving intuition; it is rather to "logical neatness." "The *actual* triangles and the 'rigid' measure cannot possibly, on his view, be of such a nature as to constrain us to accept the Euclidean interpretation of actual space." To admit that they are would be to accept synthetic judgments as determining the application of geometry, which Lewis says is just what Couturat denies.[85]

But Couturat's position requires "the thesis that experience is indeterminate." Citing Poincare's argument that the claim that rigid bodies can be displaced without distortion is circular, Lewis sees this view as too extreme. "For if experience does not possess a certain amount of determinate character, one hypothesis will apply to it as well as another." What Poincare is really claiming, Lewis says, is that there are "minute deviations from rigidity, straightness, and so forth" such that we could never be certain which geometry correctly applies to real space. Lewis does not deny such variations. Real objects always deviate to some degree from ideal conceptions. But he argues that deviation can have no meaning except as we compare the deviant to "an imagined ideally 'rigid' body." "Only as the concept of rigidity means a certain at least *imaginable* mode of behavior, can deviation from rigidity be detected or thought."[86] If "retaining the same length" is not something that we can identify in intuitional experience, then variation in length would be meaningless and unknowable. But if such notions as "rigidity" are not representable in intuition, then neither are changes in size and shape. One would be forced to the conclusion that these notions have no application at all to experience. Indeed, if experience be taken to be indeterminate, "*any* conception can be applied equally well to *any* experience"[87]—a position Lewis regards as absurd.

An alternative view that Lewis attributes to Poincare is that a non-Euclidean world "is readily imaginable and can be made up from elements of our own experience."[88] Thus, by reinterpreting terms such as "plane," "straight line," and so on, Poincare claims that we can find an interpretation of Lobachevski's geometry in terms that are familiar to us. Such a procedure Lewis regards as entirely proper, since it involves an interpretation in terms of things given in intuition. "But this is not in the least to establish that what we *at present* denote by space, plane, straight line, and so on, can have any such relations in *our* experience as they are made to have by Lobachevski. If we are asked to imagine the non-Euclidean terms as denoting what they ordinarily do, we must then refuse to accept the non-Euclidean postulates and theorems as the truth about reality, for they belie the character of our experience."[89]

Could a line that appears straight be, in fact, curved? Lewis agrees that it could, but emphasizes that this is a question about the line as a real object. "Whatever boundary of colored patches *appears* straight, is *given as* straight." To say that a real line could appear straight but in fact be curved is to say that there is some other possible experience in which it will appear as curved, and this would have to be an experience of the same real object. But the real line cannot, as a real object, be both straight and curved; "the mind which can *think* the divergence or discrepancy, can do so only as it can represent it and *correct it in imagination*, if not in perception."[90]

Considered as abstract mathematical systems, the geometries are completely independent of intuition. The price of this is that "you reduce them to meaningless words and phrases, intellectual playthings." Lewis's view of abstract mathematics is thus purely formalistic. But

> when it comes to deciding which system of propositions contains the *truths* of *existence*, reference to the *denotation* of its indefinables and to the kind of coherence which such entities may have in possible experience, must be made.[91]

When we attempt to apply these systems to our world, "the system of Euclid will be valid, and those of Riemann and Lobachevski will be false." There is no reference here to any pragmatic choice among these competing geometries; Lewis's view in 1910 is that Euclidean geometry is true of real space and the non-Euclidean geometries are false.

Poincare has denied that Euclidean space is "*the a priori form* of intuition." Lewis agrees. But, he adds,

> The Euclidean space is rather a schema of our activity, when we conform to the uniformities of the kind of experience which we have. It differs from other schemata, except time, in that it is partially exhibited in *every* experience of a 'tangible object'—every given which we can, consistently with the necessary postulate of intelligibility, regard as real in the category of space-filling objects. It is a schema which is not 'made,' in the sense of being the context which is supplied altogether by our purposes to adequately determine. So long as we live in *this* world, it is the space form of *all* experience of real 'tangible' objects.[92]

Thus, space and time are not forms of pure intuition in the Kantian sense, but they are properties of all sensuous intuition that we have.

However, Lewis recognizes that our space could change; it could evolve into some other possible form. In that case, Euclidean geometry would function like an a priori form that would render the new world unintelligible—for a while. But experiences of this new world, should we live long enough to accumulate any, could lead us to change our geometry to some new alternative that would be appropriate to this brave new world. Euclidean geometry is thus not necessary; rather what is necessary is "that *some* uniform coherence must be present in order that a world be knowable." But Lewis then goes on to say:

> The Euclidean space form is not, then, a priori necessary in the sense in which the categories of logic are; for *any* of the all-possible worlds would necessarily conform to the fundamental laws of our thinking, if knowable at all.[93]

At this point, Lewis did regard logic as absolute, as a priori necessary for our thought; the issue of alternative logics had yet to be broached.

Lewis's dissertation is his earliest work that has survived and is crucial for an understanding of his subsequent development. In an autobiographical account written in 1930, Lewis said that Royce was "my paradigm of a philosopher," and that he minimized the differences between his own views and Royce's until Royce pointed them out to him after reading his dissertation. This statement strongly suggests that at this time Lewis thought of himself as a Roycean Idealist, and the dissertation contains many features that suggest this. The description of ideas as purposive acts of will that intend a transcendent object is, of course, precisely Royce's. So is the claim that reality is necessarily intelligible and the view of logic as absolute truth and of classification as arbitrary. Echoes of his courses with Royce are clear in the reference to spatial position as a law, and to the spectrum and three-dimensional space as schemata imposed on experience. Indeed, the Roycean influence is obvious. But the dissertation is also an attack on Royce's theory of epistemology. In *The World and the Individual*, Royce had held that the "internal meaning" or purpose of the idea must become fully embodied in experience in order to become one with the "external meaning" or object of the idea, and that this process of embodiment is an infinite process of determination.[94] This is just what Lewis attacks when he insists that the idea must be able to identify its object in finite time, and that this can be done because of the limited character of finite experience. In fact, Lewis's differences from Royce are quite evident. But in what sense are these differences due to Perry?

The only explicit references to Perry in the dissertation are those to the egocentric predicament on pages 4 and 11, and Lewis nowhere speaks of the real as independent of our knowledge, which was Perry's characteristic position. But Lewis does hold that at least some aspects of the real object are presented in experience. Whether this is Perry's influence is uncertain. Nevertheless, Perry's influence is there in very important ways.

In the dissertation, Lewis insists that reality transcends any particular experience of it. This does not mean that the presentation is not a presentation of the real object, but that "we never know any object in such a way that there is nothing further to be found out about it." No one experience of the object tells us all there is to know about it; further inquiry will lead to further experience that further increases our knowledge. "The complete understanding of this presentation requires the complete satisfaction of this particular purpose whose unity is the unity of the real object."[95] That is, we want an understanding of the object that will unify all our experience of it.

> The *unity of this purpose [to know] prescribes certain relations which must hold, in actual or possible experience,* among the various parts and aspects of the object. If a presentation is to be understood, it must be referred to some object that is real for some category.[96]

Moreover,

> the purpose to *understand* the presentation of any object, is the purpose to apprehend it in such categorical relations as it may have. *From the point of view of this purpose, the presentation implies these relations of it.*[97]

What Lewis is saying is that if I classify a presentation as a presentation of a house, then further experience must reveal that the object has the other features of a house. So, Lewis says, "The real is, then, not simply the given, but the given plus that which the given implies in order that it be intelligible."[98] Thus, Lewis holds that if on the basis of a presentation, we postulate the existence of an object of a certain class, that postulate must unify our further experience of the object and so enable us to understand our experience. Suppose it does not? Then Lewis emphasizes that we reclassify the presentation as a presentation of something else. In other words, our classification is a hypothesis to give unity and coherence to our experience, and is acceptable just insofar as it does so. If it does not, the hypothesis is rejected and we seek another. But the presentation must be explicable as a presentation of something in *some* category, even if that means that it is a real illusion. It is thus obvious why the object must be intelligible; we postulate the object as intelligible in order to make experience intelligible.

What Lewis has done here amounts to a redefinition of metaphysics as the correct classification of our experience with respect to reality rather then as an argument for an Absolute Mind. Whether Lewis fully realized what he had done is unclear; he gives this position only minor emphasis in the dissertation, but Royce would certainly have understood its importance. This view of metaphysics is usually associated with Lewis's later work—specifically, with *Mind and the World Order* in which Lewis gave it full development, and is usually seen as part of Lewis's doctrine of the pragmatic a priori.

It is therefore important to note that in the dissertation it is nowhere associated with Pragmatism, and has nothing to do with logic, with respect to which Lewis is there an absolutist. Logic involves absolute truth; empirical knowledge is contingent.

Lewis apparently saw himself at this time as still an Idealist. But epistemologically he is closer to Kant (whom he had studied with Perry) than to Royce. The emphasis on intuition is obviously Kantian. Lewis does not explicitly discuss the origin of intuition, nor did his subject—"The Place of Intuition in Knowledge"—require him to do so. But, for an Idealist, intuition cannot stand by itself. If, as Lewis seems to hold, intuition is the presentation of the real object in our experience, then the issue becomes the status of the real object. Lewis never says that the real object is mental; if it is a postulate for explanatory reasons, it is of course postulated by us, but he does not say that it is postulated as being ideal. Certainly it cannot be an idea of the Absolute if the Absolute is merely a regulative ideal. But Lewis also does not say that it is independent of our knowledge; rather, he insists that it must be "akin" to our rational activity and that its unity is the unity of our purpose to know. One can read these passages in two ways. On the one hand, if the real object is our postulate to explain intuition, it will be intelligible to us, for why else would we postulate it? On the other, one can read Lewis as saying that since the postulate is the product of our reason, it must conform to the laws of constructive reason and must therefore be intelligible. These are not necessarily inconsistent readings. Lewis insists that the real is knowable in the sense that we can predict further experience of it, but that it will also have properties we cannot predict. If it is not independent of our knowledge, it is also not simply created by our knowledge—our's or the Absolute's. The best that one can say here about Lewis's theory of reality is that he has left a great many questions to be answered. If it was Lewis's intention to marry Perry and Royce in the dissertation, one has the impression that the marriage was not consummated. And that may well have been deliberate. Lewis was not the first graduate student to be faced with dissertation readers whose views were diametrically opposed. To have split the differences neatly enough to please both was no mean achievement.

Looking at the dissertation from the perspective of Lewis's later work, what is striking is how much of his subsequent philosophy is already there. The basic model of knowing as the conceptual interpretation of the given is clearly spelled out, as is the nature of the given. Lewis's concern with the egocentric predicament and his adoption of the Idealistic answer to it— that our purpose in cognition is to explain present experience in terms of a real object—are clear. So is his doctrine that the real object is an infinitely determinate individual that is knowable in our finite experience because only a finite set of its properties can be actualized. His doctrine that whatever is real must have an experiential aspect by which it can be identified and that the reality of the object implies possible experiences of it not now had are asserted. The claim that it is relations among sense qualities and not the qualities themselves that are sharable is set out, along, of course, with his view of metaphysics. In short, by 1910, Lewis had already reached a set of conclusions that would reappear in all his future work.

2

Berkeley

After receiving his degree in 1910, Lewis found himself without a job. Faced with this, the Lewises then spent the summer with Uncle Will.[1] In the fall, Royce invited Lewis to be his assistant, and that, together with such odd jobs as tending Palmer's furnace and tutoring, got them though the year. Then Lewis received an appointment as instructor of philosophy at the University of California at Berkeley—"or as it should be put, Palmer sent me there." Palmer more than anyone else handled the placement of freshly minted Ph.D.s from Harvard; he was a superb academic politician, knew everyone, and, as Lewis said, "stood *in loco parentis* in my slightly desperate financial and more personal affairs."[2] Thus, in 1911, Lewis went west again, this time for a stay of nine years, to begin his career as a philosopher.

The Berkeley department was a combination of philosophy and psychology, as was the Harvard department. It had been founded by George Howison, who was second only to Royce as the country's leading living Idealist. Howison had ruled the department with an iron hand until his retirement, which occurred shortly before Lewis arrived,[3] and his influence was still strong. For a young man who modeled himself on Royce, it was a very good place to begin a career.

In 1911, Santayana taught in the summer school at Berkeley, and on August 25 he delivered a paper before the Philosophical Union there that was entitled "The Genteel Tradition in American Philosophy"; it was published in the *University of California Chronicle* in October. This famous paper was an attack on the stultifying character of the American Protestant mind, and particularly upon Idealism. The American mind, Santayana said, is split.

> One-half of the American mind, that not occupied intensely in practical affairs, has remained, I will not say high-and-dry, but slightly becalmed; it has floated gently in the backwater, while, alongside, in invention and industry and social organization the other half of the mind was leaping down a sort of Niagara Rapids.[4]

Contrasting the vogue of the colonial mansion with the skyscraper, Santayana remarked that "the American Will inhabits the sky-scraper, the American Intellect inhabits the colonial mansion . . . . The one is all aggressive enterprise; the other is all genteel tradition."[5]

In 1912, Lewis delivered a paper before the Philosophical Union at Berkeley under the title "Professor Santayana and Idealism" that was subsequently published in the *University of California Chronicle*. This paper was a reply to Santayana's attack on Idealism, but its real target was "Naturalism," and, when it was later republished, the title was appropriately changed to "Naturalism and Idealism."[6] Here Lewis's Idealism is far more explicit than it was in his dissertation. He starts by remarking that Idealism has lately come under increasing attack. But he says that there are so many versions of Idealism that attempts to refute one often unintentionally support another. Santayana's attack on Idealism, however, is a general assault on "the general trend" of its thinking and the triviality of its conclusions. This leads Lewis to remark that

> there is, perhaps, this much of justice in Professor Santayana's attitude— that Idealism stands today just a little in need of fresh and vigorous restatement, shorn of all obsolete phraseology, and fully abreast of the best scientific and religious thinking of our time.[7]

Lewis turns first to an attack on Santayana's materialism. Santayana held that the qualitative aspects of things are "essences"—thus, "red" is an essence—which may or may not be actualized in a particular object. Taken by themselves, essences form a "realm of being" that includes all possible properties. An essence is actualized when it is joined to "matter." Essences are passive entities; matter is the dynamic agent that arbitrarily selects its essences. Lewis assails this view on the ground that Santayana's matter is an unknowable; it has no properties by which it can be identified, since any such property is an essence, and the relation of matter to essence is arbitrary. Matter cannot be described, since any description would be by essences, or identified independently of essences. "Matter," Lewis remarks, "is the universal dough which lends itself to every shape, but has no shape itself. It is the great Nothing-in-particular."[8] Santayana, Lewis says, has forgotten the "trivial truth of transcendentalism—that we can and must interpret experience in the light of constructive reason: that it is meaningless to call anything real whose nature we can never understand."[9]

Having disposed summarily of Santayana, Lewis turns to his main theme—the defense of Idealism against Naturalism. What then is Naturalism? According to Lewis, it is chiefly a negative doctrine that tries to curb the exuberance of Idealism. More exactly, the Naturalist believes that "the limits of knowledge are the (ideal!) limits of natural science" and that knowable reality is what can be explained causally and mathematically. "He seems then to be confined to the assertion that the world is full of a number of things; for further particulars consult the encyclopedias of natural science."[10]

Idealism, Lewis emphasizes, is not opposed to science. "Reality must be through and through intelligible—that is the fundamental thesis of Idealism,"[11] and so far as science strives to make the world intelligible, Idealism and science walk hand in hand. But science is not the whole truth about nature.

> There still remains the truth as to the validity of the idea, the rationality or irrationality of the will act—the truth of evaluation, of purposes and ideals. There still remains that truth which interests one who would take an appropriate attitude toward nature in general—its submission to or subversion of human interests, its kinship with our ideals or the opposite. If one chooses to use a much misunderstood term, one may say that there is a truth of final causes, over and above—though never contradictory of—the truth of efficient causes with which natural science deals.[12]

Even if the whole of nature were described scientifically in terms of natural laws, Lewis says, that would not account for progress, which Lewis identified with evolution, nor would it account for the very facts that science presupposes—that nature *is* describable by laws, that the inductive method works, that the consequences of observed facts will be observed facts. Science has its own ideals that are assumed as the basis of the enterprise, but cannot be established by science itself.

That final causes have truth means, Lewis says, that reality can only be understood when viewed in terms of ideals and values. This is not contrary to science, Lewis claims, because science is the attempt to make the unintelligible intelligible—"science finds its beginning and end in ideals." Echoing Royce, Lewis says that "the truth of values includes the truth of description; the truth of description does not include the truth of values."[13]

Idealism subsumes science. The Naturalist, however, claims that science *can* account for values and ideals. Psychology, biology, and anthropology can offer causal explanations of such phenomena; for example, integrated social groups are only possible when the conduct of the members is governed by moral rules, and such groups have a better chance of survival than disorganized groups. Science, Lewis says, "offers the only possible explanation of the fact that those reactions which we call moral or artistic or logical are increasingly present in surviving human organisms."[14] Idealism fully endorses this view. But such explanations do not account for the truth of our ideas or for their justification. The psychologist can perhaps account for our having certain ideas, or having certain feelings, but that account applies equally to true and false ideas, to the right and wrong intent. Nothing the scientist can tell us will discriminate between these because they are judgments of value. "If validity is a matter of causation, all ideas and evaluations are equally valid, since all are equally caused."[15] Appeals to evolution here, Lewis holds, are futile; the saint and the sinner are equally products of evolution.

The Naturalist, however, may turn Pragmatist, and, rejecting any absolute standards, hold that truth is simply a name for a hypothesis that works. But this, Lewis claims, is no solution unless he can explain what "working" means.

> A physical hypothesis works when you can deduce facts from it. Logic says that the hypothesis is thus rendered more or less *probable*, and reminds us that the truth may often be deduced from false premises. But Pragmatism asserts that if the hypothesis gives you the facts, it is so far true. Truth is only probability. Even the laws of probability are only probably true. Or more accurately, *probably* the laws of probability are only probable. It is probably best not to pursue this line of thought too far.[16]

But the important point for the Pragmatist is that ideas "work" when they are "useful." But "useful" is a value term. And so the Pragmatist is either forced to assume an objective standard of value or run in a circle.

The premises of Idealism, Lewis says, are

> that the real is intelligible and that the truth is free from contradictions. In Ethics, its arch principle is only the law that there shall be law; that right conduct must be rational conduct, and that good wills can never find themselves really at cross purposes. One must so act that he can will the principle of his action as a universal law of conduct. One must seek his happiness by means which do not contradict the possibility of happiness for all. One must so think that the logical consequences of his idea do not contradict the idea itself.[17]

These are not subjective standards; they spring from the "roots of human nature," from "the common rationality of mankind."

> They are ideals to be realized in the process of becoming what one means to be and attempts to become in every rational thought and action. Yet the realization of this goal is an infinite task—the vocation of humanity. The truth and objective value of these standards is revealed in the fact that to deny them or refuse them is to contradict one's self, and make life a meaningless muddle.[18]

Thus, speaking of Idealism, Lewis says, "If I should attempt further to reinstate Idealism, I should inevitably trespass" on other's turf. Again speaking of Idealism, he says, "We are often accused of being dialectical." It is quite clear here that Lewis is identifying himself as an Idealist. He goes on to assert "that the laws of constructive reason [i.e., logic] are the universal determinants and the framework of all that is knowable."[19] Further,

> Science affirms the sovereignty of Intelligence over Nature, and is itself a process by which Reason takes possession of its realm. When science supplements itself with the statement of what it implies, and what it seriously means to do and be, it becomes Idealism.[20]

This is a statement that Emerson could have made.

In this paper, Lewis talks like a full-fledged Idealist. Invoking Royce's terms, Lewis affirms the descriptive role of science, but makes it subordinate to "final causes"—to the values and ideals that govern all knowledge. Truth for Lewis is normative; science can describe, but it cannot evaluate. There is no suggestion here that Lewis sees our knowledge of value as empirical; rather it lies beyond the reach of science. The claim that the "laws of constructive reason" are "universal determinants and the framework" of our knowledge shows that Lewis regarded these as legislative for any knowledge we can attain, and marks again the strong influence of Kant in his thought. But it is notable that Lewis grounds values and ideas on the "common rationality of mankind," not on a transcendental standard, so that his claim that the principles of Idealism are proved by the fact that their denials are contradictory is an appeal to logic and human reason. This is the same method of proof by dialectical argument that Royce employed. Nowhere does Lewis invoke the Absolute; this is Idealism shorn of its metaphysical foundations. Lewis's attitude toward Pragmatism is clearly negative as is his attitude toward probable knowledge; the assertion of the regress argument is striking in view of his later use of that same argument. And Lewis is clearly a believer in human progress, not only as a possibility but as a fact, and his identification of it with Fichte's "vocation of man"[21] carries a heavy idealistic message.

In 1913, Lewis took up the challenge of Perry and his fellow realists in *The New Realism*. Lewis claims that the Idealists have downplayed their differences because of their essential agreement on "the non-existence of any alogical real, [on] the priority of epistemology, and the precedence of 'truths of appreciation' over 'truths of description.' "[22] But the Realist attack, which Lewis says is directed at subjective Idealism, requires that distinctions among Idealists be drawn, since not all Idealists are subject to the criticisms Perry has made in "the Ego-Centric Predicament"[23] and *The New Realism*[24]—namely, that Idealists believe that "all reals must be known, or that knowing is constitutive of reality, because no real can ever be discovered out of relation to a knower."[25] If this is taken to mean that Idealists believe the known to be identical with present experience, which is how Lewis construes it, then Lewis rejects this view as being a false description of at least his Idealism. The problem of knowledge for the Idealist is exactly that the knowing experience intends something not given, something that is beyond itself. Subjectivism, Lewis says, is as distressing to the Idealist as to the Realist.

Idealism does, Lewis admits, use the conception of an "ideal or limiting case of knowledge—the toilless knowledge of an absolute mind" in which thought and object would be identical. But Lewis claims that "the idealistic theory of knowledge can get on very comfortably without hypothecating the *existence* of such a case of knowing, provided only its validity as an ideal be allowed,"[26] particularly since no such case can ever occur in time. Idealists do hold that all reality is knowable, but not that all reals are presently known. The egocentric predicament can only be solved by proving that reality has some necessary relation to our ways of knowing; otherwise, we are left with either skepticism or dogmatism.

The Realist, Lewis says, holds that when something real, say x, enters into relation to a mind, it acquires a new relation, but he denies that this new relation is necessary to x as it is already constituted. Known-x of course is dependent on knowledge as one of its parts, but the claim is that x itself is independent of knowledge. But by how much does known-x differ from x? Knowing is a kind of action, Lewis asserts; hence known-x will differ from x by whatever effect the action of knowing has on x. Knowing could be a transforming activity; it could also be a selecting activity governed by our interests, in which case "all the reality we can ever hope to know will be relative to those interests." Or if knowing is "acting according to certain principles, then the world of our possible knowledge will reflect the legislation of those principles." Or it may be that there are reals that can never enter the knowing relation at all. But given the active character of knowing, we can never know what x itself is really like, independent of our knowledge. For the realist claim that knowing x does not alter x cannot be proven, since it would require comparison of known-x with unknown-x, which is obviously impossible. It is the realist who is trapped in the egocentric predicament, not the Idealist. For

> Whoever takes the principles of knowledge to be legislative for whatever can properly be called real, and holds reality to be so far dependent on knowledge, will be assured—if he makes out his case—that *known-a's* and real *a's* are not of essentially different character, and that knowledge is objectively valid.[27]

So much for the New Realism!

What is particularly interesting about this paper is that it focuses directly on Perry's views[28] and yet completely ignores his basic argument. Perry's strategy in his contribution to *The New Realism* was first to define "dependence." After reviewing a variety of possible ways in which one term may depend on another, Perry concluded that there were five basic types of dependency: relation, whole–part, exclusive causation, implying, and being exclusively implied. "Independent" is then defined negatively as what is not dependent. Perry then seeks to show that although when something x enters the cognitive relation, known-x is indeed dependent on being known, nevertheless it cannot be shown that x itself has any of the five dependency relations to being known. Thus, the independence of x can be demonstrated without having to compare known-x with unknown-x. Lewis ignores this argument entirely to argue that x can only be shown independent of being known by comparing known-x with unknown-x, which obviously cannot be done. As a former student of Perry's, Lewis certainly understood Perry's views. There is no evidence here that he had any sympathy for them.

This paper helps to clarify the kind of Idealism Lewis held at this time. With Royce and other Absolute Idealists, Lewis accepted the quest for the perfect state of knowledge as an Ideal—the limit toward which inquiry would ever approach but never reach in finite time. This is what the Absolute *would* know *if* there were an Absolute. But as against the Absolute Idealists, Lewis rejected the actual existence of the Absolute; it is only as an ideal of inquiry that such a state of perfect knowledge exists. He is here following Kant's doctrine that the ideas of reason have only a regulative role in knowledge, not a constitutive one. But what then is the "necessary relation of reality to our ways of knowing"?[29] If the real is what we postulate to exist in order to explain our experience, then the real is necessarily intelligible if our experience can be explained, and our postulates must conform to the "laws of constructive reason"—that is, to the principles of logic—since the truths of logic are absolute. An "alogical real" cannot exist, and that guarantees that the real, whatever it is, will be intelligible. The Kantian flavor of this argument is obvious. Furthermore, as Lewis had argued in the dissertation, we can always find *some* way of classifying our experience that will yield an explanation of it. Hence the real is knowable, since our classifications of it lead to expectations of possible experiences that will be confirmed. But this so-called Idealism that Lewis propounds has obvious problems. If the Absolute exists only as an ideal, what becomes of the "truths of appreciation" and how can they subsume the "truths of description"? "Appreciation" is not just the knowledge of ideals; it includes the knowledge of other minds. Royce's famous argument was that only because we are all ideas of the Absolute, and therefore share in the knowledge of the Absolute, can we know that there are other minds with experiences like ours. If there is no Absolute, except as a regulative ideal, what becomes the appreciative knowledge? Lewis suggests no answer here. It seems clear that Lewis's Idealism is, in fact, a very tenuous sort of Idealism that could easily slip over into something else entirely.

Indeed, one must ask if Lewis is really an Idealist at all. Certainly he is not an Absolute Idealist. It is equally clear that he is not a Subjective Idealist; the given is not created by the activity of mind. What Lewis seems to mean in calling himself an Idealist is that the mind plays an active role in the construction of our knowledge of the world. If experience is the conceptual interpretation of the given, as Lewis argued in his dissertation, then human thought enters into our experience and the knowledge we construct to account for it. As Lewis says, "whoever takes the principles of knowledge to be legislative for whatever can properly be called real, and holds reality to be so far dependent on knowledge" can be assured of objectively valid knowledge. This position is much closer to Kant than to either of the types of Idealism referred to earlier. Lewis is not a pure Kantian, for he differs from Kant on the forms of intuition and the categories as well as other matters, but he does appear to hold a modified form of the Kantian view. Lewis did indeed find Kant compelling.

In 1914, Lewis addressed the Berkeley Philosophical Union on the topic of "Bergson and Contemporary Thought."[30] Speaking to an audience that had already heard Lovejoy's analysis of Bergson, Lewis sought to explain what the controversy over Bergson was all about and why he had become a fad, not to present a technical analysis of Bergson's philosophy. And Lewis says he was a fad, though more so in the United States and Britain than in France. To some extent, Lewis thinks this is due to James's interest in Bergson, which introduced him to his American audience, but the basic reasons go deeper. First, Lewis says that in America of 1914, the emphasis falls on the external characteristics of people—their possessions, their wealth, their deeds—a view that Lewis terms "materialism." Religion, however, emphasizes the inner life, and so does Bergson, leading many who share this religious view to see Bergson as an ally. Second, Lewis says Bergson appeals to anti-intellectuals. Intellectuals, Lewis says, are those who "maintained the logical or analytical function of mind to be the highest, and hold that ideally all conduct should be guided by the reasoning power."[31] The anti-intellectuals are the "partisans of feeling and intuition," "those who, discarding reason, face the mystery [of life] with instinctive or intuitive insight."[32] For the Romantic, Bergson has seemed a comrade in arms. Third, Lewis points to the continuing conflict of science and religion. "The higher interests translate facts into terms of spiritual life; science tends to translate spiritual life into cold facts."[33] This conflict, Lewis says, has been particularly clear in disputes over evolution, and "the opposition between those who would view Nature in the light of life and its values and those who would look upon life from the point of view of naturalism is just as real and significant as ever."[34] Bergson is seen as a champion of the "higher interests," of "life and its values." The issue, Lewis says, is

> which then . . . is the higher point of view, and the truer—science which interprets life in terms of things or the intuition which translates things in terms of life? Which is the medium of genuine comprehension—the analytic reason which dissects wholes into parts and then arranges the fragments in imitation of the whole again, or that synthetic insight which grasps at once felt wholes and does not seek to analyze?[35]

Throughout this talk, Lewis strove to appear nonpartisan, but his antinaturalism was clear. Lewis was a partisan of "life and its values." But he made it clear that, in his view, many of those who had embraced Bergson had done so without really understanding him and often for superficial reasons. Lewis himself did not accept Bergson's philosophy, but his sympathy with those who did is clear. The "synthetic insight" to which Lewis refers is strikingly similar to the "synthetic view of many facts in their unity"[36] that Royce propounded in *The Sources of Religious Insight*. Although Lewis was not personally religious, he clearly believed that "the higher point of view" was the right one.

World War I placed Lewis, like all admirers of German thought and culture, in a difficult position, particularly when philosophers as eminent as Dewey and Santayana sought to draw connections between German Idealism and the German nationalism that led to the war. When the

United States entered the war, anti-German feeling swept the country, leading even to such absurdities as banning the teaching of German in public schools. To defend German Idealism in the face of such hysteria required considerable courage, but Lewis did so. On September 28, 1917—the year before the *Survey* was published—Lewis addressed the Berkeley Philosophical Union on the subject of "German Idealism and Its War Critics." Lewis agrees that the philosophic ideas current in Germany contribute to German militarism, but with respect to the relation of these ideas to German Idealism, he argues that the critics are simply wrong in their intellectual history. Quoting from Kant's *Perpetual Peace*, Lewis says that Kant opposed war, was a supporter of representative government, and that his morality was contrary to the subordination of the individual to the state.[37] It was after Kant that the cosmopolitanism of eighteenth-century Germany was replaced by nationalism, largely as a result of the Napoleonic Wars. But Fichte's nationalism, Lewis argues, was a call for German freedom, not conquest, and exalted intellectual and cultural achievement, not military exploit. Lewis is less sanguine in his defense of Hegel, but here, too, he argues that Hegel, even though he glorified the state and made a place for war in his system, nevertheless viewed war as an evil that served a purgative function. In any event, Lewis claims, the attempt to link present German ideology to German Idealism is mistaken. "Less than fifteen years after the death of Hegel, in 1831, German thinkers very generally repudiated him and all his works."[38] Idealism was replaced by the materialism of Feuerbach, Stirner, and Marx, and these men and their successors, Lewis says, were responsible for modern German ideology. And the materialistic movement has adopted what Lewis calls "a certain pragmatic attitude."

> In its diplomatic dealing with other nations Wilhelmstrasse seems to have taken the pragmatic oath: "We swear to tell what is expedient, the whole of what is expedient, and nothing but what is expedient, so help us future experience."[39]

Thus, as late as September 1917, with the United States already five months into the war with Germany and anti-German feeling running very high, Lewis was still sufficiently sympathetic to Idealism that he felt compelled to defend its German founders against the charge that they were responsible for German militarism.

3

Logic

It is generally agreed that the first great logician was Aristotle, whose invention of the syllogism inaugurated the study of formal logic. But there was far more to Aristotle's logic than the syllogism; it included the nature of terms, statements, and relations among statements through syllogistic reasoning and modal logic as well as demonstration, definition, and argument by analogy and induction—that is, the methodology of science or explanation.[1] This broad range of subjects continued to occupy his followers both in antiquity and through the Middle Ages, when logic was intensively studied. But the advent of the Renaissance brought both the recovery of a wide range of classical texts, and thus a renewed interest in classical thought, including Aristotle's, and the development of new scientific and mathematical theories. These developments focused attention on the questions of scientific method, methodology in general, and the relation of mathematics to logic. Bacon, Descartes, Ramus, and many others tackled these questions, and the so-called revolt against Aristotelian logic in the Renaissance was largely an attempt to develop broader and more powerful methods of reasoning suitable for the purposes of the new science and mathematics.

In the seventeenth and eighteenth centuries, syllogistic logic lost much of its luster as it became increasingly clear that the methods used in the rapidly expanding scientific and mathematical fields could not be represented syllogistically. It is true that Kant held syllogistic logic in high regard, but he also regarded it as a completed and closed subject. In England and Scotland, the repute of formal logic steadily fell. Thomas Reid remarked that the principles underlying the syllogism were "of undoubted certainty indeed, but of no great depth," and Dugald Stewart regarded syllogistic reasoning as so limited that it was trivial and useless.[2] But in the nineteenth century, several things happened to alter this picture. First, there was increasing concern over the foundations of mathematics itself. While the calculus was universally regarded as one of the greatest achievements of mathematics, the notion of infinitesimal quantities on which Newton had based it had come under close and disconcerting scrutiny as early as the late seventeenth century. The Kantian notion that Euclidean geometry was necessarily true of space received a stunning blow from the development of the non-Euclidean geometries of Lobachevski, Bolyai, and Riemann, which raised in urgent form the issue of the foundations of geometry. Moreover, the work of Poncelet, Gergonne, and others on projective geometry made it clear that there was a distinctively geometric subject matter that was not metrical, and consequently raised the issue of how projective geometry was related to the metrical geometries.[3] And puzzles over what sort of thing an "imaginary" number might be and whether its use was legitimate exercised conscientious mathematicians. In short, the nineteenth century brought serious questions about the foundations of mathematics itself.

Second, there were dramatic developments in logic. A group of young mathematicians at Cambridge under the lead of George Peacock developed the theory of symbolic algebra. Instead of limiting algebraic formulae to those that could be directly applied to numerical models, Peacock held that if algebra is viewed as a purely symbolic system, then its operations are legitimate even when they yield negative or "impossible" numbers such as the square root of minus one. This conception of algebra as an abstract formal system made possible its application to alternative subject matters. When William Rowan Hamilton showed that the complex numbers could be represented as couples of real numbers, the way was open to the development of multiple algebras—algebras of n-ads of numbers—that would result in vector and matrix algebras. But one application of symbolic algebra that had a profound effect in philosophy was its application to logic by George Boole in 1847 and 1854. It is Boole who is the real founder of mathematical logic.

Boole's conception of mathematical logic was that it was an application of mathematics to a logical subject matter. This was the conception that dominated "the algebraic tradition"—those who followed Boole and extended his work in the "algebra of logic," among whom Charles Peirce was the greatest figure. As we will see, Lewis himself wrote a history of this school. But while these "descendants" of Boole's worked, other developments were taking place that bore on the relation of logic and mathematics. As noted earlier, the discovery of multiple metrical geometries (Euclidean and non-Euclidean) and the development of projective geometry created great confusion in the field of geometry. Then the English mathematician Arthur Cayley showed that all the metrical geometries could be obtained from projective geometry by the addition of suitable definitions of distance.[4] This does not mean that metrical geometries can be *derived* from projective geometry, since the definitions of distance result from added postulates; rather what it demonstrated is that projective geometry is more general than metrical geometry. All the postulates of projective geometry are true of all metrical geometries; the different metrical geometries result from the addition of new postulates that provide definitions of distance. Furthermore, beginning in 1794 with Gauss's work on knots, a new field of geometry came into existence called topology—the study of those properties of space that are not changed by transformations that are one-to-one and continuous both ways.[5] As the German mathematician Felix Klein showed, topology bears the same sort of relation to projective geometry that projective geometry bears to each metrical geometry. Klein showed that each geometry can be specified by a group of transformations, and that the geometrical properties of a geometry are those that are invariant under the transformations of the group.[6] This led Klein to develop a classification of the geometries in terms of generality in which the less general are obtained from the more general by the addition of new postulates. This project of classification, known as the Erlanger Program, restored order to the field of geometry. It was this model of how systems are related to each other that was used by Royce in relating the system Σ to logic and geometry.

Parallel to these developments was a third course of investigation now called the arithmetization of analysis. The calculus of Newton and Leibniz employed an intuitive notion of continuity and an appeal to infinitesimal quantities. In the period after the passing of these giants, the calculus was rapidly developed despite doubts about infinitesmals, but the appearance of anomalous results gradually forced at least some mathematicians to recognize that its basic notions required a more exact analysis. By 1754, d'Alembert saw that "the theory of limits is the true metaphysics of the differential calculus,"[7] though few believed him. Not until 1812 was the convergence of an infinite series adequately investigated when Gauss carried it out.[8] But it was Cauchy in his lectures and writings of the 1820s who put the calculus solidly on the basis of limits, defined the differential quotient and the definite integral in terms of limits, and referred the continuity of functions and the convergence of infinite series to the same base.[9] But the discovery of continuous functions without derivatives made obvious the need for a clearer understanding of continuity and of the real number system.

The work of Weierstrass, Dedekind, and Cantor revolutionized this field. The definition of real numbers as limits of series of rationals by

Dedekind, along with the development of class theory by Cantor, demonstrated how little the concept of number had previously been understood. Cantor's theory of transfinite numbers, his proof that cardinal and ordinal numbers are radically different in the transfinite realm, and his proof of the cardinality of the real numbers opened the way for a new approach to a number of classical problems. The definition of continuity for the real numbers and the establishment of a one-to-one correspondence between the points on any line segment and the real numbers permitted a purely arithmetical definition of a curve, and was followed by Peano's demonstration that the points of a plane square can be put into one-to-one correspondence with the real numbers. These developments were followed by Frege's attempt to define number in purely logical terms, and so to reduce arithmetic itself to logic. Unfortunately, Frege's notation so encrypted his ideas that almost no one but Frege understood what he had done until Russell deciphered his writings and brought them to the attention of the world in 1905.[10] So here was yet another view of the relation of mathematics to logic—namely, that mathematics is merely a further extension of logic. This claim, first advanced by Frege, became the program that Russell and Whitehead sought to carry to completion in *Principia Mathematica*. Its first volume was published in 1910.

In 1909, Lewis had taken Royce's course on symbolic logic. He records that this course first aroused his interest in the subject. Lewis later commented that "it was a tough course; but no better preparation for exactly what, as it turned out, was to ensue in the development of exact logic could well have been devised."[11] In 1911, Lewis assisted Royce in the logic course, and it was then that he encountered *Principia Mathematica*. Lewis remarked, "Under the pretext that he had ordered a copy before receiving a complimentary copy, Royce put it into my hands."[12] Lewis's reaction to the *Principia* was mixed. He recognized at once the importance of the work and the method it employed. But Lewis included it under the "logistic" approach, by which he then meant the science of the types of order—an obviously Roycean view. He accepted the Frege–Russell thesis that mathematics (geometry excepted) was deducible from logic, which he believed the *Principia* established. But Lewis objected strongly to Whitehead and Russell's use of material implication and the paradoxes that this caused. Looking back in 1930, Lewis described his reaction to this situation as follows:

> Two sorts of problems were before me. First and most obviously: Is there an exact logic, comparable to this extensional calculus, which will exhibit the analogous relations in intension? And is the intensional analogue of material implication the relation upon which deductive inference is usually founded? Second, there were larger and vaguer questions: could there be different exact logics?[13]

Lewis records that he undertook to solve the first problem first, and the record supports that. But the record also suggests that it took him some time to grasp the full significance of the second problem.

Why did Lewis suddenly take up the study of logic? His prior work had been in epistemology; that is the field in which he had written his dissertation and the one he regarded as his area of research. Yet for the seven years between 1911 and the publication of his first book, he devoted himself almost exclusively to logic. For one deeply impressed by Kant, logic had a special status; it defined the "laws of constructive reason" that were legislative for human thought. Furthermore, Lewis was greatly influenced by Royce, and Royce saw in logic the absolute truth that would enable us to understand the mind of the Absolute and consequently the world. Lewis did not need to adopt Royce's metaphysics to accept the fundamental status of logic in human knowledge, and it is clear that he did. And he believed, as he would spell out in a later paper, that logic had profound metaphysical implications. Moreover, Lewis said later, "having been introduced to this subject by Josiah Royce, I had been intrigued to follow it through by observance of the insights that could so be afforded and sharpened in the field of epistemology."[14] Lewis does not say what these insights were, but in a paper written while he was still at Berkeley, he said that "the distinction of phenomenon and ding an sich rests upon the skeptical thought that the limitations of experience so far as these have to do with imagination and not reasoning may be subjective." Lewis then notes that Kant's proof of the ding an sich fails since the antinomies are based on erroneous mathematics. He continues:

> Remove all this [superficial?] junk by proper criticism and the ding an sich subsides to an inconsiderable bogey which cannot perhaps be banished but certainly can never harm or concern us from any but the purely theoretical point of view. Do this, and the idealistic house of cards, built upon the contrast of natural and spiritual, tumbles at once.
>
> Curb naturalism by a proper critique of causal and mathematical explanation, and by giving human reason its proper part in the discrimination and synthesis which makes *our* world of objects, and it becomes no longer necessary to oppose the theory of the social order—decorated with idealistic mysticism—to the theory of physical and biological nature. And a new humanism, which need possess none of the extravagances of pragmatism is here possible.[15]

What this passage shows is that Lewis believed that the analysis of infinity and continuity provided by recent logic and mathematics undercut Kant's proof in the antinomies of the ideality of appearances, leaving only the

"theoretical" doubt of skepticism. This overthrew Idealism, and if naturalism could be redefined to give an adequate role to the mind in the construction of the world as we know it, the result would be a new humanism.
For Lewis, the mind plays an active role in knowing; our knowledge is the
conceptual interpretation of the given, and the laws of constructive reason—
that is, logic—are legislative for that knowledge. Thus, the Idealism that
Lewis espoused in his early years at Berkeley—an Idealism shorn of its
metaphysical foundation—becomes a humanism that emphasises the role
of the human mind in knowledge. But it is a "humanism" without the
"extravagances" of Pragmatism, whatever they may be; Lewis had not yet
found his way into the pragmatic camp.

Lewis had learned from his studies with Royce that symbolic logic was
a subject undergoing explosive growth. Therefore if material implication
was a fallacious form of inference, as Lewis believed, its consequences
would ramify throughout philosophy. Lewis thus had every reason to be
concerned over the influence that he foresaw the *Principia* would have and
to try to remedy the situation. Furthermore, symbolic logic was a relatively
new field in which few people specialized at that time. Here was an oppor-
tunity to achieve distinction in a new and growing field that would almost
certainly become increasingly important. Lewis had thus both intellectual
and personal reasons for his decision to seek his fortunes in logic.

Lewis first voiced his objections to the *Principia* in an article entitled
"Implication and the Algebra of Logic" that he published in *Mind* in
1912.[16] Having noted Whitehead and Russell's definition of "implication"
as $(p \supset q) = (\sim p \lor q)$, Lewis focused on disjunction: "Compare, if you
will, the disjunctions: (1) Either Caesar died or the moon is made of green
cheese, and (2) Either Matilda does not love me or I am beloved."[17] Lewis
says (2) is such that at least one of the disjuncts must be true, for to deny
either is to affirm the other. Further, and most significant, the truth of (2)
can be known before knowing which disjunct is true—that is, "It has a
truth which is prior to the determination of the facts in question."[18] The
truth or falsity of material disjunction, however, requires prior knowledge
of the truth-value of the disjuncts. Thus, if, contrary to fact, Caesar had not
died, that "would not bind one to suppose the moon made of green
cheese."[19] Lewis says (1) is an "extensional disjunction"; (2) is "intensional."

To clarify his point, Lewis notes that the negation of an intensional disjunction is a denial of the disjunctive relation itself, not the negation of the
disjuncts. Thus, not-(John is a Catholic or John is a Protestant) can be read,
not as (John is not a Catholic and John is not a Protestant), but as denying
that these are the only alternatives, since John could be a Jew. The disjunction would still be false even if John were Catholic, since it is not exhaustive.

"One denies only that his statement exhausts the possibilities. The negative of intensional disjunction is, thus, the negation of the disjunctive relation itself and not the negation of either member."[20] Similarly, one knows that an intensional disjunction is true independently of knowing the truth or falsity of the disjuncts. But for the extensional disjunction, DeMorgan's laws hold:

$$[\sim(p \vee q) \equiv (\sim p \mathbin{\&} \sim q)]$$

Lewis's notion of intensional disjunction was by no means clear at this point. His basic idea seems to be a disjunction between alternatives that exhausts all possibilities. He flirts with the idea that it is dilemmatic, but retreats from such a claim since the disjuncts may both be true. But the negation of the disjunctive relation, even though the disjuncts are true, is not a viable notion.

Having distinguished intensional and extensional disjunction, Lewis then uses the rule $[(p \supset q) = (\sim p \vee q)]$ to convert each type of disjunction into an implication. Intensional disjunctions become "strict" implications—a term Lewis explains in a footnote: "We may call this kind of implication 'strict' at least in the sense that its meaning is narrower than that of the algebraic implication."[21] This is, so far as I know, the first appearance in Lewis's writing of this term. Thus, "Either Matilda does not love me or I am beloved" is equivalent to "Matilda loves me" implies "that I am beloved." And since disjunction commutes, the same disjunction gives "I am not loved" implies "Matilda does not love me." Further, Lewis says, the strict implication holds good whether the antecedent is true or not—that is, it holds in the counterfactual case.[22]

The same rule of equivalence applied to the extensional disjunction "Either London is in England or Paris is in France" gives us "London is not in England" implies "Paris is in France." But, Lewis says,

> *Any two propositions whatever* might have been substituted for "London is in England" and "Paris is in France"; the implications would have resulted in the same way. The denial of the one would imply the other; the denial of the other, the one.[23]

Moreover,

> Of any two false propositions, each [materially] implies the other; and similarly, of any two true propositions, each is implied by the other. If one of two propositions is false and the other true, the former implies the latter.[24]

These difficulties result, Lewis holds, from the inclusion in *Principia* of the postulate "$(p \supset (p \vee q))$." This principle is true extensionally but not intensionally—in the strict sense, "p does not imply that if p *were* false, any other proposition q would necessarily be true."[25] But from this postulate of *Principia*, we have

$p \supset (p \lor q)$

$\sim p \supset (\sim p \lor q)$ $\sim p / p$

$\sim p \supset (p \supset q)$ $p \supset q / \sim p \lor q$ Biconditional substitution

or, p is false implies that p implies any proposition. And

$p \supset (p \lor q)$

$p \supset (q \lor p)$

$p \supset (\sim q \lor p)$ $\sim q / q$

$p \supset (q \supset p)$ $q \supset p / \sim q \lor p$ Biconditional substitution

or, a true proposition is implied by any proposition. These are the classic paradoxes of material implication.

Material implication does not correspond to the ordinary meaning of "implies," Lewis asserts. If it did, the consequences for science would be disastrous. If an experiment testing an hypothesis were to yield an observational report "p", then since a true proposition is implied by any proposition, no conclusion could be drawn about the hypothesis; hence "no proposition could be verified by its logical consequences." Similarly, contrary to fact conditionals would be devoid of significance. But "hypotheses whose truth is problematic have logical consequences *which are independent of its (sic) truth or falsity*."[26] If they did not, the hypothetical–deductive method would be useless.

Is the system of the *Principia* false? Lewis rejects any such claim, comparing the situation to that of choosing among the Euclidean and non-Euclidean geometries. We can reject the system of the *Principia* only in the sense that "a more useful one is possible," but he goes on to say that "the present calculus of propositions is untrue in the sense in which non-Euclidean geometry is untrue."[27] Thus, as early as 1912, Lewis saw the problem of alternative logics as analogous to that of alternative geometries. But what would such an alternative system be? Lewis suggests that the removal of the principle of addition—"$p \supset (p \lor q)$"—which, he says, is the only postulate of *Principia* inconsistent with strict implication—and its replacement by the "principle of simplification" "($p \ \& \ q \supset p$)", the restriction of disjunction to the intensional variety, and the restriction of DeMorgan's laws to extensional disjunction only, would solve the problem. However, Lewis concludes that the better course would be to retain both intensional and extensional disjunction while defining implication in terms of intensional disjunction only. The result would be a richer system in which the paradoxes would not appear [the formulae "$(p \supset (q \supset p))$" and "$(\sim p \supset (p \supset q))$" would appear, but "$(p < (q < p))$" and "$(\sim p < (p < q))$" would not], "$p \,\&\, q \supset p$" would be a theorem rather than a postulate, and the "meaning of implication is precisely that of ordinary inference and proof."[28]

This article is remarkable; it shows how early Lewis had developed some of the ideas that would guide all his subsequent work. The attack on the use of material implication and the identification of it with extensionality, the call for an intensional notion of "strict" implication, and the general idea of what a system of strict implication might be are clearly spelled out. Although the concept of intensional implication is not fully clarified, Lewis's identification of strict implication on the one hand with deducibility and on the other with modality is clearly there. And Lewis had already seen the analogy of the problem of alternative logics to the problem of alternative geometries; just as the issue among alternative geometries was which applied to real space, so Lewis saw the issue among alternative formal logics as which applied to ordinary logical inference, and recognized that the choice between them must be based on utility. But he was still a long way from the concept of the pragmatic a priori.

Quine criticized Lewis's use of the term "implication" as being a confusion of use and mention. In Quine's view, one can write "$(p \supset q)$" and ("p" implies "q") but not "$(p$ implies $q)$". With respect to Lewis's early work, this criticism is anachronistic; Lewis was following the usage of Whitehead and Russell[29] (who therefore incur the same criticism from Quine).[30] But even in his later work, when he was well aware of Quine's criticism, Lewis continued to employ "implies" as he had before and denied that any confusion of use and mention was involved. As we will see, Lewis's theory of propositions lends some plausibility to his view.

In 1913, Lewis pushed his attack on *Principia* further in an article entitled "Interesting Theorems in Symbolic Logic" in the *Journal of Philosophy*.[31] Noting that discussions of the paradoxes of material implication have focused only on the two theorems "a true proposition is implied by any proposition" and "a false proposition implies any proposition," Lewis points out that many more such propositions are derivable from the postulates of the *Principia*. To demonstrate this, he lists thirty-five theorems of *Principia* that he considers appropriate for "Alice in Wonderland." The list includes not only the paradoxical theorems previously cited but also

$\sim(p \supset q) \supset p$.	If p does not imply q, then p is true.
$\sim(p \supset q) \supset \sim q$.	If p does not imply q, then q is false.
$\sim(p \supset q) \supset (q \supset r)$.	If p does not imply q, then q implies any proposition r.

and many more that he considers equally "startling." In fact, Lewis claims that the list of such bizarre theorems is infinite. As he notes, these theorems are also derivable in the systems of Schroder, Huntington, Peano, and Ladd-Franklin. They are consequences of the use of material implication.

Lewis offers an historical explanation for the prevalence of this type of implication. Boole developed the calculus of propositions from his calculus of classes, and, as a result, implication was modeled on class inclusion. The fact that the null-class is included in every class, and that every class is included in the universal class, led to the claim that every proposition whose truth-value was zero implies every other and that every proposition whose truth-value was 1 is implied by every other. But the consequences of this misplaced analogy are very serious, for "not only does the calculus of implication contain false theorems, but all its theorems are *not proved*."[32] What Lewis means by "false" here is false of the ordinary use of "implication" to mean derivability. The crucial point for Lewis is that since all the theorems of *Principia* are derived from its postulates by the use of material implication, and material implication does not correspond to derivability, "*it has not been demonstrated* that the theorems *can be inferred from* the postulates, even if all the postulates are granted."[33] Thus, in Lewis's view, Whitehead and Russell have failed to accomplish their purpose; the deductive rigor of the *Principia* is an illusion because it is based on a fallacious concept of deduction.

In a second article in the *Journal of Philosophy* that year, "A New Algebra of Implications and Some Consequences,"[34] Lewis begins the development of his own system. He starts by praising Whitehead and Russell for their contribution to "an ideal development of pure mathematics in general," free of all reliance on construction or empirical data. He describes the postulational method, and emphasizes that pure mathematics deals only with the relation between premises and conclusions. But although pure mathematics is not concerned with the truth of its premises or conclusions, it is concerned "with the fact that the postulates *truly imply* the theorems," and therefore with "the truth of the postulates in the logic." To the objection that logic, like mathematics, is only concerned with consistency, Lewis replies by distinguishing between a pure system and an applied one.

> The attempt to separate formal consistency and material truth is, in the case of logic, peculiarly difficult. For while other branches [of knowledge] find their organon of proof in logic, this discipline supplies it own. Hence, if this system is formally consistent, but contains a primitive proposition which is materially false, we shall have *false proofs* as well as materially false statements of implications, within the logic itself.[35]

What Lewis means here by "materially false" is propositions that "do not accord with the nature of valid inference." Clearly, what he has in mind is the failure of material implication to accord with derivability.

Lewis then turns to his own system of "strict implication," which, he says, "is applicable, in every proposition, to ordinary 'sound reasoning.'" This system is to be based on a relation of "intension or meaning" and will be a modal system, distinguishing necessary relations from merely contingent ones. Lewis then gives a list of sixteen postulates for his system.[36] All of them involve strict implication and strict disjunction, but they also employ material implication and material disjunction. The last four postulates are rules—modus ponens [Lewis rarely uses this term, preferring "inference," but since its meaning is standard, it will make for clarity to employ it], adjunction, meaning that if "p" and "q" are separately asserted, "p & q" may be asserted, substitution for variables—all for strict implication—and a formation rule. The inclusion of these as postulates shows that Lewis did not at this point distinguish clearly between the postulates and the rules. Among the other postulates are

P.1. $(p = q) < [(p < q) \ \& \ (q < p)]$

P.2. $[(p < q) \ \& \ (q < p) < (p = q)]$

P.8. $p \ \& \ q < p$

P.11. $[p \wedge (q \wedge r)] < [q \wedge (p \wedge r)]$

P.11 however is an error; as Parry showed, its inclusion reduces the system to Material Implication.[37] P.8 is the principle of simplification. P.1 and P.2 employ the sign "$=$," which Lewis does not list among the primitive signs, and this use leads him to a discussion of definition.

Lewis remarks: "the curious fact is that it is not essential, in strict implication, that definitions should have any meaning; it is requisite only that we should be able to get their implications."[38] Thus, taking P.1 and P.2 with "$=$" undefined, theorems involving strict implication can be inferred. In fact, P.1 and P.2 could be dropped and implicational postulates substituted for them. What then is the role of definitions? In mathematics, Lewis notes, definitions legitimize substitution "on the ground that the two expressions represent the same mathematical entity," but Lewis considers it doubtful if this is the only reason since they could be eliminated in favor of implications. Alternatively, Lewis proposes taking "$=$" as a primitive relation defined as "means the same as" and related to implication by "$(p = q) = [(p < q) \ \& \ (q < p)]$", and categorically distinct from material equivalence, which is merely likeness of truth-values. Lewis is clearly uncertain whether a definition of the defining relation can be considered legitimate. Noting that we can derive equivalences of meaning of which definitions are particular cases, Lewis comments, "Is it not possible that the usual treatment of definitions involves some confusion between mathematical and psychological requirements?" What he means by "psychological requirements" is that the use of definitions permits complex relations to be stated economically, making them easier to grasp. He then goes on to argue that definitions "are not assumptions fundamentally different in kind from other postulates. They need not stand outside the mathematical system as sanction for substitutions, but should appear *in* the system and be used exactly as other postulates."[39] What is bothering Lewis is the ambiguity involved in a proposition like "$(p = q) = [(p < q) \& (q < p)]$", where "$=$" is used both as strict equivalence and as the defining relation. He sees that there is a problem involved here, but he does not see any way to solve it. Lewis further states explicitly that, from his postulates, all the theorems of *Principia Mathematica* that are "consonant" with the meaning of strict implication—that is, those that hold when "$\supset$" is replaced by "$<$"—can be derived, but that "all theorems of material implication which are false for ordinary inference" are excluded. Thus, Lewis's system does not include that of the *Principia*; it is a different logic.

Also in 1913, Lewis published in *Mind* a paper entitled "The Calculus of Strict Implication."[40] Here Lewis comes closer than in his other papers to spelling out his objections to material implication. He starts by drawing the analogy between alternative geometries and alternative logics. Euclidean and non-Euclidean geometries are, he notes, both self-consistent, but they apply to different spaces. Whether or not we can prove that our space is Euclidean or non-Euclidean, Lewis claims that Euclidean geometry is "pragmatically the true one" because it is for us the more practical. Then, referring to his previous paper, Lewis says, "I have tried to show that the present calculus of propositions, in the algebra of logic, is to ordinary inference what a non-Euclidean geometry is to our space."[41] It is clear that in line with the algebraic tradition in which he had been trained, Lewis regards mathematical logic as the application of mathematical systems to logical subject matter. If in logic, "*p* implies *q*" means "*q* is deducible from *p*", then it is clear to Lewis that material implication cannot represent logical implication.

Lewis then discusses the two systems of logic. Since "it seems fairly evident that '*p* implies *q*' is equivalent to 'either *p* is false or *q* is true,'" he draws the contrast first between strict disjunction and "material" disjunction. Strict disjunction is now explicitly defined as meaning "it is *impossible* that *p* and *q* should both be false." He then derives the two forms of implication from these. He gives postulates for each system; those for material implication are taken from the *Principia*. The eleven postulates he gives for Strict Implication differ from his earlier list (only six are common) but are chosen to emphasize the contrast with material implication. However, the system includes postulate S.8—the fatal formula "$(p \wedge (q \wedge r)) < (q \wedge (p \wedge r))$", the consequences of which Lewis had yet to recognize. The two systems differ, Lewis emphasizes, even when their formulae appear to be duals of each other because the logical constants have a different significance in the two systems. "This" Lewis says "is because a logical calculus is a system not only *of* implications but *about* implications." Here one notes a merging of logic and metalogic. Lewis also notes that there are paradoxes of strict implication similar to those of material implication—namely, an impossible proposition implies any proposition and a necessary proposition is implied by any proposition. This is his first mention of these paradoxes, though he may have known about them earlier. They are clearly stated by MacColl in his *Symbolic Logic*; Lewis had read MacColl's article "Symbolic Reasoning VI" in *Mind* that does not mention the paradoxes so he knew something of MacColl's work, but whether or not he had read *Symbolic Logic* at this time is unknown.[42] But instead of insisting that these paradoxes of strict implication are acceptable, he indicates that they can be avoided by a change in his postulates.

Lewis then lists eight theorems of material implication that he considers particularly objectionable. These are

1. $p \supset (q \supset p)$. A true proposition is implied by any proposition.
2. $\sim p \supset (p \supset q)$. A false proposition implies any proposition.
3. $\sim(p \supset q) \supset (p \supset \sim q)$. If a given proposition does not imply any other, then it implies the negative of that other.
4. $\sim(p \supset q) \supset (q \supset p)$. Of any two propositions, if one does not imply the other, then the other implies the one.
5. $(p \,\&\, q) \supset (p \supset q)$. Of any two true proportions, each implies the other.
6. $(\sim p \,\&\, \sim q) \supset (p \supset q)$. Of any two false propositions, each implies the other.
7. $\sim p \,\&\, q \supset (p \supset q)$. Of any two propositions, one of which is false and the other true, the false one implies the true one.
8. $(p \supset r) \supset [p \supset (q \supset r)]$. If a given proportion, "p", implies another, "r", then "p" implies that "r" is implied by any proposition.

Having set these out, Lewis then draws the following conclusion.

These theorems are absurd only in the sense that they are utterly inapplicable to our modes of inference and proof. Properly, they are not rules for drawing inferences at all, but only propositions about the nature of any world to which this system of material implication would apply. *In such a world, the all-possible must be real, the true must be necessary, the contingent cannot exist, the false must be absurd and impossible, and the contrary to fact supposition must be quite meaningless.*[43]

The all-possible must be real because intensional and extensional disjunction must coincide and so any disjunction would have the force of a dilemma that "exhausts the possibilities." The true must be necessary and a priori because "$p \supset (\sim p \supset p)$" follows from "$p \supset (q \supset p)$", and any proposition implied by its denial is necessarily true. The contingent cannot exist because all facts will be necessary and the truth about them a priori. The false will be impossible because "$\sim p \supset (p \supset \sim p)$" follows from "$\sim p \supset (p \supset q)$", so a false proposition implies it own contradiction. The contrary to fact must be meaningless because a false antecedent implies any consequent. Finally, Lewis says, "this world will be marked by that ubiquity of the implication relation which is maintained by the 'coherence theory of truth' "[44] since as the eight theorems previously listed show, any true proposition implies any other. "Not only is such reasoning applicable only to a monistic universe, but it is suited only to infinite wisdom."[45] This makes evident the metaphysical reasons that underlay Lewis's aversion to material implication. One can imagine Russell's surprise at discovering that the logic of the *Principia* is that of the Absolute!

That will not be true of the system of Strict Implication that distinguishes the false from the absurd, the true from the necessary, the contingent from the necessary, the possible from the false, and denies the ubiquity of implication. "One may thus maintain that the real is not the all-possible, that reality is, in some part, contingent and not necessary, that the multiverse of things 'hang together by their edges,' and, consequently, that the system of material implication is false as an applied logic."[46] The quoted phrase is I think from James[47] and clearly shows Lewis's commitment to pluralism. But, having made this point clear, Lewis retreats, saying that given our ignorance of the real, "a decision on metaphysical grounds would thus be doubtful. Pragmatically, however, material implication is an obviously false logic."[48] On pragmatic grounds, the advantages lie with Strict Implication because it includes "possibilities, impossibilities, and necessities, not simply facts." Thus, just as Euclidean geometry is pragmatically the better choice for a description of our space, so Lewis holds the system of Strict Implication to be the better choice for a logic of our world, though, as is true in geometry, it is a choice of one from a variety of equally consistent systems.

This paper is an unusual one for Lewis. It shows that he is thinking of symbolic logic as a formal system to be applied to a subject matter. As in his earlier papers, he takes this subject matter to be ordinary inference. But what is surprising—and revealing—is that here he applies it to the "world." Lewis was normally very careful to avoid this sort of metaphysical speculation. But the fact that he uses such arguments here, and that he clearly sees the issue between Material Implication and Strict Implication as a choice between Absolute Idealism and Pluralism, helps to explain why Lewis threw himself into the task of creating an alternative to *Principia* and how his work in logic was related to his other philosophic concerns. Having rejected the notion of the Absolute as anything more than a regulative ideal, and developed a theory of the real in his dissertation that required a multiplicity of real objects, Lewis rejected monism for pluralism. Whatever logic he advocated would therefore have to be applicable to a pluralistic universe. Whether James's doctrine played a part in bringing Lewis to this position is unclear, but this position was certainly not Royce's.

One should also note here the foreshadowing of the notion of the pragmatic a priori with respect to logic and mathematics. The analogy between geometry and logic is explicitly drawn; Material Implication and Strict Implication are both consistent systems, just as the geometries are, and the issue in both cases is which is pragmatically true of the "world." Even if metaphysical or physical considerations cannot decide these issues definitively, Lewis thinks that the choices of Euclidean geometry and Strict Implication are pragmatically justified; we should adopt these systems because they have greater practical utility for us than their alternatives. But as we will now see, Lewis was not yet ready to abandon the idea of logic as absolute.

In 1914, Lewis published "The Matrix Algebra for Implications" in the *Journal of Philosophy*.[49] This paper marks a dramatic advance over his previous work. He sets out a new logical system, called the Matrix Algebra, that includes Strict Implication, Material Implication, and a new Calculus of Consistencies, and which is more general than his previous systems, in the sense that these three systems can be deduced from postulates and theorems of the new algebra. This was a new and far more ambitious undertaking than anything Lewis had tried before.

Lewis lays down the following definitions:

1. Consistency $(p \circ q) = \Diamond(p \ \& \ q)$
2. Strict Implication $(p \prec q) = {\sim}\Diamond(p \ \& \ {\sim}q)$
3. Dilemmatic Disjunction $(p \wedge q) = {\sim}\Diamond({\sim}p \ \& \ {\sim}q)$
4. Material Implication $(p \supset q) = {\sim}(p \ \& \ {\sim}q)$
5. Non-Dilemmatic Disjunction $(p \vee q) = {\sim}({\sim}p \ \& \ {\sim}q)$
6. Material Equivalence $(p \equiv q) = [(p \supset q) \ \& \ (q \supset p)]$
7. Strict Equivalence $(p = q) = [(p \prec q) \ \& \ (q \prec p)]$

The symbol "$=$" is the "defining relation" and is therefore primitive, but it is also defined because Lewis says doing so allows the deduction of further definitions. The postulates of the Matrix Algebra are

P.1. $(p \ \& \ q) \prec (q \ \& \ p)$
P.2. $(q \ \& \ p) \prec p$

P.3. $p < (p \& p)$
P.4. $[p \& (q \& r)] < [q \& (p \& r)]$
P.5. $[p < (q < r)] < [q < (p < r)]$
P.6. $(p < q) < [(q < r) < (p < r)]$
P.7. $p = \sim(\sim p)$
P.8. $(p < q) = (\sim\Diamond q < \sim\Diamond p)$
P.9. $\sim\Diamond p < \sim p$

The rules, which are here clearly separated from the postulates and are called operations, are modus ponens for strict implication, substitution for variables, "production" (i.e., if "p" and "q" are asserted separately, "$p \& q$" is asserted), and although Lewis does not say so, substitution of equivalents. P.5 is equivalent to "$[p \wedge (q \wedge r)] < [q \wedge (p \wedge r)]$" which as previously noted reduces the system to material implication. Also Lewis here introduces P.8: "$(p < q) = (\sim\Diamond q < \sim\Diamond p)$", which was to cause him considerable embarrassment when it was later included in the *Survey*. Then, for the first time in any of these papers, Lewis proceeds to prove a number of theorems.

He sets out the new Calculus of Consistencies, the postulates of which are

$$(p \bigcirc q) < (q \bigcirc p)$$

$$(p \bigcirc q) < (p \bigcirc p)$$

$$p < (p \bigcirc p)$$

$$[p \bigcirc (q \bigcirc r)] < [q \bigcirc (p \bigcirc r)]$$

$$(q < r) < [(p \bigcirc q) < (p \bigcirc r)]$$

These are derivable from the Matrix Algebra. Then comes the main act. Lewis proceeds to derive the postulates of *Principia* from the Matrix Algebra, using only the postulates, rules, and theorems of the Matrix Algebra to accomplish this. Lewis then claims that

> we can prove all the theorems of material implication from the postu-
> lates of the matrix algebra in much the same way as we have just proved
> the postulates. Also, by using the postulates and theorems of the matrix
> algebra—e.g., P.6 and Theorem 27 $\{[(p < q) < (r < s)] < [(p \supset q) < (r \supset s)]\}$—as principles of inference, we can prove that the theorems
> of material implication *can be inferred from* the postulates of material
> implication. This has never before been shown.[50]

In other words, Lewis denies that the proofs of *Principia* are valid proofs because they proceed by modus ponens for material implication; by showing that he can derive all the theorems of *Principia* from the postulates of the

Principia in the Matrix Algebra, Lewis believes he has developed the first real proof of the system of the *Principia*. Previously, Lewis had sought to develop his system by excluding certain theorems of material implication. Now he includes the whole system of Material Implication as a subsystem of the Matrix Algebra. This leads him to conclude that "the system of material implication has no value as an organon of proof, and its interest is chiefly mathematical and historical."[51]

To round out the Matrix Algebra, Lewis shows that the system of Strict Implication is derivable from it, using the eleven postulates of Strict Implication that he had given in "The Calculus of Strict Implication" the year before. He concludes that if the postulates of the Matrix Algebra are "true," it has important consequences for epistemology and metaphysics as well as logic, but he does not say what those consequences are. One can, however, assume that they were similar to those drawn in his earlier papers. And note that Lewis took the postulates of the Matrix Algebra to be "true," though whether he meant true of ordinary inference or true of our world or both is unclear.

Prior to this paper, Lewis had been intent on developing a system of Strict Implication that would be an alternative to the system of Material Implication. In the Matrix System, he attempted to create a more general system from which, by appropriate selections of matrix theorems to serve as postulates, both the systems of Strict Implication and Material Implication, as well as the Calculus of Consistencies, could be derived. This is a distinctly Roycean approach modeled on the system Σ; the aim is a general theory of order, or "logistic," that will "include" multiple subsystems in the sense that the postulates of these subsystems are theorems of the general Matrix System, although the subsystems are incompatible. This incompatibility arises, not from the subsystems containing contradictory theorems, but from the fact that the postulates of the subsystems are so chosen that some theorems assertible in one are not assertible in the other. Lewis's views of logic here continue to be strongly influenced by Royce. He was still looking for a system of logic that was absolute and would resolve the conflict among the subsystems by showing that they are the results of different selections from the more general system.

Also in 1914, Lewis reviewed Vol. II of *Principia* for the *Journal of Philosophy*.[52] The review is interesting chiefly for what it reveals about Lewis's attitude toward the work. Lewis begins by describing Whitehead and Russell's theory of cardinal number. When he comes to the theory of types, he remarks "this theory can not be made clear in brief space,—almost one is persuaded it can not be made clear in any space—but something of what it accomplishes may be explained." Having reached the point where Whitehead and Russell conclude the treatment of cardinal arithmetic by saying that "we can now adopt the standpoint of ordinary arithmetic, and can for the future in arithmetical operations with cardinals ignore differences in type," Lewis comments that "the reader's joy in this consummation is clouded only by the fact that we now leave the subject of cardinal number and pass to relation arithmetic." The fact that relation arithmetic is more general than ordinal arithmetic draws from Lewis the comment "the value of this greater generality is something which the reviewer has not yet discovered."

Lewis is, of course, critical of the extensional view of *Principia* and notes the difficulties that this made for the theory of ordinal numbers. Lewis particularly ridicules the method Whitehead and Russell used for defining the ordinal number 1 and its addition.

> Finally the authors *define* the relational sum 1 + 1 as 2, and frankly state that they do so in order to avoid troublesome exceptions. After the logical niceties of the theory of types, this procedure is something of a joke.[53]

It is in the method of *Principia* that Lewis finds its chief value, which he calls "logistic." By adherence to this method, Lewis says, Whitehead and Russell have demonstrated that mathematics can be "developed strictly from the fundamental logical relations." Whatever Lewis's criticisms of *Principia*, he accepts this thesis, which he attributes to Russell. And Lewis is careful to give ample credit to *Principia*.

> Whatever one's opinion of logistic or the particular treatment here given to mathematics, one must at least pay his respects to the logical rigor of the method and the splendid persistence with which it is maintained. The "Principia" is to intellect what the pyramids are to manual labor. And the "Principia" has the added wonder that the whole structure is balanced on its apex of logical constants.[54]

One senses in this review both Lewis's admiration for what Whitehead and Russell had accomplished and his irritation that it should have been done on what he considered an unsound basis. He was greatly impressed by the method of the *Principia*, which he adopted as his own, as he did the Frege–Russell thesis of the relation of logic and mathematics. As the Matrix Algebra shows, he no longer sought to refute the *Principia*, but rather to place it on a sound foundation. It was to be one of the chief frustrations of Lewis's life that almost no one else saw the issue as he did or appreciated what he had done.

The next year, Lewis returned to the attack on Material Implication in a paper called "A Too Brief Set of Postulates for the Algebra of Logic" in the

Journal of Philosophy.[55] He first remarks that the meaning of material implication differs from the usual meaning of implication in "Aristotlean logic," and notes that "some" have supposed it represented an advance. "For the consideration of any such persons," Lewis offers a new system from which he says "all the theorems of symbolic logic, all the theorems of cardinal and ordinal arithmetic, of statics and dynamics, and of various branches of exact science can immediately be derived." This rather startling remark is followed by setting out the following system. The propositional variables are "p", "q", and so on and are to be taken as representing *true* propositions; their negations as representing false propositions. "$(p + q)$" is defined as "One (but not both) of the two propositions, p and q, is true"—in other words as exclusive disjunction. The sign "$-<$" [Lewis actually uses "$\supset$," but to avoid confusion with its usual meaning, I have substituted "$-<$"] is introduced by the definition "$(p -< q) = (p + \sim q)$." The system has one postulate:

$$p -< (p + \sim q)$$

Although Lewis does not say so, he also assumes substitution for variables and modus ponens for "$-<$". Given this equipment, he derives

1. $p -< (p -< q)$. Any true proposition implies every true proposition, and

2. $(p + q) -< (q + p)$. Permutation

and asserts that "any other theorem in logic or in mathematics generally can be proved directly from theorem 1 by exactly the same method." He then challenges the advocates of material implication to "state their objections to our procedure."

The paper seems at first rather bizarre, and one is left wondering in just what sense Lewis believes exact science is "derived" from this system. Lewis believed that in the development of mathematics through the "logistic" method, "the 'calculus of propositions' appears as the organon of proof in general."[56] Presumably what he meant here was not that the concepts of mathematics and physics could be derived from his postulate, but that, by substituting theorems of mathematics and physics for the variables, all the *proofs* of mathematics and physics could be given in this system.

The next year (1916) Lewis published an article entitled "Types of Order and the System 'Σ'" that appeared in the *Philosophical Review.*[57] Here Lewis explicitly contrasts the method of *Principia* with that of Royce's Σ. Following Royce, Lewis defines "logistic" as "the science which treats of the types of order." The "minimum order" that must obtain among any set of entities that constitute a system is, Lewis says, "the order of logic." By further specification, one may obtain the particular type of order desired, and this can be done in two ways.

> These two methods are distinguished by the fact that in the one case the "numbers" of arithmetic or "points" of geometry are treated as (conceptual) complexes having a definite internal structure, while in the other the "numbers" or "points" are the simple and indifferent terms, the x's and y's of the system. The former mode of procedure is best illustrated by the investigations of Russell's *Principles of Mathematics* and *Principia Mathematica* of Russell and Whitehead. The other method is exemplified by Dedekind's *Was sind and was sollen die Zahlan*, by the *Augdehnungslehre* of Grassmann, and by the paper of Mr. A. B. Kempe, "On the Relation between the Logical Theory of Classes and the Geometrical Theory of Points." But this second method appears in its best and clearest form in the paper of Professor Royce on "The Relation of the Principles of Logic to the Foundations of Geometry."[58]

Here one recognizes at once the contrast between the Frege–Russell method and the formalist approach.

But much more is involved, for Royce's system is being held up as a viable alternative to the *Principia*. Since we have discussed Σ already, that description need not be repeated here. It is, however, notable that although Lewis emphasized that the more specialized systems of order employed by the calculi of classes and geometry require the selection of certain sets of elements from Σ, he nowhere indicates how these selections are to be made. Lewis credits the method of the *Principia* with rigor and with constructing the entities described from basic concepts, but he criticizes the resulting complexity. "Such a work as *Principia Mathematica* runs great risk of being much referred to, little read, and less understood."[59] By contrast, he sees in Σ "an order completely general at the start" from which special orders are obtained *simply by selection*." And he sees Royce's method as "the method of the path-finder" for in Σ new systems of order may be readily discovered, whereas "one would hardly care to invent a new geometry" by the methods of Whitehead and Russell.[60] Lewis is here following out Royce's suggestion in his paper of 1914 that the method of Σ offered an alternative to that of the *Principia*. That Lewis was still strongly attracted to this Roycean formalist approach is obvious. It is, after all, the approach in which he had been trained. It is no accident that Lewis still referred to symbolic logic as the algebra of logic.

In volume 13 of the *Journal of Philosophy*, Norbert Wiener attacked Lewis's strictures on the *Principia* and on material implication. In 1917, Lewis replied,[61] again setting out his objections to the *Principia* and trying to clarify his position. The issue, Lewis argues, is that material implication does not correspond to the logical notion of deducibility. Citing the paradoxes of material implication, and other related theorems of *Principia*, Lewis emphasizes that these are used not only as premises but also as rules of inference. By this he meant, as he explained in a footnote, that proof in *Principia* consists in (1) a material conditional statement of the form "$p \supset q$" (2) where "p" is some formula already taken as established, and (3) from the conjunction of "$p \supset q$" and "p", "q" is then separated and treated as established. Therefore, Lewis holds, all theorems proven *in* the *Principia* depend on material implications, and since material implications are not genuine implications, these are not valid proofs. Lewis admits that *Principia* is perfectly consistent in its use of this method of proof, but he holds the method itself invalid. As a result, Lewis says that the theorems of the *Principia* are not proven *in Principia*. They are provable by the use of strict implication, as Lewis has shown in his Matrix Logic, but Whitehead and Russell did not prove them.

But why aren't they proven? It is true that a material conditional such as "$p \supset q$" is true when the antecedent is false, but when used in a proof by modus ponens this is inconsequential since "q" follows not from "$p \supset q$" alone but from "$p \supset q$" and "p". And Lewis admits that such a proof is truth-preserving; no false proposition can be so derived. Lewis's objection is not that in this case "q" can be false, but that "q" can be irrelevant to "p". Thus, for Lewis

> The question always comes back to the proper meaning of "implies" which ought to figure in demonstration and proof. "Proof" requires that a connection of content or meaning or logical significations be established. And this is not done for the postulates and theorems in material implication: what is more, it can not be done without calling on principles outside the system.[62]

From "$(2 + 2 = 4) \supset$ The Danube is blue" and "$2 + 2 = 4$" we can by the method of *Principia* validly deduce "The Danube is blue." The Danube may indeed be blue, but Lewis says it is nonsense to say that this proposition is logically deducible from "$2 + 2 = 4$." In this usage, it clearly does not mean what a scientist means when he or she asks "What if p were true? What would that imply?" And that for Lewis shows that material implication will not do.

In 1918, Lewis published his first major work, *A Survey of Symbolic Logic*. The volume appeared as one of a series written by faculty members to commemorate the fiftieth anniversary of the founding of the University of California at Berkeley. As his wife remarked, "This was a break for him, for it was questionable if he could otherwise find a publisher for it, so

abstruse and unfamiliar was its subject matter, and the cost of printing its
pages of symbols so great."[63] In the preface, Lewis notes the absence of any
"comprehensive survey of the subject" that could serve as an introduction
to the current work in symbolic logic and declares his intention to provide
it. But the book is much more than this statement would suggest—a fact
Lewis hints at when he emphasizes that his treatment is "selective" rather
than encyclopedic and that in including his own system in Chapter V, "I
plead guilty to partiality."[64] Lewis has theses of his own that he wishes to
advance, most of them suggested in his earlier papers. At the same time, he
does present a survey of the development from Leibniz to the present that
is largely a history of the algebraic tradition.

This history is presented in Chapter I. Lewis begins by defining symbolic logic. The essential characteristics of symbolic logic, he says, are four:
first, the "subject matter is the subject matter of logic in any form"; second,
the medium is idiographic symbolism; third, some ideograms represent
variables having a definite range of signification; fourth, the system will
be developed deductively. Lewis is careful to distinguish symbolic logic, so
defined, from "logistic," to which he gives a Roycean definition as "the science which deals with the types of order as such."[65] Logistic is a broader
notion than symbolic logic and includes it. The importance of this distinction is suggested by Lewis's note in the acknowledgments.

> But most of all, I am indebted to my friend and teacher, Josiah Royce,
> who first aroused my interest in this subject, and who never failed to give
> me encouragement and wise counsel. Much that is best in this book is
> due to him.[66]

In Chapter VI, the consequences of this Roycean definition will be
made clear.

Lewis does not begin his history with Aristotle but with Leibniz: "the
history of symbolic logic and logistic properly begins with Leibniz."[67] Lewis
is not writing a history of logic, but of *symbolic* logic and, although the use
of symbols in logic goes back to antiquity, it is with Leibniz that we have
stated the plan for a "universal language" for the expression of science and a
"universal calculus" for reasoning. The former was a proposal for the determination of a small set of basic concepts—an "alphabet of human thought"—
in terms of which the whole of science could be reconstructed so that
"its real logical organization will be reflected in its symbolism." This Lewis
says is the program of logistic, of which he cites Peano's *Formulaire* and
Principia Mathematica as realizations. The "universal calculus" is, Lewis
says, the "precursor of symbolic logic." Lewis describes Leibniz's attempt in

De Arte Combinatoria to create a symbolism that would show the relation of analyzable concepts to their primitive constituents, and remarks of *Specimen calculi universalis* that Leibniz came close to stating the most important basic principles of symbolic logic. He is critical of Leibniz's failure to distinguish clearly between the intensional and the extensional points of view—a failure that led him into difficulties.[68] But Lewis has great admiration for Leibniz; he includes as appendices translations of two fragments of Leibniz on logic, and remarks:

> If the successors of Leibniz had retained the breadth of view which characterizes his studies and aimed to symbolize relations of a like generality, these fragments might well have proved sufficient foundation for a satisfactory calculus of logic.[69]

Of Leibniz's successors before DeMorgan and Boole, Lewis discusses Lambert, Castillon, and—briefly—Holland. None were successful, and Lewis attributes this in large part to their attempt to create a calculus of concepts in intension—something he says that "is either immensely difficult or, as Courturat has said, impossible." The success of the English logicians Lewis attributes to the fact that "they habitually think of logical relations in extension." Coming from Lewis, this may seem a surprising claim, but what he means is that a *purely* intensional calculus is impossible, not that *only* an extensional one is possible. He then deals briefly with Sir William Hamilton, and points out that, whatever Hamilton's failings, his writings aroused interest in logic in England, and his scheme of propositions focused attention on the extensional approach. "Without Hamilton," Lewis remarks, "we might not have had Boole."[70]

Lewis's treatment of DeMorgan chiefly emphasizes his work on relations. In general, Lewis regards DeMorgan as too tied to traditional Aristotlean logic and his notation, which is carefully described, as cumbersome. Lewis notes his introduction of the concept of the universe of discourse and the laws that bear his name, but sees his main contribution in relations. His introduction of the relative product, converse and contrary relations, the notion of containment for relations, the recognition that the essential feature of the copula is transitivity, and that any transitive relation can play the role of the copula are cited, but Lewis concludes that DeMorgan failed to make the breakthrough he might have made because he was too traditional in his approach to logic.[71]

As Russell remarks, modern mathematical logic began with the work of Boole.[72] It is Boole, of course, from whom modern mathematical logic descends, as Lewis points out. The fundamental ideas on which Boole built, Lewis says, are, first, the conception of elective symbols; second, the laws of thought expressed as operations on these symbols; and, third "the observation that these rules of operation are the same which would hold for an algebra of the numbers 0 and 1."[73] Boole's algebra is an algebra of classes. "1" represents the universal class, "0" the null class, "$1 - x$" represents the selection, or election, of all "X's" from the universal class, and so "x" is the class of "X's." Addition of classes gives class union, but is restricted to disjoint classes. That permits subtraction to be defined as the inverse of addition. Multiplication of classes is defined as class intersection. The "index law"—"$a \cdot a = a$"—that this interpretation of multiplication enforces restricts the algebra to the numerical values 1 and 0. The complement of "x" is "$(1 - x)$". Boole quantifies the predicate, as Hamilton had, using the symbol "v" to mean "some part of"; thus "all x's are y's" becomes "$x = vy$," or "$x(1 - y) = 0$"—"the class of x's that are not y's is null." Thus, "all x's are y's" can be written in the form of a simple linear equation. Lewis describes Boole's method of developing his functions and the processes of solving the equations. He then describes Boole's application of this algebra to propositions by letting "x" stand for the times when the proposition "X" is true: "$x = 0$" here means "X" is false at all times, "$x = 1$" that "X" is true at all times. As Boole has no symbol for class inclusion, he also has none for implication. In fact, Lewis holds that Boole's "propositions" are really propositional functions; the notion that propositions are simply always true or always false is not found in the system. Finally, Lewis describes in some detail Boole's application of the algebra to probabilities. Lewis is clearly impressed by this application, and remarks: "Suffice it to say that, with certain modifications, it is an entirely workable method and seems to possess certain marked advantages over those more generally in use. It is a matter of surprise that this immediately useful application of symbolic logic has been so generally overlooked."[74]

After a brief discussion of Jevons's work, Lewis turns to Peirce, whose contributions he says "are more numerous and varied than those of any other writer—at least in the nineteenth century."[75] Those that Lewis emphasizes are, first, Peirce's development of Boole's algebra. Boole's operations are a mixture of arithmetic and logical relations. Peirce distinguished the two sorts and completed the paradigm for each type. Thus, Peirce distinguishes logical disjunction, "$a + b$," which denotes those things that are "a's", those that are "b's" and those that are both "a" and "b", from Boole's arithmetic type of addition where "a" and "b" must be disjoint. Second, Peirce introduced the copula of inclusion, which he wrote as "$-\!\!\!<$", and stated its basic laws. He interpreted this copula as material implication, but, as Lewis notes, he was well aware of the problems that that notion involved. Third, Peirce introduced the universal and existential quantifiers, which he wrote as "π" and "Σ," respectively. As the symbols suggest, Peirce saw these as analogous to products and sums— "$\pi_x\phi_x = \phi_{x1} \cdot \phi_{x2} \ldots$" and "$\Sigma_x\phi_x = \phi_{x1} + \phi_{x2} + \cdots\cdot$" But, as Lewis notes, while Peirce thought the analogy useful, he did not identify the two, remarking that "$\Sigma_i x_i$" and "$\pi_i x_i$" "are only *similar* to a sum and a product; they are not strictly of that nature, because the individuals of the universe may be innumerable."[76] Lewis thus credits Peirce with introducing quantification into symbolic logic; he is apparently unaware that Frege anticipated Peirce by six years. But he is right in saying that it was Peirce's form of quantification that became standard in subsequent logical work.[77] Peirce also gave a very clear analysis of the notion of the real variable, from which Lewis quotes.

Fourth, probably Peirce's most important contribution to logic was his development of DeMorgan's ideas on relations into a powerful calculus of relations. Lewis describes this calculus briefly, but emphasizes particularly the theoretical basis on which Peirce built, defining a "general relative" as an aggregate of ordered pairs—a definition that Lewis calls "the first formulation of 'definition in extension,' now widely used in logistic."[78] He also credits Peirce with introducing the "law" for propositions that "If x is not false, then x is true, and if x is not true, then x is false." Fifth, Lewis briefly describes Peirce work on probability and compares it to Boole's.

To close Chapter I, Lewis briefly summarizes developments since Peirce. This includes a brief description of MacColl's work, and of Christine Ladd-Franklin's system. The chief contribution mentioned is Ernst Schroder's, who brought together the work of his predecessors in his three-volume *Vorlesungen uber die Albegra der Logik* in the early 1890s. Since Chapter II will be devoted to the Boole–Schroder algebra, Lewis merely touches on Schroder's work here. He does very briefly discuss Frege, noting that his notation so encrypted his work that its value was not recognized until Russell published the *Principles of Mathematics* in 1905. Peano and Whitehead and Russell are barely mentioned since they will receive more extended treatment later in the book. Thus, Chapter I of the *Survey* is almost entirely a history of symbolic logic in the algebraic tradition, though it is clear that Lewis is thoroughly familiar with the work being done in Europe.

In Chapter II, Lewis presents what he calls the "classic" Boole–Schroder algebra—"classic" to distinguish it from other logical algebras, several of which had appeared, and because Lewis believes "there are indications that it will serve as the parent stem from which other calculuses of an important type will grow."[79] This algebra is that formulated by Schroder in the *Vorlesungen*, together with certain additions, particularly by Paretsky. Having presented the postulates, Lewis says, "We shall develop the algebra as an abstract mathematical system: the terms, a, b, c, etc., may be any entities which have the postulated properties."[80] As a heuristic aid, Lewis briefly indicates two interpretations of the algebra—to regions of space and to the logic of classes—but the chief point of this seems to be to warrant the claim that the algebra is consistent, since applications are reserved for Chapter III. It is an important point that the theorems and proofs are presented by the use of ordinary logical terms. Thus, theorem 5.73 is given as

5.73. $ab = 1$ is equivalent to the two equations, $a = 1$ and $b = 1$.[81]

"Equivalent" and "and" are not here symbolized within the algebra, but are used to formulate the algebra. Lewis remarks regarding the *reductio ad absurdum* proof:

> But the calculus of propositions, as an applied logic, cannot be *derived* from this algebra without a circle in the proof, for the reasoning in demonstration of the theorems *presupposes* the logical laws of propositions at every step. We must, then, regard these laws of the *reductio ad absurdum*, like the principles of proof previously used, as given us by ordinary logic, which mathematics generally presupposes.[82]

This, for Lewis, is an important point to which he will return in later chapters.

The exposition of the Boole–Schroder algebra Lewis gives is brief, clear, and similar to what can be found in other works—for example, Whitehead's *Universal Algebra*. We need not therefore reproduce it here.

In Chapter III, Lewis presents four applications or interpretations of the Boole–Schroder algebra. The first is to spatial regions. Starting with Euler diagrams and moving on to Venn diagrams, Lewis shows how such diagrams can be used to draw conclusions from expressions containing as many as seven terms. The diagrams become increasingly unwieldy as the number of terms increases, but, as Lewis demonstrates, one can indeed reason with them.

The second application is to classes. As Lewis shows, the four traditional propositions are symbolized as

    A.   All a is b, $a \cdot \sim b = 0$
    E.   No a is b, $a \cdot b = 0$
    I.   Some a is b, $a \cdot b \neq 0$
    O.   Some a is not b, $a \cdot \sim b \neq 0$

He then points out that "All *a* is *b*" must hold if "*a* = 0." This gives of course the paradoxes that if "*a*" is null, "All *a* is *b*" is true, and if "*b*" is the universal class, "All *a* is *b*" is true. Lewis then stresses that the algebra of classes is extensional only, and in that application the law that the null-class is included in every class is true. "The law does *not* accord with the ordinary use of language. This is, however, no observation upon its truth, for it is a necessary law of the relation of classes in extension."[83]

Lewis then examines the square of opposition and immediate inference as they appear in this algebra. Traditionally, "A" contradicts "O" and "E" contradicts "I"—from the formulae previously given, it is obvious that these relations hold in the algebra. But the relation of contraries between "A" and "E"—that these cannot be true together but can be both false—does not hold if "*a* = 0" but holds otherwise. The relation of subcontraries—that both may be true but not both false—also fails if "*a* = 0" but holds otherwise. Similarly, the principles of immediate inference are vitiated wherever the null-class is involved. Syllogistic reasoning is easily done in the algebra, since the syllogism amounts to eliminating one term from two linear equations, but, again, it is necessary to stipulate that the classes are non-null to infer a particular proposition from universal ones.[84]

The third application is to propositions. To do this, the propositional variable "*p*" must be taken to represent the class of cases in which "*p*" is true. Then "1" will be the class of all cases, 0 the class of no cases, "$p \cdot q$" the class of cases where both "*p*" and "*q*" are true, and so forth. This interpretation leads at once to material implication, since "0" will be included in every class.[85]

The last application is to relations. Since the logic of relations is more complex that the Boole–Schroder algebra, Lewis regards this application as "relatively unimportant" for his purposes here and gives it barely a glance.

In Chapter IV, Lewis takes up systems based on Material Implication. What Lewis undertakes to do here is to compare the Boole–Schroder algebra, amended to include the postulate "for any *x*, if $x \neq 1$, then $x = 0$, and if $x \neq 0$, then $x = 1$," with the treatment of propositions and propositional functions in *Principia*, and to demonstrate that the difference between them is one of method, not result.[86] The addition of the new postulate converts the Boole–Schroder algebra into what Lewis calls the Two-Valued Algebra. The postulate is given as

$$p = (p = 1)$$

or "*p* is equivalent to *p* is true," from which we have at once

$$\sim p = (\sim p = 1) = (p = 0)$$

or "~*p* is equivalent to *p* is false." This addition compromises the status of the algebra as an abstract system for it requires "*p*" to be a proposition, but Lewis holds that no proof depends on this *interpretation* so that the system can still be treated abstractly.

Lewis calls attention to the fact that so far he has treated the logical relations "if . . . then . . . ," "and," and so forth, not as part of the algebra but as part of an ordinary logic in which the algebra is presented. But the addition of the new postulate makes it possible to prove that "*p* and *q*" is equivalent to "*p* & *q*," "*p* is equivalent to *q*" is equivalent to "*p* = *q*," and so on. Thus, each theorem of the Boole–Schroder algebra that was not stated wholly in symbols can be so stated. Using "⊃" for "if . . . then . . ." [Lewis actually uses "⊂"], he can then prove the theorems regarding material implication that he so disliked, including the paradoxes. Material Implication is a relation of truth-values, not of the meanings of propositions.

Lewis then turns to propositional functions, following Russell's lead, and redefines the quantifiers "π*x*" and "Σ*x*" as "for all values of *x*" and "for some values of *x*," respectively. All the theorems of the Two-Valued Algebra remain true when for "*p*", "*q*", and so on. we substitute "ϕ*x*", "Σ*x*ϕ*x*", or "π*x*ϕ*x*".[87] Lewis then deals with formal implication and formal equivalence, emphasizing that formal implication "is simply a class or aggregate of material implications" and that formal equivalence is "reciprocal material implication." This is followed by a description of propositional functions of two or more variables. Lewis then derives the calculus of logical classes and the calculus of relations. But, in doing so, Lewis assumes that any propositional function determines a class. Lewis is well aware of Russell's paradox, so one must assume here that for the purposes of his exposition, which Lewis regards as an elementary one, he simply ignores the problem. This interpretation is borne out by his statement that "there is, in *Principia*, the 'theory of types,' which concerns the range of significance of functions. But we shall omit consideration of this."[88] But there are differences between the calculus of classes derived from the calculus of propositional functions and that derived from the Boole–Schroder algebra. Specifically, he cites two defects of the later: the Boole–Schroder algebra lacks the notion of membership so that the relation of a member to a class cannot be symbolized, and the theorems of the Boole–Schroder algebra "cannot validly be given a completely symbolic form" while those of the class calculus derived from the calculus of propositional functions can.

Lewis then turns to *Principia*. Lewis fully admits that the system of the *Principia* is superior to that of the Two-Valued Algebra. He says that the logic of *Principia* is "theoretically sounder and more adequate" and points out some inadequacies of the earlier system—specifically, even though it can symbolize logical relations that the Boole–Schroder albegra cannot, it still assumes the logic of propositions in doing so, and thus circularity is not avoided.[89] This and other defects are removed by *Principia*, the system of which Lewis then goes on to describe briefly. He explains its notation, and basic ideas, gives the postulates for the propositional calculus, and describes the rules and method of proof. He then claims that

> we have now seen that the calculus of propositions in *Principia Mathematica* avoids both defects of the Two-Valued Algebra. The further comparison of the two systems can be made in a sentence: Except for the absence, in the logic of *Principia*, of the redundancy of forms, p, $p = 1$, $p \neq 0$, etc., etc., and the absence of the entities 0 and 1, the two systems are identical.[90]

Lewis proves this by showing that the postulates of each system can be derived from those of the other. This claim of equivalence is not entirely true with respect to propositional functions. Aside from the notational difference, the interpretation of quantifiers in *Principia* avoids all the problems about an infinity of values for the variables, and there is, of course, the theory of types, as well as the theory of descriptions. But Lewis remarks: "none of these exceptions is a *necessary* difference. They are due to the more elementary character of our presentation of the subject. We may, then, say loosely that the two methods give identical results." He concludes, "when we remember the date of the work of Peirce and Schroder, it becomes clear what is our debt to them for the better developments which have since been made."[91]

In Chapter V, Lewis presents his system of Strict Implication. The avowed purpose of this system is to avoid reliance on material implication by using a notion of "implies" "more in accord with the customary uses of that relation in inference and proof."[92] This system is neither purely extensional nor purely intensional but includes relations of both types and shows their relations. Lewis presents the basic ideas of the system that he calls "similar" to those of MacColl's *Symbolic Logic and Its Applications*.[93] These are

1. Propositional variables: "p", "q", "r", and so on
2. Negation: "$\sim p$", meaning "p" is false.
3. Impossibility: "$\sim \Diamond p$", "p" is impossible.
4. Logical product: "$p \ \& \ q$", meaning both "p" and "q" are true.
5. Equivalence: "$p = q$", "the defining relation."

He defines consistency as

$$1.01. \quad p \circ q = \Diamond(p \ \& \ q).$$

It is possible "p" and "q" are both true. He then gives the following definitions.

> 1.02. $p < q = \sim\Diamond(p\ \&\ \sim q)$. Strict Implication
>
> 1.03. $p \supset q = \sim(p\ \&\ \sim q)$. Material Implication
>
> 1.04. $p \wedge q = \sim\Diamond(\sim p\ \&\ \sim q)$. Strict Logical Sum
>
> 1.05. $p \vee q = \sim(\sim p\ \&\ \sim q)$. Material Logical Sum
>
> 1.06. $(p = q) = (p < q)\ \&\ (q < p)$. Strict Equivalence
>
> 1.07. $(p \equiv q) = (p \supset q)\ \&\ (q \supset p)$. Material Equivalence

The postulates of the system are then given as

> 1.1. $p\ \&\ q < q\ \&\ p$
>
> 1.2. $q\ \&\ p < p$
>
> 1.3. $p < p\ \&\ p$
>
> 1.4. $[p\ \&\ (q\ \&\ r)] < [q\ \&\ (p\ \&\ r)]$
>
> 1.5. $p < \sim(\sim p)$
>
> 1.6. $[(p < q)\ \&\ (q < r)] < (p < r)$
>
> 1.7. $\sim\Diamond p < \sim p$
>
> 1.8. $(p < q) = (\sim\Diamond q < \sim\Diamond p)$

1.8, Lewis says, is equivalent to

> A. $(p < q) < (\Diamond p < \Diamond q)$
>
> B. $(\sim\Diamond p < \sim\Diamond q) < (\sim p < \sim q)$

One should note that the postulate "$[p \wedge (q \wedge r)] < [q \wedge (p \wedge r)]$" of the earlier systems has been dropped; Lewis had discovered its baneful consequences. But 1.8 is still a postulate, although Lewis apparently had doubts about it. He later said, "In developing the system, I had worked for a month to avoid this principle, which later turned out to be false. Then, finding no reason to think it false, I sacrificed economy and put it in."[94]

The rules of inference of the system are substitution for variables, substitution of equivalents, modus ponens for strict implication—that is, if "p" is asserted and if "$p < q$" is asserted, then "q" may be asserted, and "production"—if "p" and "q" are separately asserted, then "$p\ \&\ q$" may be asserted. Lewis then proves a number of theorems, but in all of them, the main relation asserted is strict implication. The formula "$\sim\Diamond\sim p = (\sim p < p)$," Lewis says, "defines the idea of 'necessity'." "A *necessarily true* proposition . . . is one whose denial strictly implies it." Similarly,

$$\sim\Diamond p = (p < \sim p)$$

"An impossible or absurd proposition is one which strictly implies its own denial and is not consistent with itself."[95]

Lewis shows that "for every strict relation which is assertible in the system, the corresponding material relation is also assertible."[96] This, Lewis argues, is true not only with respect to the main asserted relation of the proposition but for the component parts as well. Hence: "All the postulates and theorems of Material Implication can be derived from the postulates and definitions of Strict Implication: the system of Strict Implication *contains* the system of Material Implication."[97]

Lewis then derives the postulates of *Principia*, and modus ponens for material implication. He makes the point he had made in an earlier paper that, although the theorems of *Principia* are derived from its postulates in that work using material relations only, they can also be derived using only strict relations. Thus, the theorems of *Principia* hold as consequences of Strict Implication whether the method of proof used in *Principia* is regarded as legitimate or not.

Lewis also presents a Calculus of Consistencies. This is a subsystem of the system of Strict Implication; all the postulates and rules are theorems of Strict Implication, given the definitions added. The primitive ideas are propositions, represented by "p", "q", "r", and so on, negation, impossibility, consistency "$(p \circ q)$", and "$p = q$". Other strict relations are then defined as

$$p \wedge q = \sim(\sim p \circ \sim q)$$
$$p < q = \sim(p \circ \sim q)$$

The postulates are

1. $(p \circ q) < (q \circ p)$
2. $(q \circ p) < \Diamond p$
3. $\Diamond p < (p \circ p)$
4. $p = \sim(\sim p)$

Substitution for variables, substitution of equivalents, and modus ponens are assumed; production is replaced by the rule that if "$p < q$" is asserted and "$q < r$" is asserted, then "$p < r$" may be asserted. The resulting calculus Lewis says is "purely a calculus of intensions."

Lewis next presents what he calls the Calculus of Ordinary Inference that is also contained in the system of Strict Implication. The primitives are conjunction, negation, strict implication, and strict equivalence, in terms of which strict disjunction and consistency are defined, but not material implication. The postulates are

1. $(\sim p < q) < (\sim q < p)$

2. $p \& q < p$

3. $p < p \& p$

4. $p \& (q \& r) < q \& (p \& r)$

5. $p < \sim(\sim p)$

6. $[(p < q) \& (q < r)] < (p < r)$

7. $(p \& q) < (p \bigcirc q)$

8. $(p \& q < r \& s) = [(p \bigcirc q) < (r \bigcirc s)]$

All these are theorems of Strict Implication. But Lewis says of the resulting system, "it *does not contain* the useless and doubtful theorems such as 'A false proposition implies any proposition' and 'A true proposition is implied by any proposition.'"[98] It will be recalled that Lewis had always claimed that material implication did not accord with ordinary inference, and that he invented the system of Strict Implication to provide a notion of implication that did. The fact that all of the theorems of *Principia* turn out to be consequences of the postulates of Strict Implication was presumably the reason for creating a distinct subsystem without material implication that would accord with ordinary inference.

Lewis then undertakes to extend Strict Implication to propositional functions. The key question here is how the modal operators are to relate to the quantifiers. Lewis takes the quantifiers as referring to actual cases. What then is the status of "$\sim \Diamond \phi x$"? Lewis's answer is that "$\sim \Diamond \phi x$" is not a propositional function but a proposition, even though it contains a variable. Then Lewis says, "we shall have the law '$\sim \Diamond \phi x < \pi x \sim \phi x$' 'If ϕx is impossible, then it is false in all [actual] cases.'" Modal operators here act in some respects like quantifiers. Since "$\sim \Diamond \phi x$" is the proposition "ϕx is impossible," it holds of all "x's", for a proposition is true of every x or of none. So in "$\sim \Diamond \phi x < \pi x \sim \phi x$", the quantifier is required only in the consequent to cover all actual cases. The modal proposition implies the extensional proposition, but not the converse. If we take "$\alpha = \hat{x}(\phi x)$" and "$\beta = \hat{x}(\psi x)$", then "$\alpha < \beta$" may be correctly interpreted "The class-concept of α, that is, ϕ, contains or implies the class-concept of β, that is, ψ. The intensional relation "$<$" implies the extensional relation, "$\supset$", but not the converse." Lewis then raises the question of what intensional relations correspond to the extensional logical sum and logical product of two classes. His answer is, "there are none." Consider, he says, the following equivalences:

$$\alpha \wedge \beta = \hat{x}(\phi x \wedge \psi x) = \hat{x}[(x \in \alpha) \wedge (x \in \beta)]$$

$$\alpha \bigcirc \beta = \hat{x}(\varphi x \bigcirc \psi x) = \hat{x}[(x \in \alpha) \bigcirc (x \in \beta)]$$

$\varphi x \bigcirc \psi x$ is a *proposition*—the proposition $\Diamond (\varphi x \cdot \psi x)$, "It is possible that φx and ψx both be true." And being a proposition, either it is true of *every x* or it is true of none. So that $\alpha \bigcirc \beta$, so defined, would be either 1 or 0. Similarly, $\varphi x \wedge \psi x$ is a proposition, either true of every *x* or false of every *x*; and $\alpha \wedge \beta$ would be either 1 or 0. Consequently, $\alpha \wedge \beta$ and $\alpha \bigcirc \beta$ are not relations of α and β at all. The product and sum of classes are relations of extension, for which no analogous relations of intension exist. This is the clue to the failure of the continental successors of Leibniz. They sought a calculus of classes in intension: *there is no such calculus*, unless it be confined to the relations $\alpha < \beta$ and $\alpha = \beta$.[99]

This argument is not clear, for

$$(\alpha = \beta) = \hat{x}(\varphi x = \psi x) = \hat{x}[(x \in \alpha) = (x \in \beta)]$$

Why isn't "$\varphi x = \psi x$" a proposition if "$\varphi x \wedge \psi x$" is a proposition? If it is, it would seem that there can be *no* intensional relations corresponding to the relations among classes. Indeed, since Lewis gives "$p \wedge q = \sim p < q$", if "$\varphi x \wedge \psi x$" is a proposition, how can "$\varphi x < \psi x$" not be a proposition? If there is a calculus of class-concepts in intension involving "$<$" and "$=$", it must involve "$\wedge$" and "$\bigcirc$".

There is an interesting contrast between the system of Strict Implication here presented and the Matrix Algebra Lewis presented four years before. In the Matrix Algebra, both the system of Material Implication and the system of Strict Implication are subsystems whose postulates are theorems of the more general system. But, by 1918, Lewis had succeeded in deriving the subsystems, including the system of Material Implication, from the system of Strict Implication. Thus, now Lewis could indeed claim that the system of Strict Implication was the fundamental system of logic, not in the sense that no other was possible, but in the sense that the others, including the system of the *Principia*, were subsystems of Strict Implication. For pragmatic reasons, one might prefer the system of Material Implication, or the Calculus of Ordinary Inference, but the system of Strict Implication was the fundamental system.

At this point, Lewis launches into a discussion of the notion of implication. "It is impossible," he says, "to escape the assumption that there is some definite and 'proper' meaning of 'implies.'"

The word denotes that relation which is present when we "validly" pass from one assertion, or set of assertions, to another assertion, without any reference to additional "evidence." If a system of symbolic logic is to be

applied to such valid inference, the meaning of "implies" which figures
in it must be such a "proper" meaning . . . This is no more than to say:
there are certain ways of reasoning that are correct or valid, as opposed
to certain other ways which are incorrect or invalid.[100]

Logic for Lewis is a normative science; some arguments are correct or right
and some are not. Here again, one sees that Lewis regards symbolic logic as
the application of a formal system to a logical subject matter. Lewis deals
with this directly. Since some mathematical systems—for example, the
geometries—are now regarded as abstract formal systems, why may not
the same be true of symbolic logic? "The answer is that a system of symbolic logic *may* have this kind of abstractness. . . . But it *cannot be a criterion of valid inference* unless the meaning, or meanings, of 'implies' which
it involves are 'proper.'"[101] There are, Lewis says, two methods of developing logic: the nonlogistic method of Boole and Schroder, and the logistic
method of *Principia* and Strict Implication. The former assumes ordinary
logic in its proofs. But in the logistic method, "its postulates and theorems
have a double use. They are used not only as premises *from which* further
theorems are deduced, but also as rules of inference *by which* the deductions are made."[102] Therefore, "if a postulate of symbolic logic, used as a
rule of inference, be false, then not only will some of the theorems be false,
but some of the theorems will be *invalidly inferred*."[103] This is the same
charge Lewis had made in his earlier papers.

What makes this problem peculiarly difficult, Lewis held, is that any
argument for a particular meaning of "implies" is necessarily circular, since
it will use one meaning of "implies" to support itself. "One must make the
Socratic presumption that one's interlocutor already knows the meaning
of 'implies,' and agrees with one's self, and needs only to be made aware
of that fact."[104] Accordingly, Lewis points to the list of theorems derived
in *Principia* that "*do not admit of any application to valid inference*." Here
Lewis presents a list of "paradoxical" theorems similar to one he gave in
his earlier papers. The reason for these "peculiar" theorems Lewis traces to
Boole's having applied the algebra of classes, in which the null-class is
included in every class, to propositions, to which Peirce added the principle $p = (p = 1)$. But, Lewis says, "*Inference* depends upon meaning, logical import, *intension*,[105] not on extension."

Lewis then discusses formal implication. The issue, he says, is the
range of the variable. According to Whitehead and Russell, "πx" [should]
be taken to signify "for all x's that *exist*." But "if $\pi x(\phi x \supset \psi x)$" refers to all
possible x's, $\pi x(\phi x \supset \psi x)$ means "It is impossible that ϕx be true and ψx
false." Thus, formal implication can be used to symbolize either a material

or strict relation, depending on the choice of values for the variables. Lewis then introduces the concept of "possible situations."

> Any set of mutually consistent propositions may be said to define a "possible situation" or "case" or "state of affairs." And a proposition may be "true" of more than one such possible situation—may belong to more than one such set.[106]

He uses this notion to resolve a problem that has arisen earlier in the *Survey*—the issue of triadic relations—where he had held that "$p \circ q \circ r$" was not equivalent to "$p \circ (q \circ r)$" but to "$p \circ (q \ \& \ r)$". Why? Suppose "p", "q", and "$\sim r$" form an inconsistent set such that "p", "q", and "$\sim r$" cannot all be true in any possible situation. Suppose that in the actual situation, "p" is true; then "q" and "$\sim r$" are not both true in the actual situation, "but it *does not* follow that q and $\sim r$ cannot both be true in some *other possible* situation (in which p should be false)—it *does not* follow that q and $\sim r$ are inconsistent, that $\sim(q \circ \sim r)$."[107] In the actual situation, we could infer "$q \supset r$", but not "$q \prec r$". Lewis does not use the term "possible worlds" here, but that is obviously what possible situations are.

In closing the chapter, Lewis tried to deal with the paradoxes of strict implication. Having attacked the systems of Material Implication on the ground that they yield paradoxical results, Lewis found that in his system of Strict Implication an impossible proposition implies every proposition, and a necessary proposition is implied by every proposition. This discovery is not original with Lewis; MacColl had noted this in 1906.[108] Rather than admit that these results are paradoxical, Lewis now tries to show that they are entirely proper. The argument is as follows.

> It will be granted that in the "proper" sense of "implies," (1) "p and q are both true" implies "q is true." And it will be granted that (2) if two premises p and q imply a conclusion, r, and that conclusion, r, is false, while one of the premises, say p, is true, then the other premise, q, must be false. . . . And it will be granted that (3) If two propositions, p and q, together imply r, and r implies s, then p and q together imply s.[109]

Then, Lewis says,

> These three principles being granted, it follows that if q implies r, the impossible proposition "q is true but r is false" implies anything and everything. For by (1) and (3), if q implies r, then "p and q are both true" implies r. But by (2), if "p and q are both true" implies r, "q is true but r is false" implies "p is false." Hence if q implies r, then "q is true but r is false" implies the negation of any proposition, p. And since p itself may be negative, this impossible proposition implies anything.[110]

The argument is then

1.	$p \ \& \ q < q$	[Postulate 1.2]
2.	$(p \ \& \ q < r) < (\sim r \ \& \ q) < \sim p$	[Antilogism]
3.	$[(p \ \& \ q < r) \ \& \ (r < s)] < (p \ \& \ q < s)$	[Transitivity]
4.	$[(p \ \& \ q < q) \ \& \ (q < r)] < (p \ \& \ q < r)$	3, $r/s \ q/r$
5.	$(p \ \& \ q < q) < [(q < r) < (p \ \& \ q < r)]$	4, Exportation
6.	$(q < r) < (p \ \& \ q < r)$	1,5, Modus ponens
7.	$(q < r) < (\sim r \ \& \ q < \sim p)$	2, 6, Transitivity

Remembering that "$q < r = \sim\Diamond(q \ \& \ \sim r)$", we have that an impossible proposition implies any proposition.

Parry criticized this proof on the ground that Lewis had gone from "$[(p \ \& \ q < r) \ \& \ (\sim r \ \& \ q)] < \sim p$" to "$(p \ \& \ q < r) < [(\sim r \ \& \ q < \sim p)]$" by Exportation, but that Exportation was not a theorem of Strict Implication. For Parry argued that, if it were, we would have

1.	$(p \ \& \ q < r) < [p < (q < r)]$	[Exportation]
2.	$(p \ \& \ q < p) < [p < (q < p)]$	[1; p/r]
3.	$p \ \& \ q < p$	[Postulate 1.2]
4.	$p < (q < p)$	[2, 3; Modus ponens]

Hence, a true proposition would be implied by any proposition. And

5.	$\sim p < (\sim q < \sim p)$	[4; $\sim p/p \ \sim q/q$]
6.	$\sim p < (p < q)$	[5; Transposition]

A false proposition would imply any proposition. That, Parry noted, "would lead to the reduction of Strict to Material Implication."[111] But Lewis's verbal argument is unclear concerning antilogism. In the first of the previous quotes, he can be interpreted as saying "$[(p \ \& \ q < r) \ \& \ (\sim r \ \& \ q)] < \sim p$," but in the second what he says is pretty clearly "$(p \ \& \ q < r) < (\sim r \ \& \ q < \sim p)$," which is correct. Parry takes Lewis to be deriving the latter from the former. Lewis's statement in the first quote is certainly unclear, so Parry's criticism may be off the mark. But there is no doubt that with respect to step 5 of Lewis's proof Exportation is applied to Transitivity, so the proof does appear to be invalid.

Lewis, however, was unaware of these problems in 1918, and concluded:

In this respect, then, in which the laws of Strict Implication seemed possibly not in accord with the "proper" sense of "implies," we have demonstrated that they are, in fact, required by obviously sound logical principles, though in ways which it is easy to overlook.[112]

In the final chapter, Lewis deals with the issues of "logistic", logic, and mathematical method. Euclid, Lewis notes, tried to deduce geometry from explicit postulates, but was unable to do so without appealing to extralogical principles—a fact that led Kant into the error of believing that mathematics required synthetic a priori principles. But modern mathematics has shown that mathematical systems can be developed as purely deductive systems that are independent of any particular interpretation. Such systems are wholly abstract; they are uninterpreted formal systems that differ from each other only in the different patterns of relations they embody. They differ then only "as *types of order*." But such systems involve logical operations by which the theorems are derived from the postulates. These logical operations may be stated in ordinary English, as in the Boole–Schroder algebra. But

> only when the logical operations also are expressed in idiographic symbols do we have logistic. In other words, *all* rigorously deductive mathematics gets its principles of operation from logic; *logistic* gets its principles of operation from *symbolic* logic. Thus logistic, or the logistic development of mathematics, is a name for abstract mathematics the logical operations of whose development are represented in the idiographic symbols of symbolic logic.[113]

The logistic method, Lewis holds, is a universal method that is applicable to any body of "exact knowledge." Nevertheless, differences within the logistic method itself require analysis. One such difference has to do with the degree to which the terms involved in the system are analyzed. Lewis takes as his example of this the difference between Peano's *Formulaire* and Whitehead and Russell's *Principia Mathematica*. He first describes Peano's work, giving the Peano axioms and pointing out that the fundamental notions—number, zero, and successor—are assumed as primitive. Lewis contrasts Peano's work with the *Principia* in which the Peano axioms are derived from those of logic and the primitives of Peano's system are defined in terms of purely logical notions. But whichever of these methods is employed, "the general method of *proof* in logistic will be the same."[114]

But there is a further difference within logistic itself that Lewis considers more fundamental. This difference has to do with two basic questions

> (1) What is the nature of the fundamental operations in mathematics; are they essentially of the nature of logical inference and the like, or are they fundamentally arbitrary and extra-logical? (2) Is logistic ideally to be stated so that all its assertions are metaphysically true, or is its principle

business the exhibition of logical types of order without reference to any interpretation or application?[115]

As Lewis notes, in *Principia*, logic is taken as fundamental and everything else is developed from the meaning of the logical constants. But there is an alternative method, which Lewis describes as follows.

> A mathematical system is any set of strings of recognizable marks in which some of the strings are taken initially and the remainder derived from these by operations performed according to rules which are independent of any meaning assigned to the marks.[116]

Thus, the system would be an uninterpreted formal calculus; no meanings would be assigned to any marks or strings, and the operations would proceed without reference to any meanings. Lewis illustrates this approach with respect to the postulates of the propositional calculus of the *Principia*, relabeling the variables as "quids" and the logical constants as "quods." Such an approach would have no metaphysical implications, whereas, Lewis says,

> If Mr. Russell is right, the mathematician has given over the metaphysics of space and of the infinite only to be plunged into the metaphysics of classes and functions. Questions of empirical possibility and factual existence are replaced by questions of "logical" possibility—questions about the "existence" of classes, about the empty or null-class, about the class of all classes, about "individuals," about "descriptions," about the relation of a class of one to its only member, about the "values" of variables and the "range of significance" of functions, about material and formal implication, about "types" and "systematic ambiguities" and "hierarchies of propositions." And we may be pardoned for wondering if the last state of that mathematician is not worse than the first.[117]

But from the formalist point of view, the approach of the *Principia* now appears as an arbitrary choice of one interpretation among many, for "nothing is essential in a mathematical system except the *type of order*."[118]

Symbolic logic, as Lewis sees it, is an *application* of a symbolic system to a logical subject matter. The circularity that Lewis has noted before, in which logic is presupposed to develop symbolic logic, results from the fact that the symbolic system, as developed in *Principia*, for example, is not truly abstract. But if the symbolic system is seen, as in the algebraic tradition it always was seen, as the application of a formal "mathematical" or symbolic system to logic, then the symbolic system itself, seen as a type of order, may be developed from principles very different from those of logic.

"We shall, in that case, regard symbolic logic as one mathematical system, or type of order, among others." "Logistic will, then, be defined not by any relation to symbolic logic but as the study of types of order as such, or as any development of mathematics which seeks a high degree of generality and complete independence of any particular subject matter."[119]

What would such an alternative system be? Lewis offers as an example the system Σ of Royce. This system, as we have already seen, is a general formal system generated from principles very different from those of symbolic logic. But, as Royce showed, from this system, by due selection, it is possible to obtain the logic of classes as a subsystem. Lewis's point here is not that the system Σ is an adequate basis for logic—it does not contain his own system of Strict Implication—but that this type of approach offers an alternative to the approach of the *Principia*, and an alternative that Lewis believes should be pursued. Which of these is the better method, Lewis says, "is entirely a matter of choice."[120] The methods of Peano, Russell, and Royce are all, in Lewis's view, variants of the "logistic" method. And Lewis concludes:

> For when mathematics is no longer viewed as the science of number and quantity, but as it is viewed by Mr. Russell or by anyone who accepts the alternative definition offered in this chapter, then the logistic treatment of *any* subject *becomes* mathematics. Mathematics itself ceases to have any peculiar subject matter, and becomes simply a method. Logistic is the universal method for presenting exact science in idiographic symbols. It is the "universal mathematics" of Leibniz.[121]

In 1920, Lewis received a letter from E. L. Post of Columbia, pointing out that his postulate 1.8—"$(p < q) = (\sim\Diamond q < \sim\Diamond p)$"—led to trouble. Lewis had held that 1.8 was equivalent to

    a. $(p < q) < (\Diamond p < \Diamond q)$

    b. $(\sim\Diamond p < \sim\Diamond q) < (\sim p < \sim q)$

(a) and (b) are equivalent to

    a' $(p < q) < (\sim\Diamond q < \sim\Diamond p)$ Transposition

    b' $(\sim\Diamond q < \sim\Diamond p) < (p < q)$ $p/q\ q/p$ Transposition

which is the form in which he gives them in his reply to Post. Post had shown that b' led to the conclusion "$\sim\Diamond p = \sim p$." As Lewis remarked, "Since the distinction of 'impossibility' from simple falsity is essential to that of 'strict' from 'material' relations, the presence of this consequence of [b'] would be to reduce the system to a redundant form of 'Material Implication.'"[122] To correct the error, Lewis replaced 1.8 by "$(p < q) < (\sim\Diamond q < \sim\Diamond p)$." But since a number of proofs in Chapter V depended on 1.8, this meant that many other theorems had to be deleted. However, Lewis still claimed that the deduction of the postulates for Material Implication could be carried out, and in his response to Post indicated how this could be done. The damage was therefore not fatal. But, for what Lewis called "similar reasons," postulate 8 of the Calculus of Ordinary Inference had to be revised from

$$8. \quad (p \ \& \ q < r \ \& \ s) = [(p \bigcirc q) < (r \bigcirc s)]$$

to

$$(p \ \& \ q < r \ \& \ s) < [(p \bigcirc q) < (r \bigcirc s)]^{123}$$

Despite the laudatory reviews by Sheffer[124] and Wiener,[125] the *Survey* had its problems.

When, in 1959, Lucie Dobbie of the University of California Press contacted Lewis about the possibility of republishing the *Survey*, he refused. "I hope that it was a good book in 1918, but to reprint it now, without extensive alterations, would be inexcusable on the part of the author."[126] He did eventually agree to having Dover Press republish the first four chapters, which appeared in 1960,[127] but Chapter V, in which he had presented his own system of Strict Implication, and Chapter VI, in which he had proposed the method of Royce's Σ as an alternative to the *Principia*, were not included. Those chapters were never republished.

Biographical Note II

Harvard

Lewis's years at Berkeley were not devoted solely to logic. He was also greatly interested in ethics and social philosophy. The lecture notes that survive from his courses on social relations between 1911 and 1920 show that he dealt with Kant, Stirner, Marx, Hegel, Fichte, Hobbes, and Royce (using the *Philosophy of Loyalty*). But the course also included economics, covering the standard topics. In these lectures, Lewis did not hesitate to express his own views. He was no advocate of laissez-faire; he believed that competition should be limited and reward proportional to services rendered. Although he saw education as the way to achieve reform, he endorsed government regulation to "prevent economic gain where no public service has been performed." "Such government regulation," he said, "must be taken out of politics and entrusted only to experts." He favored regulation by experts, not by politicians, supported a graduated income tax as well as a tax on rent. He also supported old-age pensions and the public ownership of utilities. He went even further: "possibly, the state may see to it that all children are not only educated, but properly clothed, fed, and given proper medical attention." But, he added, "this project necessarily implies some social elimination of those unfit to be parents."[1] In other words, Lewis was a Progressive; he distrusted raw competition and favored government regulation, but by experts rather than elected officials, and apparently supported some form of eugenics. This was not an uncommon combination of beliefs for a Progressive of that era. The influence of his socialist father and his early reading had not entirely disappeared.

In June 1914, Lewis was promoted to the rank of assistant professor. Clearly his teaching and publications were deemed adequate, but his salary remained low[2] and he found it necessary to supplement it with other jobs.

But his domestic life was far from satisfactory, despite the birth of his daughter Peggy on February 3, 1911.[3] Mabel had a series of serious illnesses and became increasingly unhappy over her style of life; in the spring she took the children back to Massachusetts to stay with her mother "determined not to return." But Irving fell ill with diphtheria. As his conditioned worsened, Mabel became alarmed. "I wired C, begging him to come. He wired back that he would not—the expense was too great and he felt committed to teach in the summer session."[4] Whether or not Lewis fully understood the seriousness of the situation we do not know. The child died. Mabel wrote

> C came a few days later, torn with grief. Too late! His coming was meaningless now—gave me no help. If he could afford to spend the money now, why had he not come when I had begged him to? I was shut away in my anguish. We could not reach each other. He stayed only a few days, then returned to his teaching.[5]

Mabel agonized over what to do: "Throughout the summer I wrestled with my problem: Should I go back to C or break free? In the end I decided that I could not add to C's desolation by taking away his home."[6] And so she went back. But her unhappiness continued. Lewis was clearly a traditional husband; he dominated the house, controlled the expenditure of what money there was, gave her an allowance to cover her domestic and personal needs, and expected her to play the part of a traditional wife. This was not what Mabel wanted. "Marriage to me means a union in which love—not husband, not wife—dominates. It was C's life, not *ours* that we were living. I no longer had any satisfactory place in it."[7] She tried to resume her education, and began a novel, but the demands of home and family frustrated her efforts.

In these unpromising circumstances, and with considerable soul-searching, she agreed to have another child, and in due course a son, David, was born on April 28, 1915.[8] Not long after that, Mabel came finally to a decision about her future life. As she recorded,

> Standing one morning, looking down from the window upon the ocean of roofs extending below farther than the eye could reach, I thought: So many, many roofs!—What, unknown to me, lies under each?—Perhaps problems greater than mine, perhaps pain more acute—Measured against the experiences of so many, many others, what right have I to think that my trouble is so all-important!—In the procession of life from the beginning, how puny is one individual!—What a tiny speck in infinity!—I must get my life into perspective—get my values sorted out.
>
> It is evident that, under the circumstances, there can't be two careers in our family. Which would an objective observer decide should be sacrificed? The answer is obvious. C is already established in his, has proved

its validity. Any success I might achieve can't be so assessed—has, as yet, no proof. I can, however, play an important part in shaping C's career.

Circumstance has forced me into a distasteful role.—Can't I play it as an actor should?—to the hilt while on stage, but otherwise maintaining his own untouched personality. Instead of feeling myself caged within walls, why not instead encircle that which I must set myself to accomplish: the fulfilment of C's life—and stand outside, unfettered, free in spirit? If I could keep my involvement impersonal, I could not be hurt by anything C said or did, not feel wounded and deprived.—I could learn to laugh at stings—best of all, learn to laugh at myself.

And so a new life for me began. I have ever striven to carry out the decision thus made: to protect and care for C to the utmost of my ability; to make home a place of warmth and cheer and serenity.[9]

We do not know to what extent Lewis was aware of his wife's misery, though one would think there must have been indications, or of her final decision. His attitudes were those of his time, and he probably did not understand her unhappiness. Furthermore, Lewis was a quintessential professional scholar, devoted to his work that his wife could not share, and no doubt regarded the income he earned as his primary contribution to the marriage. Throughout this period, his publications continue without interruption. Mabel was eighty years too early in her desire for a two-career family, and Lewis's low income made matters worse. She finally made the same decision that most women of that time did and sacrificed her ambitions for her family.

But then the nation went to war. Lewis enlisted as a private, although he could have gotten a commission without much difficulty. Having survived basic training, Lewis was sent to Fortress Monroe, Virginia, to teach gunnery[10] where his family joined him. Here he served out the war, reaching the rank of captain by the time it was over. The Lewises found that neither the publication of the *Survey* nor his army duty translated into either promotion or higher salary at Berkeley.[11] But then Lewis received a letter from Professor James Woods inviting him to lecture at Harvard for the academic year 1920–1921 at a salary of $4000—well above his Berkeley salary.[12] Of course, Lewis accepted.

Lewis said he left California "with reluctance," for he was leaving behind many friends and had succumbed to the beauties of the place, but, more important, he was leaving a secure position for one whose future was highly uncertain. "But for one who grew up under Royce and James and Perry, no other position in philosophy could have quite the same meaning as one at Harvard."[13] Nor was sentiment the only reason. In 1920, the Harvard Philosophy Department was still the most prestigious in the country. But it was not of the same quality as when Lewis had been a student. James had retired and subsequently died. Royce was dead. So was Munsterberg, and Palmer had retired in 1913, although he was still active.[14] Santayana had left in 1912 to make his home in Europe. Perry was still there, but the most distinguished philosopher at Harvard in 1920 was William Ernest Hocking, whose field was religious philosophy. James Houghton Woods was chairman—an able but not distinguished man.[15] In logic, Henry Sheffer was a man of real talent, but his position was only that of a lecturer.[16] The Harvard Department was living on its reputation, but it was not what it had been.

During the period Lewis was at Berkeley, the philosophic scene in the United States had become more variegated. Although Idealism was under increasing attack, it remained one of the major philosophic positions through the next several decades. William Ernest Hocking at Harvard was a leading proponent. Born in 1873, Hocking had received his doctorate from Harvard in 1904, and was particularly influenced by Royce. His *Meaning of God in Human Experience* in 1912 established him as a major philosopher of religion, but Hocking wrote on a variety of topics, including *Man and the State* in 1926 and *The Spirit of World Politics* in 1932. He was a prolific writer who addressed both popular and professional audiences. Wilbur Urban at Yale was also an Idealist. Born in 1873, he took his Ph.D. at Leipzig in 1897 and wrote on theology, cosmology, language, and particularly on values. Urban wrote the first American book devoted specifically to value theory—*Valuation*, published in 1909. He thus inaugurated a spate of books on this subject that would continue to appear for decades.[17] DeWitt Parker at the University of Michigan, John Boodin at UCLA, and Edgar Brightman at Boston University were also influential Idealists in this period. And the arrival of Whitehead at Harvard in 1924, and the publication of *Process and Reality* in 1929, brought a new variant of Idealism to the American scene. Whitehead's penchant for coining new terms, and the extreme compression of his style, made *Process and Reality* a book with a limited audience, but Whitehead's doctrines have proven to have greater staying power than those of any other Idealist and his followers are still important in American philosophy today. If Idealism no longer ruled American philosophy in the 1920s and 1930s as it had earlier, it was still very much alive and its proponents continued to address, and reach, a wide audience.

Among the rivals to Idealism, Pragmatism was one of the leaders. After the death of James, John Dewey was universally regarded as the nation's leading Pragmatist; he was also the most famous American philosopher of the era and the most widely read. Dewey's move from Chicago to Columbia did not diminish his relentless productivity or his influence. Other

Pragmatists were also important; George Herbert Mead, who stayed at Chicago when Dewey left, was a major figure. So were Charles Morris and Horace Kallen, but no one challenged Dewey's position as the leader of the movement. Of the New Realists, Perry, Montague, and Holt continued to carry the banner. Perry was the most influential; a prolific writer on a wide variety of topics, popular and technical, he continued the model of the public intellectual of James and Royce. His *General Theory of Value* in 1926 was his most famous work,[18] but he was a tireless advocate of democracy, championed intervention in both world wars, and supported a world organization to keep the peace.

But this was also the period in which Critical Realism emerged as a movement. Santayana was one of the early contributors to this movement, but the name was coined by Roy Wood Sellars. Born in Canada in 1880, Sellars took his doctorate at the University of Michigan and stayed there as a professor for the rest of his career. Sellars wrote on epistemology, cosmology, ontology, democracy, and religion, so he was no narrow specialist, but his *Critical Realism* in 1916 brought the new position to public notice. In 1920, Sellars joined with Santayana, Arthur Lovejoy, C. A. Strong, and four other philosophers to publish *Essays in Critical Realism*,[19] which was to this movement what *The New Realism* had been to Perry and his colleagues eight years before.

For the Critical Realists, the knowing process involved an organism, a "datum" or "content," and an object. Objects are independently existing entities in a real external world and are the causes of our percepts. The "content" of the percept is not our sensations, but an "essence" in Santayana's sense—that is, a pure quality (even if it is a quality of an aggregate) whose mode of being is different from that of any existent. Thus, as an essence, "red" is neither psychological nor physical; it is not a sensation but what we have the sensation of; it is static, changeless, universal, and simple.[20] Because essences are universals, they can be instanced both in our percepts and in external objects. The essence is not the object known in cognition but that by which we know the object. A cognition (proposition) is true if the essence instanced in our percept is the same as that instanced in the object; otherwise, it is false. That there are external objects to be known is an instinctive belief. As Sellars put it, "The physical world is not an inference but a retained conviction held through reflection, because it harmonizes with all the facts as no other position will."[21] This position, so its defenders claimed, could avoid the difficulties of error and illusion that plagued Neorealism, and the problems of the past and others selves that plagued Pragmatism. The philosophic scene in 1920 was more complex than it had been in Lewis's student days.

When Lewis returned to Harvard, he lived briefly in Stoneham and commuted to Cambridge; then the family settled in Cambridge in Shady Hill Square. Although they liked the house and enjoyed nice neighbors, they found the social scene at Harvard "frosty and repelling."[22] Mabel attended some college teas but found them chilly and abandoned the project. Although Palmer was gracious and Mrs. Royce was a welcome friend who lived nearby, the Lewises did not take well to Cambridge, or Cambridge to them. Lewis got along with his colleagues well enough, but, in an interesting sense, he really did not relish the company of "intellectuals." As his son put it,

> Many persons coming out of the same general sort of background as he, achieving an academic success, plunge into it; it becomes their environment. They live among academics, they socialize with academics, they are concerned with academic controversy and relationships of one field to another. In his life, dad pretty much kept these in separate compartments. . . . There was a good deal of shoe worker in him.[23]

The Lewises made other friends.

Throughout this period, Lewis's career steadily progressed. After his probationary year in 1920–1921, he was appointed an assistant professor.[24] But he had not been forgotten by his friends at Berkeley and, in 1922, was offered a full professorship there at a salary of $5000. Lewis wrote to President Lowell, explaining the situation and asking for some clarification of his prospects at Harvard. Lowell's reply offered him no assurance whatever and said, "I do not see how I can encourage you to think that it would be possible to appoint an additional professor at any time that can now be foreseen."[25] So great was the lure of Harvard that Lewis decided to stay there anyway—a decision his wife strongly supported. But Berkeley wanted Lewis back, and in the fall of 1922 renewed its offer with a salary of $6000—an excellent amount for that time. Again the Lewises agonized over the decision, but eventually decided to stay at Harvard.[26]

In January 1923, Lewis gave a series of lectures on logic at Columbia. His publications were attracting interest in the profession, and even Harvard recognized that fact. In April 1924, he was promoted to associate professor of philosophy, a permanent appointment.[27] Moreover, the social climate at Harvard, which the Lewises had found frosty when they arrived, had begun to thaw and the quality of their lives improved.

On August 5, 1925, the Lewises had their last child, Andrew.[28] Not long afterward, they moved to Lexington,[29] where they continued to live throughout Lewis's career at Harvard. Lewis rarely entertained his colleagues, but he made it a practice to invite graduate students to his home every week during the academic year. The Lewis children went to Lexington public schools, and Mabel became very active in community affairs. They were not political, and Lewis's views had become increasingly Republican, but he registered as a Democrat for the particular purpose of being able to vote against James Michael Curley in the primaries. Curley, of course, survived Lewis's opposition, but Lewis was thoroughly disgusted by the corruption of Massachusetts politics.

Lewis's teaching in the 1920s included, as one would expect, courses on logic. In 1920–1921, he taught a course on logical theory that he repeated from 1922 through 1925. He also taught a course on formal logic from 1924 through 1928. Sheffer, of course, was also teaching logic courses regularly, and Huntington in the mathematics department also worked in logic. And, in 1924, Whitehead came to Harvard. But despite this concentration of faculty talent, Harvard was not in the forefront of work in mathematical logic. Between 1916, when Sheffer joined the Harvard faculty, and 1932, when Quine submitted his dissertation, eleven dissertations were written at Harvard on "the nature of logical implication, the nature of logical systematization, or the nature of logical justification." Only Norbert Wiener's dissertation, and, of course, Quine's, were genuine dissertations *in* logic.[30] Harvard may have been the foremost center of logic in the United States, but it was not up to the standard being set abroad.

Beginning in 1920, Lewis taught a course on the "Philosophy of Evolution"; although it appeared as "Ethics" in 1921–1922, Lewis changed the name back to the "Philosophy of Evolution" from 1922 to 1930. The course was the forerunner of his later course on social ethics. In 1920, he taught a course on Post-Kantian Idealism; the next year and again in 1923 he taught a course on the *Critique of Pure Reason*, and from 1922 through 1930 he taught one entitled "The Kantian Philosophy" (except in 1923–1924 when he gave "Ethical Theories of Post-Kantian Idealism"). He also taught "Advanced Ethics" from 1920 to 1924 and a seminar on ethics in 1926–1927. And five times between 1920 and 1930 he taught a course on the theory of knowledge. These, together with various service courses, made up his schedule.[31] One should note in particular the heavy emphasis on Kant and on ethics, both of which received more emphasis in his teaching than logic or epistemology, though the latter were not neglected.

Unfortunately, notes from these courses have not survived. But there are notes from some lectures of 1922–1923 that are probably from the Philosophy of Evolution course. In lectures headed "Competition and Civilization," he covered Erasmus Darwin, Lamarck, St. Hilaire, Charles Darwin, Wallace, Lloyd Morgan, DeVries, Haeckel, and Huxley. But by far the most attention was given to Herbert Spencer. Lewis had read Spencer in his teens and regarded him as an important figure. His view is

summed up in the conclusion: "All these considerations point to one conclusion: the ethical question (in its social aspects) is the question what
extent and how we shall interfere with the otherwise 'natural' struggle for
survival."[32] As this should indicate, the equation of the struggle for survival with laissez-faire competition that Spencer advocated did not persuade Lewis; but he did not go to the other extreme of arguing, as Huxley
did, that progress depended on combating the evolutionary process.[33]
Quite clearly, Lewis's interest in social philosophy in general, and competition in particular, was part of his dominant interest in ethics.

Lewis was an excellent teacher, as the many testimonials from his students demonstrated. Williams remarks:

> He was an arresting and beguiling teacher, conversational and engag-
> ingly salty, but very learned, searching, and consecutive, and gifted above
> all with that inimitable genuineness which showed ideas growing up
> before his class with the fresh spare life and color of flowers on a New
> Hampshire hillside.[34]

Although he avoided dramatics and was intensely serious, he had well
learned from Royce the value of humor. Williams records that

> his comment on the critical realist theory that perception is mediated by
> a conscious datum between mental act and external object: it reminded
> him, he said, of the man who yelled at the intending passenger who ran
> onto the deck just as his ship drew away, "Go ahead! You can make it in
> two jumps."[35]

A course with Lewis was a memorable experience.

Throughout this period. Lewis's reputation and professional activities
continued to grow. In 1925 and again in 1927 and 1928, he lectured on
logic at Columbia[36] and in 1926 he went to Berkeley to deliver the Howison
lecture.[37] Lewis's family life had now stabilized. Whatever problems Mabel
had had with the marriage seem to have been resolved. The Lewises were
delighted with their three children, and he was now financially secure and an
established figure in his profession. And he continued to write.

4

Pragmatism

In 1914, Juliette Peirce—Charles Peirce's widow—had given or sold—maybe both—to Harvard the mass of manuscripts that Peirce had left at his death that year.[1] With Royce's death, there was no one at Harvard who was greatly interested in Peirce's papers, or in Peirce, and the papers were stored in a room in the Harvard Library. When Lewis arrived in 1920, he was given this room as an office—apparently in the hope that as a logician he would have some interest in Peirce's remains. The manuscripts were in chaos, and Lewis had no intention of devoting his time and energy to cataloguing or editing Peirce's writings—an activity that would not have been rewarded at Harvard—but he did browse through many of them. Lewis later remarked:

> This experience served to revive earlier trains of thought, particularly such as found their initiation under James's tutelage. And in Peirce basic ideas were often more roundly developed than in James, and in ways which jumped with my own bent of thinking. It finally dawned upon me, with some surprise, that as nearly as my own conceptions could be classified, they were pragmatic; somewhere between James and the absolute pragmatism of Royce; a little to one side of Dewey's naturalism and what he speaks of as "logic." When *Mind and the World Order* was published in 1929, I ventured to label its general point of view "conceptual pragmatism."[2]

In an earlier retrospective, Lewis wrote,

> At just this time it became my duty and privilege to turn over the numerous unpublished papers of Charles Peirce. Though I was not specially conscious of it, this was perhaps the means of stirring up old thoughts of

111

the time when I had listened to James, and reminding me also of what Royce used to call his "absolute pragmatism." Again, I had long been attracted to certain theses of Dewey's logic. . . . Peirce's "conceptual pragmatism," turning as it does upon the instrumental and empirical significance of concepts rather than upon any non-absolute character of truth, was at some points consonant with my own reflections where James and Dewey were not.[3]

These two passages, the first written in the early 1960s, the second published in 1930, telescope much of Lewis's development in the 1920s. But both emphasize his debt to Peirce, for whom he felt a genuine awe, and specify the time of that contact as immediately upon his return to Harvard in 1920. The latter passage, written just after *Mind and the World Order* was published, calls Peirce's position "conceptual pragmatism" (a term never used by Peirce), which is the term Lewis used to describe his own position in *Mind and the World Order*. Both passages emphasize his debt to James and Royce, as well as Dewey, and locate his adoption of Pragmatism as a development of the early 1920s.

Although discovering that he was a pragmatist surprised Lewis, the line of development that led to it is fairly clear in retrospect. When Lewis went to Berkeley, he considered himself an Idealist. But his Idealism was certainly not Royce's; his views were closer to Kant's than to either Absolute or Subjective Idealism. Lewis tells us he was drawn to the study of logic by the insights it offered in epistemology. As he saw it, the modern logical and mathematical analyses of infinity and continuity undercut Kant's proof of the ideality of appearances and showed Idealism to be false. What he then adopted was a form of "humanism" that emphasized the active role of the human mind in the construction of our knowledge of reality. He did not at that time see his position as similar to pragmatism, but the two were not that far apart, and it is not surprising that as he worked out his humanist position he found it leading him to pragmatism. This event, occurring about 1920, marked an important transformation of Lewis's work. In fact, the early 1920s seem to have been a time of great intellectual excitement for Lewis and was probably the most creative period of his career. As Lewis recalled,

I now sat down (this was in 1921) to the first draft of something concerning these [problems], which I projected as "Studies in Logic and Epistemology." These will never see the light. They grew from one box to two, and then to several. But the yeast of the newly awakened pragmatic conceptions was working too strongly. My thought changed and widened as I attempted to formulate it, and the result, instead of moving toward some unity of subject and literary coherence, spread in widening circles through the whole field of philosophy. It was a most satisfactory period to me personally, because in the course of it I squared my account with many problems and brought them into touch with one another. What I shall venture to call "conceptualistic pragmatism" proved to be, for me, the key that opened many doors.[4]

The "first draft" has not survived, but what Lewis describes fits what we know of his method of work. He wrote every day, setting down whatever came to mind,[5] and working out his ideas as they appeared. The results, if one can judge from the later manuscripts that do survive, were kept in loose-leaf notebooks—sometimes dated, sometimes not—and were then mined for material that was issued in published form—usually with extensive revision.

What were the problems Lewis was grappling with during these exciting days after his return to Harvard? Most important, he had to settle his accounts with Idealism. Doing so involved several issues. One was the absolute status of logic and, more generally, the method of proving certain doctrines absolutely true by arguing that the denial of the doctrines implied their reaffirmation. Lewis dealt with this issue in an article he published in 1921 entitled "The Structure of Logic and Its Relations to Other Systems."[6] Lewis says there are three types of logical theories: (1) the view that logic is formal and also concerned with actual ways of right thinking; (2) the view that logic is concerned with actual ways of right thinking, and which repudiates the formalist notion "for that reason"; and (3) the view that logic is formal and not concerned with the actual processes of right thinking. The first Lewis identifies as traditional logic, the second as "modern" logic— that is, Hegelian logic[7]—and the third as the new mathematical logic. Lewis considers only the third conception here and ignores the issue of the psychology of correct thinking, not because it is not important but because it is not a question of logic.[8]

The new logic treats deductive systems, of which mathematics is the best example, as formal systems. The idea that such systems can demonstrate facts from self-evident axioms Lewis says was overthrown by the discovery of non-Euclidean geometries. It is now recognized that the systems are simply a set of deductively related propositions in which the choice of postulates is governed by "deductive power and simplicity" and is quite arbitrary; different propositions can serve equally well as postulates for the same systems. The issue for such systems is their consistency, not their truth. If they are applied, then the issue of truth arises, but, in that case, their verification is "always partial and inductive."

Lewis then draws from this view of the nature of deductive systems a series of important consequences. First, "the traditional rationalistic conception that metaphysical first principles can be shown to be logically necessary, or that what is logically prior is more certain or self-evident, is a conception to which the actual structure of logical systems lends no support."[9] Given the multiple sets of postulates from which a given system can be deduced, the rationalistic view makes no sense. But does this hold true for the "fundamental principles of logic itself," since it has been held that these are "implied by the very attempt to negate them?"[10] This question leads Lewis to examine the issue of reaffirmation through denial. The denial of a fundamental principle of logic can mean one of two things. One can deny such a principle and then avoid the use of that principle in any further reasoning. This will involve no contradiction.[11] Or one can deny the principle and use it in further reasoning (i.e., stay within the system), in which case the denial of the principle will imply the principle itself and thus a contradiction. But Lewis says this proves only that "deductions *in* logic are inevitably circular . . . [that] in deducing our theorems of logic, we must make use of the very principles which the deduction is supposed to demonstrate."

To prove this, Lewis uses the example of the denial of the principle of noncontradiction, which he states as " 'x is A and x is not A' is false." The contradictory is, "x is A and x is not A." Then

1. "x is A and x is not A" implies its latter half, "x is not A."
2. "x is not A" implies "It is false that x is A."
3. "It is false that x is A" implies "That x is A and x is not A, is false."[12]

But in step 2, Lewis says we have actually reintroduced the law of noncontradiction. Hence the contradiction. That is, if we take the denial of noncontradiction as a premise, we have

1. $A \ \& \sim A$
2. $(A \ \& \sim A) < \sim A$ Simplification
3. $\sim A$ 1, 2, modus ponens
4. $A < (A \text{ v } R)$ Addition
5. $A < \sim(\sim A \ \& \sim R)$ $\sim(\sim A \ \& \sim R)/(A \text{ v } R)$ Biconditional
6. $\sim A < \sim(\sim\sim A \ \& \sim R)$ $\sim A/A$
7. $\sim A < \sim(A \ \& \sim A)$ A/R, Double Negation
8. $\sim(A \ \& \sim A)$ 3,7, modus ponens

But double negation is equivalent to the law of noncontradiction. The reasoning is therefore circular, so long as we remain within the given system of logic. Hence, the denial of any of its principles leads to contradiction.

"A *good* logic *must* be circular,"[13] Lewis says. But so, Lewis says, must a bad logic, of which he then proceeds to give an example. Using "$<$" as a symbol for "implies" in any of the several meanings of "implies," the postulates are

A. $\sim(\sim p) = p$
B. $\sim(p < \sim p)$
C. $(p < q) < (\sim q < \sim p)$
D. $[p < (q < r)] < [q < (p < r)]$
E. $(q < r) < [(p < q) < (p < r)]$
F. $(p < q) < (\sim p < \sim q)$[14]

F is clearly false as a general principle of implication. But in this system, Lewis argues, for any proposition "p", we can prove "$\sim p < (\sim p < p)$" and so prove reaffirmation by denial. Since reaffirmation by denial then holds in both "good" and "bad" logics, it does not "prove the truth of the principle thus reaffirmed."[15] "Bad" logics may be just as consistent as good ones.

What does Lewis mean here by "good" and "bad" logic? He means those that do or do not accord with our normal understanding of inference. It is not true in ordinary usage that if "p" implies "q", the negation of "p" implies the negation of "q". That "It is now January" implies "It is now winter" does not imply that "It is not now January" implies "It is not now winter." Logic in this sense is applied logic; purely formal systems are just consistent or not consistent, and are neither good nor bad.

Reaffirmation by denial also fails to prove that a proposition is necessary. There are, Lewis says, necessary propositions, and they can be proven from other necessary propositions, but they cannot be proven by reaffirmation by denial. "The use of reaffirmation through denial is never legitimate as demonstration of new truth, though it *is* legitimate, and frequently valuable, as a means of pointing out inconsistency of assumptions."[16]

What about the use of reaffirmation through denial outside of logic? Lewis's answer is that when the method is so used, it is invariably the case that what is to be proven has already been assumed; "there is always a colored gentleman in the woodpile."[17] For example, the statement "There are no propositions" is said to be self-contradictory because it is itself a proposition. But the statement does not assert that it is a proposition, and without this assumption there is no contradiction. Hence, the contradiction only results if the assumption is added, and the assumption contains the contradictory of the original statement.

Lewis then considers the issue of presupposition. This term, Lewis notes, has various meanings. Often it is taken to mean "necessary condition," but when so taken it is usually taken incorrectly, since "no general principle is a necessary condition of any particular fact or assertion unless the particular fact or assertion implies the general principle."[18] Very often, a confusion of sufficient with necessary conditions is involved. If "p" implies "q", "p" is a sufficient condition for "q", but it is not a necessary condition for "q" unless "q" implies "p". If presuppositions were necessary conditions, their number would be endless. But "presupposition" is also taken as meaning logically prior, in the sense in which mathematics is logically prior to physics. But this proves nothing about the necessary character of mathematics. The most that can be said is that where the facts of physics are well established, the application of mathematics to physics is verified partially and inductively.

A final sense of "presupposition" is psychological—the claim that certain general principles are "*necessarily assumed* by every rational mind." This, Lewis says, is what historical rationalism believed, and it will not stand examination. If there are such principles, they ought to be evident in a common logical sense. But is there any such common logical sense? Unfortunately, Lewis concludes, there is little evidence to support the existence of such agreement. And this is most apparent among those who are most versed in logic. "Precisely where we should hope to find this unanimity complete—that is, amongst students of logic—it is, in fact, most notably and lamentably absent."[19]

Up to this point, Lewis has been clearing away misconceptions about logic. He then turns to what the new logic does do—it provides a new method in philosophy whose significance has not yet been fully appreciated. "It offers the deductive procedure, *not as a method of proof but a method of analysis*."[20] By formalizing a system, we find out what is essential to it, what concepts are necessary, how they must be defined, what principles are assumed, and how its propositions are related. As Lewis notes, the use of irrationals was well established in mathematics before Dedekind and Cantor, but "what was *not* clear was the *nature* of irrationals. The problem was, as Dedekind's title put it, 'Was sind und was sollen die Zahlen?' "[21] Similarly, the point of *Principia Mathematica* was not to prove the commutative law of addition but to clarify the nature of mathematics and state its concepts and propositions precisely. And Lewis adds that Whitehead's *Principles of Natural Knowledge* undertakes to do this for physical concepts.[22]

The use of this method, Lewis says, has so far been associated with realism, by which he obviously means Russell. But the method is free of any metaphysical implications: it is equally consistent with Idealism, Realism, and Pragmatism. What it does prove is that "the idea of the traditional a priori"—of exclusive truth or indispensability of some set of first principles—has no justification. The method will be most useful "when our knowledge of proximate facts becomes fairly comprehensive, detailed, and exact." Yet even in other areas, Lewis claims, "the mental habit which this method enforces—the search for explanation through analysis and open minded consideration of alterative possibilities—has a value which should not be disregarded."[23] The position Lewis sets forth here is quite different from that he had held ten years earlier. There is nothing absolute about logic as it is conceived here. Furthermore, in attacking reaffirmation by denial, Lewis was attacking just those sorts of arguments that Royce had used to establish the absolute character of logic and that he himself had accepted. Lewis was rethinking his position.

The second issue concerning Idealism that Lewis needed to settle was the question of monism. What made this issue particularly important was the paradoxes of Strict Implication. In 1930, reflecting on those paradoxes, Lewis wrote that he had been forced to accept them when he found that they followed from principles of logic that were beyond question. Nevertheless, the existence of the paradoxes bothered him. Having early come to the conclusion that "all valid inference, being a matter of intension, rests upon the analysis of meaning"[24] and having created a logic based on intensional implication, he was perplexed by the result. On the one hand, he was now more than ever convinced that "all the propositions of logic are truths of intension, and therefore certifiable without reference to the merely factual or empirical."[25] On the other, pondering the problem of the paradoxes brought him to the conclusion that "implication is not a property of isolated propositions as such, but of systems."

> Necessary truths are all of them principles of logic, or such as can be cer-
> tified on grounds of logic alone. Without logic, nothing is derivable
> from anything; the logic of it is implicit in every deductive system. All
> necessary propositions are thus, explicitly or tacitly, present in every sys-
> tem, and indeed in every assertion conceived as having logical conse-
> quences. Inference is analytic of the system rather than of its separate
> and bare constituents.[26]

What did Lewis mean by this statement? He seems to have meant several things. First, whether or not a given proposition implies another depends not on the propositions alone, but on the system of logic in use. In his Calculus of Ordinary Inference, for example, the paradoxes of material implication cannot be derived, whereas in the system of *Principia Mathematica* they can. Second, he meant that the relation of implication is defined by the postulates of the system in which that relation occurs. "The content of logic is the principles of inference."[27] The rules of the system as a whole require a certain concept of implication. As Lewis had already shown, there were different logical systems with different concepts of implication—for example, strict implication and material implication. Third, he meant that every "system" in which the constituent propositions are held in any sense to "follow" from one another assumes a system of logic, whether this assumption is made explicitly or left implicit. These reflections led Lewis to a further question.

> If inference is analytic of systems, not of propositions in isolation, does this mean that logic compels the acceptance of a coherence theory of truth or the acceptance of that kind of unity of the world which is maintained by logicians of the "modern" or Hegelian school?[28]

This was the issue that led Lewis to publish "Facts, Systems, and the Unity of the World" in 1923.[29]

From time to time, Lewis had suggested that the new developments in logic had important metaphysical implications. In this paper, he attempted to draw such conclusions about the issue of monism versus pluralism. Instead of following most metaphysical studies by taking the world as made up of objects, Lewis chose to consider it as made up of "facts," meaning that which a proposition "denotes or asserts." These two methods of describing the world are equivalent, for "in the array of all facts, objects and their relations will be comprehended, just as all facts would be determined in the array of objects." Lewis's choice is dictated by his belief that "the *fact* is, by its very nature, the unit of knowledge"[30] and the relations among facts are simpler to deal with, being those of propositions. Moreover, Lewis takes a fact to be what a proposition asserts, whether the proposition is true or false, in order to avoid having to talk about actual and non-actual facts and because it is the relations among propositions that are his concern.

He next defines a system as follows:

1. If A is a fact of a given system—call it Σ—and A is inconsistent or incompatible with B, then B is not in Σ.
2. If C is in Σ, and C requires or implies D, then D also is in Σ. ["Implies" here means strictly implies.]
3. If E and F are facts in Σ, then Σ contains also the joint-fact E · F.[31]

To each such system of facts corresponds the system of propositions that assert those facts. Such a system will be consistent. We know, Lewis says, a lot about such systems. First "There is more than one such system." Second, one system may contain another. Third, two systems can have facts in common, but some facts in one may be inconsistent with some of those in the other. The example Lewis cites to prove this is the geometries. Whatever is implied by their common postulates alone will belong to them all, but whatever follows from the different parallel postulates will not be common. It also follows that some facts can be consistent with both a fact B and its negation, if B is independent of the other facts. "This" Lewis says "is often overlooked or even denied in metaphysics."[32]

But Lewis says the existence of facts independent of given systems does not settle the issue between monism and pluralism because it is often claimed that this independence results from the inadequacy of our knowledge and that as our knowledge becomes more complete we approach one final system "whose parts stand in relations of rigid necessity and such that no actual fact can be independent of it."[33] This claim—that every fact in our world is determined by every other—Lewis denies. To prove this, he develops the notion of "possible worlds." Any possible world is a system, but not all systems are possible worlds. To be a possible world, the following requirements must be met.

I.   If A is a fact of a given world—call it Ω, and A is incompatible with B, then B is not in Ω.
II. If C is not in Ω, then the contradictory of C is in Ω.
III. If E and F are in Ω, then Ω contains the joint-fact $E \cdot F$.[34]

The difference between systems and worlds, lies in the difference between 2 and II: for a world, excluded middle applies.

Our knowledge constitutes a system, but not a world, because our knowledge is necessarily incomplete. No matter how far knowledge advances, it can never determine the actual world; therefore *the real world is always merely one among many which must be viewed as equally possible.*[35] Furthermore, Lewis says, the world cannot have the kind of unity the monist wants. The argument Lewis summarizes as follows.

I. If any world is logically conceivable, then more than one is logically conceivable; because (a) every self-consistent system must be contained in or "true of" at least one possible world, and (b) there are systems, equally self-consistent, which cannot be true of the *same* world. II. Every possible world will contain some facts in common with any other. Hence, III, the actual world contains some facts in common with worlds which are conceivable but not actual. Therefore, IV, reality can not be such that all its facts are necessary and necessarily related.[36]

"No conceivable knowledge can ever be adequate to a world: the notion of Reality or The Universe is simply a regulative ideal of reason in the Kantian sense," Lewis concludes.[37]

The only claim here that may be puzzling is II. Lewis argues that if II were not true, there could be only two possible worlds—the world of all true propositions and the world of all false propositions. But while all true propositions are consistent with each other, this is not true of all false propositions, so they cannot describe a single possible world. Hence, there is either one possible world, or every possible world has something in common with every other. For since every proposition must be true or false of any possible world, if any two possible worlds did not have some propositions in common, one would have to contain just the negations of the propositions in the other. That would mean there is but one possible world. But there is more than one possible world. Hence, the conclusion.

Further, Lewis argues, every possible world has some mutually independent parts. For let there be two possible worlds, W1 and W2. Let the set of propositions common to W1 and W2 be A, and let the set of propositions true in W1 but false in W2 be B. A and B are contained in W1, and no proposition of B follows from a proposition of A because in W2 all propositions in A are true and all propositions in B are false. Hence A and B must be independent. The same argument applies for any two worlds, and the number of such independent systems of facts will depend on the number of possible worlds with which it has something in common. Hence "the number of independent parts in any possible world must increase as the number of mutually incompatible systems increases."[38] But there are an infinite number of such incompatible systems, for Riemann proved that the number of self-consistent geometries inconsistent with each other is infinite.

However, Lewis qualifies this conclusion by remarking that, although the world is not one in which, given any one fact, all others are then determined, it may be such that there is no fact in it not determined by some other facts in it. Any system may be formalized using different sets of postulates with no common members, so that there is no proposition that is not a consequence of some other propositions in the system. Yet some proposition may be independent of others; the postulates, for example, may be independent of each other. And some propositions of one system may belong to another, even though the two systems, taken as wholes, are inconsistent. "Thus nothing in the preceding forbids the notion that the actual world is a very tight system of interrelated facts." But, Lewis concludes, "A monism which identifies the necessary with the actual, the actual and the all-possible, is incompatible with conceptions which are logically fundamental."[39]

We have seen before good reason to believe that Lewis rejected monism, but this paper is by far his most detailed and explicit attack on the position. Whatever Lewis's attraction to Royce's work, he was certainly no Absolute Idealist. Whether James's pluralism in any respect influenced Lewis's views is unclear; Lewis makes no reference to James, and although he had certainly read *A Pluralistic Universe*, there is no evident similarity between Lewis's position and James's beyond the mere fact of rejecting monism for pluralism. What is clear is that Lewis was working out his own position in the 1920s, using the logical tools he had acquired, and exploring new ideas.

The third issue that Lewis had to deal with was the religious issue. Idealism was, among other things, a philosophy of religion, especially in the form given it by Royce. It is not clear to what extent Lewis was attracted by this aspect of Idealism, nor do we know what Lewis's own religious beliefs were, though both his son and his wife believed he was not religious at all.[40] But, in 1921, he was studying Hocking's *Meaning of God in Human Experience* and lecturing on religious feeling and religious theory.[41] In 1922 through 1924, Lewis taught courses on metaphysics. Among his papers are lectures for a course in metaphysics that, although not dated, were probably written at this time. The basic human interests, Lewis wrote, approach the character of "causes," in Royce's sense of that term. Royce had held in *The Philosophy of Loyalty*—a book Lewis assigned in his courses—that men find significance in their lives by identifying themselves with a "cause" that is at once an ideal, the realization of which they seek, and a community—the community of those loyal to that cause. For Royce, the cause unites its adherents into a superorganic entity, and eventually into that greatest of all unifying entities—the Absolute. Lewis follows Royce only part of the way. He echoes Royce in saying, "The hope of significance for one's self is the hope to find genuine 'causes' to which one is genuinely devoted," and he follows Royce in seeing these causes as social.

> So conceived, the validity of life-purposes more and more looks toward such interests as are vested in human institutions, and, finally, in the life of humanity . . . so far as this is true, the validity of the more meaningful of our purposes is concerned with the possibility of realizing social purposes—the hope of human progress in general.[42]

But what, Lewis asks, guarantees the validity of "*my* purposes"? This, he says, is the question with which the "religious mind" is primarily concerned. Lewis's answer is that the guarantee lies "in the continued and progress (sic) life of those institutions for which I have worked" or "in the life of man in society."[43] But Lewis does not follow Royce into the loving arms of the Absolute.

> In the end, we must realize that our ideal is an *ideal*, individual and perhaps not valid. But in this we merely acknowledge risks of human life in general—the scientist cannot be *guaranteed* his discovery. His purpose

has meaning if it is a genuine *possibility*. The significance is not *merely* in the end. Human life returns upon itself.[44]

Unlike Royce, for whom Absolute Idealism did guarantee our ideals, Lewis makes no such claim; he does not follow Royce to his metaphysical conclusions. Indeed, Lewis seems to have rejected any appeal to the divine.

> We have taken the weight of the world from God's shoulders and put it on our own. . . . Man invented God because he could not walk alone. . . . Our new realization shrieks to us, "You are alone. There is no help. Stand on your own two feet always and utterly—or weakly fail."[45]

This lacks something of the literary flair of Russell's "Free Man's Worship," but the message seems to be similar.

Surveying the field of philosophy at this point, Lewis was led to remark that

> no German is satisfied to discover the truth; he wants to create it. No Frenchman believes there is such a thing, and anyhow it is less important than intellectual neatness and literary form. The English glimpse the truth but are afraid to do more than poke at it. And the other nations rest in outer darkness altogether.[46]

As a comment on the relation between philosophy and national character, this is not a bad assessment of the situation at that time—or now. But one presumes Lewis did not intend to include the United States among the "other nations."

Lewis was now ready to state the conclusions to which his reassessment of his position had brought him, and he did so in 1923 in "A Pragmatic Conception of the A Priori"[47]—surely the most famous article he ever wrote. The concept of the a priori, Lewis says, involves two perennial problems of philosophy—"the part played in knowledge by the mind itself, and the possibility of 'necessary truth' or of knowledge 'independent of experience.'"[48] But traditional conceptions of the a priori have proven untenable. The reason for this Lewis locates in two errors: although what is a priori is necessary, the relation of necessary truth to mind has been misunderstood, and, although the a priori is independent of experience, its relation to empirical fact has been misunderstood. But Lewis says

> What is *a priori* is necessary truth not because it compels the mind's acceptance, but precisely because it does not. It is given experience, brute fact, the *a posteriori* element in knowledge which the mind must accept willy-nilly. The *a priori* represents an attitude in some sense freely taken,

a stipulation of the mind itself, and a stipulation which might be made in some other way if it suited our bent or need. Such truth is necessary as opposed to contingent, not as opposed to voluntary. And the *a priori* is independent of experience not because it prescribes a form which the data of sense must fit, or anticipates some preestablished harmony of experience with the mind, but precisely because it prescribes nothing to experience. That is *a priori* which is true, *no matter what*. What it anticipates is not the given, but our attitude toward it: it concerns the uncompelled initiative of mind or, as Josiah Royce would say, our categorical ways of acting.[49]

Traditionally, the prime example of the a priori was the laws of logic. "Sometimes," Lewis says, "we are asked to tremble before the spectre of the 'alogical,' in order that we may thereafter rejoice that we are saved from this by the dependence of reality upon mind."[50] And, in 1913, Lewis had listed as the cardinal principles of Idealism "the non-existence of any alogical real, the priority of epistemology, and the precedence of 'truths of appreciation' over 'truths of description.' "[51] Now he declares the alogical a "pure bogey, a word without meaning." Nothing either imaginable or unimaginable can both be and not be or violate similar laws of logic; to see this as a problem is to misconceive the relation of logic to the world. Thus falls another principle of Idealism.

Logic, Lewis says, is purely formal and prohibits only what concerns the use of terms and modes of classification and analysis. Thus, the law of excluded middle represents only our decision to make a complete dichotomy of experience for every term instead of a trichotomy or some other division. These laws Lewis calls "the parliamentary rules of intelligent thought and speech. Such laws are independent of experience because they impose no limitations whatever upon it." Their legislative character arises from the fact that they are decrees we impose on ourselves, not on the world; they represent "only our own categorical attitudes of mind."[52]

Further, Lewis says, "the ultimate criteria of the laws of logic are pragmatic."[53] Pointing to the varieties of logical systems that exist, each of which is internally consistent, Lewis says that the only bases for choosing among these are "pragmatic grounds of conformity to human bent and intellectual convenience." The same thing is true, Lewis says, of definitions. Definitions, and the analytic truths to which they give rise, are indeed necessarily true—that is, true under all possible circumstances. But definition is also arbitrary and not forced on us by experience.

If experience were other than it is, the definition and its corresponding classification might be inconvenient, fantastic, or useless, but it could not be false. Mind makes classifications and determines meanings; in so doing it creates the *a priori* truth of analytic judgments. But that the manner of this creation responds to pragmatic considerations, is so obvious that it hardly needs pointing out.[54]

This leads Lewis to consider Mill's claim that arithmetic is not a priori because one could conceive of a demon who, whenever two pairs of things were added, would sneak in a fifth, so that experience would warrant the claim that $2 + 2 = 5$. But Mill was wrong, Lewis says; he confounded pure mathematics with its physical application. Mathematical addition is not a physical process; Mill's supposition would require changes in our physics, not our mathematics, because pure mathematics prescribes nothing for experience. And this is so because we choose to make it so—we legislate it to ourselves.

> Those laws and those laws only have necessary truth which we are prepared to maintain, no matter what. It is because we shall always separate out that part of the phenomenon not in conformity with arithmetic and designate it by some other category—physical change, chemical reaction, optical illusion—that arithmetic is *a priori*.[55]

The role of the a priori in science is greater than is usually thought, Lewis says. This is shown by three considerations. First, "definition is classification." Science seeks classifications that lead to the discovery of regularities in nature. Definitions and classifications that fail to do this "can not be said to be false; they are merely useless." But this classifying–defining activity is prior to and essential to investigation. Until we can formulate our questions with precision, experience cannot answer them.[56] Second, "the fundamental laws of any science—or those treated as fundamental—are *a priori* because they formulate just such definitive concepts or categorical tests by which alone investigation becomes possible."[57] Lewis then includes an extended quotation from Einstein on the stipulative character of the definition of simultaneity in physics. "We can not even ask the questions which discovered law would answer until we have first by *a priori* stipulation formulated definitive criteria."[58] But he also notes that "such *a priori* laws are subject to abandonment" if the resulting theory does not simplify our understanding of phenomena. Third, the criteria for the real in our experience are a priori. "A mouse which disappears where no hole is, is no real mouse."[59] We define what is real and what is unreal. We determine that real things exhibit certain uniformities, and that which does not exhibit such uniformities we classify as unreal. Indeed, Lewis goes further: "An object itself is a uniformity. Failure to behave in certain categorical ways marks it as unreal." This, Lewis notes, "is one of the puzzles of empiricism." Experience contains both the real and the unreal—dream, illusion, hallucination, and veridical perceptions. There are no laws of experience per se. Only when we have sorted out the real from the unreal can we hope to find laws of the real.[60]

Scientific classification, the criteria of the real, and natural law form an interrelated and interdependent set. It is received opinion that spirits cannot be photographed. But suppose they were—what should we do?

> What we should do would be to redefine our terms. Whether "spook" was spirit or matter, whether the definition of "spirit" or of "matter" should be changed; all this would constitute one interrelated problem. We should reopen together the question of definition or classification, of criteria for this sort of real, and of natural law. And the solution of one of these would mean the solution of all. Nothing could *force* a redefinition of spirit or of matter. A sufficiently fundamental relation to human bent, to human interests, would guarantee continuance unaltered even in the face of unintelligibility and baffling experience.[61]

In addition to the principles of logic, which Lewis says "we seem fully prepared to maintain no matter what," there are categories, concepts, and laws that underlie our whole scientific enterprise. The most fundamental of these are a priori, even though "continued failure to render experience intelligible in such terms" might result in their being abandoned. Without these, we could not say what experiences are relevant to the questions we want to ask, or even formulate the questions. But no matter what our experimental findings, these concepts could be maintained. Thus, one who refused to abandon absolute space and time could maintain his belief by challenging the experimental results or adding some other "law." "And the only sense in which it could be proved unreasonable [to do this] would be the pragmatic one of comparison with another method of categorical analysis which more successfully reduced all such experience to order and law."[62]

To his views, Lewis says, it might be objected that nothing should be called a priori that could be rejected. "Such objection is especially likely from those who would conceive the *a priori* in terms of an absolute mind or an absolutely universal human nature." In reply, Lewis says:

> We wish to emphasize two facts: first, that in the field of those conceptions and principles which have altered in human history, there are those which could neither be proved nor disproved by any experience, but represent the uncompelled initiative of human thought—that without this uncompelled initiative no growth of science, nor any science at all, would

be conceivable. And second, that the difference between such conceptions as are, for example, concerned in the decision of relativity versus absolute space and time, and those more permanent attitudes such as are vested in the laws of logic, there is only a difference of degree. The dividing line between the *a priori* and the *a posteriori* is that between principles and definitive concepts which *can* be maintained in the face of all experience and those genuinely empirical generalizations which *might* be proven flatly false.[63]

Neither human nature nor human experience is fixed and absolute. Lewis holds that our categories are historical social products that have become accepted for pragmatic reasons and that they can be changed for similar reasons.

This article represents a radical shift in Lewis's position. Here he adopts Pragmatism, something one would hardly have expected on the basis of his previous statements about that position, and it is here that he declares himself an empiricist. But the shift is less radical than at first appears. Lewis has retained the constructive and legislative role of the mind, but in a new sense. He has kept a priori truth, yet redefined it. The spontaneity and freedom of mind, the essential role of the categories, the priority of logic are all here. So is the determining role of human purposes and needs in shaping our knowledge. At the same time, he has finally accepted the conclusion toward which his logical work had been leading for a dozen years—that the only basis for choosing among logics is pragmatic. And though he maintains a distinction between the a priori and the a posteriori, the difference is now one of degree only. If he will not allow the a priori to be proven false, he does allow it to be proven useless and to be abandoned. And in pointing out that classification, criteria of the real, and natural law are all mutually adjusted to give us the most useful fit to experience, he implies that analytic truths can also be abandoned when pragmatically necessary. For if analytic truth is a product of definition, and definitions can be abandoned in the face of unintelligible experience, then analytic truth has no immunity from being declared useless.

While Lewis was working out his brand of Pragmatism, he was also studying the philosophy of science. The man who seems to have made the greatest impression on him in this area was Alfred North Whitehead. Given Lewis's reputation as an empiricist, it may seem surprising that Whitehead should have exerted such an influence. But "surprise" here betokens some misunderstanding. For today's readers, Whitehead is chiefly known for two things: he was with Russell the co-author of *Principia Mathematica*, and he was the author of a panpsychic metaphysical system set forth in *Process and Reality*—the form in which his Gifford lectures were published in 1929.

But, however famous, these are only two of Whitehead's many works, and in his own time he was known for much else. Whitehead was a mathematician of enormous prestige in the early 1900s; his treatise, *Universal Algebra*, in 1898 was a book Lewis had closely studied, and his writings on geometry were well known. The original plan for *Principia Mathematica* called for a four-volume work, the first three to be written by Whitehead and Russell jointly, the fourth on geometry to be written by Whitehead alone. The fourth volume was never written; instead the researches that were to have led to it took a different turn. The work of Hilbert and Veblen had already reduced geometry to axiomatic form and sharply separated questions of the formal theory of geometry from those of its application to real space. But, beginning in 1905, came Einstein's theory of relativity, which, while it resolved the immediate crisis in physics, raised problems of a fundamental sort with respect to the most basic of physical concepts—particularly time, space, and matter. Einstein's famous definition of simultaneity forced physicists to reexamine what had seemed the most obvious and certain of the concepts they employed. One example of this process of reexamination was Percy Bridgman's *The Logic of Modern Physics*,[64] which sought to put physics on a secure basis by defining its concepts in terms of operations. In a very different way, Whitehead was reacting to the same problem.

In 1919, Whitehead published *An Enquiry Concerning the Principles of Natural Knowledge*; the next year he published his Tarner Lectures as *The Concept of Nature*; in 1922, he published *The Principle of Relativity*.[65] In these three books, Whitehead attempted to provide a new foundation for physical knowledge that would be adequate for relativity as well as all other aspects of the science. Whitehead was explicit that in these books he was not doing metaphysics or considering metaphysical questions;[66] his concern was with our knowledge of nature, where by "nature" he meant "that which we observe in perception through the senses."[67] Insofar as Whitehead dealt with the question of the relation of the mind to nature, it was as the interaction of two elements within nature, not as the relation of nature to something outside itself.

That Lewis was deeply impressed by Whitehead's views we know from his own statements. Writing in 1955, Lewis said, "I slaved over Whitehead's 1920 books."[68] Moreover, Lewis wrote an essay on Whitehead's theory of natural knowledge that was published in the Library of Living Philosophers volume on Whitehead in which he describes Whitehead's theory in some detail.[69] And among the books that Lewis left at his death is his copy of *An Enquiry Concerning the Principles of Natural Knowledge* with extensive marginalia. Thus, we have considerable evidence for the impact of Whitehead's thought on Lewis.

All we can know of the world, Whitehead held, we know through our sensory experience.[70] Nature is what we perceive by our senses. But modern science, Whitehead argued, assumes as basic a set of entitles that are not perceptibles at all and therefore are not part of nature: durationless instants of time, dimensionless points of space, and point-particles of matter occupying such spatial points at such instants. In such a scheme, change becomes impossible because change requires temporal duration.[71] Such a view Whitehead terms a "metaphysical fairy tale."[72] Instead, "the ultimate fact for observational knowledge is perception through a duration; namely, that the content of a specious present, and not that of a durationless instant, is an ultimate datum for science."[73] What Whitehead demands is that all scientific concepts must be reducible to terms "of what can be disclosed in sense-presentations."[74] This position is what Lewis terms Whitehead's "radical empiricism"—an empiricism he says that "is like no other in history."[75] The Vienna Circle went no further.

Perception, Whitehead says, is "an awareness of events, or happenings."[76] The "percipient event" is that of the perception itself that is an event in nature; everything perceived as simultaneous with the percipient event constitutes a duration—it is all nature during the percipient event. The duration itself is a "slab of nature" rather than a "stretch of time," but it contains an indefinite number of other events that comprise nature during the duration.[77] Indeed, Whitehead uses the term " 'ether of events' to express the assumption of this enquiry, which may be loosely stated as being 'that something is going on everywhere and always.' "[78] The key relation among events is extension; an event may extend over other events and be itself extended over by yet other events. Events can overlap or be separate. Time and space themselves are derived from the relation of extension among events, and all the elements of time and space—points, instants, and so on—are derived from extensive events by a process Whitehead calls extensive abstraction.[79] Events are immovable and unrepeatable; they are what is happening and their happening is what we perceive and is therefore nature.

For Whitehead, objects are not events; they are derivative entities and bear an "adjectival" relation to events. Objects are repeatables, so they can be "situated" in different events. "The essence of the perception of an object is recognition."[80] There is the recognition of the object within the specious present, the recollection of it as related to other events not in the specious present, and the memory of it as related to other specific events. In other words, "the common material objects of perception, such as chairs, stones, planets, trees, etc. are adjectival bodies pervading the historical events which they qualify."[81] Events do not move, but a continuous series of events in time, or "route," is "pervaded" by an adjective if the adjective is present at every stretch of the route. Material objects pervade such routes.

Whitehead gives particular attention to three types of objects. The first is sense objects, such as a definite shade of red, that can occur in multiple events. "The situations of sense-objects form the whole basis of our knowledge of nature, and the whole structure of natural knowledge is founded on the analysis of their relations."[82] The second type are perceptual objects, which are the ordinary objects of experience—trees, stones, cows, and so on: "A perceptual object is recognized in an association of sense-objects in the same situation. The permanence of the association is the object which is recognized."[83] But more than a constant conjunction of sense objects is involved, for the sense objects also "convey" the perceptual objects: "For example, we see both the horse and the colour of the horse, but what we see (in the strict sense of the term) is simply colour in a situation."[84]

Conveyance is not "primarily" a judgment but a sensuous perception. However, judgments supervene respecting the character of the object conveyed. If the perceptual judgment is correct (i.e., not delusive), the perceptual object is termed a "physical object."[85] At the bottom of the page on which Whitehead stated this position, Lewis wrote in the margin of his copy "What is a real object? The answer is here."[86]

The third type of object Whitehead discusses is scientific objects. Whitehead is strongly opposed to the "bifurcation of nature" and wants to show that scientific objects, like all others, are reducible to sensory experience.[87] To achieve this, he invented what he calls the method of extensive abstraction. Suppose an infinite series of events such that, for any two events in the series, one extends over the other, and no event is extended over by every event of the series; such a series is called an abstractive set or series. The abstractive series converges, but its limit does not belong to the series. Thus, although every member of the abstractive series is an element of nature, the limit, if there is one, is not. So an abstractive series of durations will converge toward an instant, but as there is no instant in nature, the series will never reach such a limit. However, the series itself, particularly the smaller end of it, may be treated as equivalent to the limit for scientific purposes. Further, other series can be formed consisting of properties of the members of the abstractive series; these series will correspond one-to-one to the members of the abstractive series and they may converge to a limit. Thus, the point of the method is to obtain the entities of classical, and relativity, physics such as instants, points of space, and so on that are not found in nature, by a limiting procedure that utilizes only entities of the sort that are found in nature. It will then follow that all types of entities employed in natural knowledge, whether common sense or scientific, are reducible to our sensory experience.[88]

Why was Lewis so impressed by Whitehead's work? Despite the difficulties of Whitehead's terminology, there is much in his theory that matched Lewis's own beliefs. In his dissertation, Lewis had sought to derive temporal and spatial relations from perceptual experience, but left the "context" of such relations unclear; Whitehead's doctrine of events provided a basis for this that Lewis needed. Lewis had made extension the fundamental property from which spatial relations are abstracted; Whitehead made extension the fundamental property from which both spatial and temporal relations are abstracted. Lewis believed that our knowledge of objects was based on regularities of our sense experience; so did Whitehead. Lewis held that physical objects were transcendent; one can certainly read Whitehead's theory of perceptual objects, and of sense-objects "conveying" the perceptual objects, in the same way, though Lewis's insistence on expectations of future experience is not obvious in Whitehead. Lewis believed in a given of perception; Whitehead's sense-objects match these very well. And Lewis had questions about the status of scientific objects such as electrons that he had yet to resolve. He was greatly impressed by Whitehead's method of extensive abstraction as a way of dealing with these issues. Lewis saw Whitehead's project as an attempt, by one of the world's leading logicians and mathematicians, to bring physics into a form in which the primitives were perceptual experiences. The attraction of this program for him was obvious; he would later find a somewhat different version of it in Carnap.

Questions about the philosophy of science of course led to questions about induction and probability, and Lewis found his answers in Keynes's *A Treatise on Probability*.[89] In 1922, Lewis wrote a review of this work that was very laudatory.[90] "The reader will easily be convinced that the method of attack is the right one and the constructive contribution is of the first importance." Four fundamental ideas, Lewis says, are developed:

> that probability is a relation of conclusion to premises like logical relations in general; that probabilities need not be numerically measurable in order to be objective and valid; that the theory of probability admits of formal treatment comparable to that of deduction; and that all induction is properly based on the notion of analogy and the rules of probability.[91]

Keynes's conception of probability, Lewis says, preserves its objectivity without making it dependent on external facts such as frequencies and frees it from psychological and subjective factors while allowing it to vary from one person to another and to be altered by new knowledge. "The probable conclusion, like the certain conclusion, is subject for logical evaluation; is a question of validity, not directly of truth-in-fact." This view Lewis finds "highly satisfactory."[92] He is troubled that the concept of probability itself is taken as unanalyzed, and that initial probabilities must somehow be directly known. This fact, together with Keynes's inclusion of rules of inference among the premises, suggests to Lewis that elements of subjectivity are not wholly excluded. He is also unhappy that Keynes accepts the Principle of Indifference, though he thinks Keynes's treatment of it avoids the worst objections to it. He praises Keynes's methods of handling problems in which direct measurement is not possible: "one feels that the refusal to reduce all to the arithmetic type is sound and promising for comprehensiveness of treatment."[93] And he expresses admiration for the way in which Keynes handles the "symbolic development" of the subject that Lewis says is "carried out much further than ever before, and with fewer errors."[94]

Lewis is particularly taken with Keynes's treatment of induction. "The important conclusions are that all induction is fundamentally concerned with analogy, and that pure induction can never establish a generalization, even in the sense of making it highly probable, unless we can find independent grounds for some *a priori* probability."[95] Lewis describes Keynes's treatment of analogy in some detail. By the use of Bayes theorem and a priori probabilities, Keynes argues that the validity of induction can be established. But the issue of a priori probabilities is one that Keynes believes involves the "structure of the natural world" and requires some "limitation on the 'independent variety of the universe.'" That leads Lewis to remark that Keynes "has made it abundantly clear that what is required for the validity of induction is some independent deduction of the categories."[96]

Lewis also continued to review a variety of books. Not surprisingly, he reviewed several books on logic.[97] By far the most important was his review of the second edition of *Principia Mathematica*.[98] Lewis notes briefly the nature of the project undertaken in the first edition—namely, the reduction of mathematics to logic—and says that is was successfully achieved for all branches of mathematics except geometry. He also notes that the fourth volume of the *Principia*, which was to have carried the project through for geometry, has not appeared and probably never will. But what receives Lewis's attention are the changes introduced in the second edition—changes due to Russell. The first of these is the introduction of the Sheffer stroke function as the single primitive in terms of which negation and disjunction can be defined, and Nicod's reduction of five of the original postulates of the *Principia* to one involving the stroke function.

The second is the elimination of asserted propositional functions by the device of quantifying their variables, thus turning them into propositions.

A more complex change made in the second edition is the restriction of the axiom of reducibility. This axiom was part of the apparatus introduced in the first edition to avoid the paradoxes, and allowed propositions about a class to be treated as statements about some propositional function that held for every member of the class. In the second edition this axiom is replaced by one holding that a propositional function "can only enter into a proposition through its values." As Lewis points out, the new substitute is not wholly satisfactory because it raises problems about real numbers and series. Lewis remarks:

> The real purpose both of the axiom of reducibility and of the proposed substitute is to be able to treat all the propositional functions which figure in mathematics in a manner which would be valid without further assumption if it were established that all such functions can be analysed into purely logical relations of their ultimate constituents.[99]

Lewis believes the difficulty in establishing this results from the attempt in the *Principia* to treat all logical functions as truth functions. This leads, Lewis says, to the view that all equivalent propositions are identical. And if logical equivalence means only equivalence of truth-value, it involves the conclusion that there are only two proposition, one true and one false.

> All mathematics will thus collapse into an immense tautology. Essentially this conclusion was accepted by Frege, and has been renewed by Wittgenstein: Mr. Russell seems to draw back from it without being willing to abandon the premises which lead to it.[100]

Lewis holds that "Logical truth, such as what is ordinarily meant by '*q* is deducible from *p*,' depends in part upon the form of '*p*' and '*q*,' and cannot be determined from their truth or falsity alone." It is therefore no surprise that the project of the *Principia* runs into difficulties. If fact, Lewis holds that the method of the *Principia* depends on considerations of form. He does not here spell out just what these considerations of form are, but apparently he is using "form" to mean that the truth or falsity of a proposition depends on its intension. In fact, Lewis believes that the logic of the *Principia* depends on the *intensional* meaning of the logical constants and, if that is the sense of "form" here, it would explain his statement that "in spite of the fact that the relations assumed as primitive are all truth-functions, the method of the work is largely dependent upon considerations of form, and is, I believe, inconsistent with the theoretical conceptions of the nature of mathematics which are expressed in it."[101]

In his Howison Lecture at Berkeley, "The Pragmatic Element in Knowledge,"[102] Lewis declared for Pragmatism more explicitly than in anything he had previously written. There are, Lewis says, three elements in knowledge: the given, the concept, and the act that interprets the former by the latter. Some like Bergson have emphasized the given; others like the Idealists have emphasized the concept, "Pragmatism is distinguished by the fact that it advances the act of interpretation, and its practical consequences, to first place." Although Pragmatism is said to hold that "the truth is made by mind," Lewis emphasizes that it differs from Idealism in that for the Idealist "mind" means the generic mind or ideal mind of the Absolute and the given "has ultimately no existence independent of mind." Lewis summarizes the fundamentals of the Pragmatic position as "that knowledge is an interpretation, instigated by need or interest and tested by its consequences in action, which individual minds put upon something confronting them or given to them."[103] The rest of the paper is an explication and defense of this position.

Lewis begins with the conceptual, and takes as his illustration pure mathematics. Recent work has shown that pure mathematics is a strictly formal structure independent of sense-experience: it is therefore a priori; given the postulates, definitions, and rules, every theorem is derivable purely by thinking. The truth about pure mathematics concerns only the logical structure, and is therefore more certain than any other type of truth we can have. *The a priori type of knowledge* is exhibited in its purest form by pure mathematics, but it is to be found in all our knowledge, although we are less aware of it. If we take the system of Newtonian mechanics and abstract the concepts from their denotation, we have a purely formal system like mathematics. When this is done, "we have generated a whole complex array of orderly relations or patterns of meaning" about which there will be a "logical truth"—a truth that is certain apart from experience"—but that concerns only the logical relations of concepts. The application of such conceptual systems to experience is essential to our knowledge, because they provide us with the system of categories by which we classify experience. And until we have such categorical concepts, we cannot acquire knowledge of the things to which they are applied because "we have no handle to take hold of them by."

Concepts represent "what thought itself brings to experience." The other element in experience is the given.

> The given is something less than perception, since perception already involves analysis and relation in recognition. One cannot express the given in language, because language implies concepts, and because the

given is just that element which cannot be conveyed from one mind to another. . . . But one can, so to speak, point to the given.[104]

The given is the "buzzing, blooming confusion," as James described it, on which the newborn infant opens its eyes. It is what is immediately before us. It is not knowledge, but the material from which knowledge is made. And the given is private to each individual. This privacy of the given does not prevent communication between two minds, however, since what is sharable is the pattern of relations among the qualities of experience rather than the qualitative aspects themselves, and these "patterns of logical relationships set up by these interconnected definitions of terms themselves constitute the conceptual meanings of the terms defined."[105] "The practical criterion of common meaning is congruous behavior."[106] If you see blue where I see red, it will make no difference so long as I act toward red things as you act toward blue things. What makes knowledge shareable is isomorphism of the relational structure of our concepts, not identity of sensuous experience.

Knowledge arises when we interpret the given by our concepts. This is something we bring to experience.

We confront what is presented by the senses with certain ready-made distinctions, relations, and ways of classifying. In particular, we impose upon experience a certain pattern of temporal relationships, a certain order, which makes one item significant of others. . . . It is by interpretation that the infant's buzzing, blooming confusion gives way to an orderly world of things.[107]

But where do these concepts come from? "The secret of them lies in purpose or interest." We invent conceptual schemes in an effort to make the world intelligible. The process is one of trial and error in which we are guided by our successes to develop better and better conceptual systems.

Lewis uses as an example the Copernican Revolution. It is possible to describe the celestial motions by either the heliocentric system or the geocentric; in theory at least, all the observational data can be made to fit either one. The choice thus comes down to the question of which system "describes the facts simply and conveniently." Similarly, he says that the choice between Newtonian mechanics and Einstein's Theory of Relativity is not just about facts, for the facts can be made to fit either, but "the really final issues are pragmatic ones such as the comprehensiveness of laws and economy in unverifiable assumption."[108] From these examples and others, Lewis concludes

that there is in [knowledge] an element of conceptual interpretation, theoretically always separable from any application to experience and capable of being studied in abstraction. . . . There is another element, the sensuous or given, likewise always separable by abstraction, though we should find it pure only in a mind which did not think but only felt. This given element, or stream of sensation, is what sets the problem of interpretation, when we approach it with our interests of action. The function of thought is to mediate between such interests and the given. Knowledge arises when we can frame the data of sense in a set of concepts which serve as guides for action.[109]

The criterion of the success of interpretation is "accommodation to our bent and service to our interests." And we find which interpretation is best by trial and error.

At this point Lewis addresses the issue posed by James's terminology in speaking of "new truth" and "old truth," of "becoming true," of "truer" and "falser." Lewis rejects this usage and tries to clear away the problems it has caused. When a new theory becomes established, as, for example, the Copernican theory, what is *new*, Lewis says, is the interpretation. The concepts themselves may or may not be new; the data may or may not be more extensive; but the crucial fact is the new application of concepts to the data. "In any case, if old principles were ever true, they must remain true—in terms of the old concepts."[110] As between two systems, both of which can account for all the data known, "the one would be better truth, the other worse, from the point of view of workability."

> Rather the point is . . . that the truths of experience must always be relative to our chosen conceptual systems in terms of which they are expressed; and that amongst such conceptual systems there may be choice in application. Such choice will be determined, consciously or unconsciously, on pragmatic grounds. New facts may cause a shifting of such grounds. When this happens, nothing literally becomes false, and nothing becomes true which was not always true. An old intellectual instrument has been given up. Old concepts lapse and new ones take their place.[111]

What is true is forever true; propositions do not become true—they are or are not true. But, at the same time, Lewis is reluctant to say that a conceptual system such as Ptolemaic astronomy is false. "Where there is more than one interpretation which can frame the given, 'truer' will mean only 'better.' And after all even flat falsity can only mean a practical breakdown which has proved complete."[112] Such rejected systems are not empirically true, but they retain their character as consistent logical systems, and are in that sense not false, but simply withdrawn from use.

5

Mind and the World Order

In 1929, Lewis published his second book, *Mind and the World Order*, in which he brought together and extended the ideas that he had been developing through the preceding years. The book, Lewis says, grew out of his investigations of logic and mathematics; he does not mention, but should have, that it evolved from the epistemological studies he had pursued in his dissertation and thereafter. These two lines of development he now sought to bringing together. Recent developments in mathematics and logic had established their "purely analytic character" and demonstrated their independence of empirical fact. Developments in physics—specifically Relativity Theory—had shown that logical consistency and empirical application were separate questions. We have, then, "a kind of double-truth"—the truth of abstract systems that are certainties, and those of empirical knowledge that are only probable. This "independence of the conceptual and the empirical" raises in pressing form the question of "the nature and validity of such empirical knowledge."[1] That is the question Lewis intends to address.

By way of preface, Lewis states the three major theses of the book:

(1) A priori truth is definitive in nature and rises exclusively from the analysis of concepts. That *reality* may be delimited a priori, is due . . . to the fact that whatever is denominated "real" must be something discriminated in experience by criteria which are antecedently determined. (2) While the delineation of concepts is a priori, the application of any particular concept to particular given experience is hypothetical; the

choice of conceptual systems for such application is instrumental or pragmatic, and empirical truth is never more than probable. (3) That experience in general is such as to be capable of conceptual interpretation, requires no peculiar and metaphysical assumption about the conformity of experience to the mind or its categories; it could not conceivably be otherwise.[2]

This position Lewis terms "conceptualistic pragmatism," and he notes specifically his debts to James, Dewey, and particularly Peirce. Lewis's pragmatism is not theirs, but he now claims explicitly to be their heir. In this context, it is striking that he does not mention Royce.

Lewis begins with a discussion of philosophic method and philosophy in general. Philosophy, Lewis holds, is and must be the business of everyone because it deals with ends and raises the unavoidable questions "What is good? What is right? What is valid?"[3] These are questions every person must face, so everyone must be their own philosopher. And everyone can, for the method of philosophy consists in reflecting on our ordinary experience in an effort to bring it to clarity. One should note here that even in 1929, Lewis considered questions of the good to be separate from questions of the right.

That the reflective method is appropriate to logic and ethics, Lewis says, is generally understood, but its appropriateness to metaphysics has not been recognized. "Metaphysics," Lewis says, "studies the nature of reality in general."[4] He rejects all forms of speculative metaphysical system building as being groundless; the determination of what specific things exist is the business of science, not philosophy. What Lewis means by metaphysics is the determination of the criteria of the real or, otherwise put, the problem of the categories. Experience is of many things: objects, dreams, hallucinations, and so on. All of these are real in *some* category—for example, we have real dreams—and are unreal in some other categories. The problem of metaphysics is to determine the major classifications of phenomena and the criteria for assigning phenomena to those categories. This is a reflective undertaking like those of logic and ethics, not a speculative or empirical investigation. The problem of metaphysics is precisely the formulation of the criteria of the various types of reality,[5] not "to triangulate the universe." Thus, the reflective method applies equally to all fields of philosophy. This is a very different view of the task of philosophy from that of Hegel and Royce.

Lewis's rejection of transcendent metaphysics is in no sense a rejection of scientific theories. "Unless the modern physicist hopelessly deludes himself, does not the existence of electrons mean something verifiable in the laboratory?" When science predicts verifiable differences in experience, they are "the 'cash-value' of the category; they constitute what it means to be real in just the way that electrons can be real."[6] Lewis goes on:

> The totality of possible experiences in which any interpretation would be verified—the completest possible empirical verification which is conceivable—constitutes the entire meaning which that interpretation has. A predication of reality to what transcends experience completely and in every sense, it not problematic; it is nonsense.[7]

One category whose particular importance Lewis emphasizes is that of mind, and it might seem that his method will not work in this case. But Lewis thinks otherwise. All our knowledge arises from the reflective analysis of experience. What we discover by such analysis is that certain components of our knowledge are not given by sense, and we attribute these to the mind. What we classify as mental—categories, criteria, purposes, and so on—are what we find in experience but not in sense. "We can discover mind and its principles only by analysis in this experience which we have."[8] It was an error of traditional rationalism to believe that such principles were innate and discoverable by direct inspection. But mind is not immediately known by itself, and although the a priori is a product of mind, it is not independent of experience in general. Here Lewis emphasizes that our categories are historical social products and, although they are prior to any given experience, they nevertheless can, and do, change over time. For the point of the a priori is to make experience intelligible, and we change categories to make it more so. The test of the a priori is pragmatic, and the a priori is just that element in knowledge that can be changed for pragmatic reasons. Philosophy cannot prove its results; it can only persuade, and the basis of persuasion is success. That scheme is persuasive that best succeeds in making experience intelligible.[9]

Lewis sees his "conceptual pragmatism" as standing between empiricism with its emphasis on what is given in sense and rationalism with its emphasis on what the mind contributes to knowledge. Both are essential, Lewis holds, and our experience is a combination of sense and purpose, qualitative suchness and conceptual systems. This is the position Lewis will attempt to defend in the remainder of the book.

Having described his method, Lewis's next task is to explain how empirical knowledge is constituted. It has, he says, five components: (1) the awareness of the given, reported in statements like "This looks round"; (2) the knowledge of objects and objective properties, reported in statements like "This is round"; (3) the analytic a priori; (4) the categorical a priori, which is the application of concepts to the given; and (5) empirical generalizations that are universal, but not a priori. The problem is to show how these components combine to form empirical knowledge.[10] We will examine them in order.

This is the first time since his dissertation that Lewis has devoted any extended attention to the given in print, and his concept of it has undergone considerable development. The criteria of the given

> are, first, its specific sensuous or feeling-character, and second, that the mode of thought can neither create nor alter it—that it remains unaffected by any change of mental attitude or interest. It is the second of these criteria which is definitive; the first alone is not sufficient.[11]

What exactly do these criteria mean? The second is the most important, but Lewis does not devote a lot of attention to it, thinking that its meaning is obvious. If, however, one looks at the examples Lewis gives, it is clear that by "mode of thought" he means voluntary thought. Thus, in discussing a pen as a perceived object, he says,

> I might then describe this object which is in my hand as "a cylinder" or "hard rubber" or "a poor buy." In each case the thing is somewhat differently related in my mind, and the connoted modes of my possible behavior toward it, and my further experience of it, are different. Something called "given" remains constant, but its character as sign, its classification, and its relation to other things and to action are differently taken.[12]

Lewis does not say that concepts can have no unconscious effect on the given, and there is nothing to suggest that that possibility occurred to him. From what he does say, the point is that one cannot alter the given element by any change of purpose or interpretation; one cannot by thinking change the given. The basic idea is, of course, Berkeley's claim that the given stands in opposition to our will.

What of the sensuous character? Lewis means here the quality of sensation or feeling that we find in a particular experience. This is not necessarily something that comes through the senses; joy and fear and pain are also given. The given cannot be described in language, because the application of words to it involves a classification that is an interpretation and therefore conceptual. In that sense, it is "ineffable." But in any perception, elements of the perception include certain "qualia." For example, in looking at a red chair, one has certain sensory qualia that we normally classify as "red." Since "red" is a class term for a range of different shades, we never see "red" as such; we see certain of the shades we classify as red displayed by the object of perception. It is the *shades* that Lewis calls the "given" and terms "qualia."[13]

Our perceptions are perceptions of objects. "We do not see patches of color, but trees and houses; we hear, not indescribable sound, but voices and violins."[14] We never perceive the given in isolation any more than we do the concept. In both cases we have an experience, and the given is *in* the experience just as the interpretation is. Both the classificatory concept and the given are abstractions from the concrete experience. When we look at a red chair, we can abstract the concept or the sensuous qualia or both, but as we find them in experience they are united. In experience, there can be no interpretation without a given; otherwise, what would the interpretation be an interpretation of?

The given element in an experience of an object Lewis terms a "presentation". Such a presentation is an event. The content of the presentation is either a particular quale or a complex of qualia. "The presentation as an event is, of course, unique, but the qualia which make it up are not. They are recognizable from one to another experience."[15] But Lewis insists they are not universals. What Lewis means here, but does not make clear, is that the qualia are prescindable from particular experiences and, as such, are repeatable, but they are not universals in the sense that "triangularity" is, nor are they essences in the sense meant by Santayana and the Critical Realists. It is this repeatability that permits qualia to serve as signs of other qualia— a fact that will play a key role in Lewis's theory. The presentation is not usually a single uniform quale; it will normally contain different qualia in juxtaposition, and the differences among them are also given.

Can verbal reports of the given be in error? Lewis's answer is yes. "It is indeed obvious that I may make erroneous report of the given, because I can make no report at all except by the use of language, which imports concepts which are *not* given."[16] My report may reflect ignorance of the proper terms or just carelessness or inadvertence. "It may require careful self-questioning, or questioning by another, to elicit the full and correct account of a given experience,"[17] but the critical point here is that verbal reports of the given must be understood in a special way. They are not classificatory statements; rather, they indicate the presence, not of objective properties, but of qualia that would lead us to ascribe such properties. It is in this indicator capacity that such statements cannot be in error, not as descriptions.

The awareness of the given is not knowledge. For Lewis, knowledge is of something objective. The given is an element in knowledge, but contemplation of the given by itself is not. Knowledge must transcend what is given in the particular experience.

Lewis deals next with our knowledge of objects and objective properties. This involves several different issues: the nature of concepts, our knowledge of reality, and the relativity of knowledge. Since such knowledge of objective things involves the conceptual interpretation of the given, he must first deal with the nature of concepts. "We shall define the pure concept as 'that meaning which must be common to two minds when they understand each other by the use of a substantive or its equivalent.'"[18] Concepts are thus identical with meanings and their existence is "a fundamental assumption of science or of any other intellectual enterprise." But this assumption does not require that the given be the same in different individuals; in fact, Lewis denies that this is the case, reusing the arguments on this point that he had previously given in his dissertation.

What common knowledge does require is "that we should share common definitions of the terms we use, and that we should apply these terms identically to what is presented."[19] This involves saying that, for both knowers, the intensions and denotations of the terms must be the same. The verification of community of meanings can be done in two ways: by definition of terms or by exhibiting denotations. The second method Lewis regards as less adequate than the first because it proceeds by comparison of specific denotata in an effort to show their common properties. As is well known, such ostensive definition is always subject to the difficulty that, at least in theory, any two objects have an infinite number of common properties, and so we can never be sure that both knowers are attending to the same property.[20] It is not clear that Lewis is entitled to this argument since he holds that what makes the identification of an object possible for us is the fact that only a finite number of its properties are ever realized in experience.

It is identity of intension that Lewis regards as the primary means of proving shared meaning. Definitions relate any given term to others; following out the chain of definitions from a term to those used to define it, to those used to define the defining terms, and so on, must inevitably lead to a circle. Since the number of terms in the language is finite, if every term is defined by other terms, circularity is certain. Any dictionary is thus circular. How then is this network of concepts related to sense? Lewis distinguishes here between meaning in the individual mind and meaning as shared. Concerning the former, he says:

> We analyse the meaning back until we come to rest in familiar imagery. But the end-terms, which for us are thus understood directly by reference to sense and feeling, have still a conceptual meaning; they are not indefinable. This conceptual meaning is sharable; our imagery essentially not.[21]

For every individual, the meaning of his terms must ultimately come to rest in sensory experience—otherwise his terms would be uninterpreted. Any two people—McGee and Walsh—must therefore anchor their terms in sensations—but not necessarily in the same sensations. McGee and Walsh can communicate if McGee's structure of interterm relations is isomorphic to Walsh's, regardless of whether or not their sensory experiences are the same. If they are isomorphic, then McGee's behavior will be congruent with Walsh's; they will mark distinctions in the same way, and use language in complementary fashion. It is the congruence of behavior that demonstrates common concepts, and this congruence does not require a sharing of the given.

This entire pattern of interrelated terms is not present to an individual's mind every time he or she uses the term. Lewis quotes Royce's doctrine about the three grades of clearness regarding the meaning of terms—an adaptation, as both Royce and Lewis noted, of Peirce's famous three grades of clearness in "How to Make Our Ideas Clear."[22] The first grade, Royce says, is "when we are able appropriately to accept or reject any object of our acquaintance as belonging or not belonging to the class in question." The second is attained when we are prepared "to classify correctly objects not precisely like those with which we have previously been acquainted." The third is attained when we have "the ability to specify the criteria by which such classification is determined." Rarely, Lewis notes, do we attain the third grade of clearness; nevertheless, "It would be an anomalous use of language to deny meaning to terms which are used without this explicit consciousness of what is essential"[23] since the use of terms is often a matter of habit that embodies prior experience in which "the mode of action was determined by clearer consciousness."

Lewis definition of the concept, then, is the following.

> The concept is a definitive structure of meanings, which is what *would verify* completely the coincidence of two minds when they understand each other by the use of language. Such ideal community requires coincidence of a pattern of interrelated connotations, projected by and necessary to cooperative, purposive behavior. It does *not* require coincidence of imagery or sensory apprehension.[24]

The possibility of our having common concepts, Lewis says, is conditioned by two things: first, the fact that human beings are fundamentally similar in their needs, interests, and powers, and, second, in their being confronted by a common reality mediated through comparable sense experience. But these considerations have led to two sorts of errors: the assumption that all humans share a set of immutable categories constituting "human reason," which has been the position of Rationalism, and the assumption that the common reality is simply exhibited to us in experience, which has been the position of Empiricism. Neither, Lewis says, will do.

Against the latter, Lewis argues that our common world is a social achievement, not a given. Sensory experience is not always the same across individuals; indeed, common concepts can be established despite radical differences in sensory inputs, as the case of Helen Keller makes clear. One cannot say, Lewis thinks, just how much commonality must exist for the construction of a common world, but the example of *Principia Mathematica* demonstrates that the whole of mathematics (geometry excluded) can be generated from an extraordinarily meager basis of seven initial concepts. Nor is there anything privileged about those seven, for other choices will yield the same system—indeed, referring to the work of Sheffer and Nicod, it can be done from one symbolic postulate and one undefined idea.[25]

Similar considerations hold against the former view that a common world requires common categories constituting human reason. If this argument holds that these categories are exemplified in our experience, then, given the fact that sensory experience differs between people, the exemplification will be very different for different knowers. To arrive at general categories in this case will require a very high level of abstraction, and such abstractions are not apt to be exemplified in simple sensory qualia. The claim that the given—the lowest level at which human experience can be detected—"already possesses a structure which reflects the nature of 'human reason'" is, Lewis says, precisely wrong.

> The reason I cannot teach my dog the calculus is not because empirical exemplifications of these primitive conceptions are not possible . . . to him, but because he is not capable of making an abstraction which is not dictated directly by instinctive interest. . . . There is no reason to think that the absence of human categories affects the content of his given experience in the least.[26]

"As Royce was fond of insisting, the categories are our ways of acting. What we can distinguish as attributable to our own acts are not, and can not be, limitations in the content of the immediate experience which is acted on."[27]

Lewis's argument thus far identifies meaning with the system of definitory relations. This leads to a view of the conceptual system as a formal system applied by the individual to his sensory experience, but since sensory experience is not sharable, the problem of communication is that, from the standpoint of another person, the individual's conceptual system must appear as uninterpreted. Does this then leave us in the position of multiple independent formal systems, none of which is intelligible to each other? Lewis thinks not. Suppose that mathematics were "a closed field." What he means by this is, if the system under consideration is arithmetic, "then no concept which occurs in arithmetic has any meaning outside arithmetic or other than an arithmetical application."[28] Here surely is exemplified Lewis's claim that "*All* meaning is relational." Would it be the case that this system would be forever meaningless? Lewis's answer is that "the characteristic order of some set of items in the experience of A can be identified by B as belonging exclusively to some set of things in his own experience." He goes on to say that a mathematician "confronted by a system in an entirely novel notation or in a language strange to him" might identify its order as just that of the complex numbers,[29] and so would be able to figure out what the system referred to. Arithmetic, of course, is not a closed field. But,

> the field of our concepts altogether is, and must be, closed in this sense. It is this fact which has been referred to as the inevitable eventual circularity of definition and illustrated by the example of the ideal dictionary.[30]

Lewis's claim that A can recognize that B's system of interrelated concepts applies to some set of objects to which his own apply and *therefore* can understand what B means assumes that the uninterpreted system has only one model. This is a very dubious assumption. But what A could know of B's conceptual system is in any case only what is exhibited in B's behavior, and behavior is what Lewis relies on to break out of the circle: it is because we "discriminate and relate as others do, when confronted by the same situation"[31] that we can identify what others mean. If I stop at red lights and go at green, it makes no difference whether you see my red as blue and my green as orange if you stop and go just as I do. This applies to verbal behavior as well as other kinds. When you use words as I do, and vice versa, we have a basis for concluding that we share common meanings.

Lewis goes on to say that we are able to understand one another because a common reality is presented to us.

> But so to put it is to reverse the order of knowledge. We have a common reality because—or in so far as—we are able to identify, each in his own experience, those systems of orderly relation indicated by behavior, and particularly by that part of behavior which serves the ends of cooperation. What this primarily requires is that, in general, we be able to discriminate and relate as others do, when confronted by the same situation.[32]

This common reality is largely a social achievement, Lewis holds. We are indeed like-minded creatures. But "like-mindedness" consists primarily of three things: "the possession of like needs and of like modes of behavior satisfying them, second the possession of common concepts, represented in behavior by discrimination and relation, and third, the capacity (evoked particularly when community in the other two respects threatens to fail) of transcending our individual limitations of discrimination by indirect methods."[33] The possibility of attaining common concepts is the criterion of like-mindedness.

This achievement of reality reflects "our common needs, our social organization for fulfilling them, and our learning from social example . . . even our common categories may be, in part, a social achievement of like-mindedness."[34] Common reality is the aim and result of social cooperation, not the prerequisite to common knowledge. It is our common concepts and meanings that create a common reality, not the other way round. It should be noted that throughout this whole argument, Lewis has assumed the reality of other minds—a not inconsiderable assumption.

Lewis is not unaware of these problems and he therefore qualifies his position, saying that he has used common meaning as the criterion of the concept "in part merely [as] an expository device." But a human being "without fellows" "would still frame concepts in terms of the relation between his own behavior and his environment."

> Knowledge must always concern principally the relations which obtain between one experience and another, particularly those relations into which the knower himself may enter as an active factor. It is the given as thus conceptually interpreted which is envisaged as the real object.[35]

Lewis entertained no Wittgensteinian doubts about the possibility of a private language. In fact, every individual's language is private in the sense that his terms are anchored in his own sensory experience. Hence, the problem of other minds and common meaning can be set aside, and the issue of knowledge addressed in terms of individual experience.

Lewis notes that "some"—that is, Russell—have distinguished two kinds of knowledge of objects: knowledge by acquaintance and knowledge about. Lewis denies that there is any such thing as knowledge by acquaintance. Simple awareness of the given qualia is not knowledge at all. It becomes knowledge "by assigning to the present given an interpretation through which it becomes related to, or a sign of, a correlation between certain behavior of my own and the realization of my purpose. This interpretation has the character of a generalization which has been learned."[36] The object itself is never given in experience. What is given is the quale. To interpret the quale is to take it as a sign of other qualia that may be expected in one's experience if the quale signifies the presence of a certain sort of object. For to say the object is, for example, an apple, is to classify it, and every classification involves generalizations of the form, "if x is an A, then if I do B, I will experience quale *Q*." Such a generalization is testable, and the "'objectivity' of this experience means *the verifiability of a further possible experience which is attributed by this interpretation.*"[37]

Qualia, Lewis reemphasizes, are ineffable; they have no names, though they are often indicated in discourse by the "looks" locution. What is important about the quale is not its character but its relations—its standing as a sign of something. It needs no verification because "it is impossible to be mistaken about it." But concepts such as "blue" involve patterns of relations. "To verify a color, we change the conditions of illumination or alter the angle so as to get rid of the sheen, or we bring the thing into juxtaposition with some object whose color has previously been tested or is accepted as a standard of comparison."[38] When we do this, the verification depends on our knowing what we should expect to experience if the thing has the objective property blue. That is, we must verify the prediction that our actions will result in the experience of certain qualia. Thus, Lewis says, "what constitutes the existence of an objective property and the applicability of a concept . . . is not a given qualia alone but an ordered relation of different qualia, relative to different conditions or behavior."[39] The predication of a property on the basis of an experience involving a quale is a hypothesis that must be verified by further experience, for different qualia can signify the same objective properties, and the same quale can signify different objects, as when the quale that is an elliptical appearance signifies either an elliptical object or a round object viewed at an angle.[40] If, Lewis points out, the denotation of any concept were a quale, then the judgment ascribing the concept could not be in error. But since such judgments can be in error, it is obvious that the concept does not denote the quale; it denotes the objective property.

What holds of the objective properties holds of objects in general. Knowledge of an object always transcends the immediately given. It begins with the immediate given, but even the application of a name to that experience involves an interpretation that hypothesizes some series of possible experiences in the future. This, Lewis remarks, is simply Berkeley's doctrine that the "idea" is a sign, together with the recognition that what is contained in one idea is only "a fragment of the nature of the real object." Similarly, conceptual knowledge, if it is knowledge of reality, always comes down to the interpretation of presented experience. Here Lewis quotes Peirce's famous maxim: "Consider what effects that might conceivably have practical bearings you conceive the objects of your conception to have. Then, your conception of those effects is the whole of your conception of the object."[41] These effects that are verifiable must be actual or possible experiences.

If the object is real, Lewis says, there "must be more to it than *could* be given in any single experience." The claim of the New Realists that in the cognitive experience the mind and the object coincide is "as wrong as possible."[42] But what does "more" mean here? It refers not only to the verifications that I will, in fact, perform, but to those predicted verifications that I *could* perform.

> The "if" clause of my prediction is allowed to remain contrary to fact. Precisely here, in this apparently commonplace fact that the meanings ascribed in our recognition of objects and predications of properties must be *verifiable*, yet are commonly not *verified* or only verified in part, is something of great importance both for understanding the relation of knowledge to our ways of acting and for the nature of objectivity or thinghood.[43]

The point here is that the real object *cannot* be translated into any series of actual verifications or experiences; it contains the *possibility* of such verifications beyond any number that can ever be actually made. This possibility is objective and real if the object is; thus Lewis appears to hold that unactualized possibilities are real, and are involved in the nature of objective reality. One can see here why Lewis considered the counterfactual conditional so important, why he rejected material implication, and why he found it necessary to create an alternative logic of strict implication.

For the object to be real, not only must there be qualia that are presentations of the object, but on the basis of these qualia it must be possible to predict that under specifiable conditions these or related qualia will occur in future experience. The existence of the real object therefore implies regularities in our experience that are lawlike. If my desk chair is a real chair, I must be able to predict future experiences of this chair, and those predictions must be verifiable and at least in part verified. If the predictions are not verified, then the chair is not real.[44]

Crucial to this view is the role of action. The predictions to which the concept of the real object gives rise involve action in the antecedent: if x is an A, and if action B is taken, then quale Q will be experienced. If, Lewis says, we were purely passive beings, our experience would be simply that of the immediately given. For such a being, there could be no distinction between the real and the illusory since this distinction is not in the given experience. Indeed, since there could be no distinction between the real and the unreal, there could be no reality. It is because we can, by action, verify or falsify predictions of this sort that the real and the illusory can be distinguished, and that the possible can be realized. "Thinghood means a stability or uniformity of appearance which can be recovered *by certain actions of my own.*"[45]

Every concept is correlated with some quale. Unless this were so, no experience could lead to predictions of future experience, since this depends on the given quale being interpreted as a sign of the content of other possible experiences. Hence, without such a correlation, "no experience could verify or fail to verify anything" since the verification consists in finding in future experience the predicted qualia. The intelligibility of experience consists in a stable relation between given qualia and "the pattern of its context in possible experience." Without this correlation, concepts could not be applied to experience or experience interpreted by concepts. But these correlations essentially involve our actions. It is our actions that create the conditions under which future experience will verify or falsify our predictions.

> The whole content of our knowledge of reality is the truth of such "If–then" propositions, in which the hypothesis is something we conceive could be made true by our mode of acting and the consequent presents a content of experience which, though not actual now and perhaps not to become actual, is a possible experience connected with the present.[46]

Human knowledge is a means by which through action we acquire valid ends. "Knowledge is pragmatic, utilitarian, and its value, like that of the activity it immediately subserves, is extrinsic."[47] We are purposeful creatures who act to attain what we value, and the function of knowledge is to guide our actions.

Lewis acknowledges that the type of theory he advances is frequently criticized for its inability to account for knowledge of the past. Lewis rejects this criticism; the fact that verification is future does not mean that past events are future. For any past event, "there is always something, which at least is conceivably possible of experience, by means of which it can be known."[48] These effects would be such things as records, letters, artifacts, and so on. If these possible effects are actualized, then we can use them to verify the reality of the past event; if they are not actualized, then the past event cannot be known. Indeed, Lewis holds that any real property, object, or event must be the basis for an infinite series of possible experiences. For suppose that all their conceivable effects were to be verified at time t such that the verification is complete—there are no testable consequences after that time. Then at $t + n$, for any positive n, there would be no way of knowing the original reality, for any records of it at $t + n$ would be a consequences that would refute the claim that all the consequences had been exhausted at t. Hence, to say the verification is complete at time t would mean that after t "its existence or historical verity would be no longer determinable." Further, since no experience can be guaranteed to be veridical, no series of such experiences can be guaranteed to be veridical, and the statement cannot therefore have been completely verified at t beyond the possibility of doubt. But Lewis has trouble with the issue of how the pastness of something presented in present memory is identified. It must be the case that "*some* kind of identifiable marks in presented experience must mean the pastness of the thing presented,"[49] but Lewis is unable to pinpoint what those marks are. Thus, on this question, he had not advanced beyond his position in the dissertation; he will return to it later.

But Lewis must then deal with the problem of the relativity of knowledge and its implications for the independence of the real. In doing so, Lewis tackles two of the major issues of early twentieth-century American philosophy. It was the claim of Idealists such as Green and Bradley that the relativity of knowledge to the mind proved Idealism to be the only viable theory of knowledge, and it was the counterclaim of Perry and the New Realists that the real is what it is independently of its being known. Lewis had come to philosophic maturity in the midst of this controversy with Royce and Perry as his mentors. Now he intended to put the dispute behind him.

Since Descartes, Lewis says, philosophy has been largely determined by the view that either knowledge is not relative to the mind, or the content of knowledge is unreal, or the real is dependent on mind. The first alternative Lewis sees as underlying realism, the second as the foundation of phenomenalism, and the third as the basis of idealism. But Lewis claims that these alternatives are false: "there is no contradiction between the relativity of knowledge and the independence of its object." If this thesis can be upheld, Lewis says, "the fundamental premises of phenomenalism and idealism fall to the ground, some of the main difficulties posed by skepticism are met, and the general attitude of common-sense realism can be re-instated."[50] This statement amounts to a declaration that Lewis is a commonsense realist.

"How can a knowledge which is relative to the knower's mind and senses be true to a reality which is independent?" Lewis's answer is "true knowledge is absolute because it conveys an absolute truth, though it can convey such truth only in relative terms." What does this mean? Lewis says:

> If relative to R, A is X, and relative to S, A is Y, neither X nor Y is an absolute predicate of A. But "A is X relative to R" and "A is Y relative to S", are absolute truths. Moreover, they may be truths about the independent nature of A . . . If A had no independent character, it would not be X relative to R or Y relative to S. These relative (or relational) characters, X and Y, are partial but absolutely valid revelations of the nature of A.[51]

Lewis illustrates this thesis with the example of Caesar's toga. Size is relative to a measure—for example, a yardstick. Given the yardstick, the size of the toga is determined by the toga; given the toga, its size is determined by the yardstick. But if the toga had no size independently of the yardstick, or the yardstick had no size independently of the toga, the relation would be entirely indeterminate. "Thus what is relative is also independent; if it had no 'absolute' character, it would have no character in relative terms."[52]

As a second example, Lewis notes that an objects's perceived size depends on its distance from the perceiver. In fact, perceived size, S, is a function of distance, d, and of the "true" size of the object, X. Hence, $S = f(d,X)$. Given d and S, we can determine X. Further, this function allows the prediction of X for any combination of d and S, and of S for any combination of d and X. But this is just what a correct interpretation ought to do. Exactly the same sort of argument holds for perceived colors and their relation to some standard that is arbitrarily determined and for shape and its relation to standard shapes. Lewis concludes:

> The concept, or conceptual interpretation, *transcends* this relativity precisely because what the concept comprises is this relational pattern in which the independent nature of what is apprehended is exhibited in experience.[53]

This, Lewis says, refutes phenomenalism. The phenomenalist's argument is that, aside from the yardstick or some similar measuring instrument, the size of Caesar's toga is either a meaningless expression, or refers to something we can never know. The logic of relativity refutes this, whatever the related terms may be.

The phenomenalist's reply, that this argument is irrelevant because its application would have to include mind as one of the terms and we do not know the mind, leaves Lewis unmoved. His answer is that I learn about my mind "through its commerce with objects." I come to understand both my mind and objective reality when I learn how to give order to the series of presentations by treating it as a function of two variables—subject and object.

> To revert to the mathematical terms, the data of appearance are the values of the function, cognition. This is a function of two variables, mind and object. I know the object by an integration of its appearance over the range of the other variable, mind or "the subjective conditions." (For example, as has been pointed out, objective change is divided from permanence of the thing by integrating with respect to those changes, in experience as given, which are due to "my own activity.") And I know mind by an integration of this function over its whole range (or the widest possible range) of variation in the objective.[54]

Of course, the mathematics is being used only as metaphor here, but the metaphor is apt. Lewis goes on to argue that the limitations of the human mind may introduce ignorance, but not error. It is one thing to say that our knowledge is false; it is very different to say it is partial or incomplete. Partial knowledge can be true, even though there are other matters about which we do not know. If our eyes were sensitive to the entire range of electromagnetic radiation, we would no doubt know more than we do, but it does not follow from that that what we do know is false. So much for phenomenalism!

Idealists, Lewis says, have concluded from the relativity of knowledge that "the conception of reality beyond all human powers to know is meaningless." This, Lewis says, is a mistake, since partial knowledge implies knowledge greater than we have. But if the Idealist challenge is put as "How can we *know* there is a kind of reality we cannot *know*?," "know" is being used equivocally. As Russell had noted, there are numbers no one will ever count. We can know that because we know the rule of succession of numbers and that the series so generated has no end. This is a different sense of "know" than "knowing" the number "7." If fact, we transcend actual experience by using possible experience—"the meaning of a possibility which transcends the actual lies in the truth of some 'If–then' proposition, the hypothesis of which is contrary to fact."[55] The conception of reality, Lewis says, is the affirmation of possibility.

The Idealist argues from the relativity of knowledge to mind that the object known is completely mind dependent. But Lewis replies that the Idealist has mistaken the logic of relative knowledge. A body moving in space has a determinate mass and velocity only relative to a frame of reference. Does that mean that mass and velocity are not properties of an independent reality? Lewis answers that the mass and velocity of the objectively real thing are functions of two variables: "the relative motion of observers and observed and the independent character of the thing observed."[56] Specify both, and the values of the function are determined; specify either and one value of the function depends on the other. Mass and velocity cannot be described apart from the specification of the frame of reference. However, given their values for one frame of reference, their values in any other frame are determinate. The parallel to the case of mind and object, Lewis says, is exact. Idealism's error, Lewis thinks, lies in having concluded from the relativity of knowledge that nothing can exist except as known. But this leaves Idealism with a peculiar problem. If its thesis were true, the Idealist ought to be able to deduce all the particular existents of the world from pure thought. Why then cannot the Idealist deduce the elephants in Africa from his premises? The fact that he cannot shows that Idealism is false.[57]

What, in terms of knowledge, does it mean to say the object is independent? It means, first, the "givenness" of the given—we do not create it and cannot alter it simply by thought. It means, second, the truth of counterfactual conditionals, where the antecedent involves our action and the consequent some result in experience—results that are "independent of any attitude or purpose of mine." It means, third, that reality transcends my present knowledge of it, that there are questions about it the answers to which I do not now know, or that I can predict the occurrence of some experience that may, or may not, occur.

> It means that we are able to interpret validly certain given items of experience as signs of other possible experiences, the total content of such further possible experience, related to the given in certain categorical ways, being attributed to the object, as constituting what we know of it and *what we mean by attributing reality to it.*[58]

Perhaps, Lewis says, Idealists have been misled by the copy theory of knowledge into believing that the independence of the real is inconsistent with their views. If so, it may be that there are no genuine issues between a sufficiently critical Idealism and a sufficiently critical Realism. But, in Lewis's view, the whole controversy between Realists and Idealists over the relativity of knowledge and the independence of the real has been a mistake.

The third component of empirical knowledge is the a priori. If knowledge is to be "valid," experience must be in some sense orderly, and that requires that "there must be some propositions the truth of which is necessary and is independent of the particular character of future experience."[59] By "necessary" here, Lewis means what is opposed to the contingent, not what is opposed to the voluntary. The a priori he affirms, echoing his earlier writings, is the freely taken activity of the mind itself and is legislative for the mind, not for something else. Lewis repeats his claim that the a priori is independent of experience just because it prescribes "*nothing* to the content of experience," and is true "*no matter what.*" The mind legislates for reality because it determines its own interpretations, regardless of what future experience may bring. This is the pragmatic theory of the a priori that he had set forth in his earlier papers.[60]

The analytic a priori plays an important role in empirical knowledge. Consider the statement "This is round." This statement involves two others: first, that if this is round, then further experiences of it will be so and so—a definitive statement embodying the empirical criteria of objective roundness, and, second, that "this present given is such that further experience (probably) *will be* thus and so."[61] The first is a priori analytic; it explicates the term "round." Without this explication, we would not have the criteria necessary to apply the concept to the particular case.

Having briefly stated his theory of the a priori, Lewis turns to the traditional concepts of the a priori. These are the psychological view of the a
priori as "natural light" or innate ideas, the view that it is distinguished by
its logical relation to experience, usually as presupposition, and the view that
the a priori is applicable to experience because experience is shaped by a
priori modes of receptivity. The idea that the human mind must contain
innate or self-evident axioms not derived from experience Lewis dismisses
summarily, and turns to the second view that the a priori is logically necessary.
Here he rehearses the arguments he had given in 1921 in "The Structure
of Logic and Its Relations to Other Systems" regarding presupposition,
deduction from self-evident principles, and reaffirmation through denial.[62]

Having disposed of the first two traditional conceptions, Lewis turns to
the third, which is Kant's view that "the possibility of knowledge is assured
by the fact that experience is not of the independent real but of phenomena
already informed by our receptivity."[63] Against this view, Lewis argues that
if it were true, the mind could never recognize the forms of intuition as its
own. Lacking that knowledge, these forms would be seen as limitations of
the given whose future continuance would be as problematic as any empirical
generalization. Lewis remarks that every beginning student of Kant asks
how Kant knows that phenomena are not things-in-themselves.

> And the only answer that can be given is that if what could be experienced
> were limited only by what existed to be experienced, then the limits of
> experience could be discovered only through experience itself. Any con-
> clusion regarding them would then be probable only, since it would be
> an argument from past to future.[64]

The issue then is how we can know that the limitations of experience are
due to the mind and are not simply those of an independent reality that
experience reveals. Lewis says this can only be done by knowing the unknowable reality or by "some criterion of what mind is responsible for in given
experience." That would have to take the form of an assertion that if something existed incompatible with our forms of receptivity, we could never
experience it.[65] But should we find ourselves in a world of, for example,
non-Euclidean geometric space or in a timeless world, how would we know
that the change was in us and not in reality? Lewis rejects the Kantian answer
not only because he believes it is not defensible but because he believes we
have a simpler alternative.

> It is an identical proposition that no conceivable experience or reality is
> beyond our powers of conception. What is beyond our powers of con-
> ception has no meaning; the word which is supposed to denote it is a

nonsense syllable. Experience does not need to be limited in order that we should be able to understand it; we can understand *anything* in one way or another.[66]

Whatever experience brings, we will find a way of understanding it either by assigning it a consistent categorical interpretation or by ruling it a hallucination, or dream, or some such. Kant made his problem more difficult than it needed to be by taking experience to coincide with the phenomenally real. "Did the sage of Konigsberg have no dreams!"[67] Lewis asks. A priori principles of categorical interpretation are necessary to limit reality, not to limit experience.

The categorical a priori is the fourth component of empirical knowledge. Whatever we find in experience will be assigned to some category in which it is real, even if it is a real dream or a real hallucination. And if worse comes to worst, we can call it a real unintelligible, meaning unintelligible at the time experienced. And since there is no time limit on investigation, we can still maintain as an ideal that "nothing can be finally and absolutely unintelligible." But Lewis notes that intelligibility is always a matter of degree; nothing is completely understood, and nothing is completely unintelligible. Ascription of unintelligibility is relative to our powers and interests. Lewis's view of the a priori is then

> the principles of categorical interpretation are a priori valid of all possible experience because such principles express the criteria of the veridical and the real. No experience could possibly invalidate them, because any experience not in conformity, which might be evidence against them, is automatically thrown out of court as not veridical in that category and hence not pertinent to them.[68]

If we are to make sense of what Lewis calls the chaos of the given, we must bring to its interpretation in any particular case a conceptual structure that permits its classification and ordering. This conceptual structure is the mind's contribution to experience. A priori truth is then conceptual whether it is purely abstract as in the case of mathematics or applied as in the case of the categories. The a priori, Lewis reiterates, imposes no restriction on experience; it is that which is true, no matter what. We discover the a priori by reflection, and this is possible because what is from the mind, what is the product of our own acts, admits of alternatives. Because our actions are freely taken, they could always have been taken differently. If, as Idealists have held, the a priori were the product of a transcendent mind and were thus unalterable, we could never distinguish it from what is determined by the independent real, and therefore we could never know that it was a priori. It is just because it is not fixed and eternal, not imposed on us by the Absolute, that we can distinguish the a priori as our own creation. Mind is revealed by choice; where there are alternatives, there is mind.[69]

As this makes clear, the a priori is changeable. The rationalist belief in an absolute human reason has led to the notion that the categories are fixed and eternal—a mistake that has caused the categories of science to be overlooked, since these are not eternal, as the history of science demonstrates. The categories used in science—the most fundamental concepts—have altered radically since antiquity. Similarly, when we look at the beliefs of "primitive peoples," by which Lewis means nonliterate peoples, we find that their categories for describing experience are often very different from ours. Nevertheless, human beings are members of one species and have much in common. There is a "fundamental likeness in our modes of thought" that is reinforced by our necessarily social and cooperative forms of life. "The human animal with his needs and interests confronts an experience in which these must be satisfied, if at all." Our thought therefore answers to criteria of the pragmatic type.[70]

To support these claims, Lewis turns to illustrative examples. He briefly rehearses the modern developments in mathematics culminating in *Principia Mathematica* and points out that choices among alternative mathematical systems, such as the various geometries, can only be made on pragmatic grounds.

Similarly, Lewis says, "there *is* an a priori truth of concepts which have concrete denotation." He cites again Einstein's definition of simultaneity and argues that fundamental definitions in physics are stipulative. We have, Lewis says, reached the point where it is generally understood that the method of science is one of hypothesis and verification. But it is still not sufficiently understood that the terms in which hypotheses are framed represent a scientific achievement. "We cannot even interrogate experience without a network of categories and definitive concepts. Until our meanings are definite and our classifications are fixed, experience cannot conceivably determine anything." The test of these categories and concepts is their ability to create an "intelligible order amongst the phenomena in question," and the satisfaction of "such criteria as intellectual simplicity, economy, and comprehensiveness of principle."[71]

Lewis notes that scientific problems are continuous with those involving the criteria of reality and natural law. The vanishing mouse appears again: "a mouse which disappears where there is no hole, is no real mouse." Is this a conclusion based on law or on criteria of the real—or both? The situation appears paradoxical, Lewis says, since natural laws are derived by generalization from veridical experience but what experience is veridical is determined by the criterion of law. But the paradox is false. What this situation shows is that "the determination of reality, the classification of phenomena, and the discovery of law, all grow up together."[72] To illustrate this, Lewis uses again the example of photographing a "spook." Something here would be wrong, but no experience could force us to reject our previously held categories or laws. "A stubborn conservatism can be proved unreasonable only on the pragmatic ground that another method of categorical analysis more successfully reduces all experience of the type in question to order and law."[73]

"It is the a priori element in knowledge which is thus pragmatic, not the empirical." Lewis writes. Pragmatists have failed to see this chiefly because they have failed to distinguish concepts from the given, and so have thought all truth was dependent on the human mind. But the given is not thus dependent; it is simply there. Since, however, the awareness of the given is not knowledge, Lewis can admit that "there can be no more fundamental ground than the pragmatic for a truth of any sort." But this does not mean, Lewis insists, that truth is merely the satisfaction of personal desire.

> Certain important ends, such as intellectual consistency and economy, completeness of comprehension, and simplicity of interpretation, occupy a place so much higher, for the long-run satisfaction of our needs in general, that they rightly take precedence over any purpose which is merely personal or transitory.[74]

That this requires the establishment of a value hierarchy is obvious, but Lewis does not further discuss that here.

When an older conceptual interpretation is abandoned, it is usually in response to new empirical data. This will not be lightly done, for it means giving up a body of theory formulated in terms of the older scheme and the "social practices" based on it. The advantages of the change must therefore be fairly clear and considerable to overcome the inertia of old ways of thought and their prestige. The Copernican Revolution serves as Lewis's example of a case in which a change in frame of reference led to an enormous simplification of the body of astronomical theory. But since the data could be explained by an alternative theory, the choice must be made on pragmatic grounds, for the point of pragmatism is "the responsiveness of truth to human bent and need, and the fact that in some sense it is made by mind."[75] We create the conceptual schemes of science, and we choose among them on the basis of our needs for understanding, simplicity, predictability, and consistency.

The fifth component is empirical generalizations. But these are of two sorts. Consider first the second generalization cited earlier as involved in

"This is round"—that this present given is such that further experiences of it (probably) *will* be thus and so." Clearly this is a generalization based on past experience. But the subject of *this* type of generalization is not the real object—it is the given itself, or a class of such presentations.

> The recognition of the *presentation* is simply the classification of it with other qualitatively similar appearances. The basis of our interpretative judgment is the fact that, in past experience, what appeared as this does, under circumstances like the present, has turned out to be, for example, a round penny—in a sufficiently large proportion of cases to warrant probable judgment.[76]

As Berkeley said, one "idea" is a sign of others; that is, one presentation signifies or is predictive of others. This sort of recognition underlies all learning; when a rat in a maze learns to turn right at the choice point, it is because the rat recognizes the similarity of its current presentation to ones it had in the past. As Lewis notes, this type of judgment is "presumably the element in human knowledge which is evolutionarily basic and is shared by us with other animals." We learn from past experience that certain appearances go together; we account for this by interpreting these appearances as appearances of a certain sort of object. But that interpretation rests on the empirical generalization that these appearances do go together. Although this sort of generalization is rarely made explicit, it is fundamental; without it, "no interpretation would be possible."[77]

In empirical knowledge we therefore have certainty with respect to two elements—the given and the a priori elaboration of the concept. But the application of the concept to the given is probable only "because such application is an interpretation which is predictive." That is, "the application of concepts in naming and recognizing objects, itself implies characters of the object which are not now presented but wait upon further experience to be revealed."[78] As Lewis summarizes his view,

> the development of the conceptual system in the abstract is a priori; the question of the applicability of one of its constituent concepts to any single particular is a matter of probability; and the question of application *in general* is the question of *choice* of an abstract conceptual system, determined by pragmatic considerations.[79]

Given this analysis, Lewis says it is dubious that there would be any advantage to us "if we *could* find a ground for a priori truth which was synthetic."

But there is a second type of empirical statement involved in empirical knowledge—those that are empirical generalizations about objects. These generalizations are not a priori. Lewis gives as an example of the difference the two propositions "All swans are birds," which is a priori analytic, and "All swans are white," which is empirical. The former proposition simply explicates our concept of "swan"; if something that we had thought was a swan turned out not to be a bird, we would withdraw the classification "swan" from it and look for some alternative. Such a proposition is definitional and legislative for our use of the term "swan." The latter proposition is empirical because our concept of "swan" does not imply any particular color; hence it "*may* be falsified by experience." These are further distinguished by the fact that the empirical proposition asserts the nonexistence of nonwhite swans, whereas, Lewis says, "All swans are birds" does not assert the nonexistence of anything but merely stipulates that anything not a bird will not be classified as a swan. Empirical generalizations are contingent because future experience can prove them false and are therefore probable only.[80]

Lewis then draws together the elements of knowledge he has discussed in a remarkable passage.

> The whole body of our conceptual interpretations form a sort of hierarchy or pyramid with the most comprehensive, such as those of logic, at the top, and the least general, such as "swans" etc., at the bottom; that with this complex system of interrelated concepts, we approach particular experiences and attempt to fit them, somewhere and somehow, into its preformed patterns. Persistent failure leads to readjustment; the applicability of certain concepts to experiences of some particular sort is abandoned, and some other conceptual pattern is brought forward for application. The higher up a concept stands in our pyramid, the more reluctant we are to disturb it, because the more radical and far-reaching the results will be if we abandon the application of it in some particular fashion. The decision that there are no such creatures as have been defined as "swans," would be unimportant. The conclusion that there are no such things as Euclidean triangles, would be immensely disturbing. And if we should be forced to realize that nothing in experience possesses any stability—that our principle, "Nothing can both be and not be," was merely a verbalism, applying to nothing more than momentarily—that denouement would rock our world to its foundations.[81]

The modern reader of this passage cannot avoid being struck by its similarity to Quine's description of the network in "Two Dogmas," and is certain to ask why Lewis did not take "the next step" by denying the distinction between analytic and synthetic truth altogether. This is the more likely in view of the fact that Lewis had previously said the difference between the analytic and the synthetic was a matter of "degree"[82] and that the a priori is what we are prepared to maintain "no matter what,"[83] thus suggesting that the criterion of the a priori was commitment. But to ask that question is to make a major mistake—in fact, several mistakes. First, it is to assume that the change from Lewis to Quine is "the next step"—that is, that it represents an advance—an assumption that Lewis certainly would not admit. Second, there is a serious ambiguity in Lewis's statement. On the one hand, in the previous passage and in "The Pragmatic Conception of the A Priori," Lewis talks as if the difference between the analytic and the synthetic were simply a matter of our determination to uphold the former "no matter what" but not the latter. But, on the other hand, Lewis also conceives of analytic statements as statements true by virtue of the relations between the meanings of the terms involved. "All swans are birds" is a definitional statement; the meaning of "swan" contains that of "bird." In this sense, the truth of analytic statements has nothing to do with commitment, for such relations among meanings are fixed and unchanging. Hence Lewis does not say, as Quine would, that a system of a priori analytic statements, such as Lobachevski's geometry, is false, since it remains true to the relations among the meanings of its terms whether or not it is applicable to real space. Rather, Lewis says it is "abandoned" as useless for the description of our space. Lewis's statement of his position is confusing because when he talks of our reluctance to abandon a given proposition, what he means is our reluctance to abandon the application of that statement to the world, but, even if the statement is withdrawn, it remains true of the meaning relations involved. Thus, if our world should change so that Euclidean geometry no longer applied to it but Riemannian geometry did, we would withdraw the former as a description of real space and substitute the latter. But Euclidean geometry would remain true of the meaning relations among in its statements. Quine, having abandoned the notion of meaning in this sense, makes no such distinction and takes all statements to be synthetic. The basic issue here is not holism, for Lewis is as holistic as Quine; the issue is meaning. Further, for Lewis meanings can change, as they have historically; more precisely, a new meaning can be given to a term in place of an old one, with the result that new analytic propositions can be created. Lewis's theory is not more rigid than Quine's, nor is it any less able to accommodate scientific revolutions. What one must ask about Quine's theory is why no empirical test is relevant to "All swans are birds"? If the answer is that we could change our conceptual scheme, Lewis's answer would be "Of course we could. So what?"

Having described the components and structure of empirical knowledge, Lewis then turns to the question of its warrant. "The only knowledge a priori is purely analytic; all empirical knowledge is probable only."[84] This sets the next problem Lewis must face—the nature of probable knowledge. As he notes, this is not an easy task. Theories of knowledge have generally held that some metaphysical basis for an order in nature is necessary for empirical knowledge. Lewis proposes to establish empirical knowledge as probable without the benefit of any such assumptions. Lewis grants that probability must rest on empirical certainty of some sort, but he believes he had found that source of certainty in the given. The fact that the application of the a priori to experience is only probable leads to the conclusion that "*Every* objective judgment is such that it can be verified only by some progression in experience. . . . Empirical knowledge depends on prediction, on an argument from past to future, on the presence of some particular uniformity in experience; and the general problem of its validity is the same which is posed by Hume's skepticism."[85] This, Lewis says, is the problem he has now to meet.

But this problem, Lewis holds, takes a different form in his theory for three reasons. First, Hume attacked the possibility of knowledge of laws, not of particular things. But Lewis argues that he has already shown that knowledge of things "requires that same kind of order or reliable relatedness which law also requires."[86] This fact Lewis says makes possible "the proof which Kant attempted in his deduction of the categories" without assuming that experience is limited by fixed categories and forms of intuition. Since what Kant meant by "experience" was experience of identifiable objects, if knowledge of laws and knowledge of objects involve the same sort of regularities in presentations, then the only alternative to the existence of such regularities is chaos. Second, because the criteria of the real are a priori, we know that "*if x* is a physical thing, then it will conform to certain general principles which can be laid down in advance because they constitute the criteria of the physical." This, Lewis says, gives us an "Archimedean point" for investigation. Whatever does not conform to the criteria of one category will conform to those of another. "We play a sort of game of 'animal, vegetable, or mineral' with experience, by which it will be impossible for it to get out of the net of our understanding, no matter what may be the content of it."[87] The third point is that Lewis has only to establish the validity of empirical knowledge as probable, not as certain. And this, Lewis says, radically changes the whole problem.

Lewis then turns to a consideration of the nature of probability. The concept of probability that Lewis adopts is logical and is that of Keynes, whose treatise he had studied and reviewed. Probability is predicated of propositions and is a logical relation between certain premises, which constitute the data or evidence on which the probability rests, and the proposition is said to be probable. This conception of probability carries with it a number of consequences. First, "given all the relevant data which there are to be known, everything is either certainly true or certainly false. Given anything short of this, what the value of the probability is, depends upon what data are thus given."[88] Probability is therefore a function of our ignorance. Second, the statement "p is probable" is always elliptical for the full statement "p is probable on the premises $q_1 \ldots q_n$." No proposition is probable alone, but only in relation to its premises. Unlike deductive logic, in which, given "p" and "$p < q$", "q" may be asserted alone, a probable proposition can never be detached from the premises containing the data on which its probability is based. Third, the statement "p is probable on the premises $q_1 \ldots q_n$" is a logical statement and therefore, if correctly calculated, a priori true. This does not mean that "p" is true, or that any or all of the "q's" are true; even if they are all false, the statement of the logical relation between them, if valid, is a priori true. Thus, for probability statements, validity and truth are the same.

Fourth, the premises "$q_1 \ldots q_n$" embody the information on the basis of which the probability of "p" is asserted. Different people may have different amounts of information; hence, the probability of "p" can vary from one person to another, depending on the information each has. But this apparent subjectivity of probability is irrelevant to the objectivity of the logical relation. If Casey has premises "$q_1 \ldots q_k$" and O'Neil premises "$r_1 \ldots r_n$", each will pronounce a different probability for "p", but in each case their statements are true if "p has probability M on premises $q_1 \ldots q_k$," and "p has probability N on premises $r_1 \ldots r_n$." Similarly, any change in the premises, as will happen with the acquisition of new information, will result in a change in the probability of "p." But if before the new information was obtained, the statement "p has probability M on premises $q_1 \ldots q_j$" was true, it is always true; the new information changes the premises by adding, let us say, "$q_k \ldots q_n$," so the new statement is "p has probability N on premises $q_1 \ldots q_n$," which is also true. *Both* statements are true because they refer to different sets of premises. The probability of "p" on a given set of premises does not change, although changes in the premises will change the probability of "p".

Fifth, if "p" has probability M on premises "$q_1 \ldots q_n$," and $M < 1$, then "p" will not always be true. What one would expect to find is that "p" is true in M proportion of cases. Hence, from a statement that "p" is probable on certain premises, one cannot deduce the truth of "p", even though the statement that "p has probability M on premises $q_1 \ldots q_n$" is true, and indeed analytically true. The truth or falsity of "p" is a matter of fact; the truth or falsity of the statement that "p" has a certain probability on certain premises is a matter of logic.[89]

The laws of nature, Lewis says, are probable only, even in such cases as Newton's law of gravitation. So are the statistical laws, which Lewis suggests may in fact not be distinguishable from other laws of nature.[90] And so is that host of empirical statements such as "potatoes are good food" without which Lewis remarks "we should most of us be dead within the week."[91] But however pervasive probability is in our knowledge, Lewis believes that statements of probability must ultimately rest on something that is certain. Otherwise, if the premises of a probability proposition are only probable, and their premises are only probable, and so on, we will find ourselves caught in a regress and nothing will be probable.[92] This, it will be recalled, is the very argument he had used against pragmatism in "Naturalism and Idealism."

Where is this certainty to be found? All empirical knowledge, Lewis says, goes back ultimately to knowledge of empirical particulars.

> And knowledge of the particular is rooted in immediate experience. The first apprehension, so to speak, is of given appearances, having a specific and later recognizable character, and of their continuity with further and equally specific experience. Coincidence of such progressions in immediacy give rise to habits of action, which may become explicit in generalizations of the form "What appears like this will turn out thus and so." Granted that such coincidence in experience can establish probability for the future, we have in the immediate awareness of the given that certainty which becomes the basis of a probable knowledge of the particular object or the occurrence of an objective property.[93]

Expressive statements of the given are not probability statements; they are, if properly understood, certain. But statements about the relations of presentations—that such a presentation as x is a sign that such a presentation as z will occur—are probability statements. These empirical statistical generalizations at the level of the given make possible the application of the concept that constitutes the interpretation. The concept predicts the occurrence of certain experiences; its application is hypothetical, and that it fits experience is only probable. "This probability is supported by a generalization from direct experience of the sort which has been pointed out," which shows that the predicted sequences of experience are realized "in a certain proportion at least of cases."[94]

This probable knowledge of particulars then becomes the basis for empirical generalizations of the sort we normally think of as laws. These generalizations are probable only, so we have a "compounding of probabilities." "But this *compound* probability has as its premises the immediate certainty of the given data in the experience of particular instances."[95]

Indeed, no matter how many probabilities must be compounded, as long as the first premises are certain the resulting probabilities will be determinate and nonzero.

As Lewis admits, this theory involves reliance on memory, but memory, Lewis holds, is "a form of empirical knowledge, parallel in most respects to perception."

> As in perception, so in the case of memory, something is absolutely given—the present recollection. And like perception, memory as a form of knowledge is an interpretation put upon this presentation; an interpretation, moreover, which in the particular case is verifiable, in those ways in which all knowledge of the past is subject to verification.[96]

Lewis admits that this introduces yet another probability into the "compound" but he claims this introduces no "new theoretical difficulty." What this does not explain is how we know the present memory is an accurate recollection of something past, and Lewis does not mention any characteristic of "pastness" here.

Other qualifications are added. Knowledge gained from reports of others is also probable; these "reports of others are a particular type of our own experience, having a probability which reflects our past experience of such reports and of their relation to our further experience pertinent to their truth."[97] Lewis admits that by the time we reach the probability of, say, a scientific law, our calculations will involve the compounding of many different probabilities, but he holds that if the probabilities are high, the resulting probability may "be very close to theoretical certainty."

Lewis concludes that our empirical knowledge is probable only, but that, given the analysis of probability he holds, "just in so far as we are rational, what we believe is absolutely and eternally true."[98] For the statement that a given empirical proposition has a certain probability is a true statement—true because the connection of premises and the proposition is a logical connection and therefore a priori. Given that our initial premises are certain, as for Lewis awareness of the given is, then we can have certain knowledge that the empirical proposition has a particular probability.

In the final chapter of *Mind and the World Order*, Lewis turns to the problem of induction. If empirical knowledge as he has described it is possible, "there must be the possibility of arguing from past to future." But "the applicability of concepts and the argument from past to future require the presence of some order and uniformity." This has generally been thought to necessitate the assumption of the uniformity of nature, a claim that has proven singularly difficult to justify. Lewis believes the reason for this is that it has been assumed that what must be justified is certain knowledge. But he claims that when it is recognized that what must be warranted is only probable knowledge, the nature of this problem is changed and its solution becomes possible.[99]

Instead of tackling this issue head on, Lewis deals first with a variety of preliminary issues. The theory Lewis has so far presented does require the existence of uniformities in experience. But Lewis now emphasizes the fact that the required uniformities are not strict; there must indeed be order, but only some order, not complete order. Those portions of experience that do not fit the order requirements of real things are simply reclassified as being something else—as dreams or hallucinations or illusions or whatever. Indeed, Lewis has repeatedly emphasized that experience in the raw contains such a mix of elements that no generalizations can be made from it until it has been categorized and the disorderly elements thrown out. Reality is far more orderly than experience, because reality is experience categorized; hence, empirical generalizations concern real things, not raw experience.[100]

Further, Lewis has argued for the importance of orderly sequences of the given that permit one quale to serve as a sign of others. But this does not mean, Lewis emphasizes, that the sequence of the given is perfectly uniform. "If within every empirical content merely as given there were that which possessed absolute uniform correlation with that further sequence which is essential to a correct apprehension, then illusion and mistake would be possible only to the inexperienced and the fool."[101] Not only would error be impossible in this situation, but such perfect uniformity would mean a completely deterministic world in which we could not vary future experience by our actions. For such a world, knowledge would be useless because it could give us no control over experience. Furthermore, Lewis notes, it is generally agreed that every real object is unique. That must mean that our future possible experience of every object will differ in some respect from our future possible experience of every other. There must accordingly be an enormous amount of nonuniformity in our experience.

By arguments such as these, Lewis seeks to establish the conclusion that "intelligibility does not require such 'through and through' uniformity [as has sometimes been claimed] but only *some* uniformity." Lewis then proceeds to state his thesis:

> What is required in the way of order if experience is to be intelligible and knowledge possible is only that there should be apprehensible things and objective facts—and to this we can conceive no alternative whatever, unless it be the non-existence of everything.[102]

Lewis's argument for this claim begins with what he calls "Principle A": "It must be false, that every identifiable entity in experience is equally associated with every other." "This Principle is," Lewis says, "what Mr. Keynes has called the 'limitation of independent variety.' "[103] It has, in fact, very little to do with Keynes's principle,[104] which applies to real objects whereas Lewis's applies to experience. All that the two have in common is the requirement that the number of "entities"—properties in Keynes's case, qualia in Lewis's—must be finite. But Lewis says it satisfies all that is necessary concerning the order of experience for the validity of empirical generalizations "based on past experience and applicable to the future." Moreover, the principle depends on the fact that "every possible experience is *ipso facto* a possibility of experience, but it is not possible that all possibilities should be actual." Both "p" and "not-p" are possible, but only one of these can be actual at one time. The requirement that actuality limit the all-possible is not a limitation on *possibility*: it is a logical necessity. That this limitation guarantees that the number of qualia is finite is not obvious.

The existence of real things and properties does not require that all possible things be actualized; "there may be no unicorns."[105] Knowledge does not require that every uniformity in experience that we define by inventing a concept to designate it should actually obtain; there could be no knowledge if that were so. What is required is that given appearances should be signs of uniformities that are designated by concepts. And that in turn requires that past sequences of experience must establish some probability with respect to future sequences of experience. In other words, it cannot be the case that all possible experiences are equally probable; some combinations of experiences must be, by Principle A, more probable than others. We need not know any particular uniformity to satisfy this principle, but we must know that, in general, there will be such uniformities. This is equivalent, Lewis says, to saying that "things *in general*" exist, and if that be so, then

> the prediction (as probable) of that future experience which means the verification of the presence of an object corresponding to a particular concept, from a given presentation with which such further experience has been associated in the past, is valid.[106]

Moreover, each such verification of the correlation between a given presentation and future experience will increase the probability of each successive verification. The argument is based on Bayes's theorem and what Keynes calls the cumulative theorem.[107] Thus, the existence of objects is "all that is required" for the validity of probable empirical generalizations or laws and of the argument from past to future, for the existence of objective properties as well as laws depends on exactly the same sort of associations between given experiences and future possible experiences. "*What* laws *must be* valid, would depend upon what things exist; but the general assumption that there are things (of some sort) includes the assumption that there are valid generalizations of the type of law." These laws need be only generalizations of the statistical type; "*No absolute uniformities* of actual experience are required." The only alternative to this, Lewis says, is "that nothing exists to be known, and that no mind exists to know it."[108]

But skeptics, Lewis says, might answer that the assumption of the existence of real objects could be a nonrational assumption based on "animal faith"—an obvious shot at Santayana and the Critical Realists. Lewis's reply is that "it is impossible to imagine any sort of experience which would not present such statistical stabilities as would validate probable prediction, and such as would represent the experience of things." To support this claim, Lewis lays down Principle B:

> In any situation (if sufficiently extended) in which there are identifiable entities which fail to satisfy Principle A—i.e., whose association is "random"—there will be other entities, systemically connected with the former or specifiable in terms of them, which do satisfy Principle A.[109]

Thus, other entities can be found by analyzing the objects into simple elements or organizing them into larger wholes, or abstracting elements from them and disregarding the remainder as irrelevant. Taking as his example a perfectly shuffled deck of cards, with every card having an equal chance of being drawn, then the stable elements of the card games will be such things as "tricks-taken, or suits, or kinds of hands such as full-houses, straights, etc." These, unlike individual cards, will not be equally probable. Or we can turn to lower level characteristics such as "the pips on the cards." Thus, Lewis says, "even with entities thus deliberately devised to approximate pure chance in certain ways, there are certain wholes which, neglecting the 'non-essential,' give rise to generalizations."[110] We cannot of course say what particular "stabilities" will be found in experience, since this depends on the given over which we have no control. But we can say that experience will contain such "stabilities" that will warrant the claims that real objects exist.

But does this really answer the question of the validity of inference from past to future? Lewis says that Principle A really covers this, but to sharpen his point he lays down Principle C:

> The statistical prediction of the future from the past cannot be generally invalid, because whatever is future to any given past, is in turn past for

some future. That is, whoever continually revises his judgment of the probability of a statistical generalization by its successively observed verifications and failures, cannot fail to make more successful predictions than if he should disregard the past in his anticipations of the future. This might be called the "Principle of statistical accumulation."[111]

Even, Lewis says, if there were a demon who deliberately manipulated our experience in an effort to deceive us, we would eventually find a way to defeat him. By ignoring enough of experience as it comes, we would arrive at repetition and uniformity. "Knowledge might be made difficult, but could not be made impossible." "In any experience such as we can, even at the worst, suppose to be our own, conception will be valid and knowledge will be possible." And this will be true, Lewis says, even if the demon has an infinite number of qualia at his disposal.

Lewis included a series of appendices to *Mind and the World Order*. The first of these, Appendix A, is entitled "Natural Science and Abstract Concepts." Starting from a comment of Max Born's about the goal of science, Lewis points out that as science develops, it departs more and more from common sense and from appearances toward a deductive system whose elements are indirectly apprehended. Increasingly, science takes laws to be the essence of things; disappearances and appearances become subsumed under transformations, so that the changes of the phenomenal world become lawful transformations of underlying abstract entities. As this process of scientific development continues, "there comes a stage when it is no longer easily possible to say whether concepts are devised, and laws discovered, to fit phenomenal facts, or whether the conceptual system itself rules and facts are reconceived in conformity to it."[112] It thus becomes possible to describe scientific truth equally as the discovery of comprehensive empirical laws or as the selection of an abstract system applicable to the facts. Taken in abstraction, such systems would be like abstract geometry. But the application of such systems to nature, Lewis emphasizes, will still depend on their fitting the data of the senses. As applied, such systems remain probable only, no matter how high the probability may be.

Appendix B is entitled "Esthesis and Esthetics." "The nearest approach to pure givenness is doubtless the esthetic experience,"[113] Lewis says. Granted that a presentation has both an instrumental sign-function and an "immediate felt quale" inseparably combined, the value of the presentation as cognitive sign is largely independent of its esthetic value. "The former is extrinsic; the latter intrinsic." All experience therefore has for Lewis an intrinsic esthetic value, whether positive or negative. But the contemplation of the immediately given does not yield aesthetic knowledge; "the object of esthetic *judgment* must always transcend the merely given." "The object of appraisal is (usually at least) to connect this quality with some thing or context as a matrix of *further* such experience."[114] Only by so doing can esthetic judgment become significant for practice.

All judgments of value, Lewis says, depend on some direct intuition of value, of the given, and about such direct valuations no error or argument is possible. But the aim of esthetics is to find enduring values by so relating the given to future possible experience that the desired values can be repeated. Thus, esthetic judgment is not really different in kind from any other form of empirical judgement. Lewis had, by 1929, already formulated ideas basic to the analysis of value he would later give in AKV.

Appendix C is called "Concepts and Ideas." In this appendix, Lewis turns to the question of ethics and of religion. Cognitively speaking, other persons are for me merely objects whose behavior is relevant to my purposes. "But so far as I desire, or feel it my duty, to treat other persons not only as behaving objects present in my environment but also as ends in themselves, I have an interest, which cannot be abstracted from, in the absolute quality of their immediate experience."[115] This poses a problem quite different from that of purely cognitive knowledge. As Lewis showed earlier with respect to cognitive knowledge, it does not matter whether what McGee calls "red" is what Walsh calls "green" so long as the relational systems in which these qualities stand are isomorphic. But with respect to ethics (and esthetics) it does matter, because the issue is precisely the quality of another's experience. Ethics therefore requires the understanding of another's mind by empathy or sympathy, an appreciation of his experience, but that this can be done—that one can know the quality of another's experience—is a postulate, and "upon such postulate, ethics must be founded."[116]

A similar issue arises with respect to ultimate reality: is ultimate reality merely indifferent to us, or does it in some sense "care" about us? If the latter, it would have to have a mind not unlike our own. This is the choice that Idealism has made; it is also the choice that Lewis rejects. At least so far as cognitive knowledge is concerned, the assumption that empathy with the inanimate is possible is devoid of meaning.

Appendix D is entitled "Mind's Knowledge of Itself." Knowledge of mind would seem to present a paradox for Lewis. If ascriptions of reality depend on something being given, then mind must be given. But mind is that to which what is not given in experience has been ascribed. How then can mind be known? But Lewis claims there is no paradox. "The activity of mind is evidenced, first, in the *feeling* of such activity."[117] One has certain feelings that are directly observable and are the ones we classify as desires, interests, purposes, and so forth. These constitute the given relevant to mind. Second, the correlation between these given feelings and certain observable happenings is that from which I learn my own activity. This correlation is, of course, not given, but an induction from many experiences. Thus, I learn through experience the correlation between feelings of attending, being interested, and so on, and further observable occurrences or alterations in what is attended to or what I am interested in. That the alterations are so correlated I learn from not attending or being interested in something. That is, "we learn the existence and nature of thought, as we learn the nature and existence of anything else, through the difference that it makes in experience."[118] What we mean by "mind" is partly revealed by just those correlations. When then I ascribe reality to mind, I ascribe an interpretation; its significance transcends any particular experience and concerns future possible experience.

The *activity* of mind is not itself given; it is learned in experience. One finds that "when we thus think, then certain contexts of the thing thought about accrue, in ways in which they do not accrue when we think of some different purpose or fail to attend or reflect."[119] But this marks no distinction from the way we learn the activity of other real things. No metaphysical agent need be assumed here. Mind is a real thing in the same sense that other things are real.

Appendix E is called "The Application of Abstract Conceptual Systems to Experience." Does the character of our experience determine what conceptual systems can be applied? Although it might seem obvious that the answer must be yes, Lewis points out that not only does the same conceptual system admit of multiple empirical models but that the same experiential phenomena can be described by different conceptual systems. Moreover, this is true even when the conceptual system marks distinctions that do not correspond to what we experience, or denies those that do. Thus, where science takes color to vary continuously along a spectrum, we see a relatively small number of distinct colors. Lewis concludes that "it is unsafe to say that *any* concept *could not* be applied to *any* empirical content."[120] Accordingly, the grounds for determining what applications are correct can only be pragmatic.

The last appendix, F, is entitled "The Logical Correlates of the A Priori and the A Posteriori." Lewis claims that a priori propositions are those that are analytic and true in intension while those that are a posteriori are synthetic and true in extension. "Propositions in intension concern what is possible, impossible, or necessary; an affirmative universal in intension states a necessity and negates a possibility. Propositions in extension concern only what does or does not exist."[121] The universal in intension implies the universal in extension, but the converse is not true. Analytic propositions are those in which the meaning of the subject term is explicated by the predicate; once we know these meanings, we know the proposition is true independently of existing things. Lewis then reviews the differences between propositions in intension and extension, focusing particularly on the problems raised by the null-class. This is familiar ground that he has covered in earlier papers. But next he turns to Russell's theory of descriptions. The singular proposition in intension, Lewis says, merely states that "the subject-concept implies (or does not imply) the predicate. The difference is only that the subject of the singular in intension is a concept such that it applies to one, and to only one, possible object."[122] But the singular in extension requires an existent. If one were to say, "The residuary legatee under this will is entitled to . . . ," where no such legatee exists, this sentence would be intensionally true as a matter of law, but false on Russell's theory. Thus, Lewis argues that Russell's theory does not fit at least some of the standard uses of singular propositions. Lewis does not deny that propositions in intension and in extension both have legitimate uses; what he most strongly objects to is the confusion of the two, and the neglect of propositions in intension. "Current revisions of tradition will all too frequently be found to have been formulated . . . as if all propositions had their meaning in extension."[123] One does not have to be told to whom he is referring.

Mind and the World Order is the book that made Lewis's reputation. His earlier work in logic had been too technical to interest more than a few people, but in this book he established himself as a major figure in philosophy, an outstanding epistemologist, and a leading Pragmatist. Reviews of *Mind and the World Order* are interesting chiefly as indications of how difficult his contemporaries found it to grasp his position. G. Watts Cunningham was baffled by Lewis's statements that, on the one hand, the a priori can be maintained in the face of any experience while, on the other, it may change over time, depending on its utility. Cunningham found this a contradiction and was unable to see how choice on pragmatic grounds could resolve the matter. Nevertheless, he recognized the importance of the book and expressed his admiration for Lewis's accomplishment.[124] Hugh Miller's review in the *Philosophical Review*[125] takes Lewis to task for claiming that all science can be systematized under a single conceptual scheme—a claim Lewis did not make—and for failing to integrate the a priori and the given! Writing in *Mind*,[126] Schiller is far more friendly to Lewis—as one would expect—but even he has trouble with Lewis's view that experience could lead us to change an a priori conceptual system. The most understanding and laudatory review is that by Charles Baylis in the *Journal of Philosophy*,[127] who begins by remarking, "It seems a safe prediction that *Mind and the World Order* will be deemed the most important contribution to epistemology in years." Having been a student of Lewis's, Baylis understood the book, and his outline of it is perceptive. So are his criticisms; Baylis particularly points out that Lewis had not dealt adequately with the problem of memory. But whether they approved Lewis's position or even understood it, reviewers gave the book attention and recognized that it was a major work. And so it proved to be, for in the next decade it was regarded as an outstanding American work in the field.

Nevertheless, Lewis soon became aware of some critical weaknesses in the book that involved problems that would occupy him for years to come. The first of these concerned the certainty of the given. Not only was the given one of the key factors of Lewis's epistemology, but it was also the anchor of his theory of probability. Lewis repeatedly said that if the premises of probable knowledge are themselves only probable, and the premises that establish those premises as probable are only probable, and so on, we have a regress that can only lead to nothing being probable. His answer to that was the certainty of the given. But Lewis had also said that immediate awareness of the given did not constitute knowledge, and that linguistic descriptions of the given could be in error. How then was the certainty of the given brought to bear on knowledge? Lewis did not provide an adequate answer to that question. Lewis's choice here is either to extend his definition of knowledge, and of propositions, to somehow enable immediate awareness of the given to serve as the premise of a probability argument, or to deny that the linguistic description of the given can be in error. He does neither. If "It looks blue" is taken, not as ascribing an objective property, but an as index of the presence of a quale, we have still the problem of how the quale is related to "blue"; what justifies the application of the term? "Blue" represents no single quale, but a class of qualia. On Lewis's grounds, its application to the given can only be probable. How can the certainty of the presentation translate into the certainty of the premise of a probability argument, which must obviously be a proposition? This was an issue Lewis would struggle with for years to come.

Second, Lewis theory of meaning was inadequate. For any given individual, the meaning of a term is given by all the terms involved in its definition, and by the presentations in experience to which the term applies. It was a brilliant insight on Lewis's part to recognize that for communication between two individuals, all that was necessary was an isomorphism between their definitional structures that would produce congruent behavior; no sharing of sensory experience was necessary. But this theory created serious problems for esthetics and ethics, as he clearly saw (Appendix B). Further,

Lewis left it very unclear what terms denote. Sometimes he says they denote qualia, sometimes the real object or real property, sometimes both. Nevertheless, the roots of his later theory of linguistic meaning and sense meaning are clearly evident here.

Third, Lewis has provided no adequate theory of memory. He was fully aware that the validity of memory was implied by his theory, but his argument for it is weak. Lewis takes memorial knowledge to be analogous to perceptual knowledge. There is, he says, "something absolutely given—the present recollection." As a form of knowledge, he takes memory to be an interpretation of this given that is verifiable. But Lewis does not explain how memorial knowledge is to be verified, what the data could be, or how we can know that a present recollection is an accurate reflection of past experience. This was another problem to which Lewis would have to return.

The fourth major problem concerns his attempt to justify induction. The conclusion Lewis wants to establish is this:

> The conclusion of which I shall hope to convince the reader is that no assumption of anything which could conceivably be false is necessary; that no sort of experience which the wildest imagination could conjure up could fail to afford a basis for intelligibility and probable judgment.[128]

But the argument Lewis presents is confusing, and one reason for that is his attempt to invoke the authority of Keynes. Lewis says of his Principle A: "It must be false, that every identifiable entity in experience is equally associated with every other," that "The principle is what Mr. Keynes has called the 'limitation of independent variety,' except that it is here applied to the identifiable constituents of experience, particularly with reference to their sequence, instead of to the qualities of objects with reference to their correlations in reality."[129] In Part III of his *Treatise*, Keynes gave a very careful and sophisticated argument for the validity of induction, of which this principle is one component. But Keynes's argument has little to do with Lewis's argument. In brief, Keynes held that if the properties of real objects are due to some underlying set of "generator properties," whose number is finite and small relative to the number of real properties that exist, then real properties can be grouped according to their generator properties. Since the number of groups will be finite, "if two sets of apparent properties are taken, there is, in the absence of evidence to the contrary, a finite probability that the second set will belong to the group specified by the first set."[130] If this is so, then, Keynes argues, inductive methods can be legitimately applied. This argument, barely touched on here, has almost nothing to do with Lewis's argument, except that Lewis adopts the idea that if the number of qualia is finite, then qualia will repeat in the course of experience. But this is only one aspect of Keynes's argument and, for Keynes, would not itself provide a justification for induction. Further, Lewis finally drops the restriction of the number of qualia to the finite and says that, even if the number of qualia were infinite, it would make no difference.[131] The issue of the finite number of qualia is a distraction from the real argument.

What then is Lewis's argument? First, Lewis believed, on the basis of the position he has established in the book, that the existence of real properties, real objects, and general laws all involve regularities in experience. If he can therefore establish the existence of real objects, he will have shown that experience involves uniformities sufficient to support induction.

> The attempt is only to show that there could not be a world of apprehensible things in which empirical generalizations should fail of valid foundation; that if there are things then laws of the type which empirical generalization seeks to grasp must hold; and hence that such generalizations may be genuinely probable and that empirical knowledge, as the only sort of thing it can reasonably be supposed to be, is genuinely possible. If this point is established, then the only alternative to the conception that our knowledge in general is valid, is the conception that there are no things; that nothing exists to be known and no mind exists to know it.[132]

But these regularities need not, and will not, be perfect. Lewis repeatedly emphasized that experience uncategorized is a welter of illusions, dreams, and what have you, that does not exhibit uniformity; it is only when experience is categorized that we can expect to find regularity. Second, Lewis believed that what set his approach to the problem apart from those of others is that he has only to justify probable knowledge. Therefore, the uniformities in experience need not be perfect; it will be sufficient if *some* uniformity can be found. Third, Lewis held, "The presentation is due to, or caused by, the object; but *knowledge* of the object is due to the presentation."[133] That is, real objects cause the qualia we experience and therefore are responsible for the regularities of experience; these qualia then serve as clues to the real object. If we then find regularities in experience, does it follow that these regularities are caused by real objects? Clearly, it does not; as Lewis says, some of them may be due to "mere coincidence."[134] But Lewis holds that if experience does show regularities—that is, if present qualia correlate with future qualia—then some of these regularities must be due to the existence of real objects. And here is the error. What Lewis's three principles show, if anything, is merely that there will be some regularities in experience. Nothing that Lewis sets forth demonstrates that these regularities are not *all* "mere coincidence." Unless Lewis *defines* the real object as a regularity in experience, the existence of a regularity in experience does not prove the existence, or even the probability of the existence, of a real object. And to *define* the real object in this way would destroy Lewis's realism. Assuming the existence of real objects as a postulate could, of course, *account* for the existence of the regularity in experience, but Lewis does not present his argument in these terms. Nor do Lewis's further principles help him here. Principle B is illustrated by card games, but the illustration is poor because cards, no matter how well shuffled, have a prior order built into them—for example, suits, numbers, and so on. And Principle C is no better. Lewis calls this the "principle of statistical accumulation," referring obviously to Bayes's Theorem, but Bayes's Theorem concerns conditional probabilities. What if the different "times" referred to in the principle are statistically independent? Then the principle fails.

What Lewis really comes down to in his efforts to prove that experience is orderly is categorization.

> By ignoring a significant proportion of the characteristics of experience as it came to us, we should arrive at such simplicity that, in terms of it, even the most disadvantageous sequence of the primary constituents— e.g., a "random" order—must afford some repetition and uniformity. Knowledge might be made difficult, but it could not be made impossible.[135]

Given a table of random numbers, one can, of course, select from the table any numerical sequence one likes, but so what? If this is the proof of the order of experience, any pretence that such an order is related to real objects or real properties is absurd, and "knowledge" loses any warrant at all.

The problem here runs very deep and exposes an underlying confusion in Lewis's thought. On the one hand, Lewis holds that the real object (or property) is the cause of regularities in experience. On the other, he identifies the real with the regularity in experience. It cannot be both; the real cannot *cause* the regularity if it *is* the regularity. The first view is realistic, the second phenomenalistic. Lewis's confusion here may represent some holdover from his earlier Idealism. By 1929, he had repudiated Idealism and considered himself a Realist, but on the crucial matter of the relation of the real object to experience, he stumbled. The result is that he ends with a Phenomenalism that is quite clearly not what he had intended.

Thus, Lewis's attempt to solve the riddle of induction failed. Lewis soon recognized that fact, and abandoned not only this argument but any further attempt to solve the problem, until he read Reichenbach.

Biographical Note III

Middle Years

The crash of 1929 left the Lewises relatively unscathed. With three children and a wife, Lewis's salary was not sufficient to have allowed the accumulation of much savings. Further, coming from the backgrounds that they did, both Lewis and his wife were extremely frugal. When automatic washing machines became available, Lewis did not buy one, although that meant Mabel had to wring the wet clothes by hand.[1] If they had any money in the market when the crash came, it was very little. But, in 1930, Lewis was promoted to the rank of full professor and the financial pressure began to ease. Moreover, in a time of very rapid deflation, an academic salary and a secure position were genuine blessings; academic salaries exhibited more rigidity than most others, and prices fell far faster. The Lewises began to save, and although Lewis considered Franklin Roosevelt benighted and deplored the New Deal, he was shrewd enough to begin investing when the recovery began.[2]

But this was also a period of devastating personal tragedy. Their daughter Peggy had been an outstanding student in high school and showed signs of real brilliance. But during her last year before graduation, she began suffering severe pains in her legs. She went through periods of agony when she was confined to her bed, followed by periods of remission when she seemed to be recovering. She entered Radcliff and managed to do very well despite her condition, and acquired a suitor to whom she became engaged.[3] But the disease returned and worsened. Finally, in October 1932, Peggy died.[4] Almost certainly the cause of her death was leukemia. How she contracted the disease, of course, no one knows, but her brother noted that there was a cluster of leukemia cases among those who had lived in Shady Hill Square, where the Lewises had resided when they returned to Cambridge.[5]

The Lewises were so distraught over Peggy's illness and death that they could not deal with the funeral; Ralph and Rachel Perry handled the whole matter for them.[6] Lewis was devastated by it. Throughout her illness, he had sought refuge in his work, but after she died he came close to unravelling. The Lewises had had four children: Irving had died as a toddler of diphtheria; now Peggy had died of leukemia. Even granting how poor the medical science of the day was, this was a terrible toll. And as events were to prove, it wasn't over.

In 1930, Lewis published his first autobiographical piece in Adams and Montague's *Contemporary American Philosophy*.[7] Here he recounts his conversations with the elderly lady heretic when he was fifteen as well as other incidents of his early life. And it is here that he describes his encounter with Kant and with James and Royce, and his introduction to logic by Royce when he served as an assistant in Royce's logic course. According to Lewis, he was immediately struck by the problem of material implication, and set out to solve it. "Two sorts of problems were before me," he says; the problem of creating an intensional logic as an alternative to the *Principia*, and the problem of what it would mean if there were different logics.[8] Lewis says he tackled the former first in the work that led to the *Survey*. He rehearses here many of his objections to material implication and his reasons for believing that strict implication was the type of implication relation that accorded with deductivity. He also says that "early in the course of these researches I formed the conviction that all valid inference, being a matter of intension, rests upon the analysis of meaning."[9] But he was surprised to discover the paradoxes of strict implication that "gave me pause." However, Lewis says he became convinced that these results are due to legitimate principles of reasoning and must be accepted, a point he supports with this argument. Let "p", "q", and "r" represent propositions, and let "p" strictly imply "q", so that "$p < q$". It is a theorem of Strict Implication {theorem 19.51 of *Symbolic Logic*} that $(p < q) < (p \,\&\, r < q)$, for any r. Then, invoking antilogism, Lewis argued

1.	$p < q$	hyp
2.	$(p < q) < (p \,\&\, r < q)$	19.51
3.	$(p \,\&\, r < q) < [(\sim q \,\&\, p) < \sim r]$	Antilogism
4.	$(p \,\&\, r < q)$	1, 2, modus ponens
5.	$(\sim q \,\&\, p) < \sim r$	3, 4, modus ponens

But "$(\sim q$ and $p)$" is a contradiction since by hypothesis "$p < q$". Because "r" is any proposition, we have that an impossible proposition implies any proportion.[10]

Thus, convinced of the soundness of his logic, Lewis realized that

> the line of division which marks off that class of propositions which are
> capable of corroboration by logic alone (necessary propositions) from
> merely empirical truths, and marks off the impossible or absurd, which
> can be refuted by logic alone, from merely empirical falsehood, is a divi-
> sion of major importance.[11]

Lewis was thus convinced that the division of the a priori and the a posteriori was fundamental.

This left Lewis with the problem of alternative logics. He says he soon
discovered not only that Strict Implication and Material Implication were
alternative systems but that a wide variety of "queer" logics could also be
created, all of which were internally consistent. That led him to conclude:

> If formal logic is capable of any exact development at all, then we are
> confronted with the task of deciding which, amongst various possible
> and actual logistic systems, is such that its principles state the truth about
> valid inference. Internal consistency and "self-criticism" are not sufficient
> criteria to determine a truth which is independent of initial assumptions
> which are themselves logical in nature. Thus logic cannot test itself—or
> rather such test does not prove truth in logic.[12]

Here again, one sees that Lewis saw the issue at that point as finding a
"true" system, meaning one that accorded with the ordinary notion of valid
inference. It was this issue, he says, that led him to epistemology. It is interesting that Lewis makes no mention of the fact that his early interest and
his dissertation had been in epistemology, and gives the impression, which
his early papers belie, that it was only after the *Survey* that he turned to this
subject. One suspects he did not wish to discuss his early Idealism now
that he had moved on.

It was to solve the problem of choosing among alternative logics that
he developed his theory of the pragmatic a priori,[13] and came to see that
what distinguishes the mind's contribution to knowledge from the given is
the existence of choice or alternatives. Lewis then describes the a priori
character of the categories, particularly of the category of the "real." The
categories, he says, "are like the reference system which the mathematician
stretches through all space and with respect to which whatever positions
and motions there are there to be described will inevitably be describable."[14] Lewis then describes briefly the theory he had put forward in
Mind and the World Order.

But in concluding his autobiographical note, Lewis remarks that he has used "knowledge" here to refer to "truths of description"; he has excluded

> "truths of appreciation," the aesthetic quality of the given, and all that depends upon sympathy and upon that communion of minds which requires coincidence of immediate experience. Evaluation can hardly be indifferent to the quality of the given. Nor can the basis of ethics be laid without reference to the felt character of experience in another mind. And the religious sense, if it is to take reality as the matrix of human values, will likewise transcend the interests of knowledge in this restricted sense. There is, then, a line of division between such interests and cognition of the type of science. And it is suggested that the foundation of these, not being found in knowledge alone, may rest upon some postulate.[15]

The influence of Royce is obvious here, though the direction in which Lewis was looking for a solution was not Royce's. Indeed, this concluding paragraph forecasts the direction of much of Lewis's future work.

Through the 1930s, Lewis continued to teach the same sorts of courses he had taught in the 1920s. He taught courses on the theory of Knowledge and on the Kantian Philosophy every year from 1930 through 1939, and from 1937 on a course on Kant. He still taught logic; he gave courses in 1932–1933, 1934–1935, 1936, and 1937. And he taught courses on ethics in 1933–1934, 1937, and 1938. The major change was in the Philosophy of Evolution course; he taught that every year from 1930 through 1937, then dropped it for 1938, and, in 1939, began teaching a course entitled Ethics and the Social Order that was a continuation under another name of the Philosophy of Evolution. These, in addition to the usual service courses, constituted his schedule of the 1930s. He also carried administrative duties. He had chaired the department from 1927 through 1929, and did so again from 1937 through 1938, and for a half-year in 1939. These duties were demanding, but not excessive, and were about the same as those of his colleagues.[16]

Nevertheless, in 1933, Lewis suffered a heart attack. Although it was judged relatively mild at the time,[17] it was a blow, both physically and psychologically. As his son recalled, "he was a devout hypochondriac."[18] He may not have had health problems as serious as he believed, but he always traveled with a large bag full of medicines, and there was no question that he had a heart condition. In 1934, grief over Peggy's death, the aftereffects of the heart attack, and overwork from his teaching and writing brought him close to what his wife called "a complete nervous breakdown." Mabel found herself called upon to give him the support he needed: "Never a religious man, suspicious of all that is mystic and 'fuzzy-minded,' he had no other source but me to turn to."[19] To recover, Lewis took a sabbatical in the spring of 1935, which they spent in California, that allowed him to regain his strength.

This trip seems to have inaugurated the Lewises's custom of summer automobile trips. Such trips were a very common vacation activity in the 1930s. Cars, and the mobility they provided, were still new enough to make exploring the country an exciting activity, and the state of the nation's highways, and cars, added an element of risk and adventure to the undertaking. Besides, Lewis and his wife were both explorers at heart. They had loved Colorado and were even more enchanted by California, and relished the chance to explore the Southwest. They usually traveled in two cars, Lewis driving one and Mabel the other, meeting at designated stopping places. Lewis was a skillful driver, though his son recalls that he did things as a driver that his son would not, but the Lewises managed to avoid any accidents. And it was at this point that Lewis became seriously interested in photography—a very common side effect of such travel. He was a good photographer, did his own developing, had his own enlarger, and made excellent pictures. It was a hobby that both provided a visual record of their travels and gave him diversion from his regular academic duties.[20]

As this suggests, the financial position of the Lewis family had improved during the 1930s. Lewis was now a full professor with an adequate and secure salary, and that allowed him to become an investor. Whether he was a shrewd investor or whether the recovery that the New Deal brought floated his boat, the Lewises were financially comfortable by 1939. They did not live high, but were well enough off to send their youngest son to Exeter in 1939.[21]

Lewis may have been a skillful driver, but as a pedestrian he was a menace. His son recalled:

> Dad had the most frightful pedestrian habits I've ever known. He would set off to cross a street in sublime disregard of the traffic, cars screeching to a halt right and left. He never wavered. This was a torment to the people who cared about him. I was always sure he would get hit, and he didn't, finally.[22]

It is doubtless fortunate that Lewis did not live in New York.

Lewis was a devoted family man. He was a man of very strong emotion that he had great difficulty expressing, but his children were never in doubt of his devotion to them. He once said to his wife that he would gladly die for them, and he would.[23] This was surely one reason, though only one, for the separation that he maintained between work and home. Although he wrote at home in the mornings, he was never unavailable to the family. His son remember:

> As a child I learned if there was something I wanted to talk to him about—I was never ever put away from addressing him—to go into his office and to stand there until at a point he would put his pen down . . . And then I would have his complete attention for as long as I wanted to occupy it.[24]

But Lewis did not talk philosophy at home; there he was a father and absorbed in the activities of his children. He had a passionate devotion to all children and his son said:

> He could not stand to hear a child cry. He was known to invade a strange house in absolute disregard of who else might be in it or object to it if he heard a child crying insistently enough. He just absolutely responded. He probably would have taken a child away from a parent that was mistreating it.[25]

Certainly the loss of two of his own children must have been partly responsible for this.

Lewis was a worker; he wrote every day on the philosophic problems that engrossed him, and wrote out his lectures, not just in outline form but often in full text. But he seems to have worked largely alone. Some philosophers carry on extensive philosophic discussions with colleagues by letter; Lewis apparently did not—at least I have found relatively few letters of that sort written to or by him. One has the impression that he worked out his ideas by himself, poring over problems again and again in his private writings until he felt he was ready to publish something. This was not from any fear of criticism, of which he apparently had none, nor was it from arrogance. Although he had a certain dignity about him, there was no trace of pretension. "He would talk as appropriate with anybody about anything in an ordinary sort of way."[26] But he was not a gregarious man, and although he read constantly and kept up with the field, he simply needed to work out his own ideas for himself.

As the 1930s drew to a close, the threat of war became increasingly real. With the beginning of the war in Europe in 1939, the issue of American intervention became the most pressing question of the day. Many in the United States were devout isolationists and fought Roosevelt's efforts to aid Britain; there were also those who believed intervention was essential, the sooner the better. Most Americans stood somewhere in the middle between these extremes. Lewis opposed American intervention, but he was not an extremist; he was also a passionate patriot, and when war came he supported the Allied cause without reservation.[27]

6

Logic II

In 1932, Lewis and Langford published *Symbolic Logic*. Cooper Harold Langford had been born in Arkansas in 1895, attended Clark University, where he received his B.A., and did his graduate work at Harvard, where he received his Ph.D. in 1924. He stayed at Harvard, serving as an instructor from 1925 to 1927, and then went to the University of Michigan, and by 1932 was a full professor. *Symbolic Logic* was less a cooperative venture than a co-authored book; in the preface the authors stated that Chapters I through VIII and Appendix II were written by Lewis and Chapters IX through XIII and Appendix I by Langford. To what extent each advised the other on their separate chapters is left unclear, but probably there was not much of an attempt to harmonize the two sections; Langford's theory of propositions, for example, in Chapter IX is clearly not Lewis's theory. The purpose of the book was to provide an authoritative treatment of logic, based on strict implication, but covering the whole field, including the paradoxes from the liar's to Russell's, that would serve both as a text and a treatise. It was to be Lewis's final effort to secure preeminence for his view of logic.

The first five of Lewis's chapters recapitulate the historical sections of the *Survey* in a condensed form. Not until Chapter VI does Lewis begin the development of his own system. As so often before, he states his intention to develop the system based on a notion of "implies" that is equivalent to deducibility, and asserts that material implication cannot meet this test. The actual system, which he, of course, calls the Calculus of Strict Implication,[1] is set forth as follows. The primitive notions are negation, conjunction, and possibility. He also includes, as previously, logical equivalence as primitive, used here as the defining relation, although he will define equivalence within the system. This has led to the charge that Lewis confused object language with metalanguage,[2] but this charge, although true, is anachronistic since Tarski's "The Concept of Truth in Formalized Languages" was not published in Polish until 1933 and in German until 1936.[3] He then defines disjunction as

$$11.01 \quad p \vee q = \sim(\sim p \mathbin{\&} \sim q)$$

Strict implication is given as

$$11.02 \quad (p < q) = \sim\Diamond\,(p \mathbin{\&} \sim q)$$

and logical equivalence as

$$11.03 \quad (p = q) = [(p < q) \mathbin{\&} (q < p)]$$

He also introduces material implication and material equivalence as

$$14.01 \quad p \supset q = \sim(p \mathbin{\&} \sim q)$$

$$14.02 \quad p \equiv q = (p \supset q) \mathbin{\&} (q \supset P)$$

The postulates are

$$11.1 \quad p \mathbin{\&} q < q \mathbin{\&} p$$

$$11.2 \quad p \mathbin{\&} q < p$$

$$11.3 \quad p < p \mathbin{\&} p$$

$$11.4 \quad ((p \mathbin{\&} q) \mathbin{\&} r) = [p \mathbin{\&} (q \mathbin{\&} r)]$$

$$11.5 \quad p < \sim(\sim p)$$

$$11.6 \quad [(p < q) \mathbin{\&} (q < r)] < (p < r)$$

$$11.7 \quad (p \mathbin{\&} (p < q)) < q \quad 124\text{--}125$$

The rules are:

1. Uniform substitution for variables.
2. Substitution of strict equivalents.
3. Adjunction—if "p" is a theorem and "q" is a theorem, then "$p \mathbin{\&} q$" is a theorem.
4. Inference (Modus Ponens)—if "p" is a theorem, and if "$p < q$" is a theorem, then "q" is a theorem.

The statement of the system is explicitly formal, independent of any particular interpretation. Lewis does not begin by setting out the truth-value propositional calculus and then adding modal notions to it, as most logicians would do today; rather, the postulates are all phrased in terms of strict implication. Lewis did not regard his system as an extension of the truth-value calculus, but as the fundamental system from which the truth-value calculus would itself be derived. This system Lewis named S1.[4]

Lewis then proves a number of theorems of S1. These include

12.3 $p = \sim(\sim p)$

12.77 $[(p < q) \,\&\, ((q \,\&\, r) < s)] < [((p \,\&\, r) < s)]$

13.2 $p < (p \vee q)$ Addition

13.5 $p \vee \sim p$ Excluded Middle

14.1 $(p < q) < (p \supset q)$

He then derives the postulates of the propositional calculus given in the *Principia*[5]. He is careful to emphasize that these derivations are in terms of strict implication, so that the postulates and theorems of the propositional calculus using material implication are strictly implied by the postulates of the system S1. The paradoxical theorems of material implication—"$(p \supset (q \supset p))$" and "$(\sim p \supset (p \supset q))$"—are therefore theorems of S1 but their strict analogues are not. Lewis also proves

15.3 $\sim(p \supset q) < (p \supset \sim q)$

15.32 $\sim(p \supset \sim q) < (p \supset q)$

From these theorems it follows that "if we take any pair of propositions, p and q, then p must materially imply q or p will materially imply that q is false." And from this it follows that, if material implication were taken as equivalent to deducibility, "no pair of propositions could be at once consistent and independent." For "if p and q are consistent, then p cannot imply that q is false: and if q is independent of p, then p cannot imply that q is true."[6]

The converse of 14.1—"$(p \supset q) < (p < q)$"—does not hold in S1.[7] This presents a problem for Lewis, since he wanted it to be the case that whenever a material implication is "asserted,"—that is, whenever $p \supset q$ is derivable as a theorem from the postulates of Strict Implication—then $p < q$ will also be a theorem. Does this then mean that the paradoxes of material implication hold for strict implication? It does not. What does hold is

15.2 $p < (q \supset p)$

15.22 $\sim p < (p \supset q)$

If "p" is true, then "p" *strictly* implies that any proposition *materially* implies "p", and if "$\sim p$" is true, then "$\sim p$" *strictly* implies that "p" *materially* implies any proposition. But the "$\supset$" in 15.2 and 15.22 cannot be replaced by "$<$". Thus, the paradoxes of material implication do not occur in Strict Implication.

As Lewis says,

> In such theorems, as deduced in the system of Strict Implication, in every
> case in which the relation ⊃ is assertible in a law (i.e., is tautological), ⊃
> can be replaced by <. But when an unasserted (non-tautological) relation
> ⊃ appears in a theorem, it cannot, in general, be replaced by <.[8]

What is asserted is the main connective, not the subordinate ones. To get
around this problem, Lewis uses "T principles." The notion is that whenever "$(p \supset q)$" is a theorem but "$(p < q)$" is not, some theorem "T" can
be found such that "$((p \& T) < q)$". This is clear since "T" can be "$(p \supset q)$"
itself, which is here a theorem by hypothesis, though usually it is a different theorem.[9] Thus, for example, Lewis gives

$$16.1 \quad [(p < q) \& T] < [(p \& r) < (q \& r)]$$
$$T = (q \& r) < (q \& r)$$

12.77, putting "$q \& r$"/"s", gives "$[(p < q) \& (q \& r < q \& r)] < (p \& r) <$
$(q \& r)$". Lewis remarks:

> Thus if we have any premise of the form of the *other* member in the
> antecedent, p < q, the corresponding conclusion of the form (p & r)
> < (q & r) can always be deduced, since the further premise needed to
> give the conclusion can always be asserted. Thus, as a principle of infer-
> ence, 16.1 can be used exactly as if the T did not occur in it.[10]

Lewis then introduces the consistency calculus that he had presented
in the *Survey*, defining "p is consistent with q" as

$$17.01 \quad (p \circ q) = \sim(p < \sim q)$$

We have then

$$17.1 \quad (p \& q) < (p \circ q)$$
$$17.12 \quad (p < q) = \sim(p \circ \sim q)$$
$$18.1 \quad \Diamond p = (p \circ p)$$
$$18.13 \quad \Diamond \sim p = (\sim p \circ \sim p) = \sim(\sim p < p)$$
$$18.14 \quad \sim\Diamond \sim p = \sim(\sim p \circ \sim p) = \sim p < p$$

A necessary proposition is one implied by its own denial.

$$18.12 \quad \sim\Diamond p = \sim(p \circ p) = (p < \sim p)$$

An impossible proposition is one that implies its own denial. As he had in the
Survey, Lewis emphasizes that "'p, q, and r are all consistent' does not mean
$p \circ (q \circ r)$ or $(p \circ q) \circ r$"—rather, it means "$p \& (q \circ r)$" or an equivalent.[11]

Lewis emphasizes that "$\Diamond p$" is given a very broad meaning—specifically, "possibly" here means "logically conceivable or the absence of self-contradiction." Hence, "$\sim \Diamond p$" means that "p" is logically inconceivable or self-contradictory, and "$\sim \Diamond \sim p$" means "It is not logically conceivable that p should be false." These are "absolute" meanings in the sense that they are not relative to any other factors. And since "$p < q$" is defined in terms of logical impossibility—$\sim \Diamond (p \,\&\, \sim q)$—Lewis remarks that it should be possible to prove that "$p < q$" is equivalent to "p and $\sim q$ implies its own denial." This is, as he demonstrates, indeed the case.[12] He also gives the important extension principle

$$18.92 \quad p = p \,\&\, (q \vee \sim q) = (p \,\&\, q) \vee (p \,\&\, \sim q)$$

Lewis then introduces a new postulate that he calls the "Consistency" postulate:

$$19.01 \quad \Diamond (p \,\&\, q) < \Diamond p$$

The addition of this postulate converts S1 into a new system, S2.[13] He proves a number of further theorems, among which are

$$19.57 \quad [p \,\&\, (q \,\&\, \sim q)] = (q \,\&\, \sim q)$$

$$19.6 \quad (p < q) < [(p \,\&\, r) < (q \,\&\, r)]$$

In S1, the proof of 19.6 took the form of the T proof 16.1. One consequence of the new postulate is that "*all* previous T-principles can now be proved, with the omission of the T."[14]

$$19.83 \quad (\sim \Diamond p \,\&\, \sim \Diamond q) < (p = q)$$

$$19.84 \quad (\sim \Diamond \sim p \,\&\, \sim \Diamond \sim q) < (p = q)$$

These two theorems show that all necessary propositions are equivalent and all impossible propositions are equivalent.

Lewis next turns to the question of existence. He has proven that there are theorems in terms of "$p \supset q$" that cannot be proven to hold of "$p < q$". But he has not shown that there are theorems of Strict Implication that would be false of Material Implication. To do this, Lewis notes that in a system of Material Implication, no two propositions can be at once consistent and independent. "That p is consistent with q means 'p does not imply the falsity of q', $\sim (p < \sim q)$. And that q is independent of p means 'p does not imply q,' $\sim (p < q)$."[15] What is needed is to find *some* propositions, "p" and "q", such that

$$\sim (p < q) \,\&\, \sim (p < \sim q)$$

Lewis introduces therefore an existence postulate by quantifying over propositions.

$$20.01 \quad (\exists \, p, q)\{ \sim (p < q) \, \& \sim (p < \sim q)\}$$

15.72 is $(p \supset q) \vee (p \supset \sim q)$. Since 15.72 is asserted for all values of "p" and "q", it is universally quantified—that is,

$$(p) \, (q)[(p \supset q) \vee (p \supset \sim q)]$$

By 11.01—the definition of "$\vee$"—this becomes

$$(p) \, (q) \sim [\sim (p \supset q) \, \& \sim (p \supset \sim q)]$$

which is

$$\sim (\exists \, p, q) \, [\sim (p \supset q) \, \& \sim (p \supset \sim q)]$$

which contradicts 20.01. "Hence the consistency of 20.01 with our previous assumptions . . . demonstrates categorically that $p < q$ in this system is distinct from $p \supset q$."[16]

Lewis then employs the existence postulate to prove the existence of at least four propositions.

> Thus to satisfy the minimum requirements of the system, there must be four distinct propositions, distributed as follows: one true and necessary, one true but not necessary, one false and impossible, and one false but not impossible.[17]

These results do not distinguish the system of Strict Implications from all other logics, but they do serve to distinguish it from a system of Material Implication.

In Chapter VII Lewis describes truth-value systems and the matrix [truth-table] method. By a truth-value system he means one in which every formula of the system is determined to be true or false by the truth or falsity of the elementary components of the formula. Lewis points out that "p", "$\sim p$", "$p \, \& \, q$", "$p \vee q$", "$p \supset q$", and "$p \equiv q$" are all truth-functional relations, whereas "$\diamond p$", "$\sim \diamond p$", "$\diamond \sim p$", "$\sim \diamond \sim p$", "$p \circ q$", "$p < q$", and "$p = q$" are not. He notes that the system of Material Implication is the only truth-value system that has been well investigated, but many others also exist. But the point Lewis wants to make concerns the notion of logical truth.

The "universal function"—the function that is always true—is 13.5: "$p \vee \sim p$"; the null function is its negative, "$p \, \& \sim p$". The universal function is always the same, regardless of the number of elements; thus, for two elements, we have

$$\text{(a)} \quad (p \, \& \, q) \vee (p \, \& \sim q) \vee (\sim p \, \& \, q) \vee (\sim p \, \& \sim q)$$

which, by 18.92, is equivalent to

$$[p \,\&\, (q \vee \sim q)] \vee [\sim p \,\&\, (q \vee \sim q)]$$

and so to "$p \vee \sim p$". These equivalences are easily demonstrated by the matrix method. "Any law," Lewis says, "being an expression which is always true, is equivalent to the universal function."[18] This, he says, is the principle of "tautology" that he derived from Wittgenstein.[19] Thus, consider the truth-table for (a):

$$[(\,p \,\&\, q) \vee (p \,\&\, \sim q)] \vee [(\sim p \,\&\, q) \vee (\sim p \,\&\, \sim q)]$$

T T T	T	T F	F T	T	F T	F T	F	F T	F	F T
T F F	T	T T	T F	T	F T	F F	F	F T	F	T F
F F T	F	F F	F T	T	T F	T T	T	T F	F	F T
F F F	F	F F	T F	T	T F	F F	T	T F	T	T F

The four lines of the truth-table show that one of the disjuncts is always true. "This represents an exhaustion of the possible alternatives as to truth and falsity; and is, therefore, true *a priori*." This is what Lewis means by a "tautology"—a proposition that is true under all possible conditions.[20]

> The *source* of this necessary truth ... is in *definitions*, arbitrarily assigned. Thus the tautology of any law of logic is merely a special case of the general principle that what is true by definition cannot conceivably be false; it merely explicates, or follows from, a meaning which has been assigned, and requires nothing in particular about the universe or the facts of nature. Thus any logical principle (and, in fact, any other truth which can be certified by logic alone) is tautological in the sense that it is an analytic proposition. The only truth which logic requires, or can state, is that which is contained in our own conceptual meanings— what our language or our symbolism represents.[21]

It is not logic alone that is tautological—the same, Lewis says, is true of mathematics. All analytic truths have this character.

Having used the truth functional systems to make this point, Lewis then emphasizes that not all logical relations are truth-functions, "and these will also give rise to analytic or tautological principles which are necessary truths." Strict Implication is of course his prime example. "The laws of the relation of strict implication, for example, are tautologies, but they are not truth-value tautologies."[22] Thus, for Lewis, no distinction is to be drawn between tautologies such as "$p \vee \sim p$" and "all men are animals." Both are true by the meanings of the terms involved: "$p \vee \sim p$" by the meanings given to the logical constants negation and disjunction, "all men are animals" by the meanings given to "all," "men," "are," and "animals." We do not have two different kinds of analytic statements, one formal and one not; both are based on the meanings involved.

Lewis then turns to the consideration of the three-valued logic of Lukasiewicz. [Lewis thought at this time the system was due to both Lukasiewicz and Tarski; when he discovered his error, he published a correction explaining the role each had played. This note was included at the end of Chapter VII when *Symbolic Logic* was republished in 1959.] Letting "*0*" mean false, "*1*" mean true, "*1/2*" mean doubtful, "*N*" mean negation, and "*C*" mean implication, the matrix is:

C	0	1/2	1	N
0	1	1	1	1
1/2	1/2	1	1	1/2
1	0	1/2	1	0

In terms of "C", disjunction, "O", is defined as "$p \, O \, q = (pCq)Cq$", conjunction as "$pAq = N(NpONq)$", and equivalence, "E", as "$pEq = (pCq)A(qCp)$". Possibility is introduced as "$Mp = (Np)Cp$", with a truth table of

p	Np	Mp
1	0	1
1/2	1/2	1
0	1	0

As Lewis emphasizes, this definition of possibility is not analogous to $\Diamond p$ in Strict Implication.[23] Lewis compares the difference between the two-valued and the three-valued systems to that between two mathematical systems, one dealing with the rationals between 0 and 1, the other involving only 0 and 1. "The analogy here is exact: the Two-valued Calculus is the system of laws which hold of the limits 0 and 1; the laws of the Three-valued Calculus must hold also of the intermediate value represented by [1/2]"[24] The two-valued calculus contains laws, such as Excluded Middle, which are not true in the three-valued calculus. This does not mean that one system is true and the other false; rather "the tautological laws of any truth-value system are necessarily true; but . . . the symbolic system itself does not tell us what it is true *of*. It is true of whatever interpretation of its truth-values will make them exhaustive of the possibilities, and for any interpretation of its relations and other truth-functions which will then be consonant with their matrix-properties."[25]

The matrix method itself never performs an inference. Rather, it proves that some propositions are tautological. But it does provide a test of whether or not inferences based on a particular implication-relation are valid. If in any truth-value system, the relation "*p*I*q*" is so defined that if it has the value 1, and "*p*" has the value 1, "*q*" also has the value 1, then the inference of "*q*" from "*p*" and "*p*I*q*" is valid.

> Thus it does not matter whether p = 1 represents "p is true" or "p is a curly wolf", nor whether pIq represents "p implies q" or "p bites q"; if the rules of the matrix game are such that when p = 1, pIq holds only if q = 1, then in the nature of the case, any q such that, for some p which always has the value 1, pIq holds, will be such that q always has the value 1.[26]

Here the operation of inference, based on this relation, will give only results assertible in the system. But the operation of inference is something outside the system that involves a particular use of the system.

Lewis points out there is a wide variety of truth-value systems, all different, and each of which could conceivably be interpreted as a calculus of propositions. Indeed, there can be four-valued systems, five-valued systems, even *n*-valued systems. Each of these will contain its own laws and will admit of various possible interpretations. There is thus not one logic of propositions but a multitude of such systems, each consistent within itself. The problem is to choose among them.

Chapter VIII is entitled "Implication and Deducibility." Logic, Lewis says, can be either a canon of deductive inference or a collection of tautologies. To be a canon of deductive inference means "to delineate correctly the properties of that relation which holds between any premise, or set of premises, and a conclusion which can be validly inferred."[27] This is the relation Lewis calls "implication". But many such relations exist, if one takes implication to mean that if "*p*" is true and if "*p*I*q*" is true, then "*q*" is true. These are not all truth-value relations.

But "there must be a truth about deducibility which is not relative to this variety and difference of systems and their relations. Either a given proposition 'q' is genuinely deducible from another, 'p', or it is not. Either, then, there is some one system which alone is true when pIq is translated 'q is deducible from p', or none of them states the truth of logic in that sense."[28] But truth-value systems also have rigor and their deductions lead to true propositions. "If the 'truth about deducibility' does not somehow include and account for this fact, then we shall have an unsolved puzzle left on our hands." Lewis believed that only in the case of strict implication, "*p* < *q*", is "*q*" deducible from "*p*". Yet he recognized that inferences in truth-value systems also lead to valid results. His problem was to explain how this can be so.

It can be so because, if "I" stands for any implication relation other than "$<$", p I q is not a tautology whereas "$p < q$" is. But, for any such relation, "I", "$[(p$ & $(p$ I $q))$ I $q]$" is a tautology. For example, if "I" is "$\supset$", we have "$[(p$ & $(p \supset q)) \supset q]$" = "$[(p$ & $\sim(p$ & $\sim q)) \supset q]$" = "$\sim[(p$ & $\sim(p$ & $\sim q))$ & $\sim q]$" = "$\sim[(p$ & $\sim q)$ & $\sim(p$ & $\sim q)]$" = "$\sim(p$ & $\sim q) \vee (p$ & $\sim q)$". Hence, "$[(p$ & $(p$ I $q)) < q]$," even if "I" = "$\supset$". It is because "$(p$ & $(p$ I $q))$" strictly implies "q" in "$[(p$ & $(p$ I $q))$ I $q]$" that the inference of "q" is legitimate from "$[p$ & $(p$ I $q)]$" in all systems, but "q" can only be inferred from p alone if "$p < q$". Thus, Lewis has not abandoned the claim that Strict Implication is the fundamental system of logic. It is because inference in other systems that use other implication relations can be proven to be valid in Strict Implication that these other systems can serve as "canons of inference." But it remains the case that their validity can only be established by the use of Strict Implication.

> In the light of all these facts, it appears that the relation of strict implication expresses precisely that relation which holds when valid deduction is possible, and fails to hold when valid deduction is not possible. In that sense, the system of Strict Implication may be said to provide that canon and critique of deductive inference which is the desideratum of logical investigation.[29]

It also explains how there can be inference in other systems, and explains the paradoxes by showing that "$p \supset q$" is not equivalent to "q is deducible from p".

One problem that may call this claim in question is the paradoxes of Strict Implication: namely,

$$19.74 \quad \sim\!\Diamond\, p < (p < q)$$

$$19.75 \quad \sim\!\Diamond \sim\!p < (q < p)$$

If we remember that "$\sim\!\Diamond \sim\!p = \sim\!p < p$" and "$\sim\!\Diamond\, p = p < \sim\!p$", and also that every tautology is expressible as "$p \vee \sim\!p$", we can show that the paradoxes really do hold. Assume an impossible proposition, "p & $\sim\!p$":

1.	p & $\sim\!p$	Hyp
2.	p	11.2
3.	$\sim\!p$	11.2
4.	$p < (p \vee q)$	13.2
5.	$p \vee q$	2, 4 modus ponens

But, Lewis says, "by (3), p is false, by [5], at least one of the two, p and q, is true; then q must be true."[30] Hence, q. Further,

1.	p	Hyp
2.	$p < [(p \,\&\, q) \vee (p \,\&\, \sim q)]$	18.92
3.	$(p \,\&\, \sim q) \vee (p \,\&\, q)$	1,2 M.P.
4.	$p \,\&\, (qv \sim q)$	18.92
5.	$q \vee \sim q$	11.2, 4, M.P.

Hence, Lewis says, "the two paradoxical theorems cited are no ground of objection to the supposition that strict implication, '$p < q$,' coincides in its properties with the relation 'q is deducible from p.'"[31] It should be noted that these proofs are not subject to the objections that afflicted the corresponding proofs in the *Survey*.

Lewis also defends Strict Implication from the objection that all necessary propositions are equivalent and all impossible propositions are equivalent. "Every tautology is expressible as some proposition of the general form $p \vee \sim p$." Different tautologies may divide up possibilities in different ways, as "Either it is raining or it is not raining" differs from "Either it is raining and hot, or raining and not hot, or not raining and hot, or not raining and not hot," but "the logical division of any proposition 'p' with respect to any exhaustive set of other alternatives, '$\sim q \vee q$,' does not alter the logical force of the assertion, p."[32]

Lewis then turns to the nature of "deducibility." The term, he says, has two meanings. (1) "'deducible by *some* valid mode of inference'; or it may mean (2) 'deducible in accordance with some principle of inference *which has been assumed or already proved*.'"[33] These are not the same; the first often occurs outside of logic itself. But, Lewis says,

> In *logic*, "deducible" may have the first meaning above, or it may have the second meaning, which is here quite different. This is the importance of the logistic method: by that method, one assumes a set of postulates and definitions to begin with; and the problem is to deduce the further principles of the system from the propositions assumed (or previously proved) *in accordance with* these same propositions as principles of inference.[33]

This second meaning Lewis terms "logistic deducibility." "The properties of strict implication . . . coincide with those of deducibility in the first or general sense . . . but the properties of strict implication do *not* coincide with those of *logistic* deducibility."[34]

What does this mean? First, Lewis is distinguishing between what is deducible in a particular system and what is always deducible. Referring back to the proof that "q" is deducible from "p & $\sim p$", it is obvious that the proof depends upon 13.2—"$p < (p \vee q)$"—and let us assume for the moment that "q" could not be derived in this system from "p & $\sim p$" without 13.2. Then Lewis's point is that until we have derived 13.2 from the postulates, "q" is not *logistically deducible* in the system. But Lewis means something more. Let it be the case that theorem "p" is deducible from postulates "A", "B", and "C", but not from "A" and "B" alone. Then "p" is logistically deducible in the former case but not the latter. "Logistic deducibility *has* no general properties, but only such as are relative to the antecedently given modes of inference."[35] That is, Lewis wants to distinguish between deducibility in general—"all valid modes of deduction being allowed"—and what is deducible in a particular system having specific postulates and rules. This is important for Lewis since the subsystems of Strict Implication depend on specifying a limited set of theorems to serve as postulates.

Lewis's position becomes clearer in the following pages as he spells out his view of logic in more detail. He assumes the notion of "proposition" here without further discussion, though that discussion is provided elsewhere. Propositions stand in certain relations, "so the truths about the relations of propositions are all of them logical facts . . . but to be a logical fact in *this* sense does not mean to be part of 'logic.' "[36] What are these relations? They are relations among the meanings of the propositions in question. The relations among propositions are not created by us—propositions have or do not have certain relations whether we pay attention to them or not. A "logic" is a certain ordering or arrangement of these logical facts. "We could not arrange facts in a certain order if the facts did not have certain relations. But facts do not arrange themselves"—*we* arrange them, and we do so by selecting from among the myriad relations of propositions those which are of interest to us. "We cannot 'relate them in certain ways'; they either are so related or they are not. We can only *select* certain relations to be our guides." And since a logic is our selection of certain facts, alternative selections are possible. If, for our purposes, relations of consistency and independence among propositions are irrelevant, then a system of material implication may be appropriate. But if consistency and independence are important to us, then the system of material implication will be inappropriate. The criterion is pragmatic: "the result of our system-making answers to pragmatic criteria."[37] We might, for instance, decide that instead of classifying propositions as true or false, we wanted to classify them as "(1) known for a fact, (2) known not to be a fact, (3) doubtful." In this case, the three-valued logic of Lukasiewicz might be more useful than the traditional two-valued logic.

"In that case, we should not (if we were consistent) *deny* the Law of the Excluded Middle; we should *ignore* it; because we should be unobservant of that principle of division to which alone it is pertinent."[38] This example makes Lewis's point very well. To deny the Law of Excluded Middle leads to contradiction—"$\sim(p \vee \sim p) = \sim p \;\&\; p$", so one could not consistently deny it; one simply creates an alternative system in which "$p \vee \sim p$" is not a theorem [like that of Fitch[39]]. Choosing among alternative logics on pragmatic grounds does not show that the systems not chosen are false, for they are true with respect to the relations they order; rather, it shows that they are not useful for our present purposes.[40]

"Inference," Lewis says, "is something we *do*, upon observation of certain relationships amongst the facts with which we are dealing." The *act* of inference is not a part of the system of logic.

> In dealing with the calculus of propositions, for example, we find A in the system, and we find the relation "A implies B" in the system; whereupon, if we choose, we 'infer B from A.' But 'B inferred from A' is nothing which happens in the system of logical facts. The three facts, A, B, and "A implies B," stand side by side in the system, and are unaffected by our inferring. Inference remains an *operation* even when implication is a relation of the system. The logistic rule which controls or allows this operation of inference reveals its externality to the facts within the system itself by being incapable of expression in the symbols of the system. The system may be discovered or delimited in terms of inference: nevertheless the fact of inference is nothing in the system.[41]

Lewis is distinguishing between the system of logic as an ordered set of relations among propositions and the actions one takes in making use of it. Logics are tools we use to make inferences that serve our purposes.

Why then is Strict Implication the "right" form of inference? Granted any logical system with an implication relation "I",

> It is a further fact that all such relations, which can give rise to inference, coincide with one another in the property that
>
> $$(p \;\&\; pIq)\, Iq$$
>
> represents a tautology; and that the relation I, in its *asserted* occurrence here, coincides with strict implication.[42]

But these conditions are not enough to determine the choice of a logic uniquely; the legitimacy of the alternative systems must be proven in Strict Implication. Given that such alternatives exist, the question becomes what pragmatic reasons there are for choosing Lewis's system over its competitors. The defect of truth-value logics, Lewis argues, is pragmatic. The fact that for any such logic the implication relation depends only on the truth or falsity of the constituents makes it useless for scientific purposes.

> Thus no relation of truth-implication [truth-value implication] has any possible use in the investigation of hypotheses. For example, in terms of material implication any known fact is implied equally by *all* hypotheses. And for *any* such relation, if *h* be a hypothesis and *f* be some known fact, then either *hIf* holds for all hypotheses equally or the truth-value of *hIf* cannot be determined until the value of h is known.
>
> Thus the only case in which any truth-implication can be known to hold, under circumstances which make that fact useful for the purposes of inference, is the case in which pIq is known to hold through knowing that the conjunction "*p* true but *q* false" is impossible under any circumstances. To know this, however, means precisely to know that *pIq* is a *tautology*—to know that $p < q$ holds.[43]

If in scientific reasoning, anything that followed from a true hypothesis also followed from a false hypothesis, confirmation or disconfirmation would be impossible. It is therefore not enough to cite "$[(p \,\&\, (pIq)Iq)]$," because in scientific practice we do not know the truth-value of "*p*". What we need is to know that if "*p*" *were* true, "*q*" *would be* true, or that "$\sim\!\Diamond (p \,\&\, \sim\!q)$". Thus, Lewis believed that only strict implication could form an adequate basis for scientific reasoning, and that truth-value systems "are 'false' or unacceptable in the sense that they have no useful application to inference."[44]

In Appendix II, Lewis returns to the discussion of the Strict Implication systems of Chapter VI. Lewis notes to begin with, "This appendix is written by Mr. Lewis, but the points demonstrated are, most of them, due to other persons."[45] Between 1918, when the *Survey* was published, and 1932, when *Symbolic Logic* appeared, Lewis's work had generated considerable interest and research. One of the most important of those who followed Lewis's lead was William Tuthill Parry, who was Lewis's graduate student and whose dissertation dealt extensively with Lewis's work. But it was not only students such as Parry, Langford, and Paul Henle who became involved; in Europe, the Polish logician Mordechaj Wajsberg and the German logician Oskar Becker made important contributions. In the Appendix, Lewis drew together their results and amplified them.

Lewis begins by setting out the postulates of the *Survey* system (amended to correct the error found by Post) as the A postulates and those used in Chapter VI of *Symbolic Logic* as the B postulates.

A.1. $(p \,\&\, q) < (q \,\&\, p)$

A.2. $(q \,\&\, p) < p$

B.1. $(p \,\&\, q) < (q \,\&\, p)$

B.2. $(p \,\&\, q) < p$

A.3. $p < (p \& p)$ B.3. $p < (p \& p)$

A.4. $p \& (q \& r) < q \& (p \& r)$ B.4. $(p \& q) \& r < p \& (q \& r)$

A.5. $p < \sim(\sim p)$ B.5. $p < \sim(\sim p)$

A.6. $[(p < q) \& (q < r)] < (p < r)$ B.6. $[(p < q) \& (q < r)] < (p < r)$

A.7. $\sim\Diamond p < \sim p$ B.7. $[p \& (p < q)] < q$

A.8. $(p < q) < (\sim\Diamond q < \sim\Diamond p)$ B.8. $\Diamond (p \& q) < \Diamond p$

                                                      B.9. $(\exists p, q) \{\sim(p < q) \& \sim(p < \sim q)\}$

Lewis then uses matrixes to explore the two sets of postulates. There are five groups of matrixes; the first, fourth, and fifth are due to Parry, the second and third to Wajsberg. The matrixes represent numerical interpretations of the postulates—that is, numerical models of the postulates. If the postulates are satisfied by a group, they are thereby shown to be consistent; if a set of postulates is satisfied by a group, but some other principle is not, the principle is independent of the postulates. Hence, the matrixes provide a useful tool for exploring important characteristics of the systems involved. All the groups have the same matrixes for conjunction and negation; they differ in the values assigned to "$\Diamond p$". One example should suffice. Group V is

p	$\sim p$	$\Diamond p$
1	4	1
2	3	2
3	2	1
4	1	3

$p \& q$ | q 1 2 3 4
p 1 | 1 2 3 4
2 | 2 2 4 4
3 | 3 4 3 4
4 | 4 4 4 4

$p < q$ | q 1 2 3 4
p 1 | 2 4 3 4
2 | 2 2 3 3
3 | 2 4 2 4
4 | 2 2 2 2^{47}

The "designated values" are 1 and 2—that is, the group satisfies the principle if, for all combinations of the values of its variables, the value of the principle is either 1 or 2.

Consider then B.2, "$p \& q < p$", and 10.01—the Consistency Postulate "$\Diamond (p \& q) < \Diamond p$".

$p \& q < p$	$\Diamond (p \& q) < \Diamond p$
1 1 1 2 1	1 1 1 1 2 1 1
2 2 1 2 2	2 2 2 1 2 2 2
3 3 1 2 3	1 3 3 1 2 1 3
4 4 1 2 4	3 4 4 1 2 3 4
1 2 2 2 1	2 1 2 2 2 1 1
2 2 2 2 2	2 2 2 2 2 2 2
3 4 2 2 3	3 3 4 2 2 1 3

```
4 4 2 2 4          3 4 4  2 2 3 4
1 3 3 2 1          1 1 3  3 1  1 1
2 4 3 2 2          3 2 4  3 4  2 2
3 3 3 2 3          1 3 3  3 1  1 3
4 4 3 2 4          3 4 4  3 2  3 4
1 4 4 2 1          3 1 4  4 2  1 1
2 4 4 2 2          3 2 4  4 4  2 2
3 4 4 2 3          3 3 4  4 2  1 3
4 4 4 2 4          3 4 4  4 2  3 4
```

B.2 holds; the Consistency Postulate does not since the value for the whole expression is 4 in two cases. Hence, the two are independent.

The point of this method is to find *an* interpretation of the postulates that shows them all to hold. Where this can be done, the system is thereby proven to be consistent. Using this method, Lewis shows first that the systems defined by both sets of postulates are consistent—Groups I, II, and III satisfy both sets of postulates. Second, the systems defined by both sets of postulates are not reducible to a system of material implication. Third, the Consistency Postulate (B.8) is independent of B 1–7 and B.9 and of A.1–7; so is A.8. Fourth, postulate B.7 is independent of B.1–6 and B.8,9, and of A.1–6 and A.8. Fifth, A.7. is independent of A.1–6 and A.8. and of B.1–6, 8, and 9. Sixth, B.9. is independent of B.1–8 and A.1–8.[48]

Are the two sets of postulates equivalent? Lewis says he has been unable to find a proof either way, but he thinks they are not. The key problem, he says, is whether or not A.8 is deducible from B.1–8. Lewis had no answer for that in 1932. He was also worried that both Parry and Wajsberg had been able to derive from A.1–8 the principle "$(p < q) < [(q < r) < (p < r)]$" that Lewis considered dubious. Since B.8 (the Consistency Postulate) is not derivable from B.1–7 and B.9, and neither is the principle Lewis considered dubious, if this principle should be derivable from B. 1–9 (and so only with the aid of B.8), then Lewis says the system S1 (B.1–7,B.9) is "the one which coincides in its properties with the strict principles of deductive inference."[49] After it was shown (1934) that S2 is distinct from S3, Lewis chose S2 as the one to be regarded as *the* System of Strict Implication, that is, the one whose "$p < q$" best represents "q is deducible from p" as ordinarily used.[50]

Oskar Becker had proposed additional postulates for Lewis's system—namely,

$$C10. \quad \sim\!\Diamond \sim\!p < \sim\!\Diamond\!\sim\!\sim\!\Diamond \sim\!p$$

$$C11. \quad \Diamond p < \sim\!\Diamond \sim\!\Diamond p$$

$$C12. \quad p < \sim\!\Diamond \sim\!\Diamond p$$

C10, Lewis notes, could be given the form $\Diamond \Diamond p < \Diamond p$. He also adds as a possible further postulate

C13. $\Diamond \Diamond p$[51]

Lewis then sets out a series of five systems. S1 is derived from B1–7; if B.9 (the existence postulate) is added to it, S1 contains the existence theorems that do not require the Consistency Postulate B.8. S2, derived from B1–8, contains all the theorems of Sections 1–5 of Chapter VI, and if the existence postulate is added, all the existence theorems as well. S3, derived from A1–8, is the amended system of the *Survey* and contains all the theorems of S2 and with the addition of B.9 all the existence theorems of S2. For these three systems, C10–C13 are consistent but independent.

S4 is derived from B1–7 and C10; it contains all the theorems of S3 and in addition the consequences of C10 and, with the addition of B9, all the existence theorems as well. C11 and C12 are consistent with S4; C13 is not. Finally S5, derived from B1–7 and C11, contains all the theorems of S4 and the consequences of C12, and with B9 all the existence theorems of S2. S5 is incompatible with C13. Obviously, the series of systems increases in strength from S1 to S5.[52]

By the time he wrote *Symbolic Logic*, Lewis had come a long way. The Roycean elements that show in his earlier work had vanished. He no longer identified "logistic" as the science of the types of order but as the method exemplified by the *Principia*. Nor is there here any attempt to derive all systems of logic from one general system, although the fact that inference in these systems is valid must be proven in Strict Implication. Probably that issue had been settled by Lukasiewicz's work. His view here is that there are multiple logics, all of which are consistent formal systems. The choice among these is straightforwardly pragmatic; we choose that system that best serves our needs. And in an interesting move that anticipates some of his later work, he separates the logical systems themselves, as selections of particular logical "facts," from the *use* of such systems for purposes of inference. At the same time, Lewis wants to preserve a preeminent position for Strict Implication, even if the decision to use Strict Implication is purely pragmatic.

In 1959, when *Symbolic Logic* was republished, Lewis added a third appendix that noted several contributions that had been made since 1932, such as that of Parry referred to earlier, but that also contained a very interesting discussion of the relation of the system of Strict Implication to the Boole–Schroder algebra. Lewis had broached this matter in his 1951 contribution to a festschrift for Henry Sheffer,[53] but the treatment in the 1959 appendix is more complete. As previously noted, there are two forms of the algebra: the general Boolean algebra (call it K1) and the two-valued algebra (call it K2) that results from the former by the addition of the postulate "$p = (p = 1)$". In both we have that "p & $\sim p = 0$" and "$p \vee \sim p = 1$". If we add the relation "$-->$" such that "$p --> q$" holds if and only if "p & $\sim q = 0$", "$p --> q$" becomes an implication relation among propositions and a containment relation among classes. Then we shall have "$0 --> p$" and "$p --> 1$" for every "p". The relation of material implication, "$p \supset q$", exactly correlates with the relation "$p --> q$" in K2.

However, if in place of "$p = (p = 1)$", we assume "for some element p, $p \neq 0$ and $p \neq 1$," a very different interpretation of the algebra is possible. If we take "0" to mean self-contradictory or impossible, and "1" to mean necessary, then we have

$$p = 1 \qquad \text{is} \quad \sim\Diamond \sim p$$
$$p = 0 \qquad \text{is} \quad \sim\Diamond p$$
$$p \neq 0 \qquad \text{is} \quad \Diamond p$$
$$p \neq 1 \qquad \text{is} \quad \Diamond \sim p$$
$$p \text{ \& } \sim q = 0 \quad \text{is} \quad p < q$$

The analogy between the paradoxes of Material Implication and those of Strict Implication is then easily explained. In K2, we have the paradoxes of Material Implication: "$0 --> p$"—a false proposition implies any proposition, and "$p --> 1$"—a true proposition is implied by any proposition. But in K1, "$0 --> p$" would mean an impossible proposition implies any proposition, and "$p --> 1$" would mean a necessary proposition is implied by any proposition. Hence, the paradoxes would not apply to contingent propositions and so the paradoxes of Material Implication would not hold true.[54]

Was it by thus reinterpreting Boole's algebra that Lewis first developed the system of Strict Implication? Lewis does not say that here, nor is there any direct evidence to support it in his early writings. But we do know that Lewis was thoroughly trained in the Boole–Schroder algebra before he encountered the *Principia* and began his quest for an alternative system of logic, and it would have been natural to utilize that training in his quest. Furthermore in a late manuscript, Lewis wrote of his work in logic that

> I should not have attempted anything in that field at all except for the concurrence of two considerations. Having been introduced to this subject by Josiah Royce, I had been intrigued to follow it through by observance of the insights which could so be afforded and sharpened in the field of epistemology. Something of that, along with other strains of thought—particularly such as derived from perusal of Charles S. Peirce's as yet unpublished

literary remains—had already appeared in "Mind and the World Order" in 1929. And—the second coincident consideration—I had, in 1911, on first reading volume I of Principia Mathematica, acquired the conviction that the foundations of that work were subtly awry, and failed to accord with the basic character of valid inference. Peirce, whose contributions to the development of exact logic were extensive, had himself, briefly but unmistakably, remarked the limitation of so-called 'material implication'; and I had been surprised that he nowhere in his work had made the correction needed to amend that matter, and delimited, in precise fashion, that relation '*p* implies *q*' whose properties exactly coincide with those of '*q* is validly deducible from *p*.' It was very simple; one needed only to reinterpret the Boolean algebra, in the final form of it due to Ernst Schroder and still current, in order to have a sufficient basis for this emendation. The coincidence of these two considerations—along with the desire for a usable text for my own classes in the subject—was responsible for my first book, "Survey of Symbolic Logic," 1918; and in 1932, when that work had been out of print for fifteen years, for the volume in cooperation with Langford, in which my own contribution, 'strict implication,' was a little better and more accurately developed.[55]

This passage, written at the end of Lewis's life, throws an interesting light on several issues in Lewis's development. First, it is clear here that Lewis took up logic because he thought it had important consequences for epistemology. This fits with the fact that his first major interest was in epistemology. That is obvious from his dissertation and his statement in 1910: "my special field of research had been epistemology."[56] Moreover, as we have seen, it was by following out those epistemological consequences that Lewis was led from his early Idealism to "humanism" and so to the conceptual pragmatism of *Mind and the World Order*. Second, it strongly suggests that he first developed his theory of strict implication by a reinterpretation of the Boole–Schroder algebra. These two facts led to the *Survey* in 1918 and later to *Symbolic Logic*. If this is the correct line of development, then one can see a unity in Lewis's work that is not otherwise visible.

There are, however, serious problems with this interpretation. If Lewis developed Strict Implication from the Boole–Schroder algebra, why was he surprised by the paradoxes of strict implication? As noted earlier, Lewis at first thought he could avoid the paradoxes by a change of postulates, but even when he realized that he could not, he said he had been greatly puzzled by them. But if he derived his system from the Boole–Schroder algebra in the fashion he indicated in Appendix III of *Symbolic Logic*, it is difficult to see why he should have been surprised by the paradoxes. Furthermore, Parry says of Lewis: "He did not remark that systems of Strict Implication are peculiar forms of Boolean algebra (adding a weaker postulate) till Wajsberg, Parry, and Henle pointed it out."[57] Parry was in a position to know when Lewis made this discovery, and his account would certainly put it after the publication of the *Survey*. It seems probable therefore that Lewis's 1963 statement is misleading and that he did not discover the relation between Strict Implication and Boole's algebra until after he had created his own system.

In the same year *Symbolic Logic appeared*, Lewis published an article on "Alternative Systems of Logic."[58] Here, Lewis went further than he had in *Symbolic Logic*. Speaking of the alternative systems of logic, Lewis said, "they are alternatives, in the sense that if one such system be taken as the canon of deduction—as it can be—then principles belonging to other systems must be abandoned as inapplicable, inexpressible, or non-significant."[59] The attempt to derive all systems of logic from a single set of general postulates has been abandoned.

This series of systems, S1 through S5, is the Lewis modal logics. In the wake of the publication of *Symbolic Logic*, many logicians were drawn to work on modal logic—indeed, Lewis is regarded by all as the *modern* father of modal logic. [There was a modal logic in antiquity and in the medieval era, and MacColl had tried to develop a modal logic before Lewis (as had Peirce), but the modern work starts with Lewis.] Many other modal systems, often called S systems, have been devised; some of them are regarded as intermediate between Lewis's systems (S4.2, S4.3 and S4.4, for example), some as further developments—S6, S7, S8, and S9, for example.[60] Moreover, there has been an explosion of work on modal logic since Kripke's papers in the 1960s, and there are a number of studies of Lewis's modal systems.[61] But *Symbolic Logic* represented the completion of Lewis's work in logic. He said later that when he finished *Symbolic Logic*, he intended never to write on logic again. He did not quite keep this resolution; as we will see, Ruth Marcus's work spurred him to further efforts. But, fundamentally, 1932 marked the end of Lewis's work in logic. He felt he had done what he could and what needed to be done. And he also recognized that he lacked the training in mathematics necessary for the ever more technical development of the subject, and that the increasingly rapid development of the field would require him either to devote himself exclusively to logic or abandon it. Lewis had other subjects that he wished to pursue, and he could not do so if he specialized in logic.[62]

In the years to come, he followed developments in logic with dismay. Writing on January 20, 1948, Lewis said:

> At the end of a winter's day, I feel moved to a reaction with no critical intent: The new logic seems destined to develop into something for which

the question of how many angels can dance on the point of a needle, will not be even a good parody. And if it makes no eventual difference to right and wrong or the love of God or of one's fellow men, or the standard of living or the size of the income tax or to living happily ever afterward, then I feel sure that at some point I am going to find it hard to bear.[63]

In a paper on the logic of imperatives in 1960, Lewis added the wry comment:

> There *is* a logic restricted to indicatives; the truth-value logic most impressively developed in Principia Mathematica. But those who adhere to it usually have thought of it—so far as they understood what they were doing—as being the universal logic of propositions which is independent of mode. And when that universal logic was first formulated in exact terms, they failed to recognize it as the only logic which is *independent* of the mode in which propositions are entertained and dubbed it "modal logic."[64]

Lewis's work in logic was surely fruitful—model logic is a major subfield within logic today, and everyone in the field views him as its modern creator. But it is only a subfield. For Lewis himself, his work failed to achieve what he had hoped. Convinced that the system of *Principia Mathematica* was fatally flawed by its reliance on material implication, he had tried to sweep the field for strict implication—and failed.

The reviews of *Symbolic Logic* were laudatory. Bronstein and Tarter declared: "The chapters written by Professor Lewis . . . are distinguished by the constructive originality and clarity for which Professor Lewis is noted."[65] Smith called the publication of the book "an event of first rate importance,"[66] and Wisdom wrote, "I believe this to be an excellent book. I very much doubt whether there exists any equally good introduction to the problems with which it deals. . . . I should like to congratulate Mr. Lewis and Mr. Langford upon a work which combines a high degree of simplicity with accuracy and liveliness with elegance."[67] But the reviews were also critical. The points that the reviewers found most objectionable were the paradoxes of strict implication, and the relativity of logic. The latter was seen as an attack on the *Principia*. Not surprisingly, several reviewers tried to reduce strict to material implication and to justify the system of material implication as the only true logic. Bronstein and Tarter claimed that Lewis's notion of possibility could be defined in the system of *Principia* as

$$\text{(a)} \quad \diamondsuit p = \sim(\exists\, q)\,(p = q\ \&\ \sim q)$$

from which the definitions of the other modal functions are easily obtained. Then, for strict implication itself, they give

$$\text{(b)} \quad (p < q) = df\,(\exists\,r)\,[(p \supset q) = (r \supset r)]$$

But McKinsey showed that these definitions have problems. Identity is defined in the *Principia* as

$$13.01 \quad (x = y) = [(\phi)\,(\phi\,!\,x \supset \phi\,!\,y)]$$

The exclamation mark after "ϕ" indicates that "ϕ" is a predicative function, but this restriction is removed in the theorem

$$13.101 \quad (x = y) \supset (\psi x \supset \psi y)$$

that holds whether ψ is predicative or not. If "ϕ" and "ψ" are taken to be truth functions, McKinsey showed that Bronstein and Tarter's definition of "$\diamond\,p$" leads to the conclusion that "$\diamond\,p\,\equiv\,p$", that is, strict implication becomes equivalent to material implication. But then Lewis's existence postulate would lead to a contradiction. If "ϕ" and "ψ" are not truth functions, McKinsey showed that "it follows that all impossible propositions are conjunctive, which is not a reasonable result."[68]

A much more comprehensive attack on *Symbolic Logic* along the same general lines was Leo Abraham's article in the *Monist* that sought to show that "material implication is the basis of all inference."[69] Fitch provided an answer to this in a note in the *Monist* where he pointed out that the system of Strict Implication is a Boolean algebra of four elements, whereas that of the *Principia* is a Boolean algebra of two elements only. The former cannot be transformed into the latter without losing the properties essential for strict implication.[70]

Writing in *Mind*, John Wisdom took issue with Lewis on the paradoxes of strict implication and held, following Everett Nelson's article in *Mind*,[71] that Lewis had wrongly defined strict implication and that it should be redefined so as to avoid the paradoxes. Wisdom also objected to the use of the existence postulate as a way of differentiating Lewis's system from the system of Material Implication. Instead, Wisdom proposed the principle

$$\sim[\sim(p < q) < (p < \sim q)]^{72}$$

Replacing "$<$" by "$\supset$", this becomes $[(p\,\&\,\sim q)\,\&\,(p\,\&\,q)]$, which is clearly false in the system of the *Principia*. Lewis did not adopt Wisdom's principle, but it did apparently become a question Lewis considered. In March 1934, McKinsey wrote Lewis that Wisdom's principle was incompatible with S4 and S5. He showed that the principle can be deduced from A 1–8 and C 13, and that from B 1–8 and Wisdom's principle, C 13 can be deduced. But C 13 leads to trouble, as McKinsey showed.

1.	$\Diamond \Diamond p$	C 13
2.	$\Diamond \Diamond (p \mathbin{\&} \sim p)$	1, $p \mathbin{\&} \sim p/p$
3.	$\Diamond \sim\sim\Diamond (p \mathbin{\&} \sim p)$	2, 12.3
4.	$\Diamond \sim(p < p)$	3, 11.02

As McKinsey noted, "it seems hard to believe that it might possibly be false that p is deducible from p." That apparently settled the question of Wisdom's principle and of C 13.[73] But the most serious criticism of Lewis's system was Ruth Marcus's proof that the Deduction Theorem does not hold for S1, S2, or S3, and does not hold unconditionally for S4 and S5. Since Lewis's systems contain two implication relations—material and strict—the relevant theorems are

MI 1.   If $A \vdash B$, then $\vdash (A \supset B)$

SI 1.   If $A \vdash B$, then $\vdash (A < B)$

MI 2.   If $A_1, A_2, \ldots A_n \vdash B$, then $A_1, A_2, \ldots A_n \vdash (A_n \supset B)$

SI 2.   If $A_1, A_2, \ldots A_n \vdash B$, then $A_1, A_2, \ldots A_n \vdash (A_n < B)$

MI 3.   If $A_1, A_2, \ldots A_n \vdash B$, then $\vdash (A_1 \mathbin{\&} \ldots \mathbin{\&} A_n) \supset B$

SI 3.   If $A_1, A_2, \ldots A_n \vdash B$, then $\vdash (A_1 \mathbin{\&} \ldots \mathbin{\&} A_n) < B$

None of these hold for S1 and S2; For S3, MI 3 and a weaker form of SI 3 do hold. For S4 and S5, MI 1, MI 2, and MI 3 hold; so does SI 1 and SI 3, but SI 2 does not hold unconditionally.[74]

Lewis had argued since he first introduced strict implication that it was *the* form of implication that corresponded to deducibility; specifically, that "$p < q$" meant "q is deducible from p". And he had chosen S2 as his preferred form of the system of strict implication.[75] "I wish the system S2, as developed in *Symbolic Logic*, Chapter V and Appendices II and III, to be regarded as the definitive form of Strict Implication." As Marcus remarked,

It appears to the author that in view of Lewis and Langford's proposed analysis, a theorem corresponding to [SI 1] should (at the least) be available. It would be a curious explication of the concept of deducibility if, although B followed from the premise A, B could not be said to be deducible from A.[76]

So far as we know, Lewis made no reply to this criticism.

In 1936, Lewis and Langford sent to *Mind* an article entitled "A Note on Strict Implication." The article is an answer to those who claimed that the relation of strict implication was definable from the implication relation of *Principia Mathematica*. "We conceive," they said, "that all valid deduction takes place through the analysis of meanings or connotations." "Today is Monday $<$ Tomorrow is Tuesday" regardless of what day this happens to be; the meanings of the terms are such that this implication holds whether today is really Monday or not. Formal implication, they held, cannot express this. They propose an alternative account based on the notion of tautology due to Wittgenstein. "Any expression is a tautology if it exhausts the conceivable alternatives," and every analytic statement is such a tautology. If "πx" and "Σx" are construed as "for all thinkable x's" and "for some thinkable x's," respectively, then letting $p = \theta x$ and $q = \psi x$, and "$\phi \hat{x}$" signifies that the function itself is referred to rather than the values of its variables, then

$$(p < q) = (\Sigma \phi, \psi)\, (\Sigma x)\, \{\phi x = p\, \&\, \psi x = q\, \&\, (\Sigma \theta)\, [\sim\!\phi \hat{x} \vee \psi \hat{x} = \sim\!\theta \hat{x} \vee \theta \hat{x}]\}$$

The relations here are among "ϕ", "ψ", and "θ", not the values of x. Galleys of this article are in Lewis's papers; the article was never published. On the back of the proofs, Lewis wrote:

> This article was suppressed. It included a point which had been conveyed to me by a German (a student of Reichenbach) who could not be referred to because he had, in the more recent phrase, 'gone underground.' I decided not to print without acknowledgement. Langford's participation was nominal. C. I. Lewis.[77]

In the *Journal of Symbolic Logic* for March 1946, Ruth Barcan (subsequently Ruth Barcan Marcus) published a paper entitled "A Functional Calculus of First Order Based on Strict Implication."[78] Previous work on strict implication, including Lewis's own, had been largely confined to the propositional calculus, and, when it had dealt with propositional functions, it had not introduced a system of quantification for strict implication. That was the innovation provided by Barcan-Marcus. Taking S2 of *Symbolic Logic* as a base, she showed that it could be extended into a first-order predicate calculus. In doing so, she used standard quantificational notions; her presentation was formal and she did not deal at all with questions of interpretation.

Dr. Barcan-Marcus sent a copy of this article to Lewis who wrote her back on October 11, 1947.[79] Lewis praised "the economy and mathematical elegance" of her work, and said he was gratified that she had correctly stated the "key-principles"

$$\Sigma x \Diamond\, \phi x = \Diamond \Sigma\, x \phi x$$

$$\Diamond\, \pi\, x \phi x < \pi x \Diamond\, \phi x$$

Lewis then referred to the difficulty of the semantic problems involved. These had led him to include the principle

$$\pi x \phi x < \Sigma x \phi x$$

but not $\phi x < \Sigma x \phi x$ or $\pi x \phi x < \phi x$. These two he says require a "correct" interpretation: "on my view, the conception [is] that there are singular statements which are true though the singular term in question denotes no existent." In the margin, Lewis adds "My conception is that what $\Sigma x \phi x$ says, could be convey (sic) by "There is at least one true statement which is a value of 'ϕx.' " One should recall that of "$\phi x \supset (\exists z)\phi z$" Whitehead and Russell wrote, "Practically, the above primitive proposition gives the only method of proving "existence-theorems," while "$(x)(\phi x) \supset \phi y$" states, "What holds in all cases, holds in any one case."[80] The principle underlying Lewis's view is made clear by his statement: "I conceive that no statement can at one and the same time be analytic and entail *existence* of a thing denoted."

In 1951, Lewis published an article entitled "Notes on the Logic of Intension" in a festschrift for Henry Sheffer.[81] Lewis begins by distinguishing extensional and intensional calculi. In the former, he says, all asserted expressions are truth-functions of the propositional variables. In the latter, the asserted expressions are of the form $\sim\diamond \sim A$ (which is true only when A is analytic), or are equivalent to an expression of the form $\sim\diamond \sim A$ or are truth-functions that are analytic, such as the theorems of *Principia* that are provable in S2. But the difference between extensional and intensional systems does not involve analyticity, since any valid calculus of logic includes only analytic propositions, but with the fact that in an extensional system it is not possible to assert that its statements are analytic, or consistent, or deducible; such assertions can only be made in a metalogic. In an intensional system, however, such assertions can be made within the system itself and the metalogic is unnecessary for this purpose.

Lewis then presents his theory of the modes of meaning of terms and propositions—fittingly enough, since the view of propositions as terms is derived explicitly from Sheffer. Lewis then states his basic thesis: "Logic can assert no expression as true unless it is true by virtue of its intensional meaning, and it can assert no expression to be false except one which is contravalid by virtue of its intension." The truths of extensional logic are due to the intensional meaning of the logical constants they contain. "To date," Lewis says, "there exists no calculus symbolizing both extensional and intensional functions of terms, distinguishing these two and relating them."[82] But Lewis qualifies this assertion; Boole's algebra can be interpreted as a logic of terms in intension, although this has not been done and would yield a cumbersome system. But, "as the existence of Dr. Barcan

Marcus' functional calculus makes sufficiently evident, there must be some intensional calculus of terms which stands related to strict implication in the same general manner that the calculus of classes in *Principia Mathematica* stands related to the extensional logic of propositions."[83]

Lewis then sketches this intensional system. The primitive notions are, first, predicate functions, symbolized by "$\phi\hat{x}$"—following Whitehead and Russell, the "$\wedge$" over the "x" indicates that the function itself is referred to, not its argument. The further primitives are negation "($\sim\phi\hat{x}$)", compound functions "($\phi\hat{x}$ & $\psi\hat{x}$)", self-consistency "($\Diamond\ \phi\hat{x}$)", and assertion "($\vdash\ \phi\hat{x}$)". The definitions and postulates are numbered to match the corresponding expression in Chapter VI of *Symbolic Logic* and are obtained from them by putting "$\phi\hat{x}$" for "p" and "$\psi\hat{x}$" for "q". The usual operations of proof are assumed. This system is "uniform" with S2; it follows that all theorems and proofs of S2 carry over to the new calculus by transliteration, providing that the corresponding proof operations are valid, which Lewis confirmed. Lewis considers the calculus to be intuitive; thus the substitution of "x is red" for "$\phi\hat{x}$", "x is damp" for "$\psi\hat{x}$", and "x contains juice" for "$\theta\hat{x}$" in the postulate of transitivity for "$<$" gives "if being red entails being damp, and being damp entails containing juice, then being red entails containing juice." This leads Lewis to conclude:

> A complete calculus of propositional functions of one variable can be derived directly from the calculus of predicates by formalization of the principle [$\vdash\ \sim\Diamond\ \sim\phi\hat{x}$ has the same logical force as $\vdash$ (Ax) $\sim\Diamond\ \sim\phi x$, where "A" is the universal quantifier.], the additional primitive idea '(Ax)ϕx,' the definition of 'S$x\phi x$' [$\sim$A$\sim$ = S], and a minimum of further assumptions which are analogous to theorems of the calculus of predicates, though not derivable from their analogues. The resultant calculus would, in general, be congruent with the functional calculus of Dr. Barcan Marcus.

Lewis asserts "the calculus of predicates could be taken as the basic branch of logic in general."[84]

This article is very brief and does not adequately reflect the degree to which Marcus's work revived Lewis's hopes for intensional logic. Among Lewis's papers are two manuscripts that deal with this issue and were probably written about the same time as the article just discussed. Although they have much in common, they differ on some important points. In the longer of the two, "Outline of a New Approach to the Calculus of Propositional Functions,"[85] Lewis attempts to develop a Calculus of Predicates corresponding to S3 rather than S2. The notion of propositional function is introduced as in the article. In "$\phi\hat{x}$", "x" is called the "subject variable" and takes as values constant expressions the substitution of which for "x" turns the function into a propositional function. "$\phi\hat{x}$" is a function of the predicate variable "ϕ"; thus, "the *values of* 'ϕx̂,' or 'ψx̂,' are *propositional functions of one* variable, *x*, or *y*." If the circumflex is removed, "ϕx" is a function of two variables, "*x*" and "ϕ". The primitive ideas are again predicate functions, negation, conjunction, and possibility. The definitions are the same as those in the article, except that the definition of consistency is omitted. The postulates are those of the article except that the postulate $\Diamond\,(\phi\hat{x}\ \&\ \psi\hat{x}) < \Diamond\,\phi\hat{x}$ is replaced by

$$11.8\quad (\phi\hat{x} < \psi\hat{x}) < (\sim\!\Diamond\,\psi\hat{x} < \sim\!\Diamond\,\phi\hat{x})$$

This is the postulate A8 of S3 with "ϕx̂" put for "*p*" and "ψx̂" for "*q*". Lewis says explicitly, "the system is that of S3, not S2." From these postulates, he proves "$\Diamond\,(\phi\hat{x}\ \&\ \psi\hat{x}) < \Diamond\,\phi\hat{x}$," and says that all theorems of Chapter VI, Sections 1–5 of *Symbolic Logic* are provable by transliteration.

Having outlined the Calculus of Predicate Functions, Lewis turns to the Calculus of Propositional Functions of one variable. The predicate variables will be used as free variables, but the subject variables will occur only within the scope of a quantifier. "Σxϕx" does not assert existence since no analytic statement can do so; it says only that there is at least one true statement of the form "ϕx". The definitions 11.01–14.02 are repeated for the Calculus of Propositional Functions without the circumflex over the *x*. The postulates are repeated, but with the tacit universal quantification of the predicate variables and the explicit universal quantification of the subject variables. Hence, Lewis says, "If F(ϕx̂, ψx̂ . . .) be a postulate or theorem of the Calculus of Predicates, π *x* F(ϕx, ψx, . . .) is assertible as a theorem of the Calculus of Propositional Functions."[86]

Since Lewis does not allow the subject variable to occur free, he has to add postulates concerning the distribution of the quantifiers and their relation to the modal operators. From these and the prior postulates, he then derives several theorems. Lewis asserts that if such "definitions" as are used in *Principia* for "(x)ϕx ∨ p" are introduced, all the "correlative" theorems that are not ruled out by the difference between "<" and "⊃" can be proven. Further, excepting those theorems, and "(x)ϕx ⊃ ϕz" and those of its consequences not derivable from "(x)ϕx ⊃ (∃ x)ϕx" "*all* theorems of Principia *as symbolized*, can be proved."[87]

In the second manuscript, Lewis attempts to create a Calculus of Predicates corresponding to S2. The development is very similar to the published article, and on many points to the longer manuscript. In concluding it, Lewis wrote:

It is my further conviction that it is this intensional Calculus of Predicates, rather than any calculus of propositions, which should be taken as basis to the whole development of exact logic. That it is uniform with S2, throughout, reflects the fact that propositions are interpretable as predicates of "the world"—the totality of the actual.[88]

This was a stronger claim than he had made in the article.

Lewis did not publish anything on the Calculus of Predicates after 1951. But he evidently hoped that others would. When Fitch published his *Symbolic Logic*, which included a section on modal logic and strict implication, Lewis wrote to him, "obviously the fate of 'strict implication' lies with you, and a few others like Parry and McKinsey."[89] He especially hoped that Ruth Marcus would carry on the work. On May 11, 1960, he wrote her, briefly sketching his ideas for a Calculus of Predicates corresponding to S2. He concluded the letter with the comment: "If it happened to please you to pick up and develop anything this may suggest, I should be pleased, and herewith convey to you all right and title. No acknowledgement would be in order."[90] She did not.

7

Positivism and the Theory of Knowledge

In the 1930s, Dewey remained the best known American philosopher, and he continued to be productive. Lewis, now officially a Pragmatist, was anxious to make common cause with Dewey, but he could not agree with him on all points. Lewis's views of Dewey's philosophy are expressed in two pieces, one written in 1930 as a review of Dewey's *Quest for Certainty*, the other in 1939 as part of a symposium of reviews of *Logic: The Theory of Inquiry*.[1] Lewis applauds Dewey's rejection of the view that security and certainty are to be found in another world and his doctrine that salvation can only be had by intelligent work in this world. He also endorses Dewey's rejection of the notion that the "norm of knowledge" is an antecedent reality—a fault of both rationalism and empiricism. Dewey, Lewis says, sees sense experience as setting the problems to be solved, and action, directed by ideas, as the means of solving them. "Knowledge here takes its place in a world which is in part its own creation. A knower, as such, is a doer, not a passive spectator of a ready-made world."[2]

Lewis states Dewey's theory of the relation of meaning and action as holding that

> the cognitive or meaning situation does not admit of bifurcation into an activity of the knower and a preformed object which is contemplated; that knowing or meaning is integral with other activities which shape the objects to which they are addressed; that meanings themselves serve to frame the situations of action into which they enter, and exercise an operational force upon what they serve to formulate. It is implied that an idea

211

or meaning, apart from some possible action and the reality in which it should eventuate, is a fictitious entity not found in human thinking. And conversely, it is implied that the objects of knowledge, without reference to meanings and the actions to which they may lead, are equally fictitious.[3]

Lewis defends this thesis as he interprets it. The knower and the object are both part of the "world-process," and the activity of the one is as important as the activity of the other. All empirical knowledge, Lewis says, leads to predictions about future experience which must be verifiable. But if the world-process were strictly determined by laws, "what boots it to know this completely inevitable futurity?" We wish to know whether or not it will rain so that we can take precautions against getting wet. But, in that case, the future cannot be determined or else our "precautions" would be without effect. "There are no such verifying or confirming experiences which can be predicted without reference to the activity of the subject."[4] Our predictions take the form of conditionals such as "if it will rain today, then if I carry an umbrella then I shall not get wet." Reference to the actions of the knower is indispensable; how else could a scientific prediction be tested except by specifying what will be observed under conditions realized by the action of the scientists? This is not a new idea for Lewis, but it is what he found most important in Dewey's work.

Yet Lewis sees Dewey's emphasis on the predictive and transformative character of knowledge as leaving out the question of justification. When scientific investigation begins with hypotheses to be tested in the future through action, the initial hypotheses are only probable. But on what ground are they probable? The warrant for their probability must lie in the past, even though their confirmation lies in the future, and Dewey has not adequately explained how this justification is found.

Furthermore, Lewis emphasizes that sense experience must do more than set us a problem; it must also provide clues or signs of what may result from our actions in the future. The "ground of our prediction must reflect some generalization—that on occasions such as this, a particular act will result thus and so—and the only possible basis of this generalization is something prior, even though the generalization be a tentative one, subject to correction in the light of further experience."[5]

Lewis also comments on Dewey's "instrumentalism"—"the subservience of cognitive activity to further interests, which are to have authority over it."[6] Lewis points out that Plato also believed in a functional theory of concepts, but one that led to an extreme emphasis on abstract knowledge that Dewey condemns, arguing that ideas must find their warrant in practical doing. Lewis finds Dewey's practical emphasis a bit extreme. "To 'make a difference in nature' is not the whole end of man. Perhaps he [Dewey] will allow us moral holidays, for the celebration of scientific insight as an end in itself."[7]

Lewis also partly endorses and partly disagrees with Dewey's view on values. Like Dewey, Lewis rejects transcendental standards of value. But Dewey's view that value standards will come from natural science draws Lewis's objections. Granting that we learn what is good by experience, Lewis argues that the ultimate criteria of the good must be brought to experience by us—"otherwise experience could no more teach us what is good than it can teach the blind man what things are red."[8] As Lewis views Dewey's theory, he has not separated the locus of the good in experience and reality from the criteria of the good, and this distinction Lewis regards as critical.

Overall, the reviews are laudatory. But while presenting his criticisms as "trivialities" with which Dewey would no doubt agree, Lewis is careful to make his own points clear. He did not retreat from the position he had staked out in *Mind and the World Order* and on which his reputation now rested.

Lewis was also concerned with clarifying just what Pragmatism was, now that he was officially a member of the club. In 1908, Arthur Lovejoy had published in the *Journal of Philosophy* an article entitled "The Thirteen Pragmatisms"[9] in which he argued that, far from being a single coherent doctrine, "pragmatism" as it was currently understood included a variety of theses concerning meaning, truth, and knowledge that were often inconsistent with each other. In 1930, Lewis published an article entitled "Pragmatism and Current Thought,"[10] in which he used Lovejoy's article as a starting point in an effort to show the coherence of Pragmatism. Lewis did not deny that there were multiple pragmatisms; so he suggested were there thirty-seven Idealisms and fifty-one realisms. All that that showed was that Pragmatism was a movement rather than a system—a movement whose origin he attributed to Peirce, who, Lewis said, "has something of the quality of a legendary figure in American philosophy." But it was a movement with a central core that gave it unity. "Pragmatism is, as James indicated, not a doctrine but a method."[11] By this Lewis referred to "the pragmatic test of significance" that requires that any significant concept make some practical difference in experience. This claim is supported by quotes from James, by Peirce's famous maxim, and by a discussion of Dewey's work. Lewis sees Dewey's functional theory of knowledge as dating from his article on the reflex arc and so predating James announcement of Pragmatism, though not, of course, Peirce's maxim. But this functional theory that Lewis believes all pragmatists share leads in two directions: one toward the empirical, the other to a view of concepts as abstractions. To illustrate these, Lewis turns to physics and cites

Bridgman's operationalism and his claim that "the concept is synonymous with the corresponding set of operations."[12] But why is it synonymous? "Their [the concepts] meaning is . . . in the operations of verification and their results; it is contained in that complex network of relationships which constitute the laws and equations and physical predications of which science consists. The concept is, thus, merely a sort of configuration or relational pattern."[13] This is the position Lewis had taken in the first part of *Mind and the World Order.* The Pragmatic test, Lewis asserts, "becomes a kind of law of intellectual parsimony" and leads us away from the subjective to the relational congruence between observers. But this does not mean that the empirical has been abandoned for the abstract.

Consider, Lewis says, an elephant sliding down a grassy slope. The physicists's account of the elephant will reduce him to pointer readings. But the purpose of this is that "we get the elephant safely into a box-car." "The function of concepts is not to *photograph* elephants but to get them into box-cars." Thus, concepts represent the tools of cognition by which we transform "the something given, with which it begins, into the something anticipated or something done, with which it ends."[14] There is thus no contradiction between the abstract and the empirical; they are part of one process. Lewis concludes:

> In one sense—that of connotation—a concept strictly comprises nothing but an abstract configuration of relations. In another sense—its denotation or empirical application—this meaning is vested in a process which characteristically begins with something given and ends with something done—in the operation which translates a presented datum into an instrument of prediction and control.[15]

One again sees here the vagueness of Lewis's theory of meaning. What is the denotation? Is it the given datum? The future result? The process by which one leads to the other? Or all of the above? And how is the connotation—the "configuration of relations"—related to the denotation? These were problems Lewis would have to solve.

But the most important development in philosophy in this period was not in the United States but in Europe; it centered around a remarkable group of men who came together in Vienna under the leadership of Moritz Schlick. Born in 1882, Schlick took his doctorate at the University of Berlin and wrote a dissertation on the reflection of light in nonhomogeneous media under the direction of Max Planck. After a stint at the University of Rostock and a brief one at Kiel, Schlick was appointed to the chair previously held by Ernst Mach at the University of Vienna. It was a fitting appointment. Although he began as a neo-Kantian, Schlick was a trained physicist, and his early publications dealt with the implications of Relativity Theory for the fundamental concepts of physical science. Even before he came to Vienna, Schlick had done important work in the theory of knowledge and had concluded that science, not metaphysics, was our only trustworthy source of knowledge of reality.[16]

Schlick was a remarkable man. Not only was he a distinguished philosopher, but he had a gift for bringing together talented people in stimulating discussions. The Vienna Circle began in 1923 in Schlick's seminar that included Herbert Feigl and Friedrich Waismann. In 1924, Schlick formed a Thursday evening discussion group with, among others, Hans Hahn (mathematics), Otto Neurath (sociology), Felix Kaufmann (law), Victor Kraft and Edgar Zilsil (philosophy), and Kurt Reidemeister (mathematics); it rapidly expanded to include the physicist Philipp Frank, the logician Kurt Godel, and the philosopher Gustav Bergmann. In 1926, Schlick engineered the appointment of Rudolph Carnap at the University of Vienna, and Carnap became at once a major figure in the circle. Although Carnap's rising star soon eclipsed those of the others in the group, it was Schlick who held it together, and, when Carnap went to Prague in 1930, the Vienna Circle continued to flourish. It ended in 1936 when a deranged student murdered Schlick.

The influences that brought the Vienna Circle into being were many, but some were clearly dominant. One was the Einsteinian revolution, which, as we have already noted, shook physical science to its roots. It is hardly surprising, in view of the sweeping changes in physics that took place throughout this period, along with the scientific backgrounds of its members, that the Vienna Circle should have focused on the physical sciences. A second influence was the work of Frege and Russell. All the members of the Vienna Circle viewed the new logic of Whitehead and Russell as marking an epoch in philosophy, but Russell's own philosophical theories—particularly his logical atomism—greatly impressed them. So, too, did the work of Poincare and Hilbert. Although they came to be known as Positivists, they drew much less inspiration from Comte than from the phenomenalism of Hume and Ernst Mach. And they were greatly influenced by Wittgenstein, whom many of them saw as carrying out what Russell had started. Wittgenstein's visits to the Vienna Circle were few, and, of course, difficult, but the *Tractatus* was intensively studied by the group, and they all were greatly influenced by it.

It is also important to note that German philosophy in the 1920s was dominated by various forms of German Idealism that were hostile to science. The antimetaphysical animus of the Positivists certainly owes a good deal to the fact that they were a marginal movement within the German philosophic establishment. Carnap's famous attack on Heidegger,[17] who was seen as exemplifying German Idealism, and Heidegger's responses,[18] are indicative of the hostility between these movements. This situation did not improve. The Nazis did not tolerate the Positivists and, under Hitler, German philosophy followed a line of development antithetical to Logical Positivism. It was in England and America that the Positivists found their audience.

Out of this combination of factors, together with the chaotic situation produced by World War I, came the general position that was called Logical Positivism. Logical Positivism was never a fixed set of doctrines; the members of the Vienna Circle were often in disagreement with each other, and they all changed their views on major issues as their own work brought new insights and problems. But certainly central to the movement was the rejection of metaphysics and the attempt to extend the reach of science over the whole domain of knowledge. This led to the classification of meaningful statements into two classes; those that were a priori and analytic, such as those of mathematics and logic, and those that were empirical. This, in turn, led to the formation of the criterion of cognitive significance: "the meaning of a proposition is the method of its verification." Put otherwise, they believed that to know the meaning of a proposition is to know when it is true. Hence, a meaningful proposition must be verifiable; one must be able to say how its truth can be established. As empiricists, they believed that verification required the comparison of the proposition with direct sensory experience. Obviously, this was an attempt to formulate the method of science in a rigorous and precise way. It led to the consequence that many propositions of philosophy are without cognitive meaning. This did not make them totally meaningless, but rather showed that they were expressions of emotions and feelings, but had no cognitive content. In this view, propositions of art and poetry were expressive statements; so were those of metaphysics and religion. They disagreed about the status of ethical propositions; most of them regarded these as devoid of cognitive meaning, but Schlick sought to create a scientific ethics free of metaphysics.

Yet the notion of verifiability contained many problems. Initially, the Positivists thought that verification must be by direct experience. But direct experience is private, whereas scientific truth is public. Neurath argued that a proposition can only be verified by a proposition. Sense experiences were captured in "protocol sentences" that were direct reports of experience such that to understand the sentence was to see that it was true. Other statements were then to be analyzed until their basis in protocol sentences was revealed, which would establish their truth or falsity. If analysis revealed no such basis, the statement was without cognitive significance. Similarly, starting from basic observational predicates of the sort occurring in protocols, it was held that all meaningful concepts and propositions could be constructed. But since protocols are reports of private experience, dispute arose over how verification could be public. Schlick continued to hold the original Vienna Circle position on protocols, but Neurath and then Carnap and others adopted the view that protocols were equivalent to statements that referred to physical occurrences and therefore were public. It soon became the view of most of the Circle that the language of all science must be a "physicalist" language. But this doctrine robbed protocols of their status as indubitable elementary statements and made them physical hypotheses subject to error. The result, as Schlick pointed out, was a coherence theory of truth. Furthermore, the verification criterion proved to be too strict. Taken literally, it made the laws of science cognitively meaningless, since there is no set of experiences that can verify a general law. The result was the weakening of the criterion to one of confirmation; a proposition is meaningful if true propositions are derivable from it.

Under the influence of Wittgenstein, the Vienna Circle adopted the view that the task of philosophy is not the creation of systems but the solution of problems through the analysis of meaning. This led Carnap to distinguish sentences of the material and formal modes—that is, statements about objects and statements about language. Many statements of philosophy, Carnap held, seem to be about objects, but they are really about language and, when translated into the "formal mode," the confusion evaporates. Thus, "Caesar is a prime number" seems to pose a puzzle, but, when translated into the formal mode, it is seen to involve the mistake of using a predicate applicable only to numbers to describe a person. In a language that is properly constructed, such confusions cannot occur because the syntactic rules would not permit it. Accordingly, the language of science should be constructed with a logical syntax that would permit only meaningful propositions.

The ultimate goal of the Logical Positivists was the creation of a unified language of science into which all the sciences could be translated. This had been Mach's objective, though for him the language would have had to have been phenomenal. As Logical Positivism developed, it became agreed that such a language would have to be physicalist—that is, its basic propositions would refer to physical objects and, as Carnap and others saw it, philosophy *was* the logic of science, which was "nothing other than the logical syntax of the language of science." The project of creating a language of unified science was promoted through the attempt to create an *Encyclopedia of Unified Science*, two volumes of which actually appeared.

The Vienna Circle was not the only such group in Europe in the 1920s. A second similar circle was the Berlin group—the Society for Scientific Philosophy—of which Hans Reichenbach, Alexander Herzberg, and Walter

Dubislav were leaders; it included Kurt Grelling, Richard von Mises, Kurt Lewin, Wolfgang Kohler, and Carl Hempel. These men were concerned with the same sorts of problems as the Vienna Circle and shared many of their views. Another such circle was the Warsaw group that included Jan Lukasiewicz, Zygmunt Zaiwirski, Stansilaw Lesniewski, Mordechaj Wajsberg, and Alfred Tarski. These philosophers were not Positivists, but they were deeply involved in logic, mathematics, and science. There were other circles as well, and frequent communication and visits among their members. This growing network of like-minded individuals set the stage for the Congresses that brought together philosophers from Europe and America and introduced Logical Positivism to the world. At the Seventh International Congress of Philosophy, held at Oxford in 1930, Schlick presented the basic position of the Circle. Also in that year the journal *Erkenntnis* was founded, edited by Neurath, Carnap, Hahn, and Frank, and in rapid order the Positivists began publishing works that won international attention. Among those who attended these Congresses from the United States were Charles Morris, Ernest Nagel, and W. V. Quine, and from England A. J. Ayer, Richard Braithwaite, and Gilbert Ryle. The 1939 Congress was held at Harvard where, of course, Lewis knew about it.

The rise of Nazism radically changed the situation in Europe. The Berlin group ended in 1933. Reichenbach went to the University of Istanbul from 1933 to 1938 before arriving in American to take a position at UCLA. Hempel left Germany in 1934 for Brussels, and then came to the United States in 1937 where he taught at the University of Chicago, CCNY, and Queens College before becoming a professor at Yale from 1948 to 1955 and at Princeton thereafter. Not all were so lucky. Grelling died in a concentration camp. So did Wajsberg, who, it will be remembered, had furnished some of the matrixes used by Lewis in *Symbolic Logic*. As the war approached, the exodus intensified. Carnap took a position at the University of Chicago in 1936. Lukasiewicz went to Ireland to the Royal Irish Academy. Tarski came to the United States in 1939 and, after two years at Harvard and two more at the Institute for Advanced Study at Princeton, settled at Berkeley. Kohler became a professor at Swarthmore in 1935. Lewin came to the United States in 1932 and landed at Cornell in 1933; subsequently he was at the University of Iowa and then MIT. Waismann and Neurath went to England; Zilsel and Kaufmann to the United States, and Godel went to the Institute for Advanced Study at Princeton in 1940. Bergmann arrived here in 1938 and took a position at the University of Iowa. Feigl came to the United States in 1930 and taught at the University of Iowa before settling into a permanent position at the University of Minnesota. Frank came in 1938 to Harvard. Von Mises arrived in 1939 and also landed at Harvard.

And so on. In other words, the Logical Positivists became part of the great tide of European intellectuals who came here fleeing Hitler—a tide that included Einstein, Szilard, Teller, Fermi, and a host of others in every field of intellectual endeavor.

The arrival of these men in the United States and their quick occupation of prestigious university positions—considerably more prestigious than those they held in Europe—only increased their influence in this country. It is difficult now, when Logical Positivism is a thing of the past, to recapture the excitement that they generated in American philosophical circles. What they brought was a clarity, a rigor, and a missionary zeal that dazzled American students accustomed to the obscurities of Dewey or the vagueness of Woodbridge. These men knew their sciences; they knew their logic; they drew sharp distinctions between cognitive and emotive, "between metaphysics and science, logical and factual truths, the verifiable and the nonverifiable, the corrigible and the incorrigible, what can be shown and what can be said, facts and theories."[19] And, perhaps most of all, they pushed philosophical analysis to the limits; they formulated their positions with a precision that allowed them to be disproven, something virtually unheard of in previous philosophy, and, when they found their doctrines inadequate, they never hesitated to change them. And they did not just propound programs; they tried to carry them out. They said science needed a measure of confirmation; Carnap tried to build one. They wanted clarification of the nature of probability: Reichenbach and Carnap wrote major treatises on probability, though they took opposing positions. They wanted a better theory of scientific explanation; Hempel tried to develop one. To American students, this was a breath of fresh air. Many American philosophers welcomed the Positivists, but for those who had viewed the Positivists askance when they were in Europe, their arrival here was anything but welcome.[20]

Just when Lewis became acquainted with the writings of the Vienna Positivists is not certain, but sources were not lacking. Feigl was at Harvard as an International Rockefeller Fellow in 1930.[21] Lewis and Feigl were well acquainted, and Lewis gave Feigl a crucial recommendation that helped to secure his appointment at the University of Iowa.[22] Quine spent the next year with Carnap and returned to Harvard "his disciple."[23] In 1934, Quine was delivering lectures on Carnap to a voluntary seminar at Harvard[24] and in 1937 and 1938 he taught courses on Logical Positivism.[25] Certainly by 1934, Lewis was citing works by Carnap, Hahn, Neurath, and Schlick. But he may well have been reading the Positivists before 1931. There is among Lewis's papers a twenty-nine page summary of the Carnap's *Aufbau*.[26] The manuscript is undated; it is also purely descriptive and gives no hint of

Lewis's opinion of the work, but the care taken in writing it speaks for itself. Further, many years later, Lewis commented:

> It is quite true that in the early documents of the neopositivists—particularly in Carnap's *Der logische Aufbau der Welt*, but also in the writings of Schlick and Reichenbach—I found an empiricism and an analytic method which were congenial to my own persuasions. I still find them so.[27]

The *Aufbau* was not Carnap's first published work, but it is certainly the one that first brought him fame. What he attempted was nothing less than the "constitution" of the natural and social sciences on the basis of elementary sensory experience. What Whitehead and Russell did for mathematics in the *Principia*, Carnap sought to do for all science in the *Aufbau*, though only in outline. But the further objective was to show how, starting with subjective experience, one could attain objective knowledge. Carnap distinguished four types of objects: cultural objects, other minds, physical objects, and the data of one's own mind. Starting with the elementary experiences of the latter, and using only the language of the *Principia* plus one additional primitive—recollected similarity—Carnap sought to show that concepts of physical objects could be "constituted" from this basis, or, conversely, that concepts of physical objects are "reducible" to the elementary experiential base. "Reduction" here does not mean that a concept of higher type is equivalent to concepts of lower type, but that any statement that contains the name of a physical object can be replaced by a statement equivalent in truth-value that does not contain it but contains only terms referring to the sensory base. Given that concepts of physical objects can be so constituted, Carnap held that concepts of other minds can then be constituted from those already shown to be constitutable, and then that concepts of cultural objects can be constituted from that base, where "cultural objects" include values, religion, customs, and so on. The project was incompletely carried out, but, in doing so, Carnap demonstrated a mastery of logic and an ingenuity in its employment that were dazzling and that seemed to promise that the project outlined could actually be done.[28]

There was much in the *Aufbau* to which Lewis was sympathetic. Lewis had been greatly interested in Whitehead's attempts to reconstruct the foundations of natural science on the basis of experience in the early 1920s. In Carnap, he found someone who had gone much further. Both men believed empirical knowledge had to be constructed on the basis of first-person experience. Both were influenced by Russell, and Carnap's attempt actually to show how empirical knowledge could be rigorously constructed from logic and a single empirical primitive notion could hardly have failed to excite Lewis's interest. Both were neo-Kantians of some variety. Although Carnap's focus was on the construction of scientific knowledge, he also included "cultural" objects, and specifically values, thus suggesting a breadth to his theory that was consonant with Lewis's views. Further, in the *Aufbau*, Carnap does not assert the strong verificationism that he later adopted, although if Lewis also read the "Pseudoproblems in Philosophy" that appeared in 1928 he would have found a full-blown verificationism there. Despite Carnap's purely extensional approach, Lewis thought the Carnap of the *Aufbau* a more congenial figure than the later Carnap.

There is among Lewis's papers a seventy-page manuscript that must have been written about this time [Lewis drew on it in his 1933 presidential address to the American Philosophical Association, so it must have been composed before that] that is an attempt to sort out the relation of his views to those of the Positivists.[29] Lewis begins with the historical context of the problem he wants to discuss. Over the last three centuries, he says, commonsense realism proved incapable of defending itself against skepticism; the only defense that appeared to offer security was Idealism; and now it has become clear that Idealism will not do. The primary motive behind Idealism, Lewis says, "has been in the defense of human ideals from the attacks of an intransigent naturalism. . . . Idealism moved to save the eternal values; and in this it has been, I think, successful."[30] But Lewis sees his own time as one in which the battle between naturalism and supernaturalism has cooled, and believed it was now possible to make a fresh start on resolving the issues.

The failure of Idealism, Lewis says, is that "the reduction of all reality to the mental is a stupendous falsehood."[31] Common men, as typified by Dr. Johnson, never accepted any such claim, as the recent resurgence of realism makes clear. But Lewis is critical of professional philosophers, who, he says, are apt to reject problems they cannot solve as being someone else's business and limit the scope of their own discipline to what they can solve. This sort of "fallacy," whether committed by scientists or philosophers, leads to an evasion of significant problems, and it is such a "professional fallacy committed by the epistemologist" to which Lewis wants to direct attention. Specifically, this is the "announcing as a sort of maxim for his science that a thing is what it is known as; and then going on to deny to known objects different kind of significance than that which is contained in the particular kind of analysis which it is the business of the theory of knowledge to make."[32] The maxim is due to James, and Lewis has no criticism of James's use of it. But not everyone has construed it as broadly as James did.

Epistemology is preoccupied with the question of the validity of knowledge. And this usually takes the form of asking what the object of knowledge is known as. Other questions could be asked, such as the cause of our experience of the object, but these do not answer the question of validity. Kant sought to approach the problem by starting with the "experience, or the mind, and explain the object of knowledge in terms of it."[33] Russell has sought to translate all the allowable terms of epistemological discourse in terms of constituents "identifiable in actual experience," which Lewis thinks is what James intended. This procedure leads to the result that terms not so translatable are meaningless. Lewis applauds this development, but with the caveat that limiting discourse to terms that refer to direct experience must not lead us to reject or ignore aspects of direct experience not representable in discourse. But this translation or analysis can be carried out in different ways; the "pragmatic or positivist maxim" is therefore ambiguous, and "if *one* such analysis is canonized as exhibiting *the* meaning, then we fall into dogmatism."[34]

Positivism and Idealism agree in rejecting an unknowable thing-in-itself. "The use of the word 'real' involves some criterion of reality. The definition of 'reality' . . . must exhibit this criterion; and the criterion must be such that it can be applied and when applied will give a definite decision as to whether what it is applied to is real or unreal."[35] We can, Lewis notes, speak meaningfully of the cause of colds, where the cause is taken to be an unknown virus, but we can do so because the relation specified is "supposed to provide a schematism for the search for this cause and a criterion by which it may be recognized when discovered."[36] By comparison, vitalists argue for an explanatory factor that cannot be distinguished from the vital processes themselves, and so could never be isolated from its effects. Lewis goes on to remark that the ascription of a cause X to an effect A where X is unobservable is meaningless; "the phrase 'essentially unobservable cause' is, in positivistic language, merely bad grammar."[37]

But now Lewis distinguishes two forms of this dictum: "as a sensible methodological restriction for science" and as a "metaphysical principle." Suppose, Lewis says,

> that there is a super-human and very powerful being, conscious like ourselves, who cherishes normal vital wholes, and who acts in conformity with this purpose to produce and restore such wholes in ways which do not exhibit any *other* detectable uniformity than this uniformity between his cherishing and process which he determines by his will. This being is not observable to us save through his effects, of which certain distinctively vital phenomena are instances.[38]

Is this hypothesis meaningless? Lewis says, "I cannot find anything essentially inconceivable in such a supposition—anything which is 'bad grammar.'"

In fact, Lewis believes most people consider such a hypothesis at some time or other. The biologist, as scientist, might exclude such a hypothesis from biology, but if he were to extend the exclusionary principle from biology to metaphysics, "then he would be, not a good scientist but a bad metaphysician."[39]

Lewis compares the hypothesis of God to the hypothesis of electrons in physics. Electrons are not observable; since color is not attributable to electrons, "it is meaningless to think of seeing an electron." Yet the hypothesis of electrons is scientifically respectable, whereas the hypothesis of God is not. Why? Citing Bridgman, Lewis notes that the electron hypothesis leads to predictions that are observable and are verified. But Bridgman's identification of the electron with its effects is not acceptable to all physicists, particularly "the more radically pragmatic or positivistic features of it."[40] Why not? Lewis thinks it is because we require a "satisfactory account of an imaginable electron" such that if our senses were sufficiently microscopic we could actually observe it.

> The point is that we feel that in reducing the electron to those effects which are observable to ordinary human beings and holding that there is nothing more to it than these items, we feel that such a positivistic view has fudged the issue. These, we feel, are its effects, not the electron itself which produces them. But when we try to specify what we mean by the electron itself, we are obliged to have recourse to conditions of observation which it is humanly impossible to realize.[41]

That these conditions are contrary to fact, Lewis says, is irrelevant, but it does require consideration of the problem of possibility. Consider the other side of the moon. We infer that the moon has another side because it behaves like a solid object. "But no human being can ever see it." On the positivist criterion, Lewis says, "the other side of the moon *consists* in those observable effects of its being a solid object."[42] But what then becomes of the question whether there are mountains on the other side of the moon? The other side of the moon must mean something more than its presently observable effects. It must mean "what we should observe if we could build a Jules Vern space ship and fly up there and investigate the moon."[43] What we therefore find is a series of counterfactual cases, running from simple ones (does my watch have another side?) to those like the other side of the moon, where the conditions in which observation could be realized are "of dubious possibility," to those like the electron where the conditions cannot be realized at all. Where, Lewis asks, in this series is the dividing line between the metaphysically acceptable and the unacceptable? Lewis suggests that this line may be drawn differently in science and in metaphysics. In science, Lewis believed the line will be determined pragmatically.

I venture the guess that the decision likely to prevail in physics will be
determined very immediately upon pragmatic grounds. If the conception
of the electron as coincident with the sum-total of those systematically
connected phenomena attributed to it which are of the order of those
observable in the laboratory enables all the predictions which the laboratory
can verify about electrons, physics will eventually extrude accept (sic) the
Bridgman point of view and repudiate the notion of the electron as a
kind of little bullet of electricity as a piece of naivety excusable only in
the layman or as metaphysical nonsense. But if the little bullet conception, as a leading idea, gives rise to predictions about electrons which
prove variable (sic) [verifiable], and these predictions would not follow
from the more positivistic conception, then physics will come to affirm
the existence of electrons as such little bullets and repudiate restriction to
that which is directly observable in the laboratory as the kind of timid
pedantry that epistemologists affect.[44]

Lewis then turns to the question of the distinction between the effects
of a thing and the thing itself. Lewis admits that if all the effects of the
object were to disappear, so would the object. In this sense, the object is
identical with the totality of its effects. There is no one effect that is essential
to the object, no essence. But, he says, the appearance of the effects depends
on conditions that go beyond the thing itself. Although Lewis is not crystal
clear here, he seems to be saying that the reality of the object consists in the
fact that under certain conditions it will produce certain effects. That is,
the possibility of producing certain effects under specified conditions marks
the object as real. That leads him to possibility and experience that is possible, but not actual. What experience is possible depends on what happens
under certain conditions. But these conditions, too, are only possible, and
so we face a problem of a regress.[45]

This is not, Lewis emphasizes, a question of logical possibility—that
is, of something being noncontradictory. This type of possibility requires
"a certain kind of basis in actuality." Probably there is no one answer to
this, Lewis thinks; there are probably a number of subspecies of possibility
with different relations to actuality. To illustrate the first subspecies, Lewis
considers the question of whether or not it is possible for him to pick up
his watch from the table. For this case, he says, "what is declared possible
would actually supervene upon a set of conditions only one of which is now
lacking, namely my intention or will."[46] That this is the case is known
empirically from past experience. There is no regress here. The second subspecies is exemplified by the problem of viewing the other side of the moon.
"I am suggesting that if we can so construct a series beginning with actuality
and ending with the space ship that the *only* conditions not actual in the

envisaged series is our own purposes or intentions, then there *could* be such a space ship if we wished; and the possibility of it is genuine in a quite clear and simple sense."[47] This approach can deal with many cases; it cannot deal with the spaceship because too many of the required conditions are not actual.

How, Lewis asks, did the Wright Brothers know an airplane was possible? Granted that they knew much of what they needed to know to build it, they did not know all they needed to know. They made, Lewis says, a probability judgment that they could overcome the remaining problems, based on their success in overcoming similar ones in the past. The combination of possibility and probability provides an adequate answer to the question of the spaceship, and many others as well. But it is not sufficient to deal with the electron. What would be required here? Lewis suggests that what we mean is that if we had a type of vision different from what we actually have, we would be able to see the electron, assuming that the notion of "seeing" the electron involves no contradiction—a reference to the uncertainty principle.[48]

This leads Lewis into a discussion of the difference between possibility and probability. Whatever is probable must be possible in the sense of non-contradictory. But Lewis says "A possibility is a cosmic fact. It absolutely exists or it does not. A probability is epistemic—is a relation between ascertained fact as premise and a conclusion."[49]

The third subspecies of possibility divides into two parts: "that in which some of the conditions of the thing are more or less definitely imaginable but not humanly possible; and that in which they are neither humanly possible nor definitely imaginable."[50] As Lewis says, the latter may be thought "beyond the pale" so he turns to the former. That involves something we might have that we know is not possessed by human nature. Lewis insists on the importance of this issue, which he takes to be that of the electron. "The assertion that X is real, or even the question about it, requires that X be so envisaged that we can tell in some sort of fashion what would be the difference between the reality of it and its unreality."[51] What Lewis proposes for the electron is that if we had some form of microvision we do not have, we would be able to observe the electron. Is this hypothesis meaningless? "I suggest that it is definitely meaningful, and is a way of ascribing a reality which may in fact obtain. To deny this is to confuse meaningfulness with what is *humanly* determinable."[52] The important point here, Lewis says, is that we specify a connection between actuality and something imagined that is contrary to fact for all humans. "Nevertheless the connection is there." This, Lewis thinks, meets the requirements of meaning for "the essence of the positivistic and pragmatic theory of meaning is—or should be—just that; a word with no denotation is meaningless; a conception which has no definiteness of denotation, no test of applicability is verbalist nonsense."[53]

This argument of Lewis's may seem far-fetched, but it is no more far-fetched than Schlick's argument against solipsism. Schlick found no difficulty in imagining a case in which humans are endowed with the ability to feel each others's pains. The fact that this is an impossibility, given the present state of human nature, does not deter Schlick from considering the proposition "I can feel somebody else's pain as well as my own" as meaningful.[54] Lewis is therefore quite correct in believing that his argument falls within the scope of the "positivist and pragmatic theory of meaning."

Kant is the philosophic father of pragmatism and positivism, Lewis says. His assertion that concepts without percepts are empty forecasts the criteria of the latter. Idealism holds that "a conception which could not humanly be tested by experience is meaningless."

> This common point between idealism and positivism illuminates and seemingly explains the "methodological solipsism" of Viennese neo-positivism which is merely the idealistic method used with more logical consistency than common sense and saved from madness Schopenhauer justly ascribed by that tongue-in-cheek word methodological. One merely argues as Berkeley does about matter, and as all idealists do about the thing itself, and one applies this style of argument to things which Berkeley and historical idealism have remained a little too sensible to apply it to. What are you but one of my ideas? Insofar as you are something more than a collection or organization of my ideas, how can I know you, or even suppose I mean anything intelligible when I try to talk about you? One thus lands in solipsism.[55]

Although Lewis admits that his view has some similarities to phenomenalism, he rejects that position, and says:

> I should, then, like to take my place with the critical realists in a class which is to be distinguished from positivism and idealism. And I should like to invite the neo- and other kinds of realists to elucidate themselves on this point. Is there any reason for the positive assertion that reality is limited to what is humanly experienceable as it is humanly experienced?
>
> The statement that it is seems to me a monstrous fallacy of anthropocentrism. And also it insults those interests which are the most frequent instigation to interest in philosophy—in the question of any other life than that presently verifiable, in any other cosmic powers than those science can observe, in any relation of human ideals to what is beyond what human observation can inductively prove. If philosophy can bake no bread for those who beg some answer to such questions, at least it need throw no stones.[56]

Despite the professionalization and specialization of philosophy that had occurred since the turn of the century, Lewis still believed that most people were drawn to the study of philosophy by religious issues.

This manuscript seems to represent a very early stage of Lewis's contact with positivism. He identifies the pragmatic maxim with the positivist criterion of cognitive meaning, and sees positivism as a position closely related to Idealism. But what is most interesting is Lewis's struggle with the issue of how statements about real objects can be translated into terms of actual experience. He resists the Positivist application of the criterion equally to both science and metaphysics; instead, he appears willing to accept in metaphysics a view of God that in evidential terms differs not at all from the vitalist principle that he rejects for science. And as the last paragraph quoted shows, Lewis was concerned that epistemology does not rule out the religious hypothesis. But it is science that poses the real problem; what does it mean to say electrons are real? Shrewdly, and accurately, Lewis sees that the answer in physics will be pragmatic, and in so doing he treats the electron hypothesis as something to be indirectly confirmed. But he doesn't put it that way; instead he invokes Royce's notion of a "leading idea" to describe the hypothesis. This is a very unRoycean use of the notion; for Royce the leading idea, exemplified by Virchow's definition of disease, could serve as a regulative principle of research, but it implied no specific testable consequences, whereas the use Lewis makes of it here does involve the implication of such consequences. But Lewis cannot leave the matter there; he feels compelled to find a way in which "direct" experience of the electron is possible, and is finally driven to consider experiences not possible for human beings as presently constituted. Granting that there must be possible experiences of the electron, no one had decreed whose possible experiences they would have to be, and invoking a nonhuman knower kept the connection of object and experience, if only just. This was not a position in which Lewis could rest content, but the fact he entertained it at all shows how critical the issue was. What Lewis needed here, but did not then have, was the notion of a theoretical construct statements about which could be indirectly confirmed.

In 1933, Lewis was chosen president of the Eastern Division of the American Philosophical Association. His presidential address that December was entitled "Experience and Meaning" and was published in the following year in the *Philosophical Review*.[57] Lewis begins by remarking that the question "How do you know?" that had dominated philosophy since Descartes is now being replaced by the question "What do you mean?," and that it is now demanded that any concept used "shall have a definite denotation," by which he means that one should be able to specify "those empirical items which would determine the applicability of the concept or constitute the verification of the proposition."[58] Among the factors that have brought about this demand for empirical meaning, Lewis lists five: Pragmatism and the pragmatic test, Neo-Realism including Russell's work, the new methodology of physics represented particularly by Einstein's treatment of definitions and Bridgmen's operationalism, Whitehead's method of extensive abstraction, and "the logical positivism of the Vienna Circle." Thus, Lewis sees Positivism and Pragmatism as having much in common. But what really concerns Lewis is "certain issues which are likely to divide those who approach these problems with the thought of James and Peirce and Dewey in mind from the logical positivists."[59]

The Positivist view, Lewis notes, divides statements into two groups: those whose meaning can be given in terms of simple statements about the empirically given, and those whose meaning cannot. The former class includes the statements of the empirical sciences. The latter class includes metaphysics, theology, value theory, and normative science, which are assigned to the same category as art and poetry. This position of the Logical Positivists, Lewis says, is not due only to the demand for empirical meaning, but also to the principle of "methodological solipsism," which demands that all knowledge be in the first person. From these first-person experiences, all knowledge is to be built up along the lines of Carnap's *Aufbau*. This represents, Lewis says, an effort to take the egocentric predicament seriously, and Lewis compares it to Berkeley's arguments carried to an extreme. Lewis is not asserting that the Positivists owe anything to Berkeley; his point is to suggest that methodological solipsism is compatible with empiricism. Citing Wittgenstein, Lewis notes that this serves to eliminate the self as anything more than "the ideas I call mine." He then summarizes what he takes to be the gist of the Logical Positivist position in three points.

First; when knowledge is envisaged, as it must be, from within the egocentric predicament, all objects known or conceived must reveal themselves as constructions, eventually, from data given in first-person experience. Also, what enters into such construction from past experience can only come in by way of present recollection. (This last is, I take it, the reason for the basic position of the relation of remembered-similarity in the program of Carnap.) Other selves and their experience, or their reports, can enter only as certain items of first-person experience upon which a peculiarly complex construction is put. Second; distinctions such as that between real and imaginary, or between that which is apprehensible to me alone and the object apprehended by us in common, must nevertheless find their genuine place and importance in such construction. The fact that we make these distinctions in practically useful ways evidences that they are not outside the egocentric predicament and metaphysical but inside it and empirical . . . Third; metaphysical issues concerning the external world and other selves do *not* turn upon such empirically applicable distinctions as those just referred to.[60]

But there is a fourth issue that Lewis finds the Logical Positivists unclear about that—of transcendence. If, Lewis says, the requirement is that knowledge is confined to what is immediately given, both knowledge and meaning are reduced to absurdity "because the *intention* to refer to what transcends immediate experience is of the essence of knowledge and meaning both."[61] Lewis does not accuse the Positivists of denying transcendence, but he finds no clear statement of their position on the matter in their writings.

This issue Lewis regards as fundamental, for it is the issue of how knowledge can be "valid" if it goes beyond what is present to the knowing experience. Lewis remarks that three solutions have been offered to this problem: the representationalist theory, in which the real object is not directly experienced at all; the identity theory, in which the object is identical with the content of the knower's experience at the moment of knowing, and the theory that while the object known must be specifiable in experience, that experience transcends the "experience of the subject of the moment of knowing"—the view held by Idealism and Pragmatism. But whereas for Idealism the present experience determines the real object with certainty, for Pragmatism the given experience of the moment of knowing is the basis of a probability judgment concerning the experiences in which the real nature of the object is expressed. Lewis does not claim that the Logical Positivists hold an identity theory, though he says he is not sure of that in view of some of Carnap's statements in the *Aufbau*, but, if they do not, they need to clarify their conception of the object known.

Lewis then goes on to elaborate his own theory of knowledge, and the meaning of saying that something is "verifiable." This term obviously involves the concept of possibility, but "possible" can be taken in several senses. First, a verifying experience is possible if I can obtain it at will, as, for example, in verifying that the object on the desk is my watch. But, second, "let us consider the other side of the moon." We believe that the moon has another side because we believe it is a solid object, but we cannot at present verify that claim [as of 1933!]. What then does it mean to say verification is possible? Lewis makes three points here. First, the reality must transcend the concept. "A construction imposed upon given data cannot be identical with a real object; the thing itself must be more specific, and in comparison with it the construction remains abstract."[62] This is Lewis's doctrine that the real object must be subject to the Law of Excluded Middle, and therefore every property or its negation must apply to it. Not all of these properties can be included in our concept of the object, so in verifying we will always find that the object has properties we did not anticipate. Second, as a criterion of *meaning*, "verification" refers "to a supposed character in what is conceived rather than to any supposed approximation of the conditions of verification to the actual."[63] That is, for a statement to be meaningful, we must be able to say what experiences *would* verify it, but it need not be the case that we can actually obtain those experiences at present. But third, the verification of *knowledge* requires assurance of truth. In the case of the other side of the moon, our description of how this is to be done must be "sketchy" because we do not know how to do it. Perhaps Lewis says what is required here is a description of a procedure "in analogy with" procedures we do know how to do.

Lewis then takes as a third example the electron. Since the electron cannot be seen, its existence is inferred from the way oil droplets behave between charged plates, from tracks on photographs, and so on. Bridgman "would say that our concept of the electron comprehends nothing more than these observable phenomena, systematically connected by mathematical equations in verifiable ways."[64] But if the electron is more than this, in what does the "more" consist? and "how direct must a 'direct verification' be?" Between the directly verifiable and the certainly not verifiable, there is a wide range that includes conceptions such as the electron as a tiny bullet.

> If those who believe in the electron as a sort of ultramicroscopic bullet cannot envisage this object of their belief in such wise that they would be able to recognize certain empirical eventualities as the verification of it, in case the conditions of such verification *could* be met, then they deceive themselves and are talking nonsense. But if they can thus envisage what they believe in, then the fact that such verifying experience is highly improbable, and even that the detail of it must be left somewhat indefinite, is no bar to its meaningfulness.[65]

Lewis draws from these examples the conclusion that "no concept has any denotation at all unless eventually in terms of sensuous data or imagery." So far as *meaning* is concerned, it is irrelevant whether the verifying experience can actually be obtained. But with respect to *knowledge*, "verifiable" requires a nonzero probability that the verifying experience can actually be attained.[66]

Lewis then applies this view to three traditional problems of philosophy. The first is immortality. We cannot, Lewis says, actually verify the hypothesis of immortality. But the hypothesis is meaningful because one can envisage what experiences would verify it. Second, he raises the question of whether the stars would go on in their courses if all minds disappeared from the universe. This hypothesis, of course, could never actually be verified; it must therefore be formulated counterfactually as "what any mind like ours *would* experience if, contrary to hypothesis, any mind *should* be there." Lewis's answer is that the hypothesis is meaningful since we can easily imagine the verifying experiences, and "*imagination* is sufficient for empirical meaning, though it requires *perception* for verification."[67] Finally, Lewis raises the issue of other selves. The Logical Positivists do not deny that other selves exist and have feelings, but they define feelings behavioristically. And here Lewis definitely parts company with the Positivists. Is the case of imagining another's pain from a toothache any different from imagining my own future pain from a toothache? Lewis thinks it is not, and since he regards it as obvious that I can imagine the latter, even though the pain is not now present, he says we can imagine the former. Therefore, the hypothesis of another's pain is meaningful. But could it actually be verified? "Any verification which I might suppose myself to make would violate the hypothesis by being first-person experience." But Lewis does not reject the hypothesis of other selves as centers of experience. Rather he concludes that meaningfulness "may even outrun the possibility of verification altogether."[68] This, of course, creates a peculiar situation for the verification theory of meaning, for Lewis is asserting the meaningfulenss of propositions that cannot be verified.

Lewis's comments in this paper did not go unnoticed in Vienna. In 1936, Schlick published an article in *The Philosophical Review*[69] that was largely a reply to Lewis. Schlick too sees the relation between Positivism and Pragmatism and holds "it will be easy to show that there is no serious divergence between the point of view of the pragmatist as Professor Lewis conceives it and that of the Viennese Empiricist."[70] Schlick rejects the notion that Logical Positivism identifies verification with present experience; he admits that some statements in Carnap's *Aufbau* can be so construed, but asserts that Carnap holds no such views now (i.e., in 1936). Schlick insists that "verifiable" means "logically possible" of verification, not empirically possible. Hence, he says, statements about the other side of the moon are verifiable; so are questions about immortality, which Schlick is willing to call "an empirical hypothesis," and statements about the stars after the extinction of human life. But Schlick rejects both Carnap's "methodological solipsism," which he regards as an unfortunate term, and the egocentric predicament, holding that experience has no owner. This represents the move toward physicalism (although Schlick does not so label it in this article) that Carnap and the Vienna Circle held. The fact that Schlick thought it necessary to reply to Lewis is an indication of the stature that Lewis had attained both here and abroad.

Whether Lewis considered Reichenbach a Positivist at this time is unclear; it is not certain just when Lewis first read Reichenbach, but he surely knew his work on probability by the mid-1930s. Reichenbach's theory of probability and induction led Lewis to change the theory he had set forth in *Mind and the World Order*, the weakness of which he now recognized. Reichenbach published his *Wahrscheinlichkeitslehre* in 1935 and a more popular presentation in *Experience and Prediction* in 1938.[71] Reichenbach's theory is a frequency theory that defines the probability of an event as the limit of the relative frequency of the event in an infinite series of trials. What particularly struck Lewis about Reichenbach's theory was his application of it to induction. Reichenbach defines induction by enumeration as "the rule by which we infer that the frequency observed in the initial section [of a series] will persist for the whole sequence,"[72] and he argues that "all inductive inferences that do not have the form of induction by enumeration must be construed in terms of the theorems of the calculus of probability."[73] Since Reichenbach holds the frequency theory of probability, and that all probable inferences "are reducible to deductive inferences with the addition of induction by enumeration,"[74] it is clear that induction by enumeration is basic to probability theory itself. But since the classic objection to this type of theory was that there is no proof in the case of empirical series that the limit of the series exists, what is the justification of this principle?

If in a given sequence, we find that the frequency of an event x is n/m, then, Reichenbach says, we "posit" that in the future the same relative frequency will hold. "The word 'posit' is used here in the same sense as the word 'wager' or 'bet' in games of chance." Now

> If the sequence has a limit of the frequency, there must exist an n such that from there on the frequency f^i $(i > n)$ will remain within the interval $f^n = \pm\delta$, where δ is a quantity that we can choose as small as we like, but that, once chosen, is kept constant. Now if we posit that the frequency f^i will remain within the interval $f^n \pm \delta$, and if we correct this posit for greater n by the same rule, we must finally come to the correct result. The inductive procedure, therefore, represents a *method of anticipation*; in applying the inductive rule we anticipate a result that for iterated procedure must finally be reached in a finite number of steps. We thus speak here of an *anticipative posit*.[75]

It is obvious here that we do not know whether or not this posit is justified. But, Reichenbach says, "the absence of proof does not mean that *we know that there is no limit*; it means only that *we do not know whether there is a limit*."[76] But if there is such a limit, this procedure will find it in the long run. Hence, Reichenbach holds that it is "a necessary condition for the existence of a limit, and thus for the existence of a method to find it, that the aim be attainable by means of the rule of induction."[77] The justification therefore is that if this method does not work, nothing will.

Further, in passages that particularly struck Lewis, Reichenbach argues that action requires two presuppositions: a wish to attain a certain aim, and cognitive beliefs that assure us that certain means will lead to the realization of the aim. Reichenbach remarks, "The justification of induction constructed may, therefore, be called a *pragmatic* justification; it demonstrates the usefulness of the inductive procedure for the purpose of acting."[78] This emphasis on the necessity of induction for action is even more explicit in Reichenbach's later book, *Experience and Prediction*, in which he argues that "inductive inference cannot be dispensed with because we need it for the purpose of action."[79] "We know," Reichenbach says, "that the principle of induction determines our best wager, or posit, because this is the only posit of which we know that it must lead to success if success is attainable at all."[80] Lewis was ever after to regard Reichenbach as a pragmatist, and Reichenbach himself suggested such an identification. Having outlined his own theory of meaning, Reichenbach asked, "Is this pragmatism?" While he hesitated to say yes, he remarked: "our conception may perhaps be taken as a further development of ideas which originated in pragmatism. It was the great merit of the founders of pragmatism to have upheld an antimetaphysical theory of meaning at a time when the logical instruments for a theory of knowledge were not yet developed to such a high degree as in our own day."[81]

It is clear that Lewis found Logical Positivism at this time both very attractive and unacceptable. He saw the verification theory of meaning as very similar to the pragmatic view, found "methodological solipsism" a version of the egocentric predicament, was drawn to Carnap's constitution theory, and to Schlick's interpretation of protocols. At the same time, he thought the Positivists view too narrow and could not accept their rejection of cognitive status for valuation, ethics, and metaphysics. He had yet to form the aversion to Positivism that marked his later work.

In 1936, Lewis read a paper before the Harvard Philosophy Club entitled "Judgments of Value and Judgments of Fact."[82] The problem Lewis focuses on is "posed, for those who would accept normative statements as meaningful, by the contention of the Vienna Circle that such pronouncements of the normative have no theoretical but only 'emotive meaning.'"[83] Lewis points out that, in the *Aufbau*, Carnap seemed to take the position that value judgments are analogous to perceptual judgments, are either true or false, and that values are not merely psychological phenomena. Lewis quotes Carnap on this point, notes that this position contradicts that of the Vienna Circle in general, and confesses he is not sure where Carnap now stands. Lewis therefore turns to the question of how judgments of fact relate to judgments of value. Immediate values are given in experience just as color is; in fact, "as given, the redness of the rose is as much feeling as the beauty of it, and is equally subjective."[84] Only by abstraction can we separate out the value aspect of experience from its other aspects; as given, they are all part of one experience.

Lewis then discusses the status of expressive statements that say what is given. He reiterates the point he had made before—that language is pre-empted by cognition, making the description of the given difficult. But Lewis here deals with the truth or falsity of expressive statements in a new way. "There is no question, for the maker of it, of its truth or falsity: as intended, it either expresses what he knows to be true, or it is a lie and he knows it."[85] One can say either that such statements need no verification, or that they are immediately verified.

> But according as one chooses either the first or the second of these alternative statements, it should be noted that one chooses a slightly different meaning of verification. In the one case, it means or includes in its meaning as verification the relation of accord between the denotative intent and that which directly meets or satisfies this intent; in the other case verification is confined to that concerning which there could conceivably be doubt or error, and hence does not apply to what is immediately and certainly determined in its truth or falsity, having no further implications.[86]

Lewis says he will take "judgment," "knowledge," and "cognition" to be verifiable in the latter sense, but expressive statements will be taken to be verified in the former. The double meaning of verification is necessary because "it would be highly paradoxical to say that such expressive statements are not true or false." *All* verification must ultimately be in terms of the accord of some statement with some immediate experience; unless verifications of the former type are allowed, no experience could ever verify anything. Expressive statements of the given are therefore true or false, but are not cognitions or judgments and do not constitute knowledge. This is a better analysis of the status of expressive statements than Lewis had previously given.

With respect to verification, Lewis holds, there is "no essential difference between the redness of the rose and the beauty of it, between sense-qualities and value-qualities."[87] The analogy continues to hold when one moves from the qualia of given experience to objective properties. Just as the attribution of an objective property (the rose is red) is predictive of future sensory experiences of the rose, so the attribution of value properties (the rose is beautiful) is predictive of future value experiences. But there is a major difference between the two cases. In the case of nonvalue qualities, our communicative needs are satisfied if we attain congruence of behavior, regardless of whether or not the given qualia are shared. This may also be the case with respect to value qualities if our intent is pragmatic and focused on cooperative behavior, since many values are extrinsic rather than intrinsic. But if the intent of the communication concerns the sharing of the immediate qualia, it may well fail.

"We arrive here," Lewis says, "at the end-point of reasonable argument."[88] So long as we restrict ourselves to "cognitive" meaning, a behavioristic account is possible, but where similarity of felt experience is required, no such behavioristic account can be adequate. But Lewis then proposes a way out of the dead-end. The word "objective" has multiple meanings, Lewis notes. In one, "that is 'objective' which belongs to or pertains to concrete objects, and that is 'subjective' which varies with states of mind." But a second meaning is "what Carnap calls 'intersubjective'—the same for all persons in question." If this latter sense obtains, then it becomes a complex case of the first. It is this second sense of objective as "intersubjective" that is critical for value; congruence of behavior is not enough—intersubjectivity is required, where this is understood to mean "the possibility of seeing it alike under appropriate conditions." Lewis then draws the conclusion:

> The predication of such intersubjective value characters has normative significance if it be granted that the intrinsically and intersubjectively valuable ought to be realized. I suggest that this last statement is a tautology, contained in the meaning of the word "ought." If this is true to the meaning of "ought" in use, then clearly questions of oughtness are, so far, questions of objective fact.[89]

Lewis is careful to point out that he is not here identifying the normative with the valuational. The normative is a question of ethics; the valuational is a question of the *summum bonum*.

But how can such intersubjectivity be verified? Lewis gives two answers.

> I have elsewhere spoken of such meanings, which include reference to the immediate quality of experience in other minds, as not subject to verification but nevertheless subject to meaningful postulation. The terms of such postulate, I have thought, possess concrete denotation; and that is all which is really essential. It is that which distinguishes the "intrinsically verifiable" (but perhaps not practically verifiable) from the intrinsically unverifiable—and which lends plausibility to the dictum that the meaningful must be verifiable.[90]

But Lewis now suggests that, as Ayer had proposed, "assertions have meaning insofar as their *probability* may be affected by empirical determining." Ayer was talking about electrons, but Lewis applies the idea to human experience.

> In view of the extraordinarily extended and thoroughly verified analogy of humans in other respects, and of the fact that all inductive reasoning is at bottom analogical, perhaps the hypothesis of like immediate experience associated with like behavior is one whose probability is genuinely affected by directly observed facts of behavior. But the experience which is the subject of this hypothesis is not to be *identified* with this behavior any more than the electron is to be identified with the behavior of molar masses observed in the laboratory.[91]

This is a very important argument for Lewis that makes its first appearance here. Lewis is making two proposals. First, he is arguing that, since all human beings share a large set of properties A_1, A_2, ... A_n, and some human beings (namely, oneself) have certain relations between immediate experiences E_1, E_2, ... E_n and behaviors B_1, B_2, ... B_n, then all human beings will (probably) exhibit the same relations between E_1 ... E_n and B_1 ... B_n. Lewis calls this an inductive argument, reflecting Keynes's emphasis on the analogical character of induction. Strictly, it is not an inductive argument; it is closer to what Peirce called a hypothetical argument. Further, the argument obviously requires clarification. Lewis cannot mean that all people have the same relations between experience and behavior; he needs an analysis of which sorts of experiences relate to which sorts of behaviors, of the varying degrees of probability attaching to these relations, and so on.

Second, Lewis is proposing that the relation of immediate experience to behavior is similar to that of electrons to laboratory observations. That is, Lewis is proposing that immediate experiences in other minds are theoretical constructs as are electrons, and that their existence can be indirectly confirmed by behavioral evidence just as the existence of electrons is indirectly confirmed by laboratory observations. The argument is so briefly stated that it is no more than a suggestion, but it nevertheless represents a major step for Lewis. The problem of other minds was one of the chief difficulties facing Lewis's theory of knowledge, and one crucial for his theory of value and of ethics. Lewis has here at least begun to formulate an attack on this problem—something he had not previously done.

What one sees in this article, and in his 1933 presidential address, is Lewis attempting to go beyond the position he had taken in *Mind and the World Order*. As noted earlier, although in *Mind and the World Order* Lewis had considered himself a realist, his attempt to prove the validity of induction collapsed into phenomenalism. But, by the 1930s, Lewis recognized this and was exploring the possibilities of indirect or partial verification—that is, of confirmation. The electron is Lewis's example, and it is also Ayer's, and Lewis now tries to apply this notion to the experience of other minds.

> The quality of experience in another mind can be "tested" if one is willing to retreat, as Mr. Ayer has done, to the position that assertions have meaning insofar as their *probability* may be affected by the empirical determining. Mr. Ayer has electrons in mind; and the analogy may be useful. The existence and conceived character of electrons is an hypothesis whose probability is affected by the experiments which verify consequences of it. Evidently Mr. Ayer would not be willing to say that the electron merely *is* or *means* the totality of this verifying and directly observable behavior of molar masses.[92]

Here it is quite clear that Lewis sees the verification of the consequences of the hypothesis of the electron as increasing the probability of that hypothesis. The electron here is not a regularity in experience, but its existence is confirmed by regularities in experience.

Taking the idea of intersubjectivity from Carnap, Lewis then applies the notion of confirmation to the experience of other minds. Congruence of behavior thus serves to confirm the existence of like sensory experience of multiple knowers, but, as Lewis emphasizes, the experience is "not to be *identified* with the behavior." Instead of regarding such sharing of qualitative experience as a postulate, as he had previously done, he now proposed to take it as a hypothesis subject to confirmation. This is a crucial step toward overcoming the division between the worlds of description and appreciation—something that had to be done if Lewis was to develop an adequate theory of ethics.

In 1936, Lewis gave a paper at Yale and at Princeton entitled "Verification and the Types of Truth."[93] He starts by noting that the question of meaning has become a central topic in current philosophy. He attributes this to the influence of pragmatism in the United States, to "Professor Moore and his analytic school" in England, to efforts to clarify the foundations of physics, and to the Vienna Circle. Lewis then notes that there is general agreement that there are two types of statements: the analytic a priori statements of logic and mathematics, and the synthetic a posteriori statements of empirical knowledge. The former are tautologies that exhaust the possible alternatives; they have no empirical content. The latter are statements of empirical matters of fact and, if true, must be empirically verifiable. So far, Pragmatists and Positivists agree, but no further. The Positivists deny that statements of metaphysics or normative statements have anything but "emotive" meaning; they are "neither analytic explications of meaning nor verifiable statements of any matter of fact."[94] Pragmatists deny this Positivist claim, as does Moore. The crucial question here, Lewis says, is the meaning of verification, and it is to this that he turns. Lewis then sketches the general procedure of verification. What is verified is a hypothesis, from which consequences are derived that predict "some empirical eventuality which can be determined by further observation or experiment."[95] If the predicted consequences occur, the probability of the hypothesis is increased; if not, it is decreased. No hypothesis is ever completely verified; the best that can be hoped for is high probability. But Lewis then goes on to note that the derivation of consequences almost always involves the use of other empirical hypotheses.

> In testing one hypothesis, we make use of other and better established hypotheses, in order to determine what consequences should follow if the hypothesis to be tested is true. . . . The important consideration here is that no one hypothesis can be tested in isolation. We test the hypothesis H by reference to its consequence C. C, however, is not a consequence of H alone, but of H together with J and K. If C fails to occur, we attribute this to the falsity of H, because J and K are better established. But if empirical principles in general are of the type called "verifiable"—always having consequences not yet tested, and never more than highly probable—then J and K of our paradigm will be themselves not theoretically certain; and all that we can be sure of, from the failure of C to occur, is that there is something false in the compound statement, HJK.[96]

This view of the role of auxiliary hypotheses in testing was nothing new. It can, for example, be found in Cohen and Nagel's book in 1934.[97]

The situation therefore is that in natural science we have at any one time some body of generalizations that we accepted as highly probable. When new facts are found that are inconsistent with this body of theory, adjustments must be made.

> In that case, the locus of the falsity in our accepted principles is not uniquely determined; a revised explanation, including what is newly discovered, can be achieved in more than one way. We are likely, for obvious reasons, to choose that revision which requires the smallest total alteration, or is most easily accepted for some other reason of the same general type—a kind of reason which is likely to be labelled "pragmatic" (though, as one with leanings to pragmatism, I regret just that use of the term).[98]

Moreover, Lewis points out a further conclusion from this picture of verification. The generalizations that constitute our scientific theories are so interrelated that each depends on others.

In the light of such considerations, the conclusion may be drawn that the whole body of empirical principles or accepted pronouncements is a vast and interrelated network, every item of which is mutually interdependent with every other, in the end; and the final test of empirical truth is simply that of complex consistency and of such mutual support within the system as a whole.[99]

This holistic position that Lewis has sketched is uncomfortably close to the coherence theory of truth—a theory that Lewis rejected as leading to the "block universe." The key question is the empirical verification of the consequences. But Lewis notes that "the predictions which we make, for the purposes of testing hypotheses, are propositions." Can any such proposition be proven absolutely true or false? The answer is clearly no: "the supposition that there are any statements of objective fact whose truth can be fully determined in any given experience is, in fact, difficult or impossible to defend."[100] No statement of objective fact can ever be more than probable. What we can be absolutely certain of is our experience. "What we absolutely find true, in the verifying experience, is not such assertion of objective properties, but is just that something looks or sounds or feels in such and such a determinate fashion."[101] Statements of the given imply nothing about the future; they merely state "an observed relation of accord between the intended denotation of the language used and the determinate content of an experience which meets or satisfies that intent."[102] These statements are certain. Verification depends on such statements of the given, for if the consequences of an hypothesis are to be verified, they must ultimately come down to a confrontation between such consequences and what is given in experience.

Lewis then points out that statements of the given are expressive statements that do not admit of "verification"—that is, of confirmation. They are therefore of the sort the Vienna Circle—or at least the members of the Circle other than Schlick—claims have only emotive meaning, and regard as subjective. To twist the knife, Lewis adds that they are "the expression of the sort of thing which Professor Prall calls an 'aesthetic surface,' which poetry and art attempt to convey." But these expressive statements are the basis of verification "because the truth of whatever is verifiable comes down eventually to the truth of just such statements of the experience in which it must be verified."[103] Accordingly, the line that the Positivists have drawn between statements that are cognitively meaningful and those that are merely emotive breaks down. As Lewis notes, this fact has implications for aesthetics and ethics, but he has no time to pursue these in this paper.

Lewis exploits in this paper the theory of expressive statements he had set forth in "Judgments of Value and Judgments of Fact," and uses it rather neatly to undercut the Positivist view of verification. But in sketching the picture of the interrelations among scientific statements, Lewis makes it clear that he understands very well that when logical consequences are drawn from a statement, they are actually drawn from the conjunction of that statement with some set of auxiliary hypotheses. The fact that the consequences of a statement are relative to the choice of auxiliaries had important implications for the theory of meaning that Lewis would develop within the next few years.

In March 1938, Lewis was working on a draft of "On Empirical Knowledge."[104] In it, he attacks Critical Realism for having substituted a belief in animal faith for Descartes's goodness of God. The theory he considers bankrupt when it takes the apprehension of essences for knowledge because essences are not constituents of objects. "Pragmatism," he says, "is antecedent to such metaphysical distinctions—though pragmatists would not generally agree with the logical positivists that such metaphysical distinctions are meaningless."[105] Pragmatism is not entirely neutral with respect to metaphysics because metaphysical theories are supposed to be true or false. "But this pragmatic doctrine is independent of metaphysical theories in the sense that it asks merely what would verify the cognitive judgment, and takes the correct answer to that question . . . to exhibit the meaning of 'knowledge' and the distinction of knowledge from error."[106]

The point on which Lewis's theory of empirical knowledge differed most sharply from that of the Positivists was the status of values. But are values objective? There are, he noted, two meanings of objective—the agreement of others, or Community, and verification by future experience, or veracity.[107] Veracity, he declares, is the better criterion because of the variability of other people. Yet Lewis is worried about the alleged lack of community regarding values, a charge he regards as spurious. He argues that what leads people to believe there is less community regarding values is the fact that, as he had detailed in *Mind and the World Order*, our concepts and language of nonvalue predications are designed to achieve agreement despite interpersonal differences in the given, and the fact that values have a closer connection with action than do other predicates, "making it more important for the individual to insist on his own evaluations."[108] Lewis then argues that in a given experience the value and nonvalue qualia are given together and are only separable by abstraction. As given, the agreeableness and the color are part of one item of experience and are equally presentations.

Community is not determined by inspecting another's experience, but by the pattern of relationships in which the particular experience stands— just as he had argued in *Mind and the World Order*. The degree of community attained is probably overestimated because of our need for cooperation.[109]

Further, "the names of non-value characters come predominantly to denote, not some quale by which the individual identifies that character in his experience, but a *stable pattern of relations* in which that quale is reliably to be found." Thus, "red" comes to be defined, not by "looks red" but by a certain "range of frequencies of vibratory motion."[110] Even colorblind people come to agree on such a use of "red." This method of definition permits the development of community with respect to such predicates much more fully than identification by qualia. Such scientific definitions allow cooperation and justly deserve praise, but they do not change the fact that "in the end, we must all live in whatever world our experience discloses."[111] Science deals with means; values deal with ends, and ultimately ends are the more important.

There is, however, an important difference between the use of terms such as "red" and value terms. "There is a certain sense in which it may be said that the objective denotation of 'red' or 'colored' as property of an object rules its expressive denotation of a directly inspectable appearance."[112] Primarily, "red" is taken to refer to an objective property, and only secondarily to a quale. "In the case of value-terms, however, this relation of the objective to the expressive meaning is reversed; the expressive use of "good" rules its objective use."[113] "Good" or "agreeable" is taken to refer first to the felt quale and only then to the object. This fact justifies calling values subjective. But this characteristic of values does not impugn their verifiability or their shareability in community.

Lewis sums up his view as follows:

> The basic predications of value are expressive statements, formulating a positive mode of the value-quality of given experience. These are true or false, but with respect to them there can be no error, and verification is not pertinent to them. Most predications of value, however . . . are judgments of the objective property of some kind of thing . . . the judgment that the thing has value or is valuable is implicit prediction of certain specific qualia as capable of being realized in direct experience under certain conditions. Such value-judgments, like other judgments, are verifiable and are a form of knowledge.[114]

The parallel to nonvalue properties could not be clearer. By 1939, Lewis had formulated the basic outlines of his value theory. It should be noted that in discussing community of value, Lewis makes no reference to the sort of confirmation procedures he had sketched in "Judgments of Value and Judgments of Fact."

A second issue on which Lewis disagreed with the Positivists was the question of other minds and the behaviorism that the Positivists claimed provided a solution. In a paper read at a meeting of the Eastern Division of the American Philosophical Association in 1940, and published as "Some Logical Consideration Concerning the Mental,"[115] Lewis dealt with the issue of our knowledge of mind. Instead of attempting a general definition of mind, he focuses on the content of consciousness as an essential characteristic of mind, and asserts:

> It is one such essential feature of what the word "mind" means that minds are private; that one's own mind is something with which one is directly acquainted—nothing more so—but that the mind of another is something which one is unable directly to inspect.[116]

If privacy is thus granted to be an essential characteristic of mind, one can rule out behavioristic and brain-state theories as irrelevant. We have no direct acquaintance with our brain states, and mental states are not the same as behavior. Such a view of mind does, however, raise the question of the existence of other minds in a very clear way.

Lewis focuses first on the question of our knowledge of our own minds. Some terms, he says, refer to what is presented to our minds in experience—to appearances or data. Such use of terms he labels as having "phenomenal meaning." But terms are also used to refer to things that, though they may appear, are those things to which appearances are attributable—in other words, physical objects. Phenomena of consciousness, Lewis holds, are of the former class; "when given, [they] are entities whose identity and character it is impossible to mistake,"[117] though language may fail to express what is intended. To the latter class belong the brain states or behaviors of psychologists, and of Logical Positivists. The behaviorists and physiological psychologists sometimes talk as if the phenomena of consciousness did not exist, but Lewis considers such a view absurd. The behaviorist view, and the physiological one, are analogous to the definition of a specific pitch as "harmonic motion within a certain range of frequencies." Such a correlation of pitch to rates of vibration may become so well confirmed that scientists define pitch by rates of vibration. This is what Lewis terms a "definition by description"—a definition "by reference to some non-essential character but one uniformly found present in all actual cases of the thing in question and found absent in all other cases which are actual."[118] Examples would be "Man is the animal that laughs" and "Men are featherless bipeds." What distinguishes such definition by description is that the relation of definiens to definiendum must be established by induction, and cannot be established by logical analysis alone. Such definitions may suffice with respect to existing things, but not when all thinkable things are included. But the fact that definitions by description must be established by induction shows that they must relate two independently specifiable things. Hence, if there were no independently specifiable phenomena of consciousness, they could not be correlated with brain states or behavior. Furthermore, no such correlations strong enough to serve as definitions by description of the phenomena of consciousness have ever been found. For in a definition, "If we know what we mean by 'A' and if what we mean by 'A' is expressed by 'XYZ,' then it could not conceivably happen that XYZ should be determined as present but there could be rational doubt whether what is presented is A."[119] Behavioristic and brain-state definitions of the mental cannot meet this test.

Lewis then turns to other minds.

> All of us who earlier were inclined to say that unverifiable statements are meaningless—and I include myself—have since learned to be more careful. This dictum is unclear; and in the most readily suggested interpretation of it, is too sweeping to be plausible. Also, the main point here does not have to do with verification at all. With empiricists in general and pragmatists in particular, such reference to verifiability as essential to meaning is only a roundabout way of pointing out that unless you are somehow prepared to recognize the factuality you assert, in case that factuality should be, or could be, presented to you, your verbal expression is not a matter-of-fact statement because it affirms nothing intelligible.[120]

Lewis asserts that belief in other minds meets this requirement. So far as *meaning* is concerned, we can envisage the conscious experience of another "by empathy, in terms of our own." That is, we can envisage what that experience would be in terms of our own experience, and for the statement to be meaningful that is enough. But:

> We significantly believe in other minds than our own, but we cannot *know* that such exist. This belief is a postulate. At least I should have said this earlier; and did say it. But I now think this statement was a concession to an over-rigorous conception of what deserves the name of "knowledge."[121]

Lewis now argues that verification may be "indirect" or "incomplete"; it may be a "confirmation" as probable, as opposed to a decisive verification.

> It may be that there is no fundamental difference, by reference to its verifiability, between the belief in other minds and the belief, for example, in ultra-violet rays or in electrons. It might even be that the belief in other minds, though always incompletely verified and incapable of becoming otherwise, is supported by inductive evidence so extensive as to be better confirmed than some of the accepted theses of physical science.[122]

Lewis's argument here is a development of the view he put forward in "Judgments of Value and Judgments of Fact." In the earlier paper, Lewis held that the analogies among human beings were so extensive that like mental states might be inferable from like behavior. Although the argument is not spelled out, Lewis seems to have meant that the hypothesis that "S has mental state X" could be confirmed if we have the further hypothesis "If S has mental state X and if conditions C_1, C_2, . . . C_n are met, then S will exhibit behavior Y," and if in fact the conditions C_1, C_2, . . . C_n are met and S does exhibit behavior Y. Lewis has now abandoned that claim because "no one could recognize these specificities of his own mentality in terms of behavior, because neither he nor anyone else can state precisely what character of behavior is unexceptionally present when there is pain or heard music or the seeing of green, and unexceptionally absent when there is not this specific mode of consciousness."[123] Lewis's argument now is that the analogies among people are so great as to justify empathetic understanding—that I am justified in believing that your toothache feels like mine. This is not, it should be emphasized, a blind faith in empathy; it is rather an inference of the form "Since people exhibit so many analogies of all sorts—physical, behavioral, linguistic, etc.,—it is reasonable to believe that if I experience X under conditions C_1 . . . C_n, others will have the same (or similar?) experiences under those conditions." Since if I burn my hand, I experience pain, I am justified in assuming that if you burn your hand, you will experience a pain similar to mine. This is not the sort of argument that can confirm a hypothesis; it is rather what Peirce called a hypothetical argument[124] in which from a large number of observed similarities among the members of some set of things we infer other non-observable similarities. As in the earlier piece, the argument is inadequately developed; people may have similar experiences when burned, but not when kissed. But Lewis is still grappling with the problem and seeking a basis for knowledge of other minds. To call this empathetic understanding is a rather peculiar choice of words, since "empathy" usually connotes an identification of one's self with another. What Lewis is actually proposing is a hypothetical understanding that is clearly subject to review in cases of incongruent behavior rather than some sort of intuitive insight or immediate grasp of the experiences of another. That the argument furnishes some support for the conclusion is obvious; that it furnishes adequate support is not so clear.

C. I. Lewis—Early Years. Courtesy of Andrew Lewis.

Mabel Maxwell Graves, High School Graduation Picture. Courtesy of Andrew Lewis.

Josiah Royce, 1887. Courtesy of the Harvard University Archives.

William James, ca. 1900. Courtesy of the Harvard University Archives.

Ralph Barton Perry, n.d. Courtesy of the Harvard University Archives.

Alfred North Whitehead, n.d. Courtesy of the Harvard University Archives.

Bertrand Russell in 1916. Courtesy of the William Ready Division of Archives and Research Collections, McMaster University Library.

Mabel, Irving, and C. I. Lewis at Berkeley. Courtesy of Andrew Lewis.

Peggy Lewis—shortly before her death. Courtesy of Andrew Lewis.

Moritz Schlick, 1930s. Courtesy of the Minnesota Center for Philosophy of Science.

Rudolph Carnap, 1920s. Courtesy of Archives of Scientific Philosophy, Special Collections, University of Pittsburgh.

Hans Reichenbach, 1935. Courtesy of Maria Reichenbach.

Lt. David Lewis. Courtesy of Andrew Lewis.

PVT. Andrew Lewis. Courtesy of Andrew Lewis.

C. I. Lewis—Middle Years. Courtesy of Andrew Lewis.

Mabel Lewis—about 1950. Courtesy of Andrew Lewis.

C. I. Lewis—1960s. Courtesy of Andrew Lewis.

W. V. Quine, 1970. Courtesy of the Harvard University Archives.

Biographical Note IV

War Years

On December 7, 1941, the Lewises's lives, like those of so many others, were interrupted by war.[1] Although Lewis had opposed intervention in the European war, he was a fervent patriot and the attack on Pearl Harbor and the German declaration of war settled all questions of our involvement. Lewis himself was too old to serve, but his sons were not. The oldest son, David, had attended Lexington public schools. Because of his interest in the theater, he began his college career at the University of North Carolina, which had an outstanding drama school, but after a year transferred to Berkeley where he finished his college education. A dynamic and handsome man, he had gone to work for Texaco and was moving up rapidly in the company in what promised to be a very successful business career when the war intervened. He went into the artillery, as his father had, and taught in the artillery school, before being sent to Okinawa as a battery officer. At that point the Okinawa campaign was over and the island was being used to prepare for the invasion of Japan. When the atomic bomb ended the war, it appeared that he had been spared, but he had not. Soon after returning to the United States, he began having severe headaches. He was hospitalized and diagnosed with encephalitis, a disease endemic to Okinawa. The physician in charge of the case told the Lewis family that the case was hopeless, but, as his brother recalled, "my mother would not let him die. . . . My mother went out and sat in his room almost day and night and spooned soup into him and sort of dragged him back by the ankle."[2] Very slowly, David recovered. But then he suffered a seizure, which resulted in a fractured hip. The surgery to repair the hip was poorly performed; the pin inserted into the hip was bent, and thereafter he could walk only with great difficulty and pain. David spent the rest of his life in a wheelchair. He was not physically able to resume work and, since he received a full disability from the army, he did not have to. He lived out his life in California, dying at the age of sixty-five.[3]

The younger son, Andrew, finished Exeter, started Harvard, and then joined the infantry where he became a machine gunner in the 86th Division. Fortunately for him, the 86th did not see combat until the war in Europe was nearly over, but once in action they went through some heavy fighting; in one day a third of Andrew's company was lost. Because this division did not have a great deal of combat experience, it was sent to the Pacific to prepare for the invasion of Japan. As Andrew recalled, "Then they dropped the big bomb and essentially, I think, saved my life. A machine gunner is not a good thing to be. [Pause] It's a good thing, it's not a healthy thing."[4] This reaction to the use of the atomic bomb was universal among the men scheduled for the invasion. As Andrew remarked of the Japanese awaiting the invasion, "they would not have been hospitable."[5] Given the fact that the army estimated American casualties in the planned invasion at one million, it is very likely that the bomb saved the lives of both Lewis brothers.

The impact of these events on Lewis and his wife can only be imagined. Lewis was extremely proud of his sons' military performances. But the cost was terrible. Of their four children, one died of diphtheria, one died of leukemia, and one was crippled for life by encephalitis and botched surgery. Granting the state of medicine at the time, this was still a terrible toll. Andrew was the only one to survive whole. After finishing Harvard, he worked briefly for the Harvard administration as a scholarship and financial aid officer, worked briefly in educational broadcasting, then became a writer for the television program "Omnibus," and then a writer of film scripts. His film *Klute* won an Oscar for Jane Fonda and an Oscar nomination for the film itself.[6]

Through the 1940s, Lewis taught Ethics and the Social Order and the Theory of Knowledge. From 1940 through 1944, he taught formal logic. He gave the course on Kant from 1940 to 1948, and again in 1950, and Kantian Philosophy from 1940 to 1943. He also taught Ethics from 1940 through 1943 and from 1945 through 1950, and in 1948 taught a course on the Theory of Meaning. In 1949 and 1950, he taught a class on Epistemology. And, of course, he did his stint teaching service courses. He also served as department chairman from 1943 through 1947.[7] But, in 1948, Lewis reached the mandatory retirement age of sixty-five. James Conant, then president of Harvard, asked Lewis to stay on for an additional five years. This was a very unusual request and showed the respect in which Lewis was held by the university. He was greatly pleased by the compliment and agreed. Harvard further showed its appreciation by appointing him Edgar Pierce Professor of Philosophy—a chair that had been held by Perry and subsequently by Quine.[8]

The recognition of Lewis's work was not confined to Harvard. He received an honorary degree from the University of Chicago, among others, and was awarded the Nicholas Murray Butler Medal by Columbia University. In 1944, he was chosen as the seventh Carus lecturer, and—perhaps most gratifying—Harvard raised his salary to $12,000, which for that time was exceptional. Lewis was elected to membership in the American Philosophical Society as well as several other prestigious organizations.[9] Mabel was extremely proud of Lewis's accomplishments and made sure her sons understood that their father was an important man.

During the war, with the children grown, Mabel had become increasingly involved in volunteer activities. She had joined the Unitarian church and was active in its social service organization. Like women the country over, she sewed for the Red Cross. She also became involved in the support of the Baldwinville Hospital for handicapped children, and helped to organize a summer camp for diabetic boys. She worked with the Florence Crittenden Circle in its efforts to help adolescent girls. But some of her activities had a political aspect. She became a crusader for birth control in a state where the law prohibited the sale of contraceptives. She also championed the cause of migrant laborers, and even campaigned to improve the conditions in which prisoners of war were housed.[10] Thus, Mabel made a fulfilling and active life for herself. These activities were very typical of those of energetic middle-class women of that time.

The war, with its gasoline and rubber rationing, curtailed the Lewises's motor trips, but they resumed after the war. With David in California, they had an additional reason for these cross-country ventures, but they enjoyed traveling and seeing new sights. Lewis continued his photography, at which he had become quite expert. But, interestingly, the Lewises's travels were confined to the United States. Although Lewis was invited to Oxford, and later received other foreign invitations, he never went, to his wife's disappointment. Why I do not know, but it suggests a certain provincialism that is surprising in one who enjoyed travel and exploration as much as he did.

In July 1948, Lewis set down some remarkable reflections that reveal a good deal about his personal values.

> The individual farmer in the nineteenth century probably represents something near to the limit of the level of human life which could be achieved by individual sharing in a store of social learning without serious loss of individual power to satisfy the individual needs and interests.

That period, in the American agrarian community probably represents the high-water mark in approximation to the ideal of "individualism" in the whole of human history; past, present and future.[11]

The farmer, Lewis remarked, "could come close to doing *anything* necessary to maintain himself and his family."[12] Of course, Lewis recognized that this was an exaggeration, and he then detailed some of the things the farmer could not do for himself, but his point is that the farmer was nearly self-sufficient.

"Those of us with the background of such agricultural living" may be inclined to doubt "whether the general level of life has really been raised above that of our childhood memory."[13] One can almost hear his Uncle Will applauding in the background. But Lewis admits that it has, noting particularly the pleasures of more specialized work. The individualism and liberty of the earlier era had great appeal to Lewis, and he raised the question of whether such an era of individual freedom could ever come again. If so, the hope for it lies in technological advance that, by making material goods plentiful and cheap for all with less work, would remove the need for social controls. Should this be possible, Lewis believed the greatest period of "stress and strain upon the native endowment of humans" will be in the next millennium. The "great problem" will be the danger of wars "instigated by political leaders who need them as an alibis for the demagogic promises they have made, in order to maintain themselves in power, and find that they cannot fulfil."[14] If we can survive that danger,

> the hope is that those too stupid to acquire the technological skills essential for the most economical production of material goods, and otherwise of too low-grade mentality to find satisfaction in non-material goods will drink themselves to death or fail, through sex-perversions, to reproduce their kind. Social interference with the natural reproductivity of those who are too stupid to be educable to this level, will probably be necessary. The types which, it must be hoped, will be obsolescent, are not racial, but they show too high a correlation with race to hope that what is desirable can be achieved without elimination of the biologically predominant strains of some races—those which, for one or another reason presently survive without having been exposed for more than a short period to the stresses and strains of a high-level civilization, and which might now persist without biological alteration because of those social forces of present civilization which prevent much working of "natural selection."[15]

Civilization cannot be maintained, Lewis thought, if the benefits of technology and medical science are extended to those with high birthrates and those who could not achieve such a level on their own. It is obvious who Lewis is talking about here, and one should bear in mind that after World War II questions of decolonization and the development of so-called underdeveloped countries were prominent. Thus, one notes that the racist and eugenicist strains evident in Lewis's early writings are still there. Lewis did not believe in equalitarianism.

> I find such attitudes in myself. I believe that Anglo-Saxons are intrinsically of higher worth than Australian aborigines, that people of high IQ are, by and large, better people than morons. . . . I would suggest, however, that the valid thought herein contained is not to be expressed in any dictum of equality; but rather in the recognition that the moral claim of any other sentient being on us is *absolute*.[16]

The intrinsic worth of conscious beings Lewis held to be their capacity to realize the good in their own persons—to experience what is good as being good.[17] Thus, Lewis's prejudices were offset by his belief in the Law of Compassion and did not lead to the consequences one might have expected. Equal treatment was essential, not because all people were equal, but because all had equal moral claims.

Lewis is not a Social Darwinist in any ordinary sense; he clearly does not see economic competition as the social form of natural selection, as many Social Darwinists did. He is no advocate of unrestricted competition, and his panacea of plentiful goods for all owes something at least to his early radicalism. But, at the same time, he regards the operation of natural selection on human populations as necessary and desirable, and is willing to employ eugenicist means to help it along. The eugenicism and racism of the Progressivism of his youth are still part of his overall view.

8

The AKV

As the 1930s ended, Lewis was working on a number of related problems—verification and confirmation, the status of expressive statements of the given, valuation, and our knowledge of other minds. In his writings on all of these subjects, he was reacting, usually explicitly, to the challenge posed by the Positivists. But he had yet to meet the most critical challenge that they posed. When Lewis said in his 1933 presidential address to the APA that the central question of philosophy had changed from "How do you know?" to "What do you mean?," he was acknowledging that the Positivists had changed the terms of philosophic debate. It was not that Lewis had ever been unconcerned with meaning; his intensional logic was based on it, and in *Mind and the World Order* he had discussed meaning at length. But Lewis had not formulated his theory of meaning in a precise way, and, as noted earlier, there were a number of questions he had yet to answer. Faced with the rigor and precision of the Positivist analysis, Lewis needed to develop and codify his own ideas. And, in 1940, this became even more urgent.

Lewis regarded the distinction between analytic and synthetic statements as fundamental. In 1936, responding to an attack on the distinction by Leonard,[1] Lewis had used the following argument. Suppose there were no distinction between analytic and synthetic propositions. Then analytic propositions must be probable as empirical propositions are. But, referring to his treatment of probability in *Mind and the World Order*, Lewis says that to say "X is Y" is probable is to say

(1)   On data R, "X is Y" has probability a/b.

This, Lewis says, is an analytic statement; the statements constituting R are synthetic, but the assertion (1) is analytic. Suppose it were not. Then we should have to say that

On data M, the statement "On data R, 'X is Y'
has probability a/b" has probability c/d.

If this statement too is only probable, we will have a regress, with the result that all probability statements will become meaningless, destroying any claims for the truth of both analytic and synthetic statements and so all knowledge. Thus, in Lewis's view, analytic statements are essential to empirical knowledge.

But, by the early 1940s, a new and more formidable attack on the analytic–synthetic distinction arose. Quine had become critical of certain aspects of Carnap's work, particularly the division between the analytic and the synthetic. In 1940–1941, Carnap, Tarski, Russell, and Quine were all at Harvard, and the issue was hotly debated. Carnap later recalled a lecture he gave to a group of faculty members.

> My main thesis was that mathematics had no factual content and, there-
> fore, is not in need of empirical confirmation, but that it nevertheless has
> a very important function in empirical science as an instrument of
> deduction. I thought that this was an old story and at any rate a purely
> academic question. But to my great surprise, the audience responded
> with vehement emotions. Even before I had finished my lecture, excited
> objections were raised. Afterwards we had a long and heated discussion
> in which several people often talked at the same time. . . . I thought: are
> we now back with John Stuart Mill? The attacks by Tarski and Quine
> were even more spirited, but also more disconcerting. Many others
> rejected my view.[2]

Thus, the great debate over analyticity was already under way. Whether or not Lewis was present at Carnap's lecture, he could not have avoided knowing what was going on. Carnap was teaching an "Introduction to Analytic Philosophy," a "Seminar on Logic," and "Principles of Empiricism" at Harvard that year. Philip Frank was teaching "Introduction to the Philosophy of Physical Science," and Bertrand Russell gave a "Seminar in Semantics."[3] In this atmosphere, the dispute over the analytic–synthetic distinction was no secret. Like Carnap, Lewis believed the analytic–synthetic distinction fun-damental. As was typical of him, he did not debate the issue publicly, but turned to the task of formulating a theory of meaning that would support the distinction.

Lewis first presented his theory in a paper entitled "The Modes of Meaning" in PPR.[4] But his full exposition of it did not appear until 1946. In 1945, Lewis delivered the Carus Lectures at Berkeley. With considerable amplification, these were published the next year as *An Analysis of Knowledge and Valuation*, a book that soon became known as the AKV. This was Lewis's major work, published when he was sixty-three and nearing retirement. But it was less a summation of his life's work than the next step he had marked out for his career. In 1932, having finished his work in logic, Lewis set out to write a book on ethics. But, as he records in the preface to the AKV, he found that to deal with ethics he had first to deal with valuation, and to do that he had to deal with empirical knowledge. Although Lewis had already written a book on epistemology—*Mind and the World Order*—he had not dealt with valuation in it. To extend his theory of empirical knowledge to include values required revisions. Furthermore, Lewis had to deal with the Positivist attack on the cognitive status of value statements. If he was to show that valuations were a form of empirical knowledge, he had to demonstrate that value statements were verifiable just as nonvaluational statements were. Believing that the Positivist doctrine was not only wrong but socially destructive, Lewis determined to provide a full answer to it. Accordingly, the work on ethics was postponed, and the AKV is really a prolegomenon to ethics. Book III deals with valuation and Book II with empirical knowledge. "To make it clear that empiricism in epistemology and naturalism in ethics do not imply such relativism and cynicism has been one main objective in the writing of this book."[5] This was the first time, so far as I know, that Lewis described his ethical position as "naturalism," and marks how far he had moved from his early polemics against it.

Book I of the AKV is entitled "Meaning and Analytic Truth." Here Lewis presents his new theory of meaning in detail, and uses it to support the analytic–synthetic distinction.

> The attempt to delineate that fundamental sense of 'meaning' in which meanings can be neither manipulated nor altered, while at the same time acknowledging the scope and importance of choice with respect to our ways of classifying and of convention in the modes of linguistic symbolism represents a major motive for including there the contents of Book I.[6]

But the theory of meaning underlies much more than the defense of analyticity. In Book II, Lewis recasts his theory of empirical knowledge in terms of the new theory; the confirmation of empirical statements depends on the fact that their meaning (in one sense of meaning) lies in statements referring to immediate experience. In fact, Books II and III are both based on the theory of meaning developed in Book I.

Lewis's targets in the AKV were the Positivist and the Quineans. As was his custom, Lewis does not name names; he refers to his opponents only as "conventionalists," "relativists," "subjectivists," and particularly "nominalists." In keeping with his own view of how such controversies should be conducted, he simply lays out his own position in elaborate detail and deals with the "objections" he thought would be raised against it. His criticism of nominalism for identifying meaning with linguistic convention, however, is pointed, if restrained. But, on occasion, the passion underlying his efforts shows through, as when he writes that relativism and subjectivism are "an expression of that immoralism and that repudiation of principle which is a major threat to all our civilization."[7]

In the introductory section, Lewis stresses the relation among knowledge, action, and value that characterizes pragmatism.

> The primary and pervasive significance of knowledge lies in its guidance of action: knowing is for the sake of doing. And action, obviously, is rooted in evaluation. For a being which did not assign comparative values, deliberate action would be pointless; and for one which did not know, it would be impossible.[8]

The "general formula" of perceptual knowledge is: "Such and such being given, if I act so and so, then the sequent experience will include this or that (specified) eventuality."[9] What is given is some sense presentation that serves as a sign of future sense presentations, whose realization is contingent on our action. Lewis particularly stresses the importance of action in this formula. For a being incapable of action, experience would be merely a series of appearances. Such a being could have no concept of reality beyond this passing show. "Epistemologically the possible is, thus, the antecedent to the real." Possible experience exists only for an active being for whom what will be experienced depends on what it does.

> For us, the surface of the presented is set against that immensely deep and wide and pervasive background of "the rest of reality," which is not now experienced and mostly will not be. It is so set because, being active, our experience could proceed from here and now in various ways which are equally genuine alternatives. The world contains not only what *is* felt and what in fact *will* be given in experience but also all that *could be*.[10]

Because we are not only active but free to act as we choose, the contrasts between appearance and reality, self and other, fact and illusion, are possible at all. "At the root, the objectively actual is the verifiable; and the verifiable is that the predictable experience of which can be realized if the appropriate routine of verifying activity be adopted. Without this sense of action, no sense of a world of things beyond experience could arise."[11]

By "action" Lewis means something done by us with the anticipation of a desired outcome. This eliminates involuntary behavior from the category of action. But it includes habitual behavior so long as it is directed toward a valued end and is corrigible. The question "Why did you do that?" asks for a justification rather than a causal explanation; to ask for the latter makes sense only when what is done is not corrigible. It is action that is corrigible for which we hold ourselves, and are held, responsible. By "knowledge" Lewis means an "assertive state of mind" that intends something beyond itself, that claims truth and so is subject to appraisal as correct or incorrect, and that is justified by some ground. Knowledge is thus normative. "Epistemology is not psychological description of such mental states, but is critique of their cognitive claim"[12]—that is, of their claims to truth and justification. Thus, knowledge and action both involve valuation; one cannot make sense of the former without invoking the latter.

Although empirical knowledge—knowledge of the world—is the prototypical form of knowledge, Lewis notes that there are two types of statements that are not constituents of empirical knowledge in the usual sense, but have cognitive functions. "We shall recognize," Lewis says,

> three types of apprehension: (1) of directly given data of sense (not excluding the illusory); (2) of what is not thus given but is empirically verifiable or confirmable; (3) of what is, implicitly or explicitly, contained in or entailed by meanings.[13]

The first does not constitute knowledge because it cannot be in error, although the expression of this content might be regarded as subject to *linguistic* correctness or incorrectness. But, Lewis says, "Any formulation of it (if statements of the given, merely as such, are to be recognized) will be independent, for its truth, of anything further and not contained in just this given experience itself."[14] Thus, Lewis seems here to ascribe certainty to both the awareness of the given and to statements reporting the given. The second and third types of apprehension are included as knowledge. Empirical statements, which are the second type, are clearly subject to error, but so are statements of type three. This does *not* mean that they are subject to empirical confirmation, but that we may make errors about our own meanings and their relations. But "it is such knowledge, representing the explication of our own intended meanings, which is found in logic and the mathematical, and includes the analytically true in general."[15]

In Book I, Lewis presents his theory of meaning. There are, he says, two types of true statements—those true or false on the basis of empirical evidence, and those true or false by virtue of meaning. Lewis identifies analytic statements with a priori statements, since a statement can only be true or false a priori if it is true or false on the basis of meaning alone, and he identifies synthetic statements with a posteriori statements. He rejects the notion that there is no distinction between the analytic and the synthetic. He also rejects any division in kind between logical truths and other analytic statements.

Lewis defines a *term* as "an expression capable of naming or applying to a thing or things, of some kind."[16] He explicitly distinguishes naming from denoting. Denoting for Lewis means referring to an existing thing or things; naming includes reference to both existing and possible things. Thus, the term "unicorn" names a possible but not actual animal. This distinction is crucial for Lewis's theory of meaning. The theory is stated as follows.

(1) The *denotation* of a term is the class of all actual things to which the term applies.

(2) The *comprehension* of a term is the classification of all possible or consistently thinkable things to which the term would be correctly applicable.

(3) The *signification* of a term is that property in things the presence of which indicates that the term correctly applies, and the absence of which indicates that it does not apply.

(4) Formally considered, the *intension* of a term is to be identified with the conjunction of all other terms each of which must be applicable to anything to which the given term would be correctly applicable.[17]

The denotation is the class of actual or existent things to which the term is correctly applied. What a term denotes is usually said to be an existent that is included in the denotation. This ambiguity in the use of the term "denotes" is awkward, Lewis agrees, but harmless, although it means that what a singular term denotes is identical with the unit class that is its denotation. A term that denotes no existent has the null-class for its denotation.[18]

The comprehension of a term is the classification of all possible things to which the term is correctly applied. Lewis restricts "class" to refer to collections of existents, and uses "classification" to refer to the collection of all possible referents. Thus, the denotation is a subclass of the comprehension. The term "unicorn" has the null-class for its denotation because there are no actual unicorns, but since there could be such a beast, the comprehension of "unicorn" is not null. On the other hand, "round square" has both a null denotation and a null comprehension.

The connotation or intension of a term "is delimited by any correct definition of it." If any term "T" is such that whatever is nameable by "T" is also nameable by "A" and "B," and whatever is nameable by the compound term "A & B" is also nameable by "T," then "T" and "A & B" have the same intension. Lewis notes that traditionally an attribute required for the application of a term was said to be "of the essence" of the thing named. Lewis rejects the notion that things have essences, but he believes that things have properties that are essential to being named by a particular term. Such an attribute he calls the "signification" of the term. Thus, to be correctly termed a "square," something must be a closed plane figure with four equal sides and four right angles.

Lewis is careful here to clarify the relation of signification and intension. Signification refers to a property in objects; intension to terms. Thus, "man" signifies the property of animality whereas it connotes the term "animal." Further, Lewis says that the intension of a term represents "the meaning it expresses in the simplest and most frequent sense which is the original meaning of 'meaning'; that sense in which what we mean by 'A' is what we have in mind in using 'A,' and what is often times spoken of as the *concept of A*."[19] But Lewis is explicit in holding that the intension of a term is the conjunction of all those terms that must apply to whatever the given term applies to.

Abstract terms "name what some other term signifies." Thus, "roundness" names that attribute signified by "round thing." The signification of an abstract term is that which it names. Terms that are not abstract are concrete. A "singular term" is one whose intension "precludes application of it to more than one *actual* thing." The comprehension of a singular term "is the classification of *all* the things consistently thinkable as being the one and only member of that class."[20] Nonsingular terms are general.

Lewis then extends this analysis of the meaning of terms to the meaning of propositions by holding that all propositions are terms, as are propositional functions. A proposition, Lewis says, "is a term capable of signifying a state of affairs."[21] This is not an entirely new idea for Lewis; in his paper "Facts, Systems and the Unity of the World" in 1923, Lewis had taken propositions as signifying "facts" that were states of affairs. But now he gives a more extensive meaning to this view. In saying that a proposition is a term, Lewis identifies it with a participial phrase such as "Mary baking pies now" or "that Mary is baking pies now." This state of affairs may then be asserted—"Mary is baking pies now," questioned—"Is Mary baking pies now?," postulated—"Suppose that Mary is baking pies now," and so on. In other words, Lewis separates the proposition, which may be simply entertained, from the various uses to which the proposition may be put. This involves a rudimentary speech act theory of which Lewis would later make important use. And it also allows him to extend to propositions the theory of the meaning of terms. Usually Lewis attributes this theory of propositions to Sheffer, though here he also credits Charles Morris.[22] It should also be noted that the proposition "that Mary is baking pies now implies that Mary is baking" involves no confusion of use and mention; so much for that Quinean criticism.[23]

What then is the denotation of a proposition? When a term denotes a thing, it denotes the whole thing, not just the attributed character; hence, by Excluded Middle, one of every pair of mutually exclusive terms must apply to it. To carry out the analogy for the proposition, Lewis makes the denotation of the true proposition the actual world, and the denotation of the false proposition nothing. Thus, all true propositions denote the same thing, and all false propositions denote the same thing. The important extensional property of any proposition is simply its truth-value. Lewis is quite aware of the relation of his position to Frege's, and regards this as a further confirmation of his view.

The comprehension of a proposition includes "any consistently thinkable world which would incorporate the state of affairs it signifies"[24]—in other words, a classification of possible worlds. The connotation or intension of a proposition is whatever the proposition entails: "all deducible consequences of a proposition, taken together, exhibit the intension of it discursively." Two propositions have the same intension only if each is deducible from the other. Alternatively, the intension of a proposition comprises "whatever must be true of any possible world in order that this proposition should be true of or apply to it." It is then easy to define an analytic proposition as one true in every possible world, a self-contradictory proposition as one true in no possible world, and a synthetic proposition as a proposition true in some possible worlds. Equivalently, an analytic proposition can be defined as one having universal comprehension and zero intension, a self-contradictory proposition as one with zero comprehension and universal intension, and a synthetic proposition as one whose comprehension and intension are neither zero nor universal.[25]

In dealing with propositional functions, Lewis now introduces the notion of a statement function. "X is a man" is a statement function; "X being a man" is a propositional function. Substitution of a term or expression converts these into statements and propositions, respectively. Lewis notes that any propositional or statement function can be put in a form in which the variable becomes the subject of the predication. Recalling that any propositional function can be construed as having one subject, whether a single variable or an n-tuple, Lewis notes that "ϕx" can be given as "x" characterized by being a "φ." "The abstract sense of such a phrase—the cognate abstract term—is the name of the *characteristic* which predication of this phrase to anything attributes."[26]

The denotation of a function (propositional or statement) is the class of existents (individuals or *n*-ads) of which the function is truly predicable. The comprehension is the classification of consistently thinkable things characterized by the predicate. The intension "comprises all that attribution of this predicate to anything entails as also predicable to that thing." The signification is the property that anything must have in order that the predicate should apply to it.[27]

Lewis attacks the view that "logic should be, or at least could be, developed in terms of extensional meaning exclusively"—a view that he says has gained ground in the last fifty years. This view, which, Lewis says, "is about as wrong as anything could be" is based on two premises—that the fundamental sense of meaning is denoting, and

> Second, that all other facts which can be known and all other statements which can be assured are finally derivative, logically and epistemologically, from facts about individuals and singular statements which express these; and that no statement which, when properly construed, is a statement about an individual, can be true if the individual meant does not exist.[28]

The first premise Lewis rejects on the ground that names correctly apply to whatever a term *comprehends* and are not restricted to those things denoted by the term. The second premise is rejected on similar grounds.

> Things merely thought of can be named; and concerning anything thought of, and required by our manner of thinking of it to have certain essential characters, there is a truth which can be told—as well as any number of statements about it which would be false. If this were not so, then nobody could make a plan concerning the execution of which there could be doubt, or entertain any expectation in which he could conceivably be disappointed.[29]

Lewis points out that intensional meaning meets Leibniz's requirement that two expressions having the same meaning must be substitutable *salve veritate*, whereas extensional meaning does not. The claim that extensional meaning alone suffices for logic Lewis regards as refuted by these considerations.

Lewis asserts that meanings "must come before the linguistic expression of them"; after all, other things besides language can express meanings. In fact, "one might well think that words are only surrogates for presentational items of other sorts." Citing Peirce, Lewis says, "The genuine significance

of meaning is that in which A means B if A operates as representing or standing for B or as calling B to mind." The critical point here is that meaning is
prior to and independent of language. Language is one vehicle through which
meanings are expressed, but it is not the only such vehicle. Lewis does
believe that all meanings can be expressed in language, but the two are distinct, and the relation of language to meaning is conventional only. Nevertheless, since it is through language that meaning is communicated from
one mind to another, the ways in which meaning is expressed in language
must be analyzed.[30]

Lewis holds that a linguistic expression—defined as the association of
a verbal symbol with a fixed meaning—always means the same thing wherever it is used. This amounts to a denial of the notion that the meaning of
an expression can vary with the context in which the expression is used.
Lewis believes this notion is the result of confusing the various modes of
meaning. In some contexts, the truth of a statement may depend on the
extension, in others on the intension. Thus, for example, "all men are featherless bipeds" is true in extension but not in intension, whereas "Aphrodite
was beautiful" is true intensionally but not extensionally. But to support
his claim of invariable meaning, Lewis needs more than this.[31]

Lewis distinguishes elementary expressions from complex ones; elementary expressions have "no symbolized constituent, the intension of which is
a constituent of the intension of the expression in question." Complex
expressions are those not elementary. The point of this distinction is to
show how holophrastic meaning depends on the meanings of elementary
expressions. But, to do this, Lewis has to decide what elements of a sentence
have meaning. His answer is that all do, including syncategorematic words.
The view that the latter do not have meaning Lewis attributes to a failure to
recognize the variety of things that can be named. Further, if syncategorematic words have no meaning, how can they modify categorematic words
to produce new phrases? "All words," Lewis says, "are either substantives or
predicables." He then deals in turn with adjectives, verbs, adverbs, prepositions, and articles, arguing that each type has a definite meaning, which may
be relational as in the case of prepositions or attributive such as adjectives. It
follows that all words have all four modes of meaning. This frees Lewis to deal
with the meaning of complex expressions without having to bother with a
class of meaningless constituents.[32]

The meaning of a complex expression is the resultant of the meanings of
its elementary constituents and the syntax that combines them. In such a
complex expression, the elementary constituents do not modify each other
but modify the complex expression itself. Thus, in "the kennel where
Harry's dog sleeps," each word contributes a fixed meaning to the whole,

and only so can the whole have a fixed meaning. What Lewis is after here is a way of explaining the meaning of analytic and contradictory statements—that is, those with zero or universal intensions. Lewis does this by defining two expressions as analytically comparable if

> (1) at least one of the two is elementary and they have the same intension, which is neither zero nor universal; or (2) if, both being complex, they can be so marked off or analysed into symbolized contents that (a) for every constituent distinguished in one there is a corresponding constituent of the other which has the same intension, (b) no constituent distinguished in either expression has zero intension or universal intension, and (c) the syntactic order of the corresponding constituents is the same in both, or can be made the same without altering the intension of either whole expression.[33]

He can then define synonymy as "two expressions are synonymous if and only if (1) they have the same intension and that intension is neither zero nor universal, or (2) their intensions being zero or universal, they are analytically comparable."[34] By distinguishing between the analytic meaning of a complex expression and it holophrastic meaning, Lewis is able to avoid the consequence that all analytic propositions have the same meaning. For although their holophrastic intensions may be zero or universal, their analytic meanings are different.

Lewis summarizes this discussion by asserting his commitment to analyticity: "Analytic truth is a priori, incapable either of proof or disproof by any empirical fact or set of such observable facts. Analytic truth and empirical truth can have no effect upon each other."[35]

Lewis then considers the question of whether or not analytic statements rest on linguistic conventions. "Every analytic statement is such as can be assured, finally, on grounds which include nothing beyond our accepted definitions and the principles of logic,"[36] Lewis asserts. And since the principles of logic themselves are certified by definitions, it is clear that analytic statements rest on definitions. But are definitions matters of convention? Lewis's answer is that while language is a matter of conventions, meanings are not. To develop this point, he turns to an analysis of definition. Definitions specify the meanings of expressions in the sense of intensional meaning and, since intensions determine both comprehension and signification, three of the four modes of meaning are thereby fixed. But definitions cannot specify denotation, since denotation depends on questions of fact.

There are, Lewis says, three types of definitions: (1) symbolic conventions, (2) dictionary definitions, and (3) explicative definitions. Lewis claims that symbolic conventions and dictionary definitions are not analytic statements. This can be made clear by using the following notation. The word spelled c-a-t is used to name an animal. To name the word so used, Lewis puts it in single quotes; thus 'cat' is used to name the word spelled c-a-t. To refer to the symbol used as a word, Lewis uses French quotes; thus, <<cat>> names the symbol 'cat' that names the term used to refer to cats. A symbolic convention is hortatory; it says, in effect, "Let us use <<A>> as an abbreviation for <<BC>>." This is obviously not an analytic statement. Dictionary definitions of the form "<<A>> symbolizes the meaning symbolized by 'BC'" are empirical statements about the use of words, and are subject to verification or falsification by observation. This is shown by the fact that dictionary definitions can be in error if the lexicographer makes a mistake. Explicative definitions of the form " 'A' has the same meaning as 'BC' " are analytic statements; they are statements of relations among meanings and meanings are what they are and their relations are fixed, regardless of linguistic conventions.

> One may use the symbols <<birds>> and <<bipeds>> as one chooses, but having chosen the meanings usually assigned, one can not then alter the analytic truth of "all birds are bipeds" any more than one can create a biped with four legs, or alter the orbit of Mercury by calling it 'Neptune.' The analytic relationships of meanings are determined by the meanings themselves, and the manner of such determination is beyond the reach of any linguistic convention.[37]

Having dealt with definition, Lewis then considers whether "analytic truth is a question of logic, a formal matter, a matter of *rules*." If explicative definitions are construed as rules, Lewis finds this unobjectionable, but he adds that the correctness of a definition depends on "a simple and direct observation that it adequately and accurately explicates the meaning in question." This appeal to direct apprehension of meaning cannot be avoided by arguing that definitions are conventional rules of language, for reasons already given. Nor can it be avoided by appeal to logical rules. "The only final test of the validity of logical rules, is the test of them as analytically true statements." Thus, any appeal to logic as a way of validating analytic statements is circular.[38] Logical theorems depend for their truth on the intensional meaning of the logical constants and on syntax; given those meanings, the theorems are analytic and independent of any question of fact. It is this fact about logic that accounts for its utility. Whenever we plan, or commit ourselves to some course of action, we reason about alternatives that are not actual—about possible states of affairs or possible worlds. "Logic must hold of whatever *could* be; and a logic whose assurance was confined to existential fact, would be of little or no service to any human being."[39] It is precisely because logic is analytic, and therefore true of all possible worlds, that it is useful.

But if all principles of logic are analytic, are all analytic statements principles of logic? The answer is no, but the decision as to which analytic statements belong to a logic is pragmatic. Instantiations of logical principles are not usually classed as logical principles; rather, we take as such principles only the most general statements that depend on the logical constants. Logic does not include the explication of meanings in general. The goal of logic is always to arrive at a

> sufficient critique of the consistency and validity of discourse and of thought; as a canon of inference. But if, on this principle, we look for any absolute distinction between analytic statements belonging to logic and those not so classified, we shall find that there is none: there is only a difference in the degree or the frequency of usefulness for purposes of attesting consistency and validity.[40]

This is Lewis's doctrine of the legitimacy of alternative logics. Depending on what set of logical constants we choose, we get different logics, and any choice among these is pragmatic.

Chapter 6 is the key chapter of Book I, because it is here that Lewis gives his theory of analytic truth. Lewis begins by spelling out his view that meaning is prior to language.

> The original determinations of analytic truth, and the final court of appeal with respect to it, cannot lie in linguistic usage, because meanings are not creatures of language but are antecedent, and the relations of meanings are not determined by our syntactic conventions but are determinative of the significance which our syntactic usages may have.[41]

Lewis believes that thought is conceptual—that is, involves meanings—before it is linguistic, and that thinking can be done independently of language. Conceptual thought can be expressed in language, but it could be otherwise expressed through different sorts of symbolic systems. There is no linguistic turn in Lewis.

Intensional meaning, Lewis says, has two aspects that are joined in language but that must be distinguished; "linguistic meaning" and "sense-meaning." By "linguistic meaning," Lewis means in the case of terms all the terms that would be correctly applied to anything to which the original term was applied, and in the case of statements all the statements deducible from the given statement.[42] The former he illustrates by the example of an Arabic dictionary. One who knew no Arabic could work out the entire pattern of linguistic relationships between a given term and the others in the dictionary with which it had any definitional relationship and yet not know what any of these terms *meant*. He would know the linguistic meaning of the term, but he would not know the sense-meaning. It is thus the sense-meaning that is the more important. This fact has been obscured, Lewis says, because "many logicians have of late been somewhat preoccupied with language"[43] and have therefore neglected sense meaning. By "many logicians," Lewis means Carnap and Quine, though others, of course, qualify.

Sense-meaning is "*a criterion in mind*, by reference to which one is able to apply or refuse to apply the expression in question in the case of presented, or imagined, things or situations."[44] What this means is a schema (in Kant's sense), "a rule or prescribed routine and an imagined result of it which will determine applicability of the expression in question."[45] By saying that the criterion is "in mind" Lewis meant "entertained in advance of instances of application which are pertinent"—that is, predesignated. Meaning, Lewis says, arises from "the sensuous criteria of recognition." We have in experience various presentations. Only when we can recognize these presentations and treat them as signs do we have meanings. Even animals without language must have this capacity since they can think. But, in order to do this, they must be able to imagine the presentation signified. "Only through the capacity called imagination could one have in mind, in advance, a workable criterion for applying or refusing to apply an expression under all circumstances of presentation."[46] Nominalistic objections that one cannot have a general image of a triangle are met by appropriating the Kantian notion of a schema. One cannot imagine a chiliagon, but one can imagine the procedure of counting the one thousand sides. The schema here is the means of verification that the presentation actually matches the imagined result. Verifiability requires a procedure by which a certain result is brought about in our experience. Such a procedure must be hypothetical— "*if* such and such conditions are satisfied, *then* the finding so and so will determine applicability or truth." But finding "so and so" can only serve as evidence if we already know what to look for and can recognize it when we see it. And that requires that we have in advance an image of what the "so and so" will be.[47]

Goodman once said that Lewis's problem was how language related to the world. Lewis's answer is sense-meaning. The relation of *words* to the world is entirely arbitrary. But the relation of *concepts* to the world is not arbitrary. Thinking involves classifying, identifying, accepting, and rejecting, and this is true for organisms without language as well as those who have it. Sense-meaning is what ties conceptual thought to presented experience; the only way we can know that something is a dog is by having "in mind" (in imagination) what presented experiences would be evidence that something is a dog, and knowing how to obtain those presented experiences in the given case. That, for Lewis, is the fundamental sense of meaning—"something which even a creature without the language habit would have to entertain in order to use his intelligence for the successful conduct of life."[48] Without the ability to recognize in experience what we conceive, intelligent activity would be impossible. This does not require language. When we bring language into the situation by assigning certain words to certain concepts, then we can use language to express the conceptual relations we have in mind. But it is not the relations among the words that are crucial; it is the relations among the concepts (meanings) and sensory experience that count.

None of this means that linguistic meaning is not important. Language can, if we like, be completely abstracted from questions of sense-meaning and treated as a formal calculus, whose relational patterns we can study. Logic has often been so treated and, for certain purposes, this is a legitimate procedure. But when logic is employed in the guidance of action, reference to sense must be restored. Furthermore, language not only facilitates the manipulation of meanings, but plays an essential role in communication. Given the fact that the workings of another's mind are not observable, language is our best medium for the exchange of ideas. However, it is far from perfect. Since interpersonal comparison of sensory experience is not possible, we cannot know that another's experiences are the same as our own, even when the same words are used. To the extent that the "schematism of application involves overt behavior, common meaning presumes community of test-routine," but we cannot be certain of identical results. "What may be thus in another's mind, we can only argue to from the observed similarity of his behavior, including his use of language, and from his observable similarities to us in other respects. Such a conclusion may be regarded as inductively justified if we are content to class as probable a conclusion from observed similarities to similarity in a respect which can never be directly observed. . . . Otherwise, we shall have to regard the supposition of such community as a postulate."[49] The problem of other minds is still very much with Lewis.

Lewis then comes to the point toward which the whole discussion has been aiming.

Insofar as the problems in which we are interested are epistemological ones, the final and finally important consideration is the fact that interpretation of meaning as linguistic significance can afford no sufficient clue to the determination of analytic truth, whereas interpretation of it as sense meaning may indicate an obvious source and criterion of it.[50]

Treating logic as an abstract formal system does nothing to explain analytic truth. Lewis attacks the idea that analytic truth is a matter of convention. Conventions are important; the relation of symbols to meanings is conventional. So are the rules of syntax. But analytic truth is a matter of relations among meanings, and those relations are not conventional. It is true, Lewis notes, that the holophrastic meaning of all analytic statements is the same, and this fact has been seen as suggesting the conventionalist view. But when analytic statements are viewed in terms of analytic meaning, they do not say the same things. "All cats are animals" asserts a relation between the intentional meaning of "cat" and that of "animal," and neither term has either zero or universal intension. Moreover, in a sense that is obvious, "all cats are animals" says something that is different from what "all squares are rectangles" says, and that difference cannot be ignored.

The answer to the problem of analytic truth is provided by sense-meaning. If "All squares are rectangles" had no criterion of application, we would never know whether or not it applied, whereas we do know that it always applies.

> What we know in advance of any particular occasion is that by virtue of the criterion of applicability of 'square' and of 'rectangle,' "not a square or else a rectangle" will always apply. We do not require examination of particular instances, because *a sort of experiment in imagination is sufficient.*[51]

Similarly, we know that "round square" never applies, because the sense-meaning of "round" excludes that of "square."

> This experiment in imagination—which we must be able to make if we know what we mean and can recognize squares and rectangles when we find them—is sufficient to insure that the intensional meaning of 'square' has to that of 'rectangle' the relation prescribed by 'all—are.'[52]

It is the "compatibility or incompatibility of sense-recognizable characters and the inclusion of one in another or its exclusion by another, [that] is thus the root of the matter."[53] Inclusion Lewis likens here to the relation of one plan to another: does one's plan to visit Chicago include a plan to visit Cleveland? Thus, the schema for verifying that something is a square also verifies that it is a rectangle; a figure cannot be the former without being the latter, and so the sense-meaning of "rectangle" is included in that of "square." Statements are analytic when the sense-meaning of one term includes that of another. This is a relation among *meanings*, not the linguistic expressions with which they are conventionally associated, and is unaffected if those conventions are changed. And relations among meanings are matters of fact that are as they are and are independent of any decision or convention of ours. Analytic statements do say something, even though their holophrastic meanings are the same; they do have applications—to all possible worlds—and they are true and a priori.[54]

Lewis's appeals to imagination and thought experiments are not likely to be popular today. But before they are dismissed, it would be well to consider them more closely. All empiricists agree that empirical statements must be tested against observation. But what is tested against what? If we are testing the acidity of a solution, we may use the statement: "If this solution is acid and I dip this piece of litmus paper in this solution, it will turn red." If we carry out the test, what precisely is compared with what? We cannot compare the color of the paper to the word "red"; they have nothing in common. We compare the color of the paper to our image of what the color should be. The word "image" here is not important; what matters is that we have a mental representation of the expected color, derived from prior experience, that we match to the color of the paper. That representation is an instance of what Lewis calls imagination, and his use of it is fully justified. For the question Lewis asks repeatedly is, if you do not have such a sensuous representation in mind when you do the test, how could you recognize the result when you get it? That question has to be answered, and Lewis's answer seems to be correct.

Further, Lewis offers a definition of the "inclusion" of one sense-meaning in another—something Quine and others have denied is possible. Consider the procedure by which one would determine that some figure is a square. Could that procedure be followed out without simultaneously determining that the figure is a rectangle? If not, the sense-meaning of "rectangle" is included in the sense-meaning of "square." Or consider "Every even number is a multiple of 2," or "Every dog is an animal," or "Every sister is a female." Could one determine that something was an even number, or a dog, or a sister without simultaneously determining that it was a multiple of two, or an animal, or a female, respectively? If not, why are the sense-meanings of the latter not included in the sense-meanings of the former? And would one really have to collect empirical data to make these determinations? Or would simply thinking about the sense-meaning be enough?

Oddly, Lewis gives no examples of analytic statements from mathematics or logic. Since he certainly held them to be analytic, one must ask how he would deal with a statement such as "$2 + 2 = 4$"? Lewis says that the test procedure or schema must be sense-recognizable.[55] What this includes is suggested by the following passage.

a sense-meaning, when precise and explicit, is a schema; a rule or prescribed routine and an imagined result of it which will determine applicability of the expression in question. We cannot adequately imagine a chiliagon, but we easily imagine counting the sides of a polygon and getting 1000 as the result.[56]

Since Lewis held a formalist view of mathematics, counting would represent a procedure for interpretation that is sense-recognizable. Presumably, "2" and "4" can then be defined by counting. If so, it would seem that a recursive procedure such as the standard definition of addition would also be sense-recognizable; thus, we could have

(a) $m + 1 = m'$
(b) $m + n' = (m + n)'$

where the prime stands for "successor of." If "equality" is then defined by counting, we would have

$$(1') + (1') = ((1')')'$$
$$\text{by (b)}\quad ((1') + 1)' = ((1')')'$$
$$\text{by (a)}\quad ((1')')' = ((1')')'$$

Clearly "2 + 2 = 4" is then analytic. This is, of course, speculative, but it seems likely that something of this sort is what Lewis had in mind.

Finally, without mentioning names, Lewis turns to the subject of ideal languages and the claim that whether a statement is analytic or synthetic is relative to the language system. We can construct formal languages so that some statements are derivable in one and not in another. But this, Lewis holds, is irrelevant to the question of what statements are analytic. Further, Lewis holds that ideal languages are created for some purpose, such as demonstrating sufficiency for mathematics.

> But the only kind of goal which makes this kind of game worth playing is one dictated by conformity of what is derivable from accepted definitions according to accepted rules with what are recognized as analytic truths, or some class of these. And the problem notably suggested by this reasonable intent of such procedure, is simply the question: *why are these results accepted as analytic truths, or some class of such?* That is the problem having epistemological importance. The language system as thus skilfully devised is itself acceptable or not by reference to some antecedent criterion. If we had no *other* way of determining analytic truth, antecedent to such efforts, the efforts themselves would be pointless. And if we have such antecedent tests of worth in a language system, the question of root importance, which has still to be answered, is what these criteria are and what is the source of such validity as they have.[57]

These comments, obviously directed at Carnap, remind one of Quine's later criticism of his method of defining analyticity.

What of Lewis's theory of meaning can still stand? The obvious objections are to his theory of propositional meaning. Lewis defined the intension of a proposition as all the propositions that are entailed by it. But as we have seen what is entailed by a proposition is either very little if the proposition is taken alone, or depends on what auxiliary propositions are assumed, so that the consequences of a proposition are relative to the choice of auxiliaries. Lewis knew this, yet he apparently failed to see its implications for his theory of intension. Different choices of auxiliaries can lead to contradictory consequences, for example, "that Mary is baking pies now and that Mary bakes only on hot days" implies "that this is a hot day," whereas "that Mary is baking pies now and that Mary bakes only on cold days" implies "that this is a cold day." Lewis's theory of propositional intension cannot survive this problem.

Lewis gave an alternative definition of propositional intension: the intension of a proposition is what must be so in any possible world in which that proposition is true. This does not mean that the intension is the set of possible worlds in which the proposition is true, but rather that its consequences in any possible world must be true. Hence, the problem of deriving consequences from the proposition is not evaded, and one is still faced with the fact that what consequences are derivable is relative to the choice of auxiliary hypotheses.

What about Lewis's theory of the meaning of terms? The intension of a term is all those terms that must apply to (be true of) whatever the given term is true of. So the intension of "dog" is all terms that must be true of whatever is correctly called a dog. The signification is then that property that anything must have for "dog" to be correctly applied to it. The problem is that Lewis is thinking in terms of the classical theory of genus and differentia. As Wittgenstein argued, and Rosch and her successors have shown, for at least many terms there is no one property shared by all and only those things to which a given term applies. In many cases, classification is by prototype, and similarity to a prototype is a multidimensional phenomenon. Further, prototypes for the same classification vary by time and place. In the United States, the prototypical bird is the robin; in Israel it is the sparrow; in ancient Egypt it was the duck. Classes defined by prototypes tend to be fuzzy sets, which means that a term like "bird" does not carry with it a clearly defined set of terms constituting its intension. Not all birds fly, but most do; does "flying creature" belong in the intension of "bird"? It is not clear how to answer that question. There are some characteristics that all birds do have, such as being bipeds, but that are not exclusive to birds.[58] It is, of course, anachronistic to criticize Lewis on these grounds since neither Wittgenstein nor Rosch had published when he wrote the AKV, but from a current perspective his theory of term signification and intension is inadequate.

But Lewis's theory of sense-meaning could be easily adapted to fit the prototype theory. In this case, the prototype would be the imagined result and the schema would contain the rules for comparing the given object to the prototype and determining if the similarities are sufficient to justify classification. Thus, Lewis could well argue that the procedure for determining whether or not something fits the prototype of "swan" would also show whether or not it fits the prototype for "bird," so the change to classification by prototype does not invalidate his claim that sense-meanings can establish analytic truth. There will be difficulties, no doubt, over borderline cases when the similarities to the prototype are not sufficient to provide a clear decision, but, for most cases, Lewis's theory would be sufficient.

There are other features of Lewis's theory of meaning that stand up. Lewis is right in holding that meaning relations obtain primarily among concepts and only secondarily among words. Contemporary cognitive science clearly demonstrates the role of mental representations in cognitive processes, and language acquisition studies show that language is used to express what is thought. In the present state of our ignorance concerning the actual processes of thought, it is not possible to provide an adequate theory of the relations among concepts, but one can expect with some confidence that this will be achieved. The problem, like so many others, has moved beyond philosophy into science, and the answers when they come will come from cognitive science, psychology, and linguistics. But the fact that there obviously are statements that are analytic in Lewis's sense, like those previously cited, strongly suggests that the notion of analyticity is not as vacuous as many philosophers now believe. Further, Lewis's theory of sense-meaning has the virtue of tying concepts to sense experience. "Imagination" is not a respectable term in modern philosophy. But if I am told "John's car is red" and I test this by looking at John's car, how would I know that the sense impression I receive is one of "red" if I did not already have in mind some image of something red? Propositions are in words; sense experience is not. The link between the word "red" and the experiences we call experiences of red has to be some mental association such that upon presentation of the word "red" I can visualize what a red thing would be—otherwise, as Lewis said, I could not recognize a red thing when I saw it. No terminological gymnastics can avoid this fact and Lewis was right to assert it.

Lewis was right to emphasize the importance of comprehension. It is simply the case that words are used to refer to possible but not actual entities. One need not here invoke golden mountains or present kings of France.

Every decision analysis poses a choice between possible outcomes of action, all but one of which will never be realized. Counterfactual statements play an essential role in life. One of Lewis's strengths was that he refused to ignore real problems just because his own theory was not wholly adequate for their solution—something that cannot be said of many of his successors. No theory of meaning that ignores possibility can be true of actual usage or behavior.

Lewis's theory of meaning, both of terms and propositions, must by today's standards be judged inadequate. Particularly with respect to analytic truth, Lewis made a heroic effort to establish the concept of a secure basis. In doing so, he gave the position he had taken in *Mind and the World Order* a more rigorous formulation that was designed to meet the growing attack on analyticity led by Quine. That his theory of sense-meaning captures some part of a criterion for analyticity seems clear from the examples to which it applies, but it is not clear that it captures the whole.

Book II, "Empirical Knowledge," opens with a prefatory chapter in which Lewis sketches out the theory that will follow. All knowledge, Lewis says, has empirical significance since it involves meanings that are sense-representable; this has been shown to be true of analytic statements in Book I, and the same will be shown for synthetic statements in Book II. Empirical or synthetic knowledge must rest on sensory experience; the problem is to explain how. There are, Lewis says, three types of statements that comprise empirical knowledge: "formulations of what is presently given in experience," terminating judgments, and nonterminating judgments.[59] Each type receives here a preliminary discussion that will be amplified in later chapters.

Statements of the first type, Lewis admits, pose problems. They are rare in ordinary discourse because "language is largely pre-empted to the assertion of objective realities and events."[60] Knowledge could get on without the formulation of statements about the given, but the analysis of knowledge cannot. If one says "This is red and round," the statement will normally be interpreted as a statement about objective properties of something, not about what is given in experience. To describe the given, Lewis suggests, locutions such as "looks like," "feels like," "tastes like," and so on must be used. This usage constitutes what Lewis calls an "*expressive* use" of language in contrast to the objective use. Lewis explains this as follows:

> It is essential to remember that in the statement or formulation of what is given . . . one uses language to *convey* this content, but what is *asserted* is what the language is intended to convey, not correctness of the language used. If, for example, one says, "I see a red round something," one assumes but does *not* assert "The words 'red' and 'round' correctly apply to something now given." This last is not a given fact of present experience but a generalization from past experience indicating the customary

use of English words. But one does not have to know English on order to see red; and that the word 'red' applies to this presently given appearance, is not a fact given in that experience.[61]

To call a presentation "red" or "round" involves a classification of the presentation, and any such classificatory judgment draws on past experience and is fallible. Lewis's dilemma is that he wants to indicate the character of the given without classifying it, but the only words available for the purpose are classificatory terms. He therefore tries to find a way to use these terms in a nonclassificatory way, and to do this he resorts to terms like "looks," "seems," and so on. Consider something red. There are innumerable shades of red, and no language contains separate terms for all of them. What is experienced is one such quale, or some combination of such qualia, that have been previously classified as red. The expressive statement "this looks red" means that "this"—the presentation—is a quale that has been classified as red. The expressive statement does not itself classify the qualia as red but assumes it, on the basis of prior classifications. The quale is directly given in experience; the expressive statement simply reports that, and the use of "looks," "seems," and so on indicates that the statement is to be understood in an expressive sense. One cannot be in error in asserting such a statement because it is directly verified by what it reports. One can, of course, lie to others about what one has experienced, so there is a sense in which the statement can be false, but the perceiver would know he was lying.

Lewis was constantly frustrated by the fact that the language does not provide precise enough terminology to name every quale, and his opponents took full advantage of that fact. His reply:

> the impossibility of their [the given] accurate expression in language would, then, merely constitute a comment upon the inessential character of language in its relation to cognitive process; and upon the errors which lie in wait for those who substitute linguistic analysis for the examination of knowledge.[62]

But Lewis made his views clear enough so that his readers should have been able to understand him.

Lewis's description of the given in AKV marks a change from his earlier position in *Mind and the World Order*—a change toward which he had been working in the 1930s. In making a statement of the given "one uses language to *convey* the content, but what is *asserted* is what the language is intended to convey, not the correctness of the language used." Since Lewis holds that statements cannot constitute knowledge unless it is possible for them to be in error, he denies the status of knowledge to expressive statements of the given. These statements are fundamental for empirical knowledge in that they provide the data on which empirical knowledge rests, but they are not themselves part of knowledge.

The second category of statements involved in empirical knowledge contains what Lewis calls terminating judgments. These statements assert that if certain conditions are fulfilled, then certain experiences will result. They are conditional statements of the form "S being given, if A then E," where "A" is some action taken, "E" some experience had, and "S" a sensory cue.[63] Statements of this sort, being predictions, can be false if the predicted consequent does not occur when the antecedent is true. But terminating judgements are statements about experience, not about the objective world. The antecedent and consequent must accordingly be formulated in expressive language. That means that they can be decisively verified; the predicted experience does or does not occur and, being the occurrence of a given experience, we can be certain about it. This is why they are called terminating judgments; the process of verification terminates when the predicted experience occurs or does not occur. Nevertheless, since the predictions can be false, they constitute knowledge.

Lewis then turns to the consideration of a series of problems about terminating judgments. The first of these is why such predictions of further possible experience should require a hypothesis of action. The reason that this seems to be a significant question, Lewis says, is because we have been raised in the belief that nature is governed by deterministic laws. Quantum indeterminacy does not affect this, since we are here concerned with molar phenomena. But even if physical determinism is correct, it applies to physical objects, not to experience. The whole point of knowledge, and particularly of scientific knowledge, is to enable us to control our own experience. Let it be the case that a calamity is predicted to occur; what is not thereby predicted is what our experience of that calamity will be, and the point of knowledge is to enable us to avoid our experience being a calamity. Because we can act so as to modify what our experience will be, we can control the effects on us of even predetermined events. Even if determinism were extended to include what would happen to us, Lewis remarks, "there is still one thing we can always do about an 'inevitable experience,' which is to 'be prepared for it.'" Further, Lewis says "anticipatable *experience* is subject to a sort of indeterminacy principle: foreknowledge itself and our active attitude can alter the quality of it."[64] Even if some experiences were predictable, how we should meet them is not. Lewis concludes:

> there is nothing which could be known, the knowledge of which might not enable us to avoid efforts which are fruitless, and enable us also to

ameliorate our lot and improve the quality with which future experience might otherwise affect us, by choosing between alternatives of action which still are open.[65]

It is obvious that Lewis assumes that the human will is free. That there should be a problem about free will, he regards as due to the general acceptance of the principle "Every event has a cause," from which determinism is taken to follow.[66] Citing Hume, Lewis points out that all observation warrants respecting physical causation is a correlation between the occurrence of an event termed the cause and the occurrence of an event termed the effect.[67] The only case in which we seem to observe a cause compelling an effect is in actions that we will, but even here what is actually observed is a given "oomph" of initiation followed by a bodily movement; we cannot observe the one "compelling" the other.[68] Accordingly, Lewis holds that all causal statements, including the laws of nature, are really probability statements based on the strength of the correlation of events. Such statements do not show that the will is determined or compelled.

The maxim "Every event has a cause" is not a provable empirical statement, nor is it a metaphysical truth or a constitutive principle.[69] Rather, Lewis holds it to be a regulative or pragmatic principle governing empirical investigation. It amounts to a hunting license for the investigator of any particular phenomenon to seek for a cause. As such, it is useful because it encourages the hunter to believe there is game in the woods,[70] but it does not guarantee that there is a cause there to be found or that the investigator will find it. Not every event has a cause; the universe is an event for which, Lewis says, there is no cause.[71] But since the objective of science is causal explanation, the maxim has a useful pragmatic role to play.

If determinism is then a false or unprovable dogma, there is no problem of the freedom of the will because there is no reason to deny it. We assume free will in every deliberative decision or choice. Arcane arguments that we could not have chosen otherwise have no basis but the mistake of taking a regulative principle to be constitutive.

The second question is the question of the nature of the connection between the antecedent and consequent of terminating judgments. If a terminating judgment is symbolized as "If S, then $A - -> E$," what is the nature of the relation $- ->$? Lewis holds that this relation is not a logical relation, but one learned from past experience by induction. It cannot be a strict implication because "E" is not deducible from "A". Furthermore, Lewis argues at length that it cannot be either a relation of material implication or of formal implication because it must support contrary-to-fact conditionals. It is crucial for the function of terminating judgments such as "If

S, then if *A*, then *E*" that "*E*" *would* occur if "*A*" *were to* occur, whether "*A*" does occur or not occur. Hence, Lewis argues the relation in question must be "real" or "matter-of-fact" relation such as a causal relation, or the sort of relation found in natural laws.[72] Such a relation can only be learned from experience, not from logic. But Lewis does not specify just what the relation "– –>" is. The most likely interpretation is that he is thinking of the sign relation, which, as Berkeley pointed out, must hold between presentations if one is to predict the other. The sign relation itself is a relation in a mind, but it must be based on a real correlation between the terms related if one is to signify the other. That correlation must be established by induction. Thus, Lewis's theory of terminating judgments assumes the validity of induction.[73]

This point leads Lewis into a digression on the importance of counterfactuals to the concept of reality. Lewis holds that "belief in objective reality is only as strong as the correlative belief that although certain hypotheses are now false, they have certain consequences (which *would* be found true if the tests *were* made) *and not others*."[74] Without counterfactuals, Lewis thinks that the alternative is skepticism. For, without counterfactuals, we should have no grounds for belief in the existence of an objective reality that is independent of being experienced. Possibility, as Lewis has remarked before, is intrinsic to the idea of the real. And Lewis comments in a note that "it is not altogether an accident" that those who reject metaphysics also deny the significance of hypothetical statements that are not formulated in terms of material or formal implication. That, he says, "would be a way of begging the question at issue by apparently rigorous but actually specious logical analysis. It would argue away the issue by refusing to state it; by refusing logical standing to that meaning of 'if–then' in terms of which alone the actual significance of common sense assertions of objective belief can be expressed."[75] The target of these remarks is clearly the Logical Positivist. Lewis then brings the discussion of judgments of objective reality back to that of terminating judgments by holding that the confirmation of the former is only possible by the testing of the latter, and that there must be terminating judgments that will never be tested, since all possible tests exceed what can be realized in actuality, but are nevertheless true. Reality requires "possibilities of experience which never become actual."[76]

There is an important point here that Lewis takes as obvious but one that needs to be clarified. A terminating judgment is a conditional of the form, "If *S*, then *A* – –> *E*." Lewis has stipulated that the antecedents "*S*" and "*A*" and the consequent "*E*" must be phrased in expressive terms. But the relation symbolized by "– –>" is not so phrased; it represents a "real" connection. A terminating judgment is not an expressive statement of the given; its antecedent and consequent are such statements, but the terminating judgment itself is not. It is rather a consequence of the objective statement for whose confirmation it is employed.

But if terminating judgments are learned from induction and if "– –>" is a "real" connection, does this not convert terminating judgments into nonterminating judgments? In fact, Lewis uses the expression "terminating judgment" in two senses. In the first, a terminating judgment has some generality. The terminating judgment is a consequence of an "objective belief," "R", such as "a real thing of a certain kind is before me." Thus, what I judge is: "For every occasion o, when Ro, if So and Ao, then Eo." Taking the objective belief as premise, I infer the terminating judgment in the general form. This type of terminating judgment is derived from the nonterminating judgment, but is itself general. But the instances of the general terminating judgment—the specification that this is an occasion "o" such that if "So" and "Ao", then "Eo"—is not general but entirely specific. It is this form of the terminating judgment that is decisively verified or falsified.[77]

What Lewis wants to capture in the concept of terminating judgment is the relation between one sense-presentation and another when the former serves as an indicator that the occurrence of the latter is probable. He regards this as fundamental for animal learning and the basis of "animal faith"; without it, not even a rat could learn. Such a relation must be learned from experience by induction; it therefore must have *some* generality, but instances of it can be wholly specific. Unfortunately, Lewis uses "terminating judgment" for both the induced principle and for its instances and does not clearly distinguish them. What the relation "– –>" is, Lewis can no more explain than can anyone else, and he is too honest to pretend otherwise. Beyond saying that it is a matter-of-fact relation that supports counterfactuals, he does not attempt to go further. But he does cite on several occasions Berkeley's statement that one "idea" must serve as a sign of a future "idea." The relation of antecedent to consequent must be such that the former can serve as a sign of the latter.

The third category of statements involved in empirical knowledge is that of "nonterminating judgments." These are statements that assert the objective reality of some state of affairs. Such statements can never be completely confirmed because they have an infinite number of consequences, and no matter how many of these are verified, it always remains possible that in a future test some consequence will turn out to be false. Nonterminating judgments therefore are at best only probable. It is true, Lewis notes, that the more confirmations of such a judgment we have, and the fewer disconfirmations, the greater the probability of the nonterminating judgment will be, but it can never reach certainty. The testable consequences of nonterminating judgments are terminating judgments. In fact,

Lewis says that nonterminating judgments must be translatable into terminating judgments. This is a bit misleading. What Lewis means is that the
set of terminating judgments deducible from a given nonterminating
judgment constitutes the sense meaning of the latter. This nonterminating
judgment should, however, have other consequences that are not terminating judgments that would be part of its linguistic meaning, but not
directly relevant to its confirmation. But because the number of terminating judgments implied by the nonterminating judgments is infinite, the
confirmation of the nonterminating judgment can never be complete.

Nonterminating judgments contain terms such as "red" and "round"
and object terms such as "tree" and "house." In nonterminating judgments
these terms refer to objective realities, and so the judgments are statements
about the real world. The terms and the statements involved have, of course,
sense-meaning, as we saw earlier, and that sense-meaning is exhibited in
the terminating judgments. "A sense meaning is a criterion of possible *confirmations*, and would be exhibited *in extenso* by the totality of terminating
judgments implied or included in objective attribution of the property or
character to be tested."[78]

Lewis's theory of empirical knowledge is a theory of the relations among
the three classes of statements previously described. Nonterminating judgments are statements about the real world. They require confirmation,
which can only come though terminating judgments that constitute their
sense-meaning and that are their implications in terms of direct experience.
Because the number of terminating judgments implied by a nonterminating
judgment is infinite, the confirmation of the nonterminating judgment can
never be complete and it can, at most, be probable. But Lewis holds that it
can be probable only because the verification of the terminating judgments
can be certain, and that depends on the fact that expressive statements of the
given are certain. "If anything is to be probable, then something must be certain. The data which eventually support a genuine probability, must themselves be certainties."[79] If statements of the given were only probable, then
Lewis believes we should need a ground for their probability, and the result
would be a regress.

It is generally understood, Lewis says, that the verification of one, or
indeed any finite number, of terminating judgments does not verify but only
partially confirms a nonterminating judgment. But what happens if a terminating judgment turns out to be false? Does this falsify the nonterminating
judgment? Lewis's answer is that it would if the relation of nonterminating
judgments to the consequent of the terminating judgments were strictly
logical. But Lewis notes that the falsification of one terminating judgment
does not lead us to reject the nonterminating judgment. The reason for

this is that in terminating judgments, it is only the probability of the consequent that is asserted. The nonterminating judgment strictly implies the terminating judgment, but the terminating judgment is a conditional, stating that if the antecedent is true, then probably the consequent is true. Lewis is far from clear on this point. In one place he says, "The consideration which should give us pause here is the fact that we can no longer regard any terminating judgment, 'When S is given, if A then E,' as strictly implied by an objective statement, 'P', which is believed."[80] That is, he seems to imply that the relation of the nonterminating judgment to the terminating judgment is a probability relation. But this is not the case, as he makes clear in other statements. Specifically, Lewis says "The analytic consequence of 'P' which we wish here to express is not the probability of a relation '$-->$', between 'S_1A_1' [the antecedent] and 'E_1' [the consequent], but a *relation of probability* between them."[81] Thus, the situation may be put as follows, where "P" is the nonterminating judgment, "S" the initial presentation, "A" the actions, "E" the predicted presentation, and "H" the probability of "E", and "M" the probability of "not-E:"

$$\text{If } P, \text{ then when } S \text{ and } A, \text{ then } H(E)$$

and

$$\text{If not-}P, \text{ then when } S \text{ and } A, \text{ then } M(\text{not-}E)$$

"P" strictly implies "When S and A, then $H(E)$"; the probability qualifies the consequent only—not the whole judgment. By Bayes theorem, it follows that

> the degree of confirmation, when the test result is positive, is the higher according as this positive result is the more *im*probable if the statement tested be *false*; and that when the test result is negative, the statement tested is the more improbable according as the negative result is the more improbable if the statement should be true.[82]

The probabilities "H" and "M", however, must be estimated directly, Lewis says; there is no mathematical method that will give them.

The last question that Lewis deals with here is actually the most difficult. Lewis has specified that the antecedent of a terminating judgment must contain reference to some action as a condition of further experience. And Lewis has assumed that "actions" are specifiable in terms of given experience in the expressive language.[83] But other conditions must be included in the antecedent—are they, too, capable of expressive formulation? Suppose the test involves the use of some apparatus that must be in proper working condition. Can we be certain of the state of this apparatus? Clearly, the answer is no, since a statement about the condition of the apparatus is a nonterminating judgment.

> That being the case, the test result will have to be weighed in the light of what we *can* genuinely assure at the time of test. And this will be what we can assure by some direct observation, formulatable in terms of what can be actually given. The appropriate hypothesis of the test, as actually carried out, is *not* then a physical condition of the apparatus but only such assurance of this as direct observation can give.[84]

Thus, the actual condition, as it will appear in the antecedent of the terminating judgment, is that the "apparatus *appears to be* a standard test apparatus in good working order." This requires the hypothesis that the appearance that the apparatus is in good working order should carry a nonzero probability that the apparatus *is* in good working order. "And if there are *no* appearances at the time of test which are indicative of any objective conditions essential for a test and give a certain degree of confirmation or disconfirmation, then it can never be determined that there *is* such confirmation or disconfirmation, because we should never know as even probable that a test having this result was actually carried out."[85] Lewis concludes that the conditions of test can be stated in terms of appearances and that real-object statements need not be included.

In summary, Lewis sets out his theory as follows:

> Let P = A sheet of real paper lies before me.
> S_1 = A visual sheet-of-paper presentation is given.
> A_1 = I [seem to] move my eyes.
> E_1 = A seen displacement of this presentation follows.
> S_2 = I seem to feel paper with my fingers.
> A_2 = I [seem to] act to pick up and tear it.
> E_2 = A torn-paper presentation follows.

Using the logical symbols, "$X - \!-\!> Y$" for "If X, then in result Y", "$h(X)$" for "In all probability, X," "Xo" for "It is the case that X on occasion o," "$(o)Xo$" for "For any occasion o, Xo," and "$<$" for a consequence relation certifiable a priori, Lewis gives

1. $P < (S_1 \,\&\, A_1 - \!-\!> h(E_1))$
2. $P < (S_1 \,\&\, A_2 - \!-\!> h(E_2))$
3. $P < (S_2 \,\&\, A_1 - \!-\!> h(E_1))$
4. $P < (S_2 \,\&\, A_2 - \!-\!> h(E_2))$
5. $(o) \, (Po < (S_1 o \,\&\, A_1 o - \!-\!> h(E_1 o)))$

6. $\sim P < (S_1 \,\&\, A_1 --> h(\sim E_1))$
7. $P \,\&\, S_1 \,\&\, A_1 < h(E_1)$
8. $\sim P \,\&\, S_1 \,\&\, A_1 < h(\sim E_1)$
9. $S_1 \,\&\, A_1 \,\&\, E_1 < h(P)$
10. $S_1 \,\&\, A_1 \,\&\, \sim E_1 < h(\sim P)$
11. $S_1 \,\&\, A_1 \,\&\, E_1 < (S_2 \,\&\, A_2 --> h(E_2))$[86]

The validation of empirical knowledge, Lewis argues, requires not only verification but justification. We may adopt a belief that happens to be true without having any rational basis for believing it true, or we may have good grounds for believing something true that is in fact false. In neither case do these beliefs constitute knowledge. Only beliefs that are both justified on rational grounds and true qualify as knowledge. For a priori beliefs, justification and verification coincide; since these beliefs are true on the basis of our own meanings, there can be no other justification for them than the relations among meanings that make them true. Similarly, for statements of the given, the justification and verification are one; nothing beyond the given itself is required for both. But for empirical knowledge, justification and verification are distinct.[87]

If a proposition is ever true, it is always true. But statements are assertions of propositions and are made at particular times when their verifications lie in the future. The warrant for assertions therefore cannot be their verifications because their verifications are yet to occur; what justifies us in making an assertion at a particular time is our past experience. Furthermore, the grounds that justify our asserting a statement at a given time do not logically imply the future verification of the statement. If they did, the statement would be certain when asserted and would therefore be a priori, whereas in fact it may be falsified by subsequent tests. Empirical knowledge is probable knowledge; for empirical statements, justification can never guarantee truth.

"The value ascribed to [empirical] knowledge," Lewis says, "is not its value for its own sake, but its value for the achievement of what is desirable and the avoidance of what is undesirable."[88] We do not seek knowledge for pure contemplation but for pragmatic reasons; empirical knowledge is utilitarian knowledge whose point is to guide action. Because this is so, and because action takes place at a particular time, the beliefs that serve as premises for action cannot be known to be true at the time the action is taken. Rational action must therefore be based on justified belief since no other basis is available.

Lewis must therefore discuss the nature of the grounds that justify empirical belief, the kind of warrant that these grounds provide, and the "sense in which a ground sufficient for the judgment may be supposed to be presented to the maker of the judgment." These grounds require the possibility of generalizations from past experience. As Lewis notes, this requires dealing with the problem posed by Hume. But Lewis points out that whatever the theoretical difficulties involved, all animal action is based on such generalizations. Unless such generalizations can be made with some degree of confidence, action itself would be wholly irrational. Picking up a point he had made in *Mind and the World Order*, Lewis holds that even our knowledge of physical things assumes the reliability of such generalizations. But such generalizations also involve the question of the reliability of memory, for past experience as it is used by us now is past experience as we remember it, and unless memorial knowledge has some degree of credibility, generalizations from past experience have no basis.[89]

As Lewis remarks, the picture of knowledge that is emerging in his pages is one of enormous complexity. It has, he says, a "many-storied character," rising from the statements of the given experience at the base to the most abstract theories at the top. Lewis is well aware that the knowledge of a society is a social product, but he also emphasizes that each person's knowledge rests, and can only rest, on that person's own experience. We do learn from others; indeed, most of our knowledge comes from others. But the reports and statements of others are for each of us simply a part of our own experience, and one that must be evaluated in terms of the reliability of our informants. Knowledge is always at root first-person knowledge, no matter how complex it becomes. Luckily for us, we do not have to marshal all we know in order to act. A man walking down stairs does not have to know all the physical and biological principles involved in his action in order to perform the feat; he just walks down the stairs. But those who want to understand knowledge and its relation to action must analyze the whole complex structure.[90]

As has become clear, this structure is largely a structure of probable knowledge, and so Lewis turns to the subject of probability. Lewis had similarly devoted a chapter of *Mind and the World Order* to this subject, but his views of it have significantly changed since then. There are, Lewis says, two competing concepts of probability. One is the a priori or logical theory that he had learned from Keynes. The other is the empirical or frequency theory, particularly in the form given it by Reichenbach. What Lewis tries to do is to find a way to combine them.

The a priori theory, Lewis holds, is a logical theory that applies to statements. Thus, " 'P' has probability a/b on data D" means that, given the data "D", it follows that "P" has probability a/b. The relation of "D" to "P" is "logical"—that is, rules of probability inference determine the probability of "*P*" if "*D*" is given. These rules are not those of deductive logic yet they are a priori rules all the same, and the inference of the probability is valid if the rules are correctly applied. Because the probability of "*P*" depends on "*D*", "*P*" will have different probabilities for different choices of data, but the connection is still logical; for any given body of data "*D*", there is but one probability for "*P*". This relativity of probability to the data means that no statement of the form "*P* had probability a/b" is meaningful; the data on which "*P*" has the probability a/b must always be specified. Hence, the correct form is " '*P*' has the probability a/b relative to data '*D*.' " It also means that one must distinguish between the validity of the probability inference and the truth of the probability statement. A probability inference can be valid even though the statements forming the data are false. Thus, as Lewis put it, "A probability determination which follows from its premised data according to correct rules of probability inference is valid; and a valid determination is true when the premises of it are true."[91] On the a priori theory, probability statements are not subject to confirmation; the statements composing the data are subject to confirmation, but the probability statement itself is a priori.

The frequency or empirical theory of probability applies to events and identifies probability with the long-run frequency of such events in some reference class. The difference between an event and a proposition Lewis brushes aside; an event or state of affairs is what is expressed in a proposition. Lewis takes probabilities as applying to individual instances and regards the standard frequency position that probability does not apply to individual events as absurd.[92] On the frequency theory, Lewis takes the statement "*P*" to be a statement function of the form "ϕx" (*x* has the property ϕ); the property "ϕ" he calls the *quaesitum* property. But *x* also has another property "ψ", which Lewis calls the *reference* property. Both "ϕ" and "ψ" determine classes that are called the "quaesitum class" and the "reference class," respectively. Then the probability of "*P*"—that is, of "ϕx" "is said to be the frequency of members of the quaesitum class, having the property ϕ, amongst members of the reference class, having the property ψ."[93]

The frequency theory also involves relativity to particular data—in this case, to the choice of the reference class. This choice is arbitrary in the sense that there will always be alternative choices of a reference class, and the frequency of the quaesitum property will vary from one reference class to another. Thus, the relativity to the data characteristic of the a priori theory also appears in the frequency theory.

More important for Lewis is the problem of the long run in frequency theory. The fact that probability on this theory is the frequency in the long run raises the issue of inference from past to future. As Lewis notes, the frequency theory is based on

> the presumption, namely, that the incidence of any property in a well defined class, as found in a sufficiently large number of past observed cases, will be approximately indicative of incidence of that property amongst instances of that class in general. We shall hereafter refer to this principle . . . as the *Rule of Induction*.[94]

It will be recalled that in *Mind and the World Order* Lewis attempted to give a justification of induction. There is no such attempt here. He explicitly refuses to be drawn into such an attempt, and states: "our attempted explanation, would, as a basis for probability formulations, be circular, since it could not itself be justly expressed except in terms of *probability*."[95] This is the influence of Reichenbach.

But the issue of the long run involves more than the problem of induction. The critical problem is the issue of convergence. The series involved is not a mathematical series for which methods of testing convergence are well known; it is an empirical series for which mathematical arguments are irrelevant. Whatever the frequency of "ϕ" in a given reference class has been up to some time "t", there is no mathematical reason to assume that it will not change radically after "t"; the question is an empirical question. Indeed, Lewis notes, such a claim is an example of a nonterminating judgment that cannot be more than probable. If, therefore, one identifies the frequency "a/b" of "ϕx" with the probability "a/b" of "ϕx", then the statement "the probability of ϕx is a/b" is only probable, and the statement asserting the probability of that statement is only probable, and so on. Obviously, we have a regress that is vicious, since without some starting point in a definite probability, none of the probabilities in the series are determined. This, Lewis says, "would not provide a solution but only the beginning of a perpetual stutter."[96]

But Lewis is not prepared to reject the importance of frequency for probability; rather, he wants a theory that will combine elements of both the a priori and the frequency theories, and he finds it in "the thesis that *a probability is a valid estimate of a frequency from the given data*."[97] This thesis combines an a priori notion that probability is determined by inference from a given body of data with the frequency notion that what matters is the frequency of the quaesitum property in the reference class. Lewis now terms the former— the probability coefficient—the "expectation," and introduces the concept of "reliability," which he defines as "the degree of assurance with which we can argue from the data given to the case whose probability is judged."[98] Reliability is not expectation; Lewis calls it a different "dimension" that is largely independent of expectation but nevertheless is essential to the understanding of probable knowledge. Reliability refers to the degree of assurance we have that our estimate will be accurate. It is Lewis's version of variance.

What then is reliability? Lewis claims there are three determinants. The first is "adequacy," which refers to the amount of pertinent data on which the estimate is based. The rule here is that additional pertinent data always increase the reliability of the estimate. The second is "proximateness," meaning the closeness of the analogy between the data and the case in question with respect to properties that may affect the quaesitum property. This really involves several issues. Since the reference class is infinite, we can observe only a limited number of its members; it is therefore important to determine how closely the observed members of the reference class resemble the rest of the members of the reference class—that is, how homogeneous is the reference class. But we must also ask that the members of the reference class (taken as a whole) resemble the instance (or instances) in question. "Proximateness" is Lewis's term for those resemblances; the greater these resemblances the greater the proximateness. The third determinant is "uniformity," by which Lewis means how closely the frequency of the quaesitum property in the reference class matches the frequency of the quaesitum property in all "properly chosen" subsets of the reference class—that is, chosen according to the rules of "fair sampling." Adequacy and proximateness often conflict; trying to increase the amount of data usually means including more cases that are dissimilar to the case in question. Lewis holds that this is not a serious problem in practice because the rate of increase in reliability falls as the size of the body of data increases.

The significance of reliability for the a priori theory is to point out that failure to include pertinent data leads to inaccurate estimates, and that more recent experience provides a sounder basis for estimates than older experience. For the empirical theory, the significance is to call attention to the fact that estimates of probability that are modest may still be highly reliable and therefore highly useful. Expectation and reliability represent two dimensions of the process of probability determination, and the fact that they can vary largely independently of each other means that a focus on one alone can be highly misleading.[99]

The theory that Lewis has constructed is an ingenious combination of the a priori theory and the frequency theory. But it is still an a priori theory; the estimate depends only on the data and the rules of inference; if the inference is valid, and the statements comprising the data are true, the probability statement is a priori true. At the same time, the expectation is an estimate of a long-run frequency. That estimate cannot be certain if it is made on empirical grounds, since the statement that the series of ratios converges to a limit as the number of cases goes to infinity is a nonterminating judgment.

By making the estimate a question of inference from the data, in the manner of the a priori theory, Lewis can produce a certain estimate of the expectation—*if the statements comprising the data are certain.* Whether they can be certain and, if so, how, Lewis has yet to explain. And by introducing the concept of reliability—his version of variance—Lewis has brought in an important consideration that deserves attention.

Lewis then turns to the principle of indifference, which had usually been associated with the a priori theory of probability and which had helped to give that theory a bad name. Lewis's point is that the principle is actually of little importance. In those cases where there is good reason to believe that the alternatives are, in fact, equally probable, Lewis notes that no one objects to the use of the principle. Similarly, where past experience shows that the alternatives are not equally probable, no one uses it. The only cases in which its use is questionable are those in which we are completely ignorant of the probability of the alternatives. And Lewis remarks, "complete ignorance of all relevant empirical facts is completely fictitious in the case of a meaningful empirical question." It is the failure to recognize that what a probability question requires is only some empirical basis for a valid *estimate* of a frequency rather than *knowledge* of a frequency that has led people to exaggerate the importance of the principle of indifference. The only cases that can legitimately be characterized as "the equal distribution of ignorance" are those in which we have no data at all, and there are few if any reasonable examples that can be so described. The principle of indifference is really a non-issue, and constitutes no legitimate objection to the a priori theory of probability.[100]

Having dealt with the nature of probability, Lewis returns to the question of knowledge. Lewis has shown that empirical knowledge is confirmable and justifiable, and has demonstrated that the justification of empirical knowledge is in terms of probability. It follows that empirical knowledge is never more than probable. Yet "knowledge" has often been used to mean "certain belief." Is empirical "knowledge" as Lewis has described it therefore knowledge at all?[101] Lewis sees this an involving two questions: Is probable knowledge really empirical? And is it truly knowledge?

In answer to the first, Lewis points out the difference between hypothetical and categorical probability knowledge. The statement " '*P*' has probability *a/b* on data '*D*' " is actually hypothetical; it is equivalent to "If data '*D*' are true, then '*P*' has probability *a/b*." This statement asserts nothing empirical; the relation of antecedent and consequent is logical on Lewis's theory, and the antecedent is not asserted. But if one adds to this hypothetical the statement "the *D*'s are true," then the statement " '*P*' has probability *a/b* (on data *D*)" is categorical, and since the statements comprising *D* are empirical, the statement as a whole is empirical. Thus, although Lewis holds an a priori theory with respect to the relation of the data to the statement for which probability is claimed, the empirical nature of the data make the resulting probability statement empirical also.[102]

With respect to the issue of certainty, Lewis agrees that certainty is the ideal of empirical knowledge, but it is an ideal never actually reached, and in fact impossible of attainment. Since nonterminating judgments cannot be completely confirmed, empirical knowledge can never be more than probable. Therefore, if the term "knowledge" is to have any application to empirical matters at all, it must be construed as including probable beliefs. The content of empirical knowledge is "believed-in matters of fact." "Empirical knowledge, then, is belief; justified belief, warranted belief, rational belief."[103] It follows that empirical knowledge can be false, and this certainly does violence to some traditional understandings of the term "knowledge," but Lewis sees no alternative to such a construal of the term.

But this analysis leads to further problems. For a statement of the form "On data *D*, it is probable that *P*" to constitute empirical knowledge, it must be the case that the statements comprising "*D*" can be asserted. But Lewis asks, "Is there any ground sufficient to warrant such belief as credible which is actually in mind? And second, in such cases, is it possible to attest the truth of these supporting premises of the judgment?"[104] The first of these questions Lewis thinks is answerable by the fact that much of what we are said to "know" is not actually in mind in any explicit sense. Knowledge becomes habitual once we have it and we can and do act on the basis of such habits without having to think of them directly. As Lewis has shown in detail, the structure of our knowledge forms a pyramid so vast that holding all parts of it before the mind at once would be impossible; nevertheless, we can act on the basis of this body of knowledge without the whole of it being present to our mind and so may be said to "know" it.

It is the second problem that Lewis sees as the serious one. This is not, as one might have thought, the question of the certainty of the given; Lewis does hold that expressive statements of the given are certain, but they are not enough to "attest" the truth of the premises. "No empirical judgment can be validated solely by reference to immediately given facts of sense. It is also necessary, in order to justify any empirical judgment—even the terminating one 'If S, then if A then (probably) E'—that some generalization of the sort derived from past experience should be afforded. . . . In fact, the terminating judgment 'S being given, if A then (probably) E' is itself such a generalization, or the extension of such a generalization to the present case."[105] That raises the problem of the validity of memory. Any terminating judgment involves the relating of the given to past experience and a prediction on that basis of future experience. This involves both the problem of memory and the problem of induction. Lewis does not attempt to solve the problem of induction; instead he says, "as Reichenbach points out, what can be assured is only that if acting on probabilities does not advantage us then no manner of directing our activities will do us any good: acting in accord with probabilities is that procedure which will achieve success if success if achievable."[106] Consequently, the question for him involves the validity of memory.

Lewis notes that philosophers have generally avoided the problem of memory—an avoidance that he considers a "bit of a scandal." But the difficulty of the problem makes it clear why others have been so shy. Our past experience is known to us only though our present memories of it. These present memories cannot be compared to our past experiences to assess their accuracy because the past experiences no longer exist. What we have therefore are simply present memories. If we could assert that present memories are infallible, there would be no problem, but present memories are often wrong—a fact that can be established by comparing them to records, or to testimony, or from contradictions among our memories. Granted that some memories are false, how can we know which are false and which are true?

Since inconsistencies among our memories can prove some of them false, Lewis considers the possibility that memory requires a coherence theory of truth. To make the case as strong as possible, Lewis considers not just consistent systems but "congruent" ones, where the definition is

> A set of statements, or a set of supposed facts asserted, will be said to be congruent if and only if they are so related that the antecedent probability of any one of them will be increased if the remainder of the set can be assumed as given premises.[107]

Congruence is a stronger relation than consistency but weaker than that in which each statement in the set is logically deducible from the others. But none of these relations alone guarantees that the statements of the set are true. Lewis points to the example of the various geometries, all incompatible with each other, of which at most only one can be true. Nor is the situation changed if the set is expanded to include all the statements we can imagine that are consistent with its members. What we would then have would be a description of one among a plethora of possible worlds with no way to tell which one was actual. Congruence alone is not enough.

In the course of this discussion, Lewis makes a very important point.

> What are put forward as consequences of some single belief or hypothesis are seldom drawn from that assumption alone but require also collateral suppositions which commonly are unexpressed just because they are taken for granted. A sufficiently meticulous examination of the actual premises of such inductive inference would oblige us to recognize a more

and more comprehensive foundation for it. This would be evident, for example, whenever a hypothesis within any science is to be examined: much more than is likely to be stated explicitly will be involved in our assumptions determining what consequences this hypothesis under consideration will be taken to have. Perhaps we should find ourselves unable to stop short of the whole body of accepted principles of that science. For reasons which thus become obvious, we might well think that the eventual basis of all our inductive inferences and all our truth-determinations, is a totality of acceptable belief; a vast and intricate hypothesis, which is at one and the same time the ideally indicated basis of particular beliefs which are acceptable, and the presumption which is corroborated by the total congruence of acceptable beliefs within it.[108]

Lewis is here describing the coherentist position, and goes on to point out that even within the geometries some postulates are independent of others, but the passage makes it clear that he understood the fact that in science the consequences of a hypothesis are derived with the help of auxiliary hypotheses. Since Lewis usually spoke of the consequences of single statements, it is important to note that he was well aware of the role played by auxiliary hypotheses. That being the case, his statements about deriving consequences from single hypotheses must be understood to mean not that no auxiliaries are involved, but that they are taken for granted.

If congruence alone will not do, what does our belief in the reliability of memory rest on? Lewis's answer is: "all that is needed is initial assumption that the mere fact of present rememberings renders what is thus memorially present in some degree credible."[109] This assumption of prima facie credibility allows any particular memory to be impugned but not the whole of our memories at once. Given this assumption of prima facie credibility, "the congruence of such items with one another and with present sense experience will be capable of establishing an eventual high credibility, often approximating to certainty, for those items which stand together in extensive relations of such congruence."[110]

But why should one grant the assumption of prima facie credibility? Lewis's answer is that the alternative is total skepticism.

To doubt our sense of past experience as founded in actuality, would be to lose any criterion by which either the doubt itself or what is doubted could be corroborated; and to erase altogether the distinction between empirical fact and fancy. In that sense, we have no rational alternative but to presume that anything sensed as past is just a little more probable than that which is incompatible with what is remembered and that with respect to which memory is blank.[111]

To reject all memory would be to reject all knowledge, for even the recognition that what we now experience is a tree requires the grasping of the similarities of present experience to remembered experiences of trees. All classification, all recognition, presupposes veridical memory. So does induction by enumeration, since if we could not trust our memory of past cases, no such procedure would be possible. There can be no reasoning from past to future without credible knowledge of the past. Without memory, we would simply experience a transient phantasmagoria of color and sound devoid of meaning. The alternative to credible memory is total skepticism of the moment.

If we grant Lewis's theory of memory, the principle of induction, and the certainty of the given, probable knowledge becomes possible, for the statements comprising the data, even if they are terminating judgments, will have some degree of credibility, and that is sufficient to block any regress of probabilities. Terminating judgments are then possible, and the foundation of empirical knowledge as Lewis envisions it can be made secure.

Lewis's theory of empirical knowledge is a heroic attempt to deal honestly with the full complexity of the problems involved. And many aspect of it are brilliantly done—for example, his treatment of memorial knowledge. But the same problem that undercut his theory of analytic truth plagues his theory of empirical knowledge. Lewis continues to hold that a nonterminating judgment implies a specific set of terminating judgments, and that the terminating judgments of that set exhibit the sense meaning of the nonterminating judgment. This is the more remarkable because Lewis recognized explicitly that the consequences of a given statement are rarely derived from that statement alone but from the conjunction of that statement with other (auxiliary) statements. Why Lewis did not see that this made the composition of the set of terminating judgments relative to the choice of auxiliaries and so destroyed the principle that nonterminating judgments can be separately confirmed or disconfirmed by specific sets of terminating judgments I am at a loss to explain. But the fact is that he did not see it and the damage to his theory is fatal.

Lewis's treatment of justification, his recognition of the essential role of possibility in the definition of the real, and his efforts to explicate the way in which sense experience is related to our conceptual formulations are all admirable. At the same time, his theory of probability is not one that has proven convincing. It represents an attempt to combine two different concepts of probability that are incompatible, and fell stillborn from his pen. Given the importance of probability for his theory of empirical knowledge, this was an unfortunate failing, though much of what he wanted his theory of probability to accomplish can be done equally well by more orthodox theories. Particularly impressive was his recognition that Reichenbach was right in holding that probability and induction are inextricably linked and that no such proof of induction as he had attempted in *Mind and the World Order* was possible. Lewis's answer here was fully pragmatic—if there is a right answer to be found, Reichenbach's method will find it, and if there is not no other approach will do any good.

It is important to note that in his table of contents, Lewis called the final section of Book II " 'Deduction' of the basic validity of memory and induction."[112] And what he presents really is a "deduction" in Kant's sense. Unless memory has prima facie credibility and enumerative induction is valid, empirical knowledge is impossible. Since, in fact, we do have empirical knowledge, therefore memory must be prima facie credible and enumerative induction legitimate. Lewis cannot *prove* the validity of empirical knowledge, but he can present a Kantian type of deduction of its fundamental principles, and this he believed was the most that could be done. Having done this, he was now prepared to deal with the problem of valuation.

Book III of the AKV is concerned with valuation. For Lewis, valuations are a form of empirical knowledge; the point of the preceding chapters has been to develop the theory of empirical knowledge that he will now apply to valuation. Lewis regards subjectivist and relativist theories of value, and emotivist theories in particular, as not only wrong but perverse. Such a view, he says,

> is one of the strangest aberrations ever to visit the mind of man. The denial to value-apprehensions in general of the character of truth or falsity and of knowledge, would imply both moral and practical cynicism. It would invalidate all action; because action becomes pointless unless there can be some measure of assurance of a valuable result which it may realize. And this negation, if it be carried our consistently, likewise invalidates all knowledge; both because believing is itself an active attitude which would have no point if it were not better to be right than wrong in what one believes, and because knowledge in general is for the sake of action. If action is in general pointless, then knowledge is also futile, and one belief is as good as another.[113]

Having thus set out what he considers the stakes to be, Lewis began the presentation of his own theory. As one might expect, the first order of business is to lay out the terminology he will use. As the quoted passage shows, one of the key terms is "action." It is the failure to distinguish action from behavior that has led some to believe that value judgments are not cognitive. By "action" Lewis means behavior that is deliberated, subject to critique, decided on, and therefore alterable on reflection—in other words, conduct.

Action therefore essentially involves values. Behavior that is not subject to control is not action. "Sensible action," Lewis says, is action for the sake of attaining something valued or avoiding something disvalued, where a choice is implied among alternative possibilities. The "intent" of an action is the expected result of it; a "sensible intent" is one in which the expected result has comparative value—that is, is valued in comparison to possible alternatives. "That *part* of the intent for the sake of which it [the action] is adopted, we shall call its purpose." Thus, the purpose is narrower than the intent. Purposes also may be sensible or not, and the purpose and intent may conflict on this score. One could take an action for the purpose of achieving an immediate gratification, although the total result of the action—the intent—might be anything but sensible. An action is "successful" if it is sensible and "*so far as* the purpose of it is verifiably achieved." Thus, an action may be successful even if only a part of the hoped for result was achieved or achieved only in some measure. But where the expected value is attained, not by the expected means, but by some unexpected coincidence, the action is termed "fortunate" rather than successful.[114]

Success is the hoped-for result of action, but Lewis emphasizes that what is most important about an action is its "practical justification," meaning that the intent of the action is an expectation that is a "warranted empirical belief." The point here is that at the time the decision to act is made, its success lies in the future and its attainment therefore cannot be certain; the decision must rest on the justification.[115]

Lewis then reemphasizes the importance of the fact that value apprehensions are empirical and comments:

> those who would deny the character of cognition and the possibility of truth to value-apprehensions, must find themselves, ultimately, in the position of Epimenides the Cretan who said that all Cretans are liars. Either their thesis must be false or it is not worth believing or discussing; because if it should be true, then *nothing* would be worth believing or discussing.[116]

This is Lewis's first published use of the Epimenides paradox in this connection, and although it is not here fully developed, one can see here the root of the idea of the pragmatic contradiction of which he would make extensive use later on.

Lewis then begins the application of his theory of empirical knowledge to valuation. "First, there is expressive statement of a value-quality found in the directly experienced." These expressive statements function just like those previously considered; they are not subject to error "unless merely linguistic error in the words chosen to express it." Since one could lie about immediate value apprehensions, such statements can be true or false, but they do not constitute knowledge and "the apprehension expressed is not a judgment."

Second, "there are evaluations which are terminating judgments." Given the possibility of expressive statements of the value-given, the application of the idea of terminating judgments poses no new problems. And, third, there are nonterminating judgments of value. These admit only of confirmation, not verification. As is true for empirical knowledge generally, the terminating judgments of value constitute the sense-meaning of the nonterminating judgments. Like their nonvaluational counterparts, these three types of valuational statements are all empirical. They are, however, different from each other, and Lewis believes it has been the failure of philosophers to draw these distinctions that accounts for most of the confusion afflicting value theory. Lewis emphasizes in particular that many well-known statements of value theory, such as "a thing is constituted good by being an object of an interest" of Perry's theory, are not empirical statements at all but definitions of value and therefore analytic statements, but in this case false because they incorrectly explicate the meanings involved.[117]

But Lewis notes that, in a certain respect, nonterminating judgments of value do differ from nonterminating judgments of other qualities. Statements about qualities such as roundness and hardness are tested not only against direct presentations but by measurement and experiment—for example, by measuring the distance of the perimeter from the center or by the scratch test—and it is the latter tests that are regarded as definitive. But this is not true regarding values.

> For value-predications, this relation between the expressive and the objective meanings appears to be reversed: a thing *is* valuable according as it may *appear* valuable; objective value is at bottom derivative from direct appreciation; beauty is not finally determinable apart from the delight of some beholder; and nothing is good except relative to some possible felt goodness.[118]

Lewis therefore introduces a new set of distinctions designed to clarify the nature of value. The first division is between "intrinsic" and "extrinsic" values. "Intrinsic" value refers to "the content of some actual or possible experience," for only experience can be valuable "for its own sake." "Extrinsic" values are of two sorts: "those which are to be found in experience of that object itself to which the value is attributed, and are here called inherent values, and those which are realizable in the experience of something else to which the object in question may be instrumental, which are here called instrumental values."[119] An object is valuable insofar as it conduces to intrinsic values in our experience; the experienced value is intrinsic, the value of the object that produces this experience is extrinsic, but inherent in the object. And an object that is purely instrumental to the production of something else that has inherent value is said to have instrumental value.

The notion of instrumental value poses a further problem. Tobacco is a means of inducing lung cancer; does that mean that tobacco has instrumental value? Lewis restricts the term "instrumental value" to those things that are instrumental to the inherently valuable, among which cancer is not to be found. For those things "good for" the production of something that has no value, he uses the term "utility," thus providing a category into which economic values can easily be fitted.

Lewis is careful to point out that so far he has said nothing about ethics. For Lewis, valuation is empirical, whereas ethics is not. "Good" is a category of value theory; values will, of course, play a role in ethics, but the two subjects should not be confused. Even the notion of the good life, which Lewis takes to be "the final end by reference to which all values are to be appraised,"[120] belongs to value theory. Further, Lewis believes that value theory is no more relativistic or subjectivistic than empirical knowledge generally. It is this conception of value theory that Lewis now has to develop.

Lewis identifies his position as "a naturalistic or humanistic conception of values"; since it holds that the natural bent of the natural man stands in no need of correction in order validly to be the touchstone of *intrinsic* value."[121] No redemption from sin or illumination from above is necessary for the correct understanding of values on this view. But this rejection of transcendental standards does not mean any adoption of Protagorean relativism or of the "cynical or nihilistic" view of Positivism. What sets his position apart from these alternatives is that for him valuations are empirical cognitions, and that the ultimate test of value is a "quality unmistakably identifiable in the direct apprehension of it when disclosed in experience." The problem of characterizing this quality Lewis finds baffling and irritating because, on the one hand, everyone knows what it is, yet on the other, "we here arrive at a point where we realize that between words and what they signify there is a gap; and more words will not build a bridge across it."[122] Lewis has wrestled with this problem of the description of the given throughout his career.

Lewis rejects the notion that the value experienced is a distinct quale, nor is it a dimension in the mathematical sense. "What is found directly good in life" is enormously variable and allows no simple description. Values do admit of some ordering, but there are different modalities of value that are not directly comparable—for example, colors and sounds. His thesis is rather "that value-disvalue is a mode of experience as it comes to us, and that values so disclosed are genuine and determine an ultimate kind of value-truth." Value as immediately found has the status of the apparent: "Its *esse* is *percipi*."[123] There cannot be an illusion of enjoyment or pain; to feel enjoyment is to enjoy, to feel pain is to be in pain. To charge that such appearances are "subjective" is a mistake. All apprehension of the empirical is by apprehension of appearances.

> When the content of appearance is considered as such—as appearance—it is more appropriately recognized as neither subjective nor objective, or as both without distinction. Subjectivity and objectivity, in any distinctive sense, are a "later" classification of apprehended content; a classification by reference to the relation of this content to reality or to further possible experience.[124]

Thus, Lewis holds that experience simply is and is prior to any such classification. It is the interpretation put on the presentation that will determine the classification. This is reminiscent of James's view in *Radical Empiricism* and of Chauncey Wright's earlier doctrine.

The meanings of the terms "subjective" and "objective" as applied to value presentations require clarification. Every presentation is potentially an evidence of some objective state of affairs, and could serve as a clue to a correct interpretation. And it may well be that the state of the organism is an element in the state of affairs to which the presentation provides a clue. In cases of illusion, for example, the condition of the subject may be highly relevant. This is not something unique to the apprehension of values, but is true of all perception. Hence:

> Where this reason why a given presentational content is affected with a particular value-quality, is such a reason which is personal or peculiar to the individual, the value-quality as affecting this given content may be said to be subjective; and where there is no such preponderant influence of what is personal, but the factors responsible are to be found in the objective situation, together with the capacities of apprehension shared by humans generally, the value-quality apprehended as affecting the given content of presentation may be said to be objective.[125]

All perception is conditioned by the nature and state of the perceiving organism as it is by the conditions of perception and the nature of the thing perceived. These are all part of the objective state of affairs in which perception takes place. Neither subjectivity or objectivity has any relevance to the value-quality found in a particular experience; that quality is as it is. The relevant question is whether the factors influencing the particular presentation are idiosyncratic to the individual perceiver or are common to humans generally. If the factors affecting the presentation are idiosyncratic, it is usually termed subjective; if not, objective. But this leads at once to two questions: are all value apprehensions subjective? and "does subjective character of direct value findings make them misleading or an unreliable basis for the judgment of independent value-facts?"[126]

In answer to the first question, Lewis concedes that disagreements with respect to value are more common than those regarding other types of phenomenal qualia. There probably are greater differences among individuals in their experience of phenomenal qualities than we know, since we only become aware of them when they are revealed by incongruent behavior. But given the close connection of value qualities to conduct, Lewis suggests that there is a greater likelihood of our becoming aware of differences in values than of differences of other qualia. Furthermore, there is a greater commonality of language in the description of colors and shapes than in the description of values. For both these reasons, interpersonal differences with respect to values are more likely to be noticed than those respecting other sorts of properties. But if there were not very substantial commonalities among people with respect to values, the result would be chaos in our interpersonal relations—a result that does not occur.

But the crucial question is the second one, and to this Lewis replies, "there is no necessary connection between subjectivity and any misjudgment of pertinent objective fact."[127] Consider a nearsighted man. His visual experiences will differ from those of people with normal eyes. But the judgments he makes, the predictions of future experiences that he constructs, will be in terms of his own visual experience and just as likely to be confirmed as the judgments of his more fortunate fellows. The reasons we have come to believe that subjectivity of immediate experience leads to error are several. First, there is a holdover from "prescientific psychology" that viewed anything derived through the five external senses as an accurate copy of the external world, whereas whatever was affected by "internal" factors was dismissed as unreliable. Second, Lewis points out that the subjective–objective distinction is often confused with the veridical–illusory distinction. Whenever our directly apprehended data lead to judgments that are born out by experience, we explain this fact by saying that they are objective, and whenever these data lead to judgments that are not born out by experience, we explain that by saying that they are subjective. Thus, we make subjective experience unreliable by *defining* experiences that lead to unreliable results as subjective. In fact, subjective experiences, especially when recognized as such by the person involved, are no more likely to lead to errors of judgment than those of people in general. Finally, if our value-findings had no significance and did not correlate to the objective value-properties of things, we could never learn from experience how to improve our lot in life, nor could we learn how to do anyone else harm. But Lewis sees such consequences as patently false.

Value qualities attach to the presentations we have in experience, and particularly to those that become the foci of attention. It is these that are most apt to acquire sign functions. But the value of the presentation also qualifies the "fringe" as well as the focus, to use William James's well-known terminology, and the value-quality of the fringe serves as a context for the focal presentation. As Lewis puts it, "value-quality is not simply a function of the presentation, but tends to be determined in some part by the relation of that presentation to the context of it."[128] That context will be composed of several types of factors. One will be the organic condition and feeling of the organism, whether it is well or ill, depressed or euphoric. A second will be anticipatory associations, whether habitual or cognitive, triggered by the presentation, as when the smell of coffee in the morning stimulates thoughts of breakfast. Third, there will be various private associations, as when the sight of a gardenia brings suddenly to mind the image of one's first love. And finally there will be those associations of the presentation to what are thought to be real-world objects and events, particularly those arising from experience and from community conventions. Thus, the context may be in part composed of elements that the subject brings to the experience, a fact that Lewis regards as crucial for the understanding of esthetic experience.

There is, Lewis says, no single characteristic that marks off what has esthetic values from all others. Esthetic values are intrinsic, but not all intrinsic values are esthetic—just as esthetically valuable objects have inherent value but not all inherent values are esthetic. The criteria involved in distinguishing the esthetic are therefore complex, and can be classed as those of degree, attitude, and association. Most things we encounter in experience have a utilitarian purpose, but they often have other properties that may provide us with immediate gratification. It is among those things where the degree of immediate gratification is high relative to their utilitarian properties that one should look for the esthetic. But this alone is not enough; esthetic values also involve a question of attitude.

The typical attitudes that we take toward what is presented to us may be classified as the "moral or active," the cognitive, and the esthetic. The active attitude is utilitarian and is concerned with how things can be used to attain ends.

> Esthetic values are not the goals of action; and the attitude which elicits them is amoral and free of such concern. They are those which are grasped by absorbtion in the presented in its own inherent quality and for the sake of the value so realizable in immediate experience. It is inimical to esthetic apprehension that in our confrontation with the thing we should be distracted by the thought of something else or something further.[129]

The esthetic attitude is one in which attention is absorbed in the contemplation of what Lewis's colleague David Prall called "the esthetic surface"[130]—that is, in presented experience as such. It is an "amoral" attitude in the very broad sense of "moral" as meaning "active"; it is the contemplation of the presented experience apart from its significance for action. Recalling James's description of the stream of thought as having "flights" and "perches," Lewis associates esthetic contemplation with the perches and action with the flights. The esthetic attitude involves a complete absorption in present experience, not concern for future experience.

The differences among attitudes are not absolute—there is always an overlap between them. "In a broad and literal sense, all direct apprehensions are esthetic." The comfort of a well-fitting shoe and the balance of a well-made ax are immediate gratifications, but our normal attitude toward such things is utilitarian rather than esthetic. Nor is the esthetic attitude more aristocratic "such as might mark a discriminating taste in wines but not an equal discrimination exercised amongst the various brands of canned beans," for esthetic values must be universal. Rather, "the distinctively esthetic values must not only possess a goodness which is inherent but possess it such wise and in such degree as to solicit the esthetic attitude of absorbed contemplation, and hold us free from all distractions of further and utilitarian aims." Only when the degree of immediate gratification is high will the esthetic values have this arresting power.[131]

The esthetic attitude is also different from the cognitive. It is true that both require one to be disinterested and dispassionate. "If by its utilitarian purpose, cognition is a thinking which is motivated by our wishes, still it must, in order to serve them, refuse to be wishful thinking."[132] Knowing is for acting, and our cognitive interest in immediate experiences is as clues to future experience. There are, Lewis admits, those who make knowledge an end in itself, but to do so "divests knowledge of it natural and pragmatic significance." Those who do so are the scholars. "The ivory tower is characteristically the refuge of the practically defeated and of those who become disillusioned of the utilities of action."[133] Lewis was a quintessential academic, but as noted before, "there was a lot of the shoe worker" in him. The reference to well-fitting shoes and the comparison of wine tasting to bean tasting indicate that he had a certain distrust of intellectuals.

Esthetic values are no more subjective than any others. Reiterating a point he has made before, Lewis says:

> What is given is empirically aboriginal, and neither subjective nor objective. These terms have no application until what is given is weighed in relation to the interpretation put upon it. That which induces expectations which later experience will confirm is by that fact "objective"; and that which leads us to believe what further experience would disprove, is by that fact "subjective." But the content of immediate awareness, abstracted from any supplementation by the interpreting attitude, is significant neither of the subject nor of the object. It is apprehended, not by introspection nor by extrospection, but simply by *spection*, unqualified by any further relationship either to the external world or to those dominant interests and that cumulativeness of conscious content which mark the continuity of the self.[134]

This statement of the relation of subjectivity and objectivity to future success and failure is inconsistent with Lewis's earlier statement and reflects precisely that way of defining subjectivity that he had previously criticized.

Thus far, Lewis's description of the esthetic has been extremely inclusive, to the point that almost anything having a high positive value might be included. He now tries to narrow the category to the distinctively esthetic by introducing further qualifications. The first qualification is that the distinctively esthetic should be a source of enduring realizations of value rather than transitory ones. A second is that they should be "what Bentham calls the fecund pleasures"—that is, those that give rise to other intrinsic values or enhance our realization of them or are reinforced by derivative goods. Further, Lewis claims that esthetic values are noncompetitive in the sense that they are not exclusive; an increase for one subject does not decrease the value available for others. These are not goods that set one person against another. "Such values are pure; the enjoyment of them may be serene, and their contemplation free from practical care."[135]

Lewis is well aware of the importance of technique in art and recognizes that critics may evaluate esthetic works on the basis of technical excellence, novelty, or virtuosity. But, for Lewis, attention to such matters should not only not overshadow the intrinsic gratifications received but may even detract from them by introducing distracting considerations. Lewis remains wedded to the notion that the standard of esthetic value must be the unselfconscious appreciation of the common man. The esthetic enjoyment of nature is not the appreciation of technique but of inherent value, and the same should be true of man-made art.

Having discussed esthetic experience, Lewis turns to esthetic judgment. Apprehensions of immediate esthetic values are not judgments because they cannot be in error; like all apprehensions of the given, they are certain. But statements about the esthetic values of objects are nonterminating judgments and, like all such judgments, are subject to error. The inherent values of objects are potentialities for the production of intrinsic values in experience and are objective. The failure to make this distinction, Lewis says, has led to emotivism. The presence of an inherent value in an object does not require that every individual will have the same intrinsic value on its presentation, or that every presentation to a given individual will result in the same intrinsic value. In the case of esthetic values, as in the case of all other objective qualities, there are subjective conditions—that is, conditions of the subject—that may affect his experience of the object. The value found in experience is *evidence* of the value in the object, and in the case of esthetic value it is the best evidence. But to *identify* intrinsic values in the experience of the subject with inherent values of the object is to make the latter subject to the idiosyncratic conditions affecting the former and reduce all values to subjectivism. Failure to understand this distinction leads to the belief that subjective conditions create values. It is true that those who are trained in the arts are better judges of esthetic value than those who are not, and that some are more gifted in esthetic valuation than others. So much is true also of physics: the untrained find quantum mechanics tough going. But this no more proves that esthetic values are created by esthetic training than it proves that particle spin is created by training in physics. In both cases, what is being judged is objective, and the better trained make better judgments.[136]

Confusion is further apt to arise from the fact that there is a certain sense in which the immediate value of an experience can be said to be assessed. To explain this point, Lewis uses the example of comparing the color of a presented apple to that of one seen in the past. The color of the presented apple is directly given rather than judged. But the color of the past apple must be remembered, and the comparison of it to the present apple as more or less red does involve a judgment. In this same way, Lewis says, the comparison of the value of a presentation to that of as past presentation with respect to the degree of esthetic value involves a judgment, although the apprehension of the presented values does not. Worse yet, such a comparative assessment of value in present experience may be confused with the objective value of a presented object, so that what does not require judgment is confused with what does. These distinctions are difficult to keep straight, but their confusion plays havoc with esthetics.[137]

Lewis distinguishes between esthetics, which he regards as an empirical science, and the theory of esthetics, or what today would be called metaesthetics.[138] His concern is with the theory of esthetics; esthetics itself is the concern of the esthetician. But Lewis regards as appropriate to the theory of esthetics the consideration of certain aspects of esthetic objects. If one compares a symphony, a poem, and a play with a painting, a building, or a sculpture, there is an obvious difference between the two types of objects. Paintings, sculptures, and buildings are physical objects; symphonies, poems, and plays are not. The symphony is an abstract object that is realized in various performances of it; the poem is a similarly abstract object that is instantiated in multiple printed or written or spoken forms; the play is also something abstract realized in performances. These performances and renditions are of variable quality, some better than others. Even in the case of the painting, the sculpture, and the building, each physical object is one member of a class of replicas, either actual as is usually the case with paintings, or potential as may be the case with buildings. And what is realized by these replicas is something abstract, just as with the symphony or poem. Lewis even goes so far as to apply this analysis to natural object like a landscape.

> there is no natural object which would inevitably solicit and reward esthetic contemplation if we merely open our outward senses to it. *Something* is essential which is not literally a physical property of it but associated with these: it is by that fact that genuinely esthetic values are to be distinguished from inherent values of a "lower" order, like the gratefulness of water to the thirsty man.[139]

The printed poem is a pattern of physical symbols. But these are merely the means by which the poem is conveyed from one mind to another. The meanings involved are related to the physical marks on the page by a complex of linguistic and social rules, yet it is only through the physical object that these meanings can be communicated. These meanings constitute the poem itself.

> What needs to be observed here is that the esthetic actuality—the poem— is *physically presented*, when conveyed by the printed page or by a reader's voice, but that this esthetic entity is not, either spatially or in any other appropriate sense, to be located within the physical object or event which serves to present it. Some of the properties of the poem—the language pattern of it—genuinely characterize the print on the page or the temporal sequence of the sounds. In much larger part, however, the "poem itself", being constituted by the meanings thus physically symbolized, lies in the *context associated with* this physical entity which presents it.[140]

This abstract entity associated with the physical object, Lewis says, is the "esthetic essence" and is that to which esthetic judgment is really addressed. This "essence" is not, he assures us, anything transcendental or mystical. Lewis even proposes an ordering of esthetic objects on the basis of the extent to which the esthetically essential lies in the physical properties of the thing or in the associated context. The proposed scale would run from literary objects at one extreme to natural objects at the other.

This argument certainly involves problems. What evokes an esthetic response is a concrete object, whether a building or a musical performance, not something abstract. And what does Lewis mean by "esthetic essence"? Clearly, he wants to emphasize that a poem or symphony is an abstract object that can be realized in multiple physical forms. But it is obvious that he means something more than this. The "essence," he says, "is in some part literally embodied, or capable of being embodied, in some physical thing which is the instrument of presentation, and in some part belongs to a context of this object, which is associated with it in some manner which is not subjective merely."[141] What this "context" is, Lewis never is able to say. Gottschalk takes it to be "a complexus of common properties, found in all aesthetic instances of anything properly bearing the title of that work of art."[142] But it is difficult to square this with Lewis's claim that the degree to which the esthetic essence lies in the physical properties of the object varies by type of object. One suspects that what he means is, in the case of the poem, the pattern of relationships among the meanings that a New Critic would have regarded as essential to the poem—a kind of meaning gestalt. This is consistent with his view that such an "essence" is found even in natural scenes like a sunset, where presumably it is not just the concrete scene but the gestalt created by its elements that has the esthetic quality. It can hardly be said that Lewis was clear on this point, but no one else has been much clearer.

Lewis's foray into esthetics was necessary for this book because he could hardly claim to have treated valuation if he had ignored esthetics. Furthermore, he had earlier considered the possibility that esthetics might be the science of values in general—a position from which he had retreated by the time he wrote the AKV. In his treatment of esthetics, Lewis was greatly influenced by the views of his colleague David Prall, as he acknowledged in his preface. Following Prall, he distinguishes esthetic experience from esthetic judgment, and regards esthetic experience as the absorbed contemplation of "the esthetic surface"—Prall's term. And, like Prall, he viewed esthetics as an empirical study. Lewis's concept of value is different from Prall's, who held an interest theory of value, and Lewis develops the subject in his own way, but unlike many writers who have classed esthetics and ethics together, Lewis sharply divides them, assigning esthetics to the theory of value, but giving ethics a quite different status.[143]

Having dealt with esthetic values, Lewis turns to the question of the *summum bonum*. In doing so, he sets forth principles that lie at the very heart of his philosophic vision. The most basic fact about human beings for Lewis is our temporality; we live in time, but, unlike other species, we are aware of that fact. This creates the fundamental necessity of human life to shape our actions to the realization of future goods and the avoidance of future ills, and it is awareness of the future and uncertainty about what it will bring that creates "concern" or anxiety, and presents us with the necessity of balancing our desire for present gratification against our desire for future gratification. It is because life has this character that we find rationality imperative, for "to be rational, instead of foolish or perverse, means to be capable of constraint by prevision of some future good or ill; to be amenable to the consideration, 'You will be sorry if you don't,' or 'if you do.' "[144] It is this characteristic of life that makes consistency imperative and so gives rise to logic, that requires adherence to principles and rules and the following of norms. The temporal character of human life, the fact that what we do now will have consequences for us later, is the reason why we must be rational, and must govern our actions by imperatives. Hence, such imperatives require no warrant beyond the nature of life itself; they are constitutive of rationality. To deny them, as the Cyrenaic does, is to contradict oneself "not formally but pragmatically," for he who would live by the injunction "Have no concern for the future" thereby expresses concern for the future.

Similarly, Lewis says,

> We may observe that the fundamental dictum of justice, "No rule of action is right except one which is right in all instances, and therefore right for everyone" is likewise not a principle acceptance of which either requires to be or could be inculcated by argument where natively the recognition of it should be absent. Logically considered, it is a tautology: it merely expresses a formal character of the correct or justified, implicit recognition of which is contained in acknowledgment of the distinction between right and wrong. Given this moral sense, recognition of the principle is mere selfclarification; and where the moral sense should be lacking, argument for this or any other principle of action would be pointless. This moral sense may be presumed in humans; and creatures who lack it can only be lured by some kind of bait or driven by some kind of goad.[145]

In this passage one can hear echoes of the moral sense doctrine of the Scots. Lewis holds that it is a generic trait of human beings to be sensitive to the distinction between right and wrong. He takes what he calls the "fundamental dictum" to be an explication of the meaning of that distinction, and therefore analytic. If the distinction were not already present in humans, no argument could inculcate it. Human nature itself is its basis.

It is a life found good in the living of it that is the *summum bonum*. "That fact," Lewis says, "is a datum of the human attitude to life." This claim does not lessen the intrinsic value of immediate experience; rather, it adds a new dimension to the process of valuation. Presentations are still "good for their own sake," but they are also to be valued in terms of their contribution to the good life. But this two-dimensional mode of valuation raises an obvious question of consistency; what are we to say about an experience that has high intrinsic value but is subversive of the good life? Lewis's answer is that value as immediately found "is subject to no critique." It is what it is and cannot be diminished. "But the *aim to realize it*, and the value of *having* that particular experience, are still subject to rational criticism by reference to the value which it may contribute instrumentally to any whole of experience in which it is included."[146] The struggle of human life, as Lewis sees it, is not between innate depravity and divine grace but between the desire for maximum satisfactions now and for the best complete life. Prostitutes may provide one with immediate intrinsic values, but frequenting them may be subversive of the good life.

The good life constitutes a whole of which particular intrinsic values are parts. But the relation is a special one; the good life forms a gestalt that has its own intrinsic value, while the particular intrinsic values of different experiences are components of the gestalt. These particular values are said to be "contributory" to the value of the whole, but they are contributory in a second sense of influencing one another. Thus, a course of training in art appreciation is an experience that has its own value, but it may also increase the value one finds in viewing paintings. The values found in the immediate experience of the painting are what they are, but they would have been less without the training.[147]

Lewis considers Bentham's view of the good life as an alternative to his own, but rejects it.[148] He agrees with Bentham that some values are capable of being ordered, but such an ordinal scale does not provide an interval level of measurement, and without that the hedonic calculus is impossible. But the critical objection is that for Lewis the good life is not an aggregate of separate pleasures but a gestalt. The whole here is not just a collection of particular values but has it own characteristic value that is not only qualified by its components but qualifies them in turn.

Lewis does not restrict life to the physical existence of the individual: "life is bounded, not by the physical limits of it, but by its horizon." "No man so brutish that he does not prospectively live in what he does and may do for his children; and there is none who feels no concern for any contribution he may make to the lives of others who will come after."[149] The inclusion of such ends adds a goodness (or badness) to a life, even though their realization lies beyond its temporal boundaries. As against Bentham, Lewis also insists that future goods must be considered as if they were present goods— that is, temporal distance should not lead to any discounting of a good. The reason, Lewis says, is that "one who followed this rule [of discounting by temporal distance] would, so far as his actions so decided affect the matter, be self-condemned to a less good life than he could otherwise achieve."[150] Presumably what Lewis means here is that if goods are discounted by their futurity, one would be more inclined to seek a present good in preference to a future good that would, if it should be realized in due course, be found to be greater than the previous good for which it was sacrificed.

The good life, Lewis says, is both cumulative and consummatory.[151] It has the character of the value of a musical composition, or a novel. While each note of the musical piece has its own value, the value of the whole is not a simple sum of the values of the parts but something greater—something that is progressively realized during the performance but not completely attained until the performance is over. The same can be said of the novel, or a drama; whatever the value of the separate lines, the value of the whole cumulatively unfolds during the reading and is consummated only at the end.

Lewis holds that this is particularly true of the life of action. When a goal is attained as the result of purposeful striving, its attainment constitutes an achievement whose value is quite different from what it would be if the goal were fortuitously acquired. The entire process of striving and attainment constitutes a gestalt in which the striving is infused with the value of the anticipated result and the value of the result is enhanced by the successful effort of attaining it. The value of the achievement is not an additive combination of its separate components but arises from their interrelations in a gestalt.[152]

Furthermore, if life is to be found good in the living of it, the ends sought must be ones that are highly valued and worth the striving to gain them. Verging on ethics, Lewis says

> We shall not here discuss, in the full scope of it, that final riddle of ethics that if duty be done towards another for *one's own* sake, then the peculiar significance of morally just action is lost to it; but that if it be done without regard to self-interest, then there may accrue to it a value findable in the first person.[153]

Lewis's point here is that an unworthy end diminishes the value of the action, just as a worthy end enhances it. But one notes that he already saw this particular issue as the "final riddle" of ethics—a riddle that would occupy him for the rest of his life.

How are we to determine the intrinsic value of our lives? This is not a question of something immediately given, for the whole of one's life cannot be present at once in immediate experience. Furthermore, the whole will include not only past experiences but anticipations of future experiences, as when a young person makes a plan for his or her life. Since, as Wittgenstein pointed out, death is not an event in life because it is not lived through, there can be no final retrospective summing up; the evaluations of a life must be made in midstream. This judgment is a nonterminating judgment and is subject to the same sorts of errors that all nonterminating judgments are subject to. But the difficulty here is particularly great.

> There is a kind of possible error to which assessment of the value of an experiential whole is especially liable—not specifically because it is *value*-quality which is in question, but because it is a difficulty affecting determination of any quality of a whole which runs beyond what can be apprehended at one moment, and it is a quality of that whole which is affected by the character of it as a *Gestalt*.[154]

Lewis invokes the term "synthetic intuition" to refer to the type of synthetic "envisagement" required; it is the same sort of synthetic process "by which we hear a symphony" rather than an aggregate of distinct notes. One is reminded here of Royce's synthetic insight in *The Sources of Religious Insight*. The value assessment so arrived at is something that has to be confirmed and can never provide certainty.[155] This is one case in which an intrinsic value is not indubitable, but it is also one in which the value can hardly be given.

In daily life, we do not usually weigh actions in terms of such a final value, but in serious decisions—precisely those that do affect the foreseeable course of our lives—we do. Granted that any such estimate of how our current conduct will affect the final evaluation must be probable at best and speculative at least, "the moral concern for the whole of life sets that end to which all particular aims must be subordinated, and constitutes the rational imperative."[156]

In concluding the book, Lewis deals with questions of utility and of instrumental value. But doing so leads him into a discussion of potentiality, about which he says:

> If we could envisage all reality and the whole of history, and be certain about it, there would be no occasion to refer to the potentialities of things in their relation to experience—whether value-potentiality or any

other kind. Instead we should then evaluate objects in that absolute fashion having reference only to their actual instrumentality in conducing to goods or ills found in experience. We should discard all reference to any conditions beyond the actual; and neither potentiality nor probability would be a concept for which we should find any application.[157]

This statement certainly seems to imply that, for Lewis, possibility is an epistemic category only, not an ontological one, or, put otherwise, that Lewis believes there are no real unactualized possibilities. Such a view is inconsistent with a number of other statements Lewis has made about possibility, and it is inconsistent with what he goes on to say in the next paragraph. For Lewis insists that properties such as solubility are real properties of substances like salt. A potentiality, Lewis says, is formulatable by an if–then statement asserting a "*real connection*"; "the salt has this property not only when or if it is put in water; it equally has it when not put in water, and if it is never put in water." But if in the completely envisaged reality supposed, this salt were never put in water, how could it still be soluble unless potentialities are real? Similarly, Lewis continues to insist on the truth of counterfactuals.

> Thus the attribution of any property to an unexamined object—or to an examined one for that matter—asserts a real connection between a hypothetical operation or observable circumstance and a certain observation or experience in result; and asserts the truth of this if-then statement of such real connection independently of the factual truth or falsity of either clause of it.[158]

Moreover, Williams records Lewis as holding

> that the causal and predictive connections which hold together the experience world, especially the conditionality required by the fundamental pragmatic scheme, "If circumstances x obtained, then if operation y were performed, then observation z would ensue," are similarly more than either rules of language or mere material or statistical associations. That just such conditionalities are indeed the ultimate hard facts—that there must be real *potencies*, as he used to assure neoscholastic friends—is the principle which he sometimes cited as his "realism."[159]

These statements cannot be made consistent with the claim that potentialities would vanish with complete knowledge of reality. They reveal either an ambiguity or a confusion in Lewis's thought that has serious consequences. This is the same ambiguity that showed itself in his early claim that real objects are identical with regularities in experience. In both cases, the issue is whether the actual, even if infinite, can exhaust the possible. If possibility is epistemic only, it reflects the limited character of our knowledge and would vanish if our knowledge were complete; the real would be nothing but our total experience; the meaning of nonterminating judgments would be nothing but the complete set of verified terminating judgments. This would reduce Lewis's position to a form of subjective idealism, or at best a phenomenalism. Yet Lewis frequently asserts that the reality of objects lies in their potentialities for experience, and that those potentialities remain real whether or not they are ever actualized. If that is so, then unactualized potentialities are real, and real objects are not just the sum of the actual experiences they produce. This problem is not a new one for Pragmatism. Indeed, in many ways it is *the* problem of Pragmatism. Peirce struggled with it and finally came down on the side of real unactualized possibilities; James struggled with it; Royce failed to face the issue squarely and never resolved it. Neither apparently did Lewis. What his position requires is the commitment to real unactualized possibilities, but, in 1946, either he did not clearly understand that or he misspoke. Whichever it was, he continued to treat objectivity in terms of potentiality, just as if unactualized potentialities were real, even though he sometimes denied them.

Lewis's main objective here is to demonstrate that many of the problems of value theory are apparent only and result from the complexity of value predications. Thus, he notes that in the case of utility and instrumental value there is a dual type of predication. On the one hand, these are predicated in the sense of a simple possibility that that of which they are predicated will conduce to the production of some effect. But, on the other hand, they are predicated "relative to circumstances known to be or assumed to be actual." Thus, one might say that a gold nugget no one will ever find "has no value," not because the potential is not there but because in the actual conditions it will never be realized. The latter sort of predication can be termed "value-in-fact," and obtains when the conditions of realization or nonrealization are either actual or highly probable. The confusion of these two modes of predication leads, Lewis says, to many errors.[160]

Among these are problems of the relativity of values to persons. When values are said to be relative to persons, whether to an individual or a class, or to all persons, the predication is one of value-in-fact, "connoting conditions actually affecting whatever persons are in question."[161] Thus, an object may possess a given potentiality for producing experience of intrinsic value, but this potentiality may not be realizable for certain people under certain circumstances. A man without legs will not find shoes useful, not because they have no potential utility but because in his circumstances the utility cannot be realized. A person who has been trained in music will be able to appreciate a composition that an untrained person will not. Herein Lewis finds the cause of a crucial type of error in value theory.

> It is because a thing which has value to one may have no value to another that value in general is sometimes denied to have the character of an objective property of the thing valued, and is said to be relative or subjective. . . . It is a simple and obvious consideration that a thing may genuinely have a certain potentiality for realizations of value in experience, though these can *not* be realized within the limits of actual conditions affecting some individual or individuals. . . . This merely signifies that S has certain incapacities, or is affected by certain circumstances, within the limits of which the potentialities which the object has for conducing to satisfactions cannot be realized.[162]

The fact that in certain conditions an object has no value to one person although it has value for someone else in different circumstances does not prove anything about the subjectivity of value.

These considerations, Lewis believed, enable us to deal with the problem created when some object having inherent value fails to produce intrinsic value for some people. But the theoretically more difficult question is raised when an object devoid of objective value nevertheless does produce experiences having intrinsic value in some people. Lewis notes that some values are comparative, as one might say that one tool is better than another or than others of its kind. But a tool that has comparatively little value may still be regarded by someone as having some value, even if it is a deviant one such as sentimental value. As Lewis notes, it is hard to think of any object totally devoid of any value at all. The value an object has for a particular person may be completely subjective—associations, for example, with a friend—yet for that person it does have real value, even if it has none for anyone else. Differences in valuation among people are, after all, what makes economic exchange possible, since some will pay dearly for what others regard as worthless.[163]

Lewis then raises the question of limitation of value predictions to those affecting human beings only and ignoring animals. This may seem surprising in a book written in the 1940s, and one might wonder if Lewis was some sort of protoanimal rights advocate. In fact, this concern reflects an older tradition rooted in the farm experience of an earlier generation. The question of the proper treatment of animals was often raised in nineteenth-century books on "moral science" and was a practical as well as a moral issue for those who grew up on farms where animals played a major part in the farm economy. But Lewis's view also reflects his adopting of what he called the "Law of Compassion" that he learned from Schopenhauer,[164] and that would later play an important part in his ethics.

The complexity of value predications also leads to what Lewis calls the "Fallacy of the Epithet," whereby the names given to things carry valuational implications that are false to the facts. "Because all things are subject to correct naming in various ways; and the logical distinction of essential from accidental is not one which is rooted in the nature of things but is itself relative to the chosen manner of naming them," the use of different names can persuade people of the essential properties of the object. But, as Lewis asserts, to think that the essence of an object can be determined independently of how it is named "is falsely to believe that reality itself determines what distinctions we shall observe and apply, and that classifications are metaphysically instead of pragmatically determined." This sort of fallacious use of value terms is obvious in propaganda and advertising. The sudden change from "used cars" to "preowned cars" is a typical example, but it is not confined to unscrupulous money-changers. "We may be reminded that Plato, who was the first to recognize the value-significance of names—the idea or essence of a thing is the good of it—himself conducted one of the most successful propaganda campaigns in history, rendering the name of his opponents (literally connoting wisdom) a permanently derogatory epithet."[165]

If value realizations are subject to conditions, it makes a difference to what degree those conditions are subject to our control. Lewis notes that positive values will be greater in proportion to the amount of control we have over their realization, and negative values will be greater the less control we have over their realization.

As a final example of the problems of value predications, Lewis considers social values. To solve this problem, Lewis says, Bentham proposed his calculus, but Lewis rejects that solution because he denies that values are measurable on a scale that will allow additivity. But Lewis does believe that values can be ordered. There is a problem of comparability—musical values are not directly comparable to color values. But all values are comparable in terms of contributory value—that is, their contribution to a good life; at least in theory such an ordering can be done. That leaves the problem of interpersonal comparison. Lewis's answer is that we can only know the value orderings of another person through empathetic identification.

> We have to "put yourself in the place of" the other person—whatever the epistemological hazards of doing so—and gauge value as realized by him on the supposition of whatever fundamental likeness to yourself seems justified by the evidence of his behavior and other pertinent circumstances.[166]

Supposing this to be possible, how should these different experiential worlds be weighted? Lewis proposes that they should be given equal weight, not only for ethical reasons, but because doing so would be the only way to make the valuation impersonal. If the question is one of choosing among two proposed social goods, Lewis poses the issue as:

> Supposing that you have envisaged the experience of all these persons involved, as accurately and adequately as you are able to do, which of these two objects would you prefer if the experience of all these persons were to be your own; as, for example, if you had to live the lives of each of them *seriatim*?[167]

Lewis admits that the idea of actually carrying this out for all people of a society is "fantastic," but his point is that it is theoretically possible, and that our actual estimate of the social values of a thing will be accurate only to the degree that it approximates what the result of such a procedure would be.

Lewis's goal in Book III is to develop a theory of valuation as a part of empirical knowledge. For him, questions of values are questions of fact, and the theory of empirical knowledge he developed in Book II is extended to apply to valuation. Despite the differences between direct experiences of intrinsic value and experiences of nonvaluational qualia, expressive statements of the former are treated like expressive statements of the latter. Nonterminating judgments of value face the same problems of confirmation as their nonvaluational counterparts; they are confirmed by the terminating judgments of value that constitute their sense-meaning. He does not deny that questions of value differ in some respects from other empirical questions, but he claims that these differences are not such as to differentiate valuation from empirical knowledge in general. But all this is, in Lewis's mind, a prolegomenon to the study Lewis devoted the rest of his life to—ethics. The question of the good, Lewis held, was a question of value and therefore empirical; but the questions of ethics are of a different order. "What is right and what is just, can never be determined by empirical facts alone."[168]

Reviews of the AKV were in general laudatory, but not uncritical. Book III on values drew the least criticism; it was Lewis's theory of meaning, particularly his treatment of propositions as terms, and his theory of empirical knowledge that drew fire. Lewis's claim that nonterminating judgments are translatable into terminating judgments led to the charge that this reduced his realism to phenomenalism and required the translation of statements about the past into statements about the future. Stace even suggested that Lewis's position was an early form of Positivist verificationism. What Lewis thought of these criticisms we do not know; he rarely answered his critics.[169]

But there was one critique of his position to which he did reply—that of Chisholm.[170] The point of attack for Chisholm is Lewis's statement that "an objective and nonterminating judgment must be translatable into judgments of the terminating kind." Chisholm takes this to mean "that any ordinary thing statement has, as analytic consequences, statements which refer solely to sense-data." Chisholm objects that the appearance of an object depends on both the character of the object itself and the conditions of perception, and that it is not possible to describe both of these in terms of appearances without circularity. Thus, consider the "thing statement"

> (*P*)   This is red.

and the sense datum statement

> (*R*)   Redness will appear.

"*P*", Chisholm says, does not entail "*R*" unless it is conjoined with a further statement

> (*Q*)   This is observed under normal conditions; and if this is red and is observed under normal conditions redness will appear.

"*P* & *Q*" imply "*R*", but "*P*" alone does not. Consider an alternative statement

> (*S*)   This is observed under conditions which are normal except for the presence of blue lights; and if this is red and is observed under conditions which are normal except for the presence of blue lights, redness will not appear.

"*S*" is consistent with "*P*", but "*P* & *S*" implies "not-*R*"; therefore it is impossible that "*P*" alone entails "*R*".

"*Q*" and "*S*" are "thing statements"; could they be reformulated in expressive terms? Chisholm argues that even if they could, it would make no difference, for if "*Q*" can be so reformulated, so can "*S*", and the previous argument still holds. Nor can "*Q*" or "*S*", when formulated as expressive statements, be held to be implied by *P*. Hence, it cannot be shown that any sense datum statement is implied by a thing statement alone. Rather, the thing statement must be conjoined with another thing statement such as "*Q*" in order to imply "*R*". One would then have the problem of testing "*Q*", and so on.

Lewis admired Chisholm and perfectly understood the consequences of his argument. "If that objection can be sustained [Chisholm's], then I agree with him in thinking that the type of empiricism of which my account is one variant—verification-theories and confirmation-theories of the meaning of empirical statements of objective fact—will be altogether indefensible."[171] But Lewis was not about to concede, because he believed that the only alternative to his own type of empiricism was skepticism. Lewis's first point is that some conditions of perception, such as the angle of perspective from which something is seen, are evident in the presentation itself and do not require further statements of objective fact. But this will not do for all such cases. To deal with the others, Lewis says,

> the given appearance may not be discernably different from that of some other kind of object, under conditions other than those which actually affect this observation—so that the appearance could "deceive" us under conditions which, for all we know, may presently obtain—but because the condition which would lead to this "deception" is one which is exceptional, there is a high correlation between just this given character of the appearance and the objective property it leads us to ascribe to the thing observed; in which case it remains the fact that the given appearance is a valid *probability*-index of the objective property.[172]

On the basis of this assertion, Lewis then attacks Chisholm's argument. The rule that if " 'P' entails 'R', then for any 'Q', 'P & Q' entails 'R' " is a true principle of ordinary logic, but it does not hold when probability statements are involved. Since probability statements are relative to their premises, it is quite consistent to hold that on premise "P & Q", "R" is highly probable, and also to hold that on premise "P & S", "not-R" is highly probable; the premises being different in the two cases, the probabilities may be different. Thus, Chisholm's argument does not hold against Lewis's theory, and Lewis reasserts his claim.

> Objective statements of fact are said to *entail* such probability-consequences because it is consequences of this sort which *are contained in what it means*—in one sense of meaning—to assert the objective statements from which they are derivative. It is such probable eventuations of experience, as results of possible ways of acting when certain appearances present themselves, which represent what we learn when we learn objective facts; and there is no directly testable content of any belief in an objective state of affairs beyond what could be specified in such predictions.[173]

Actually, Lewis is here reiterating and elaborating arguments he had already given in the AKV, where he had argued at length that such conditions of observation as the state of the test apparatus must be incorporated into the test hypothesis in expressive terms.[174]

Biographical Note V

Retirement

Lewis reached the age of seventy in 1953 and after completing the five additional years he had promised Conant, retired. He spent the next year at Princeton as a Hibbens Research Fellow,[1] teaching an advanced seminar and also writing. But with his retirement now final, the question of where the Lewises would spend their final years had to be settled. Partly because Mabel thought Lewis needed a milder climate, partly because David lived there, but chiefly because they had always loved California, they decided to make that their final home and purchased a house in Menlo Park at 68 Yale Road—a choice that occasioned some comment among their Harvard friends.[2] Although the move meant abandoning her many activities in Massachusetts, Mabel showed no reluctance, and was soon involved in a variety of church and social service activities in California. Lewis was at once appointed a lecturer at Stanford, so he continued to teach, and, of course, to write. Their move did not betoken any radical change in lifestyle.

Lewis had more requests to lecture and teach than he cared to accept, but, in 1954, he did give the Woodbridge Lectures at Columbia that were subsequently published as *The Ground and Nature of the Right*. In 1956, he gave the Mahlon Powell Lectures at the University of Indiana that were published as *Our Social Inheritance*. In 1957, he taught at the University of Southern California and in the summer of 1958 at Michigan State.[3] But his teaching at Stanford ended in 1957. His wife wrote:

> He taught the spring quarter there [Stanford], but he had found his students so ill-prepared, so unwilling to do the assigned work, so unused to any mental discipline in abstract, intensive thinking, he no longer found any satisfaction in trying to teach them. He was encountering

young people who, from their earliest school years, had been the victims of permissive education. They refrained from any unpleasurable exertion. I think what broke the camel's back was a student's contemptuous refusal to study such an old fogy as Kant. C decided that he could spend his time more profitably in writing, and gave up teaching.[4]

But he continued to lecture. He was invited to lecture at the University of Kyoto in Japan, but once again declined to leave the country.[5] He did, however, accept an invitation to lecture at Wesleyan in 1959. Lewis had given lectures there in 1952 and had enjoyed doing so, so he agreed to come back. But on the trip east, he suffered his second heart attack.[6] Despite that, he went on to Wesleyan and gave the lectures. Although not published in his lifetime, they were subsequently published as "Foundations of Ethics" in 1969.[7]

It is a testimony to Lewis's stature in the field that Paul Schilpp and his advisors decided to devote a volume of the Library of Living Philosophers to Lewis. This was a very considerable honor—it placed Lewis in a galaxy that included Russell, Whitehead, Einstein, Moore, Dewey, Santayana, Broad, and Carnap, among others. Lewis agreed, but at the cost of having to write a brief autobiographical note that would introduce the volume. Lewis hated doing that. On December 28, 1959, he wrote to Schilpp[8] and vented his feelings. "As I have told you, my autobiography is all written. As I have not told you, it is the worst piece of writing I ever did. I can't hope to do much better: I hate the idea of it. It happens that shortly ago I reread it for the first time. I now hate it worse."

Most of the content of this autobiography has been included above. Lewis describes himself as "an upcountry New England Yankee" and recounts his early life and education, his undergraduate years at Harvard, his teaching stint at the University of Colorado, his return to Harvard for graduate work, his years at Berkeley, and his final return to Harvard in 1920. He describes his work method—he spent part of every day at his desk writing on whatever came to mind. In his papers, there are many loose-leaf notebooks—unfortunately almost all from his later years—that contain those daily productions he considered worth saving. He describes his major publications, and tells us that when *Mind and the World Order* was republished in 1956, he reread it and was "less dissatisfied than I expected to be." Only two points, he says, gave him real regret. One was his treatment of the given, which he says is "the most difficult—the most nearly impossible—enterprise to which epistemology is committed." Still determined to uphold his position to the end, Lewis includes one last attempt to state the matter correctly. The other point is the last chapter of *Mind and the World Order*; he retracts nothing of what he said there, but comments that "I wish only that my discussion in the book had less the air of 'proving;' and more that of simply calling attention to: I come to think that matters so fundamental are, just by being thus fundamental, beyond the reach of anything appropriately to be regarded as proof." This is a bit disingenuous, since he had, in fact, tried to prove the principle of induction in *Mind and the World Order*, but after reading Reichenbach had recognized that the principle could not be proven.[9]

As previously noted, in 1932, after *Mind and the World Order* and *Symbolic Logic*, Lewis turned to ethics. "From the early years of my teaching I had thought of ethics as the most important branch of philosophy,"[10] but he found it necessary to revisit epistemology in order to establish in the AKV his thesis that valuation is a form of empirical knowledge. He says very little of his work on ethics after AKV, barely mentioning *The Ground and Nature of the Right* and *Our Social Inheritance*, but, of course, Lewis still hoped at that point that he would complete his "Foundations of Ethics" on which he was then working.

The most interesting part of the "Autobiography" is his account of his early years, particularly of his relations to Royce, Perry, James, and Peirce. The importance of the two former is brought out in a letter to Morton White on December 10, 1955, in reply to White's invitation to Lewis to participate in a Royce Centennial. In it, Lewis said "There is no one to whom I owe so much as to Royce for my own philosophical development, though my debt to Ralph Perry is close second. And in both cases I owe a personal debt which can't be paid."[11] This confirms what we have already seen to be the case.

The 1950s were a period of Republican rule and unremitting Cold War. Lewis was a Cold Warrior. He disapproved of professors "hiding behind the ivy" and had no hesitation in condemning the Soviet Union. But he had contempt for McCarthy and opposed the loyalty oath that at that time was required by law of university professors in California. His son recalled:

> I remember my mother saying, with respect to the loyalty oath. . . . Well, if they believe in it why shouldn't they swear to it? And Dad responding that this was an invasion, he felt, and that if it came right up to it he would not render a loyalty oath. What the hell do you want? I have served my country and I don't need to be interrogated.[12]

On the other hand, Lewis did oppose the appointment of Robert Oppenheimer as William James Lecturer at Harvard. Apparently the committee at Harvard wrote Lewis asking his opinion of the appointment. On March 3, 1957, he wrote back strongly advising the committee to "drop your activities in this matter at once."[13] Otherwise, he said, it would cause a "stink" that would damage Harvard, the Harvard Philosophy Department, and possibly Oppenheimer. He then went on to say that he had known Oppenheimer for some years and had followed the Oppenheimer security clearance case closely. "I give you credit for being smart men. If so, and if you had known Dr. Oppenheimer as well as I do, I think you would have read something 'between the lines' which would quite alter your opinion about it [the appointment] and him." He goes on to say that Oppenheimer is a "notably moral man" and that his scientific colleagues have "unshaken confidence" in him. The letter is peculiarly oblique. Lewis was a strong anti-Communist, but it is not clear whether he opposed the appointment because he considered Oppenheimer too far left or because of the controversy he thought it would cause. But there is no doubt that he did oppose it.[14]

Lewis was not a man noted for his humor, but he did have his moments. In December 1959, he was having trouble getting the *Palo Alto Times* delivered to his house. On the 16th he wrote the paper as follows.

> Please run ad below under HELP WANTED daily until I get action from it. Will report response to you daily if desired. Bill me at above address.
>
> > Very truly yours,
> > C. I. Lewis

> PRIZE of 2 dollars paid to anyone who will induce *Palo Alto Times* to resume daily delivery of paper to 68 Yale Road, M. P.[Menlo Park]. More persuasive power than I have required.[15]

One presumes that delivery was restored.

His wife found among his papers an interview Lewis had given to his granddaughter Wendy (David's oldest child) in connection with some school project. The questions are hers, the answers his.

> How did you happen to be a professor?
>   My uncle asked if I would rather or go fishing.
> Why did you take philosophy as your subject?
>   It looked like a gravy racket to me.
> What is philosophy?
>   Philosophy is a blind man in a dark closet looking for a black cat that isn't there.
> Why is philosophy?
>   Yes, if it doesn't rain.

What is philosophy used for?
     To make square pegs fit round holes.
Who made it up?
     It came from the mouths of babes.[16]

On May 5, 1961, Lewis wrote:

> We live for the sake of our children. And our children have found it out.
> They see no reason to change that happy arrangement and grow up. The
> welfare state in which nobody ever grows up is the projected ideal. It can
> be realized as soon as all our thinking, as well as all the work, can be
> turned over to robots. Progressive education can then be prolonged to
> age fifty, at which time everybody becomes entitled to a pension. The
> Politboro will provide management, and surplus spinsters can man the
> control panels.[17]

It is obvious that Lewis did not approve of the direction in which the
country was going. He felt that he had made it on his own (which he had)
and that anyone with ability and desire could do the same. Like so many
who have risen from poverty to success, he had little sympathy for those he
had left behind.

During the 1950s, Lewis developed, or indulged, his love of music. He
and his granddaughter Wendy often listened to music together. His taste was
for symphonic and chamber music, and he was particularly fond of lieder.
Although he did not play an instrument and had long since given up singing
himself, he collected records and played them at home. He also continued
to play the stock market with considerable success. This was an ideal time
since the American economy was exceptionally prosperous. Whether he was
a smart investor or a lucky one, the result was that the Lewises had a comfortable income and, when he died, he left enough to maintain Mabel in
comfort until she died at the age of one hundred and two.[18]

9

After the AKV

EPISTEMOLOGY

In 1949, Lewis delivered a paper before the Association for Symbolic Logic entitled "Some Suggestions Concerning Metaphysics of Logic."[1] The paper was published eight years later, but it belongs to the earlier period, and both the content and the context of its delivery show that it was addressed to the analytic–synthetic controversy. Lewis asserts that his subject is the relation of the conceptual and the existential. And, he says, "the general thesis which these [arguments] seem to me to support is that the conceptual and the existential are irreducibly different categories," both necessary for any theory of logic, but that within logic itself "there are only such truths as are certifiable from conception alone and are independent of existential fact." Logic is concerned only with what is deducible from what, not with any question of material truth.[2] Having laid down that dictum, Lewis says that it is desirable to identify the ground on which the logically true is distinguished from the logically false. This cannot be done by reference to language. In the first place, linguistic entities are universals. In the second place, "the meaning associated with a symbol and essential to its being a linguistic entity, must be a psychological or mental entity." Lewis says he wants to avoid questions of mind, but that meanings are clearly mind-dependent—"no minds, no meanings." "This meaning as characterizing different psychological events, and the same for any occasion of its entertainment, is the concept."[3] In the third place, meanings serve as the criteria

319

determining what is referred to, and do so by specifying the character of the actual thing essential to its being referred to by the meanings. The concept is prior to language and is the fundamental constituent of language: "We do not first have marks and sounds and then invent or try to discover concepts for them to convey, but devise language to convey what is conceptually entertained." The relations among meanings "are as they are";[4] they are not created by language but underlie the use of language.

The intension of an expression is the criterion of classification that has to be satisfied; the denotation depends on the accidents of actuality—that is, it is meaning as application, the actual things picked out as satisfying the criterion. Lewis then briefly set out his theory of the modes of meaning. In doing so, he distinguishes the statement "S" from the proposition, which he now writes as "that S," that is, "that Mary is baking pies now." This "formulation of their relations in intension," Lewis says, "never requires quotation marks; and one superficial objection to the logic of intension thereby loses its superficial plausibility."[5] This comment is directed at Quine's charge that in Strict Implication Lewis had confused use and mention. Lewis's answer is "that today is Monday implies that tomorrow is Tuesday" involves no such confusion.

On December 29, 1951, a symposium was held at a meeting of the Eastern Division of the American Philosophic Association in which Reichenbach and Goodman attacked Lewis's theory of the certainty of expressive statements of the given and Lewis defended it. Reichenbach led off.[6] There were, he said, three arguments for Lewis's position. The first stems from the procedure by which such "report propositions" or "phenomenal propositions," as he calls them, are introduced. According to Reichenbach, they are introduced when we find that an observation report in a physical language is false; we then retreat to saying that, even though it is false, what we saw was so and so. Thus the phenomenal report—"I saw so and so"—appears certain, since to reach it we have, as it were, subtracted out what was false. It should be noted that Lewis nowhere used this procedure for introducing such statements. The second argument is that observation cannot lie, and that the only source of error for phenomenal propositions is misstatement—that is, a failure of linguistic formulation such as using the wrong word. So if we exclude errors of linguistic formulation, there are no other sources of error for phenomenal propositions. The third argument is that if, as Lewis does hold, empirical knowledge is probable, then in order that any propositions have nonzero probabilities, some propositions must be certain.

Reichenbach attacks the last argument first. Let "s" be the sentence "The probability of event E is p." If "s" is not certain but only probable, let "q" be the probability "s" is true. Then the probability of "E" is "$q \cdot p$." Now if the statement "'s' has probability q", is only probable—say with probability "r"—then the probability of "E" is "$r \cdot q \cdot p$." And so on. Clearly the product ". . . $r \cdot q \cdot p$" goes to zero as the number of terms increases. But Reichenbach argues that this argument is incorrect, for "E" may still be probable even if "s" is false. That is, if "s" is false, the probability of "E" may not be "p" but something else entirely, say "p^*." In that case, the probability of the event "E" is not "$p \cdot q$" but "$(p \cdot q) + (1 - q) \cdot p^*$." This expression need not be smaller than "p" and can be larger. But the sentence asserting *this* probability of "E" may itself be only probable. Clearly, if each sentence asserting a particular probability of its predecessor is itself only probable, we will have, not Lewis's product "$p \cdot q \cdot r \ldots$" but a series of sums of products with no reason to think it convergent at all. Thus, it does not follow that unless some proposition is certain, no proposition can have nonzero probability.[7] Furthermore, Reichenbach points out that Lewis's product "$p \cdot q \cdot r \ldots$" is not the probability of the event "E" but the probability that each of an infinite series of sentences is true, which can hardly be anything but zero.

Reichenbach attacks the second argument for Lewis's position by arguing that on Lewis's theory

> report sentences cannot *strictly imply* predictions; i.e., any implications to the future cannot be analytic implications, or, what is perhaps the same thing, strict implications in the sense of Lewis's famous term, or even synthetic nomological implications, when I use this term to denote the form of implication represented by the laws of nature. So the implications from report sentences to predictions of further report sentences must be probability implications.

But Reichenbach says such relations work in both directions. "If the phenomenal sentence a, in a certain context, makes the phenomenal sentence b highly probable, whereas non-a would make non-b highly probable, then conversely, the verification of b will make a highly probable, whereas the verification of non-b would make a highly improbable."[8] That means, Reichenbach says, that other phenomenal sentences contribute indirect evidence for or against the given phenomenal sentence. Reichenbach then gives an example *in physical object terms* in which a given individual sentence could be refuted by the indirect evidence of other sentences; to uphold the given sentence in the face of such evidence, he says, "is equivalent to predicting that the class of observation sentences . . . will be so extended as to turn the negative indirect evidence into positive evidence."[9] Reichenbach claims that this principle, which he calls the "principle of *inductive consistency,*" holds in the same way for cases in the phenomenal language. He concludes:

> I arrive at the result that phenomenal sentences cannot be absolutely certain, because retaining an individual sentence against any possible indirect evidence may lead to the abandonment of inductive consistency. This argument I regard as a conclusive proof against the thesis [Lewis's thesis].[10]

Finally, Reichenbach attacks the argument that error for phenomenal sentences can arise only from poor linguistic formulation by arguing that we would only recognize such an error from inconsistencies among our phenomenal sentences, and that the argument that the error was the result of poor linguistic formulation is a psychological explanation for its being in error.

Reichenbach then attacks the notion of a phenomenal language, arguing that knowledge requires a physical object language. But in doing so, he states an important principle of his philosophy: "Our knowledge is built up, not from facts, but from what we know about facts; and knowing refers to language. Phenomenal knowledge must somehow be given in linguistic form . . . and for this very reason it can be false."[11]

Goodman's turn was next.[12] Using an argument that he had first used in his dissertation in 1940,[13] Goodman sought to prove that not all phenomenal sentences are certain. Consider the following three sentences.

1. At time t_1 this patch is red.
2. At time t_2 this patch is blue.
3. Between t_1 and t_2 this patch did not change color.

All three are phenomenal statements; the use of time coordinates is irrelevant since they could be easily replaced by phenomenal terms. But Goodman says that since the three are inconsistent, one at least must be false. Hence, not all phenomenal sentences are certain. But Goodman does not deny that there is a given; what he denies is that anything given is true. For what is given is experience, whereas "truth and falsity and certainty pertain to statements or judgments and not to mere particles or materials or elements."[14] Moreover, Goodman points out that Lewis's own theory does not require certainty of phenomenal statements; what it requires is credibility, and that can be compatible with the withdrawal of some phenomenal sentences, just as some memorial sentences can be rejected, even though all memorial statements have prima facie credibility.

But Goodman notes that these arguments miss the heart of the matter, which is "the problem of relating language to what it describes." He therefore sketches a theory of signaling in which a particular experience may serve as a signal for a future experience; a statement "*p*" asserting the existence of a red patch in the visual field could signal a future statement-event that will occur when a similar patch occurs at a future time. Goodman does not try to elaborate this into a theory of language; his point is only to suggest that such a signaling relation may underlie language, and that the explanation of how language relates to experience may require some such device.

Lewis's replies are both a defense of his own system and an answer to his two critics.[15] He has already made his case in print and does not try to repeat it here. Yet he is bothered by his critics: "this dissent with respect to something which, if correctly stated, should be obvious gives me pause."[16] This is the first time Lewis publicly expressed his frustration at the refusal of his critics to admit his theory of the given. And it is more than just frustration, because Lewis reiterates his belief that the only alternatives for a plausible theory of knowledge are empiricism of the sort he espouses, or the coherence theory of truth, and that is not enough.

> We have nothing but experience and logic to determine truth or credibility of any synthetic judgment. Rule out datum-facts afforded by experience, and you have nothing left but the logically certifiable. And logic will not do it.[17]

Lewis then takes up Reichenbach's paper. Reichenbach's theory, Lewis says, is a modern and sophisticated form of the coherence theory of truth phrased in terms of probability. As to his argument with respect to the regress of probabilities unless some statement is certain, Lewis asserts that Reichenbach would have to show that the series he defines does not converge to zero, "and I question whether such proof can be given."[18] Lewis is adamant in reasserting his position that nothing is probable unless something is certain. This answer is not a strong one. Given the nature of the series of probabilities defined by Reichenbach's argument, it is doubtful that it can be shown to converge to any limit. Lewis also rejects Reichenbach's "argument from concatenation." It is true, he notes, that by the use of Bayes theorem, "we may proceed in either direction, determining the probability of a 'consequence' from the probability of a 'ground,' or of a 'ground' from a 'consequence.'" But this requires the assignment of numerical probabilities as the priors. "These must literally be determined *before* the use of the rule will determine the probability of anything." And if that determination is by a rule, what will determine that? And so on, ad infinitum. "The supposition that the probability of anything whatever always depends on something else which is only probable itself, is flatly incompatible with the justifiable assignment of any probability at all."[19]

Lewis notes that both Reichenbach and Goodman require that "protocols" (that is phenomenal statements) be consistent. Lewis replies "there is no requirement of consistency which is relevant to protocols." "The careless observer's protocols, the insane man's direct experience, and the content of the dreamer's dream must not be corrected or eliminated in the interest of consistency; to do that would be simple falsification of the facts of experience."[20] The problem is to explain the experience we have, including its inconsistencies. To throw out protocols because they are inconsistent is to falsify the data.

Lewis has time and space to deal only briefly with Goodman's remaining points, but his objection is clear enough. Goodman's proposed theory of signaling is concerned with prediction only.

> However plausibly such reformulation could be carried out, it would fail to satisfy me because of a conviction I have concerning the task of epistemological study; the conviction, namely, that a principal business of epistemology is with the *validity* of knowledge. And validity concerns the character of cognition as warranted or justified.[21]

Even if Goodman's proposed signaling theory could deal with prediction, it would not provide justification. "It is," Lewis says, "on account of that point that I have felt it necessary to depart from or to supplement other pragmatic theories." It is because he regards the certainty of the given as essential to justification that Lewis stands by his view. For the alternative to an empiricism rooted in experience is in Lewis's eyes skepticism, and that is "an intellectual disaster."[22]

Public arguments of this sort were not to Lewis's liking, but reviewing the three papers, even though his opponents had twenty pages to make their arguments whereas he had only seven to answer them, it seems clear that Lewis won the argument. Lewis is right to deny that protocols must be consistent, and even Goodman's triad of contradictory statements does not pose a real problem for him. Think of the well-known phenomenon of the duck–rabbit: at one moment it looks like a duck, at the next is looks like a rabbit, yet the linear figure remains unchanged. This is true of all reversible figures—the rat–man, the face–vase, the young woman–old woman, the Necker cube, and so on. Even with respect to colors, the white triangle illusion shows that a color patch that does not change can look different from second to second. Reichenbach and Goodman insist on applying to protocols criteria that hold of statements of objective fact. Once that error is eliminated, most of their arguments evaporate. Reichenbach's probability argument remains a problem for Lewis, but not a vital one; at best it would eliminate one ground for Lewis's belief that protocols *had to be* certain, but it does not show they are not. And underlying the whole discussion was a fundamental difference that was never made explicit. Reichenbach and Goodman believed all knowledge had to be in language; Lewis believed knowledge was conceptual and often inadequately formulated in language. In this sense, as so often in such debates, the contestants talked past each other.

It is also significant that, in his replies, Lewis refers to expressive statements of the given as "protocols." This was the term used in the early debates of the Vienna Circle for statements "which express the result of a pure immediate experience without any theoretical addition."[23] I know of no other occasion on which Lewis used this term to describe his own view, and his decision to do so in a debate with Reichenbach, who had been a member of the Berlin Group in the 1920s and 1930s, and Goodman, whose dissertation had been inspired by the program of the *Aufbau*, was surely no accident. Lewis was telling them that the original position held by Schlick and others had been right all along.

Lewis's papers are generally free from expressions of his personal feelings, but occasionally when he was feeling low he wrote personal comments that are worth preserving. In a fragment written sometime in 1952, he wrote:

> A scientist is supposed to tell the rest of us something which we do not know but which, if we doubt it, he can prove. A philosopher is supposed to tell us something which we already know but have failed to recognize as a fact, hence something which if it be doubted nobody can prove. Being a scientist is a delightful business; it gives a man authority. And if a scientist happens to be wrong, nobody but another scientist can find it out. Being a philosopher is a miserable business. There is no authority in philosophy. And if a philosopher is wrong, anybody can find it out.[24]

It may not be an accident that this dour reflection was written in 1952. Six years before, Lewis had published the AKV; now central doctrines of that book were under attack. Lewis was well aware of the assault on analyticity that was under way at Harvard, and he may well have felt himself under siege.

In May 1947, a three-way correspondence had begun among Quine, Morton White, and Nelson Goodman on the issue of the analytic–synthetic distinction.[25] All three were at that point skeptical of the distinction, with Goodman being the most opposed to it and Quine still hoping to find a "behavioristic criterion" of synonymy. The two defenders of the distinction against whom their comments are directed were Lewis and Carnap, whose views were seen as similar. The upshot of this correspondence was the agreement among the three that White would write "a survey article" dealing with the problem. The result was a paper entitled "The Analytic and the Synthetic: An Untenable Dualism" that White read before the Fullerton Club at Bryn Mawr College on May 14, 1949, and that was published the next year.[26]

White cast the paper as a Deweyian attack on a dualism that was untenable, and fully acknowledged the influence of Quine and Goodman. He carefully limited his target to statements traditionally seen as examples of essential predication such as "All men are rational animals" and did not discuss logical statements such as "$p \vee \sim p$." However, he points out that analytic statements of the sort he is discussing can be obtained from logical statements by the substitution of synonyms for synonyms—that is, "Every P is P" yields "Every man is a man" and then "Every man is a rational animal," if "man" is synonymous with "rational animal." Thus, the root problem is the explanation of synonymy. White deals rather summarily with the use of formal languages to define analyticity and synonymy, pointing out that such languages are arbitrary creations of philosophers in which what is taken as analytic depends on the creator's "formal fancy." Such formal languages offer no help in defining the questionable terms in natural languages.

White then considers two statements often used to justify the analytic–synthetic distinction. (1) "Analytic statements are those whose denials are self-contradictory." But the denial of "All men are rational animals"—that is, "Some men are not rational animals"—is not obviously self-contradictory, unless "men" is substituted for "rational animals" which takes synonymy for granted and so begs the question. Nor will less formal criteria of self-contradictoriness do, for these boil down to feelings of discomfort in the presence of the sentence alleged to be self-contradictory. Such criteria could at most offer a difference of degree between analytic and synthetic statements and that will not support the traditional dualism.

The second statement is: (2) "If we were presented with something which wasn't a rational animal, we would not call it a man." White argues that this would require "us" to distinguish the responses of speakers to calling something not a rational animal a man from their responses to calling something not a featherless biped a man, and that, at best, one could by such methods only find a distinction in degree of certainty in the responses. That again would undercut the traditional sharp distinction. Moreover, White points out that this whole argument hinges on the use of contrary to fact conditionals, which are "just as much in need of explanation as the notion of *analytic* itself."

In this article, the only advocate of the analytic–synthetic distinction that White addresses by name is Lewis. "Lewis is led to say that whether 'All men are rational animals' is analytic in a natural language . . . depends on whether the *criterion in mind* of *man* includes *the criterion in mind* of *rational animal*."[27] That is to be determined by an "experiment in imagination" that will show whether or not a nonrational animal that is a man is consistently thinkable. But White argues that this leads to a "private, intuitive insight" that offers no way to explain the analyticity of "commonly understood statements." Lewis's examples of the inclusion of the sense-meaning of rectangle in that of square or of one plan in another are for White something one either sees or does not see, since this "inclusion" relation for Lewis is "sense-apprehensible," and he regards this as an appeal to intuition. White does say, however, that "Lewis has dealt with this matter more extensively than any recent philosopher who advocates a sharp distinction between analytic and synthetic, and his arguments are too complex to be treated here." In any event, White says his differences with Lewis involve the issue of intensionality and "that is a large matter."[28]

White's article was merely the opening gun. In 1951, Quine brought up the heavy artillery when he published "Two Dogmas of Empiricism."[29] Lewis rarely mentioned his opponents by name, but in his notes for "Proseminar Lectures on Practical Philosophy in 1952,[30] Lewis spoke about Quine by name. Because of the importance of the conflict between the two men, I will quote it at length. Lewis made what he called "Point (1): What is a priori is certifiable by reference to relations of our concepts—our meanings entertained—which relations can be determined as holding by reference to the concepts themselves."

This dictum is itself an example of the point I want to make. Prof. Quine would not accept it without a lot of talk, because (a) he probably doesn't like the word 'concept', being suspicious of what I have in mind when I use it, and (b) he doubts, without being certain about it, that my notion so expressed would stand up to certain requirements he sets store by. I have entirely similar suspicions of his vocabulary and of his clarity about certain requirements the significance of which I think is fundamental. We should like to debate certain issues concerning the nature of logic and the a priori. But we have difficulty in finding sufficiently precise words (concepts) which we can both agree to use to start with.

We both agree that the questions we should like to debate are questions of discoverable truth, and we both think that truth of questions of this sort [is] important. We are very much less far apart than many others who are interested in these questions. But—let us face the fact—we are both aware that to reach any mutually satisfactory mutual understanding to start from, and one of us persuade the other from there on, would take more time than either of us could spare. We both of us in fact entertain the thin hope that some of you who listen to us and read what we write will go on from where we leave off; and each of us secretly believes—I am foolish enough to let the secret out—that someday those who interest themselves will come to agree that he had the truth of this matter. Neither of us, as a fact, grasps with a absolute clearness and correctness, the full pattern of implications (in my good sense of 'implications', not his bad sense) of his own conceptions. I take it that if, per impossible, we did, we should come to full agreement. But that doesn't enable us fully to agree now.

This is, so far as I know, the only time Lewis ever referred to Quine or his writings on analyticity. And in lecturing to a class, Lewis would not have criticized a colleague. Nor is there any reason to believe that he harbored any animus toward Quine. His son recalls that he regarded Quine with "affection and respect. Whatever academic or theoretical philosophical differences they may have had, this was of no particular consequence in terms of their personal relationship and I know that Dad had enormous respect for Quine's mind."[31] Nevertheless, the issues between them were of fundamental importance.

"Two Dogmas of Empiricism" is the most influential single article published by an American philosopher in the twentieth century. This article was the outcome of the debate over analyticity that had raged since 1939 and was explicitly directed against the views of Lewis and Carnap.[32] Quine states the two dogmas in question as follows:

> One is a belief in some fundamental cleavage between truths which are *analytic*, or grounded in meanings independently of matters of fact, and truths which are *synthetic*, or grounded in fact. The other dogma is *reductionism*: the belief that each meaningful statement is equivalent to some logical construct upon terms which refer to immediate experience.[33]

Quine deals with the initial dogma first. Pointing out that analyticity could be defined if synonymy could be defined, and vice versa, he argues that neither concept can be given a clear definition. But, in doing so, Quine rejects the use of intensional entitles. "A felt need for meant entities may derive from an earlier failure to appreciate that meaning and reference are distinct," Quine says, and asserts that "the primary business of the theory of meaning [is] simply the synonymy of linguistic forms and the analyticity of statements: meanings themselves, as obscure intermediary entities, may well be abandoned."[34] Having made this crucial move, Quine shows that appeal to definition will not serve to clarify either questionable notion since definitions themselves presuppose synonymy. He then considers two possible ways of defining analyticity and synonymy. The first is substitution salva veritate in an *extensional* language, which is easily shown to be inadequate. The second is Carnap's method of defining analytic sentences in formalized languages as those true by semantic rules. As Quine shows, this requires an explanation of why something is a semantic rule beyond the fact that it is labeled as such, and no satisfactory explanation is available. Quine concludes that the distinction between the analytic and the synthetic is untenable: "that there is such a distinction to be drawn at all is an unempirical dogma of empiricists, a metaphysical article of faith."[35]

From Lewis's point of view, this attack on the analytic–synthetic distinction fails. Lewis would be the first to agree that substitution salva veritate in an *extensional* language is no criterion of synonymy, and he had already rejected the idea that stipulating certain sentences in a formal language as analytic could accomplish anything. For Lewis, Quine's error is the rejection of intensional entities; Lewis had always held that synonymy and analyticity were intensional relations and that they could not possibly be defined extensionally.

It is Quine's attack on the second dogma that was devastating for Lewis. As Quine puts it, "the dogma of reductionism survives in the supposition that each statement, taken in isolation from its fellows, can admit of confirmation of infirmation at all."[36] This is a fundamental principle of Lewis's theory of meaning; it is precisely what is asserted by the claim that a nonterminating judgment is confirmable or disconfirmable by a specific set of terminating judgments. Quine gives the argument against this principle in a very compressed form, but it will be useful to expand it. A statement alone has little in the way of logical consequences. What is usually meant by the logical consequences of a statement is its consequences when conjoined with some set of auxiliary hypotheses. Letting "h" be the hypothesis and "$a_1 \ldots a_n$" the auxiliaries and "C" the consequence, the inference has the form

$$h \,\&\, a_1 \,\&\, \ldots \,\&\, a_n --> C$$

It follows by modus tollens that, if C is false,

$$\sim C --> \sim h \, v \sim a_1 \, v \ldots v \sim a_n$$

The falsity of "C" can be accommodated by rejecting any hypothesis of the disjunction; hence, "h" can be preserved by suitable adjustments of the auxiliaries. "h" cannot therefore be disconfirmed by "$\sim C$." Further, we may have multiple theories, each of which is confirmed by a given set of empirical statements, in which case the choice among them will be made on grounds of simplicity, utility, consistency with other theories, and similar criteria.

Hence, it cannot be said that "*h*" is confirmed by any specific set of empirical statements. Quine's famous metaphor for this situation is that our knowledge is "a man-made fabric which impinges on experience only along the edges. . . . A conflict with experience at the periphery occasions readjustments in the interior . . . no particular experiences are linked with any particular statements in the interior . . . except indirectly through considerations of equilibrium affecting the field as a whole."[37] Any statement within the network of knowledge can be rejected, including those of mathematics and logic, if doing so provides a simpler and more usable theory that fits experience better.

White's paper and particularly "Two Dogmas" had disastrous consequences for the position Lewis had advanced in the AKV. Although Lewis did not attack Quine or White directly, there are passages in his writings that deal explicitly with the analytic–synthetic issue. In his reply to Asher Moore's paper in the Schilpp volume, Lewis noted that during his lifetime Kant's notion of the synthetic a priori had been replaced by the conviction that all a priori statements are analytic. But Lewis says that although *Principia Mathemetica* seemed to support this view,

> the exclusively extensionalist logical theory which is built into that work is incompatible with taking this distinction [analytic–synthetic] as finally valid; and that those who carry forward this exclusively extensionalist conception of the logical, and refuse to recognize any significance in the logic of intension, are bound eventually to challenge the validity of this distinction between the analytic and the synthetic. And in result . . . they are then left with no ground for distinguishing a priori from a posteriori, and no clear conception of the foundation of logic and mathematics as distinct from physics and psychology.
>
> Exactly this process of attrition has now begun; though perhaps the consequences, for logic and for theory of knowledge, have not yet been squarely faced. So far as the history of thought suggests, there is no theory of the possible validity of knowledge which is compatible with such a radical empiricism as is implied by repudiation of analytic truth. . . . The suggestion is that we are back with the Sophists; or if not, must at least begin all over again, and from scratch.[38]

Lewis made no bones about the consequences of this debate for his own philosophy. "I wish to acknowledge that the whole body of my philosophic conceptions, in logic, epistemology, theory of value, and even ethics, depends on the validity of this distinction; and if that plank is pulled from under me, the whole structure will come tumbling down."[39] This is a precisely accurate appraisal. The fundamental issue between Quine and Lewis was the existence of conceptual meanings and their relations, and the ascendency of Quine's views after the publication of "Two Dogmas" marked the eclipse of Lewis's philosophic work.

But even more devastating for Lewis's position in the AKV was Quine's attack on the second dogma. If the logical consequences of a proposition are relative to the choice of auxiliary hypotheses, Lewis's theory of intensional meaning becomes untenable, his theory of empirical knowledge fails since there is no set of terminating judgments that constitute the sense-meaning of a nonterminating judgment, and the attempt to show that valuation is a type of empirical knowledge suffers the same fate. Lewis knew very well that the consequences inferred from a hypothesis required the use of auxiliary hypotheses; he had made this point himself on a number of occasions. But he had not drawn the conclusion Quine drew. So far as I know, Lewis never attempted to answer Quine's argument, or commented on it. Indeed, Lewis ignored Quine's attack on the second dogma and continued on with his work as though it had never happened. Lewis obviously knew about it, yet whenever he acknowledged Quine's work at all, he was concerned only with the attack on the first dogma. And there is a deep irony here, for Lewis's position in *Mind and the World Order* was in some ways closer to Quine's than the position he took in the AKV. In his efforts to meet the challenge of the Positivists in the 1930s and 1940s, Lewis had recast his views in a more rigorous, and rigid, form that in some ways resembled theirs. Now having just completed his monumental efforts to answer them, he suddenly found himself outflanked. By 1952, the AKV was in ruins, and Lewis left epistemology behind, remarking to Victor Lowe that he had done what he could in epistemology and would now leave the field to younger men.[40] In his later years, Lewis did occasionally deal with topics in the theory of knowledge, but he published very little on the subject.

By 1953, Lewis had also become tired of wrangling about the given. In a letter on March 28, 1953, to Professor Thomas Hill of Macalister College,[41] he commented: "the fact is that—irrationally—I have got sick of that topic, though realizing that I have never stated what I think about it in any way I should now regard as the best I could do." Lewis now proposed to designate anything that can be "discovered directly in experience" as "found"—a usage that harks back to the AKV where Lewis spoke of value-qualities as found in experience. The "found" then is to be the general term for the directly experienced; the "given" should be restricted to those found qualities that "exhibits the phenomenological qualities usually accepted as sanctioning objective reference"—that is, those to which cognitive significance is usually assigned. However, Lewis is careful to point out that to classify something as "given" is not to assert that it has cognitive status—that is, objective reference; it is only to say that it is the sort of quale that usually functions in that way.

Why does Lewis introduce this new distinction? The reason is that in questions of valuation, the evidence against which judgments of objective value are tested is "feelings of satisfaction and dissatisfaction." Calling these "found" rather than "given" will, he believes, avoid any suggestion that these qualities have objective reference.

But he could not let the issue go. In his "Replies" in the Schilpp volume, he wrote:

> I have reached the point of exasperation about this topic. As it appears to me, no conscious being capable of self-observation and abstract thinking, can fail to be aware of that element in his experience which he finds, willy-nilly, as it is and not otherwise; or to recognize that, without this, he could have no apprehension of an external world at all.[42]

He also continued to emphasize the key role of counterfactuals in knowledge. In a letter to Victor Lowe in 1953, Lewis discussed this topic. Chisholm and Goodman, he said, overlooked the obvious interpretation of them. As Lewis puts it,

> "If I should do A, then E" is equivalent in force to "The premise 'I do A' plus other premises of the (actual or hypothetical) case, are sufficient for the inductive conclusion, "E will follow." . . . I know what *would* have happened only in that manner in which I know what inductive conclusions are justified by presumption resumption of the contrary to fact-condition and other pertinent presumptions (actual or hypothetical). If there is any possibility of valid inductive conclusions, then whatever makes these conclusions valid to infer from their premises makes them *valid* to infer *independently of the question* whether the premises are true or false.[43]

That is, Lewis holds that given "I do A" as a premise, if there is a valid "inductive"—that is, probability—inference from "I do A," with or without auxiliary hypotheses, to "E will follow," then the conditional is true whether or not "I do A" is true. This is exactly what strict implication means, and the so-called problem of counterfactuals is the result of the failure of those who cannot see that. As Lewis comments, "Most of those who have gone into print on this topic are trying to make the matter amenable to a truth-value logic. Their trouble is due to the fact that *no* principles of valid *inference* are capable of statement in terms of a truth-value logic." Thus, the whole "problem of counterfactuals," as Lewis sees it, is due to his old bete noir, material implication.

As this suggests, Lewis's aversion to Positivism did not diminish. There is among Lewis's papers a remarkable letter that Lewis wrote to Stephen

Pepper in reply to a request for his evaluation of Carl Hempel,[44] who was being considered for an appointment. Lewis notes that many philosophers would disagree with his views and even think him prejudiced. But Lewis does not flinch from his duty. Concerning Positivism, he writes:

> I have become more and more convinced that the neo-positivism which he represents is not only an unsound philosophic view but one whose effect is meretricious and runs counter to all that is best in the whole tradition of western thought. I believe its influence is now on the wane, but not yet in such measure that I would withhold any discouragement of it of which I am capable.

Lewis agrees that Hempel is an excellent representative of Positivism, but he thinks Positivism itself should be rejected. He then turns to Hempel himself.

> I think that while Hempel has an immense—even astounding—facility in absorbing whatever stands in the forefront of new and creative thinking, he has no intellectual originality or creativity himself. Consonantly, he may be the best of all expositors . . . but nobody will ever acquire real insight or catch any genuine philosophic disposition from him. I feel obliged to account him a high-level trivializer of philosophic thinking.

The letter is not all negative. Lewis says that Hempel "has real critical capacity, at his own less-than-highest level." He praises his ability as a teacher, his intellectual honesty, and his social skills. He sums it up by saying, "though I think he lacks qualities without which I can rate no man as tops, I think he may be the best second-rate man I know of." This is a remarkable letter concerning a man who, as Lewis notes, was the least doctrinaire of the Positivists, and Lewis confessed that he knew his view was prejudiced. But it is a letter that makes very clear the depth and strength of Lewis's aversion to Positivism.

Lewis was an empiricist; two of his major works had been devoted to the epistemological study of empirical knowledge. Yet when all was said and done, he did not believe that the validity of empirical knowledge could be proven. Citing Reichenbach, he wrote, "The validity of Induction is the postulate of an intelligible world. And about that, Reichenbach has said the last word; if it isn't true, you have no alternative to it which holds any promise whatever."[45] Lewis equates the rule of induction to the basic rule of conditioning that underlies animal learning—that if A has been followed by B in the past, it will continue to be followed by B in the future. The fact that animal learning is adaptive must reflect the fact that such associations are due to the nature of the real world; otherwise, adaptation would fail and the animal would perish.

Lewis then draws the analogy to Kant's Deduction of the Categories. Kant had held that, without the categories, knowledge of the world was impossible; hence, the categories must be assumed as valid. Lewis's point is that without induction and credible memory, knowledge of the world is impossible, and therefore the validity of induction and memory must be assumed. Just as the consistency of logic cannot be proven without assuming logic, so the cogency of empirical knowledge cannot be proven without assuming induction and the credibility of memory. Lewis's empiricism is at last a Kantian empiricism, resting on a " 'deduction' of the basic validity of memory and of induction." And this is precisely what he had called it in the AKV when he entitled Section 11 of Chapter XI " 'Deduction' of the basic validity of memory and of induction."[46]

METAPHYSICS

On January 1, 1959, Lewis wrote a letter to Victor Lowe[47] concerning his determination never to publish his views on metaphysics. "I have not, and shall not, commit to print what are to me my most valued metaphysical conclusions. I believe . . . a number of very unfashionable things." But Lewis does give one hint at what he believes.

> If I were younger, I might startle the natives by some quite novel 'speculations.' I should say, for example, that what figures to us as the distribution of matter, is a question merely of those space-time volumes, within which there are, for our senses—directly or indirectly—observable events which are, for our understanding, clue to other discoverable events within the same volume and in contiguous volumes. It is not necessary to suppose that *an sich* there is any distinction of objects from 'empty space.' But the natives will remain unstartled, and no doubt it is better so.

On January 29, Lewis received a three-page letter from Victor Lowe in reply to his earlier letter.[48] Lowe pleaded with Lewis to publish his metaphysical conclusions, pointing out that it would be far better to have his own statement of what he believed than to leave it to others to speculate. Since Lewis's letter hints at metaphysical doctrines of the sort Whitehead had advanced in 1919–1922, and since Lowe was a Whiteheadian, he must have been salivating at the prospect of getting Lewis to publish, but Lewis kept his secret. This is the only letter Lowe ever wrote to Lewis to which he received no reply.[49] Lewis had made his decision.

Lewis's statements at first appear to represent a marked change from his earlier views. In his early papers, he had clearly expressed an interest in metaphysical issues, such as monism, when he was working his way free of Idealism. By the time he wrote *Mind and the World Order*, he appeared to have abandoned speculative metaphysics entirely, and to define metaphysics as a reflective inquiry whose objective was to determine the criteria for classifying something as real. But he had never accepted the Positivist view that metaphysics was merely a pleasant form of myth-making. It is also clear that, in the 1920s, he had studied Whitehead's books on the nature of natural knowledge intensively, but not as metaphysics—he took them to be what Whitehead said they were—reconstructions of scientific knowledge. It is not a long step from there to regarding such a reconstruction as dealing with ontology and, by the 1950s, Lewis seems to have seen ontology as part of metaphysics. There was also the question of the status of ideals and values—questions that Lewis had been concerned with since at least 1910. Lewis's interest in metaphysical issues was not therefore a development of his later years; these issues had been with him throughout his career.

In a paper written in 1949 but not published until eight years later,[50] Lewis spelled out several ontological theses.

> Only individuals exist. . . . Neither concepts nor intensional meanings exist. But a concept is real if there is a psychological instance of its entertainment, or if it is logically (and consistently) constructible from element-concepts which are entertained.[51]

Lewis accepts the fact that this commits him to the reality of concepts never entertained, but asserts that this is the mode of being of most of the natural numbers. The reality of the concept does not entail that the corresponding character is instanced in some existent, nor vice versa. It is this fact that allows us to think and act deliberately—that is, to choose among alternatives, with all but one never realized.

Lewis asserts, as against nominalism, that individuals can only be thought of as identified by their characters. He rejects the notion that individuals can be identified by ostensive definition on the ground that the number of characters of an individual is infinite. Only when the learner "guesses correctly the *rule of discrimination* which the one who points is using in determining when to point and when not to point" will he know what the thing is, and "that criterion is the concept."[52] Then, harking back to a point made in his dissertation years before, Lewis says:

> The intention to identify an individual as meant can, in any case, succeed only on account of the logically accidental limitations of what exists. An

individual is apprehendable only as *that which* satisfies certain conditions specifiable in terms of characters it incorporates. The specified characters must be finitely enumerable, but the individual, being subject to the law of excluded middle, is infinitely specific.[53]

What this passage leaves unexplained is why, if the number of actual characters of the thing is finite, ostensive definition cannot work as well as intensional definition.

This paper is an unusual one for Lewis, who generally avoided metaphysical issues. It does show that Lewis recognized two modes of being—existence and reality—but it does little to explicate his concept of reality. It is clear that Lewis considered himself a realist, and that he rejected nominalism, and his assertions about the conceptual character of meaning and logical truth are explicit. But there is much here that requires a clarification it did not receive in subsequent papers.

In 1954, Lewis delivered a paper before the Pacific Division of the American Philosophical Association that was published the next year in the *Philosophical Review* as "Realism or Phenomenalism."[54] The paper is interesting as an attempt by Lewis to clarify his own metaphysical position. He notes that philosophy has retreated from problems of metaphysics to problems of epistemology, then to problems of meaning, and then to problems of language without any apparent success is solving its ultimate questions, but only the raising of more and more issues. The ultimate problems remain, however, and the one Lewis deals with here is the issue among Realism, Idealism, and Phenomenalism. This problem is both metaphysical and epistemological, but Lewis believes these aspects of it are separable; the metaphysical issue is the relation of subject and object and therefore transcends experience; the epistemological issue is the validity of knowledge and is an issue within experience. Experiences serve as signs or predictors of future experiences, and the verification of these predictions takes place within experience itself. The critique of cognition therefore appeals to nothing beyond belief, and the standards by which the validity of belief are judged are not subject to further critique; "any supposed demonstration of their acceptability must be circular" like the demonstration of the validity of logic.

Truth, however, concerns the relation of subject to object.

"Snow is white" is true just in case snow is white. The epistemological problem is how we know that snow is white; how well it is evidenced by experience and how in experience it may be further corroborated or disconfirmed. And the remaining problem is the metaphysical one, what snow being white is.[55]

The independence of the reality is something forced on us by "the presence of that which is as it is and not otherwise and must be accepted as we find it"—that is, the given. To deal with this fact of life, we "posit" the presence of an independent reality, and this is as true of Idealism as of Phenomenalism or Realism. What distinguishes Idealism, Lewis says, is its attempt to uphold the validity of values by anchoring them in a reality more ultimate than our everyday world. "The primary interest of idealism has never been in any distinctive thesis concerning common knowledge, but rather in the validity of values: in supporting the conviction that human ideals of the good and the right find some sanction in a reality more ultimate than the everyday world of our common thinking and doing."[56] But for the Idealist, no less than the Realist, that reality is an independent factuality.

What is the independently real? Traditionally, Lewis says, this was the problem of substance, but today is has become "whether an object is merely a bundle of attributes—that and the surd of existential fact." Lewis rejects this view, noting that it fails to answer the question of how the attributes are related. Lewis draws his own answer from Whitehead—that "an object is an event; some continuous volume in space-time comprising a history of enduring." "What we recognize as an object is so recognizable only by some persistence of character."[57] Either something in the object is unalterable, or it exhibits some law of alteration permitting prediction of future characters. Such an object exhibits a lawlike character both with respect to the phases of its own life history and in its relations to other objects. Further, Lewis argues, whatever qualifies as an object is an individual and therefore has, as the Law of Excluded Middle shows, an infinity of attributes. That means that we never fully know such an object: "We *posit* individuals, though we shall never verify the individuality of any object by full acquaintance."[58] It is because only a finite subset of these attributes are ever actualized that we can identify an object at all.

The properties of objects are universals, but universals are of several kinds. The properties of objects are different from the qualia of sense-presentations. The latter are "discriminable to sense only by reference to their content." What Lewis means here is that in a given presentation, a quale classed as "blue," can be discriminated from the shape and other qualia of the presentation by being selected by attention—in other words, its is pre-scinded (though Lewis does not use this term) and since such a prescinded quale may occur in different presentations, it is a kind of universal. But it is not a universal in the sense that "triangularity" is a universal that can be instanced in a variety of shapes. A blue quale is never the same as the objective quality "blue." "The objective color of a thing is a potentiality or dispositional trait inherent in the nature of this object, and evidenced in various

observable ways, including a variety of effects upon human eyes under specifiable conditions,"[59] among which effects would be the quale "blue."

All this leads Lewis to propose

> that we know objects only as we know certain objective properties of
> them, which are potentialities or reliable dispositional traits resident in
> the nature of them as they objectively exist, and whose manifestations
> are variously observable; directly in the presentational content of human
> experience to which they give rise, and indirectly through the observable
> interactions of objects with one another. We never know or can know all
> the properties of any individual thing, but what we do or may know is
> metaphysically veridical.[60]

Our knowledge of objects is mediated by appearances, but it is not a
knowledge *of* appearances but of objects. Lewis comments, "I do not know
whether so conceiving the matter is appropriately to be classed as phenomenalism or as realism. My preference would be for 'realism.' "[61]

In 1954, Lewis published "A Comment" in *The Philosophical Review*
that was a reply to an article by Everett Nelson.[62] What is important about
this piece is that in it Lewis rejects phenomenalism. Lewis protests "against
any suggestion that a verification theory of meaning implies phenomenalism." He says that this error lies in thinking that "in identifying the conceptual and implicative significance of "This object is an apple" with the
empirical eventuations which would attest its believability, one must somehow be reducing the substantial apple to the sum of its various appearances
in experience."[63] Further, Lewis says,

> There are, in my opinion, metaphysical presuppositions which are essen-
> tial to epistemology, for example, the nature of knowledge itself pre-
> supposes a reality to be known which transcends the content of any
> experience in which it may be known. And my own metaphysical con-
> victions are, as it happens, realistic.[64]

That Lewis considered himself a realist is clear, but what sort of realist?
Although his secret metaphysics remained secret, occasional passages in his
unpublished papers indicate that his metaphysics was largely derived from
Whitehead's books of the 1919 to 1922 period. Thus, in August 1960, Lewis
laid out a series of numbered claims. First, "Time is the first intellectual construct, logically considered."[65] The past and future do not exist; what we
directly observe is the passage of time. The specious present contains the
lapsing and dawning of time. We project experience beyond the present by
the "pervasiveness of the possible confirmation of the remembered." "There

is no ground for the belief in actual existences except, finally, memory." The second claim is "we are aware of our own conscious experience as having temporal spread . . . as a 'stream of consciousness' in time." "We construct the external world as a physical continuum in time." We cannot prove the existence of the external world because any such proof would be circular. The third is that "we are all aware of ourselves as continuing consciousnesses in time," and we discover our separateness from the external world by ignorance and error. Fourth, the proof of our existence "can never be any better expressed than it was by Descartes," where "think" is taken to mean awareness. Fifth, "we directly observe ourselves as feeling, thinking, believing, doubting beings. We believe in the existence of our fellows as expressing, thinking beings by analogy." Sixth, Lewis says, "we believe in *any* object, anything existing outside our experience, and independently of it, only by analogy." What Lewis means here is that we recognize objects only by their similarity to things experienced in the past, and we recognize future experience as confirmatory only by its analogy to past experience. Finally,

> Some other things we see, hear, feel, and so on, behave like other men who feel, think, doubt, believe, and say what they think, just as we do. If they cannot validly be believed to be what they seem, by analogy—then *alles geht los*; we have no fellows, and the world around us is so full of the illusory that we may as well curse God and die.[66]

He returned to the priority of time later that year.

> Kant was right that time is inexorably the form of intuition in which alone anything *is* for us; and Whitehead is right; without happenings there would be nothing. And an object is something that can be *again*— for a creature with a past and a future endowed with memory and the will to do. The ultimate form of reality is passage—from remembered past to anticipatable future. Space is constituted out of items which persist or are recoverable in time's passage. Without time and its arrow—nothing.[67]

We cannot imagine "time-in-experience" without the arrow; a recovery of something past could not be a *re*-covery if it were not for the arrow. "Spatial interval is, in terms of our experience, constituted out of time interval, not vice versa."[68]

Two years later he described events in clearly Whiteheadian terms. "An event is the occupant of a specifiable and continuous location in space-time—what happens then and there." Events can contain other events, can overlap, or can be completely separate. An individual thing is an event. We discriminate individuals in terms of what interests us and name them accordingly. "The existential occupant of any specifiable event, as defined above, would appear to be a thing in its own metaphysical right." An attribute, Lewis says, is a property of a thing. But attributes do not exist; rather "attributes *inexist* in individuals which are characterized by having them."[69]

Moreover, in a manuscript written in June 1962, Lewis returned to his "secret metaphysics." "The main types of entities which are referred to, mentioned, and are or could be ingredient in a total reality or 'world' are individuals, events, and states of affairs." Lewis's description of events is Whiteheadian—a point made very clear by his note: "We take advantage here of much which Whitehead has said, with the utmost precision." Individuals coincide with actual events that are their "lifetime endurance" and are known by their attributes. States of affairs are assertables. Individuals exist or do not exist. Attributes exist by *inexisting* in their instances. Lewis then summarizes his theory of propositions as signifying states of affairs that are predicated of the world.[70]

These passages are all too brief, but they do show the lasting influence of Whitehead on Lewis. In a letter to Charles Hendle, Lewis remarked, "I slaved over Whitehead's 1920 books." But he also says that "nobody but Whitehead himself can impart prophetic quality to the obscurities of "Process and Reality."[71] It was not the Whitehead of *Process and Reality* but the Whitehead of *An Enquiry Concerning the Principles of Natural Knowledge*, *The Concept of Nature*, and *The Principle of Relativity* that influenced Lewis. One can understand why Lowe should have been so eager to learn more about Lewis's "secret metaphysics."

In a piece written in 1963, Lewis toyed with an even more radical idea. "External objects exist independently of our observing them or thinking about them; and as so existent have characters in some part discoverable to us."[72] But not all their characteristics are discoverable to us. By the Law of Excluded Middle, the real object must be infinitely determinate, and we can know at most a finite number of its attributes. From what we know of the limitations of our senses, and the different senses of other creatures, we must suppose external objects to have characteristics we can only discover by inference from our experience. This is old news to Lewis, but he then goes on to say that by analogy we may attribute characteristics to reality beyond what we can even imagine. Primitive humans ascribed sentience to the world at large, and although we have now narrowed the scope of that attribution radically,

> the final stage of such sophistication appears to be the thought that con-
> sciousness itself has its degrees, as each of us can corroborate within his

own conscious experience; that a lower degree of such consciousness may correlate with the complexity of observable modes of behavior, as these approximate to our own; and that we have no way of precluding the supposition that some degree of consciousness may be correlated with any kind of objective thing we can discriminate. The further thought that our modes of such discrimination of objects may be adventitious to the being of what we discriminate as objective individual things, may lead us to the conviction that panpsychism cannot be precluded as a metaphysical conception, though equally it can never be corroborated. More importantly perhaps, but perhaps more vaguely also, it may suggest the thought of a cosmic consciousness, conjoint with all that observably—or even unobservably to us—exists. At the limits, this is Kant's thought of things in themselves.[73]

Physicists, Lewis remarks, "are, without their realizing it, the most extreme Kantian metaphysicians." The world they describe "would be totally unbelievable if it were not that pragmatically it works." What Lewis has in mind here is the entities postulated by quantum mechanics that defy our efforts to imagine them, though not our mathematics.

Does this mean that Lewis was a panpsychist? This is the only passage I know of in which Lewis even considered such a metaphysical hypothesis, and what he says here hardly amounts to an endorsement of it. He was of course familiar with such theories; James and Peirce both adopted panpsychist theories as did Whitehead. But on the evidence available here, one can hardly conclude that Lewis was doing more than speculating on its possibility.

As we have already seen, the issue of the status of potentiality was an important one for Lewis, and he continued to be concerned with it. In his last year, he wrote: "The *proof* of a potentiality is the *observable realization* of it,"[74] and in September: "What is a potentiality? It is something which is possible of realization at times when it is *not* realized."[75] But more interesting is his discussion of Peirce's famous diamond. In "How to Make Our Ideas Clear," Peirce had posed the following question: "Suppose, then that a diamond could be crystallized in the midst of a cushion of soft cotton, and should remain there until it was finally burned up. Would it be false to say that the diamond was soft?" Peirce's answer to that in 1878 was that it would not be false, but would involve "a modification of our present usage of speech with regard to the words hard and soft, but not of their meanings. For they represent no fact to be different from what it is; only they involve arrangements of facts which would be exceedingly maladroit."[76] The issue here is that of unactualized possibilities. Peirce himself later repudiated this answer as nominalistic and held that the diamond would have been hard whether or not its hardness was tested.[77] Lewis was apparently not aware of Peirce's later change of position and criticized Peirce's 1878 answer on grounds similar to those Peirce later adopted—Lewis held Peirce's early answer to be positivistic.

> Common-sense realism *postulates the object* (the diamond) antecedently to our finding out, as the ground of what will disclose itself in subsequent investigation. In case of disparity between cognitive expectancies and further experiential findings, it is our antecedent expectancies which are to be repudiated or amended, the object *being already as it is and not otherwise*, regardless of our cognitive predictions. The independently real world is postulated as the *to be* cognized; not cognition as the ground of reality.

And, Lewis adds, "Mill spoke of objects as 'permanent possibilities of experience.' We would amend this to 'objects are what we postulate as the *grounds* of permanent possibilities of experience.'"[78] Lewis thought Peirce's early position left the objective hardness of the diamond indeterminate, and rejected that view. Since, by hypothesis, the diamond is never tested, this would appear to mean that Lewis accepted the notion that the unactualized possibility of the experiences of the diamond's hardness was real. One could surely wish for a more definitive statement by Lewis on this issue, but this seems to be the clearest we have, and it does appear to put him on the side of the reality of unactualized possibilities.

Given the limited amount that we know about Lewis's metaphysics, why did he want to keep it secret? It is obvious that Lewis's metaphysics is heavily indebted to Whitehead's books of the 1919–1922 period. But it does not appear to be identical to Whitehead's doctrine. Lewis takes objects to be events and describes them in ways that seem at first inconsistent. Thus, he says, "A thing-object, individual—is a four-dimensional space-time volume, whose space-time are (sic) related in law-like ways. Events within it are related causally—i.e., in ways which are predictable. The appearances it presents to us are correlated with anticipatable further experiences of it."[79] But he also says, "'objects' represent congellations (sic) of characters which arise by association together on a sufficient number of different occasions of observation so that presentation of a partial colligation of this total congellation arouses expectation of the others as to be disclosed—usually upon condition of some governable way of behaving on occasion of the presentation of this partial colligation."[80] In the first passage, Lewis seems to identify objects with events, and this is borne out in other texts: "The distinction of objects from events is in the manner of their abstraction only. And [an] object is an event having space-time boundaries, and an event is a closed and continuous space-time volume, defined by [its] space-time boundaries. An object is an event defined by description of the content of the event-volume which is its lifetime locus."[81] This would appear to deny that the object is just a coagulation of properties. The resolution of this apparent problem is this: "The space-time localized syndrome of observable symptoms, is, on the side of the Universe, an event-object; on the side of our apprehension, as a syndrome repeatable in more than one space-time locale, it is a concept of a recognizable thing."[82] Evidently, what Lewis is contrasting is the metaphysical object, which is an event, with the epistemic object, which is a colligation of observable properties. This is necessary for Lewis because, for him, objects are individuals to which Excluded Middle applies, whereas for Whitehead objects have an adjectival relation to events and therefore could not be subject to Excluded Middle. But if for the Universe the object-event is a "localized syndrome of observable symptoms," then objects may not differ from the empty space-time in which the syndrome is localized. But this does not explain how an object, which for Whitehead has an adjectival relation to events, can itself be an event. But whatever the differences between Lewis and Whitehead, it is clear that much of Lewis's metaphysics finds its origin in Whitehead's writings.

Whitehead's books of the 1919–1922 period were presented, not as metaphysics, but as a reconstruction of natural knowledge on the basis of sense experience—a project with which Lewis had great sympathy. But after the publication of *Process and Reality* in 1929, Whitehead became known as a panpsychist metaphysician and he acquired disciples, such as Charles Hartshorne and Victor Lowe among others, so that, by the 1950s, what was remembered about him was his work in logic and his process metaphysics. Lewis was an empiricist and a realist; he had long since rejected Idealism. I think he knew that to publish a metaphysical doctrine with obvious links to Whitehead would immediately lead to his being called an Idealist, and that to clear himself of that charge would require more controversy than he wanted and would distract him from his work on ethics. I suspect that is the reason he chose to leave the natives "unstartled."

RELIGION

Lewis was not a religious philosopher; unlike Royce, whose philosophic writings were steeped in religious belief and Christian theology, Lewis rarely mentioned religion and was certainly not a theological advocate. But Lewis did sometimes deal with religious topics, and these passages are important because of the close connection between religion and ethics that has generally obtained in philosophy, and particularly in those influenced by Idealism, as Lewis was.

In September 1950, Lewis wrote: "a man's spiritual interests are those dictated by his love for others, and his consequent willingness to sacrifice his private interest for the sake of good to them."[83] Love, Lewis says, is an attitude in which one finds his own interests "fulfilled in the realization of good in the life of another." This attitude is more than simply respect; it is one in which "respect is replaced by self-identification." In words that clearly echo Royce, Lewis wrote:

> To appreciate the reality of another life with that poignancy with which the spiritual reality respected would be felt if it were first-personal, is to make it first-personal; to enjoy the good of another as he enjoys it, and to suffer the evils which affect him as one suffers one's own.[84]

This is the love that we attribute to an "all understanding God" who would appreciate fully the lives of his people. Such an "all-embracing self-hood" would overcome all the conflicts of finite interests. This greater self-hood "must remain as the vision of the only valid ideal of self-hood, in the realization of which there could be the perfection of integrity and of peace within one's self." Lewis draws from this the conclusion that "a God who pities must suffer, for He lives in us." And in the margin he wrote, "Buddhism is the religion of escapism; Christianity the religion of the love of life."[85]

By this period, Lewis had long since rejected Idealism, but he is obviously using Roycean ideas to define what God would be. Whether Lewis was a believing Christian, as these passages suggest, or some sort of Cosmic Theist, is not clear, but it does seem that he held some sort of religious belief. There is a two-and-a-half-page undated manuscript among Lewis's papers that may date from this period in which Lewis invoked Royce's concept of loyalty for religious purposes. "The emotive attachment to reality as valuable in itself, and the residence of all value, is the religious emotion," he wrote. "It is, as Royce has pointed out, that attachment which expresses itself as loyalty."[86] Lewis identified loyalty with love. Although usually exhibited as loyalty to persons, it can be accorded to "an old and faithful dog." Lewis then wrote:

> One who stands before a giant redwood, following the pillar of it up to the branches framed against the sky and conscious of the centuries through which it has stood in quiet and in storm, may accord a spontaneous love and loyalty to this existence, this being, in whose presence we stand. So too one who lifts his eyes to the mountain-tops or contemplates the solitude of the desert, may find himself in a presence which speaks to him saying

"Quiet," and fills him with a strength which is not emotion but a purga-
tion of emotion and a release from the smallness of himself. For the
moment he lives outside and beyond himself, and this greater being into
which he is lifted up fills him with love and loyalty and accords the sense
of reunion with that in which he lives and moves and has his being.

One receives "the intimation of that immortality which belongs to all that
is—so it be lifted up and find itself in the eternal."

He so feels and envisages, from afar, the most real being, and is content
with so much as he may now see and feel of it; because it is not meet that
he should feel and see it in its infinitude and eternity, but only that it
speak to him and that in the word it speaks he may find peace.[87]

The religious need, Lewis says, is man's need to live beyond himself.
Without such love and loyalty, "his life is missing and his death is final."
With it, he can find meaning in what he does, and there is no death "for
he lives in that to which he is devoted; in what he loves and that to which
he would be loyal."[88]

This is the most explicitly religious statement that I have found in
Lewis's writings, and might well have been written by Royce, or even
Emerson. It does seem clear that he was some sort of theist and that he
regarded such belief as essential to give meaning to life. Whether he was a
believer in literal immortality is left ambiguous: one can read the text that
way, or as meaning that one lives on in the work or institutions or causes
to which one is loyal.

In an undated note that seems to have been written in 1962, Lewis came
as close to stating his religious convictions as in anything else I have seen.

Your conception of God is your conception of that, in the real at large,
in the absence of which you would find purposeful human living pointless. Your belief in God is your belief in the security of those aims and
purposes without some eventual security of which you would find your
living and doing meaningless. The only rational alternative to faith in
this God you worship—perhaps ignorantly—would be to curse this god-
less world and die. And your faithfulness to this faith, in what you do, is
such service as you may give to God.[89]

This is probably as accurate statement of Lewis's belief as there is. He did
not apparently believe in God in any conventional sense; it is not clear that
he believed in a personal god at all. What he wanted was an assurance that
human ideals had some sort of objective validity. This is what he recognized

that Idealism had provided, and when he abandoned the belief in the Absolute as anything more than an ideal, he did not mean simply a subjective ideal. What is obviously called for here is some statement of the metaphysical basis for believing these ideals true. But unless one takes Lewis's few remarks about panpsychism as indicating that he had returned to Idealism—a hypothesis that has little warrant in his writings—he left no indication of what that metaphysical basis might be.

Against such statements, one must put his wife's assertion that he was not a religious believer, his son's conviction that he was not religious at all, and other statements in which Lewis appears to deny any belief in God. These need not be contradictory if the denials are taken as referring to the orthodox conception of God and Lewis's own profession to a sort of Cosmic interest in human welfare. But, as we will see, the issue is by no means easy to resolve.

PHILOSOPHY

At various times, Lewis also reflected on just what the field of philosophy was—reflections that show his dissatisfaction with the way the field was developing. When it was suggested that the Harvard Department might offer a course in Existentialism, Lewis strongly objected.[90] On February 19, 1954, he wrote that the only philosophers who seem to have a clear idea of what philosophy is are the Positivists, and on their view "most of philosophy is the bunk, consisting of conundrums to be answered by a pun, and the rest is amateur science."[91] He attacked the Positivists's reduction of genuine problems to questions of linguistic convention and their ignoring of "essences or universals." But Lewis believed that Positivism was now fading and "I confess that I should like to do any little thing I can to expedite the process of its obsolescence."[92]

What then is philosophy? One view is that philosophy synthesizes knowledge from all fields and provides a perspective on life and the world. Lewis agrees that this is something that should be done and that any acceptable conception of philosophy should do justice to it. The other main view is that philosophy is the study of the normative—specifically, logic, ethics, and the theory of value. But this view leaves unclear the status of metaphysics and epistemology. Lewis did not solve the issue; instead he turned to justifying the importance of the study of the normative, noting that, with the atom bomb, the question of morality now involves the survival of mankind.

In May 1961, Lewis vented his frustrations with contemporary philosophy.

I build on Peirce. The jibbering semanticists of neo-philosophy have added noting else that is constructive to it. They are not even trying to. They don't even understand it. They have no story of the nature of knowledge to tell. Somebody should notice the complete absence of any constructive ability in their 'philosophy' eventually, and cast them out for the jabbering nincompoops they are.[93]

Unfortunately, Lewis does not name names. But what did he mean when he said he built on Peirce? He meant by it the theory of sense-meaning. "In AKV, we have attempted to development (sic) this Peircean concept of concept, under the head of 'sense-meaning' of concepts, in contrast to the merely 'linguistic meaning' of the verbal expression."[94]

In October 1961, Lewis was led to examine the current state of philosophy. Lewis is concerned that philosophy's role in supplying a general conspectus and critique of human learning was becoming increasingly difficult in view of the ever growing specialization of learning. He admits, "I have no recipe," but he does have a negative conclusion—that no one specialty, such as physics, should be allowed to usurp this role. But Lewis also sees a positive role for philosophy, based on the fact that humans are deliberative, self-governing creatures. "The critique of human controllable activity at large, and human thinking at large—if there be any such critique—stands over and above and intrinsically antecedent to, any specialization of human thinking and doing whatever."[95] And whatever specialist attempts to instruct the rest of us presumes some basic community of understanding in terms of which his or her recommendations can be made to appear reasonable. Critique must be a part of the community of common sense. The crisis over the definition of philosophy was not a new development, even in Lewis's time. Thus, while Lewis still believed that it was part of the role of philosophy to provide a synthesis of human knowledge, his main concern was with its normative role as a critique of deliberate activity—in other words, as ethics.[96]

10

Ethics

Lewis described the AKV as a prolegomenon to ethics. After its publication in 1946, he focused on writing what he intended to be his last major work—the book on ethics. It never appeared, although he worked on it from 1946 until his death in 1964. What he did publish were some articles on ethics and three series of lectures. The *Ground and Nature of the Right*, the Woodbridge Lectures delivered in 1954 at Columbia,[1] was published in 1955; *Our Social Inheritance*, the Mahlon Powell Lectures delivered at the University of Indiana in 1956,[2] was published in 1957; and "Foundations of Ethics," four lectures delivered at Wesleyan University in 1959, was posthumously published in 1969.[3] These were popular lectures and none of them constitute an adequate presentation of Lewis's position. One must therefore try to piece together Lewis's theory from such materials as he did publish with the help of the manuscripts he left at his death.

To understand what Lewis was attempting to do in ethics, one has to put it into the context of ethical theory in the United States during the late 1940s and the 1950s. Writing in 1950, Arthur Pap commented that current theories about the meanings of ethical terms could be described as naturalistic, emotivist, and intuitionist.[4] In 1953, Philip Rice commented that "a decade ago," empiricism or naturalism in ethics and value theory (Santayana, Perry, Dewey) was dominant. But now attacks from the analytic movement "constitute a kind of invasion from such centers of philosophic concentration as Vienna, Oxford and Cambridge." On the "right," Rice saw the attack coming from nonnaturalists led by Moore, Broad,

Ross, and Ewing; on the "left" were the emotivists led by Carnap, Ayer, and Stevenson—that is, the Positivists. And now, he added, there was a new assault from the natural language philosophers, led by Toulmin, Hampshire, Strawson, Hare, and Hart.[5] In addition, Utilitarianism remained a position with many adherents, and some still argued for a return to Kant. Thus, ethics had become a battleground, and Lewis did not fit into any of the opposing camps.

It will be useful to look briefly at some of these conflicting views, since they constitute the context for Lewis's work and the opponents he faced. Although John Dewey died in 1952, so great was Dewey's influence that anyone in this period who discussed "Pragmatic Ethics" discussed Dewey's theory, as if there were no others. Dewey rejected any supernatural or transcendental standards in ethics; his position was thoroughly naturalistic. He also rejected the classical psychology that viewed human beings as passive creatures that had to be kicked into action by some stimulus. Human beings, Dewey held, are energetic, active creatures; man "is an active being and that is all there is to be said on that score."[6] The problem of socialization is the problem of channeling this energy, which Dewey calls impulse, into "habits." Such a habit "includes a sequence of acts following upon some clue, internal or external; it leads to the satisfaction of needs; and it is in itself energetic—quite literally, it is energy harnessed for a particular purpose."[7] Human action is always goal oriented, a search for those things that satisfy human needs. These are the ends sought; more exactly, what is sought is an end-in-view—our present concept of what will satisfy our needs and desires, and our habits are those modes of action that lead to such satisfactions.

Unfortunately, desires are many and satisfactions are few. A problem situation thus arises, one in which old habits fail to work, because either of environmental change or conflict among habits themselves. Following Peirce's famous doubt–belief model, Dewey holds that the problem situation evokes inquiry and reflection in an attempt to find a way out. The method of inquiry is the scientific method; the problem must be diagnosed, alternative hypotheses developed as to how to resolve it, and these must be tested to determine which works the best. Upon that discovery, a new habit is formed that allows action to flow smoothly into satisfaction. "The good is that which satisfies want, craving, which fulfils or makes complete the need which stirs to action."[8]

Not only are human beings by nature active; they are also social. Human life is possible only in a group. As members of a group, we are subject to the demands of its members, and make our own demands on them. "'Right,'" Dewey holds, "is only an abstract term for the totality of demands which others make upon us, and which we must acknowledge and accommodate to survive as members of the group."[9] Right and good are indeed different, but both are natural facts of human life. So, too, Dewey takes a "motive" to be, not the cause of an act, but an element in an action that is seen as having a tendency to produce certain consequences, and is "virtuous" if those consequences are ones we regard as good.

Dewey's theory denies any division of the moral and the natural; the moral *is* part of the natural. Not only does he deny transcendental standards of morality, he also rejects universal principles of morality. What is good, right, or virtuous depends on the particular problem situation. "In quality," Dewey says, "the good is never twice alike."[10] What resolves one problem situation may not resolve another. What has generality are the methods by which such situations can be resolved, but even these are constantly changing as human knowledge advances. For Dewey, nothing could be more absurd that the attempt to establish a universal categorical imperative.

A second major position of the period was intuitionism, of which A. C. Ewing is a good example. In *Principia Ethica*, G. E. Moore had claimed that "good" was indefinable—more exactly, that the concept of "good" could not be analyzed into other concepts. "Good," for Moore, is a simple unanalyzable quality like yellow; we learn it from experience, but we cannot reduce it to some combination of other qualities. Specifically, the attempt to define "good" in naturalistic terms is what Moore called the naturalistic fallacy. Ewing adopted this view; the fundamental ethical concepts—"good" and "right" (or "duty") are indefinable in Moore's sense.[11] If they were not—if they were definable in naturalistic terms—ethics would be reduced to a natural science, such as psychology, and would no longer be ethics.

Given the total set of terms, either of a theory or a language, not all of them are definable by others without circularity. It is therefore no criticism of ethics that its primitive terms are not capable of explicit definition. Like science, Ewing holds that ethics begins from basic judgments and seeks to create a coherent system that accounts for them. What corresponds to the observations of science are "intuitions" in ethics, where by "intuition" is meant that one knows something "otherwise than by simple observation or reasoning." Ewing holds that some ethical judgments are true, and "it is very hard to see how we can know anything to be intrinsically good or bad except by intuition. What argument could prove it?" Again, in comparing the consequences of alternative actions, "we just see that one set of consequences or one act is preferable to a suggested alternative after having viewed them as a whole, paying attention to their relevant factual aspects."[12]

Intuitions can be in error, Ewing holds, just as perceptions can be delusive, and therefore they must be tested. What constitutes tests in this case are making certain all aspects of the case are considered, that those making the decisions have the relevant knowledge and experiences, that whatever reasoning is involved is carefully analyzed, that conceptual confusions are cleared away, that operative prejudices are avoided, and that the judgment is consistent with other established ethical judgments. An intuition, Ewing says, "must be regarded as a rational judgment, though one not based on argument, even if capable of confirmation by it, and not as a mere feeling."[13] Thus, for Ewing, ethical propositions are true or false, and although they are not verifiable in a scientific sense, if they withstand the test of cool, judicious, and comprehensive examination and are consistent with our established ethical propositions, they may be taken for true, though future examination may find them mistaken.

The term "emotive" as applied to value and ethical statements was first employed by Ayer in *Language, Truth and Logic*. This was, for most English-speaking readers, the book that introduced them to Viennese Positivism, of which Ayer was the leading English exponent, and Ayer's presentation of the position was abrasively strong. "We shall set ourselves to show that in so far as statements of value are significant, they are ordinary 'scientific' statements; and that in so far as they are not scientific, they are not in the literal sense significant, but are simply expressions of emotion which can be neither true nor false."[14] Ayer draws no distinction in this regard between statements of value and statements of ethics or aesthetics; the same analysis applies to all. Ayer first argues that ethical statements are not reducible to non-ethical—that is, scientific—statements. He rejects the utilitarian definition of "good" as pleasure on the ground that it is not contradictory to say that pleasant things are wrong, as it would be if the utilitarian definition held, and he rejects absolutist and intuitive theories on the ground that they are unverifiable. Instead, Ayer holds that, in ethical judgments, "the function of the relevant ethical word is purely 'emotive.' It is used to express feeling about certain objects, but not to make any assertion about them."[15] But statements that merely *express* emotion (as distinct from statements that *describe* emotion) cannot be either true or false. On the verification criterion of meaning, therefore, such statements "do not say anything" and are meaningless.

The position Ayer advanced was that of most members of the Vienna Circle from the 1920s on. It is remarkable that the Positivists, faced with the rise of Hitler, should have adhered to a doctrine that made moral statements cognitively meaningless. This was certainly not due to any sympathy for Nazism; Carnap was a Socialist, Neurath was even further left, and none of them were Fascists. Yet, although Hitler's rise to power cost some of the Positivists their lives and forced the others to flee their country, they continued to promote a doctrine of moral relativism that meant quite literally that moral condemnations of Nazism were meaningless. And they and their followers continued to maintain these views through the war and the subsequent cold war. Those who hold externalist theories of intellectual history owe us an explanation of this case, for it is hard to think of a more graphic illustration of brilliant men being so bound by the requirements of their theory that they were unable to find an intellectual basis on which to condemn the greatest evil of their time.

The book that became the classic statement of the emotivist theory in the United States was Charles Stevenson's *Ethics and Language*, which appeared in 1944. Stevenson's presentation of his theory is less abrasive than Ayer's and concentrates on the linguistic analysis of ethical propositions. His argument is that ethical statements involve both descriptive and emotive meanings, where the latter is defined as "a meaning in which the response (from the hearer's point of view) or the stimulus (from the speaker's point of view) is a range of emotions."[16] Stevenson presents two "patterns" of how ethical statements should be analyzed, but the second is equivalent to the first in its bearings on ethical questions,[17] so we may restrict our attention to the first, namely—

"This is good" means "*I approve of this; do so as well.*"[18]

"I" here refers to the speaker who utters "This is good." "I approve of this" is a factual statement having descriptive meaning; it describes the psychological state of the speaker, and is subject to verification in the usual ways. "Do so as well" is an imperative that calls on the hearer to adopt the same attitude toward "this" that the speaker holds. Since imperatives are neither true nor false, this component of the "pattern" is not verifiable, nor should it be, for its function is not to describe a state of affairs, but to modify an attitude. For Stevenson, ethical statements thus combine factual beliefs and attitudes. Ethical disagreement can arise on either score. When disagreement occurs, protagonists will support their view by advancing "reasons" for holding them.[19] If the disagreement is rooted in beliefs about the act or thing under discussion—for example, about its properties or consequences—the dispute may be resolved since factual beliefs are subject to test, but the resolution will occur only if the differences in attitude are eliminated by the change in beliefs. "But if any ethical dispute is *not* rooted in disagreement in belief, then no *reasoned* solution of any sort is possible."[20] That does not mean that the dispute can never be resolved, but that it can only be resolved by persuasion that will alter one party's attitude.

Belief and attitude can thus vary independently of each other, and while Stevenson believes that in many cases differences in attitude are due to differences in belief, this is not always the case.

It was Stevenson's analysis that became the center of the controversy over emotivism.[21] Some construed the emotivist theory as a denial that moral reasoning was of any use. "There can be little doubt that the present preoccupation with the problem of moral reasoning is itself largely due to the challenge which the emotive theory has offered to the whole notion of rational justification in moral discourse."[22] But everyone in the field found themselves in the position of having to answer Stevenson.

The trend to linguistic analysis evident in Stevenson was carried further in R. M. Hare's *The Language of Morals*. For Hare, the problem of ethics is the problem of how to answer the question: "What shall I do?" This is a question everyone faces constantly. What the question demands is an imperative answer—"Do this." Thus, ethical statements must be prescriptive; they are "commands," under which term Hare includes all imperatives. But, unlike Stevenson, Hare defends the view that ethics rests on a rational basis. Imperatives have a logic of their own, and Hare lays down two rules governing that logic.

(1) No indicative conclusion can be validly drawn from a set of premises which cannot be validly drawn from the indicatives among them alone.

(2) No imperative conclusion can be validly drawn from a set of premises which does not contain at least one imperative.[23]

The second principle establishes the claim that "ought" cannot be derived from "is"; an imperative can be derived only from other imperatives. And since imperatives cannot be either true or false, it follows that ethical statements are neither true nor false.

Moral and ethical reasoning takes the form of the practical syllogism.[24] The minor premise is a descriptive statement that sets out the facts of the case in such a way as to justify the application of the major premise. This major premise is an ethical principle—that is, an imperative—and from the two the specific imperative conclusion is derived. But what justifies the major premise? Such a justification would involve citing the effects of the act prescribed and other ethical principles from which it might be derived. If the demand for justification is pressed, more and more effects and principles must be invoked. "Thus, if pressed to justify a decision completely, we have to give a complete specification of the way of life of which it is a part." But if even this justification is not sufficient for the critic, "then there is no further answer to give him, because we have already, *ex hypothesi*, said everything that could be included in this further answer."[25] In this situation, one must simply decide which culture to subscribe to, and proceed accordingly. This sounds very much like cultural relativism; different "ways of life" have differing principles and there is no way to decide among them. But Hare denies that.

> To describe such ultimate decisions as arbitrary, because *ex hypothesi* everything which could be used to justify them has already been included in the decision, would be like saying that a complete description of the universe was utterly unfounded, because no further fact could be called upon in corroboration of it. . . . Far from being arbitrary, such a decision would be the most well-founded of decisions, because it would be based upon a consideration of everything upon which it could possibly be founded.[26]

The problem with this argument is obvious. There is only one universe (or so it was believed when Hare wrote) but there are multiple ways of life. Hare seems to be saying that having adopted one's form of life, one has a rational reason for the decisions one makes, but it is unclear that the decision to subscribe to the particular form of life is rational since there are alternatives. Yet Hare also appears to hold that ethical principles are universal; "To ask whether I ought to do A in these circumstances is (to borrow Kantian language with a small though important modification) to ask whether or not I will that doing A in such circumstances should become a universal law."[27] If so, then ways of life will collide, and what to do when that happens is unclear.

Hare includes a detailed analysis of the ethical terms "ought," "right," and particularly "good," whose primary function is taken to be to commend.[28] But to make his argument complete, Hare needs to show that all morally evaluative judgments entail imperatives. Hare solves this problem by definition. "I propose to say that the test, whether someone is using the judgment 'I ought to do X' as a value judgment or not is, 'Does he or does he not recognize that if he asserts the judgment, he must also assent to the command 'Let me do X?' "[29] This is a rather swift way of settling the matter.

These are only a few of the major ethical works of the time, but, in the diversity of views they represent, they should convey a sense of the context in which Lewis worked. Lewis did not usually attack his opponents by name, but he was so strongly opposed to emotivism that in his private writings he made an exception in this case. Among the books Lewis left at his death was his copy of *Ethics and Language*. In it there are several marginalia that are not complimentary—for example, "I have always feared that Stevenson is a little light-minded" on pages 102–103.[30] The most interesting of these is the following.

> I disapprove of my own attitude in disapproving Stevenson—though I approve my disapproval. My original reaction to his view was emotive; and I disapprove of emotive attitudes as a basis of any act or of the *adoption* of any attitude. I disapprove of attitudes which are not dispassionately approvable—And fear them in myself.[31]

Only Lewis, reading a book that espoused a doctrine he loathed, would have written such a comment.

In one of his manuscripts, Lewis attacked Stevenson's thesis directly. "Mr. Stevenson says that '["]X is good" means "I approve of X—do you so likewise." ' " Lewis agrees that if I believe "X is good" I also approve of X, but he denies the converse. " 'I approve of X' is true when and only when I *think* X is good. . . . But the point is that my thinking it good didn't make it so." He draws the analogy between "X is good" and "A is true": "The truth of A does not depend on my, or anybody's, belief in it; and the goodness of X has no dependence on my or anybody's approval of it."[32] The analogy is exact, since for Lewis statements such as "X is good" are empirical statements that are verifiable or falsifiable. As for "Do you so likewise," Lewis agrees that in some cases the judgment "X is good" may carry such a corollary, but not in all. "Since we make all our purchases in a competitive market, the more people who *don't* approve the things I think good, the cheaper I can buy." However, the *assertion* that "X is good" does carry the exhortation to agree, but not because this is part of the meaning of "X is good"; rather, it is part of the intention involved in the act of assertion. But this is true of all assertions, not just of those concerning goodness.[33]

Lewis did not *publicly* attack Stevenson by name, but he did publicly and repeatedly attack emotivism with a vehemence he used against no other doctrine.

> It is a curious and dreadful fact that just at the time science has put into the hands of men the most powerful instruments for control of their environment—ambivalently capable of use for human betterment or for the suicide of civilization—we should be told, by some of those who celebrate science as the outstanding triumph of the human mind, that appraisals of the good and bad and assessments of the right and wrong have nothing more fundamental as their basis and their sanction than our emotive drives and our subjective persuasions of attitude.[34]

Lewis described the Emotivists as "cynics" and "skeptics,"[35] and accused them of "poisoning of the very wellsprings of truth and endeavor" and undermining the defense of Western Civilization.[36] Lewis was a Cold Warrior who accused academics of "hiding behind the ivy"[37] because they would not take an anti-Communist position. He never accused the Emotivists of being pro-Communist, but he regarded their doctrines as subversive.

When at the end of the AKV, Lewis wrote: "Valuation is always a matter of empirical knowledge. But what is right and what is just, can never be determined by empirical facts alone"[38] he left many philosophers bewildered. Most writers of the time either merged value theory with ethics or saw a much closer relation between them than Lewis seemed to allow. Lewis was counted a Pragmatist, and Pragmatic ethics was naturalistic, yet he appeared to be rejecting naturalism without adopting any of the other views that were prominent at the time. Writing in the *Philosophical Review*, Morton White pointed out that Lewis had divided knowledge into the analytic and the empirical. How, White wondered, could he possibly justify an ethics that was neither. White considered Lewis's announced intention to create such a system "an insurmountable task in the light of his epistemological commitments."[39] Similarly, in an extended article in *Ethics* in 1948, Robert Browning concluded:

> Evidently Lewis desires a universalistic normative ethics, but it is most difficult to see how he can validate other-regarding imperatives within the bounds of his perspective. We do not say success is impossible, but one concludes that this most ably undertaken venture is not yet consummated and seems to be temporarily halted.[40]

Browning's piece even led Asher Moore to attempt to demonstrate that "there cannot be any such thing as a universal normative ethical principle because the notion of such a principle is a self-contradictory notion."[41] Lewis had in effect challenged the field. It was clear, as Browning said, that he intended to create a universal normative ethics. With the possible exception of utilitarianism, none of the other major positions of the time gave support for such a venture—least of all Dewey's Pragmatism. The question was whether or not Lewis could made good on the challenge.

Perhaps if Lewis's critics had looked at the AKV and his earlier work more closely, they would have been less surprised. Lewis was a pragmatist. For him, man's purpose in life is to attain the *summum bonum*—a life found good in the living of it. This is possible only through action. The point of knowledge is the guidance of action so that the good life may be achieved. But knowing is itself a form of action, and so must be subject to the same sort of critique to which all action is subject: does it lead to the good life? To do so, knowing, and doing, must be right, for it is only right action that can achieve this result. And right actions are actions that it is imperative for individuals to perform. In reply to Browning and White, Lewis remarked:

> I think my critics must somehow have overlooked this basic thesis of pragmatism. Otherwise they could hardly have been so mystified over the question how a pragmatic theory of knowledge could be made consistent with the recognition of valid imperatives of action. They might better have asked how pragmatism in epistemology could be compatible with anything else.[42]

All knowledge, according to Lewis, is based on imperatives: " 'Knowledge' is itself a normative word. Cognition which is not valid is not knowledge but error or baseless fancy." "We arrive at the undeniably correct statement that warranted beliefs represent what is *right* in the way of believing."[43] One should bear in mind that Lewis had been teaching courses on ethics throughout his entire career. This was in no sense a new subject for him. But his concern with ethics was not a concern with ethics in the narrow sense but with the normative basis of all knowledge—logic, science, empirical knowledge generally, and valuation. The shift of focus after the publication of the AKV—if there is a shift—was not to a new subject but to the foundations of all his previous work.

Lewis often says that his view of the normative is based on what he took to be human nature. As Lewis sees it, the essential facts about human beings are: (1) that they are free and active beings (2) who not only live in time but know that they live in time, and (3) are capable of making deliberate decisions that permit them to govern their own actions. Not only is this a capacity of human beings; (4) it is a necessity for human beings because they are so poorly equipped with instincts that they must decide for themselves, "What shall I do?" Furthermore, like all sentient beings, (5) humans find their experience to be either grievous or gratifying; they seek to avoid the former and obtain the latter. (6) They are impulsive, and seek instant gratification. But because they are aware of time, they learn (7) that greater gratifications can be had in the future by resisting the impulse to immediate gratification. To be rational means to Lewis to subordinate present gratification to future and greater gratification. Rationality requires that human beings govern themselves, and (8) that governance is exercised through rules or imperatives. Imperatives therefore are intrinsic to human nature, and no further explanation of their existence is required. But that does not determine which imperatives are valid.

Since Lewis believes that all knowledge is for action, it is important to be clear about what he means by action.

> There is first the envisagement of something as possible for us to bring about; sometimes more than one such possibility. In any case, there is the alternative of doing or not doing. There is then attentive consideration, briefly or at length, terminating in decision. Criticism of action mostly turns upon the characters of the decision or of what is so decided. But the decision is not the doing, since we may decide to do something tomorrow or next week and meantime change our minds. The "doing itself" is the indescribable oomph of initiation, the fiat of the will, accompanied by expectation of something as about to follow. This fiat of willing is the commitment because, prior to that, any deliberate act can be altered or cancelled, but after that the act and all its consequences are out of our hands.[44]

Lewis divides actions into elementary and complex. An act is elementary if "there is no physical first part of it which can be done without doing the whole of it."[45] Complex acts are composed of a series of elementary acts, even though a single decision may determine the entire series. We know how to do complex acts by knowing how to do the constituent elementary acts, but the connection between the fiat and its physical enactment is inscrutable.

Since the fiat of the will is indescribable, the only way in which an act can be identified is by its consequences. Usually the first consequence is some movement of a part of the body, but what we generally refer to as the consequences are somewhat more remote. Thus, in "He signed a contract," it is not the movement of the hand that we use to identify the act but the completion of the signing process. The consequences of an act are therefore crucial since only by them is the act identified. Only the consequences make the act important[46]—an action that had no consequences would be of no interest to anyone. Lewis invokes the terms "intention" and "purpose" that he had defined in the AKV: the intention is all the consequences expected to follow upon the act; the purpose, the consequences for the sake of which the act is done.[47]

Lewis notes that all decisions to act are, to some degree, general, for every act is a *way* of acting under certain conditions. This is why actions can be habitual; any decision to act can be extended to cover a class of like cases.[48] Hence, the manner in which a deliberate act is decided can be formulated as a rule. Such a rule is subject to critique on the issue of whether or not it should be adhered to in all like cases. And the critique of actions will be both moral and cognitive; was the intention of the act morally right or wrong, and were its predictions of consequences true or false? Lewis equates rules and general imperatives.[49] All rules are normative; they define what ought to be done in given circumstances. Lewis takes the term "ought" to have imperative force, so that it makes no difference whether the imperative or indicative form is used. Thus, the rule that one ought to drive on the right and the imperative "Drive on the right!" are, in his view, equivalent. That means that conforming to an imperative has the same force as following a rule; both require a conscious conforming of one's behavior to a stated norm.

Since Lewis believes that an act can only be identified by its consequences, if an act is right or wrong, there must be some characteristic of its consequences that makes it so. The relevant characteristics are good and bad. Broadly speaking, Lewis says, "to do that the consequences of which are justifiably expected to be good rather than bad, is the objectively right way to act; and the doing of that which justified belief would indicate to have bad consequences rather than good, is the objectively wrong way to act."[50] This, of course, requires definitions of "good" and "bad," and here Lewis invokes the theory of value he had laid out in Book III of AKV.

This way of stating the matter, however, has consequences that can be misleading. Lewis had argued in AKV that valuation was a form of empirical knowledge. Since in the passage just quoted, he appears to have defined the rightness and wrongness of an action in terms of good and bad, why does this not reduce Lewis's ethical theory to an empirical theory? The answer is that, as Lewis puts it, "the good solicits but the right commands."[51] The goodness or badness of the consequences of an act are necessary conditions for the act being right or wrong, but they are not sufficient. They tell us why an act may be desirable, but they do not tell us why we are or are not obligated to do it. Specifically, an act may offer us immediate gratifications, yet have long-run consequences that are grievous either to ourselves or to others. It is only by conformity to a rule or imperative that we can override the allure of the immediately gratifying. In general, an ethical judgment for Lewis carries an imperative force that is not accounted for by the mere fact that the consequences of the act in question may be good. Ethical principles are imperatives.

But Lewis has a further reason for rejecting a purely empirical theory of the right. As is well known, utilitarianism is subject to the criticism that the greatest good for the greatest number may result from an unjust act, such as sacrificing an innocent person to increase the good obtained by others. Lewis apparently believed that all empirical theories are subject to similar difficulties. It was to rule out such actions that Lewis separated ethics from valuation and insisted that the ethical critique of action must be the final arbiter of rightness and wrongness. It is therefore essential for his theory that the justification of imperatives should not rest on empirical grounds.[52]

Conformity to imperatives is the rightness of action. But Lewis distinguishes between objective rightness and subjective rightness. Objective rightness requires both that the intention of the act must be right and that its prediction of the goodness of the consequences must be accurate. Subjective rightness concerns only the intention with which the act is done; the act is subjectively right if the intention is right. Further, Lewis holds that the allocation of praise or blame depends only on the subjective rightness of the action, not its objective rightness.

Lewis's notion of objective rightness involved an ambiguity that he did not resolve until October 1958. He had previously distinguished between objective and subjective rightness. But with respect to "This is right," two different significances

> of [objective] 'right' are here involved in the very statement of the case: (1) that which, on completest investigation, would show itself as satisfying the criteria of right; that which would *prove* right to do; and (2) that which to the best knowledge and belief of the doer, in the circumstances requiring him to decide his action, appear to satisfy the criteria of rightly done.[53]

At first,[54] Lewis rejected the first of these meanings of right and held that it was the latter that defined objective rightness. But he then resolved the issue by expanding his typology. He now admitted three senses of right. First, an act can be said to be right just in case its consequences are good or better than any alternative. This would be "absolute rightness" because it assumes that the doer's knowledge of the consequences is omniscient. Second, an act is "objectively right" if the doer's expectation that the consequences will be good is a justified belief at the time of action—that is, if based on all the evidence available, it is highly probable that the consequences will be good. In a sentence that reveals why this had seemed a problem to him, Lewis says, "we thus have the paradox of empirical believing that its aim or end—truth or conformity to fact—is not the right-making property of it."[55] Because one cannot know its truth when one adopts a belief, it can only be the relation of the belief to the available evidence that makes it right to believe. Third, an act is "subjectively right" if the doer's intention in performing the act is to bring about good results.[56]

What then are the imperatives that govern human action? It is here that Lewis's debt to Kant is most apparent. Kant held that in the case of the Holy Will, no imperatives applied; one whose will was holy would, of course, conform to the moral law. But for human beings, who are not purely rational beings but whose will is subject to impulses and inclinations arising from our animal nature, the dictates of reason must assume an imperative form that enables us to override impulse. Lewis does not invoke the Holy Will, and his definition of reason is very different from Kant's, but he sees the problem of morality, and the normative in general, as the struggle between reason and impulse, and the implement by which impulse is subdued as imperatives, which, like Kant, he takes to formulate an obligatory command of reason.[57] Rationality, as Lewis defines it, involves the subordination of present goods to greater future goods. On Lewis's view of human nature, this is difficult because we are creatures of impulse, and not only do our desires for present gratification interfere with the pursuit of more adequate future ones, but they often conflict among themselves.[58] Our immersion in time, our need to pursue a course of action that will lead to maximum gratification in the long run, imposes on us the imperative of consistency. By this, Lewis means "practical consistency"; we cannot simultaneously pursue courses of action that cancel each other; further, we must be able to follow a plan or a rule that we believe will maximize our long-run gratification despite temptations to do otherwise. One species of practical consistency is logical consistency.[59] Logic, as Lewis pointed out in AKV, arises from our need to function in time, not the converse.[60] Thus, the first imperative of action is: "Be consistent!" This is an imperative of *action* because, as all Pragmatists hold, thinking is a form of action. Which among the various systems of logic we choose to use is a purely pragmatic matter; we use the one that best serves our purposes in a given situation. But the imperative to be consistent applies to all systems of logic, even though the rules of the systems may differ. Lewis thoroughly agrees with Peirce that logic is a normative science. To say that an argument is valid is to say that the steps of the argument are right.

But the successful pursuit of long-run gratification involves more than being consistent; it involves having justified empirical beliefs. The effectiveness of any course of action depends on accurate knowledge of the environment, the ends sought, our capacities, and the means employed. Here, too, the action involved is mental, but it is still action and subject to critique, for, unless our empirical beliefs are correct, the proposed course of action will fail. But, as Lewis had discussed in detail in the AKV, empirical knowledge rests on the validity of memory and induction. There may be a limited amount we can do about memory, but there are imperatives that must be obeyed if enumerative induction is to be valid. Specifically, our estimates of the probability of our empirical beliefs must be reliable. Thus, the critique of empirical knowledge involves the imperative to "Be cogent!," meaning that all the right procedures of induction must be followed, and particularly that all the relevant evidence must be considered.[61]

As Saydah has pointed out,[62] Lewis's use of the term "cogency" is often ambiguous. At times he applies it to all concluding and believing, and seems to subsume consistency under cogency; at other times he separates the two and restricts cogency to empirical belief. The ambiguity is rarely troublesome, but in what follows I will take cogency to be distinct from consistency.

Concluding and believing are mental acts; there are also imperatives that apply to ways of doing. Lewis's classification of the modes of right doing is taken directly from Kant;[63] he divided right doing into the technical, the prudential, and the moral. The technical receives the briefest treatment; it is the rightness of an instrumental action for the attainment of some end. Thus, Lewis says there is a right way to make sponge cake and a wrong way. But whether or not a given technical act is right to do depends chiefly on whether or not the end is one that ought to be pursued, so Lewis takes the real question to be the character of the end. At times Lewis talks as if the end justifies the means, but he is well aware that there can be ethical questions concerning the means themselves. This is particularly evident in his discussion of professional action, which he includes under the technical. A doctor's treatment of his or her patient and a lawyer's treatment of his client involve ethical considerations beyond those concerning the end sought.[64]

The technical imperatives are hypothetical imperatives: if one wants to achieve this particular end, then do . . . ! These imperatives are based on past experience with methods for attaining the desired ends, and "the rightness of the directives themselves derives from the presumed goodness of the results and the reliability of achieving such results by following these directives."[65] The general principle of the technical right is to use the most effective means to the end sought. The prudential and moral imperatives Lewis takes to be both categorical; the former is to maximize one's long-run goods, and the latter is Kant's Categorical Imperative.

What is the justification for these imperatives? Lewis accepted the view that propositions involving "right" cannot be derived from propositions that do not involve "right."[66] Thus, he agrees with Moore, Hare, Ewing, and the non-Naturalists that "ought" cannot be derived from "is." He believed that some imperatives can be derived from others, but, of course, the fundamental imperatives cannot. Lewis changed his position on the justification of these imperatives during the course of the 1950s. In his Proseminar Lecture on "Modes of Evaluation" in 1952, Lewis took the position that the basic imperatives of Consistency, Cogency, Prudence, and Morality are analytic a priori statements.

> With something of that intellectual ingenuity which Whitehead and Russell displayed in tucking all Peano's postulates for arithmetic into definitions of the arithmetical entities—leaving no synthetic statements in arithmetic—all the rational imperatives can be shown a priori by tucking them into definitions; eventually into definitions of the different kinds of correctness. It will then follow that they ought to be conformed to, because, by definition, "correct" means ought to be conformed to.
>
> Pure mathematics leaves any application of mathematics at the mercy of discernable character of this which makes mathematics practical to apply. Arithmetic and any geometry needs a Kantian 'deduction'—or would if their applicability could be doubted.
>
> The pure and analytic-founded logic of practice still needs such 'deduction'—proof of applicability to human living in this world. That 'deduction' is afforded by the fact that humans find decision making inescapable, and are (sic) also find it impossible to escape the implication of some 'correctness' to be achieved and a constraint to seek it in any deliberate decision. The last fact is simply a datum of human life.[67]

Lewis is again following Kant here in holding the imperatives of skill and prudence to be analytic a priori, but whereas Kant regarded the imperative of morality as synthetic a priori, Lewis, having rejected the notion of the synthetic a priori, claims that it, too, is analytic a priori.

But how can an imperative be a priori true? Lewis holds that for every imperative there is a corresponding indicative sentence that is equivalent in meaning. "I think we should also become clear that for every form of indicative statement there is some axiological correlate—some dictate of the form the repudiation of which is irrational."[68] Thus, he takes "Be consistent!" as equivalent to "One ought to be consistent," and the latter as indicative and true.

The fundamental ethical imperatives are therefore analytic a priori "in the same sense that the principles of logic are analytic," and their denials are self-contradictory. But "that such a particular decision is right, is a synthetic statement, just as 'this figure is a triangle and has three sides' is synthetic."[69] Thus, in 1952, Lewis saw the problem of ethics as analogous to the problem of geometry. The basic imperatives themselves were a priori analytic; their application to particulars was synthetic, involving the classification of actions as falling under the concepts of the a priori system. This gave to ethics a familiar and well-understood structure.

The validity of the basic imperatives cannot be proven any more than the validity of the postulates of geometry can. "Any argument to convince of the conclusion that these are valid imperatives can only be a *petetio prin-cipii*. It need not be, for that reason, without point."[70] A Kantian deduc-tion is not without point because it demonstrates the applicability of the imperatives to human life. Kant's deduction of his categories showed that they must apply to phenomenal experience because without them scien-tific knowledge would be impossible; so, Lewis held, a Kantian deduction of the imperatives shows that unless they apply to human life, there are crucial aspects of human experience that cannot be accounted for.

> Kantian fashion . . . I shall seek to remind the reader of peculiarly human features of human experience and products of the human men-tality which would be unintelligible or non-significant if there are not valid imperatives our recognition of which is humanly obligatory.[71]

Human life requires deliberative decision, and such decision must be either correct or incorrect. But Lewis holds that such deliberative behavior would be impossible if there were no imperatives that defined what is or is not correct to do.

In 1952, and indeed through the publication of *The Ground and Nature of the Right* in 1955, Lewis held that the basic imperative was what he called the Law of Objectivity, which, he said, was "the law of life."[72]

> So conduct and determine your activities of thinking and doing, as to conform any decision of them to the objective actualities, as cognitively signified to you in your representational apprehension of them, and not according to any impulsion or solicitation exercised by the affective qual-ity of your present experience or immediate feeling merely.[73]

To this, he added the corollary:

> Conduct yourself, with reference to those future eventualities which cog-nition advises that your activity may affect, as you would if these pre-dictable effects of it were to be realized, at this moment of decision, with the poignancy of the here and now, instead of the less poignant feeling which representation of the future and possible may automatically arouse.[74]

To these, Lewis adds the claim (a) that "the peculiarly human kind of life is *imperatively* social."[75] From this claim, together with the Law of Objectivity, arises the imperative (b) to so deal with others as if the effects of our actions on them were to be realized in our own person. This imper-ative divides into two: the Law of Compassion—"recognize, in your action affecting any sentient being, that claim on your compassion which comports with its capacity to enjoy and suffer,"[76] and the Law of Moral Equity: "No manner of thought or action is valid for any of us except as, in the same premises of circumstance and evidenced fact, it is valid for all of us."[77] The Law of Compassion, that Lewis says he derived from Schopenhauer,[78] applies to all sentient life—animals, children, the insane, and the retarded; the Law of Moral Equity to what Lewis calls our "full peers." The latter, Lewis says, is equivalent to the principle of equality before the moral law— "there shall be no law for one which is not law for all."[79] These principles serve to divide acts into those that are permissible and those that are not. An act is wrong if it violates *any* such principle, and an act is right only if it violates *no* such principle.[80]

Lewis's view of the status of the Law of Objectivity seems to have changed over time. In his Proseminar Lectures in 1952, he regarded it as *the* fundamental imperative. This principle, he says, "is an implication of the cognitive capacity itself. Without it, knowledge would be of no effect."[81] To know, Lewis says, is to take the qualia of experience as significant of some reality. "The very nature of human cognition, as subject to deliberation and to the distinction of knowledge from mistake, implies the imperative to that correctness which is so distinguished and is the mark of knowledge."[82] "Knowledge" itself is a normative concept that distinguishes what in our beliefs is correct from what is not. The Law of Objectivity is the "general root" of all the rational imperatives. One cannot repudiate it and still have knowledge, for knowledge is correct cognition of the actual; without the Law of Objectivity there could be no science and no empirical knowledge of any sort.[83] The same applies to moral imperatives.

> The valid directives of action, including any moral imperatives which are genuine, have this same root. The *sine qua non* of their significance is some kind of objective facts due respect for which requires conformity to them.[84]

Thus, with respect to justice, the Law of Objectivity implies "that other persons, and their joys and sorrows are as real as we are and as our own."

> The dictate to respect them as the actualities they are, instead of acting toward them as prompted by the greater poignancy with which we feel our own joys and sorrows, as compared with our fainter empathetic feelings of the weal and woes of others; that dictate is the very root of any principle of justice.[85]

Lewis does not claim that the Law of Objectivity alone is sufficient to establish all the other rational imperatives, but he takes it as the fundamental imperative and a necessary condition for the others. This appears still to be his position in *The Ground and Nature of the Right.*

The Law of Objectivity involves, on the one hand, Lewis's claim that every objective fact involves an imperative for action. Thus, "The stove is hot" yields the imperative "If you don't want to be burned, don't touch the stove!" Since doing takes place in an environment of objects, it must be carried out in accordance with the properties and relations of those objects. On the other hand, it involves Lewis's doctrine that inherent values are objective properties of things that are empirically determinable. As the corollary spells out, Lewis regards it as imperative to seek greater future values rather than lesser immediate ones. So far as the individual is concerned, ethical conflict is largely a question of the effort to bring impulses under rational control and establish an order of precedence among them.[86] Lewis was not a New Englander for nothing.

To the rationale for imperative (a) we will return in a moment, but that its conjunction with the Law of Objectivity yields imperative (b) is questionable. What Lewis means is that since other humans are objectively real, their properties and relations, including their capacities for grief and gratification, must be taken into account in our conduct. But it is very hard to see how this implies (b). Why should we not so act as to ensure that the effects of our actions on others are *not* visited on us? Suppose I sell to A an article X that I don't want in return for money that I do want. The effect on A is that he has X and less money. But this is just the effect that I do *not* want visited on me. Yet this example embraces economic exchanges generally, which Lewis could hardly rule out as immoral. Nor does the Law of Compassion follow from any of this—obviously, since it involves all sentient beings, whereas the principles taken as premises apply only to human beings. As for the Law of Moral Equity, although the relation to (b) is obvious, it does not follow from (b). Acting toward others as though the effects of our actions are to be visited on us may provide a psychological reason for holding that an act is "valid," by which I think Lewis means "right," only if under like conditions it is right for all, but the one does not imply the other. Lewis's arguments in *The Ground and Nature of the Right* were not convincing, as the reviewers of the book made clear.[87]

What underlies Lewis's arguments, but is not made explicit, is his belief in empathetic knowledge. We have earlier seen Lewis's struggles with the problem of other minds. The point in his philosophy where this is critical is in his ethics. The doctrine that we must act toward others as if the effects of our actions on them were to be visited on us assumes that we can know what these effects are, and that we can know it with sufficient accuracy so that we can realize—make real to ourselves—the griefs or gratifications that they feel. Lewis does believe that this is possible. To use his example, I do not now feel the pain of tomorrow's toothache, but I can well imagine it. So, equally, I can imagine the pain of another's toothache, even though I will never feel it.[88] It is the assumption of such interpersonal empathetic knowledge that gives content to Lewis moral imperatives. Lewis had previously considered two justifications for such knowledge: one was to adopt a postulate to that effect, the other was to base it on the similarity among humans. Which is invoked here is not clear. Obviously, the latter requires some notion of what similarities are generic and what are idiosyncratic. As Lewis put it, "the problem of statement [having the consequences of our actions for others visited upon ourselves] is to eliminate what is personal *in the manner of weighing* without eliminating what may be personal in *what is to be weighed*."[89] "What is to be weighed" is the good or bad effects in the experience of the person suffering the act; "in the manner of weighing" is what is idiosyncratic to that particular person.[90]

In his 1952 lectures, Lewis took the Law of Objectivity as the basis of social ethics, about which he gave an extensive discussion. The law, he holds, implies respect for the moral autonomy of other humans. He insists that there is a "right of privacy" involved in autonomy—"an area of action in which we are left free to pursue our own best good in our own way."[91] He takes this to be an essential feature of a just society and part of the explanation of our civilization and its progress. It is the denial of this freedom of the individual that marks totalitarian societies. Accordingly, Lewis says, a just society is not one in which each seeks to do what is best for every other, since that would lead to the sort of problem sometimes found in family conferences when each tries to choose what the others want with the result that nobody does what he or she wants.[92] Further, Lewis holds, a just society does not require the abrogation of prudence. Lewis formulates the imperative of justice as "so act as to respect the interests of others whom your action may affect, as you would call upon others to respect your own."[93] Justice does not require altruism.

Lewis then states a principle concerning the relation of the individual to the society: "The greatest need of any human individual is for human fellowship; and to find one's place in a good society, and to function successfully in it . . . a lone last survivor of the human race, whatever his material circumstances, would surely wish to be done and join the others."[94] Accordingly, "self-concern and concern for others . . . must overlap."

> To conserve the highest ends of others must include conserving their autonomy and the privilege of a private and peculiar concern for their own individual ends. And to conserve one's own interest must include

conserving those spiritual and deep interests which one has in others and in mutually satisfying relationships with others.[95]

Given the degree to which the quality of the individual's life depends on his membership in a society, it is in the self-interest of the individual to protect and further the society to which he belongs. This is what Lewis calls the "higher prudence." The success of the society depends on the devotion of its members. But as Lewis notes one has here the problem of the "free rider"— the person who uses the society to further his or her own interests while contributing nothing in return. But Lewis holds that such behavior violates Kant's Categorical Imperative since if all behaved that way, society would collapse. What the Categorical Imperative requires here is that each should contribute: "He who would benefit is morally obligated to contribute."[96]

The right of privacy is closely linked to the concept of liberty. It is one of man's privileges to be able to choose his own ends and to strive to attain them. This is a mark of free men—those not only not compelled by others but having open to them concrete possibilities for realizing their own ends. This freedom is more than individual, for "the freedom he enjoys will include much which can only accrue to him through the attainments of his social order and by reason of its legacy from the past."[97] This is also a social freedom—a freedom of the group, or the race, to pursue its own chosen goals. Since social living is a necessity for human beings, "the disparity between our native inclinations and social requirements" is an inevitable feature of social life and the source of the problem of social control. At the individual level, this requires "control of primal emotive urges and natural inclinations by intelligent understanding of what individual well-being and welfare of the organized group require."[98] This, as Lewis has repeatedly argued, requires self-criticism and self-restraint so that desired future experiences may be attained, but he now adds that one's own behavior must be weighed as a type of behavior open to others in the group and must be compatible with group living and the attainment of group goals. In other words, rational conduct is conduct that fits social requirements.

Lewis does not attempt to specify the details of a desirable social order, but he does indicate certain features that it must have. Above all, it must provide individual liberty. "The crux of this problem [of social order] concerns social institutions founded upon liberty; for civilization arises and progresses by the initiative of free men, freely cooperating in society." What then is liberty?

Liberty is the rational creature's ownership of himself. It consists in the exercise by the individual of his natural capacity for deliberate decision and self-determined action, subject only to restraints which find a sanction in that rationality which all men claim in common. As such, liberty is essential to personality.[99]

Liberty as here defined is identical with rational self-government; it is not a freedom to do as one lists or to indulge one's emotions, but to do what is dictated by rational decision. "Any restriction of action which is implicit in such rationality cannot be accounted a curtailment of the liberty of the individual since it springs from imperatives of his own nature."[100] Liberty is the freedom to be rational. One is reminded of John Winthrop's definition of civil liberty as the liberty to do that which is "good, just, and honest."[101] Lewis was no libertine.

Lewis holds that the moral autonomy of the individual and that person's freedom of decision are both ineradicable facts and inalienable rights. The determination of which liberties should be universally accorded and which denied he considers "the major problem of a just and desirable social order, supposing that the major principle of social justice—equality of all men with respect to liberties allowed and restraints imposed—is met."[102]

Although Lewis believes in government by consent of the governed and in choice of governors by free elections, he rejects any notion of a social contract. If the justification for society involves the benefits that accrue to individuals from belonging to it, then at some point that adherence to the contract will become so costly that it will be canceled. If it is not, then adherence to the social order must rest on some antecedent obligation to honor contracts that cannot be part of the social contract itself. To live in any social order is to agree to be bound by some principles that operate to one's disadvantage. "The reality of an obligation is tested only when it hurts to fulfil it. And when it hurts, it cannot be validated on the ground of self-interest."[103] Instead, Lewis derives the principle that legitimate government must rest on the consent of the governed from the fact "that self-conscious personality cannot exist without self-determination." But what does "consent" mean here? Lewis explicates it as meaning that "no man can rationally claim the advantages of cooperation while dissenting, by his actions, from those restrictions by which alone this cooperation is possible and may attain those common ends for the sake of which it is undertaken."[104]

Lewis accepts that public institutions must enforce justice and equality before the law, and that this requires respect for the interests of others. But it does not require love, nor does it require that one show the same consideration for the ends of others as for one's own. Lewis holds that "the fundamental liberty to be an individual includes [the] right to a measure of privacy."[105] The maximum social good is not won "by the continual attention of each to the maximum good of all"; rather each must give special concern to his or her own interest while respecting the right of others to do the same. "There is no social good or welfare which is not constituted out of individual goods or welfare." Lewis's individualism would not permit him to accept such a principle as the utilitarian doctrine of the greatest good to the greatest number.[106]

For Lewis, then, what is socially good is constituted by all members of society fulfilling their own prudential aims. This is possible only when each has an area of privacy—an area of freedom of action for the individual. What limits that freedom? Lewis says there is no a priori answer to that question. Each society has its mores, and they will determine what the rewards and obligations of that society are. Those who live in the society are bound to conform to its mores and contribute to it. In

> the best human society, each individual will be appointed a committee of one to give special attention to what will be best for himself; every family a committee specially charged to look out for their family interest, and every lesser community, whether an included political community or economic unit or unit of those specially interested in some particular good cause, will be appointed a committee to make the interests which thus naturally lie closest to them, their first order of business.[107]

Such a decentralized society, Lewis believes, will be far more efficient than a centrally managed one. There should be "some peculiar concern on the part of each for his individual interests and the ends represented by his natural loyalties and his particular function in this social organization."[108] Justice and prudence, Lewis believes, are not necessarily opposed to one another.

Lewis finds this illustrated by the relation between competition and cooperation. By cooperative activity he means "the success of one person or party engaging in it furthers the like success of others also. And a mode of activity is competitive if, or insofar as, the success of one person or one party engaging in it prevents or militates against the like success of others."[109] He then divides competitive activities into those whose purpose is to preclude the success of others, and those not intended to preclude other's success—as, for example, in perfect competition. Lewis believes humans are by nature competitive animals, and that it is neither possible nor desirable to ban competition from society. He also believes that there is a historical trend away from the most brutal forms of competition toward the less brutal. But, at any given time, the balance between cooperation and competition must be determined by the balance of social costs and social benefits.[110]

Many activities are both competitive and cooperative. He uses the example of games in which there must be cooperation to maintain the rules of the game, but there is also competition to win. Lewis sees a loose correlation between these activities and the types of ends sought. He says competitive activities are usually directed toward material ends, while cooperative activities usually involve nonmaterial ones. He admits that the correlation is far from perfect; social prestige is an obvious example of a competitive goal that is not material.[111] The existence of civilization, Lewis says, depends on the outlawing among members of the society of the most destructive forms of competition. This does not mean outlawing competition; social control is largely exercised by graded rewards, and such rewards are competitive.[112]

Competitive motives are always prudential. And "in the absence of social interference, or the threat of it, any competition always tends to take the most brutal possible and most destructive form."[113] That, Lewis notes, is what makes the elimination of war so difficult. War has been socially profitable in the past; it has led to "securing to the most effective social groups, a privileged status in relation to available natural resources."[114] But

> Western civilization appears to have decided that the social costs of international warfare are not worth the profit. Or more accurately, they see the cost; they hope—whether they admit it or not—that the process by which the best people in the world may remain or become dominant in history will still go without it. War *will* go on, until they are cured of this schizophrenia—wanting to eat their cake and have it too.[115]

Lewis had not studied Herbert Spencer for nothing.

The chief social profit of economic competition is the creation of more material goods at less cost in terms of human labor. The chief cost is the maldistribution of wealth. The successful have yachts, the unsuccessful barely subsist. As a result, Lewis says,

> the institution of economic competition is now on trial. We are moving—whether we like it or not, and very rapidly—in the direction away from the laissez-faire conception of justice and toward socialism. We would like to keep the social profit of the highest possible economic efficiency but do away with, or considerably mitigate, the natural effect of it in inequalities of the distribution of wealth. Until we cure ourselves of that wishful thinking we shall not know whether we want to go where we are now headed or not.[116]

Not all forms of competition are ruthless. Lewis distinguishes what he labels "professional competition" as particularly praiseworthy. The professional has a high degree of autonomy combined with strong obligations to the society. This also involves "a considerable degree of subordination of the economic motivation to motivation by the non-material goods of public recognition, and a recognition of leadership, on the part of others, in what the professional competence touches, and in prestige in the group itself which exercises the professional and social function in question."[117]

Lewis goes on to say that the crux of the social problem does not lie in persuading the ablest people to contribute to society because these people enjoy what they do and will do it for modest rewards. The real problem, he believes is "how well would the economically mediocre and the economic bums perform any necessary economic function under socialism?"[118] The naivete of these remarks is almost beyond belief.

If the social good is constituted by individual goods, there must be some rule for determining how these individual goods are to be weighed against each other. In the AKV, Lewis had made a compelling argument against the possibility of a utilitarian calculus on the grounds that goods could not simply be summed. Although Lewis does not deal extensively with the problem of interpersonal comparisons of values, he does say that we should adopt the principle: "Each to count for one, and none for more than one."[119]

Prudence and justice are the two categorical imperatives that govern the relation of individuals to society. Yet Lewis recognizes that there are actions not governed by either.

> The moral man will, I say, often find himself bound to go beyond such higher prudence and contribute to the well-being of others, in ways for which there is no recompense for him beyond such satisfaction as he may find in preserving his own integrity. But any action he so takes is *not* an obligation to others, and is not a *duty* in any literal sense of 'duty'. It is a free gift of good will.[120]

Such actions Lewis regards as having no prudential or moral worth beyond that covered by the imperatives. But if they are neither prudent nor just, are they right? This was a problem Lewis would have to return to.

Lewis's social ethics hardly ranks as a significant contribution to social thought. He is clearly a believer in some type of free-market capitalism and opposed to socialism, but there is little here dealing with the major economic or social problems of his time. Although Lewis had taught economics and had read Marx, there is no discussion of the relation of labor and capital, of unemployment, or of the role of the state in the management of the economy. Similarly, there is no discussion of race relations, crime, bureaucracy, gangs, or other social issues prominent at that time.

Perhaps Lewis thought such questions lay beyond the scope of ethics, but his remarks on competition and cooperation hardly bear that out. One has the sense that Lewis was a disgruntled conservative for whom the New Deal economy looked all too much like socialism.

After the publication of *The Ground and Nature of the Right* in 1955, Lewis abandoned both the claim that the fundamental imperatives are analytic and that the Law of Objectivity is *the* fundamental imperative. I have found no statement as to why he changed his mind, but the reasons are perhaps not far to seek. The Law of Objectivity assumes that we have true, or at least highly probable, empirical knowledge; how else could one conform one's actions to "objective actualities?" It therefore assumes at least the imperatives of consistency and cogency, and cannot be the premise from which they are derived. Lewis did not abandon the Law of Objectivity entirely; it remained as a legitimate imperative of action. But after *The Ground and Nature of the Right* he did not regard it as fundamental.

His abandonment of the claim that the fundamental imperatives are analytic comes, I suspect, from an ambiguity in this claim. On the one hand, Lewis says that the imperatives themselves are analytic; on the other, he says that the claim the imperatives should be adhered to is analytic. These are not the same. Thus, Lewis says,

> If one still insists that there is a difference between cogency, or prudence, or justice and their ought-to-be adhered-to-ness, and that statements such as "Cogency ought to be adhered to in thinking and believing" is a synthetic statement, then I offer the following as definitions, faithful to common meanings: Cogency is correctness in thought and belief. Correctness is rightness. What is correct or right is what ought to be adhered to. I will not claim that the like questions about prudence and justice can be dealt with thus summarily and with a like plausibility without a good deal of further discussion, though it is my conviction that they can be so dealt with in the end and after notice of certain further problems concerning them.[121]

Furthermore,

> Repudiation of the ought-to-be-adhered-to-ness of right, in any of its modes, is always a self-inconsistent attitude which vitiates and declares non-significant decisions which [we] necessarily are nevertheless obliged to make, and make with a sense of them as justified and unjustified, right or wrong.[122]

Here it is the denial of the claim that the imperatives must be adhered to that is declared self-contradictory, though it is not the logical negation of the claim itself, but the consequences of negating it that Lewis cites. But does the negation of the imperative itself result in a contradiction? If the prudential imperative is taken to be

> Always seek to maximize your long-run goods.

The negation is

> Sometimes do not seek to maximize your long-run goods.

This is not obviously self-contradictory, as it ought to be if the imperative is analytic. Lewis clearly does hold that the statement "Whatever is correct ought to be adhered to" is analytic, but what is missing here is the demonstration that prudence and the other imperatives are forms of correctness. That is not obvious from the imperatives themselves, and it is not clear how Lewis thought he could "tuck" them into definitions. Lewis seems to have recognized this problem shortly after 1952, and abandoned the claim that the basic imperatives were analytic. Instead, he turned to a new method of demonstrating their a priori character—the pragmatic contradiction.

Lewis's theory of the pragmatic contradiction is based on his theory of the proposition. Lewis held that propositions are terms such as "Mary baking pies now" or "that Mary is baking pies now." Propositions admit of multiple uses; they can be used to question, assert, command, and so on. When asserted, a proposition becomes a statement: thus "Mary is baking pies now" asserts the proposition, "Mary baking pies now." This separation of the act of assertion from the proposition itself is important because the "act of asserting has what may be called pragmatic implications which are not, strictly and properly, implications of the proposition asserted."[123] Thus, "John being here today" does not imply that "It is true that John is here today," but the act of asserting it does. The act of assertion expresses the speaker's belief that the state of affairs signified by the proposition obtains—that is, that John is here today. "No speaker can make any assertion without thus implying the correctness of the belief expressed. In this sense every assertion (act of assertion) has the corresponding normative implication of correctness of a belief."[124] Whoever makes an assertion, but also rejects the imperative to believe what he asserts, "contradicts himself pragmatically." Lewis cites the example of Epimenides the Cretan, who said, "All Cretans are liars." This statement is not logically contradictory; had a non-Cretan uttered it, there would be no problem. But the assertion of it by a Cretan involves a pragmatic contradiction since the act of assertion implies what the statement denies.[125]

Lewis emphasizes that the paradox of Epimenides is not truly the paradox of the liar because it does not involve a logical contradiction. But consider

    (a) This statement is true.
    (b) This statement is false.

(a) lacks meaning "because it applies to itself a predicate 'is true' whose applicability under these circumstances, is intrinsically impossible to determine." But (b) is contradictory. "This statement" refers to the whole statement (b). If we substitute for "This statement" what it refers to, we have " 'This statement is false' is false," which, if true, is false and, if false, is true.[126] The paradox of the liar is a logical contradiction; the pragmatic contradiction is not.

Lewis's two favorite examples of the pragmatic contradiction are Epimenides and the Cyrenaic, who said, "Catch pleasure as it flies; have no thought for the morrow."[127] But Lewis points out that the Cyrenaic's assertion is the assertion of a principle governing how one should behave tomorrow, and therefore pragmatically contradicts the proposition it asserts. In this case, we have an imperative that leads to pragmatic contradiction, whereas Epimenides's statement is a declarative. Lewis views the notion of the pragmatic contradiction as equally applicable in both cases. Furthermore, Lewis holds that a statement whose denial leads to a pragmatic contradiction is "pragmatically a priori."[128] It need not be a priori in the sense of being analytic, but just as the negation of an analytic statement leads to a logical contradiction, so Lewis holds that a statement whose denial leads to a pragmatic contradiction is pragmatically a priori. This claim seems clear with respect to the Cyrenaics, but not with respect to Epimenides. "All Cretans are liars" contradicts the truth implication of its assertion only because the speaker is a Cretan. It is very hard to see how this statement can be a priori since there would be no contradiction if it were uttered by a non-Cretan. Lewis does not deal with this issue.

There is a problem with Lewis's theory of the pragmatic contradiction that needs to be discussed; it involves the assumption that there is a logic that is applicable to imperatives. That claim has been the subject of debate, which in modern times began with Ernst Mally's *Grundgesetze der Sollens* in 1926. It was Mally who introduced the term "deontic" ("deontik") by which such logics have since been called.[129] But the work from which more recent studies date is von Wright's "Deontic Logic" in 1951. Von Wright viewed deontic logic as a type of modal logic[130] and saw the deontic notions of obligation and permission as analogous to the modal notions of necessity and possibility. In his system, the deontic operators are pre-fixed to the names of generic acts—thus, to "theft" rather than to names of individual acts of theft. He then defines performance-values (by an agent) and performance-functions whose values are uniquely determined by the performance-values of acts of the same agent. As he states, "the concept of performance-function is strictly analogous to the concept of a truth-function in propositional logic." We then have sentences stating that an act, A, is either permitted or obligatory, and such sentences can be true or false. Von Wright developed truth-tables for deontic sentences, defined analytic and contradictory deontic sentences, and showed that the decision problem is solved for this system.[131]

The 1950s and 1960s saw a rapid increase in work on deontic logic. Whereas von Wright had regarded imperativeness and commitment as concepts of deontic logic, other writers disagreed. A lively debate followed over deontic logic,[132] which even led to the claim by Everett Hall that an imperative statement has two different negations and that therefore a three-valued logic is necessary to deal with it[133]—a view that, while not unique to Hall, has not won favor.

It is not clear how much of this literature Lewis read, but he does cite von Wright as having demonstrated that "there is not one logic of science and a quite different one—or none at all—for morals. The logic of imperatives is fundamentally no different from the logic of the indicative; the logic of simple assertion."[134] Although in a footnote Lewis says he is not convinced von Wright's position is correct on some technical issues, it is not surprising that Lewis should have taken this position. Citing a paper of Henry Leonard,[135] Lewis says that "there are propositions formulating states of affairs, which remain identical in whatever syntactic mode they are entertained or considered—the indicative, the imperative, the inter-rogative, the optative, or any other."[136] This is Lewis's own analysis of propositions as terms that can be put to various uses. It was therefore nat-ural for him to hold that the use of the proposition does not affect its role in logic. What von Wright has established, he says, is "that what has been called necessary truth or apodeictic, since the time of Aristotle, is the ana-logue, in any logic of imperatives, of that which is commanded or obliga-tory."[137] Thus, Lewis views imperatives and statements of obligation as equivalent, and he believes the rules of ordinary logic apply to imperative inference.

This has important consequences for the theory of pragmatic contra-diction. The imperatives that Lewis considers are general imperatives of the form "Be consistent!" Such an imperative may be taken to mean "Always be consistent!" As the denial of this imperative, he uses, "Never be consistent!"

or "Be inconsistent!" But "Never be consistent!" is the contrary of "Always be consistent!," not the contradictory. The denial would be "Sometimes do not be consistent!" Lewis's use of the pragmatic contradiction usually depends on taking the contrary to be the denial. While it is true that a universal sentence and its contrary cannot simultaneously be true, nevertheless, if the contradictory were used, some of his arguments would not hold.

Lewis believes that moral reasoning involving imperatives conforms to the rules of logic (meaning, of course, the rules of strict implication) and takes the form of the practical syllogism. What Lewis says on this issue is often confusing. Thus, he notes that "some import of goodness or badness represents the middle term which is common to any rule of right doing and any case to be decided under that rule." Again, he says, "It takes two things, then, to determine the rightness of action: a rule or directive of right doing, or something operative in the manner of a rule, and a judgment of goodness to be found in the consequences of the act in question."[138] Thus, using the prudential imperative as major premise, one could argue

So act as to maximize your possible realizations of the good,
as against the bad, in your life as a whole!

Marrying Susie will not maximize the good in your life.

Therefore, Don't marry Susie!

This is analogous to a second figure AOO syllogism except for the fact that the major and the conclusion are imperatives. But consider

Tell no lies!

Telling Susie you love her is a lie.

Therefore, Don't tell Susie you love her!

Here the analogous form is the second figure EIO. But "good" does not occur in either premise. However, Lewis says that a maxim such as "Tell no lies!" is an empirical generalization based on our experience of the effects of the action in question, and therefore "serves in place of a prediction of the good or bad results likely to accrue in the particular case to be decided."[139] But the Categorical Imperative does not mention the good or the bad and is not an empirical generalization. However, the inference

Act only on that maxim which will enable you at the same time to
will that it be a universal law!

It ought to be a universal law always to vote for the candidate of the Democracy.

Therefore, always vote for the candidate of the Democratic Party!

is analogous to a first figure AAA syllogism. Lewis would have disagreed with the politics of this inference, but presumably he would have considered it valid. But it could be objected that the premises of this inference make no mention of good or bad. One might, however, rewrite it as two inferences:

> Act only on that maxim which will enable you at the same
> time to will that it be a universal law!
>
> Any maxim of an act that you could will to be a universal law
> serves the social good.
>
> Therefore, act only on that maxim that serves the social good!

and

> Always vote for the candidate who will further the social good!
>
> The social good is always furthered by the candidate
> of the Democratic Party.
>
> Therefore, always vote for the candidate of the Democratic Party!

These are all analogous to first figure AAA syllogisms. Presumably, Lewis would have found them acceptable, at least in form. Thus, Lewis believed that the rules of ordinary inference could be applied to imperatives, and that the pragmatic contradiction was a valid form of argument.

As noted earlier, Lewis held that "the peculiarly human kind of life in *imperatively* social."[140] His interest in social ethics had always been strong, as his teaching record and his 1952 lectures demonstrate. In 1957, he published *Our Social Inheritance*, in which he sought to approach ethics from an evolutionary perspective, drawing no doubt on the Philosophy of Evolution course that he had taught for so many years. To emphasize how special human evolution has been, he compares it with that of other species. Evolution as a biological process is responsible for the origin and development of all species, as Darwin showed, yet the rapid evolution of human society that has taken place in the last few thousand years has not been the result of any change in human biology. From a strictly biological point of view, human beings are no different now from what they were in the Stone Age. Environmental factors have played an important role in the development of other species, as well as in human development, but the environmental changes that have been most important have been those introduced by man himself. To an increasing extent, the physical environment in which humans live is an environment they themselves have created. There are other species that exhibit forms of social organization, ranging from hunting packs to ant colonies, but these modes of organization appear to be the result of internal programming—ants do not change their social organization over time. But human social organization has changed radically in kind over a very brief period of time—far too brief to be accounted for by any change in genetic makeup. Thus, human social evolution appears to be unique among the earth's species. To what do we attribute this special character?

Man's mode of life depends on his biological characteristics, and particularly on two things: man alone has hands with opposable thumbs, and man's central nervous system permits more complex responses than those of other animals. "No effect which any organism can produce in the external world can come about otherwise than by the displacement of something: it moves some object from the place or position in which it is to another."[141] Man's hand has given him an ability to grasp that has permitted him to manipulate objects as no other organism can. And this physical ability has been used by a brain with unique powers. But it is not simply man's greater ability to learn that is crucial; it is the content of what is learned. Because man has greater manipulative power than other creatures, more possible responses are open to him. That, in turn, creates a need for foresight concerning the results of alternative responses, and hence the need for planning. Only such a creature can develop the ability to imagine what will or can be, and so develops the capacity for deliberation and long-range purposes and ideals.[142]

A further distinctive feature of human beings is language—something Lewis takes to be different in kind from animal cries and beyond animal capacity. Language is essential to group communication and coordination, to the development of common plans, group consensus, and the directing of attention to what is not present. Language permits us to be advised of what we will never experience, or need to experience.[143] This allows us to learn by being told in addition to learning by doing ourselves. "Through language, the small child can learn about elephants in Africa, the blind can come to know as much as others about the heavenly bodies, and we can discover the microbes of disease and learn what to do about them, though they are beyond our senses."[144] This makes possible the education of the young, and so the transmission from one generation to another of what has been learned. Because knowledge can be stored in linguistic form, it can be preserved and passed on, so that a new generation can add to the stock already held. Thus, knowledge is cumulative, and so is the power it conveys. Ideas are the capital stock of the race that permits the transformation of its material conditions.

What cannot well escape us is that in the few thousand years for which we can tell the story of man in any detail and with any assurance, the

conditions and the manner of his living must have altered in larger measure than in all the millennia preceding. And the changes which have
come about in the two hundred years since Watt invented the steam
engine are, in turn, something like as considerable in effect as all that
took place in two thousand years before.[145]

This remarkable progress is indeed due to the character of the human
individual.

His freedom of choice is the necessity of decision and the responsibility
for what is chosen and decided. This freedom and this responsibility,
whether as privilege or as burden, are part of his inheritance as human;
and the acceptance and exercise of them are the vocation of man.[146]

But the critical factor in human social evolution is the nature of the
social order that humans have created. Human knowledge is too great to
be held by any one person; it must be held and passed on by society as a
whole. And the utilization of that growing stock of knowledge has required
increasingly complex forms of social organization. Man's own capacities
have not greatly[147] changed in thousands of years; it is his society that has
changed, and as bearer and user of his accumulated knowledge that is the
key to his future. As the growth of knowledge accelerates, social organization becomes more complex, and departs ever more from the conditions in
which his native endowment was formed. To be a civilized man becomes
an ever more complex and demanding task, which must create ever more
stresses. If "the understanding which man most needs is self-conscious and
self-critical understanding of himself, [then] this time it is beyond all
doubt that the requirement is to understand himself as a social animal, if
he wishes to control his future history."[148]

Judged on the basis of his evolutionary history, man is the most successful species on earth. But survival only proves the ability to survive; it
would be an example of the naturalistic fallacy to argue that survival proves
greater worth.[149] Yet men do, in fact, regard the human race as superior to
all other species. Is this merely an example of chauvinism in which we take
our own characteristics as the standard of worth? Lewis argues that the fact
we can ask this question shows that we can transcend such a limited perspective. "The requirement to make assessment of worth and of validity
beyond the bounds of what is merely subjective and relative to himself, is
one which the self-conscious being cannot set aside."[150] And this requirement arises with respect to any basic issue of social policy or any choice
among social systems—an obvious reference to the Soviet Union. Even
with respect to our remarkable evolutionary history, the question still

remains whether or not it represents progress toward "the common goals of the human will."

The molding of the individual into a group citizen begins at birth and is the task of education. And the function of education is "the imparting of information and the inculcation of mores." Education is a lifelong process through which men come to share in the cumulative social heritage and pass it on. The power of this inherited capital is illustrated in the technological and economic field. Were it not for human stupidities, our technological prowess is already such that it could satisfy the basic wants of the entire population of the earth. Not only that, but the specialization of social functions in today's society is approaching the point at which it will be possible for everyone to make a living by doing what he or she most likes to do—a situation currently most nearly realized in the professions. And if technology and economics best exemplify the power of our social inheritance, science best demonstrates its cumulative character and its manner of transmission.[151] Science, too, best illustrates how the cognitive limits of the individual are transcended, for although every new discovery occurs in the mind of one person, it is society that records and transmits that ever-growing stock of knowledge and makes it "a permanent possession of mankind." In view of these considerations, Lewis says, "The positive force which operates to give him [man] his peculiar power and determine his destiny lies in his capacity to create and maintain a social order which preserves and transmits the conquests of the human mind, and by doing so progressively enlarges and secures to men the possible realization of their common aims." It is in the continued working of the social system that "our surest hope for the future lies."[152] There is, Lewis says, one goal common to all mankind—the improvement of human life. Only a moral failure can put that goal in jeopardy.

The learned modes of directing conduct to projected ends and conviction of right and wrong in governing actions constitute the morals of individuals, and at the social level they constitute the mores of the social group. If there is any overall direction or progress in human history, it must reflect "some community of moral sense." Morals and mores, Lewis says, are the crucial factors that set the goals sought and determine how they are sought, and they are themselves products of critical reflection and assessment. But critical judgments take two forms: the appraisals of the good and bad, and of right and wrong. The sense of good and bad is primordial and represents the earliest form of consciousness, for "to seek the good and to avoid the bad is the basic bent of conscious life." The laws of learning depend on that. What distinguishes this in humans is the extension of this process to experiences distant in time through deliberation and self-criticism. The basis of the sense of right and wrong lies in our knowledge of the good and bad of the consequences of our conduct. Because man can learn from his past experience what the consequences of his actions will be, and because he can judge future consequences as good or ill, he is capable of governing his actions to achieve desirable results, and hence lead a rational life.[153]

The ability to predict future experience on the basis of past experience is cognitive, and evidences intelligence. The ability to derive rules of conduct and guide action by them is rationality. We may go astray on either count; we may be stupid and fail to understand our situation, or we may understand very well what the results of action will be, yet act irrationally. It is because we do not always act to achieve anticipated goods rather than to gratify present impulse that behaving rationally becomes an imperative. Such an imperative is, of course, prudential; specifically, it directs us to "so act as to maximize your total probable realizations of satisfaction over time."[154] But the prudential is the "beginning of moral wisdom." For, Lewis says,

> Given the basic capacity to subordinate immediate feeling to the dictates of the cognitive recognition of objective actualities, and given the intelligence to appreciate the gratifications and griefs of others as realities fully comparable to our own, the imperative to respect the interests of others as we would call upon others to respect our own, is a dictate of rationality.[155]

In a footnote, Lewis comments that while prudence is rational, if one recognizes that "his contemplated act will not conform to what he would call upon any other man in his situation to do, and he does not recognize that consideration as constituting a claim upon his conduct, then we *shall* account him irrational."[156] Lewis equates this imperative to the Golden Rule and views refusal to acknowledge it as perverse. But he also avers that his imperative needs social reinforcement and social consensus for its support.

This is a criterion of "morally right action and [is] definitive of justice." It sets two further criteria of right action, one formal, one contentual. The formal criterion is that of universality and impersonality: "whatever is a right way of acting is right in all instances; right for anybody to adopt, in the same premises of action." The contentual criterion refers to *what we could be satisfied with* as a universally prevailing practice"— that is, actions are to be judged by their good or bad consequences, and assessed from the point of view of the person upon whom those consequences fall. The formal criterion is a priori and due to rationality. In a footnote, Lewis says that the only proof of such ultimate principles is an argument from pragmatic contradiction.[157] But what will accord with this a priori principle, or not accord with it, is a question of empirical fact that must be settled a posteriori. The gap between them must be bridged by maxims such as "Do not steal!" and "Tell no lies!" that we have learned from experience and that may, under certain conditions, satisfy the fundamental imperative. Lewis says,

> while the roots of the moral sense must lie in something common to all men and significant of their native endowment, correct moral practice, like correct technological practices of any sort, or correct practice in an art, is something which has to be learned and developed through relevant experience.[158]

The native moral sense requires clarification and enhancement by "the critical processes implicit in social living and common thinking, and may stand in need of social reinforcement." Thus, Lewis admits that morals may vary among societies. "The morals of primitive peoples", he says, are "relative to their ignorance." At any particular period of history, "prevailing morals are relative to the stage of human development"[159] as are science and technology. Thus, while Lewis recognizes that the morals of different societies may differ, he interprets this from a progressionist point of view. As "primitive" societies develop and become civilized, presumably their mores will develop toward ours.

Given this progressionist perspective, it seemed clear to Lewis that there were universal moral principles that could be discovered by empirical research. In his view, the point of descriptive studies of the ethics of other societies was not just to describe them because, like Mt. Everest, they were there; what we might look for, and perhaps eventually find, is some higher order of generalizations about "what it [is] thus right to do, in the case of any social order at any other time and place."[160] If this cannot be done, "why study cultural anthropology?" If anthropology does not yield lessons that supply some guidance to the actions we should take now in our own situations, Lewis considered it a "waste of time." "The next time a Bay of Pigs episode comes up, we shall know who not to summon to our aid."[161]

In an extended footnote in *Our Social Inheritance*, Lewis claims that any principle that cannot be repudiated without running into a pragmatic contradiction is "pragmatically a priori."[162] The example used is "Be consistent." Lewis says:

> a decision without intent to adhere to it would not be a genuine decision. But one who should adopt the decision, "Disregard consistency," would be deciding to disregard his decisions as soon as made.

And adherence to *that* decision would require that it be promptly disregarded.[163]

The imperative, "Be consistent," cannot therefore be repudiated and so is pragmatically a priori.

The social order is conservative; it selects and preserves. If it is not to stultify and solidify at a particular point, its conservatism must be balanced by the free inquiry and criticism of individuals, for only so can new ideas be introduced and mistakes eliminated. The "preservation of individual liberties in thought and action" is therefore essential to social evolution. "Free societies progress," Lewis claims, "and those in which critical thinking is relatively suppressed must inevitably be retarded in like measure."[164] This is as true regarding morals as it is regarding science and technology. A crucial feature of the mores of any society is whether or not they permit or even encourage the reconsideration of themselves. If they do not, the mores may freeze and prevent further progress. If they do, then new ways of achieving "human betterment" are possible, and progress may continue. Lewis takes the latter to be the case in Western civilization, and the chief reason for its dramatic success.

Finally, Lewis says "without the primacy of moral principle, there could be no right or wrong as between us and the social order we would defend, and any who would seek to displace and destroy our cherished institutions."[165] The reference here is obviously to the Soviet Union. But his point is not simply political, for Lewis concludes:

> Either the historic process in which we find ourselves involved is just the boiling up of its own particular kind of brew, and we float momentarily on the surface of it, or there is a power operative in human history which makes for the right and the good, and we have our privilege of participation and a valid end toward which to move. But whatever should be our confidence, or lack of it, in the attainment by men of the goals which represent their common aims, we still have no alternative but to conduct ourselves on the assumption of their validity and the possibility of their furtherance. Otherwise the common vocation of man would lack significance.[166]

Clearly, Lewis does believe in a social evolutionary process that is progressive and apparently linear. What Lewis understands by social evolution is the evolution of the social structure and of the knowledge, including the mores, that it makes possible. In this process, individual freedom of thought produces the variations while the accepted body of belief plays a selective role by incorporating "whatever practices are found to be conducive to human betterment" and rejecting the rest. It is because man seeks "human betterment," and because man has devised a type of social structure that selects, preserves, and transmits whatever makes for "human betterment," that there is progress. The point of the book is that progress can be and has been achieved by purely human agencies.

But is the evolutionary process providential? When Lewis refers to "a power operative in human history which makes for the right and the good," is this power supernatural—a World Spirit working through history? Despite this one rhapsodic passage, I think the answer is clearly no. Nowhere in the book does Lewis appeal to supernatural agents; his claim is that human evolution is progressive because of the nature of human society and human nature.

> There is nothing in man's make-up or in the kind of life which he alone among the animals can live, or in the problems he must learn to solve, which does not take its color from the character of the human creature as reflective, self-conscious and capable of deliberation in decision, self-determining and self-critical in action.[167]

Thus, Lewis had apparently not changed from his early view that the realization of our ideal of progress cannot be guaranteed.

To achieve this continual progress is the vocation of man. The invocation—twice in the book—of Fichte's famous title, *The Vocation of Man*, is quite deliberate, but the significant point is the way in which Lewis's vocation of man differs from Fichte's. It will be recalled that in Book III, "Faith," Fichte first developed the vocation of man in this world. "My vocation," Fichte says, "[is] to moral activity,"[168] to listen to and obey the voice of conscience in order to bring about a better state for humanity. "It is the vocation of our race to unite itself into one single body, all the parts of which shall be thoroughly known to each other, and all possessed of similar culture."[169] And this state of universal peace and well-being is, Fichte claims, "attainable *in life*." But, for Fichte, this is not enough. "But when this end shall have been attained, and humanity shall at length stand at this point, what is there then to do?"[170] Fichte's answer is that man's true vocation lies in the spiritual world in service to God. The attainment of earthly utopia is thus merely a first step in the soul's endless service to the will of God.

But, in Lewis's book, there is no second step. The vocation of man for Lewis is the acceptance and exercise of his freedom and responsibility; this will make possible the attainment of the ideal state of peace and prosperity here on earth. Lewis's point is that this is possible, not because of divine guidance, but because human social evolution takes the unique form it does. Because our inherited stock of ideas constitutes our social capital, because we have devised a social structure capable of preserving, transmitting, and augmenting that capital, human beings *can* achieve human betterment through purely naturalistic means. This is Lewis's answer to Fichte, Hegel, Spencer, and all those who saw progress as providential.

In the preface to *Our Social Inheritance*, Lewis wrote:

> I should like to record the fact that what is here put forward represents a direction of thinking to which I was first drawn by Josiah Royce. If my thoughts have now strayed from the path to which his counsels pointed, still I hope he might not be displeased with them.[171]

Lewis's thoughts had indeed strayed from the path of his old mentor. One can only wonder what Royce would have thought of them.

In *Our Social Inheritance*, one sees Lewis once again seeking to derive a criterion of morally right action. But he makes no mention of the Law of Objectivity. Lewis says the "prudential sense is, so to say, the beginning of moral wisdom." He does not claim to be able to "trace out" the psychological development of morality from prudence, but he claims the result must be this:

> (A) Given the basic capacity to subordinate immediate feeling to the dictates of the cognitive recognition of objective actualities, and given the intelligence to appreciate the gratifications and griefs of others as realities fully comparable to our own, the imperative to respect the interests of others as we would call upon others to respect our own, is a dictate of rationality.

Or, as he puts it a few sentences later: "(B) A way of acting, to be right in a given case, must be one which would, in the same premises of action, be right in every instance and right for anybody."[172] This, he claims, is equivalent to the Golden Rule and to Kant's Categorical Imperative.

Do these arguments hold? Let us look first at the prudential imperative, which Lewis gives as "So act as to maximize your possible realizations of the good, as against the bad, in your life as a whole."[173] He takes this to imply "Do no act which will sacrifice a future and greater good to any lesser and more immediate good." Lewis's proof of this imperative is by pragmatic contradiction; he takes the negation of it to be the doctrine of the Cyrenaics, which he states as follows: "Take no thought for the morrow; catch pleasure as it flies; gratify every momentary impulse, so far as you can; never subordinate any good of the moment from concern for a later good."[174]

The Cyrenaic view does involve a pragmatic contradiction because it denies that there should be any principle governing future behavior, whereas the assertion of the position propounds just such a principle. The final clause of Lewis's version of the Cyrenaic position—"never subordinate any good of the moment from concern for a later good"—is opposed to the prudential imperative. But it is not the *act of assertion* of this imperative that conflicts with the prudential imperative, but the final clause of the imperative itself. Further, note here that Lewis takes the negative of the prudential imperative to be the contrary. If, instead, one takes the negative to be the contradictory, one would have: "Sometimes do not act so as to maximize your possible realizations of the good, as against the bad, in your life as a whole." This demand for moral holidays does indeed follow from the Cyrenaic position, but it robs the pragmatic contradiction of much of its force.

But even if one grants Lewis the prudential imperative, does it follow from the prudential imperative, the premises of (A), and the fact that human life is imperatively social that it is "imperative to respect the interests of others as we would call upon others to respect our own"? On the contrary, what does appear to follow is that one should use others to further one's own interests. Since one must live in society, one's self-interest will certainly involve the welfare of the society on which one is dependent, but the leap from the recognition of others's thoughts and feelings as real to respecting them as we do our own involves a subordination of self-interest that is not explained or justified by the premises. Moreover, the passage from (A) to (B) is open to the same questions raised earlier. It is not clear that respecting the interests of others as our own implies that a way of acting that is right for one is "in the same premises" right for all. I may respect someone's interest in wealth as I do my own, yet deplore the acts by which he acquires it.

It is fairly obvious that (B) and the conclusion of (A) are modeled on the Categorical Imperative. But is it the case, as Lewis claims, that the Categorical Imperative and the Golden Rule are equivalent? Lewis makes this assertion on several occasions. Yet the claim is dubious. Kant stated the Categorical Imperative in several different forms; the one Lewis usually cites is the Principle of Universal Law, but I include also, though he does not, the Principle of Humanity as an End.[175]

(1) Act only on that maxim whereby thou canst at the same time will that it should become a universal law.[176]

and

(2) So act as to treat humanity, whether in thine own person or in that of any other, in every case as an end withal, never as means only.[177]

The Golden Rule is

>   (3)   As ye would that men should do to you, do ye also to them likewise.
>   [Luke 6:31]

And, to add to the confusion, Lewis states "still another formulation":

>   (4)   Do no act which contravenes any rule which you would call upon
>   other men to respect and conform to.[178]

Neither (1) nor (2) is equivalent to (3). (1) concerns maxims, (3) concerns particular acts. (1) and (2) forbid suicide, as Kant argued at length; (3) does not. In fact, (3) concerns only acts affecting other people; it makes no mention of acts concerning oneself alone, whereas (1) implicitly, and (2) explicitly, applies to acts that affect only oneself. (4) concerns rules, of which (3) makes no mention. The equivalences that Lewis claimed to hold do not, in fact, do so.

What is striking in all these arguments is what Lewis does not say. In his 1952 Proseminar Lectures, Lewis had asserted "the greatest need of any individual is for human fellowship; and to find one's place in a good society, and to function successfully in it . . . a lone last survivor of the human race, whatever his material circumstances, would surely wish to be done and join the others." Accordingly, "self-concern and concern for others must overlap." Lewis had here at least the beginning of a way of bringing prudence and justice together. Why did he not use it in 1956? Since, as will be noted, he reiterates the last survivor argument after this time, he had apparently not abandoned his earlier position. And it can be argued that this view is implicit in *Our Social Inheritance*. But why is it not explicit? It was not because Lewis was naive about conflicts between self-interest and the social good. But the fact is that he did not believe he had a solution to the problem of how prudence and justice are related. His 1952 position, which he termed the "higher prudence," represents a form of enlightened self-interest. But Lewis wanted something more. As he had remarked in the AKV,[179] an act that benefits others loses its moral worth if it is done out of self-interest. Lewis wanted to protect the freedom of the individual to pursue his or her own ends; he also wanted to ensure that such a freedom for one individual would not jeopardize the freedom of others to do the same. Making fellowship the supreme interest of the individual still leaves it a form of self-interest. Something beyond this was necessary as a basis for morality.

Lewis made no secret of his debt to Kant. "I derive much of what is fundamental in my own view"[180] from Kant's ethical writings. Having outlined Kant's argument for the Categorical Imperative, Lewis then says, "It is this line of thought, which might be called Kant's rationalism in his theory of the right, which commends itself to me as sound, and which I should like, if so be I can, to clarify and further."[181] That Lewis meant what he said is clear in a paper he gave at Pomona College.

> What we require is what Kant called a "deduction": a demonstration that there are principles of practice which apply in human experience because in the absence of them—without recognition of them as valid in practice—there would be no fully human experience. At least, that is the kind of deduction I would attempt.[182]

Lewis believed such a deduction possible because without the distinction between right and wrong "there could not be that kind of experience characteristic of the animal which finds that he has to make deliberate decisions and that he cannot live by doing always and only what he feels inclined to do." The actual deduction Lewis summarized as follows:

(1) We can govern conduct only by reference to generalities, to implicit rules of conduct.

(2) Any valid rule of conduct must hold good of all instances to which it is relevant. Hence it must be as valid for our own conduct as for that of others, in the same premises of action.

(3) The categorical imperative of action is such a rule—the clearest and most general, since it dictates only adherence to ways of acting which do not contravene any rule recognized as thus universal, impersonal, and valid.

(4) To negate this categorical imperative would be to decide to disregard valid rules in general—to adopt as a rule the rule of disregarding rules of conduct. That would be the ultimate in pragmatic self-contradiction. The categorical imperative can be repudiated only by such pragmatic self-contradiction. It is *a priori* in the sense that, for any creature which is rational and must make his own decisions of conduct, it is nonrepudiable.[183]

It is clearly the first form of the Categorical Imperative—the Principle of Universal Law—that Lewis has in mind here. But does the proof by pragmatic contradiction in (4) hold good? Note first that Lewis here takes the negation of the Categorical Imperative to be the contrary: "Never act only on that maxim which will enable you at the same time to will that it be a universal law." If the contradictory were used, that is, "Sometimes do not act only on that maxim which will enable you at the same time to will that it be a universal law," the argument of (4) would not follow. But does the argument of (4) hold using the contrary? The *assertion* of the contrary is the assertion of a rule that, by (2), must be universal. Thus, the contrary of the Categorical Imperative would have to be interpreted as meaning that one should never act according to a maxim one could wish to be a universal law. This is certainly contrary to what Lewis took the Categorical Imperative to mean. "It is simply the law that there shall be law—that there is that which is right; that this law, this rightness, is universal to rational beings; and that whatever it is that is right for one such rational being—the rule or maxim he so accepts—must, if valid, be right for all."[184] Note first that here the terms "rule" and "law" are being used interchangeably; more exactly, "law" is being employed to mean "rule," not natural law. It is nonsense to say that it is right to obey the law of gravity; right and wrong apply only to rules or man-made "laws." Second, Lewis takes "right" and "rule" to be correlative terms. A rule defines what it is right to do, and right action is action according to a rule. Thus, the Categorical Imperative not only means that action should be in accordance with a universal rule; it also means that there is universal rightness and universal wrongness. One may therefore conclude that here by using the contrary Lewis has made his case. Yet it wasn't enough. For, as Lewis recognized in the 1959 Wesleyan lectures,

> I should wish it to be observed that in that kind of *reductio ad absurdum* which I think holds against any theory which is skeptical of the validity of normative judgments, I appeal to certain premises as implicit. . . . The *reductio ad absurdum* which proceeds by exposing an implicit pragmatic contradiction must, in the end, appeal to such self-consciousness of active and self-governing creatures.[185]

In discussing Kant, Lewis notes that Kant had distinguished the prudential imperative as hypothetical from the moral imperative as categorical. But a hypothetical imperative becomes categorical if the antecedent condition always obtains, and since the antecedent of the prudential imperative is "If you want to be happy . . . ," and men always do want to be happy, the prudential imperative is, in, fact categorical. But Kant recognized this, Lewis says, and he therefore drew the distinction another way; the prudential imperative was contingent, whereas the moral imperative was necessary. Kant held that the prudential imperative could be set aside when it conflicted with the moral. But the moral imperative could never be set aside "because the recognition of it is the very essence of being rational; and this rationality is the very essence of human mentality."[186]

But Lewis holds that both the prudential and the moral imperatives are categorical, and essential to rationality. As Lewis put it in 1959,

> I have said that there is no final proof of the validity of any species of norms except by appeal to what is involved in being human, and an active self-governing being. In the case of the moral, I can only say finally that one who does not acknowledge it as imperative to behave in that same way in which he would call upon other men generally to behave is irrational, as one who denies the law of contradiction is irrational, and one who should find prudence a matter of no concern is irrational.[187]

If the Categorical Imperative is understood as implying the rule that conduct must be rule-governed, then it simply states what Lewis takes to be essential to rationality. Hence, to deny it is irrational. And since the prudential imperative is also a categorical rule of self-governance, its denial is similarly irrational. And if one understands a "valid rule" to be universal—that is, to contain no reference to particulars—then what is required of any man by the rule is required of every man to whom the rule applies. For Lewis, the essence of human nature is rationality—the governance of oneself by acting according to deliberately chosen rules.

But having reached this point in his argument, Lewis had still not solved his problem, for, as he admitted, even an egoist could accept the Categorical Imperative as Lewis understood it, if he had a strong enough stomach to endure the consequences. Worse yet, "even the emotivist could crawl under the Kantian tent,"[188] though Lewis doubted he could be comfortable there. Lewis still faced the problem he had propound in the *Ground and Nature of the Right*: the issue, he said, "could be settled if we had a rule or valid directive of prudential decisions, a rule of justice, and a rule for weighing prudence and justice one against the other."[189] Lewis had what he considered a valid prudential imperative, and he could well argue that the Categorical Imperative was a valid moral rule—that is, a rule of justice—but how was one to be weighed against the other? Lewis wanted an ethics that would permit the subordination of self-interest to the common good, but he also insisted that prudence had to be given its due. In the first place, Lewis regarded the social good as constituted by the goods of the members of the society, so the social good could only be determined by the prudential aims of its members properly constrained by respect for others. But he does not say here, as he had in 1952, that the highest prudential aim is to be a member of a society. And, in the second place, Lewis was too much an individualist to tolerate any theory that did not give an adequate place to self-interest. Being morally right was, he held, a necessary condition for an action's being right, but he also believed that other claims, such as those of prudence, had to be included.[190] But was it possible to hold that a right action had to be both morally and prudentially right? In September 1960, he wrote, "Justice is that character of an action by which it conforms to a correct adjudication as between [our] own interests and interests of others. Justice includes 'justice to oneself.' Or does it?"[191] What about gift-giving? If one gives something to another without thought of reward, can such an act be *both* moral and prudent? Lewis notes the various forms of reward that gift-giving in fact achieves—gratitude, pride, and so on. But these do not solve the issue. "There are acts which not only satisfy every obligation to others, but are gift-giving to others, in ways that sacrifice the doer's own interest and definitely important interests of the doer. These include those of which the words 'above and beyond the call of duty' are commonly used."[192] These are cases of heroism or martyrdom. Lewis had previously held that such acts represented a "free gift of good will" and had no moral worth beyond that given by the imperatives except the feeling of integrity that the doer might experience. But, at this point, he recognized that heroism and martyrdom cannot be so easily dismissed. Can such actions be judged wrong because they are imprudent? As Lewis sees it, "If we are to follow common-sense in the conclusion that heroism and martyrdom for a genuine and well-judged cause have their occasional and real instances, then the supposition that prudence is 'imperative' in the same sense that morally required action is, is wrecked."[193] Lewis was here on the horns of a dilemma that he had made for himself when he elevated prudence to co-equal categorical status with morality.

His way out—at least here—is to argue for "the right of the individual to do as he freely decides, as long as he does not thereby infringe the equal right of others." But this requires reducing the prudential from the status of an imperative to that of an advisory principle. Lewis is then forced to say that prudence is not an obligation except where "to be imprudent would also be a disregard for claims of others on the doer, and be immoral."[194] This was not a satisfactory solution for Lewis.

In April 1961, Lewis was still struggling with the relation of prudence and morality. On the one hand, Lewis wrote, "Self-interest is the drive of conscious life; without it it is doubtful that there could be a conscious life." It is from the conflicts of self-interests that moral problems arise.

> Any attribution of a valid claim to the interest of another requires, both logically and psychologically, antecedent attribution of validity to the claims of the doer's own self-interest, assessed in that manner in which

the rightness of prudent doing is assigned a weight. The claim of justice
is of something owed to others because they likewise owe it to us.[195]

Yet, in the same month, Lewis was writing of the need to expand ethics to
include "all valid principles of the right to do."

> We find the point [need for a wider view] in an unexpected place—the
> possible justification of self-sacrifice. Can genuine sacrifice—above and
> beyond any *obligation* to others—ever be genuinely right. If so, then
> there can be something finally justified to do—if we be so minded—
> which is *not* an obligation to others, and is *not* prudentially justified,
> which is nevertheless finally justified.[196]

But justified how? If such acts are neither prudentially right nor morally
right and yet are right, what is the justifying principle? Lewis does not say,
but he has here reached an impasse that does not appear resolvable within
the categories he had previously used.

Why does Lewis raise this issue now? Eight years earlier he had been
content to view such actions as free gifts of good will. What happened to
change his mind? In 1958, J. O. Urmson published an essay on "Saints
and Heroes"[197] in which he argued that traditional ethical theories were
inadequate because they contained only a triadic classification of acts into
the obligatory, the forbidden, and the permitted. This classification scheme,
Urmson held, failed to provide for actions of supererogation—those that,
like the actions of the hero and the saint, go above and beyond the call of
duty. Urmson's paper aroused considerable interest and controversy, and
led to a number of further publications. It is particularly important that
among the traditional theories Urmson criticized as unable to accommodate acts of supererogation was Kant's ethics, a claim that Kant scholars
now seem to agree is correct.[198]

We do not know if Lewis read Urmson's paper. He does not mention
Urmson by name and his terminology varies from Urmson's; he does not
use the term "supererogatory" and he refers to martyrs rather than saints.
But Lewis was a Kant scholar, and it would be surprising if he did not read,
or at least hear about, Urmson's paper, both because of its relevance to
Kant and because of its bearing on his own theory. If this is the case, it
would explain why he should have revisited this problem in 1960, only
two years after Urmson published.

Lewis does not discuss the relevance of this issue for Kant, but for his
own theory, though the connection is obvious. At least since 1912, Lewis
had held that the Categorical Imperative was the fundamental principle of

morality. But what did Lewis take the Categorical Imperative to be? Kant gives at least four different formulations of the Categorical Imperative.

> Act only on that maxim whereby thou canst at the same
>   time will that it should become a universal law.
>   (Principle of Universal Law—PUL)[199]
>
> So act as to treat humanity, both in thine own person or in that
>   of any other, in every case as an end, never simply as
>   a means. (Principle of Humanity as End—PHE)[200]
>
> So act that the will could at any time regard itself as
>   giving in its maxims universal laws.
>   (Principle of Autonomy—PA)[201]
>
> So act as if you were always by your maxim a legislating
>   member of the universal kingdom of ends.
>   (Principle of the kingdom of ends—PKE)[202]

Kant says that these formulations are equivalent, but though he doubtless saw the PHE, the PA, and the PKE as simply explicating the meaning of the PUL, there is more to it than that. The PUL is a purely formal principle asserting the universality of the moral law. What the PHE adds to this is the end "which serves the will as the objective,"[203] namely, rational being itself. It is the fact that the Categorical Imperative has this objective that makes it rational for a rational being to act in accordance with the PUL. The PA further adds to this picture of rational beings the "unique dignity as makers of their own laws" so that "rational nature [is] not only an objective end but also one that can motivate." And the PKE adds the assertion that the Categorical Imperative can actually be realized in a community of rational beings.[204]

Lewis usually quotes the Categorical Imperative as being the PUL; the other formulations are rarely mentioned. Since the PUL is a purely formal principle, Lewis has to provide a reason why one should adopt it. The answer Lewis gives is not Kant's; rather his answer depends on empathy; we should act as though the consequences of our actions on others were to be visited on ourselves. But this leaves Lewis with two problems. First, it is by no means clear that we have, or can have, such empathetic knowledge and, as we have seen earlier, Lewis vacillated between taking empathetic knowledge as a postulate and trying to provide an inductive argument for it. But, second, if my motive for conforming to the Categorical Imperative is empathetic knowledge, then that is really a matter of self-interest. If I feel your pain as I do my own, then it is in my self-interest that you not be in pain. But my empathy for you, be it never so great, does not justify my subordination of my own interests to yours. Yet it is just this sort of subordination that Lewis seems to regard as essential to morality.

Lewis continued to wrestle with the problems of self-interest. Why, Lewis asks, should one not take self-interest as the final end?

> That is the final riddle of ethics; and a conception which does not unriddle it is not an acceptable conception; as also one which should repudiate the significance of such empathetic feeling as a fact presumed in ethics, must likewise be less than faithful to the pertinent facts. The activity of social empathy is a *necessary* condition of the validity of moral obligation but not a *sufficient* condition of the validity of moral imperatives. The *further* required condition, or conditions, of validly moral obligation, represent the major question of ethical theory.[205]

Lewis does not have an answer to these questions.

In September and October 1963, Lewis was still struggling with the question of how self-interest and the good of others can be reconciled. "The final surd of ethical theory is doubtless the question of any sanction for the subordination of what may finally appear to us as our own individual best-good to the best-good of all whom our action may affect."[206]

In several brief pieces written at this time, Lewis takes an unexpected turn. In one written in October, Lewis returns to the issue of sacrifice, remarking that a mother may well prefer to die in place of her child. Then, reflecting the current concern over nuclear war, Lewis raises the issue of whether or not, if one were the last human being alive, one would wish to continue to live.

> What I am trying to say is that I cannot believe there is any conscious life at the human level for which a felt conviction of community of value with another, is itself less than an indispensable good for the goodness of anything else which could be aimed at. And if what has just been said be said by any other to be what he intends by the postulate of God, or that this is the last and final significance of the Kantian postulate of God, required for consistency in any moral connection and the validity of any valuing, then I would agree with these others, and with Kant, in saying, "I believe in God, because I can do no other. I believe in conscious life as the final and only repository of value in anything." And I believe that the postulate of some end resident in conscious living as such, is the postulate which has no significant negative for a creature.[207]

Lewis then goes on to say that he feels obliged to include this "confession"

> because I do not know how else to convey the overwhelming conviction that no man livith to himself alone; and the consequence of that for any

discussion of egoism and altruism which, as I conceive it, has any point or is even tolerable. There is none who can be satisfied with satisfactions which are merely "his own feelings." His satisfactions and his dissatisfactions are to be shared; to be appreciated by others who are like-minded and right-minded. Otherwise he cannot live with himself. Life outside some community of what he appreciates and depreciates is not worth living.[208]

In these passages, Lewis seems to be doing two things. First, as we have seen, Lewis had always wanted human ideals to have objective validity, and this had led him to espouse a rather vague and unorthodox belief in the divine. But, second, Lewis seems here to be searching for a way to harmonize self-interest and the good of others by the claim that membership in and the welfare of the community of others is the supreme self-interest of the individual. This was the position he had taken in his 1952 lectures and had called the higher prudence. Something close to this view was implicit in *Our Social Inheritance*, but here he is explicit. But if this passage is read as saying that membership in a community is a precondition for having any interests at all, then Lewis can argue that the welfare of others must dominate self-interest because without membership in the community the self has no interests—life is not worth living.

Obviously, Lewis could have made this argument without invoking God. If it is a fact of human life—and clearly Lewis thinks it is—that there are no real satisfactions that are not shared satisfactions, then he has an argument for morality dominating prudence that does not require divine support. But Lewis chose to link the two arguments, perhaps just because visions of that great mushroom cloud in the sky were so common in 1963, but also because he had never been able to rid himself of some form of cosmic theism. Lewis could never quite accept the idea that human life has no significance beyond what humans themselves give it. That is I think the characterological inheritance that he drew from his New England past.

December 1963 found Lewis working on a preface to a projected volume of "Essays on Ethics" and apologizing for the fact that the book would not be the "Foundations of Ethics" that he had hoped to write. He intended to summarize briefly the points he had made in AKV, *The Ground and Nature of the Right*, and *Our Social Inheritance*, show the connections among them, and indicate "the conspectus upon Ethics which represents the collation of them, in a resultant theory of the moral." The preface runs only four pages before breaking off. Lewis knew he would never live to write the book.[209]

Lewis then turns to the issue of the relation of the moral and the prudential. "We are generally agreed about that: What is finally right to do is what is morally right, whether it is also prudentially dictated or not." But, as Lewis notes, we don't always conform to this principle, and we don't always feel "any sense of sin" when we do not. "So what about that?"[210] But, here again, Lewis has no answer, and the discussion moves to other issues.

Lewis never finished his book on ethics; a month after he wrote the paper last cited he was dead. It is pointless to ask whether or not he could have finished it, since the question cannot be answered. But it is important to note several points about his ethics. For Lewis, ethics was but one species of the normative. In his view, all knowledge was normative, and the same issues of the validity of imperatives lay at the foundations of all fields. He himself had established the existence of alternative logics and the fact that any choice among them could only be pragmatic. Any proof of logic, he said, was circular. But viewed as an activity, as concluding, logic rested on the imperative to be "consistent," where "consistent" was construed broadly. Similarly, he had learned from Reichenbach that empirical knowledge could not be proven true but rested on the principles of enumerative induction and the credibility of memory, neither of which could be empirically proven without circularity. For these he had furnished a Kantian deduction in the AKV, and as activity—as "believings"—he rested empirical knowledge on the imperative of cogency. Right doing, he held, rested on the imperatives of the technical, the prudential, and the moral. All these were justified by the argument of pragmatic contradiction. But Lewis frankly stated that that argument itself rested on further principles. "I have said that there is no final proof of the validity of any species of norms except by appeal to what is involved in being human, and an active, self-governing being."[211]

Does this, as some have suggested and Lewis himself hinted, make his whole philosophy circular? Saydah has argued that it does not if Lewis's arguments are taken, not as assuming the existence of human beings, but as a Kantian deduction of the *possibility* of a human type of experience. There is no doubt that he did make this argument in "Pragmatism and the Roots of the Moral" in 1956.[212] But, in 1959, in "Foundations of Ethics" he takes a different position. Lewis points out that his arguments from pragmatic contradiction "appeal to certain premises as implicit." The argument, he says,

> appeals to facts about the common nature of man which are open to all of us in a reflective examination of the kind of creatures that we are, and which I think that any such examination which is judicious must compel us to recognize as the truth about ourselves. The *reductio ad absurdum* which proceeds by exposing an implicit pragmatic contradiction must, in the end, appeal to such self-consciousness of active and self-governing creatures.[213]

If this leads his readers to claim that his whole argument is circular, Lewis says, "I shall not attempt to fend off that accusation, but instead will ask, 'What other kind of proof would you ask for, touching the very foundations of the right and valid?' " An ultimate premise, Lewis claims, can only be supported by demonstrating "some *reductio ad absurdum* of denying it." But, he adds, "it is nevertheless the fact that even such proof by the method of *reductio ad absurdum*, when addressed to ultimates, must be, in a queer kind of way, a begging of the question."[214] To support this, Lewis cites the example of logic; any proof of logic would have to assume logical principles in the proof.

> But is it anything against the necessary truth of logic that you can't prove it without begging the question? And is it anything against the validity of the distinction between right and wrong that the first principles of the right—in any particular sense of 'right'—cannot be proved without somehow begging the question? It is in recognition of such considerations that I have said that there is no final proof of the validity of any species of norms except by appeal to what is involved in being human, and an active, self-governing being. In the case of the moral, I can only say finally that one who does not acknowledge it as imperative to behave in the same way in which he would call upon other men generally to behave is irrational, as one who denies the law of contradiction is irrational, and one who should find prudence a matter of no concern is irrational.[215]

Saydah's argument is that Lewis does not assume the existence of human beings; rather he seeks to show that the *possibility* of a human type of experience depends on the existence of something that is self-conscious and self-governing—that is, governed by the basic imperatives. Rationality is then defined in terms of this deduction and the *reductio*. "The imperative to be consistent is not based on the fact that man is rational; instead, rationality is defined in terms of consistency, cogency, and objective rightness, all of which are shown to be imperative before a concept of rationality is developed."[216] This argument is attractive because it is designed to rescue Lewis from the charge of circularity. But I cannot see that this is what Lewis says in the passages previously quoted. Lewis appeals to the self-consciousness *of* an active and self-governing creature. To be self-governing means for him to be governed by imperatives. And this, he says, is a fact about the "common nature of man." In these passage, he is clearly talking about what reflection on this common nature shows, and such reflection is the self-consciousness referred to in the last clause. The *reductio* begs the question because it appeals to this common nature of man—to "what is involved in being human, and an active, self-governing being." But I find no evidence here that Lewis is talking about any experience other than that of actual human beings, or that he is arguing for the possibility of human experience rather than reflecting on actual human experience. If Lewis's position in 1959 was what Saydah takes it to have been, why didn't he say so? If he has a way to avoid circularity, why does he admit that his argument is a *petitio principii*? Perhaps it is because the issue of circularity is the wrong issue to raise.

What is involved in being human? I think Lewis's clearest statement of this is in the AKV, where he says:

> Life is temporal; and human life is self-consciously temporal. Our ultimate interest looks to possible realizations of value in direct experience; but the immediacies so looked to are not what is immediate now but extend beyond that to the future. It is thus that human life is permeated with the quality of concern. The secret of activity is to be found in such concern; of activity, that is, so far as it goes beyond unconscious behavior and animal compulsions, and attempts some self-direction of the passage of immediacy. It is only by such concern and such attempt of self-direction that we entertain any clearly conscious interests and seek to make appraisals. This is also the root of what we call our rationality and of that imperative which attaches to the rational. It is through such concern that we are constrained now to take that attitude, and now to do that deed, which later we shall be satisfied to have taken and to have done.[217]

I take this to mean that our awareness that we live in time is the source of our "concern"—that is, anxiety—about the future; this drives us to action and to the effort to control our destiny. This is what it means to be rational: "To be rational, instead of foolish or perverse, means to be capable of constraint by prevision of some future good or ill; to be amenable to the consideration, 'You will be sorry if you don't,' or 'if you do.'" Such constraint requires consistency in its observance.

> The final and universal imperative, "Be consistent, in valuation and in thought and action"; "Be concerned about yourself in future and on the whole"; is one which is categorical. It requires no reason; being itself the expression of that which is the root of all reason; that in the absence of which there could be no reason of any sort or for anything.[218]

He subsequently cites the Cyrenaic's denial of this imperative and claims it leads to pragmatic contradiction. But he then says,

> The validity of this categorical imperative to recognize genuine imperatives of thought and action, does not rest upon logical argument finally. Because presuming that the one to whom the argument is addressed will

respond to considerations of consistency and inconsistency, presumes the validity of precisely what is argued for. The basis of this imperative is a datum of human nature.[219]

The validity of this imperative cannot rest on any logical argument any more than it can rest on a pragmatic contradiction, because the ability to recognize either sort of argument as having any force assumes the imperative to be consistent. It is only because human beings have this ability to recognize the imperative nature of consistency that *any* argument has *any* force. And that ability must be assumed to be a "datum of human nature." No Kantian deduction can circumvent this problem because the ability to recognize such a deduction as commanding assent assumes the imperative of consistency. In the final analysis, human knowledge of any sort must rest on the abilities and capacities of human beings and their situation in the world.

Biographical Note VI

Final Years

In 1960, Lewis was seventy-seven years old. Honors continued to accrue. In the spring of 1961, the American Council of Learned Societies gave him a tax-free award of ten thousand dollars—an extraordinary honor that brought a flood of congratulatory letters and telegrams and surely helped financially.[1] He continued to work every day at the book on ethics and to seek ways to solve the problems that kept him from finishing it. But Lewis was in declining health. He had two heart attacks, and had never fully recovered from the second. He had angina since at least 1958[2] and his condition was not improving. On November 14, 1961, he wrote to Leonard about his situation: "As you know, I am busy trying to write 'Foundations of Ethics,' feeling that, as things are with me now, I am working against the clock, but could have no better occupation whether I complete this task or not."[3] He also told Schilpp, who was editing the volume on Lewis in the Library of Living Philosophers, that if he didn't hurry up with the book, he might no longer qualify.[4]

By 1963, Lewis was visibly failing. He was on an extremely restricted diet and his activities were sharply curtailed. In the fall, swelling in his feet forced him to give up his daily walks.[5] Lewis was well aware of the situation and it bothered him, but he accepted it as what life brings. In January 1964, he commented, "I am a little sick all the time lately."[6] He records having had three or four spells not unlike "mystic experiences." "The presentations were definitely of myself at the time of death. But they are of a sort a believing mystic would treasure as 'revelation.' Outside these passing states I never have had any slightest temptation to *believe*."[7] Clearly, Lewis is here denying any belief in the supernatural. Lewis goes on to record some dream experiences, and the fact that often when he went to bed with a problem in mind, he would wake up with the solution but no recollection of how it had been obtained. This is not an uncommon experience for people who do intellectual work, but the presentiments of dying were a different matter.

Lewis was, in fact, near death and seems to have known that. Finally, he agreed to enter the hospital where his physician believed treatment would improve his condition. He faced the situation with grim humor. When the nurse adjusted the oxygen mask over his face and asked if it helped his breathing, he replied, "I'm tired of breathing. I think I'll stop."[8] He did. Lewis died on February 3, 1964—the anniversary of his daughter Peggy's birth.[9]

11

Conclusion

The lifetime of C. I. Lewis spanned a period of radical changes in science, religion, and philosophy, both here and in Europe. Lewis was born twenty-four years after the *Origin of Species* was published, yet the battle between science and religion continued to rage throughout his lifetime. It was this issue that made Idealism the reigning philosophy of the late nineteenth century and inspired the Pragmatism of Peirce, James, and Dewey. But science itself was revolutionized by Einstein's work in the early twentieth century, at the same time that the struggles of mathematics with problems concerning its foundations culminated in *Principia Mathematica*. The Realist revolt against Idealism that marked the beginning of its eclipse and the emergence of Logical Positivism as an attempt to bring scientific rigor to philosophy transformed the philosophic scene, bringing new issues, new methods, and new controversies. Few who had been trained for the issues of the nineteenth century could deal effectively with the very different issues of the 1940s and 1950s.

Lewis was one of the few. Trained by Royce and James, he found himself confronting Whitehead and Russell. There had been no mathematical logic in the United States before Peirce, and few here had any appreciation of what Peirce had done. Luckily, Royce was one of the few, and, through him, Lewis was prepared to contest the ground with Whitehead and Russell. Lewis first opposed *Principia Mathematica* because of what he took to be its support of monistic determinism. The alternative he proposed emphasized intensionality over extensionality, possibility as well as fact. That emphasis on possibility led Lewis into pluralism, Realism, and eventually Pragmatism, and so to a defense of freedom in the pragmatic conception of the a priori. Retaining James's empiricism in his commitment to the given, Lewis upheld the creative role of the mind in its freedom to create and choose among a priori systems, so that knowledge became an interpretion of the given to further the pursuit of human values. The real then is what we must suppose to explain our experience. The Idealistic emphasis on the creative and legislative role of mind, the impossibility of an alogical reality, and the priority of epistemology was thus preserved within a Pragmatic empiricism.

At first, Lewis approved of the Positivist attempt to make empiricism rigorous and of Carnap's constitution theory. Lewis took the egocentric predicament seriously; unlike Dewey, he was never willing to take other minds for granted and insisted that knowledge had to be built up from a first-person basis. But when it became clear that the Logical Positivists had rejected that course and were seeking to extend the reach of science to include all knowledge, Lewis was forced to take up arms to defend values and morality against their scientistic imperialism. By making value theory an empirical theory, he hoped to outflank them, but he intended to meet them head-on on the question of ethics. Death cut short his effots.

Lewis's opposition to the extensionalism of *Principia Mathematica* proved prescient. In Quine, he saw extensionalism gone berserk. Quine's denial of the existence of conceptual meanings and his substitution of language for thought Lewis regarded as leading to a total relativism in which even "truth," let alone "good" and "right," would become meaningless. Looking at Quine's later work—*Word and Object*, "Ontological Relativity," and "On Empirically Equivalent Systems of the World"—one might well conclude that Lewis was right.

One can see in Lewis's work the struggle to preserve and develop the ideas and ideals of Peirce, James, and Dewey in a philosophic climate that was increasingly hostile. As committed as they had been to the free creative role of the mind in knowledge, to the concept of knowledge as a human creation for the furtherance of action to serve human values, and to the moral critique of conduct, he was the one American philosopher who was able to defend these views effectively against the onslought of a naturalism that he believed had become a dogmatic worship of science. He was the last of the great American Pragmatists and the only important American systematic philosopher of his time. And if he was not the first American analytic philosopher, he was certainly the grandfather of that movement in this country.

Today, "Pragmatism" has become an honorific term, appropriated by a bewildering variety of philosophers who have little in common with the pioneers who created the movement. But at least this Neo-Pragmatic movement has sparked renewed interest in Peirce, James, and Dewey. It is high time that it brought a renewed interest in Lewis, who, of all the pioneers, was the most systematic, the most thorough, and the most precise. Now that Positivism is dead, behaviorism is defunct in psychology and dying in philosophy, now that the French disease is fading into a bad memory, and the linguistic fetishism that has plagued philosophy is beginning to ebb, perhaps it is time to study again the work of the last great Pragmatist.

Notes

Notes to Introduction

1. Ralph Henry Gabriel, *The Course of American Democratic Thought* (New York: Ronald Press, 1956), Part I. Frederick Rudolph, *The American College and University* (New York: Vintage, 1965), Chs. 1–11. Richard Mosier, *Making the American Mind: Social and Moral Ideas in the McGuffey Readers* (New York: King's Crown Press, 1947).

2. George H. Daniels, *Science in American Society* (New York: Knopf, 1971), Chs. 5–9.

3. Elizabeth Flower and Murray G. Murphey, *A History of Philosophy in America* (New York: Putnam's, 1977), II, 517–525.

4. Flower and Murphey, *History*, I, Chs. 4–5. Bruce Kuklick, *The Rise of American Philosophy* (New Haven: Yale University Press, 1977), Ch. 1.

5. Flower and Murphey, *History*, II, Ch. 9. Bruce Kuklick, *Churchmen and Philosophers* (New Haven: Yale University Press, 1985), Chs. 13–15.

6. Herbert Spencer, *Social Statics* (New York: D. Appleton, 1915), 150.

7. Flower and Murphey, *History*, II, 528–535.

8. Lester Ward, *The Psychic Factors in Civilization* (Boston: Ginn and Co., 1901), 286.

9. Flower and Murphey, *History*, II, Ch. 8.

10. Charles S. Peirce, *The Collected Papers of Charles Sanders Peirce*, eds. Hartshorne and Weiss (Cambridge: Harvard University Press, 1934) 5.402.

11. Murray G. Murphey, *The Development of Peirce's Philosophy* (Cambridge: Harvard University Press, 1961), 156.

12. Kuklick, *Rise*, 159–166.

13. Ibid., Ch. 9.

14. William James, *The Principles of Psychology* (New York; Henry Holt, 1910), I, 288–289.

15. Kuklick, *Rise*, passim. Flower and Murphey, *History*, II, Ch. 11.

16. Kuklick, *Rise*, Chs. 11–12.

17. Josiah Royce, "The Relation of the Principles of Logic to the Foundations of Geometry" in *Royce's Logical Essays*, ed. Robinson (Dubuque: William C. Brown Co., 1951), 379–441.

18. Ibid., 427–428.

19. Ibid., 385.

20. Josiah Royce, "The Principles of Logic" in *Logical Essays*, 373–374.

21. Ibid., 374.

22. Ibid., 375.

23. Ibid., 365.

24. Josiah Royce, "Introduction to Poincare's Foundations of Science" in *Royce's Logical Essays*, 280–281.

25. On Royce, see Bruce Kuklick, *Josiah Royce* (Indianapolis: Hackett, 1985) and Kuklick, *Rise*, which contains a detailed discussion of the interaction between James and Royce. On Σ, see Kuklick, *Royce*, Ch. 10, and Murray G. Murphey, "The Synechism of Charles Sanders Peirce," unpublished Ph.D. dissertation, Yale University, 1954, Ch. 3.

Notes to Biographical Note I

1. C. I. Lewis, "Autobiography" in *The Philosophy of C. I. Lewis*, ed. Schilpp (LaSalle: Open Court, 1968), 1.

2. Mabel Lewis, "Some Family Data." Manuscript in possession of Andrew Lewis.

3. Lewis, "Autobiography," 1.

4. Ibid., 2.

5. Mabel Lewis, *As the Twig Is Bent* (privately printed, 1969), 39. Courtesy of Andrew Lewis.

6. M. Lewis, "Some Family Data," 23.

7. Mabel M. Lewis, *As We Go On* (privately printed), 30. Courtesy of Andrew Lewis.

8. Andrew Lewis, Interview, September 15, 2001.

9. M. Lewis, *As the Twig Is Bent*, 39.

10. Andrew Lewis, Interview.

11. M. Lewis, *As the Twig Is Bent*, 38. Andrew Lewis, Interview.

12. C. I. Lewis, "Student Record," Harvard University Archives.

13. M. Lewis, *As the Twig Is Bent*, 40.

14. Ibid., 6–7, 10–11, 25.

15. Lewis, "Student Record."

16. Lewis, "Autobiography," 3.

17. Ibid., 3–4.

18. Ibid., 4. C. I. Lewis, "Logic and Pragmatism" in *Contemporary American Philosophy*, eds. Adams and Montague (New York: Macmillan, 1930), 31. The books cited are John Marshall, *A Short History of Greek Philosophy* (London: Percival and Co., 1891), Eduard Zeller, *A History of Greek Philosophy* (London: Longmans, Green and Co., 1891), Friedrich Ueberweg,

Grundriss der Geschichte der Philosophie (Berlin: E. E. Mitler and Sohn, 1894–1902), Herbert Spencer, *First Principles* (New York: D. Appleton and Co., 1896).

19. Lewis, "Autobiography," 4.

20. Lewis, "Student Record."

21. *The Tourist's Guide Book to the State of New Hampshire* (Concord: Rumsford Press, 1902), 292–293.

22. Andrew Lewis, Interview. Lewis, "Student Record."

23. Lewis, "Autobiography," 7.

24. Lewis, "Student Record."

25. Lewis, "Autobiography," 5.

26. Ibid., 6.

27. Ibid., 7.

28. Ibid., 7–8.

29. M. Lewis, *As the Twig Is Bent*, 43–47.

30. Andrew Lewis, Interview.

31. CI&I, 1.

32. Ibid., 4.

33. Ibid., 25. M. Lewis, *As We Go On*, 30.

34. CI&I, 19, 21–22.

35. Lewis, "Autobiography," 8–9.

36. Ibid., 9.

37. Lewis, "Logic and Pragmatism," 31–32.

38. Lewis, "Autobiography," 9.

39. Ibid., 10.

40. Ibid., 9–10.

41. Ibid., 11.

42. Ibid., 12.

43. Ralph Barton Perry, *Present Philosophical Tendencies* (New York: Longmans Green and Co., 1916), 143.

44. Immanuel Kant, *Critique of Pure Reason*, trans. Kemp Smith (London: Macmillan, 1956), A592–593, B620–621.

45. Ibid., A644, B672.

46. Ibid., A686, B714.

47. Lewis, "Autobiography," 12.

48. C. I. Lewis, "Realism and Subjectivism" in CP, 36.

49. Kant, *Critique*, A664, B692.

50. Ibid., A669–671, B697–698.

51. Ibid., A657–658, B685–687.

52. Lewis, "Autobiography," 12.

53. Box 19, f.1, f.3, S.C.

54. *Encyclopedia of Philosophical Sciences*, ed. Ruge (London: Macmillan, 1914), I, reprinted in "The Principles of Logic" in *Royce's Logical Essays*, 310–378.

55. Ibid., 312.

56. Ibid., 321.

57. Ibid., 322–330.

58. Ibid., 332.

59. Ibid., 333.

60. Ibid., 336–351.

61. Ibid., 354.

62. Ibid., 354.

63. Ibid., 365.

64. Ibid., 368.

65. Ibid., 372–378.

66. C. I. Lewis, "Philosophy 15—Logic," Box 19, f.1. S.C.

67. CI&I, 30–34.

68. Lewis, "Student Record."

69, Andrew Lewis, Interview.

70. Ibid.

71. CI&I, 37.

72. Ibid., 41–42.

73. Ibid., 58.

74. Ibid., 42.

75. Lewis, "Logic and Pragmatism," 32.

Notes to Chapter 1

1. C. I. Lewis, "The Place of Intuition in Knowledge" (Cambridge: Unpublished Harvard Ph.D. Dissertation, 1910), 4.

2. Ibid., 11.

3. Ibid., 16.

4. Ibid., 3.

5. Ibid., 1.

6. Ibid., 1–3, 16.

7. Ibid., 3.

8. Ibid., 16.

9. Ibid., 20.

10. Ibid., 21.

11. Ibid., 23–24.

12. Ibid., 25.

13. Ibid., 26–27.

14. Ralph Barton Perry, "The Ego-Centric Predicament," JP 7:5–14 (1910).

15. Lewis, "Place of Intuition," 28.

16. Ibid., 28.

17. Ibid., 29.

18. Ibid., 30–32.

19. Ibid., 34.

20. Ibid., 33.

21. Ibid., 34.

22. Ibid., 35.

23. Ibid., 36.

24. Ibid., 37.

25. Ibid., 38.

26. Ibid., 43.

27. Ibid., 42.

28. Ibid., 46.

29. Ibid., 56.

30. Ibid., 56–57.

31. Ibid., 59–60.

32. Ibid., 69.

33. Ibid., 71–72.

34. Ibid., 75–76.

35. Ibid., 78.

36. Ibid., 78–81.

37. James, *The Principles of Psychology*, I, 258ff.

38. Lewis, "The Place of Intuition," 80.

39. Ibid., 87.

40. Ibid., 87.

41. Ibid., 90.

42. Ibid., 91–92.

43. Ibid., 92.

44. Ibid., 93.

45. Ibid., 94.

46. Ibid., 95.

47. Ibid., 96.

48. Ibid., 99.

49. Ibid., 101.

50. Ibid., 101.

51. Ibid., 103.

52. Ibid., 104.

53. Ibid., 106.

54. Ibid., 106.

55. Ibid., 108.

56. Ibid., 109–110.

57. Ibid., 114.

58. Ibid., 115.

59. Bertrand Russell, "The Notion of Order," *Mind*, New Series, 10:30–51 (1901).

60. Lewis, "Place of Intuition," 116–120.

61. Ibid., 115.

62. Ibid., 117.

63. Ibid., 133.

64. Ibid., 121.

65. Ibid., 124–125.

66. Ibid., 125.

67. Ibid., 127–128.

68. Ibid., 128.

69. Ibid., 129–130.

70. Ibid., 133.

71. Ibid., 134.

72. Ibid., 133.

73. Ibid., 139.

74. Ibid., 136.

75. Ibid., 137.

76. Ibid., 136.

77. Josiah Royce, *The Spirit of Modern Philosophy* (Boston: Houghton Mifflin Co., 1897), 402.

78. Lewis, "Place of Intuition," 139–140.

79. Ibid., 139.

80. Ibid., 142.

81. Ibid., 143.

82. Ibid., 144.

83. Ibid., 145–146.

84. Ibid., 147.

85. Ibid., 147–149.

86. Ibid., 149–152.

87. Ibid., 155.

88. Ibid., 157.

89. Ibid., 158.

90. Ibid., 160–162.

91. Ibid., 164.

92. Ibid., 165.

93. Ibid., 166.

94. Josiah Royce, *The World and The Individual* (New York: Macmillan, 1901), I, 335–342.

95. Lewis, "Place of Intuition," 134.

96. Ibid., 136.

97. Ibid., 137.

98. Ibid., 138.

Notes to Chapter 2

1. CI&I, 42–47.

2. Lewis, "Autobiography," 13.

3. CI&I, 49.

4. George Santayana, *The Genteel Tradition*, ed. Wilson (Cambridge: Harvard University Press, 1967), 39–40.

5. Ibid., 40.

6. C. I. Lewis, "Naturalism and Idealism," CP 20.

7. Ibid., 21.

8. Ibid., 24.

9. Ibid., 25.

10. Ibid., 22.

11. Ibid., 23.

12. Ibid., 26.

13. Ibid., 27.

14. Ibid., 28.

15. Ibid., 30.

16. Ibid., 31–32.

17. Ibid., 32–33.

18. Ibid., 33.

19. Ibid., 33.

20. Ibid., 33–34.

21. Johann Gottlieb Fichte, *The Vocation of Man*, trans. Smith (Chicago: Open Court, 1916).

22. C. I. Lewis, "Realism and Subjectivism," JP 10:43–49 (1913). (Reprinted in CP 35–41), 35.

23. Perry, "Ego-Centric Predicament."

24. Ralph Barton Perry, "A Realistic Theory of Independence" in Edwin Holt et al., *The New Realism* (New York: Macmillan, 1912), 99–151.

25. Lewis, "Realism and Subjectivism," 35.

26. Ibid., 36.

27. Ibid., 39.

28. Ibid., 35. See *The New Realism*, 118.

29. Ibid., 37.

30. C. I. Lewis, "Bergson and Contemporary Thought," CP 42–54.

31. Ibid., 46.

32. Ibid., 47.

33. Ibid., 49.

34. Ibid., 50.

35. Ibid., 53.

36. Josiah Royce, *The Sources of Religious Insight* (New York: Charles Scribner's Sons, 1912), 90.

37. C. I. Lewis, "German Idealism and Its War Critics," CP 55–65, 57–58.

38. Ibid., 63.

39. Ibid., 64.

NOTES TO CHAPTER 3

1. Flower and Murphey, *History*, I, 366.

2. Ibid., I, 372.

3. Murphey, *Development*, 185–186.

4. Ibid., 190.

5. Eric T. Bell, *The Development of Mathematics* (New York: McGraw-Hill, 1945), 454–455.

6. Ibid., 444. Murphey, *Development*, 192.

7. Bell, *Development*, 289.

8. Ibid., 291.

9. Ibid., 292.

10. Ibid., 273–280.

11. Lewis, "Autobiography," 12–13.

12. Ibid., 13.

13. Lewis, "Logic and Pragmatism," 35.

14. C. I. Lewis, "Preface—and Confession," December 15, 1963, 1–2. Box 2, Vol. 2. S.C.

15. C. I. Lewis, ahl. #0N3. 70–71, Box 19, f. 4. S.C.

16. C. I. Lewis, "Implication and the Algebra of Logic," *Mind* 21:522–531 (1912). CP 351–359.

17. Ibid., 523.

18. Ibid., 524.

19. Ibid., 523.

20. Ibid., 524.

21. Ibid., 526.

22. Ibid., 529.

23. Ibid., 527.

24. Ibid., 529.

25. Ibid., 528.

26. Ibid., 529.

27. Ibid., 530.

28. Ibid., 531.

29. Alfred North Whitehead and Bertrand Russell, *Principia Mathematica* (Cambridge: University Press, 1950), Vol. I, 7, 94.

30. W. V. Quine, "Whitehead and the Rise of Modern Logic" in *The Philosophy of Alfred North Whitehead*, ed. Schilpp (New York: Tudor, 1951), 141.

31. C. I. Lewis, "Interesting Theorems in Symbolic Logic," JP 10:239–242 (1913).

32. Ibid., 242.

33. Ibid., 242.

34. C. I. Lewis, "A New Algebra of Implications and Some Consequences," JP 10:428–438 (1913).

35. Ibid., 429.

36. In these early writings, Lewis's notation varies from one paper to another, due in large part to the unavailability of suitable typographical symbols at the time. I will therefore use the notation that he settled on in 1932, with the exception of replacing "·" by "&" to avoid confusion with punctuation marks. p, q, r, etc. will be propositional variables; "∼" will mean negation, "&" will mean conjunction, "v" material disjunction, "Λ" strict disjunction, "⊃" material implication, "<" strict implication, "o" consistency, "≡" material equivalence, "=" strict equivalence, and "◇" possibility. Thus, "◇ p" means "possibly p," "◇∼ p" means "possibly not p," "∼◇ p" means "not possibly p" or "p is impossible," and "∼◇∼ p" "not possibly not p" or "necessarily p." Some later writers who have used this infixative notation have employed the symbol "□" to mean necessity. Lewis did not use this symbol, so neither will I. To avoid further confusion, I will use "Strict Implication" in caps to refer to the system of strict implication and in lowercase to refer to the relation itself, and will similarly distinguish Material Implication from material implication.

37. William Tuthill Parry, "The Logic of C. I. Lewis" in Schilpp, *Philosophy of C. I. Lewis*, 143.

38. Lewis, "A New Algebra," 436.

39. Ibid., 438.

40. C. I. Lewis, "The Calculus of Strict Implication," *Mind* 23:240–247 (1913).

41. Ibid., 240.

42. C. I. Lewis, "Notes on Philosophy 15—1909," Box 19, f.1., S.C. Hugh MacColl, "Symbolic Reasoning VI," *Mind*, 14:74–81 (1905). Hugh MacColl, *Symbolic Logic and Its Applications* (London: Longmans, Green and Co., 1906).

43. Lewis, "Calculus of Strict Implication," 244.

44. Ibid., 245.

45. Ibid., 246.

46. Ibid., 246.

47. William James, *Essays in Radical Empiricism* and *A Pluralistic Universe* (New York: Longmans, Green and Co., 1943), 86.

48. Lewis, "Calculus of Strict Implication," 246.

49. C. I. Lewis, "The Matrix Algebra for Implications," JP 11:589–600 (1914).

50. Ibid., 598.

51. Ibid., 598.

52. C. I. Lewis, "Review of *Principia Mathematica*," JP 11:497–502 (1914).

53. Ibid., 501.

54. Ibid., 502.

55. C. I. Lewis, "A Too Brief Set of Postulates for the Algebra of Logic," JP 12:523–525 (1915).

56. Lewis, "A New Algebra of Implication," 428.

57. C. I. Lewis, "The Types of Order and the System Σ," PR 25:407–419 (1916). CP 360–370.

58. Ibid., 408.

59. Ibid., 418.

60. Ibid., 419.

61. C. I. Lewis, "The Issues Concerning Material Implication," JP 14:350–356 (1917).

62. Ibid., 355–356.

63. CI&I, 67.

64 SSL, vi.

65. Ibid., 3.

66. Ibid., vi.

67. Ibid., 5.

68. Ibid., 6–16.

69. Ibid., 18.

70. Ibid., 35–37.

71. Ibid., 43–51.

72. Bertrand Russell, *Our Knowledge of the External World* (London: George Allen and Unwin, 1952), 49–50.

73. SSL, 52.

74. Ibid., 71.

75. Ibid., 79.

76. Ibid., 100.

77. Hilary Putnam, "Peirce the Logician" in *Historica Mathematica* 9:290–301 (1982).

78. SSL, 93.

79. Ibid., 118.

80. Ibid., 120.

81. Ibid., 130.

82. Ibid., 167.

83. Ibid., 187.

84. Ibid., 189–198.

85. Ibid., 213–219.

86. Ibid., 222, 286.

87. Ibid., 235.

88. Ibid., 287.

89. Ibid., 281.

90. Ibid., 286.

91. Ibid., 290.

92. Ibid., 291.

93. Ibid., 292. MacColl, *Symbolic Logic*.

94. Lewis, "Logic and Pragmatism," 35n.

95. SSL, 304.

96. Ibid., 307.

97. Ibid., 314.

98. Ibid., 319.

99. Ibid., 323.

100. Ibid., 324.

101. Ibid., 324.

102. Ibid., 324.

103. Ibid., 325.

104. Ibid., 325.

105. Ibid., 328–329.

106. Ibid., 333.

107. Ibid., 334.

108. MacColl, *Symbolic Logic*, 13.

109. SSL, 336.

110. Ibid., 336.

111. William Tuthill Parry, "Implication" (Cambridge: Unpublished Harvard Ph.D. Dissertation, 1931), 113–116.

112. SSL, 338–339.

113. Ibid., 343.

114. Ibid., 351.

115. Ibid., 354.

116. Ibid., 355.

117. Ibid., 356.

118. Ibid., 356.

119. Ibid., 362.

120. Ibid., 362.

121. Ibid., 372.

122. C. I. Lewis, "Strict Implication—An Emendation," JP 17:301 (1920).

123. Ibid., 302.

124. Henry M. Sheffer, "Review of *A Survey of Symbolic Logic*," *American Mathematical Monthly* 27:309–311 (1920).

125. Norbert Wiener, "A Review of *A Survey of Symbolic Logic*," JP 17:78–79 (1920).

126. C. I. Lewis to Lucie Dobbie, Box 1, F. 6. S.C.

127. C. I. Lewis, *A Survey of Symbolic Logic* (New York: Dover, 1960).

Notes to Biographical Note II

1. C. I. Lewis, "Lecture Courses on: Philosophies of Social Relations, Logical Theory, University of California, Berkeley, 1911–1920," Box 19 f.4. S.C.

2. CI&I, 60.

3. M. Lewis, *As We Go On*, 30.

4. CI&I, 53.

5. Ibid., 54.

6. Ibid., 54.

7. Ibid., 58.

8. Ibid., 60–62. M. Lewis, *As We Go On*, 30.

9. CI&I, 63.

10. Ibid., 70–72.

11. Ibid., 79.

12. Ibid., 86.

13. Lewis, "Autobiography," 15.

14. Kuklick, *Rise*, 217.

15. Ibid., 255–256.

16. Ibid., 457–458.

17. Andrew Reck, *Recent American Philosophy* (New York: Pantheon, 1962), 158.

18. Ibid., 21.

19. Durant Drake et al., *Essays in Critical Realism* (New York: Gordian, 1968).

20. Flower and Murphey, *History*, II, 799.

21. Drake, *Critical Realism*, 212.

22. CI&I, 92.

23. Andrew Lewis, Interview.

24. CI&I, 90.

25. Ibid., 93.

26. Ibid., 97.

27. Ibid., 102.

28. Ibid., 103.

29. Ibid., 106.

30. Burton Dreben, "Quine" in *Perspectives on Quine*, ed. Barrett and Gibson (Cambridge: Basil Blackwood, 1990), 81–84.

31. Harvard University Catalogues. Harvard Archives, Harvard University.

32. C. I. Lewis, "Lectures on Competition and Civilization: Harvard 1922–1923," 125. Box 20, f.2. S.C.

33. Thomas H. Huxley, "Evolution and Ethics" in *Evolution and Ethics and Other Essays* (New York: D. Appleton and Co., 1894), 83.

34. Donald C. Williams, "Clarence Irving Lewis 1883–1964," PPR 26:159–172 (1965), 163.

35. Ibid., 163.

36. CI&I. 110.

37. Ibid., 104.

NOTES TO CHAPTER 4

1. Victor Lenzen, "Reminiscences of a Mission to Milford, Pennsylvania," *Transactions* of the Charles S. Peirce Society, 1:3–11 (1965).

2. Lewis, "Autobiography," 17.

3. Lewis, "Logic and Pragmatism," 42.

4. Ibid., 43–44.

5. Lewis, "Autobiography," 17.

6. C. I. Lewis, "The Structure of Logic and Its Relation to Other Systems," JP 18:505–516 (1921). CP 371–382.

7. Lewis, "Logic and Pragmatism," 40.

8. Lewis, "Structure of Logic," 505.

9. Ibid., 506.

10. Ibid., 506–507.

11. Cf. Frederick Fitch, *Symbolic Logic* (New York: Ronald Press, 1952) where Excluded Middle is not a theorem.

12. Lewis, "Structure of Logic," 508.

13. Ibid., 508.

14. Ibid., 509.

15. Ibid., 508.

16. Ibid., 511.

17. Ibid., 510.

18. Ibid., 511.

19. Ibid., 513.

20. Ibid., 514.

21. Ibid., 514.

22. Ibid., 514.

23. Ibid., 516.

24. Lewis, "Logic and Pragmatism," 37–38.

25. Ibid., 39.

26. Ibid., 39.

27. Lewis, "Structure of Logic," 507.

28. Lewis, "Logic and Pragmatism," 40.

29. C. I. Lewis, "Facts, Systems, and the Unity of the World," JP 20:141–151 (1923). CP 383–393.

30. Ibid., 142.

31. Ibid., 143.

32. Ibid., 144.

33. Ibid., 144.

34. Ibid., 145.

35. Ibid., 145.

36. Ibid., 147.

37. Ibid., 147.

38. Ibid., 149.

39. Ibid., 150–151.

40. Andrew Lewis, Interview.

41. C. I. Lewis, "Religious Feeling and Religious Theory (Part II. 'The Meaning of God in Human Experience;' Hocking)," 3–43. Box 19, f.5. S.C.

42. C. I. Lewis, "Lecture Courses on Metaphysics: Lecture 22," n.d., 127–129. Box 21, Vol. 3. S.C.

43. Ibid., 131–133.

44. Ibid., 133.

45. Ibid.

46. Ibid.

47. C. I. Lewis, "A Pragmatic Conception of the A Priori," JP 20:169–177 (1923). CP 231–239.

48. Ibid., 169.

49. Ibid., 169.

50. Ibid., 170.

51. Lewis, "Realism and Subjectivism," 43–44.

52. Lewis, "A Pragmatic Conception," 170.

53. Ibid., 170.

54. Ibid., 171.

55. Ibid., 172.

56. Ibid., 172–173.

57. Ibid., 174.

58. Ibid., 174.

59. Ibid., 174.

60. Ibid., 174.

61. Ibid., 175.

62. Ibid., 176.

63. Ibid., 176.

64. Percy Bridgman, *The Logic of Modern Physics* (New York: Macmillan, 1927).

65. Alfred North Whitehead, *An Enquiry Concerning the Principles of Natural Knowledge* (Cambridge: University Press, 1919); *The Concept of Nature* (Cambridge: University Press, 1920); *The Principle of Relativity* (Cambridge: University Press, 1922).

66. Whitehead, *Principles of Natural Knowledge*, vii, 13, 28.

67. Whitehead, *Concept of Nature*, 3.

68. C. I. Lewis to Charles Hendle, December 10, 1955. Box 1, f.2. S.C.

69. C. I. Lewis, "The Categories of Natural Knowledge" in *The Philosophy of Alfred North Whitehead*, 701–744. CP 113–147.

70. Whitehead, *Principles of Natural Knowledge*, 85.

71. Ibid., 2, Chapter 2.

72. Ibid., 6.

73. Ibid., 8.

74. Lewis, "Categories of Natural Knowledge," 707.

75. Ibid., 707.

76. Whitehead, *Principles of Natural Knowledge*, 68.

77. Ibid., 68–77.

78. Ibid., 25.

79. Ibid., 75.

80. Ibid., 82.

81. Whitehead, *Principle of Relativity*, 33.

82. Whitehead, *Principles of Natural Knowledge*, 88.

83. Ibid., 88.

84. Ibid., 88.

85. Ibid., 89–90.

86. C. I. Lewis, Box 27, Vol. 19, p. 90. S.C.

87. Whitehead, *Concept of Nature*, Chapter 2.

88. Ibid., Chapter IV. Whitehead, *Principles of Natural Knowledge*, Part III.

89. John Maynard Keynes, *A Treatise on Probability* (London: Macmillan, 1948).

90. C. I. Lewis, "Review of Keynes *A Treatise on Probability*," PR 31:180–186 (1922).

91. Ibid., 180.

92. Ibid., 180.

93. Ibid., 182.

94. Ibid., 183.

95. Ibid., 183.

96. Ibid., 185.

97. C. I. Lewis, "Review of Rupert Lodge, *An Introduction to Modern Logic*," JP 17:498–500 (1920); "Review of Harold Smart, *The Philosophical Presuppositions of Mathematical Logic*," JP 23:220–222 (1926); "Review of N. O. Losskig, *Handbuch der Logik*," JP 24:665–667 (1927).

98. C. I. Lewis, "Review of *Principia Mathematica, by A. N. Whitehead and B. Russell*," *American Mathematical Monthly* 35:200–205 (1928). CP 394–399.

99. Ibid., 204.

100. Ibid., 204.

101. Ibid., 204–205.

102. C. I. Lewis, "The Pragmatic Element in Knowledge," CP 240–257.

103. Ibid., 241.

104. Ibid., 248–249.

105. Ibid., 247.

106. Ibid., 248.

107. Ibid., 250.

108. Ibid., 252.

109. Ibid., 253–254.

110. Ibid., 256.

111. Ibid., 257.

112. Ibid., 255.

Notes to Chapter 5

1. MWO, ix.

2. Ibid., x.

3. Ibid., 2.

4. Ibid., 4.

5. Ibid., 14.

6. Ibid., 32.

7. Ibid., 32.

8. Ibid., 30.

9. Ibid., 23–30.

10. Ibid., 274–275.

11. Ibid., 66.

12. Ibid., 50.

13. Ibid., 53–58.

14. Ibid., 54.

15. Ibid., 60.

16. Ibid., 62.

17. Ibid., 62–63.

18. Ibid., 70.

19. Ibid., 76.

20. Ibid., 79.

21. Ibid., 81.

22. Ibid., 86. Charles S. Peirce, "How to Make Our Ideas Clear," in Peirce, *Collected Papers*, 5.388–5.410.

23. MWO, 87.

24. Ibid., 89.

25. Ibid., 94, 107.

26. Ibid., 101.

27. Ibid., 101–102.

28. Ibid., 104.

29. Ibid., 110.

30. Ibid., 109.

31. Ibid., 111.

32. Ibid., 111.

33. Ibid., 113.

34. Ibid., 115.

35. Ibid., 117.

36. Ibid., 119.

37. Ibid., 120.

38. Ibid., 129.

39. Ibid., 130.

40. Ibid., 122–123.

41. Ibid., 133.

42. Ibid., 135.

43. Ibid., 136.

44. Ibid., 137.

45. Ibid., 139.

46. Ibid., 142, 144.

47. Ibid., 145.

48. Ibid., 148, 151.

49. Ibid., 153.

50. Ibid., 155.

51. Ibid., 166–168.

52. Ibid., 169.

53, Ibid., 173.

54. Ibid., 175–176.

55. Ibid., 182.

56. Ibid., 185.

57. Ibid., 191.

58. Ibid., 193.

59. Ibid., 196.

60. Ibid., 193–197.

61. Ibid., 285.

62. Ibid., 198–212.

63. Ibid., 214.

64. Ibid., 215.

65. Ibid., 216.

66. Ibid., 219.

67. Ibid., 221.

68. Ibid., 227.

69. Ibid., 232–233, 236.

70. Ibid., 234–239.

71. Ibid., 250–259.

72. Ibid., 261–263.

73. Ibid., 263–264.

74. Ibid., 267.

75. Ibid., 269–271.

76. Ibid., 290.

77. Ibid., 290–291.

78. Ibid., 292–294.

79. Ibid., 298–299.

80. Ibid., 302–305.

81. Ibid., 305–306.

82. Lewis, "Pragmatic Conception of the A Priori," 176.

83. MWO, 197, 244.

84. Ibid., 309.

85. Ibid., 310–319.

86. Ibid., 320.

87. Ibid., 322–323.

88. Ibid., 330.

89. Cf. Keynes, *Treatise*, Part I.

90. MWO, 355. Keynes, *Treatise*, Part III.

91. MWO, 334.

92. Ibid., 328.

93. Ibid., 335–336.

94. Ibid., 336.

95. Ibid., 336–337.

96. Ibid., 337.

97. Ibid., 338.

98. Ibid., 341.

99. Ibid., 346–347.

100. Ibid., 349–353, 365.

101. Ibid., 354.

102. Ibid., 366–367.

103. Ibid., 368.

104. Keynes, *Treatise*, 253–254.

105. MWO, 369.

106. Ibid., 372.

107. Keynes, *Treatise*, 234–237.

108. Ibid. MWO 373–378.

109. MWO, 382–383.

110. Ibid., 384.

111. Ibid., 386.

112. Ibid., 397–398.

113. Ibid., 402.

114. Ibid., 403.

115. Ibid., 407–408.

116. Ibid., 409.

117. Ibid., 419.

118. Ibid., 421–422.

119. Ibid., 423.

120. Ibid., 431.

121. Ibid., 435.

122. Ibid., 439.

123. Ibid., 440.

124. G. Watts Cunningham, "Review of *Mind and the World Order*" in *International Journal of Ethics* 40:550–556 (1929–1930).

125. Hugh Miller, "Review of *Mind and the World Order*" in PR 40:573–579 (1931).

126. F. C. S. Schiller, "Review of *Mind and the World Order*" in *Mind* 39:505–507 (1930).

127. Charles Baylis, "Review of *Mind and the World Order*," JP 27:320–327 (1929).

128. MWO, 348.

129. Ibid., 368.

130. Keynes, *Treatise*, 253–264.

131. MWO, 390.

132. Ibid., 378.

133. Ibid., 414.

134. Ibid., 372.

135. Ibid., 388–389.

NOTES TO BIOGRAPHICAL NOTE III

1. Andrew Lewis, Interview.

2. Ibid.

3. CI&I, 117.

4. Ibid., 111–117.

5. Andrew Lewis, Interview.

6. CI&I. 118.

7. Lewis, "Logic and Pragmatism," 31–51.

8. Ibid., 35.

9. Ibid., 37–38.

10. Ibid., 38–39.

11. Ibid., 39.

12. Ibid., 41.

13. Ibid., 45–46.

14. Ibid., 47.

15. Ibid., 50.

16. Harvard Catalogues 1930–1940. Minutes of the Division of Philosophy and Psychology. Harvard Archives, Harvard University.

17. CI&I, 126.

18. Andrew Lewis, Interview.

19. CI&I, 127.

20. Andrew Lewis, Interview.

21. Ibid.

22. Ibid.

23. Ibid.

24. Ibid.

25. Ibid.

26. Ibid.

27. Ibid.

Notes to Chapter 6

1. SL, 123.

2. J. Jay Zeman, *Modal Logic* (Oxford: Clarendon Press, 1973), 79.

3. Alfred Tarski, "The Concept of Truth in Formalized Languages" in Tarski, *Logic, Semantics, Metamathematics* (Oxford: Clarendon Press, 1956), 152n.

4. SL, 500.

5. Ibid., 136–139.

6. Ibid., 144.

7. G. E. Hughes and M. J. Cresswell, *An Introduction to Modal Logic* (London: Methuen Co., 1968), 228.

8. SL, 245.

9. Hughes and Cresswell, *Modal Logic*, 229.

10. SL, 147.

11. Ibid., 156.

12. Ibid., 161–162.

13. Ibid., 500.

14. Ibid., 171.

15. Ibid., 178–179.

16. Ibid., 179.

17. Ibid., 189.

18. Ibid., 209.

19. Ludwig Wittgenstein, *Tractatus Logico-Philosophicus* (London: Routledge and Kegan Paul, 1949), 4.46.

20. SL, 210–211.

21. Ibid., 211.

22. Ibid., 212–213.

23. Ibid., 215.

24. Ibid., 219.

25. Ibid., 222.

26. Ibid., 227.

27. Ibid., 235.

28. Ibid., 236.

29. Ibid., 247.

30. Ibid., 250. Theorem 19.74 is $\sim \Diamond\, p < (p < q)$

31. Ibid., 251.

32. Ibid., 249–252.

33. Ibid., 252–253.

34. Ibid., 253.

35. Ibid., 255.

36. Ibid., 256.

37. Ibid., 257.

38. Ibid., 260.

39. Fitch, *Symbolic Logic*.

40. SL, 257–262.

41. Ibid., 258.

42. Ibid., 259–260.

43. Ibid., 261–262.

44. Ibid., 262.

45. Ibid., 492n.

46. Hughes and Cresswell, *Modal Logic*, 240.

47. SL, 494–495.

48. Ibid., 494–495.

49. Ibid., 496.

50. Parry, "Logic of C. I. Lewis," 135.

51. SL, 497.

52. Ibid., 500–501.

53. C. I. Lewis, "Notes on the Logic of Intension" in *Structure Method and Meaning*, eds. Henle, Kallen, and Langer (New York: Liberal Arts Press, 1951), 25–34.

54. SL, 508–511.

55. C. I. Lewis, "Preface—and Confession," 1–2.

56. Lewis, "Student Record." Harvard Archives.

57. Parry, "Logic of C. I. Lewis," 142.

58. C. I. Lewis, "Alternative Systems of Logic," *Monist* 42:481–507 (1932). CP 400–419.

59. Ibid., 482.

60. Hughes and Cresswell, *Modal Logic*, 340–346.

61. Cf. Zeman, *Modal Logic*.

62. Lewis, "Preface—and Confession," 1–2.

63. C. I. Lewis, "The Conceptual and Material in Logic and Philosophy," 1948, 168. Box 13, Vol. 30. S.C.

64. C. I. Lewis, "The Logic of Imperatives," 139. Box 5, Vol. 9. S.C.

65. Daniel Bronstein and Harry Tarter, "Review of *Symbolic Logic*," PR 43:305–309 (1934), 309.

66. Henry Bradford Smith, "Review of *Symbolic Logic*," JP 30:302–306 (1933), 302.

67. John Wisdom, "Review of *Symbolic Logic*," *Mind* 43:99–109 (1934).

68. J. C. Chenoweth McKinsey, "A Note on Bronstein's and Tarter's Definition of Strict Implication," PR 43:518–520 (1934).

69. Leo Abraham, "Implication, Modality and Intension in Symbolic Logic," *Monist* 43:119–153 (1933), 153.

70. Frederick Fitch, "Note on Leo Abraham's 'Transformations' of Strict Implication," *Monist* 43:297–298 (1933).

71. Everett Nelson, "Intensional Relations," *Mind* 39:440–453 (1930).

72. Wisdom, "Review," 103.

73. J. C. Chenoweth McKinsey to C. I. Lewis, March 26, 1934. Box 22, f.6. S.C.

74. Ruth Barcan Marcus, "The Deduction Theorem in a Functional Calculus of First Order Based on Strict Implication," JSL 11:115–118 (1946). "Strict Implication,

Deducibility and the Deduction Theorem," JSL 18:234–236 (1953). Parry, "Logic of C. I. Lewis," 145–147.

75. SSL (Dover Edition), vii.

76. Marcus, "Strict Implication," 235. Parry, "Logic of C. I. Lewis," 145–147.

77. C. I. Lewis and C. H. Langford, "A Note on Strict Implication," submitted to *Mind*. Box 18, Vol. 1. S.C.

78. Ruth Barcan (Marcus), "A Functional Calculus of First Order Based on Strict Implication," JSL 11:1–16 (1946).

79. C. I. Lewis to Ruth Barcan (Marcus), October 11, 1947. Quoted by permission of Professor Marcus.

80. Whitehead and Russell, *Principia*, I, 131, 133.

81. Lewis, "Notes on the Logic of Intension," 25–34. CP 420–429.

82. Ibid., 28.

83. Ibid., 29–30.

84. Ibid., 34.

85. C. I. Lewis, "Outline of a New Approach to the Calculus of Propositional Functions," Box 21, 2. S.C.

86. Ibid., 353.

87. Ibid., 357.

88. C. I. Lewis, "Calculus of Propositional Functions," December 19, 10. Box 21, 2. S.C.

89. C. I. Lewis to Frederick Fitch, June 2, 1952. Fitch Papers, Yale University Library.

90. C. I. Lewis to Ruth Marcus, May 11, 1960. Quoted by permission of Professor Marcus.

Notes to Chapter 7

1. C. I. Lewis, "Review of John Dewey's *The Quest for Certainty*," JP 27:14–25 (1930); "Meaning and Action," JP:36:572–576 (1939).

2. Lewis, "Review of *Quest for Certainty*," 16.

3. Lewis, "Meaning and Action," 572.

4. Ibid., 573–575.

5. Lewis, "Review of *Quest for Certainty*," 19–20.

6. Ibid., 20.

7. Ibid., 23.

8. Ibid., 24.

9. Arthur Lovejoy, "The Thirteen Pragmatisms," JP 5:29–39 (1908).

10. C. I. Lewis, "Pragmatism and Current Thought," JP 27:238–246 (1930). CP 78–86.

11. Ibid., 239.

12. Ibid., 242.

13. Ibid., 243.

14. Ibid., 245.

15. Ibid., 246.

16. Herbert Feigl, "The Wiener Kreis in America" in *The Intellectual Migration*, eds. Fleming and Bailyn (Cambridge: Harvard University Press, 1969), 632–633.

17. Rudolph Carnap, "The Elimination of Metaphysics through Logical Analysis of Language," in *Logical Positivism*, ed. Ayer (New York: Free Press, 1959), 60–81.

18. Michael Friedman, "Overcoming Metaphysics: Carnap and Heidegger" in *Origins of Logical Empiricism*, eds. Giere and Richardson, Minnesota Studies in the Philosophy of Science (Minneapolis: University of Minnesota Press, 1996), Vol. 16, 45–79.

19. John Passmore, "Logical Positivism" in *Encyclopedia of Philosophy*, ed. Edwards (New York: Macmillan, 1967), Vol. 5, 52–57.

20. Ibid., 52–57. Feigl, "Wiener Kreis in America," 630–673. A. J. Ayer, "Introduction" to *Logical Positivism*. Joergen Joergensen, *The Development of Logical Positivism* (Chicago: University of Chicago Press, 1951). *Origins of Logical Empiricism*, eds. Giere and Richardson.

21. Feigl, "Wiener Kreis in America," 643.

22. Ibid., 650.

23. W. V. Quine, "Homage to Rudolph Carnap" in W. V. Quine, *The Ways of Paradox* (Cambridge: Harvard University Press, 1966), 41.

24. Peter Hylton, " 'The Defensible Province of Philosophy': Quine's 1934 Lectures on Carnap" in *Future Pasts*, ed. Floyd and Shieh (Oxford: Oxford University Press, 2001), 257.

25. Harvard Catalogues, Harvard Archives. Ralph Barton Perry to C. I. Lewis, Perry Correspondence, December 31, 1935. Folder I–L. Positivism. Harvard Archives, Harvard University.

26. C. I. Lewis, "Carnap: Logische Aufbau der Welt, Summary." Box 22, F. 4. S.C.

27. C. I. Lewis, "The Philosopher Replies" in *The Philosophy of C. I. Lewis*, ed. Schilpp, 664.

28. Rudolph Carnap, *Der Logische Aufbau der Welt* (Berlin-Schlachtensee:Weltkreis-Verlag, 1928). English translation, *The Logical Structure of the World and Pseudoproblems in Philosophy*, trans. Rolf George (Berkeley: University of California Press, 1967).

29. C. I. Lewis, "Positivism, Phenomenalism, and Idealism," Box 18, f.3. S.C.

30. Ibid., 4.

31. Ibid., 6.

32. Ibid., 14.

33. Ibid., 18.

34. Ibid., 22.

35. Ibid., 24–25.

36. Ibid., 26.

37. Ibid., 29.

38. Ibid., 29–30.

39. Ibid., 31.

40. Ibid., 32.

41. Ibid., 33–34.

42. Ibid., 35.

43. Ibid., 36. The question of the meaningfulness of statements about mountains on the other side of the moon had been raised by Schlick in "Positivismus und Realismus," *Erkenntnis* 3:1–31 (1932). Although Lewis does not refer to Schlick, it is likely that his article prompted Lewis to use this example.

44. Ibid., 39. Both "extrude" and "accept" are written in the manuscript as shown.

45. Ibid., 42–44.

46. Ibid., 46.

47. Ibid., 48–49.

48. Ibid., 53–54.

49. Ibid., 57.

50. Ibid., 59.

51. Ibid., 62.

52. Ibid., 63.

53. Ibid., 64.

54. Moritz Schlick, "Meaning and Verification" in *Readings in Philosophical Analysis*, eds. Feigl and Sellars (New York: Appleton-Century-Crofts, 1949), 164.

55. Lewis, "Positivism, Phenomenalism, and Idealism," 66–67.

56. Ibid., 68.

57. C. I. Lewis, "Experience and Meaning," PR 43:125–146 (1934).

58. Ibid., 125.

59. Ibid., 126.

60. Ibid., 129–130.

61. Ibid., 131.

62. Ibid., 138.

63. Ibid., 138.

64. Ibid., 139.

65. Ibid., 140.

66. Ibid., 140–142.

67. Ibid., 144.

68. Ibid., 146.

69. Schlick, "Meaning and Verification."

70. Ibid., 150.

71. Hans Reichenbach, *The Theory of Probability* (Berkeley: University of California Press, 1949). *Experience and Prediction*, (Chicago: University of Chicago Press, 1938).

72. Reichenbach, *Probability*, 429.

73. Ibid., 432.

74. Ibid., 433.

75. Ibid., 373, 445–446.

76. Ibid., 473.

77. Ibid., 474.

78. Ibid., 481.

79. Reichenbach, *Experience*, 346.

80. Ibid., 400.

81. Ibid., 69.

82. C. I. Lewis, "Judgments of Value and Judgments of Fact," CP 151–161.

83. Ibid., 152.

84. Ibid., 154.

85. Ibid., 155.

86. Ibid., 155.

87. Ibid., 156.

88. Ibid., 158.

89. Ibid., 159.

90. Ibid., 160.

91. Ibid., 160–161.

92. Ibid., 160.

93. C. I. Lewis, "Verification and The Types of Truth," CP 277–293.

94. Ibid., 280.

95. Ibid., 281.

96. Ibid., 282–283.

97. Morris R. Cohen and Ernest Nagel, *An Introduction to Logic and Scientific Method* (New York: Harcourt, Brace and Co., 1934), 219–221.

98. Lewis, "Verification and the Types of Truth," 283.

99. Ibid., 284.

100. Ibid., 288.

101. Ibid., 290.

102. Ibid., 291.

103. Ibid., 292–293.

104. C. I. Lewis, "On Empirical Knowledge," March 1938. Box 15, Vol. 42. S.C.

105. Ibid., 16–17.

106. Ibid., 17.

107. C. I. Lewis, "Relativity of Values," August 1939, 31. Box 15, Vol. 42. S.C.

108. Ibid., 47.

109. Ibid., 50.

110. Ibid., 51.

111. Ibid., 53.

112. Ibid., 57.

113. Ibid., 58.

114. Ibid., 56.

115. C. I. Lewis, "Some Logical Considerations Concerning the Mental," JP 38:225–233 (1941), CP 294–302.

116. Ibid., 226.

117. Ibid., 228.

118. Ibid., 231.

119. Ibid., 230.

120. Ibid., 232.

121. Ibid., 232.

122. Ibid., 233.

123. Ibid., 230.

124. Peirce, *Collected Papers*, 2.623–624.

Notes to Biographical Note IV

1. CI&I, 156.

2. Andrew Lewis, Interview.

3. CI&I, 168–174. M. Lewis, *As We Go On*, 1–24. Andrew Lewis, Interview.

4. Andrew Lewis, Interview.

5. Ibid.

6. Ibid.

7. Harvard Catalogues. Minutes of the Division of Philosophy. Harvard Archives, Harvard University.

8. Andrew Lewis. Interview.

9. CI&I, 152–176. Andrew Lewis. Interview.

10. CI&I, 161ff.

11. C. I. Lewis, "Introduction: Subjective and Objective Right," August 1948, 11. Box 14, Vol. 36. S.C.

12. Ibid., 12.

13. Ibid., 13.

14. Ibid., 16.

15. Ibid., 16–17.

16. C. I. Lewis, "Two Basic Problems of Ethics," October 1937, 110–112. Box 15, Vol. 42. S.C.

17. Ibid., 31.

NOTES TO CHAPTER 8

1. C. I. Lewis, "Dr. Leonard and others . . . ," August 31, 1936. Courtesy of Andrew Lewis.

2. Rudolph Carnap, "Intellectul Biography" in *The Philosophy of Rudolph Carnap*, ed. Schilpp (LaSalle: Open Court, 1963), 64–65.

3. Harvard Catalogue 1940. Harvard Archives, Harvard University.

4. C. I. Lewis, "The Modes of Meaning," PPR 4:236–249 (1943–1944), CP 303–316.

5. AKV, viii.

6. Ibid., x.

7. Ibid., 406–407.

8. Ibid., 3,

9. Ibid., 16.

10. Ibid., 18–19.

11. Ibid., 21.

12. Ibid., 10–11.

13. Ibid., 30.

14. Ibid., 26.

15. Ibid., 31.

16. Ibid., 39.

17. Ibid., 39.

18. Ibid., 39–40.

19. Ibid., 43.

20. Ibid., 46.

21. Ibid., 48.

22. Ibid., 49n7.

23. Parry, "Logic of C. I. Lewis," 145.

24. AKV, 57.

25. Ibid., 56–57. For Tarski's views on the analytic–synthetic distinction, see Alfred Tarski, "A Philosophical Letter of Alfred Tarski," JP 84:28–32 (1987), and White, *Philosopher's Story*, 52–55, 118–119.

26. Ibid., 63.

27. Ibid., 64.

28. Ibid., 67.

29. Ibid., 69.

30. Ibid., 72–73.

31. Ibid., 73–77.

32. Ibid., 78–82.

33. Ibid., 85.

34. Ibid., 86.

35. Ibid., 94.

36. Ibid., 96.

37. Ibid., 110.

38. Ibid., 111–113.

39. Ibid., 122.

40. Ibid., 126.

41. Ibid., 131.

42. Ibid., 132.

43. Ibid., 133.

44. Ibid., 133.

45. Ibid., 134.

46. Ibid., 134.

47. Ibid., 136–137.

48. Ibid., 139.

49. Ibid., 143.

50. Ibid., 146–147.

51. Ibid., 151.

52. Ibid., 152.

53. Ibid., 152–153.

54. Ibid., 153–157.

55. Ibid., 135, 156.

56. Ibid., 134.

57. Ibid., 166.

58. Ludwig Wittgenstein, *Philosophical Investigations* (Oxford: Basil Blackwell, 1953), Part I, ss68–71. Eleanor Rosch and Carolyn Mervis, "Family Resemblances: Studies in the Internal Structure of Categories," *Cognitive Psychology* 7:573–605 (1975). Eleanor Rosch, "On the Internal Structure of Perceptual and Semantic Categories" in Timothy Moore, ed., *Cognitive Development and the Acquisition of Language* (New York: Academic, 1973), 111–144.

59. AKV, 171–184.

60. Ibid., 173.

61. Ibid., 183.

62. Ibid., 204.

63. Ibid., 184.

64. Ibid., 209.

65. Ibid., 210–211.

66. C. I. Lewis, "Chapter IV: On Kant. Appendix. Freedom of the Will," November 5, 1961, 30–31. Box 3, Vol. 4. S.C.

67. Ibid., 36.

68. Ibid., 37.

69. C. I. Lewis, "Chapter IV. On Kant. Appendix," November 1, 1961, 69. Box 3, Vol. 4. S.C.

70. Lewis, "Freedom of the Will," 36.

71. Lewis, "Appendix," 70.

72. AKV, 227.

73. George Pappas, "C. I. Lewis's Theory of Knowledge" (Philadelphia: Unpublished Master's Thesis, University of Pennsylvania, 1966), 34–35, 52.

74. AKV, 215.

75. Ibid., 226n.

76. Ibid., 229–230.

77. Ibid., 219.

78. Ibid., 192–193.

79. Ibid., 186.

80. Ibid., 237.

81. Ibid., 250.

82. Ibid., 237–238.

83. Ibid., 203–204.

84. Ibid., 244.

85. Ibid., 244.

86. Ibid., 248–249.

87. Ibid., 254.

88. Ibid., 256.

89. Ibid., 260–264.

90. Ibid., 262.

91. Ibid., 269.

92. Ibid., 270, 311n.

93. Ibid., 271.

94. Ibid., 271, 273.

95. Ibid., 273.

96. Ibid., 289.

97. Ibid., 291.

98. Ibid., 292.

99. Ibid., 298–303.

100. Ibid., 306–314.

101. Ibid., 315–317.

102. Ibid., 318–320.

103. Ibid., 323.

104. Ibid., 325.

105. Ibid., 327.

106. Ibid., 325.

107. Ibid., 338.

108. Ibid., 350.

109. Ibid., 354.

110. Ibid., 354.

111. Ibid., 358.

112. Ibid., xix.

113. Ibid., 366.

114. Ibid., 366–370.

115. Ibid., 371.

116. Ibid., 373.

117. Ibid., 374–379.

118. Ibid., 381.

119. Ibid., 392.

120. Ibid., 395.

121. Ibid., 398.

122. Ibid., 400.

123. Ibid., 406–407.

124. Ibid., 408.

125. Ibid., 416.

126. Ibid., 418.

127. Ibid., 421.

128. Ibid., 426.

129. Ibid., 438.

130. David Prall, *Aesthetic Analysis* (New York: Thomas Crowell Co., 1936) 6, 9. *Aesthetic Judgment* (New York: Thomas Crowell Co., 1929), Chs. 4, 5, 10.

131. AKV, 440.

132. Ibid., 441.

133. Ibid., 442.

134. Ibid., 444.

135. Ibid., 447–450.

136. Ibid., 460–461.

137. Ibid., 461–465.

138. Ibid., 446–449.

139. Ibid., 475–476.

140. Ibid., 474.

141. Ibid., 478.

142. D. W. Gottschalk, "C. I. Lewis on Esthetic Experience and Esthetic Value" in *The Philosophy of C. I. Lewis*, 567.

143. David Prall, *A Study in the Theory of Value* (University of California Publications in Philosophy, Vol. 3, #2, 1921), 179–290, Chapter 3. Prall, *Aesthetic Judgment*, Ch. 16.

144. AKV, 480.

145. Ibid., 482.

146. Ibid., 483–485.

147. Ibid., 486–487.

148. Ibid., 488–494.

149. Ibid., 503.

150. C. I. Lewis, "Acts and Active Attitudes II," August 8, 1952, 90. Box 11, Vol. 25. S.C.

151. AKV, 496.

152. Ibid., 498–499.

153. Ibid., 500.

154. Ibid., 506.

155. Ibid., 508.

156. Ibid., 510.

157. Ibid., 512.

158. Ibid., 513–514.

159. Donald C. Williams, "Clarence Irving Lewis 1883–1964" PPR 26:159–172 (1965), 168–169.

160. AKV, 517–520.

161. Ibid., 528.

162. Ibid., 522–523.

163. Ibid., 524–527.

164. C. I. Lewis to Charles Hendle. Francis Wayland, *The Elements of Moral Science* (Boston: Gould and Lincoln, 1867), 395–396.

165. AKV, 537–538.

166. Ibid., 545.

167. Ibid., 546–547.

168. Ibid., 554.

169. Paul Henle, "Review of *An Analysis of Knowledge and Valuation*," JP 45:524–532 (1948). C. J. Ducasse, "C. I. Lewis's Analysis of Knowledge and Valuation," PR 57:260–280 (1948). W. T. Stace, "Review of *An Analysis of Knowledge and Valuation*," *Mind* 57: 71–85 (1948).

170. Roderick M. Chisholm, "The Problem of Empiricism," JP 45:512–517 (1948). CP 317–323.

171. C. I. Lewis, "Professor Chisholm and Empiricism," JP 45:517–524 (1948), 518.

172. Ibid., 520.

173. Ibid., 524.

174. See earlier, 495–497.

NOTES TO BIOGRAPHICAL NOTE V

1. CI&I, 178.

2. Ibid., 181.

3. Ibid., 184, 186, 189.

4. Ibid., 188.

5. Ibid., 189.

6. Ibid., 191.

7. Lewis, "Foundations of Ethics," in V&I, 3–82.

8. C. I. Lewis to Paul Schilpp, December 28, 1959. Box 1, f.8. S.C.

9. Lewis, "Autobiography," 17–19.

10. Ibid., 19.

11. C. I. Lewis to Morton White, December 10, 1955. Box 1, f.2. S.C.

12. Andrew Lewis, Interview.

13. C. I. Lewis to Harvard Veritas Committee, March 27, 1957, Box 1, f.4. S.C.

14. Lewis was not alone in his opposition. See the *New York Times* for March 25, 1957, and for April 7, 1957.

15. C. I. Lewis to *Palo Alto Times*, December 16, 1959. Box 1, f.8. S.C.

16. CI&I, 193–194.

17. C. I. Lewis, "The Logic of Directives," May, 1961, 139. Box 5, Vol. 7. S.C.

18. Andrew Lewis, Interview.

Notes to Chapter 9

1. C. I. Lewis, "Some Suggestions Concerning Metaphysics of Logic," in Sidney Hook, ed. *American Philosophers at Work* (New York: Criterion Books, 1957), 93–105. CP 430–441.

2. Ibid., 93.

3. Ibid., 95.

4. Ibid., 96.

5. Ibid., 99.

6. Hans Reichenbach, "Are Phenomenal Reports Absolutely Certain?," PR 61:147–159 (1952).

7. Reichenbach, *Probability*, 76ff, 321.

8. Reichenbach, "Phenomenal Reports," 153.

9. Ibid., 155.

10. Ibid., 155.

11. Ibid., 157.

12. Nelson Goodman, "Sense and Certainty," PR 61:160–167 (1952).

13. Nelson Goodman, "A Study of Qualities: An Essay in Elementary Constructional Theory" (Cambridge: Unpublished Harvard Ph.D. Dissertation, 1940).

14. Goodman, "Sense and Certainty," 162.

15. C. I. Lewis, "The Given Element in Empirical Knowledge," PR 61:168–175 (1952). CP 324–330.

16. Ibid., 168.

17. Ibid., 169.

18. Ibid., 172.

19. Ibid., 172–173.

20. Ibid., 173–174.

21. Ibid., 174.

22. Ibid., 175.

23. Carl G. Hempel, "On the Logical Positivists' Theory of Truth," in Paul Horwich, ed., *Theories of Truth* (Aldershot: Dartmouth, 1994), 81.

24. C. I. Lewis, "Fragments" 1952, 251. Box 13, Vol. 34. S.C.

25. Morton White, *A Philosopher's Story* (University Park: Pennsylvania State University Press, 1999), 338–357.

26. Morton White, "The Analytic and the Synthetic: An Untenable Dualism" in Sidney Hook, ed., *John Dewey: Philosopher of Science and Freedom* (New York: Dial, 1950), 316–330.

27. Ibid., 323.

28. Ibid., 323–324.

29. W. V. Quine, "Two Dogmas of Empiricism," PR 60:20–43 (1951). Reprinted in Quine, *From a Logical Point of View* (Cambridge: Harvard University Press, 1953), 20–46.

30. C. I. Lewis, "Proseminar Lectures on 'Practical Philosophy,'" 1952. Box 11, DN9, 29–31. S.C.

31. Andrew Lewis, Interview.

32. Quine, "Two Dogmas," footnotes 7, 15. See also the Quine–White–Goodman correspondence in White, *Philosopher's Story*, 338–357.

33. Quine, "Two Dogmas," 20.

34. Ibid., 22.

35. Ibid., 37.

36. Ibid., 41.

37. Ibid., 42–43.

38. Lewis, "The Philosopher Replies," 659.

39. Ibid., 659.

40. C. I. Lewis to Victor Lowe, April 5, 1953. Box 1, f.16. S.C.

41. C. I. Lewis to Thomas Hill, March 28, 1953. Box 1, f.16. S.C.

42. Lewis, "The Philosopher Replies," 664–665.

43. C. I. Lewis to Victor Lowe, April 5, 1953.

44. C. I. Lewis to Stephen Pepper. December 10, 1954. Box 1, f.1. S.C.

45. C. I. Lewis, "Ethics and the Logical: Chapter 2," June, 1962. Box 4, Vol. 5a, 64–65. S.C.

46. AKV, xix.

47. C. I. Lewis to Victor Lowe, January 1, 1958. Box 1, f.16. S.C. Lewis misdated the letter as 1958; it was written in 1959. See Victor Lowe to John Goheen, June 9, 1966. Box 1, f.16. S.C.

48. Victor Lowe to C. I. Lewis, January 28, 1959. Box 1, f.16. S.C.

49. Victor Lowe to John Goheen.

50. Lewis, "Suggestions Concerning Metaphysics of Logic," 93–105.

51. Ibid., 101.

52. Ibid., 103.

53. Ibid., 103.

54. C. I. Lewis, "Realism or Phenomenalism," PR 64:233–247 (1955). CP 335–347.

55. Ibid., 238.

56. Ibid., 239.

57. Ibid., 240.

58. Ibid., 242.

59. Ibid., 244.

60. Ibid., 245–246.

61. Ibid., 247.

62. C. I. Lewis, "A Comment," PR 63:193–196 (1954). CP 332–334.

63. Ibid., 194.

64. Ibid., 194.

65. C. I. Lewis, "Belief in Other Humans," 122. August 8, 1960. Box 6, Vol. 10. S.C.

66. Ibid., 125.

67. C. I. Lewis, October 9, 1960, E 10. Box 25, f.8. S.C.

68. Ibid., E 10.

69. C. I. Lewis, "Logic," May 1960, 127. Box 4, Vol. 5. S.C.

70. C. I. Lewis, "Ethics and the Logical. Chapter two," June 16, 1962, 41–44. Box 4, Vol. 5a. S.C.

71. Lewis to Hendle.

72. C. I. Lewis, "The Metaphysics of Common-Sense Realism," 1963, 83. Box 2, Vol. 2x. S.C.

73. Ibid., 85–86.

74. C. I. Lewis, "Potentialities and Contrary-to-Fact-Conditionals," July 1963, 31. Box 3, Vol. 2xa. S.C.

75. Ibid., 173.

76. Peirce, *Collected Papers*, 5.403.

77. Murphey, *Development*, 397.

78. C. I. Lewis, "Good and Bad in Experience," June–July 1963, 35. Box 2, Vol. 2x. S.C.

79. C. I. Lewis, "Saved Jottings—1958–59," February 28, 1959, 131. Box 6, Vol. 12. S.C.

80. C. I. Lewis, "Analytic and Synthetic," in "Rejects . . . But Worth Saving," July 6, 1963, 89. Box 2, Vol. 2. S.C.

81. C. I. Lewis, "Chapter IV: On Kant. Appendix. Freedom of the Will," 30–31.

82. Lewis, "Analytic and Synthetic," B.

83. C. I. Lewis, "Man's Spiritual Interests," September 12, 1950, 219. Box 13, Vol. 33. S.C.

84. Ibid., 219.

85. Ibid., 220.

86. C. I. Lewis, "On Loyalty," 113. Box 12, Vol. 26. S.C.

87. Ibid., 113–114.

88. Ibid., 115.

89. C. I. Lewis, "Your conception of god. . . . ," 1962?, 174. Box 4, Vol. 5a, S.C.

90. Andrew Lewis, Interview.

91. C. I. Lewis, "What Is Philosophy?" February 19, 1954, 166. Box 11, DN10. S.C.

92. Ibid., 2.

93. C. I. Lewis, "Experience and the Good," April–November 1961, 42. Box 3, CN3. S.C.

94. Ibid., 54.

95. C. I. Lewis, "Experience and the Good," October 5, 1962, 94–96. Box 3, Vol. 3x. S.C.

Notes to Chapter 10

1. C. I. Lewis, *The Ground and Nature of the Right* (New York: Columbia University Press, 1955).

2. C. I. Lewis, *Our Social Inheritance* (Bloomington: University of Indiana Press, 1957).

3. C. I. Lewis, "Foundations of Ethics," in V&I.

4. Arthur Pap, "What Are 'Critical Meanings'?" *Ethics* 60:131–134 (1949–1950).

5. Philip Rice, "Ethical Empiricism and Its Critics," PR 62:355–373 (1953).

6. John Dewey, *Human Nature and Conduct* (Carbondale: Southern Illinois University Press, 1983), 84.

7. Ibid., x.

8. John Dewey, *Theory of the Moral Life* (New York: Holt, Rinehart and Winston, 1960), 37.

9. Dewey, *Human Nature*, xv.

10. Ibid., 146.

11. A. C. Ewing, *Ethics* (New York: Free Press, 1953), 79–82.

12. Ibid., 121.

13. Ibid., 123.

14. Alfred Jules Ayer, *Language, Truth and Logic* (London: Victor Gollancz, 1948), 102–103.

15. Ibid., 108.

16. Charles Stevenson, *Ethics and Language* (New Haven: Yale Press, 1944), 59.

17. Ibid., 209, 229.

18. Ibid., 21.

19. Ibid., 30.

20. Ibid., 138.

21. Cf. "A Symposium on Emotive Meaning" with papers by I. A. Richards, Max Black, and Charles Stevenson, PR 57:111–157 (1948). Cf. also the exchange between Stevenson and Richard Brandt in the same volume.

22. Henry Aiken, "Moral Reasoning," *Ethics* 64:24–37 (1953–1954), 25.

23. R. M. Hare, *The Language of Morals* (Oxford: Clarendon Press, 1952), 28.

24. Ibid., 56.

25. Ibid., 69.

26. Ibid., 69.

27. Ibid., 70.

28. Ibid., Chs. 5–11.

29. Ibid., 168–169.

30. Copy in Box 25, S.C. Lewis's copies of Moore, Ewing, and Hare are also in Box 25.

31. Ibid., 97n12.

32. C. I. Lewis, "Miscellaneous Writings on Ethics," Fall, 1956, 37–38. Box 9, Vol. 18. S.C.

33. Ibid., 39–40.

34. C. I. Lewis, "Ethics and the Present Scene," in Lewis, V&I, 20.

35. Ibid., 14. C. I. Lewis, "An Attempted Answer," in V&I, 62. 70. C. I. Lewis, "Values and Facts," in V&I, 89.

36. Williams, "Lewis," 170.

37. C. I. Lewis, "Course Lectures on 'Social Ethics'" 1945–1946, 6. Box 14, Vol. 38. S.C.

38. AKV, 554.

39. Morton White, "Value and Obligation in Dewey and Lewis," in PR 58:321–329 (1949), 329.

40. Robert W. Browning, "On Professor Lewis's Distinction between Ethics and Valuation," *Ethics* 59:95–111 (1949), 111.

41. Asher Moore, "A Categorical Imperative?" *Ethics* 63:235–250 (1953), 235.

42. C. I. Lewis, "Practical and Moral Imperatives," in V&I, 128.

43. C. I. Lewis, "Pragmatism and the Roots of the Moral," in V&I, 104, 106.

44. C. I. Lewis, "The Rational Imperatives," in *Vision and Action: Essays in Honor of Horace M. Kallen* (New Brunswick: Rutgers Press, 1953), 149–150.

45. Ibid., 150.

46. C. I. Lewis, "The Right and the Good," in S.C. 30. GNR 47, 53.

47. Lewis, "The Rational Imperatives," 151.

48. Ibid., 153.

49. C. I. Lewis, "Pragmatism and the Roots of the Moral," in V&I, 119–125.

50. GNR, 79–80.

51. Lewis, "Pragmatism and the Roots of the Moral," 106.

52. J. Roger Saydah, *The Ethical Theory of Clarence Irving Lewis* (Athens: Ohio University Press, 1969), 46–47.

53. C. I. Lewis, "What Good Is Ethics?" October 23, 1958, 33. Box 7, Vol. 13. S.C.

54. C. I. Lewis, "Miscellaneous Jottings on Ethics," March–June, 1959, 27. Box 7, Vol. 14. S.C.

55. C. I. Lewis, "Chapter Five: Right Doing and Right Thinking," July 1960, 65. Box 6, Vol. 10. S.C.

56. Lewis, "The Right and the Good," 38.

57. Immanuel Kant, "Fundamental Principles of the Metaphysics of Morals" in *Kant's Critique of Practical Reason and Other Works*, ed. Abbott (London: Longmans Green and Co., n.d.), 30.

58. Lewis, "Pragmatism and the Roots of the Moral," 120–122.

59. Ibid., 121–122.

60. AKV, 480.

61. Lewis, "Rational Imperatives," 156–157.

62. Saydah, *Ethical Theory*, 18–19.

63. Kant, "Metaphysics of Morals," Section 2.

64. Lewis, "An Attempted Answer," 76.

65. GNR, 81.

66. Ibid., 84.

67. C. I. Lewis, "Validity of Imperatives VII," October 19, 1952, 26. Box 11, Vol. 25a. S.C.

68. C. I. Lewis, "Validity of Imperatives VII," October 19, 1952, 25. Box 11, Vol. 24. S.C.

69. C. I. Lewis, "Modes of Evaluation VIII" October 26, 1952, 72. Box 11, Vol. 25. S.C.

70. C. I. Lewis, "On the Ground and Validity of Moral Principles," June 26, 1953, 11. Box 11, Vol. 24. S.C.

71. Ibid., 12.

72. C. I. Lewis, "The Social Contract and the Good Will. XI" December 5, 1952, 110. Box 11, Vol. 24. S.C.

73. GNR, 89.

74. Ibid., 89.

75. Ibid., 90.

76. Ibid., 92.

77. Ibid., 93.

78. Lewis to Hendle.

79. GNR, 92.

80. Ibid., 94.

81. Lewis, "Validity of Imperatives," 39.

82. Ibid., 40.

83. Ibid., 52–53.

84. Ibid., 54.

85. Ibid., 50.

86. Lewis, "Pragmatism and the Roots of the Moral," 188–122.

87. Rollo Handy, "Review of *The Ground and Nature of the Right*" PPR 18:273–274 (1957). Charner Perry, "Review of *The Ground and Nature of the Right*," *Ethics* 66:137–139 (1956). J. D. Mabbott, "Review of *The Ground and Nature of the Right*," *Mind* 67:109–111 (1958).

88. Lewis, "Experience and Meaning," 145–146.

89. Lewis, "An Attempted Answer," 76.

90. GNR, 94. OSI, 92. Saydah, *Ethical Theory*, 82.

91. Lewis, "The Social Contract and the Good Will," 119.

92. C. I. Lewis, "Competition and Civilization XII," December 7, 1952, 138. Box 11, Vol. 24. S.C.

93. Lewis, "Social Contract," 122.

94. Ibid., 124.

95. Ibid., 125.

96. Ibid., 129.

97. OSI, 54.

98. Ibid., 58–59.

99. C. I. Lewis, "The Meaning of Liberty," *Revue Internationale de Philosophe* 11:14–22 (1948), 14.

100. Ibid., 16.

101. John Winthrop, "Speech to the General Court July 3, 1645" in Perry Miller and Thomas Johnson, eds., *The Puritans* (New York: American Book Co., 1938), 207.

102. C. I. Lewis, "Lecture 20: Social Ethics 1945–1946," 77. Box 14. S.C.

103. C. I. Lewis, "On Principles," August 1950, 122. Box 13, Vol. 33. S.C.

104. Lewis, "The Meaning of Liberty," 20–21.

105. Ibid., 17–18.

106. C. I. Lewis, "Social Ethics Lecture XX," 1945–1946, 75. Box 14. S.C.

107. Lewis, "Competition and Civilization," 138.

108. Ibid., 139.

109. Ibid., 143–144.

110. Ibid., 143.

111. Ibid., 145.

112. Ibid., 147.

113. Ibid., 154.

114. Ibid., 156.

115. Ibid., 157.

116. Ibid., 156–158.

117. Ibid., 158–159.

118. Ibid., 160.

119. AKV, 545–546.

120. Lewis, "The Social Contract," 133.

121. Lewis, "Modes of Evaluation," 71.

122. Ibid., 72.

123. C. I. Lewis, "Introduction," August, 1948, 22. Box 14, Vol. 36. C.S.

124. Ibid., 24.

125. Lewis, "An Attempted Answer," 67–73.

126. C. I. Lewis, "First Draft of Chapter Two: The Field of Ethics," August 1948, 39–51. Box 14, Vol. 36. S.C.

127. Lewis, "An Attempted Answer," 67–73.

128. OSI, 100n.

129. Risto Hilpinen, *Deontic Logic: Introductory and Systematic Readings* (Dordrecht: R. Reidel, 1971), 1.

130. Georg H. von Wright, "Deontic Logic," *Mind* 60:1–15 (1951).

131. Georg H. von Wright, *An Essay in Modal Logic* (Amsterdam: North Holland, 1951), 36. Hilpinen, *Deontic Logic*, 8.

132. See Hare, *Language of Morals*, 191–197. Krister Segerberg, "Some Logics of Commitment and Obligation" in Hilpinen, *Deontic Logic*, 148–158. A number of articles appeared on the problem of the logic of imperatives—see B. O. A. Williams, "Imperative Inference," *Analysis* 23, supplement (1963); Nicholas Rescher and John Robison, "Can One Infer Commands from Commands?," *Analysis* 24:176–179 (1963); Hector Neri Castaneda, "Imperative Reasonings," PPR 21:21–49 (1960); B. F. Staley, "Intentions, Beliefs, and Imperative Logic," *Mind* 81:18–28 (1972); Alfred MacKay, "Inferential Validity and Imperative Inference," *Analysis* 29:145–156 (1969); R. M. Hare, "Some Alleged Differences Between Imperatives and Indicatives," *Mind* 76:309–326 (1967).

133. Everett Hall, *What Is Value?* (London: Routledge and Kegan Paul, 1952), 126–128, 189–190.

134. Lewis, "The Categorical Imperative," V&I, 188–189.

135. Henry Leonard, "Interrogatives, Imperatives, Truth, Falsity, and Lies," *Philosophy of Science* 26:172–186 (1969).

136. Lewis, "The Categorical Imperative," 189.

137. Ibid., 189–190.

138. GNR, 75.

139. Lewis, "Pragmatism and the Roots of the Moral," 114.

140. GNR, 90.

141. OSI, 22.

142. Ibid., 26–28.

143. Ibid., 35.

144. Ibid., 37.

145. Ibid., 39–40.

146. Ibid., 16.

147. Ibid., 46.

148. Ibid., 42.

149. Ibid., 46.

150. Ibid., 49.

151. Ibid., 60–69.

152. Ibid., 71–73.

153. Ibid., 77–87.

154. Ibid., 91n.

155. Ibid., 92.

156. Ibid., 92n.

157. Ibid., 97–100.

158. Ibid., 103.

159. Ibid., 104.

160. C. I. Lewis, "Chapter One: Introduction. About Philosophy in General and Ethics in Particular," January 19, 1964, 48–49. Box 2, Vol. 2. S.C.

161. Ibid., 49–54.

162. OSI, 100n.

163. Ibid., 100–101n.

164. Ibid., 108.

165. Ibid., 109.

166. Ibid., 110.

167. Ibid., 13.

168. Fichte, *The Vocation of Man*, 108.

169. Ibid., 120.

170. Ibid., 129.

171. OSI, 7–8.

172. Ibid., 92–93.

173. Lewis, "An Attempted Answer," 71–72.

174. Lewis, "The Categorical Imperative," 198.

175. Paul Guyer, "The Possibility of the Categorical Imperative," PR 104:353–385 (1995).

176. Kant, *Kant's Critique*, 38.

177. Ibid., 47.

178. Lewis, "An Attempted Answer," 75.

179. AKV, 500.

180. Lewis, "The Categorical Imperative," 178.

181. Ibid., 186.

182. Lewis, "Pragmatism and the Roots of the Moral," 116.

183. Ibid., 125.

184. Lewis, "The Categorical Imperative," 185.

185. Lewis, "An Attempted Answer," 79–80.

186. Lewis, "The Categorical Imperative," 185.

187. Lewis, "An Attempted Answer," 82.

188. Ibid., 78.

189. GNR, 74.

190. C. I. Lewis, "More on the Technical, Prudential, and Moral," September–October 1960, 181. Box 6, Vol. 11a. S.C.

191. C. I. Lewis, "Chapter One: The Field of Ethics," September 12, 1960, 138. Box 5, Vol. 8. S.C.

192. Ibid., 142.

193. Ibid., 146–147.

194. Ibid., 148–151.

195. C. I. Lewis, "Chapter One: The Field of Ethics," April–September 1961, 131. Box 5, Vol. 8. S.C.

196. C. I. Lewis, "Wide View and Narrow View," April 1961, 2–3. Box 5, Vol. 8. S.C.

197. J. O. Urmson, "Saints and Heroes," in A. I. Melden, *Essays in Moral Philosophy* (Seattle: University of Washington Press, 1958), 198–216.

198. Paul Eisenberg, "From the Forbidden to the Supererogatory: The Basic Ethical Categories in Kant's *Tugendlehre*," *American Philosophical Quarterly* 3:255–269 (1966); Marcia

Brown, *Kantian Ethics Almost Without Apology* (Ithaca: Cornell University Press, 1995); Paul Guyer, *Kant on Freedom, Law, and Happiness* (Cambridge: University Press, 2000), 324–329.

199. Kant, *Kant's Critique of Practical Reason*, 38.

200. Ibid., 47.

201. Ibid., 52.

202. Ibid., 57. The names of the principles are taken from Guyer, "The Possibility of the Categorical Imperative." See also Herbert J. Paton, *The Categorical Imperative* (London: Hutchinson Library, 1948), 129ff. Paton holds that there are five versions of the Categorical Imperative, Guyer believes there are four.

203. Guyer, "Categorical Imperative," 371.

204. Ibid., 389–391.

205. C. I. Lewis, "Logical and Ethical Directives," July 1962, 207. Box 4, Vol. 5a. S.C.

206. C. I. Lewis, "We Approach the Normative Finalities," September–October 1963, 87. Box 3, Vol. 2xa. S.C.

207. C. I. Lewis, "Terminology about 'Probable' and 'Improbable,'" October 1963, 50–51. Box 2, Vol. 1. S.C.

208. Lewis, "Confession," October 1963, 52. Box 2, Vol. 1. S.C.

209. C. I. Lewis, "Preface—and Confession," 4.

210. Lewis, "Chapter One: Introduction. About Philosophy in General and Ethics in Particular," 58–59.

211. Lewis, "An Attempted Answer," 82.

212. See earlier, 389–390.

213. Lewis, "An Attempted Answer," 80.

214. Ibid., 81.

215. Ibid., 82.

216. Saydah, *Ethical Theory*, 64–65.

217. AKV, 479–480.

218. Ibid., 481.

219. Ibid., 482.

NOTES TO BIOGRAPHICAL NOTE VI

1. CI&I, 194.

2. C. I. Lewis to Henry Leonard, February 1, 1958. Box 1, f.5. S.C.

3. C. I. Lewis to Henry Leonard, November 14, 1961. Box 1, f.16. S.C.

4. Andrew Lewis, Interview.

5. CI&I, 195.

6. C. I. Lewis, "Comments on his Writing, Dreams, and State of Health," July 12, 1964, 3. Box 2, Vol. 2. S.C.

7. Ibid., 3.

8. Andrew Lewis, Interview.

9. CI&I, 196.

Name Index

Subject Index